New York and the International Sound of Latin Music
1940–1990

NEW YORK

—— and the ——

International Sound

of Latin Music

—— 1940–1990 ——

BENJAMIN LAPIDUS

University Press of Mississippi · Jackson

The University Press of Mississippi is the scholarly publishing agency of
the Mississippi Institutions of Higher Learning: Alcorn State University,
Delta State University, Jackson State University, Mississippi State University,
Mississippi University for Women, Mississippi Valley State University,
University of Mississippi, and University of Southern Mississippi.

www.upress.state.ms.us

Designed by Peter D. Halverson

The University Press of Mississippi is a member of
the Association of University Presses.

First printing 2021

∞

Library of Congress Control Number: 2020028468
Hardback: 978-1-4968-3128-6
Trade paperback: 978-1-4968-3129-3
Epub Single: 978-1-4968-3130-9
Epub Institutional: 978-1-4968-3131-6
PDF Single: 978-1-4968-3132-3
PDF Institutional: 978-1-4968-3127-9

British Library Cataloging-in-Publication Data available

CONTENTS

Contents

ACKNOWLEDGMENTS

This book started as an idea in 2010. After winning a series of internal and external grants over the years, I was able to start my research in 2012 and my writing in 2014. There is so much material that had to be left out of the story, but this means that I or someone else will have to find other avenues of sharing it. It's easy to feel alone and even futile when tackling such a large project, but the encouragement and interest from the musicians and collectors who shared their time with me really made me feel like it was a worthwhile endeavor. I am truly grateful for the help of numerous historians and collectors, including David Cantrell, José Raphael Méndez, Andy González, René López, Henry Medina, Jaime Jaramillo, Barry Cox, Mark Schwartz, Carlos Flores, Mike Reyes, Phil Schaap, Raúl Fernández, Olavo Alén Rodríguez, Cristóbal Díaz Ayala, Gregorio Marcano, William Cumpiano, John Sotomayor, Felix Romero, Mark Sanders, Ben Young, Mario García Hudson, Tomas Peña, and David F. García for their insights and sharing materials with me. Richard Blondet helped me obtain innumerable archival resources, helped with fact-checking the manuscript, and offered great suggestions and encouragement throughout the process.

So many musicians and dancers gave me their unconditional support and took great care and time to provide me with important historical details and some sat for long or multi-day interviews including Andy and Jerry González, Paquito Pastor, Joe Quijano, Alphonso Joseph, Margo Bartolomei, Gerardo "Taboada" Fernández, Cándido Camero, Johnny Rodríguez, Sonny Bravo, Gilberto "Pulpo" Colón Jr., Ben Bierman, Gene Jefferson, Frank Anderson, Enid Lowe, Ernesto "Chico" Álvarez, Paquito D'Rivera, Juan Ángel González, Vincent Livelli, Rubén Rodríguez, Oscar Hernández, Mauricio Herrera, Román Díaz, Larry Harlow, Eddie Palmieri, Gabriel "Chinchilita" Machado, Johnny Colón, Vincent Livelli, Dr. Ira Golwasser, Andrea Brachfeld, Sergio Rivera, Ronnie Baró, Juan Colón, Crispín Fernández, Felix Sanabria, Bobby Sanabria, Rubén González, Andy Kaufman, and Felix Romero. Sonny Bravo, Ben Bierman, Frank Anderson, and Enid Lowe took the time to review what I had written or transcribed and add missing data or corrections when necessary.

Elena Martínez of City Lore generously shared interviews of Gene Jefferson, Frank Anderson, and Enid Lowe that she had filmed with Bobby Sanabria and

Berta Jottár. Veronica González at the Díaz Ayala Archives made herself available for this research project and others for many years offering her archival insight, assistance, and encouragement. Felix Romero, Carlos Flores, Milford Graves, Jane Oriel, Chick Corea, Gregorio Marcano, Izzy Sanabria, Olavo Alén Rodríguez, Sonny Bravo, Patrick Dalmace, Gabriele Saplana, Gary Gene Jefferson, Enid Lowe, and Richard Blondet shared some important historical details and photos. Amanda Moreno and Gladys Gómez-Rossie at the Cuban Heritage Collection of the University of Miami helped me find and get permission to use some great photos. Kenny O'Banyoun at Concepts and Designs helped enlarge and sharpen some archival photos. Dr. Michael Eckroth took on the Sonny Bravo piano transcriptions with aplomb and cleaned up my scores. Ronaldo Whittaker gave me some last-minute Panamanian leads. Robin Moore and Lisa Farrington wrote letters of recommendation on my behalf for the NEH HSI fellowship award that supported the research and writing for this book in 2013–14. Gregg August checked one of my transcriptions and cooked some great pasta. Andy McCormick provided great legal advice.

A number of people looked at the manuscript in various stages. Over the period of one year, Evan Rapport, a brilliant scholar, musician and friend for almost thirty years, graciously read and commented on each chapter, providing me with tremendous insight and encouragement. Teresita Levy read the manuscript before it was submitted for blind peer review and offered some good advice. My parents, who first introduced me to Latin music and jazz, also read through the manuscript and offered some insightful comments. My John Jay colleagues Peter Manuel and Ben Bierman read various drafts of the text at different stages. My mentor Steve Blum also provided his unequaled insight and valuable assistance after I received the comments from the blind peer review process. Barbara Rodríguez read a few sections and made some useful comments. A number of friends such as Aaron Weistrop, David Font-Navarrete, John Gutiérrez, and David García helped me work through some important concepts. I also extend thanks to my blind peer reviewers whose comments were helpful in making the manuscript better. Jacob Marini helped me apply for and successfully win an NEH award in 2013; this was a long process and he was more than generous with his time. Over the years, a number of awards from the John Jay College Office for the Advancement of Research including

NATIONAL ENDOWMENT
FOR THE HUMANITIES

a Mid-Career Award and a scholarly incentive award made this work possible. In addition, an award from PSC-CUNY allowed me to complete and edit the manuscript. The Diaz Ayala travel grant also facilitated travel and research in the best archives for Latin music.

A 2013–14 fellowship from the National Endowment for the Humanities allowed me to research and write this book. Any views, findings, conclusions, or recommendations expressed in this book do not necessarily represent those of the National Endowment for the Humanities.

This book is dedicated to the memories of Andy and Jerry González, Gerardo "Taboada" Fernández, Al Quiñones, Manuel Martínez Olivera *El llanero solitario*" (The Lone Ranger), Alberto Serrano, Eddie Rodríguez, Ray Mantilla, Mario Rivera, Lewis Kahn, Melba Alvarado, Joe Quijano, Walter Gene Jefferson, Sergio Rivera, Canute "Bunny" Bernard Jr., Ronnie Baró, and Ray Santos whose contributions to Latin music and jazz are explored within the text. With the exception of Mario Rivera, El Maestro Ray Santos, Ray Mantilla, and Joe Quijano (Al Quiñones and Melba Alvarado were not musicians), I shared the bandstand with these men who were encouraging and always willing to share musical and historical knowledge with me. Mario Rivera welcomed me into his home when I was in high school and for many years showed me and countless others the serious study required to be a professional musician. This book is also dedicated to my children Ari Miguel and Ilan Andrés, who like to ask me cosmic musical-historical questions that often end with videos and/or music on the stereo as well as us playing music together. It's also for future generations of musicians and fans of Latin music. Lastly, it is my sincere wish to honor my musical colleagues who are out there every day playing this great music and keeping Latin music alive, evolving, and thriving in New York City and beyond.

Fig I.1. José Rafael Méndez speaking at the Arsenio Rodríguez street-naming ceremony. In the background l-r: Bobby Sanabria, Nelson González, Eddie Montalvo, Larry Harlow, Roberto Marrero, Alfredo "Chocolate" Armenteros, Andy González. Photo by Benjamin Lapidus.

Fig I.2. Lázaro Martínez (Arsenio's grand-nephew), Alfredo "Chocolate" Armenteros, Xiomara Travieso Martínez (Arsenio's niece). Photo by Benjamin Lapidus.

INTRODUCTION

ARSENIO RODRÍGUEZ WAY

Standing at the Crossroads, Thursday, June 6, 2013

It's a beautiful day and a crowd is gathered on Dawson Street between Intervale and Longwood Avenues in the Bronx for a special occasion: a street naming ceremony in honor of the legendary Afro-Cuban musician and composer Arsenio Rodríguez. We are standing at a literal and figurative crossroads, we are looking forward and back as well as to each side. This event is the culmination of two years of detective work, political maneuvering, and the desire to honor Rodríguez within the community that he called home at one point and sang about in his songs such as "*La gente del Bronx*" (The People of the Bronx). The attendees include musical luminaries from Arsenio Rodríguez's bands, his non-Cuban disciples, one Hollywood celebrity, living family members, local politicians, and fans who danced at his live performances. Everything goes off without a hitch, but for a moment it seems like the paper sign that is covering the new street sign won't come off. With one last tug and a lot of laughter, the sign is revealed and everyone claps.

This event was the last of three incredible acts that brought together an ethnically diverse community unified in its love of Afro-Latin music made in New York City. Spearheaded by collector José Rafael Méndez, the first achievement was to put a tombstone on Rodríguez's grave where there had previously been none. Méndez, a Puerto Rican New Yorker, tracked down Rodríguez's heirs in New York and Cuba, ran a media campaign, and paid for the permit to secure the headstone. Larry Harlow, the legendary salsa musician known as *El judío maravilloso* (The Marvelous Jew) and an acknowledged Rodríguez disciple, paid for the headstone. In the preceding fall, on September 1, 2012, a collectors' convention sponsored by the Caribbean Cultural Center of New York convened a panel of musicians who worked with Arsenio Rodríguez. Cuban, Puerto Rican, and Panamanian musicians from his bands were on the panel and some of Rodríguez's family visiting from Cuba were in the audience. Walking into the panel discussion, visitors were greeted outside by Méndez's poster boards, which included maps and photos of Arsenio's different addresses during his time living in New York.

Although Arsenio Rodríguez died in the United States in 1970, it is noteworthy that there is no statue or public monument to his achievements in Cuba where he and his music were born, developed, and flourished. And despite the appreciation of his musical legacy in Colombia, Puerto Rico, Los Angeles (where he lived his last days), or Miami, home to the largest Cuban community outside of Cuba, his memory was never honored in this way in any of these locations. Why was he only honored in New York City when there is no doubt that both his music and style influenced popular music throughout the Americas?

New York City remains the place where Arsenio's impact and musical legacy have perhaps been the greatest. Today, there is no doubt that Arsenio Rodríguez's musical spirit lives on in New York City. His legacy is pronounced in the *rumbas, bembés, toques de santo, son montuno, mambo,* distorted and amplified *tres* sound and tuning of countless *treseros* (tres players), and the particular swing and musical swagger of generations of New York musicians who play Afro-Latin music. However, Rodríguez's personal and musical trajectories and his connection to New York City exemplify the musical goals and aspirations of many musicians steeped in Spanish Caribbean music who came to New York City specifically to create innovative music for a knowledgeable dancing public and to improve their craft amongst the best musicians in the field of Afro-Latin music. Rodríguez could not have continued to achieve his musical vision without coming to New York City on multiple occasions and eventually settling here.

Arsenio Rodríguez was a musical genius with supreme gifts, but there have been many other musicians in New York City who have been important in the development of the international sound of Spanish Caribbean music. Many of these musicians came to New York City before Rodríguez, and many have come and continue to come since his arrival. This book is about how interethnic collaboration among musicians, composers, dancers, instrument builders, and music teachers in New York City set a standard for the study, creation, performance, and innovation of Latin music. The Latin music scene developed in a parallel fashion and intersected with the music scenes in Cuba, Puerto Rico, Panama, and the Dominican Republic.

Before Arsenio Rodríguez's arrival, the first recording of Cuban music was actually made in New York City. And in the ensuing 120 years, while the story of Spanish Caribbean music is tied to specific genres and musicians who were physically based in the Spanish Caribbean, it is very much a story about New York City, as many of these musicians recorded in New York and called New York their home.[1] Furthermore, many current practices in Afro-Latin music were codified and standardized in New York City. This book aims to address and fill in some important pieces and overlooked gaps from extant histories of Latin music in New York City.[2]

NEW YORK AS A FOCAL POINT FOR MUSICAL EXCHANGE IN CARIBBEAN MUSIC

In his important introductory essay to *Mambo Montage: The Latinization of New York City*, Augustín Laó-Montes makes some powerful statements about Latinidad and New York City that are self-evident and relevant: first, he declares that "New York is the capital of mambo and a global factory of latinidad"; second, that "New York is a Latino metropolis and a mecca of the Black Atlantic"; third, that "New York is a montage of Latin American, Caribbean, and Afro-diasporic cultures"; and fourth, Laó-Montes "encourages reading the 'city-as-text' and 'writing the text as city.'"[3] In many ways, this book is about the last statement if it is reshaped to be *listening* to the city as music and writing/performing/recording the *music* as city.

The aforementioned coming together of many musicians from a variety of backgrounds illustrates another of Laó-Montes's points that, as "the largest and most important world city of the U.S. Empire, New York has been an important site and reference point for Latin American and Caribbean political developments and cultural expressions since the last part of the nineteenth century."[4] In *The Transformation of Black Music*, Samuel Floyd Jr. provides an excellent framework for the study of black music:

> Historical and diasporic landscapes are dotted with examples of musical transactions—variable time frames in which instances of prevailing musical practices and structures drive and react to cultural, social and political transformations. Such transactions range in size and duration from small to large and from short to long, and they interact with, overlap, and/or influence one another. When effective and influential musico-cultural transactions take place among musical agents, musical objects, and ideas about cultural locations, these transactions create broad ranges of particular activity that we might call "moments." Musical agents, such as composers and performers, are indispensable in the creation of moments because they initiate the emergence of the transaction.[5]

The moments and transactions among musicians that Floyd refers to are the centerpiece of this study of Latin music in New York City. One immediate result of this large Caribbean diaspora is that New York became part of the circum-Caribbean flow of music so that national borders and identities became less specific in musical performance and were not limited to a particular geographic location. Laó-Montes describes New York City in these terms, writing that "We can now speak of a transnational field of exchanges or a space of flows between the world city (New York) and a multiplicity of Latin American and Caribbean locales."[6] In the same way that blues forms and conventions were codified in the setting of urban recording studios and under commercial considerations, specific genres of Spanish Caribbean music were codified in New York City.

Throughout this study one can identify what Samuel Floyd Jr. and Martha Buskirk identified as "readymade" musical elements such as riffs or vamps that are transformed and given new meaning "within new frameworks over time and space."[7] Latin music as performed by musicians in New York City from 1940 to 1990 allowed for one area of cultural expression with many different participants from distinct racial, national, and ethnic groups. Laó-Montes writes:

> Beneath most conceptions of latinidad lies a nationalist common sense. Latin American nationalisms always involved a relationship between region (Latin America as the Big Motherland) and nation (nationalities as small motherlands). Latino/a discourses build from that historic entanglement of region and nation by developing a sort of pan-Latino nationalism in which latinidad appears as an association of nationalities . . . Latinidad is shaped and defined by racial discourses, processes of racialization, and racisms . . . Latinized people(s) are subject/ed to (and engage in) several systems of racial classification and racist inequality.[8]

This study demonstrates how Latin music reconciled these seemingly insurmountable divisions and has succeeded in including a variety of voices. However, it is important to point out that neither the musicians nor the audience for Latin music is monolithic, and it does not form "one community with shared cultural roots," as César Miguel Rondón has suggested.[9] There were venues throughout the city that catered to a variety of musical tastes, specific genres, and distinct audiences. The musicians and dancers shared a common goal of musical excellence and innovation, yet their experiences were quite different. Some musicians traveled back and forth to New York City from their home countries throughout the period of this study or resettled permanently in their home countries sharing their musical information and standards with their fellow musicians who in turn made new innovations. This fact supports Laó-Montes's assertion that "New York is a key site for the globalization of latinidad."[10] Thus, the line delineating national styles was further blurred in the process. Laó-Montes correctly asserts that "The 'Latino' category collapses the differences between and among colonial/racial subjects, colonial immigrants, and immigrants in the U.S. empire."[11] Understanding the full implications of this notion, I have chosen to use the term *Latin* music throughout this book, rather than *salsa*, which I view as music from a specific a period of time, namely 1960–75, as articulated by Juan Flores. In addition, practicing musicians choose to use the term *Latin music* as an umbrella term encompassing *salsa*, regional music (Cuban *son*, Dominican *merengue*, Puerto Rican *bomba, jíbaro, plena*, and *cumbia*). Musicians will always refer to specific genres by name, but the term Latin music implies a particular set of performative expectations and cultural familiarity for the musicians who make the music.[12]

This study identifies a number of important individuals and themes that have not been properly recognized and appropriately credited with the major innovations that took place between 1940 and 1990. In doing so, this study challenges the dominant narrative of modern Afro-Latin music that has narrowly focused on the accomplishments of a handful of musicians and left out the innovations of many other musicians. In some ways this study can be considered a counternarrative, because it aims to include the contributions of particular women as teachers and performers who have previously been absent from any history of Latin music in New York. It also challenges the mythmaking and inaccuracies that overlook the labor of entire ethnic groups who helped change the music in New York. Often, smaller elements in these historical retellings seem to take on nationalistic qualities when, in fact, the musicians did not necessarily view them as such.

The music would not sound like it does and it would never have reached as many people as it has without these unacknowledged individuals and their tangible contributions to arranging and performance techniques as well as codifying musical education. All of this helped to create and perpetuate a specific and identifiable New York City Latin music aesthetic that was emulated internationally.

This study is largely based on archival research, oral history collected in interviews, and musicological analysis focused on musical transcriptions. To date, most studies of Latin music in New York have not examined how and why inter-ethnic music making was achieved in musically tangible and identifiable ways. Similarly, no study of New York's Latin music scene has ever examined exactly how music education, folklore, or instrument making were connected to the evolution of an identifiable sound. As demonstrated in the following chapters, musicians specializing in Spanish Caribbean music in New York studied and synthesized as many sources as possible to cultivate a personal sound that was grounded in tradition, including classical, jazz, and Spanish Caribbean folkloric music. Specific arranging techniques, harmonic concepts, instrumental techniques, and even specific musical instruments contributed to forging an original sound that became a standard for contemporaries, not only in New York and the United States, but beyond the continental shores as well.

New York City is an important site in the history of the transnational Latin music scene because there was no other place in the Americas where such large numbers of people from throughout the Caribbean region came together to make music under one banner. The uniqueness of the New York sound from 1940 to 1990 can best be explained as the melding of jazz and North American music, folklore, and Spanish Caribbean popular dance music (Cuban, Puerto Rican, Dominican) into something distinct from what these genres sounded like in their home countries.

BEYOND ARSENIO RODRÍGUEZ

The history of Latin music is still visible around the city today. In addition to Arsenio Rodríguez, there are streets named after some of the greatest Spanish Caribbean musicians in the world who made their homes in New York City: Vocalists Lupe Victoria Yolí a.k.a. "La Lupe" and Frank Grillo a.k.a. "Machito" from Cuba; composer Mike Amadeo and *cuatro* virtuoso Yomo Toro from Puerto Rico; East Harlem's own Ernest "Tito" Puente; and Bronx piano legend Charlie Palmieri. All of these musicians called New York City their home whether they were born in New York, Puerto Rico, or Cuba. They created long-lasting and memorable art in New York City that still makes people dance and reflect.

It takes a little digging to uncover the history of how, what, and why this happened in New York, but the recordings, venues, magazines, newspapers, instruments (and their builders), and the musicians and dancers themselves, tell an amazing story that weaves together many seemingly disparate strands: *jíbaros* (country folk of Puerto Rico) and *santeros* (followers of a Yoruba-derived religion from Cuba), doo-wop and chachachá, jazz and folkloric music from throughout the Caribbean. As detailed in subsequent chapters, these elements combined coherently on recordings from throughout this time period. Some experiments became standards and others novelties, but each reflected their New York City confection. In *Lost Sounds*, David Brooks argued convincingly that sound recordings fomented

> The integration of minorities into the social mainstream. Jews, Italians, and others who would hardly have been welcomed into the neighborhood in person carried their cultural values into many a genteel Victorian parlor through the medium of recordings.

In the case of Latin music in New York City, it was the music itself that had the power to "gradually break down [the] social barriers" that Brooks attributed to the recordings.[13] As shown throughout this study, this does not dismiss or diminish the historical facts of segregation and racism that Latinos, African Americans, and Jews experienced as New Yorkers nor does it fantasize a utopian past where all was peaceful between these ethnic groups. However, the music was a unifying force, and band makeup was based on musical merit and often independent of color and nationality. In an interview, Mario Bauzá described himself performing in a Pan-Caribbean group in New York City that played American music led by the trombonist Hi Clark:

> There was another trumpet player in the group called—they used to call him Chico [Guerreo?], a Puerto Rican trumpet player. And they had a guy by the name of Napoleon, played tenor, from Santo Domingo. Who—he had a West Indian guitar player named Lufu. He had another practically, everybody was West Indians or Latin or something like that.[14]

Thus, a band made up of West Indian, Cuban, Dominican, and Puerto Rican musicians was accepted professionally as long as the musicians' performance fulfilled the expectations of the bandleader and the audience.

This book relies heavily on interviews that I conducted as well as interviews conducted by others. The first two chapters of this book explore the unsung heroines and heroes who worked in music education and folkloric music, along with the history of Spanish Caribbean instrument makers in New York City. I explore many of the concepts that these educators emphasized in formal and informal training, as well as the influence of jazz and other rhythmic innovations, the connection to modern Cuban music, inter-ethnic collaboration, and family lineages.

Chapter 1 details the longstanding formal and informal Latin music education settings and networks in New York City, as well as some of the ways in which the musicians benefited from them. From the 1920s through 1950s, three Puerto Rican women, Maria Luisa Lecompte, Eduveges Bocanegra, and Victoria Hernández, taught some of the greatest pianists to emerge from the New York scene. Similarly, the Panamanian pianist Nicolás Rodríguez and the Cuban flautist Alberto Socarrás imparted musicianship, theory, and piano lessons to countless musicians who were influential performers, composers, and arrangers. The Afro-Latin folkloric music scene in New York was an incubator for musical innovation and preservation; musicians from across ethnic groups have studied, performed, and recorded ritual and folkloric genres. *Batá* drumming, rumba, bomba, and plena are but a few genres where inter-ethnic collaboration was actively encouraged. New York City, unlike sites within the Caribbean, offered a wide range of formal and informal study opportunities for musicians from throughout the Caribbean.

Chapter 2 details the important history and role of craftsmen based in New York City who produced and repaired traditional instruments used in the performance of Latin music. These individuals came from Cuban, Puerto Rican, Dominican, and Jewish communities, but their instruments physically represented the actual sound of Latin Music to New York and the world on widely disseminated recordings. Many of these instrument makers also sold their instruments beyond New York City and the United States. Builders and musicians in New York City worked together to create and modify the tools used to forge the sound of Latin music and diffuse both the instruments and their aesthetic throughout the world.

Chapter 3 is an in-depth study of Elio Osácar a.k.a. Sonny Bravo, whose career as an arranger and performer began in the 1950s. It also examines the rise, fall, and return of Típica 73, a pan-ethnic salsa group representative of the period 1973–80 that featured musicians from Panama, Dominican Republic, Cuba, Puerto Rico, and New Yorkers of Cuban, Puerto Rican, and Mexican descent. Key band members such as Sonny Bravo and Johnny Rodríguez represented important New York–based familial and musical lineages, but the group covered contemporary Cuban songs and pushed the boundaries of tradition through their instrumentation and performance. Their success was a direct result of musical innovation and negotiation. The band came to an abrupt end after a career-defining trip to Cuba, where they recorded with Cuban counterparts. Upon their return to the United States, they were branded as communist sympathizers. Today, despite continually shifting policies toward Cuba it is quite common for Cuban groups to perform in the United States and for US-based artists to work with Cuban-based artists without the concomitant bomb threats and politics of the period before the 1990s. It is important to examine Típica 73 within this greater musical and geopolitical context. This chapter presents musical transcriptions of Bravo's arrangements and solos and places his music and his family, via his own father's musical career, within the historical context of early twentieth-century Cuban migration to Tampa, Miami, and New York. There are numerous issues and claims surrounding the development and history of Spanish Caribbean music in New York City, but they are not usually backed up with the kind of musical evidence in this chapter. Many of the social and musical changes and political forces from the era can be seen through transcription and analysis, further demonstrating how unique New York City was compared to other locations in the circum-Caribbean.

The second section of the book consists of four chapters dedicated to four ethnic groups, three of which have been subsumed, overlooked, and underrepresented in the written history of Latin music in New York City, as well as one group whose musical contributions remain misunderstood. Each of these different ethnic groups—Panamanians, Puerto Ricans, Jews, and the Cubans who arrived in the Mariel Boatlift of 1980—made distinct and valuable contributions to Latin music in New York. Chapter 4 covers the overlooked legacy of the Panamanian musical community of Brooklyn and the greater New York metropolitan area. These musicians came to New York prepared to play any type of music and the chapter explores how Panamanian musicians positioned themselves and were positioned both musically and socially by their Latino and non-Latino colleagues in New York. As Latinos of Black West Indian descent, the New York Panamanians encountered racism among both Latinos and African Americans, but worked with these groups of musicians and others in a variety of settings. Numerous Panamanian musicians such as Princess Orelia Benskina, Nicolás Rodríguez, Walter Gene Jefferson, Frank Anderson, Victor Paz, Mauricio Smith, and many others successfully negotiated classical, jazz, Broadway, Caribbean, and Latin music scenes (often simultaneously) and created a considerable body of work that has not been previously analyzed or contextualized.

Chapter 5 examines New York–based Puerto Rican musicians and how they drew upon jazz to realize new creative possibilities that shaped the cosmopolitan sound of Latin music in New York. The Puerto Rican connection to jazz was extensive and encompassed a variety of styles and eras. Previous scholarship such as Ruth Glasser's excellent study, *My Music Is My Flag* (1998), focused on some of these same themes surrounding New York–based Puerto Rican musicians, but her work was limited to the time period of 1917–40. This chapter challenges the debate over salsa's patrimony and development, by demonstrating how particular Puerto Rican musicians in New York City were fluent in jazz and incorporated it into Latin music. Much discourse has unfortunately centered on pitting Puerto Rican against Cuban musicians or looking only at commercial or sociocultural considerations when considering Latin music in New York. Proficiency in both jazz and Latin music allowed Puerto Rican musicians to innovate in ways that did not happen in Puerto Rico or elsewhere.

Chapter 6 continues my previous work on the understudied, multidimensional relationship of New York Jews with Latin music.[15] This chapter details the historical depth of Jewish New Yorkers' involvement in Spanish Caribbean music by examining performance venues and events beyond the Catskills and the Palladium Ballroom as well as the specific contributions of Eydie Gormé, Abbe Lane, Barry Rogers, and the dancer Ira Goldwasser. Lane and Gormé, two female performers who both enjoyed long and commercially successful careers, have been omitted from every narrative of Latin music in New York. Finally, the chapter explores Jewish self-representations in Latin music and portrayals

of Jews by non-Jews in Latin music. While there have been Jewish performers
of Latin music throughout the Americas, Jewish New Yorkers' ongoing and
nuanced relationship to Latin music has been unique and distinct.

Chapter 7 discusses the immediate musical impact of the Cuban dancers
and musicians who arrived in New York City through the 1980 Mariel Boatlift.
The activities of Orlando "Puntilla" Ríos, Gerardo "Taboada" Fernández, Gabriel
"Chinchilita" Machado, Manuel Martín Olivera, Roberto Borrell, Daniel Ponce,
and others had long-term effects on the folkloric and Latin popular dance music scene in New York, the greater United States and generations of non-Cuban
musicians. Unlike previous waves of Cuban arrivals, the overwhelming majority
of these musicians were Afro-Cuban and they strengthened and reinvigorated
the Afro-Cuban ritual music and folkloric scenes in New York City and beyond.
Their personal stories also reveal the extent to which they became a part of the
fabric of New York City's jazz and Latin popular music scenes. Cuban musicians
of the Mariel generation changed the landscape of Latin music in New York in
profound ways that were not available to them in Cuba.

The conclusion draws the main themes together and offers ideas for a clearer
and more coherent overview of Latin music in New York, as well as ideas for
future scholarship. Cuban author Leonardo Padura Fuentes has presented ten
points to defend the position that salsa might or might not exist as a genre.[16]
Using this as a model, the conclusion presents ten themes from throughout
the book that show how musicians based in New York City shaped the international sound of Latin music. All of these are not treated in each chapter, but
they recur throughout and overlap considerably.

ELEGGUÁ THE TRICKSTER

I often wonder if I have listened to the same records that are used by some to illustrate points about the history of Latin music in New York. When I have spent
time as a youngster or as an adult with musicians and collectors such as Mario
Rivera, René López, or Andy González, they have each emphasized close, con-
centrated listening to recordings. I am a professional musician, and when I have
done this kind of listening by myself or in the company of the aforementioned
individuals, I hear artistry, hard work, attention to craft, history, and years of
training regardless of whether it's folkloric or dance music. I also pay attention
to clave adherence, solo improvisations, and vocal improvisations, among other
things. I fully recognize and support the need for scholarship of New York City's
Latin music—and of all music—that is informed by social, racial, ethnic, gender,
and cultural analyses; but music in and of itself never sounds "impoverished"
or lacking in technique, as suggested by Rondón. There is no doubt that this

positivist approach reflects my training as an ethnomusicologist; something that sounds "rich" to one listener may be "poor" for another, and this is because music is not a universal language; it is not mutually intelligible worldwide. Some scholars of Latin music in New York have focused exclusively on lyrical content, which sometimes speaks of violence and difficult circumstances, but what would specifically characterize an instrumental sound or arrangement to be what Rondón labels as a "poor" *sound*? In addition, the ongoing debate over the exclusive Cuban paternity of Latin music in New York makes even less sense from a listening standpoint. Everything produced in New York can't be compared to its Cuban analogue because the context is so distinct. I say this as a staunch defender and researcher of Cuban music. Cuban music in Cuba and Latin music in New York were developed in different places by different musical protagonists. Sometimes they intersected, but often they didn't, and this is important to remember. To think otherwise denies the validity and history of interesting innovations that New Yorkers have made to Latin music, some of which have been imitated in Cuba and elsewhere. It also denies the actual history of Cuban music (and Puerto Rican music), much of which has been recorded in New York City since the nineteenth century. Some musicians continued to connect with Cuba and other islands in unseen ways after 1959, as was the case for Sonny Bravo and Típica 73, who maintained close relations with their Cuban counterparts and shared billing at international performances. Similarly, multitudes of non-Cuban ritual drummers and folkloric musicians stayed connected to Cuban musical practices through playing music in ritual settings and in the secular settings of New York's parks.

Rondón's privileging of Cuban music and musicians seems to miss this point completely when he discusses how New York musicians were cut off from Cuba as a musical source. In his discussion of the 1960s, he offers the Joe Cuba hit "Alafia" (1966) as an example of removal from Cuba when it proves to be quite the opposite.[17] It is in fact, filled with Cuban language and folklore beyond its obvious title. The song's title is derived from the Yoruba expression *Ache Alafia ni* (may the divine energy bring you peace) and the rest of the song has other *cubanismos* (aspects of Cuban speech and culture) including the assertion that the composer is black ("*chocolate*"), not a *negro ñañamboro* (*abakuá* spirit dancer), but that he still has a good sense of clave and enjoys rumba. In this way, the Afro–Puerto Rican composer Jimmy Sabater is at once distancing himself from and positioning himself and his band with respect to his New York Afro-Cuban predecessor Machito who had a hit with the song "Negro Ñañamboro." The song's choral refrain is a common ritual refrain for the Yoruba and Santeria spirit of the wind and the graveyard known as *Oyá*.

This is much more than a New York Puerto Rican resignification of Cuban music, because the song demonstrates that musicians were indeed steeped in these folkloric traditions to such an extent that they became their own, and that they were quite comfortable and knowledgeable working within and beyond the scope of folklore and its expectations. In addition, the musical arrangement uses jazz harmonies and instrumentation (through the vibraphone) to expand upon the *son montuno* format. Furthermore, Sabater riffed on Machito as a framework that was established and recorded in New York City, rather than in Cuba. Thus the Joe Cuba performance of "Alafia" should be viewed as what Samuel Floyd Jr. called a "moment" in the Afro-Latin diasporic landscape of New York City, which is part of a longstanding and ongoing circum-Caribbean flow, and the musico-cultural transaction in play is the transformation of the "Negro Ñañamboro."[18] Here is Elegguá, the trickster. As the song lyrics suggest: "*El que sabe sabe sabe, el que no, que se quede bruto*" (He who knows, knows, knows; He who doesn't stays stupid). The music speaks for itself if we are listening to what it says.

FINAL THOUGHTS

The goal of this book is to offer a new understanding of exactly how Spanish Caribbean popular music was made and formally transmitted among musicians in New York City from 1940 to 1990. A different history is revealed by looking beyond the repeated tropes of a few major protagonists. Talking to musicians and listening to the recordings demonstrates that for every individual musician who has been championed in the history books of this music, there were many other contemporaries who have not been credited for their equally important contributions. Furthermore, many dates that have been repeatedly given as definitive firsts for Latin music have turned out to be incorrect.

Latin music collectors and musicians in New York seem to have a better sense of the historical chronology of Latin music in New York because they deal with primary sources like recordings, but scholars have largely dismissed their importance. Directed listening is something that both musicians and collectors practice regularly. Recordings are transcribed and analyzed, but also shared among musicians for their musical information and history. Collectors and independent researchers are constantly finding new information that has previously eluded those who write and publish the history of Latin music. Thanks to one determined independent researcher and collector, Richard Blondet, we now know that the Fania All-Stars' performance at Yankee Stadium, celebrated as the first time that Latin music was played in the "House that Ruth Built," was not the first time this happened. Although undated, an advertisement, most likely from sometime between 1952–56, shows otherwise (see figs. I.3 and I.4).[19] Most likely, Johnny Seguí and Miguelito Valdés took to

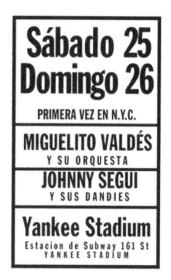

Fig I.3. Advertisement enlargement from unknown Spanish-language newspaper for performances at Yankee Stadium in 1946 or 1956. Photo courtesy of Kenneth O'Banyoun.

the stage at Yankee Stadium and became the "first" Latin musicians to perform there—until someone discovers evidence of an even earlier performance by another group of musicians. The written history of Latin music in New York City is still missing many key pieces and often-repeated statements of fact are simply incorrect.

This project is the culmination of thirty years as a professional musician and many more as a New York City resident, along with many years as a scholar. On a personal note, I have performed, recorded with, and lived close to many of the musicians in this study, both as a teenager and as an adult; our conversations have provided the initiative to document their history and the unwritten history of Latin music in New York City. Like most New Yorkers, I have lived in multiple parts of the city. When I first moved to New York City at the age of fourteen I lived in Brooklyn, and soon relocated to Manhattan. My neighborhood was filled with Latin music, musicians, food, *botánicas*, and other expressions of Latinidad. Thinking back on this experience as a young man resonates when I read Laó-Montes explain that:

As the oldest and most cosmopolitan world city of the Americas, New York is a borderland of global latinidad and a crossroads of Latino/American and Caribbean diasporas. Indeed, New York can be described as a microcosm of world cultures. This is partly motivated by metropolitan imperial desire (i.e. New York Centrism) but it also reveals the character of the city as a global crossroads, a City of Elegguá.[20]

Fig I.4. A closeup of the collage. Photo courtesy of Gregorio Marcano.

Elegguá is the Yoruba orisha of the crossroads. Religious ceremonies in the Yoruba tradition of *la regla de ocha* begin and end with Elegguá, who is associated with children, crossroads, and being known as the trickster; these beliefs came to the New World, Cuba, and the United States through slavery and subsequent migration. It's hard not to see through the lens of Yoruba cosmology when reflecting on the Arsenio Rodríguez street-naming ceremony discussed earlier. A group was gathered at the crossroads to commemorate and mark an important person and history, but the trickster had to make everyone sweat and laugh when removing the paper sign covering initially appeared to be a problem. Latin music in New York has opened up many worlds to me, and it began even before I moved to New York City. In my early years I was exposed to Latin music through my father's record collection and his piano playing. I continue to pursue my interest in the topic as a performer and scholar with a childlike curiosity that reminds me of how immense the world is. There is always more to learn and more to listen to; this often makes me feel like a child. It is my hope that this work will be of use to students and will open them up to further study. At the same time it is directed to musicians and fans of the music as well as scholars; I consider myself to be a member of each of these groups.

New York and the International Sound of Latin Music
1940–1990

CHAPTER 1

LATIN MUSIC EDUCATION IN NEW YORK

As I discuss in the introduction, it is a common misperception that musicians performing Spanish Caribbean popular music in New York City lack formal musical training and that the "university of the streets" is the principal locale for disseminating musical information and technique. Nothing could be further from the truth. This chapter details the formal and informal Latin music education settings and networks in New York as well as the ways in which musicians benefited from them. Some of the institutions explored include the East Harlem Music School, the Harbor Conservatory, and New York City public schools such as Music and Art High School in Manhattan and PS 52 in the Bronx that served as meeting grounds for musicians, and provided both rehearsal and performance opportunities for aspiring musicians. Private instructors taught theory, solfège, and instrumental technique to the most prominent musicians in Latin dance music.

Informal listening sessions among collectors of Latin music in New York City also served as educational opportunities and basic training for a number of musicians. Ensembles dedicated to specific genres of Cuban, Dominican, and Puerto Rican folkloric music can be seen as important incubators for Latin popular music groups in New York City, but they have also functioned as a primary site for Latin music education. Mentoring of younger musicians by older musicians has remained a constant of the New York Latin music scene and is responsible for maintaining the intergenerational characteristic of many bands, but also ensures the passage of musical history and technique from one generation to the next. In addition, many musicians have spent considerable time in New York helping fashion the New York "sound" before moving back to their home countries, recognized as heroes and acknowledged by subsequent generations as legends whose advice, teaching, and performance are sought out and emulated. Finally, interviews with a number of musicians who have attained artistic success in New York and beyond reveal the importance of New York as an educational hub crucial for success as a musician dedicated to playing Latin music.

PRIVATE STUDIO INSTRUCTION BY THREE PUERTO RICAN WOMEN

The first group of educators associated with performers of Latin music in New York City did not teach Spanish Caribbean popular music or necessarily encourage its practice, yet they taught a substantial number of Spanish Caribbean popular musicians who would go on to achieve professional and artistic success. These early educators who served the Spanish Caribbean community included three Puerto Rican women: Victoria Hernández, Maria Luisa Lecompte, and Eduviges Bocanegra. Hernández was the sister of Rafael Hernández, the great Puerto Rican musician, composer, and recruit in the 369th Infantry orchestra, whose unit became world famous as the "Harlem Hellfighters." In 1928 Victoria Hernández founded a record label, Disco Hispano. A year earlier, in 1927, she "Opened the Hernández record store on Madison Avenue. She sold 78-rpm records, pianola rolls, maracas, guitars, and guitar strings. A room at the back of the store housed a piano to teach students."[1] Hernández helped handle her brother's business affairs and can be seen as an early example of Puerto Rican women asserting their musical and business independence in post–World War I New York City. Although Hernández was intimately familiar with Latin popular music, with her own students she emphasized basic musicianship, technique, and appreciation for musical works of the Western canon. This personal bias in music education can be seen in a 1981 interview with Max Salazar, in which she states: "During the mid-to-late 1930s, two of my students were Tito Puente and Joe Loco. Tito told me to tell his mother that he liked to play drums instead of the piano."[2]

Puente and fellow percussionist Joe Quijano were two of many musicians who studied with another classically trained Puerto Rican female musician based in New York City, Maria Luisa Lecompte de Varona, the mother of Machito pianist Luis Carlos Varona, whom she also taught to play piano.[3] Lecompte's husband was a Cuban concert violinist named Luis Humberto Varona. The couple lived at 234 W. 114th Street. Lecompte was born in Puerto Rico and, after studying violin with her father, spent time at the Conservatory of Music in Havana, Cuba, and later lived in Santiago de Cuba.[4] Lecompte came from a family of professional musicians in Puerto Rico, and she performed there extensively as early as 1901.[5] According to Callejo Ferrer's 1915 study of musicians on the island of Puerto Rico, she was the only woman who "occupied a preferred post in the opera orchestra."[6]

LeCompte's music school was located at 112 E. 116th Street, between Park and Lexington avenues. Percussionist and bandleader Joe Quijano took the subway from the Bronx to 116th Street to study piano and solfège in Lecompte's storefront music school and later studied with Eduviges Bocanegra in the

Bronx.[7] Quijano remembered other students who studied with both Victoria Hernández and Maria Luisa Lecompte included Charlie and Eddie Palmieri, Paquito Pastor, Hector Rivera, and Arte Azenzer.[8] In addition to studying solfège, Quijano worked with the Hanon method, Alfred Burgemüller's books, and loose sheets of Chopin as well as pop songs from the era such as "Beautiful."[9] Lecompte taught one student at a time for three dollars per lesson. Quijano recalled that he only worked on classical music with Lecompte during the one year that he was her pupil, but at that time he knew that her son, Luis Varona, taught and played Latin popular music. An advertisement for Lecompte's school in *La Prensa* notes that she used the "plan of the Paris Conservatory" for piano, violin, and solfège and harmony.[10]

Lecompte organized public recitals for her students in New York City. A 1938 article in *La Prensa* describes a concert program to be given at Casa Valencia by Lecompte's fifth- and sixth-year students; the program included works by Chopin and Beethoven, but the theme of the program was "*Armonías Americanas*" (American harmonies) and was conceived by the director of the Pan-American League of Students of New York.[11] Assemblyman Oscar García Rivera spoke at the event. A review of the concert with a picture of the best student, Viola Echevarría, who was elected "*La reina de la música*" (the queen of music), said that it was a success and that after the awards were handed out, and remarks were made, all the participants danced to the house band.[12]

Another public recital was held one afternoon at the El Toreador club/restaurant and the reviewer indicated that each of the participants, all with Spanish names, earned "repeated applause."[13] Another review of one of Lecompte's annual student recitals at El Torreador states that her husband Luis Varona performed some of his own compositions on violin with Lecompte accompanying him; the couple is publicly acknowledged for "their important work of developing, in the metropolis, the musical education of so many students, children and adults in our colony [Spanish-speaking neighborhood]."[14]

It is interesting that Lecompte held her recitals in places such as El Toreador and Casa Valencia, the latter of which was a cabaret located at 300 W. 45th Street that would later became the Cuban Casino. Despite the fact that these venues were not recital halls, their location in midtown Manhattan, away from the center of the Latino community, meant that they were also intended for non-Latino audiences and thus deemed "respectable."

Scholar Lorrin Thomas writes that Lecompte was aware of the political movement of the *colonia hispana* of the late 1930s and the plight of Puerto Ricans.[15] Lecompte and Varona can be seen performing on a program commemorating the sixty-second anniversary of the proclamation of the Republic of Puerto Rico that was sponsored by the New York delegation of the Nationalist Party of Puerto Rico on September 23, 1930.[16]

Lecompte's obituary states that she taught piano and violin for twenty-five years in Cuba, Puerto Rico, and New York, "graduating 7 students" in addition to being a member of the Chopin Society, the Association of Music Teachers of New York, and the Ateneo of Puerto Rico.[17] Her "advocacy for the social better-ment of [Spanish-speaking people] and children's education" is also singled out in the obituary.[18] Lecompte was also socially minded as an active performer in New York City; she lent her musical talents to noble causes such as performing the Puerto Rican national anthem at the opening of the Festival of the Associa-tion for Blind Hispanic Americans.[19]

Lecompte's student Quijano also studied for one year with the piano teacher Eduviges Bocanegra, who taught lessons in her third-floor apartment at the corner of Kelly Street and Longwood Avenue across from PS 39.[20] Quijano did not know if Bocanegra played Latin dance music, but he did recall that "she would whack you with *timbal* sticks" to correct his hand positions at the piano.[21]

Another pianist who had visited, but not studied at, Lecompte's school is Paquito Pastor. Pastor, who grew up on 111th Street between Park and Madi-son avenues, also remembers that Luis Varona taught piano at Lecompte's school and that Gil Suarez was one of his students. Pastor recalled not having the one dollar that Varona charged per lesson, but he knew that Varona was a great teacher because Varona would walk around the room and hear that the student was playing the wrong notes and identify them.[22] Pastor studied at the New York Schools for Music for one dollar a lesson, though the initial rate was thirty-five cents a lesson. Throughout his youth Pastor's teachers pushed classical repertoire by DeFalla and Albeñiz, and some of his teach-ers such as Billie Cane and Josefina Andrade also pushed classical repertoire even though they played with Latin dance bands. Generally speaking, Pastor felt that pianists who played Spanish Caribbean dance music did not want to teach him or any up-and-coming young players "because they were thought to be competition."[23]

Pastor also studied with the legendary Puerto Rican pianist and educator simply known as Bocanegra in the 1970s, and he remembered her large apart-ment, and excellent piano, to be located either on Tiffany near Prospect Avenue or on Longwood Avenue.[24] He remembered Bocanegra as a "very methodical" teacher and that she was able to solve his technique problems in "four or five lessons."[25] Pastor had pain in his fingertips from playing loudly and extending them outward in dance band situations. Bocanegra used a ruler to emphasize that he curl his fingers to play correctly and emphasized classical music and technique. Pastor also confirmed that Eddie Palmieri was a student of hers. Pas-tor recalled that her husband had been a musician and that Bocanegra herself played in bands in the 1940s and early 1950s. Like Lecompte, Bocanegra also organized public recitals for her students that were also written about in *La*

Prensa. In these reviews, her students were singled out for their "surprisingly advanced execution of musical pieces."[26]

Margo Bartolomei was another student of Bocanegra for roughly two to three years from the age of eleven or twelve. As an adult, Bartolomei would achieve fame as part of the mambo dance team of Augie and Margo that I discuss later. She recalled that Bocanegra "knew some *danzas* . . . I used to play boogie woogie for her and she said 'I liked the way you played that' and not to give up the classical."[27] Bartolomei recalled that her lessons with Bocanegra were given in Spanish and focused entirely on classical music such as Beethoven, the Hanon book, the Eslava book, and learning scales. Bartrolomei also remembered learning the *danza* "*La bella trigueña*" in her lessons with Bocanegra.

Not much else is known about Eduviges Bocanegra Pino. The 1920 census of Puerto Rico lists her as a twenty-nine-year-old black single woman, with the occupation of piano teacher, and a resident of Guayama.[28] Other documentation has her living at 244 W. 136th Street in Manhattan.[29] An April 14, 1941, article in *La Prensa* documents one of Bocanegra's own performances in New York sponsored by the Department of Children's Literature at the New York Public Library on 174 E. 110th Street, indicating that she was going to perform a selection of "danzas by Puerto Rican composers."[30]

Bocanegra's student Paquito Pastor recalled being rebuffed by a renowned Cuban composer and music publisher with legendary musical technique with whom he wished to study. However, he did study solfège or *solfeo* with a Puerto Rican teacher named Adolfo Mesorana on West 116th Street in the 1950s.[31] Mesorana's advertisement in *La Prensa* announces instruction for every instrument but focuses on "preparation of singers for radio, television, theaters, etc., and modern orchestrations."[32]

Santiago Mesorana (unrelated) was another Puerto Rican musician who taught at Juan Mas's music school at 727 Avenue of the Americas. As chronicled in the *New York Post*, students received private lessons from 6:30–8pm on Mondays, Wednesdays and Fridays before the full ensemble rehearsed. The music school provided instruction to "boys and young men, 11 to 21, of Puerto Rican and other Spanish background," and they performed as the Banda Hispana Los Granaderos, which was formed in August 1958. Mas explained, "the main reason for forming the band was to combat delinquency" and that playing a "musical instrument is the best thing for mental and physical soundness." By Mesorana's estimation, "80 percent of the boys have never touched a musical instrument before they came here, [but] they all soon develop great interest and the desire to play the music."[33] Mesorana's most well-known student would be Hilton Ruiz, who I profile in the chapter on Puerto Rican musicians. At the age of eight, Ruiz debuted at Carnegie Hall performing a solo recital of Mozart and Chopin.[34]

PRIVATE STUDIO INSTRUCTION IN MIDTOWN MANHATTAN WITH THREE MEN: OSVALDO ALÉN, NICOLÁS GOODWIN RODRÍGUEZ, AND ALBERTO SOCARRÁS

In the 1950s a gifted Cuban pianist named Osvaldo Alén ran a music instruction studio in midtown Manhattan and raised his family on the West Side of Manhattan. The focus of Alén's lessons was classical music and light-classical Cuban genres such as *contradanza* and *zarzuela*. Born in Cienfuegos, Cuba, Alén had been the organist and choral director of the cathedral in his hometown. After relocating to Havana and performing in various nightclubs, he signed a contract in 1955 to become a regular performer at El Liborio, one of New York's most celebrated Cuban restaurants. The contract covered moving costs and transportation to New York City, paid $75 per week, and included meals. Alén was also active as a performer beyond El Liborio and can be seen in nightlife photos from various newspapers playing with numerous Latin American and Caribbean musicians (such as his contemporary Noro Morales), actors, politicians, and celebrities in a variety of circumstances.[35]

Alén's studio was located at 1687 Broadway, Suite #2, at the corner of 53rd Street; his business card advertised modern courses of music, piano, voice, and repertoire. While it is unclear if he taught any Cuban popular music, it is known from concert programs and newspaper clippings that he performed a wide range of Cuban music including popular and light-classical genres. The studio space that Alén taught in was also used to host press events for visiting Cuban artists such as Tony de la Fuente and Roberto Gormes. Although Alén also performed at El Rancho, boxer Patsy Álvarez's restaurant, and in Carnegie Hall on a number of occasions, he was best known for his tenure at El Liborio.[36] In New York, Alén also performed in patriotic concerts to help the Cuban rebels and continued to perform in concerts that supported the new revolutionary government.

Alén's son, the distinguished Cuban musicologist Olavo Alén, recalled an interesting story involving his father and the new Cuban leader, Fidel Castro.[37] When Castro came to the United States on April 15, 1959, he was disappointed that President Eisenhower would not meet him; and after finishing his obligations at the Council of Foreign Affairs he and his entourage headed into Central Park, looking for someone welcoming the group before it headed to El Liborio for dinner. Upon entering the restaurant, half of the clientele turned their backs and remained seated while the other half stood at attention. Osvaldo Alén immediately started playing the Cuban national anthem. Castro later approached Alén to thank him for his patriotism and asked him about returning to Cuba.

Fig 1.1. Osvaldo Alén performing at El Liborio 1958. Photo courtesy of Olavo Alén.

Alén replied that his teaching studio was thriving and that he was planning on staying in New York City. The Cuban leader left with the promise that if Alén ever needed anything in the future that he should not hesitate to ask. Shortly after this encounter, Alen's studio caught fire and was destroyed. For many Cubans living outside of Cuba it seemed that the increasing US-Cuba hostilities would make it difficult to get back into Cuba with their families.

Up to that point, Alen's three sons were New Yorkers and attended local public schools on the Upper West Side. Alén taught his sons, and in the late 1950s two of them performed Ignacio Cervantes's "La Camagüeyana" for four hands live on WHOM. With the clock ticking and looking at the uncertainty of the situation, Alén packed his family and returned to Cuba. After the family's arrival, another chance encounter with Fidel Castro led Alén to become a music educator and also helped him secure a good piano. All three of Alén's sons would go on to have musical careers, two as performers and one as one of Cuba's preeminent musicologists.

Two teachers stand out as having had the greatest impact on at least two generations of Latin music performers: Nicolás Goodwin Rodríguez and Alberto Socarrás. As demonstrated below, their instruction was sought out by musicians of different ethnicities to improve their musicianship and technique.

Although Nicolás Goodwin Rodríguez is discussed as a performer in the chapter on Panamanians, here is a quick introduction. He was born September

Fig 1.2. Alberto Socarrás (from *Cuba Musical*, 1929).

10, 1906, and after gaining a solid musical education and experience as a musician he left Panama and began playing with Jelly Roll Morton (1929–30). Rodriguez subsequently recorded with Benny Carter (1932–34), played with the Spike Hughes Orchestra (1933), and later joined Don Redman (1938–43).[38] He worked briefly with Louis Armstrong, but devoted the remainder of his time to teaching and also performing Latin music. Throughout his career in the United States, Rodríguez's first name was listed as Nick or Nicholas.

Alberto Socarrás Estacio (1903–1987) was a Cuban flautist who is widely regarded by jazz historians as being the first musician to record a jazz flute solo when he appeared on Clarence Williams's "Shootin' the Pistol" in 1927. He also worked as a sideman with Benny Carter and Erskine Hawkins, and as musical director with Cuban artists such as Anacaona and others. Prior to arriving in New York, Socarrás was something of a musical prodigy in his native Manzanillo, Cuba, where he studied with Segismundo Estrada Palma and Angel Castro Virella before entering Rafael Inciarte's Children's Academy as first flautist in the children's band. Throughout this time, he continued his studies in solfège and theory with his mother, with whom he had been studying since the age of nine. In 1916 Socarrás joined the municipal band, played flute in the Teatro Popular, and was clarinetist for what must have been his family's band, Familia

Estacio. In 1920 Socarrás left Manzanillo and toured with a Cuban zarzuela company before picking up the saxophone in 1923 and working in different bands at the Campoamor, Fausto, Cubano, [and] Plaza [hotel] theaters. He left for New York in April 1927 and was hired by Clarence Williams one month later as a porter, working in his office, and making records with him.[39] Socarrás achieved great success in New York and can even be seen playing the flute in the dance lesson scene of the Lana Turner and Ricardo Montalbán feature film *Latin Lovers* (1953).[40] However, Socarrás is best known in the community of Latin musicians as a specialist in solfège.

STUDYING WITH RODRÍGUEZ AND SOCARRÁS

Some of Nicolas Rodríguez's noted students include Paquito Pastor, Oscar Hernández, Gilberto "Pulpo" Colón Jr., Sergio Rivera, Michael LeDonne, John Henry Goldman, Benjamin Bierman, and Guillermo Edgehill. Conversations with these musicians indicate that Rodríguez approached each student uniquely and tailored his lessons to what he thought the student needed, but also what the student was seeking from him. World-renowned arranger, pianist, and bandleader Oscar Hernández studied with Rodríguez when he was eighteen years old. Hernández began playing at the age of fourteen and was mostly self-taught. Up until that time, Hernández believed that one had to play the piano as forcefully as possible, like his then idol Eddie Palmieri.[41] Hernández's first professional performance was with Joey Pastrana at Club Union on New Year's Eve in 1971, and he continued to work professionally with many bands on the circuit. In 1973 Hernández was playing with vocalist Ismael Miranda five or six times per week, and around this time, he remembers, Victor Paz or Mauricio Smith suggested that he study with Nicolás Rodríguez. It's noteworthy that both Paz and Smith were friends of Rodríguez and that all three were Panamanian. However, what is more important is that both Paz and Smith were two of the best-prepared musicians who played Latin music on the scene. Both also taught countless students and were well studied in classical instrumental technique. Hernández remembers Rodríguez's studio as being located on 52nd Street between 8th and 9th avenues, across from the Cheetah Club.

For Hernández, Rodríguez was "strictly known as a teacher," and while he was aware of his classical background and Juilliard affiliation, he did not know that Rodríguez had an extensive career as a jazz musician.[42] Although Hernández studied with Rodríguez for no more than a year, he remembered that Rodríguez would repeatedly joke with the young pianist and ask which was heavier, "a pound of lead or a pound of feathers?"[43] Referring to the *montunos* that Hernández was playing night after night, Rodríguez pointed out that "repetition causes tension."[44] He urged Hernández to use the "normal weight of [his] body" and imparted the concept of "relaxing technique" and playing in a relaxed fashion so that the player would be "throwing the natural weight of the hand" on the keys.[45] This was revolutionary for Hernández, and much later he further explored "The Taubman Method" with Maria del Pico Taylor, a disciple of Dorothy Taubman, based at Temple University.[46]

Hernández's close friend Gilberto "Pulpo" Colón Jr. also studied with Nicolás Rodriguez but got there through a more circuitous route. Colón was born and raised in New York but spent a number of years living in Puerto Rico; he self-identifies as Puerto Rican and not as a Nuyorican. Colón started studying music formally at PS 111 in Queens as a snare drummer in fourth grade. Colón moved to the Bronx in 1963 and by fifth grade he started with the trumpet, but he continued to study drum set privately. Through seventh to ninth grade Colón continued with trumpet and private drum lessons. In school he showed an Anglo teacher Cortijo's music with a conga and he was amazed that the teacher could write out the rhythm but not feel it. Colón's reading improved and he was most impressed by trombonist Johnny Colón's marriage of jazz, blues, and boogaloo that represented the new sound of Latin music made in New York City. Colón was playing second trumpet in the school band at Roosevelt High School and befriended Oscar Hernández, who at the time was playing first trumpet. To this day, Hernández remains his biggest influence. On breaks, Colón and Hernández would take turns "banging out tunes" on a school piano in an auditorium.[47] In 1968 Hernández started studying with a Puerto Rican pianist named George Gould, who was a student of Larry Harlow.[48] Colón had been studying with another teacher, but soon followed in his *compadre*'s footsteps and switched to study with Gould as well. Gould taught both young pianists to play Mozart and Bach, but did not teach them Latin music.

Colón then studied with Charlie Palmieri, who also did not want to teach the young pianist any Latin music. At twenty dollars per lesson, Palmieri started Colón with finger exercise methods such as Hanon, Czerny, and then Clementi's sonatinas; successful completion was met with the reward of a Gm6 (G-B♭-D-E) montuno played with both hands in octaves. This did not deter the aspiring pianist, and Palmieri came to see Colón play a year into his studies. Later he would send Colón to sub for him in Tito Puente's band. Colón still felt that he wanted to learn more Latin music from Palmieri, and he continued studying with him for two years until Palmieri told him he was no longer teaching. Sometime before Colón's lessons with Palmieri ended, Palmieri suggested that Colón should study with Alberto Socarrás.

Colón studied with Socarrás from 1970 to 1973.[49] Socarrás did not want Colón to be a singer, but asked his student to sing slowly and to hear pitches. One aspect of Socarrás's lessons was to trade phrases while snapping the *son clave* or a 6/8 pattern. If the pitches were off and not in tune, Socarrás would pick up the flute to be sure that his student was more precise with his intonation. Generally speaking, each lesson was based on specific exercises in the Hilario Eslava book.[50] This book, most likely what Socarrás himself learned with, remains the main instruction book in Cuba and the Spanish-speaking world. During Colón's lessons, Socarrás stressed the importance of clave when improvising *"para que no choque,"* (so it would not cross the clave), but not in relation to the piano or the montuno. Colón felt that Socarrás primarily emphasized 3–2 clave, which was not in vogue at the time that he was studying with him. Colón also felt that his main purpose in studying with Socarrás was to improve his musicianship and not necessarily to focus on clave.

Other prominent students of Socarrás included Joe González, Ronnie Baró, Omar Castellanos, Ronnie Amoróz, and Rubén Rodríguez. Percussionist Joe González remembered "making it through to the second book" before ending his lessons.[51] Whereas vocalist Ronnie Baró remembered studying with Socarrás from 1978–82/83 and that during their lessons he used all of the books by Eslava, Pozoli, and Dannhauser and with a moveable "do."[52] Baró related that his training with Socarrás was so thorough that, when some musicians in the Cuban university system came to visit Socarrás in New York, they told Baró and his teacher that in Cuba he would be at a doctoral level in sight singing and musicianship.[53]

Colón explained that with "Socarrás, for all intents and purposes, I got my reading and my ear to a point where I started doing recordings. So it paid off and I started understanding what not to do. I might have not readily understood what to do, which is ok, I got that from Ray Maldonado, but he [Socarrás] taught me what not to do."[54] For Colón, these lessons really paid off during recording sessions for Fania Records that required sight-reading at $75/song. Colón would schedule his lessons with Socarrás to be right before his piano lessons with Nicolás Rodríguez, since their studios were two blocks away from one another. Although the two teachers had worked together on the bandstand and in the studio in the 1950s, Colón recalls reconnecting Socarrás and Rodríguez as their student in common, and that Rodríguez would subsequently hire Socarrás on lounge gigs.[55]

As noted above, Colón came to study with Nicolás Rodríguez through his friend Oscar Hernández between 1972 and 1974. Rodríguez gave Colón lessons in Spanish. Colón was eighteen when he began with Rodríguez and was impressed with his new teacher's sight-reading abilities. Rodríguez was impressed with his student's persistence in getting through reading a piece of music. Colón felt that the ability to never say no and to continue through a piece of music is a lesson that has stayed with him to this day, saying, "he [Rodríguez] taught me, *métele*, it's better to make a mistake than to sit there and be [a wimp]."[56]

Colón subsequently taught piano at Johnny Colón's music school and taught this concept for sixteen years. Rodríguez also worked on Colón's touch, "where the finger hits on the key," and how to produce the best possible sound.[57] Colón felt that his lessons were the next step from the three- and four-note phrasing learned with Charlie Palmieri. Rodríguez focused his student on achieving richer tone in a variety of velocities and how to relax and play from his shoulders. Interestingly, Colón's colleagues felt that he was getting "wimpy" from playing "pianistically" on live gigs as a result of his studies, but he could see and hear the results himself in the recording studio: "I didn't have to bang no more and when I had to do a run, if I relaxed then it came out easier. . . . Nick took my playing to another level."[58]

In other conversations with Rodríguez's former students, some spoke of Rodríguez's concept of physical positioning vis à vis the keyboard.[59] Colón explained it as follows: "He would tell you, you gotta sit between middle C and E, and D hits your belly button. That breaks, that splits the keyboard in half. When you're going to play on the left hand side of middle C, anywhere to the left, you shift, you put all your weight on your left *muslo* [thigh], you lift your right one up and *boom*, come back to the middle."[60] This allowed the player to play comfortably on each side of the keyboard without any disadvantages. Colón said that Rodríguez developed this technique when he was playing with Louis Armstrong after watching stride pianists shifting with the chair. As Colón explained it, the positioning was applicable to any style of music and worked well with the performance of Latin music.

Colón did work on some Latin music with Rodríguez, but the focus was more on playing extensions in that context and exploring chord voicings that Colón could use in playing a solo ballad or comping. More importantly, Rodríguez also taught Colón things about life that he needed to hear at that time. According to Colón, other notable pianists who studied with Nicolás Rodríguez included Alfredo Rodríguez, Lino Frías, Joe Mannozzi, Elvis Cabrera, Nestor Sánchez, Willie Rodríguez, and Sergio Rivera.[61] Colón felt that all of them were great pianists, but that Nicolás Rodríguez was able to teach each of them what he needed to improve and become even better.

Colón also verified the claim that Rodríguez put himself through school with his piano playing and that he "grew up real poor" in Panama.[62] In 1975 Colón played in Panama with Kako and brought back something for Rodríguez from a relative in Panama, further strengthening the bond between teacher and student.

So how would a talented musician like Colón improve his Latin piano playing and musicianship if these were not the main focus of his lessons and studies with Rodríguez and Socarrás? In 1977 or 1978, Colón was playing a José Febles arrangement of a Puerto Rican *aguinaldo* in Oakland, California, with

Hector Lavoe's band. The song shifted between 2–3 and 3–2 clave, and during the performance Eddie Montalvo screamed out that Colón was *cruzao* (crossed)—literally playing a piano ostinato in the wrong clave—in front of 15,000 people.[63] Trumpeter Ray Maldonado explained to Colón how to listen to the *cáscara* (shell of the timbales) pattern of the timbal part in 2–3 and 3–2 if he ever got lost again.[64] From that point on, Colón practiced transitioning between the two and listening more carefully. Playing with Nicky Marrero in his small group Ensalada de Pulpo also helped Colón deepen his understanding of playing in clave.

Trumpeter Ben Bierman is another musician who studied with both Rodríguez and Socarrás. Bierman toured with Johnny Copeland and other blues acts, but also played with a variety of Latin bands in New York including Conjunto Barroco, Rey Reyes, and others. He was studying with Vincent Penzarella when someone suggested that he study with Rodríguez sometime in 1980 or 1981. Bierman hooked up with Rodríguez when he was already in his seventies and the lessons took place in a studio on 73rd and Amsterdam Avenue in a side room of "an African American Broadway musical director and vocal coach" named Danny.[65] Bierman studied with Rodríguez for three years in the early 1980s and he was aware that in his heyday his teacher had worked all the time playing lounges, shows, jazz, and Latin gigs. Other students and friends told him that Rodríguez had paid his tuition for Juilliard all in cash because he was playing so many gigs. At Juilliard, Rodríguez studied with a disciple of the music theorist Percy Goetschius (1853–1943), who first published in 1889. Many years later, as Bierman familiarized himself with Goetschius's work, he would "appreciate, on an emotional level, the connection between Nick [Rodríguez] and . . . the early American tradition . . . the late 1800s, represented by Goetschius."[66] One particular aspect of the system that Rodríguez imparted was to treat diminished chords as incomplete dominant chords, indicated in figured bass as oV9.[67] Bierman was unsure if Rodríguez had learned Goetschius's system orally, but Rodríguez would dictate music theory notes and rules to Bierman, who would write them down. The lessons cost ten dollars each and began with scales and rules, then built up to chorales that teacher and student would analyze together. Like Bierman, Paquito Pastor wanted to study advanced arranging when he began lessons with Nick Rodríguez, but Rodríguez also "started [him] on four-part harmony."[68] Pastor studied with Rodríguez for six months and said that "everything he [Rodríguez] taught me I remember and I use it."[69]

Rodríguez insisted that his student write the chorales away from the piano. For a street-educated musician, Bierman felt that the process of learning the nuts and bolts of music theory from the bottom up as an adult provided him with new insights. Rodríguez also started from scratch at least five times, and Bierman enjoyed this approach when compared to other previous teachers like Adolph Sandoli. Bierman did not cover Latin or jazz in his lessons with Rodríguez; the focus was strictly on classical four-part writing. They also talked about reharmonizations of standards, and Bierman remembers that Rodríguez would constantly work on reharmonizing "Tenderly" in the styles of Art Tatum and Willie "The Lion" Smith. Rodríguez spoke often of Willie "The Lion" Smith, who he greatly admired and whom he aspired to play like. Often, Rodríguez proudly recounted to Bierman that Willie "The Lion" Smith had heard him play one night and that Smith told Rodríguez that he was a "very interesting musician," and suggested that they "should get together and talk about music sometime and share ideas on music."[70] Bierman started studying with Rodríguez in Manhattan but when Rodríguez moved to Brooklyn in 1987, he would study at Rodríguez's house on E. 44th Street and Foster Avenue. Bierman's musicianship improved greatly, he said:

> For me, more than being able to go back [to the beginning], what the lessons with Nick did for me were to help me write parts, to do inner voices, and how to handle writing for horns. . . . I knew chords really well by the time I went to Nick. I was pretty good, I had been writing pretty nice arrangements and I knew what I was doing, but it really helped with how to manipulate, particularly inner voices and gave me a lot of freedom away from the piano, and it helped my ear. I liked it 'cause it was old school. Same with Socarrás. They were old school, they did everything . . . I felt really lucky to have met them. I feel really fortunate to be with them and have them give me that education.[71]

Like Gilberto "Pulpo" Colón Jr., Bierman also studied with Socarrás for about a year at the suggestion of Penzarella. Socarrás covered alto, tenor, bass, and treble clefs in the lessons. Bierman recalled that every exercise they worked on in the Eslava book would be performed straight and while snapping 3–2 clave. Socarrás would rephrase the exercises when singing them in clave and encouraged his student to do the same, but he would never talk about or comment on the clave. The focus of singing the exercises in clave was to focus on phrasing. This demonstrates one way that New York–based Latin musicians would use European classical materials to teach and learn Spanish Caribbean music. For Bierman, Socarrás's delivery was always easy and floating. Bierman said:

> What I appreciated about them [Socarras and Rodríguez] was how effortless the negotiation [between classical and Caribbean] was. Of course they worked hard at it, right? So it's not like easy or something but it was totally natural. There was nothing about it that had to be intellectualized or [that] had to be questioned. They didn't even talk about it. It wasn't even discussed. It wasn't an issue, the differentiation between styles.[72]

Bierman's personal observation sums up the heart of this study: Spanish-Caribbean musicians in New York City have been able to negotiate a wide variety of musical styles that are often bound to specific racial and national divisions. Here in New York City, musical-culture borders are not always specific or limited to a map or a geographic space. Musicians in this scene were able to reconcile these musical and stylistic differences, because they needed to in order to earn a living, but also because they did not see the same divisions and differences that a simple black/white dichotomy presents. Spanish Caribbean musicians were able to move back and forth across musical borders easily and reconcile seemingly disparate worlds.

PLAYING SITUATIONS AND REHEARSAL BANDS AS EDUCATIONAL SETTINGS

Being a jazz and blues player, Bierman enjoyed playing *típico* (smaller, traditional Latin dance music) gigs more than larger salsa ensembles. Similar to "Pulpo" Colón's experience, for deeper understanding of clave-based music Bierman asked questions at rehearsals and on gigs and in this way his education in Latin music was largely informal or on the job training. Bierman noted that Latin players were welcoming to him and other non-Latino players. They were totally open to sharing information and explaining concepts. Trombonist Rick Davies echoed Bierman's feelings about getting musical help, including improvisation and rhythmic concepts from fellow instrument players like Jimmy Bosch.[73]

However, this treatment was not reciprocal: jazz players were not as welcoming to Latin musicians even though they could play jazz at the highest level.[74] Although some Latin musicians were playing club dates with jazz musicians, "the worlds were really separate."[75] This was unjustified as Bierman remembered seeing the Latin soloists outplay the jazz soloists at the Village Gate's Salsa Meets Jazz nights.[76] Ray Santos emphasized this point about Latin players and their abilities compared to non-Latin players, explaining why he "carefully indicates all the articulations and accents" in his arrangements:[77] "It's not like Latin players where you just give 'em a piece of paper with no phrasing or accents and they know exactly what to do. When you write for a band of students or non-Latino players you have to put the articulations in carefully and try and get the phrasing as close as possible."[78] There were bands with mixed players. Bierman played in a Latin club date group with tenor saxophonist Al Acosta, subbing for trumpeter Al Torrente. Bierman also played in a jazz big band at Lehman College with Willie Ruiz, Rubén Rodríguez, and a number of Latin musicians.

Reading and rehearsal bands like Lynn Oliver's were another setting where musicians from Latin and jazz worlds would meet. Alex Stewart explains the purpose, function, and idiosyncrasies of these bands, including intricacies of race, in his study of the New York City jazz big band scene. In describing how Oliver amassed such a coveted collection of music, Stewart writes: "Lynn Oliver, whose rehearsal studio was frequented by Gerry Mulligan, Horace Silver, the Basie Band, and many others, built a formidable library by photocopying the charts of every band that passed through."[79] Many Latino and Latin musicians such as Mario Rivera, Crispín Fernández, Al Acosta, and others paid the five-dollar fee to sit in the horn section of Oliver's reading band as a means of honing their craft and working on jazz section playing and sight reading. Stewart observes that "to play Latin jazz, musicians are expected to improvise fluidly, even over difficult chord progressions."[80] Clearly, New York–based Latin musicians put the time into mastering rhythmic and harmonic aspects of the music, more so than those who only played straight-ahead jazz. Ray Vega further highlighted the responsibility of the Latin jazz musician to be intimate with all aspects of both Latin and jazz music, emphasizing that for the successful musician, "if you're gonna do it for real, it's a question of [acquiring a deep] historical perspective."[81]

LATIN MUSICIANS AND FORMAL JAZZ AND CLASSICAL EDUCATION

As I detail in chapter 5 on Puerto Rican musicians, iconic musical architects such as Tito Puente and Ray Santos (Puente from 1945–47 and Santos from 1948–52) both studied music formally at Juilliard, not only, as some seem to assume, at "UCLA," satirically known as the University on the Corner of Lexington Avenue. Puerto Rican piano virtuoso Ricardo Ray, brother of trumpeter Ray Maldonado, was also a student at Juilliard. His classical chops are always on display during live performances, where he is known to please audiences with excerpts of Bach and other classical piano repertoire between salsa songs.

INFORMAL MUSICAL EDUCATION: CHICO ÁLVAREZ

Despite the presence of formal education opportunities for musicians performing Latin music in New York, the "university of the streets" remained a powerful force. Many musicians have described "on the job" learning opportunities in Latin music that they had as youngsters growing up in New York City. In the documentary *From Mambo to Hip Hop*, percussionist Benny Bonilla describes walking from bar to bar, asking if he could sit in with each group, staying to play the whole night, and feeling grateful for the opportunity.

Ernest "Chico" Álvarez Perraza (b. 1947), a Cuban vocalist, bandleader, and visual artist whose work is visible on hundreds of seminal album covers, had a similar experience. Born in 1947 at 127 or 125 Atlantic Ave in Brooklyn, Álvarez had a fascinating childhood moving back and forth between Eastern Cuba, Havana, Bridgeport, Connecticut, and New York City. Like Sonny Bravo's family history, detailed in chapter 3, this movement provided Álvarez with a unique cultural background. His US merchant marine father came to the United States in 1941 from Antilla, Cuba, and became a citizen in 1945.[82] Álvarez's mother and family had come to New York City as exiles in the 1930s, because the dictator Machado had Álvarez's great grandfather assassinated and his grandfather had a death warrant placed on him. In 1933, with Machado gone, the family went back to Havana. His mother returned to New York in 1945 and the Álvarez Per- raza family lived in Chelsea. In 1948, at the age of one, Álvarez and his mother returned to Havana until 1957. Álvarez attended Saint Patrick's Academy, a Catholic military school in Harriman, New York, for a semester and returned to Cuba for the summer. Both he and his family were unhappy with the school, and in 1958 he started school in Antilla, living with his paternal grandmother and aunt until 1962. Álvarez would visit New York every summer (1957–61), mastering English. As a result he was fluent in Cuban and North American mu- sical and popular culture. More importantly, while his mother was listening to Cuban music on radio programs such as *Caravana Cubana*, he fell in love with the music of Elvis Presley, the Platters, the Flamingos, Fats Domino, Bill Haley and the Comets. Back in Oriente he performed with a small combo dedicated to this music, but he also studied music theory with a teacher named Catalina. This pop music was also heard in Antilla, and Álvarez was Americanized to the point of being able to sing "'Rock Around the Clock' without an accent . . . they called me '*el americanito*'. . . . I'm a city kid in the summer and a country boy in the rest of the year there."[83]

Although he was a rock and roller, he was steeped in Cuban music of the day, such as Vicentico Valdés and José Fajardo, as well as Cuban carnival music. After the revolution American music was viewed negatively, and by 1961 it was removed from the jukeboxes and the radio, but Álvarez was too young to un- derstand why. In 1962 he left Cuba for good and arrived in New York, hearing Sam Cooke, Dinah Washington, Brook Benton, Aretha Franklin, the Drifters, and Ben E. King. Álvarez attended junior high school at PS 3 through ninth grade but had fights every day, so in 1963 his mother sent him to live with her relatives in Bridgeport, Connecticut, in the middle of the year. He would go on to graduate from Bridgeport Central High in 1965. During this time his interest in his Cuban identity surged, largely because he was living with Cubans who arrived in the 1960s and "never assimilated," as opposed to his parents' genera- tion of the 1940s, so "everywhere was Cuban and *pachanga* was the deal."[84] *El liceo cubano* was the main place to hear the groups of the day, like Joe Cuba, Joe Quijano, Charlie Palmieri, Johnny Pacheco, Joe Quijano, Joe Valle, Carlos Pizarro, and the venue also featured a local Cape Verdean and Puerto Rican house band called Los Melody Boys.

Álvarez was listening to Ray Barretto, Orlando Marín, Charlie and Eddie Palmieri: "All this Cuban music, it's not called salsa yet, that's how I got into it, via New York. It's like I rediscovered it. And I would hear [something familiar], Oh, I remember hearing that in Cuba. The New York bands would cover all the big hits in Cuba."[85] Álvarez would see bands at the Palladium like Monguito El Único singing with Johnny Pacheco during the summer of 1964 and knew he wanted to be involved with it. In October or November 1964 a dance was held with Charlie Palmieri's band in the Puerto Rican section of Bridgeport at a Polish venue called Sokol Hall.

Palmieri and a few of his musicians were lost and stopped Álvarez on the street asking him for directions and offered him a ride to the venue. Álvarez noticed that the car held congas and other instruments, so he struck a deal with them to carry in some of the instruments in order to avoid paying the entrance fee. Carrying a conga inside, Álvarez's Puerto Rican friends took note of their friend's closeness to the star, Palmieri. The band's singer, Victor Velásquez, and the timbalero had come in another car and were late and lost. Even though he was a rock and roller, Álvarez told Palmieri that he could cover for the singer and offered to sing "Vuela la paloma," "Cachita," and "Guantanamera." The high schooler climbed onstage, impressing his friends and the neighborhood girls, and was handed a cowbell. Never having played a cowbell in his life, the con-guero said "'Just play this [the cáscara pattern]. I said, 'oh no, that's too compli-cated.' So he says just play this [son cowbell pattern]" (see musical examples 1.1 and 1.2).[86] After singing his part for "Vuela la paloma" successfully, the conga player took a solo and sang the timbal bell pattern to Álvarez, who learned it on the spot. Seeing the timbalero and the singer rush in, he felt relieved because he doubted that he could hold the pattern all night. Eager to leave the stage, Álvarez was asked by Palmieri to stay and sing *coro* (background vocals) for the rest of the night. Then Palmieri asked the youngster:

> "Do you know how to play clave?" I said, "No." Charlie takes the clave and he shows me what to do, he says . . . but he didn't tell me nothing about 2–3 and 3–2 or none of that shit. So when the tune starts, I start on the wrong side and he says "No, no, no!" And he sings it to me and I flip it around and I play the clave straight through the whole number. This is my initiation, man, it's like a crash course in Cuban music. So at the end of the night you know, that's it, I went home and I was in heaven. All the guys from the neighborhood there from the East side, said "¡coño!" this guy knew Charlie Palmieri.[87]

Musical Example 1.1. Cáscara pattern (2–3 clave)

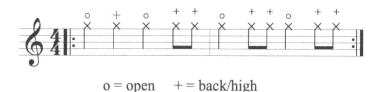

o = open   + = back/high

Musical Example 1.2. Son cowbell pattern (2–3 clave)

After that, Álvarez joined a rock band that played "El Watusi," and he continued learning and singing more Latin music. Upon graduating, Álvarez returned to New York City, where he continued to manage being a Cuban in two worlds, Italian and Puerto Rican; then he moved to Hoboken, New Jersey. At this time he started to develop his conga playing by going to the Central Park rumba. Among the largely Puerto Rican crowd of drummers, he remembered seeing Carlos "Patato" Valdéz there but not knowing who he was at that time. Álvarez was a self-taught conga player, but credits Marcelino Valdés with showing him proper two-hand technique. Álvarez started playing congas with local Cuban combo groups of four musicians in Hoboken and Union City. Álvarez played bongó at Catalino's Steakhouse, where he accompanied pianist Facundo Rivera, bassist Marcelino Váldes and Los Jimaguas, twin brothers who played congas and timbales. Álvarez would also accompany pianist Fernando Muléns and bassist Mariano Sánchez at La Roca on Lincoln Street. He also played congas with Las Hermanas Cano, two sisters who played piano and saxophone at a club called La Choza; the vocalist was Welfo. Álvarez gained his chops this way before working with bands like Baby González and his conjunto.[88] Álvarez even auditioned for Arsenio Rodríguez's band in 1968 at Freddy Grant Studios on Saint Nicholas and 168th Street, but Arsenio's brother said that Álvarez couldn't cut it, because they wanted someone who sounded like Arsenio's brother Kike and Álvarez played in a New York style.

By his own admission, Álvarez's professional career as a vocalist started accidentally, but fits nicely with the Charlie Palmieri story from his high school years. Around 1970, as a working percussionist, Álvarez was playing an engagement with Baby Gónzalez on the same bill with Tito Rodríguez. González had car trouble and was not there in time so Álvarez took over the vocal duties while playing congas, since he knew the tunes. Álvarez stayed to hear Rodríguez's set because he was one of his favorite singers. The two started talking after the show and Rodríguez said to him:

> "I was listening to you before," and he said, "you should start singing, forget about the conga drum. You ain't no Ray Barretto and you ain't no Mongo Santamaria." And he said, these are the words I'll never forget, and he said . . . "conga players are a dime a dozen, there's one born every minute. You ain't no Mongo, you ain't no Ray Barretto, but you got a good voice, man, you should start singing."

Although Tito Rodríguez did not mentor Chico Álvarez formally, this type of informal advice was a common pattern in Latin music. Álvarez stuck with the congas for a few more years, but by 1972 he had heeded Rodríguez's words and eventually abandoned the congas. He became an art director at United Artists when the two men crossed paths again and Rodríguez remembered him. Álvarez continued doing artwork for albums and magazines and sang with Miguel Pérez's Típica New York, a band that included Cachao, Felo Brito, Gonzalo Fernández, Henry Fiol, Ralph Irizarry, Andrea Brachfeld, Dave Valentín, and later Ronnie Barró. Then he started singing with Havana Brass and Ocho. He finally started his own band, Mayombe, in 1976–78. Álvarez also sang with Hector Rivera's Conjunto La Llave. At the same time he focused on his own graphic arts studio, where he made artwork for thousands of album covers. In 1980 he sang with Chihuahua Martinez's Orquesta Metropolitana, as well as Sublime and Novel. In 1981 he made a record with Nosotros, with whom he had been working from 1979–81. For Álvarez the Latin music scene burned brightest "in the 60s and 70s, it was Union City, Hudson County, Newark and Essex County, and New York City, the Tri-State area, in Connecticut, too."[89] Álvarez remembers many dances for Cuban social clubs in the area such as *El liceo cubano*, *Hijos y amigos de fomento* (previously called VFW), *Club cubano de Elizabeth*, *Club cubano de Passaic*, and *Salón Amistad*, the Masonic lodge, as well as Madison Manor. These events included a superstar group from New York, a local Cuban group, and a small combo playing rock like Los Safari. There were no large clubs except for Catalino's Steakhouse (owned by Puerto Rican Sarín Rosario and his Peruvian wife), which would have shows featuring megastars like Olga Guillot, Roberto Ledesma, Orlando Contreras, Vicentico Valdés, La India de Oriente, Rolando La Serie, and Celio González who would play with the house band.

Lastly, Álvarez wrote album reviews, liner notes, and other short pieces for a variety of outlets, but started focusing on radio, where he has been active for thirty-one years. He was invited to one of Al Angeloro's live radio broadcasts of a jam session on WBAI and later Angeloro asked him to fill in for him; he subsequently was given his own show. Álvarez was given another time slot on Tuesday mornings before Gary Null's show. He was then moved to Saturday afternoons and finally Sundays where he has been ever since, even winning an award for his special on Arsenio Rodríguez.

JOHNNY COLÓN, THE EAST HARLEM SCHOOL OF MUSIC, AND THE HARBOR

The school for me, was my life.

—JOHNNY COLÓN

Johnny Colón has undoubtedly been one of the single greatest forces in Latin music education in New York City. At the age of five Colón did his first radio appearance on WHOM. Shortly after, he started studying Puerto Rican music and boleros with Puerto Rican guitarist Ramón Cortijo.[90] As a youngster growing up in East Harlem, he formed a quartet with Ángel René (bongó). Colón also performed as a doo-wop vocalist during the genre's heyday, particularly songs by the Moonglows, the Spaniels, the Flamingos, and the Cadillacs.[91] Eventually, Colón would go on to record the best-selling, but not the best-paying album, *Boogaloo Blues* in 1967. This album would bring Colón international fame and fans.

The Johnny Colón music school started in Colón's mother's house in 1962. Colón's mother encouraged her son to share his knowledge and Colón would "just show them what I had, what I thought I knew" on a variety of instruments.[92] Lenny Castro, Harry DeAguiar, and George Haskins were among some of his first students. Colón was politically conscious and active in protesting and demanding better conditions in his community. He wrote a concept paper for a neighborhood music program and submitted it to local officials. When it was tossed in the garbage, a kindly administrator alerted him and he hung onto it. After Colón released *Boogaloo Blues* and gained professional success, doors started to open where they were previously closed. An administrator named José Aguayo from the New York City Youth Bureau took an interest in making the program a reality. Politicians did not want Colón to have an after-school program in their district, so the school was started on 94th and Park Avenue, as a pilot project in summer 1972. Colón hired some of the most highly regarded musicians on the scene, including Sonny Bravo, Steve Guttenberg, Leopoldo Pineda, Manny Oquendo, Andy González, Victor Venegas, Nicky Marrero, Ron Davis, and other luminaries. Oscar Hernández substituted for Bravo and Gilberto "Pulpo" Colón Jr. substituted for Hernández.

While there was no curriculum in the beginning, there was a good deal of mentoring, as exemplified by teachers like Marrero bringing students like Jimmy Delgado to gigs and recording sessions. Initially, the program was given "funding for 19 kids, [and] the first year we ended up with 45," and when the program was funded the following summer they were given enough money for "45 kids, more or less, and we ended up with 150 and the thing just kept growing to the extent that now parents would come and bring their kids and they wanted to take a class."[93] Sonny Bravo recalled his involvement as a teacher at the school:

> I taught beginner, intermediate, and advanced theory classes, as well as beginner, intermediate, and advanced piano classes, and also gave private piano lessons. The theory classes were rudimentary. The beginner and intermediate piano classes were rudimentary as well. The advanced piano classes, as well as the private lessons covered Afro-Cuban genres/styles. Some classes were in English, some were in Spanish, and some were bilingual.[94]

Gilberto "Pulpo" Colón Jr. also taught beginner piano, intermediate piano, advanced piano including *montunos*, and some of his students included Victor Santos, Carlos Jiménez (a young Cuban), Ricky González, and Sergio George.[95] González and George would both go on to become artistic and commercial giants as composers, producers, and pianists.

When the school moved into PS 121 in 1973 or 1974, a local politician named Bobby Rodríguez wanted them removed. The school needed a letter of approval from the New York Board of Education (BOE) at 110 Livingston Street, but the BOE defended the school and the program continued. Colón still felt like he did not know what he was doing, but he led the workshop band. Ron Davis took over the workshop band from Colón and a group called Orquesta Yambú came out of the program. The bass player for the group, Tito Nieves, would go on to be one of the most commercially successful salsa singers. Trumpeter Pete Nater was also in the workshop band. Future eight-time Grammy® nominee and percussionist Bobby Sanabria would later run the workshop band.

Orlando Marín asked Colón if he could help their mutual friend Charlie Palmieri find work in New York.[96] Colón often ran school fundraisers at the March Ballroom and the Corso club, and they had a little more money in the budget. Colón had been a fan of Palmieri since the elder musician gave him career advice as a sixteen-year-old at the Yorkville Casino, when he told him that there was room for everyone to be a musician. Now was Colón's chance to "pay it forward . . . and so we hired him; I didn't know what Charlie was going to do, I just knew I had to hire him."[97] In 1979 Colón and his wife cut their salaries in half to give Palmieri his $10,000 salary. Colón made Palmieri the program director and he was in "charge of the classes, program wise and personnel wise."[98] Palmieri proved to be unsuccessful as an administrator and shifted to teaching piano lessons and running the workshop band, which he excelled at. Around this time, Palmieri was writing arrangements and recording at a studio near the school until his passing.

Colón's wife, Stephanie, had been working at Union Settlement, and left her position to join her husband's school. A Hungarian/Irish American who brought her children to live in El Barrio for diversity, she was described by Colón as a genius. Through her successful grant and budget proposals the school was able to increase its funding. In 1978 Colón's program at PS 121 had 3,000 students going through the doors every week. Nevertheless, the headaches of running a non-profit, such as being dependent on the city's budget, made it difficult to run the program and pay teachers consistently; teachers were paid, but receipt of payment required flexibility.

In the summer of 1978, when they moved into the police precinct at 104th Street, Colón and his wife decided to add more structure to the program. Students were given simple tests of rhythm or theory based on the John Brimhall books used in Colón's program.[99] There were three theory tests, but most of the students failed the first level, because their teachers had been "teaching them the mechanics and not so much how to process it with your eyes and your head."[100] Colón also emphasized "love and respect" for every student and this premise was carried through to practice and learning. As a result of this attitude, Colón and his wife acted like family members when students and families had emergencies or needed help, all while fulfilling their responsibilities to the music school and later to the high school they started.

The East Harlem Music School Workshop Band was sixteen pieces (or more) and had many notable members, including Pete Nater, Jimmy Delgado, Tito Nieves, Alex Cruz, George Haskins, Ricky González, Rubén Rodríguez, José Rodríguez, Robin Loeb, Harry Aviar, and Joe Dejesús. The workshop band got so good that they started getting calls for events. They charged nothing to non-profits, but they charged money for weddings and parties. Half of the money that came in went to repair instruments, make T-shirts, and cover transportation to gigs. The other half went to the students. At the apex, they would earn $400. When Charlie Palmieri ran the workshop band they did not play for money, mainly because the students were older and already working as musicians. The purpose was to improve their performance. The best students in the workshop band went on to play and record with Tito Puente, Larry Harlow, Eddie Palmieri, Machito, and Ray Barretto, who always asked Johnny Colón for recommendations when he was looking for musicians.

At one point the workshop band was invited to play at an event for the Agency for Child Development. The director of HRA (Human Resources

Administration) and the commissioner were so impressed that they agreed to fund Stephanie's idea for a high school to educate dropouts in East Harlem. In the winter of 1978, they started a straight academic program high school that became an alternative site high school: The East Harlem Music School High School. The Board of Education sent three or four teachers and one or two paraprofessionals that the board paid for. Many of these students succeeded in going to college, particularly Antioch College. Before going to the high school, the students were required to study three weeks of music theory with Colón. This was how Colón could tell if "they were going to be responsible, account-able, and committed to coming in and doing the work, so this was kind of test for them. And of course my rules were you couldn't be late, you couldn't be absent, you couldn't give me attitude, and you have to pass your tests."[101] Students who did not make it through Colón's three-week class were given other chances to try. Colón admitted some kids who did not pass the test, "because they were there every day trying" and were not good test takers.[102] Some of these students went into music and became music teachers in the New York City school system. To this day, students stop Colón on the street and thank him for helping them use music to get through life even if they did not become professional musicians. Later, Colón's ideas about music and education were validated through published studies of the effects of music on the brain and learning improvement.

Colón's wife died on October 1, 1994, but he kept both the high school program and the music school running for another two or three years. The loss of his wife was emotionally devastating and the grant-writing and fund-raising responsibilities became too much to bear by himself. Since then Colón has focused on getting paid what he deserves for his music and securing good gig opportunities at Lincoln Center, various park concerts throughout New York City, and at venues like Le Poisson Rouge.

The legacy of Colón's school is felt deeply to this day, as many of the best musicians on the scene were associated as students and faculty. In many ways, the school would also leave its imprint on subsequent music programs at the New School and Manhattan School of Music, where Jerry González, Bobby Sanabria, and Sonny Bravo have taught lessons and led ensembles. Sanabria has led and recorded with two Afro-Latin big bands for many years at both of these institutions. It is also notable that Marc Anthony, one of the biggest-selling and most award-winning artists on the scene today, got his musical start as a six-year-old kid hanging around Johnny Colón's neighborhood music program.[103]

Another important program that has helped develop many musicians is the Harbor. "The Harbor was founded in 1937 by Anthony 'Tony' Drexel Duke as a small, innovative summer camp for economically disadvantaged boys from New York City."[104] It became a year-round program in 1960 and, after moving locations including Long Island, Kingston, and Connecticut, the program settled on 104th and Fifth Avenue in 1977. Cuban American musician Ramón Rodríguez started the Latin music program at the Harbor Conservatory in 1970, and in 1979 he and Louis Bauzó also started Raíces, a Latin music archive. Numerous notable musicians have taught or continue to teach in the program, such as Louis Bauzó, Jose Madera, Johnny Almendra, Sonny Bravo, Yrving Yeras, David Oquendo, and others.[105] The school has offered private lessons, group lessons, big band, and even dance classes over the years, in addition to hosting workshops from visiting international performers. In the documentary *Mi Mambo*, Ramón Rodríguez acknowledges that Latin music pedagogy was historically informal:

> It has always been taught as an oral tradition. You would have to try keep up with the musicians at rumbas in the parks, in the springtime and the summertime or catch them in between gigs, in between sets at clubs to try to get them to teach you a lick or two at that time. It was never formally taught in a conservatory setting . . . and we were the first school to bring it out of the street and teach in the conservatory setting of writing it down, transcribing it, putting it down on paper . . . the tip of the iceberg.[106]

Rodríguez, a classically trained pianist, started teaching at the age of fourteen and quickly found that he needed to modify his approach to reach young people and communicate basic musical concepts. Interactions with notable professional musicians are frequent during ensemble rehearsals and in workshops. The big band features many professional musicians who see it as an opportunity to work on large Latin ensemble repertoire.[107] Many of the students in the music program are also adults. Folklore is also an important aspect of Latin music; for percussionist Louis Bauzó, who studied at Juilliard: "In terms of the Afro-Caribbean experience, folklore is essential and is something else that we teach here. It shows the roots of a lot of the modern dance steps that are used today in some of the different styles of music like the mambo and the chachachá."[108] Teachers like dancer Alma Cruz insist that the students learn all styles of Caribbean folkloric dance. Students also work on classical music as a foundation. Rodríguez feels that students are fortunate "[because] all three divisions of the Harbor Conservatory work together to put on big productions at the end of the year." For Rodríguez, the end result is: "The kids leave here, get tortured by us and they go out to the street bands and they play like nothing, it's a piece of cake. What we're teaching them here is five times as hard as what anything they are going to play out in the street, in most situations."[109] Rodríguez and Bauzó are very involved in academic advising as well, pushing the students to pursue excellence not only the arts, but in their education, and to apply to colleges and conservatories. Ultimately, the goal is that the students continue to appreciate the arts and learn from the discipline of the arts how to apply themselves to any learning and life situation.

RENÉ LÓPEZ: A MUSIC COLLECTOR WITH AN INFORMAL BUT RIGOROUS LISTENING SALON

In New York City, record collectors have served as an additional important source of musical instruction and education. This has been René López's mission. López's uncle, Catalino Rolón, played maracas and sang with Xavier Cugat. In 1936 or 1937, Rolón started to travel to Cuba as a musical booking agent, later bringing artists such as Benny Moré and Orquesta Aragón to play at the Palladium. Rolón also personally helped many musicians in the process of coming to the United States, in some cases permanently. In this way, René grew up surrounded by Cuban, Puerto Rican, and Mexican popular and folkloric music that his uncle cultivated in the theaters and clubs of the Bronx and Manhattan. René moved to Puerto Rico in 1954 at the age of fourteen and visited Cuba for the first time in 1957. His life as a collector and folklorist began in the mid-1960s, when López bought 65–75 percent of a record collection from Suaritos, the owner of a jewelry store on 116th Street. Since the 1940s, jewelry stores had also served as record stores. Eddie Palmieri, a friend of René's, bought the first record by Conjunto Modelo from Cuba in Suaritos's store on 116th Street.

When new members joined Eddie Palmieri's group, La Perfecta, Palmieri demanded that the musicians spend time with René at his home and with his records. While René worked during the day as a radiology technician at Lenox Hill Hospital, young musicians like Nicky Marrero, Joe Santiago, Jerry and Andy González, Charlie Santiago, Willie García, and Heny Álvarez listened to René's records and hung out with legendary musicians such as Israel "Cachao" López, Justi Barreto, and Machito every Tuesday and Wednesday until 3:00 or 4:00 in the morning. This cycle of intense listening and analysis lasted from 1967 into the 1970s.

Another benefit of these listening sessions was that Cuban trumpet icon Alfredo "Chocolate" Armenteros lived close by and he, too spent a lot of time in René's house talking music and sharing intimate knowledge about what happened on the recording sessions and what was and was not captured on the recording. Chocolate, who had played with many groups in Cuba as a young man and with other groups around the world, explained to René and the younger New York musicians exactly who the musicians were on the recordings and why Arsenio shouted out their nicknames to be recorded forever thereafter.

He also explained the secret and comic messages of Arsenio's songs known only to those who were in his bands or lived near him. On an extra-musical level, Chocolate explained various aspects of Afro-Cuban culture and offered personal insights into the daily life of Afro-Cubans that gave birth to Arsenio's music and to that of his contemporaries, with many of whom Chocolate had worked.

René continued searching for records and recordings of concerts that were transmitted on short wave radio. Pablo Menéndez, a young American man living in Cuba since the 1960s, visited New York in 1974 and brought René some Cuban records, which he shared with his musician friends. René traveled to Cuba in 1978, where he recorded the new style of *batárumba* (a fusion of Afro-Cuban sacred *batá* drumming and secular *rumba*) played by the folkloric groups Afrocuba de Matanzas and Los Muñequitos. Musicians in New York shared these field recordings. René worked with Sheldon Gold as a consultant for the ICM agency to bring the Cuban group Grupo Folklórico Nacional on a tour from Canada to New York, and in 1977 he helped when Los Papines came to New York and played for JazzMobile on 42nd Street. Manny Oquendo and Conjunto Libre (with Andy and Jerry González) went to Cuba during this time to perform. At the same time, René began to work with Fania Records when they formed the Bárbaro Records label to put out records in New York that were made by Cuban groups in Cuba.[110] Throughout the years, Rene López has traveled to Cuba on various occasions as a folklorist, recording interviews with musicians. He also worked as an advisor to Sandra Levinson at the Center for Cuban Studies and later, in the 1980s, worked for the Smithsonian as an adviser and producer. From 1977 into the 1980s, López served as an adviser on musical folklore at the state and national levels, working for the New York State Council for the Arts and the National Endowment for the Arts. René is a concrete example of how the musical connection and exchange of information between New York and Cuba never ceased to exist.

A significant historical achievement of his participation in the music scene and a direct outgrowth of the intensive listening sessions held in his house was the Grupo Folklórico Experimental Nuevayorquino and the two records by them that Rene and Andy Kaufman produced in 1975. This group consisted of the aforementioned younger musicians along with masters of Cuban and Puerto Rican folkloric and religious music such as Julito Collazo, Virgilio Martí, Corozo (vocalist of Cuarteto Mayarí), and members of Los Pleneros de la 110 such as Victor Montañez, Marcial Reyes, and Ismael Rivera (Mon Rivera's brother). This group has since reformed with some of the original members and a few new members who are active on today's Spanish Caribbean popular and folkloric music scenes. This group helped give birth to Fort Apache, Conjunto Libre, and various other folkloric groups.[111]

DANCE

Like their musician counterparts, dancers also studied technique. The successful mambo dance team of Augie and Margo (Augie Meléndez and Margo Bartolomei) were no exception. As indicated in Meléndez's obituary:

> In the 1950s, '60s and '70s, Augie and Margo were among mambo's most famous exponents, appearing on television, on concert stages and in nightclubs worldwide, often accompanied by renowned bandleaders like Xavier Cugat. . . . In Las Vegas, Augie and Margo opened for many major entertainers, including Frank Sinatra, Dean Martin and Sammy Davis Jr.; they also performed at the White House for Presidents John F. Kennedy and Richard M. Nixon and in London for Queen Elizabeth II.[112]

While they showed their stuff locally at the Palladium ballroom, their training is seldom spoken of. As I note in chapter 6 on Jewish musicians and dancers, Ira Goldwasser recalled first meeting Rodríguez at Katherine Dunham's dance school. Juliet McMaines points out that they studied at Dunham's school for two years on a scholarship and then studied ballet for many years at the American Ballet Theater School and at Ballet Arts.[113] By her own admission, Bartolomei explained that whatever they learned in their classes they would incorporate into their mambo dancing.[114] In an interview with filmmaker Lex Gillespie, Augie summed up their approach to mambo dancing, saying "our style is ballet with Latin and modern jazz."[115]

Millie Donay and Pedro Aguilar, a.k.a. "Cuban Pete," another well-known pair of Palladium mambo dancers, also studied at Dunham's school.[116] Aguilar had been a boxer prior to becoming a dancer and Miguelito Valdés suggested he switch to dancing after seeing Aguilar's face after a fight.[117] Like Augie and Margo, he and Millie had incorporated many elements from beyond Cuban music into their dance. This led to "two White House performances, for Presidents Dwight D. Eisenhower and Lyndon B. Johnson, a command performance for Queen Elizabeth II of England and a performance at Madison Square Garden for Prime Minister David Ben-Gurion of Israel."[118] Thus, the New York Palladium-style mambo that these dancers innovated and made popular around the world involved formal study that many people were unaware of, and this study helped create new ways of coordinating dance and music that were a direct result of being in and studying in New York City.

Since 1977 many percussionists have learned hand percussion and set techniques at Drummers Collective, where instructors included Frankie Malabé, Eddie Bobè, Gene Golden, John Amira, and others. Students such as jazz drummer Conor Guilfoyle came from as far away as Ireland to study with these

Fig 1.3. 1970s Drummers Collective advertisement from *Latin NY* magazine featuring Gene Golden. Photo courtesy of Izzy Sanabria.

musicians and master the idiom. As seen in figure 1.3, *Latin NY* magazine advertised workshops that focused on musicians in the rhythm section.[119]

INSTRUCTIONAL MATERIALS PUBLISHED IN NEW YORK CITY

Several important Latin music method books have been published in New York City. In 1930, 1933, and again in 1970, Efraín Ronda published *La antorcha* [The Torch], a bilingual method book for the Puerto Rican cuatro.[120] In 1942 Phil Rale published *Latin-American Rhythms for the Drummer*, which covers a variety of Afro-Latin percussion instruments and rhythmic patterns. Another early attempt at a Latin music instruction book, albeit less serious, was bandleader Xavier Cugat's *Meet Mr. Cugat* (1943), which included, as suggested by its longer title, "bringing Latin America to you in music and rhythms, including instructional material for the maracas and other rumba instruments and original songs and caricatures."[121]

In 1954 Henry Adler published *How to Play Latin American Rhythm Instruments* by Humberto Morales, with a chapter by Ubaldo Nieto.[122] This book is possibly the first-ever bilingual guide to Caribbean percussion. In 1955 Humberto's brother, the celebrated virtuoso pianist Noro Morales, published a method book, *Latin-American Rhythms and Improvisations for Piano*. The flautist Esy Morales, another brother of Noro and Humberto, also published a method book on how to play flute in Latin music.[123] In 1972 Roger "Montego Joe" Sanders published a conga and bongó method book in New York that covered techniques and rhythms.

In addition to releasing influential recordings without didactic intentions, the drum manufacturer Latin Percussion made a number of albums by acknowledged masters with illustrated booklets dedicated to students who wanted to learn to play Latin music. These included *Understanding Latin Rhythms Vol. I* (1974) with Bobby Rodríguez (bass), Louis Mangual (bongó), José Mangual (bongó, maracas, güiro), Milton Cardona (claves and congas), José Mangual Jr. (congas, percussion), Carlos "Patato" Valdéz (congas and shekere), Porfirio Fernández (tambora), and Manny Oquendo (timbales); *Understanding Latin Rhythms Vol. II / Down to Basics* (1977) with Charlie Santiago and Nelson González (percussion) and Joe Mannozzi (piano); *Drum Solos* Vols. 1–3 (1978) with Sal Cuevas (bass), Charlie Santiago and Eddie Montalvo (percussion), Joe Santiago (bass), and Gilberto "Pulpo" Colón Jr. (piano).

These publications led the way for future method books such as John Amira and Steven Cornelius's 1992 book and CD of sacred batá drum transcriptions and audio examples as well as a similar book, *The Drums of Vodou*, by the distinguished master of Haitian folklore and ritual drumming, Frizner Augustin, who had moved to New York in 1972.[124] Frankie Malabe's teachings would eventually be compiled into *Afro-Cuban Rhythms for Drumset*, a book with a CD that was published by Alfred in 1994. The aforementioned players assumed the responsibility of creating a body of teaching materials for Caribbean music.

PUBLIC EDUCATION AND LATIN MUSIC IN NEW YORK CITY

A number of the musicians profiled earlier in this chapter attended junior high school at PS (Public School) 52 at 681 Kelly Street. Many of them bonded through stickball, music, and hanging around the local candy store run by Eddie and Charlie Palmieri's father called the Mambo Candy Store. Some of these musicians included Benny Bonilla (percussion), Manny Oquendo (percussionist),

Ray Barretto (percussionist), Tony Pabón (trumpeter and vocalist), Charlie Palmieri (piano), Eddie Palmieri (pianist), Orlando Marín (percussionist), "Long" Joe Rodríguez (percussionist), Ray Coen (piano), Joe Quijano (vocalist and percussionist), Larry Acevedo (trumpet), Hector Rivera (piano), "Professor" Joe Torres (pianist), and Rudy Romero (percussion). Other notable graduates include the mambo dancer Tony "Peanuts" Aubert, Latin music archivist and collector Henry Medina, and former Secretary of State and General Colin Powell. In the film *From Mambo to Hip Hop*, Marín explains: "we rehearsed right in the auditorium . . . They would let us rehearse here [in the auditorium] and we performed Friday nights in the gym. This was the beginning of the era of the mambo dancing." According to a profile of PS 52 musicians, Alex Friedman wrote that "Johnny Pacheco rehearsed flute in a classroom. Willie Colón, Pete 'El Conde' Rodríguez, Ray Santos, and Barry Rogers played there."[125] Young drummers showed each other the foundational rhythms of Latin music on parked cars by the school. In "A South Bronx Latin Music Tale," Percussionist Adolfo "Lefty" Maldonado explained to folklorist Elena Martínez:

> The key to it was all the brass players came from a school band. So without that even if we are doing the street stuff and the piano players are taking their private lessons, see it all clicked. It's a magical thing. We were doing it from the records, because the percussionists were doing it from the records. And the piano players were doing a private thing because their mothers wouldn't let them go out and play stickball. And the trumpets and the brass guys were doing it in schools. And this phenomenon, this incredible combination got together. But one without the other wouldn't make it. So the school had a lot to do with it.[126]

From this quote it is possible to see how the hierarchy of music education worked for young Puerto Rican musicians in the 1940s and 1950s and how shared information was ultimately combined in Latin dance music ensembles. In 1980 a group of locals led by Al Quiñones, Fred Demera, Eduardo Rivera, and Victoria Medina started a non-profit organization called 52 People for Progress and 52 Park, dedicated to renovating the playground next to the school. Once the site was renovated, Quiñones brought numerous Latin legends from the musical community associated with the neighborhood to perform there in addition to having theater, sports, and children's events.[127]

Music and Art High School, now known as the Fiorello H. LaGuardia High School of Music and Art and Performing Arts, was an important early training ground for a number of musicians who would go on to have major impacts and successful careers performing Latin music. In some cases, the school's program was a natural fit for people like Andy and Jerry González, who began their musical education with their father, a vocalist who sang with Augie and Moncho Meléndez, a local musical group that Jerry González described as a "somewhat like La Playa Sextet with guitars and no piano."[128] The group performed Irish and Puerto Rican music at weddings at the Casino Puerto Rico on 130th Street. Some of the repertoire at these events included "When Irish Eyes Are Smiling" accompanied with Latin percussion and rendered as a Puerto Rican *danza*. Two of the trumpeters in the group were high-level professionals, Tony Cofresí (Tito Rodríguez) and Papi Román (Ray Barretto). Augie Meléndez was friendly with the director of the Samuel Gompers Automotive High School Band teacher, Mr. Alteri, who had trained Cofresí, Roman, and U.S. Navy trumpeter Eliezer Rodríguez, among many other fine trumpeters in the Bronx. As youngsters, both boys with their friends would sneak into a local amusement park in the Bronx called Freedomland to see their musical heroes Israel "Cachao" López, Victor Paz, Mario Rivera, and Mike Collazo performing with Tito Rodríguez, as well as Tito Puente and Bobby Rodríguez, and others.[129]

Andy González (1951–2020) played bass with the Latin jazz group at Samuel Gompers after getting his start on violin in elementary school. He played for two years in the chamber orchestra in fifth and sixth grades before switching to bass in the middle of fifth grade. In junior high school, Andy began playing Latin jazz and studied with jazz bassist Steve Swallow for three years. He recalled taking the train to Swallow's apartment on 18th Street, where they worked on "jazz bass, playing melodies on bass, and dealing with chord structures."[130] González also remembered working through a book of major and minor scales in all keys written out specifically for bass. Swallow turned González on to Pablo Casals and Scott Lafaro, wrote out the second movement of the Bach Cello Suite in D minor, and helped González prepare for his audition at Music and Art. Once admitted to the school, González played bass in the school orchestra in tenth through twelfth grades. He remembered a particular class where he recorded a live gig that was broadcast from the school. González also remembered playing with other classmates such as Mongo Santamaria's son, Monguito, José Mangual Jr., Rene McClean, Onaje Allen Gumbs, Stafford Osborne, Nelson Samañego, a Puerto Rican alto saxophonist, DJ Cousin Brucie, Eric Bibb (son of Leo Bibb), Wilbur Bascomb (son of Ted Bascomb, bassist for Erskine Hawkins), Allison Dean, and Janis Ian, who was in his homeroom and dropped out sophomore year just after recording "Society's Child." At the age of sixteen, González participated in his first recording session with Monguito Santamaria; none other than Julio Andino was present to encourage and assure the nervous young man, putting his hand on his shoulder and telling González that he could do it and that he played well.[131]

Andy González joked that the school was also a "den of iniquity" because students raised funds for Hanoi during the Vietnam War, but that it was a "very hip" place. Elder brother Jerry González graduated from the school in 1967. Andy González remembers spending time with pianist and French horn major Llewelyn Matthews in high school, who he described as a genius that would write big band scores a la Oliver Nelson while riding the subway.[132] For both brothers, Matthews's dedication provided them with guidance and direction that kept them off of the streets.[133] Once he graduated in 1969, Andy went on to work with Eddie Palmieri, Ray Barretto, Dizzy Gillespie, and many others.

Andy González is widely known as a serious collector of Latin music.[134] He began collecting records in seventh grade and by ninth grade had an immense collection, particularly when record stores got rid of monaural LPs. For González, intense listening allows for depth of understanding, particularly when it comes to the role of the bass in Cuban and other Latin music. From an early age, González would listen to older recordings by Cuban son groups like Sexteto Boloña and modern bomba and plena groups like Cortijo. He would notice that the bass player did not play half notes in the plena, but would play rhythmic counter lines and seek to incorporate this into his own playing.

Earlier, I discussed the importance of René López as an educator through the sharing of his collection with Andy and Jerry González and many other musicians. According to Jerry Gonzalez, the brothers met López when they were in high school.[135] The listening sessions sometimes focused on particular instruments from recordings as early as the 1930s, which opened the brothers up to many creative possibilities they felt were missing from the music of their era.[136]

It is important to point out Andy González's relationship with percussionist Manny Oquendo, with whom Gónzalez spent a great deal of time and with whom he co-led Conjunto Libre. Oquendo also mentored other important musicians such as trombonist Barry Rogers. The two spent an entire summer listening to 78s during their residency with Eddie Palmieri at Kutshers. Andy has in turn mentored many younger musicians including Luques and Zaccai Curtis, Carlos Abadie, and others.

Like his younger brother Andy, Jerry González (1949–2018) also graduated from Music and Art in 1967. He played Antonio Carlos Jobim's "Desafinado" at his audition and remembered being intimidated by the kids who were playing the Haydn Trumpet Concerto.[137] González remembered how little he knew at the time that he started:

> I was one of the few token Puerto Ricans that made that school. A lot of good musicians came out of that school. It was a good school, better than Evander Childs or Dewitt Clinton. I appreciate it now more because I reflect on how lucky I am. It'd be a whole different ball game if I hadn't gone to that school, too. They had high standards. Didn't even know about the Arban, which is the trumpet bible. It's a conservatory method of training classical trumpet

players. I didn't even know that book existed. And another one called the St. Giacome's. I actually stole the books from the school and just practiced every day to catch up with those people.[138]

González took to the daily schedule, with the first half of the day devoted to music history classes and ensemble rehearsals. He also excelled in math and science classes in the second half of the day and loved "to go to that school, I wouldn't miss a day."[139]

Jerry González eventually attended the New York College of Music, an institution that would become part of NYU. As a fitting end to his time at Music and Art, the last page of the school's 1967 yearbook featured a photo of a desk carving that says "Latin jazz," Jerry González's handiwork.[140] In college, he paid his tuition from playing gigs with the Beach Boys and wound up being in a combo with none other than jazz legend Kenny Dorham, who was seeking to finish his own college degree.[141] The intense listening that the González brothers practiced led to their unique vision of Latin jazz. As he once explained to me, he was listening to a live recording of Thelonious Monk performing "Evidence" with Steve Lacy and he thought it was a natural fit for using the rhythmic structure of Frank Emilio Flynn's "Gandinga, Mondongo y Sandunga."[142] These types of connections were part and parcel of the González brothers' musical training and development with Oquendo, López, and the bandleaders who hired them. In later years, González gave back to the next generation and taught percussion in the jazz program at the New School.

Another important Latin musician to come out of Music and Art High School was flautist Andrea Brachfeld. Brachfeld was born in Utica, New York, in 1954 and started on piano at the age of six. Her teacher encouraged her to move toward jazz early on. Her family settled in Spring Valley, New York, for kindergarten through seventh grade, and she picked up flute at the age of ten. In eighth grade, after a year in Paris as part of her NYU professor father's sabbatical, Brachfeld successfully auditioned for Music and Art on piano and flute, graduating in 1972. At the school, Denise Bevers, a bass student of Richard Davis, turned her on to Eric Dolphy's *Out to Lunch* and she was forever hooked on jazz.[143] At about sixteen or seventeen years old, in 1970 or 1971, she met another flautist, Karen Joseph, and started studying with Jimmy Heath at Jazzmobile. As part of Joe and Rigmoe Newman's Jazz Interactions program, Brachfeld also studied with Yusef Lateef and took classes with Barry Harris. By her own admission, she felt that she was still in a "musical fog" in terms of knowing what she wanted to do with music.[144] She earned admission to NYU, Brooklyn College, Manhattan School of Music, and an award from Jazz Interactions that included a full scholarship to Berklee College of Music, but she was still unsure of her path forward. Praise for playing came from *Down Beat* magazine and the musical community but, undecided about what to do next, she continued with Jazzmobile and Manhattan School of Music, from which she would graduate. Although she was encouraged by her Latin neighbors to pursue playing the flute in Latin bands, Brachfeld was not interested and wanted to pursue jazz. Sometime around 1974, after stopping by Lloyd MacNeil's gig at the Tin Palace, Mauricio Smith asked her if she wanted to work in the Latin scene. He encouraged her to work but warned her, "don't stay in this field [of Latin music], use it as a stepping stone."[145] Before this she had played Latin music with a group called the Benito Sextet, but Smith hooked her up with Mike Pérez's Típica New York. The flute player was Felix Wilkins, originally from Panama and discussed in the Panamanian chapter, and he did a couple of gigs with her, where he "trained" her. By her own admission, during these gigs she had to learn the correct feel of Latin music, having come from a jazz background. In her own words, Brachfeld explains:

> I had to play loudly and I had to play high, so I gathered that I really needed to get my chops together. And it was really a process that I did by ear. It was really more than that. After the fact I realized that it was two-bar phrases and to play more simply. And I realized how much more difficult it was to play over a montuno than to play over changes per se, because you have to come up with so many more ideas within a very limited harmonic structure . . . that was interesting . . . it really opened me up creatively.[146]

All of this instruction happened on the bandstand and was never given in a formal lesson or any similar situation. Brachfeld credits the musicians around her as being particularly helpful and giving her tons of records to listen to, such as Louie Bauzó, Dave Chamberlain, Johnny Almendra, and José Madera. Then percussionist Phil Martínez called her to work with Charanga 76, with whom she began playing up to "nine gigs a week."[147] After Charanga 76, Brachfeld had been working a lot with Andy González and Conjunto Libre. González called her to do the band's first record, but she decided not to do it. Another classmate from Music and Art, Dave Valentín, did. Throughout this period, Brachfeld played gigs with Joe Cuba, Joe Quijano, Típica Ideal, Charanga America, subbed with Típica Novel, and sat in with groups like Tito Puente and Machito, with whom she remembers "talking a lot about Charlie Parker."[148] She also hung out with Irakere and Los Papines when they came to New York. Brachfeld toured nationally and internationally with many bands during this time. Sometime around 1978, Brachfeld remembers:

> At one point I was working at Sam Goody's as a cashier and Billy Taylor was in my line. He looked up and he said, "What are you doing here?" I said, "I'm

earning a living." He said, "You're not supposed to be doing this, you're supposed to be playing music." And typical of him, because he helped so many
people, he said, "Well, we're looking for the leader for an Afro-Cuban band
for CETA, Comprehensive Educational Training Act, because Jazzmobile had
gotten a grant and they had two bands, they had a big band and then they
had the Latin band." . . . And he said "We're auditioning right now . . . go up
there and toot a couple of notes and you've got the job."[149]

Brachfeld held that job for about a year in 1979. Throughout this period she
continued to play and work with many jazz musicians, such as Mark Helias,
Charles Eubanks, Jay Clayton, Frank Clayton, Jeff Andrews, Adam Nussbaum,
Peter Fisch, Rob Schneiderman, and Kenwood Denard, among others. Then she
got a call from Venezuelan bandleader and businessman Renato Capriles about
coming to play in Venezuela for an extended engagement. In 1980 Brachfeld
went to Venezuela for a month and wound up staying for two and a half years,
becoming a superstar before returning to the United States. Capriles created
a band around her called La Inmensa. During this time, Brachfeld met and
played with many jazz musicians who came to town like Gary Burton, Chick
Correa, and others. Brachfeld taught jazz at the Yamaha school in Caracas and
had students like Otmaro Ruiz. In Venezuela, she married Nelson Hernández
and became pregnant before returning home and giving birth to a daughter. For
Brachfeld, the scene had changed and there weren't as many gigs, but she did
play and record with Charanga 76 again. Latin record companies offered her
recording contracts, but she declined. Brachfeld returned to school, earned a
master's degree in education, and began a career teaching and taking care of her
family. Eventually, Brachfeld made her way into the Latin jazz scene, combining
her Latin music experience and her love for jazz once her daughter reached the
age of fifteen. She traveled to Cuba in the mid-2000s for musical research and
connected with Orlando "Maraca" Valle and Bobby Carcassés, with whom she
has performed and recorded. In general, Brachfeld has always felt that she had
to prove herself to many men as a serious musician, but this seems to have been
in the jazz scene and not in the Latin scene. She conceives of her own back and
forth between the jazz and Latin continuum like "an infinity sign."[150]

   A few other Latin music giants who graduated from Music and Art need
to be mentioned. Dave Valentín (1952–2017) was a contemporary of Brachfeld
and the González brothers at Music and Art and would eventually become one
of the best-known Latin jazz flute players in the world. Larry Harlow, better
known as "El judío maravilloso," was another Music and Art graduate, as were
Elias "Phoenix" Rivera (son of Mario Rivera), and Chris Rogers (son of Barry
Rogers). Hence, the school has been an incubator for Latin musicians for quite
some time and over the course of at least two generations.

OTHER TYPES OF INFORMAL MENTORSHIP

Among musicians it is common knowledge that iconic Latin music performers also studied and/or worked with non-Latin musicians in a variety of genres. In some cases these were formal lessons or joint practice sessions. Although he is known primarily as a Latin jazz musician and sideman for Tito Puente and others, Hilton Ruiz was a student of piano legend Mary Lou Williams. Ruiz recorded and performed with a number of jazz greats such as Rahsaan Roland Kirk, among others. Puerto Rican bassist Bobby Rodríguez originally came to New York City to immerse himself in the jazz scene. He would go on to perform with the Fania All-Stars and his own groups as a bassist, but he recorded two albums of Latin jazz in New York City and studied trumpet with Art Farmer. Puerto Rican bassist Julio Andino performed and recorded with Cab Calloway. Mario Rivera was known to practice extensively with George Coleman and Dizzy Gillespie.

As I discuss in the Puerto Rico chapter, Eddie Palmieri formally studied classical piano with the likes of Margaret Bonds and Claudio Saavedra, but his interest in jazz harmony and its applications to Afro-Latin dance music and later Latin jazz was cultivated and expanded through one-on-one lessons for twenty-five years with guitarist Bob Bianco, where he delved into the Schillinger system.[151] One of Palmieri's trademark techniques is to maintain a tumbao (montuno ostinato pattern) in his left hand while soloing with the right hand. This makes him sound like two piano players and reflects his years of classical technique.[152] Latin performers mentored jazz musicians as well, and in this way, the Latin sound in New York City was a two-way street with musicians potentially moving in both directions or staying closer to one side. Such was the case with Doc Cheatham in the Machito band and Steve Sacks in the Angel Canales band. Marty Sheller, Pat Patrick, Marshall Allen, Ed Diehl, and Sonny Henry worked with bands led by Mongo Santamaria and Willie Bobo. Both Herbie Hancock and Chick Corea came through Willie Bobo and Mongo Santamaria's groups. And four female non-Latina flute players apprenticed in a variety of bands becoming powerful soloists on the New York City Charanga scene: the aforementioned Andrea Brachfeld, Karen Joseph, Carla Poole, and Connie Grossman. Bassist Rubén Rodríguez was an admirer and follower of Sonny Bravo's cousin Bobby Rodríguez. He eventually took his hero's seat in Tito Puente's band, but also enjoyed an extended tenure with Roberta Flack. Seasoned veterans have also coached newcomers, as is the case with vocalist Rafael "Chivirico" Dávila mentoring both Tito Rodríguez and Bobby Cruz. Cruz began as a guitarist and sought out Dávila to help him develop his voice.[153] Dominican multi-instrumentalist Mario Rivera was an important mentor to a number of musicians including Michel Camilo, Howard Levy, Paquito D'Rivera,

Fig 1.4. L-r: Pete Yellin, Chick Corea, Milford Graves, Noel Carter, Bill Fitch at Linden Manor Ballroom, Jamaica, Queens, NY, 1960–61. Photo courtesy of Milford Graves.

and many more. Puerto Rican saxophone virtuoso Ivan Renta practiced regularly with Mario Rivera upon arriving to New York City. I myself spent countless hours visiting Rivera's house during high school, to soak up both jazz and Latin music recordings and playing techniques. For a musician such as Rivera it was crucial to excel in all genres, and he pushed me and anyone else who he allowed into his home to work on technique and study music seriously.

In *Salsa: The Rhythm of Latin Music* (1989), Charley Gerard calls attention to the reciprocal relationship between trumpeter and arranger Marty Sheller and percussionist Franky Malabe, friends since the 1950s working in Harvey Averne's band:

> Malabe played an important part in his [Sheller's] learning about the music. Coincidentally, Malabe credits Sheller with introducing him to jazz . . . Sheller and Malabe often got together to play jazz and Latin records. After awhile, Malabe learned that Sheller took a special delight in being able to figure out where the clave was in rhythmically confusing performances. Malabe brought out of his record collection the selections in which it was difficult to hear the "one." At first, Sheller would be completely confused by the rhythm. Malabe would then show him where the beat started and tell him to follow along with the clave. Eventually, Sheller told me, he was able to hear the clave in any music from the oldest son montunos to the most modern Tito Puente arrangement. At this point, Malabe played him some batá music and, at first, Sheller felt like he "was back to Square One."[154]

Many jazz musicians have been active as performers of Latin music before reaching international success as jazz musicians. These include Pete Yellin, Pete "La Roca" Sims, Milford Graves, and others mentioned above.

In subsequent chapters we will see how, during their breaks, working Latin musicians would run to catch their contemporaries playing at neighboring jazz venues, but it also happened the other way. In a recent interview, Chick Corea explains:

> "Four doors up from Birdland on Broadway was the Palladium, where you could hear people like Tito Puente, Machito, Ray Barretto, Eddie Palmieri," Corea recalls of his first gig upon arriving in New York in the early '60s. "I used to jump out of my gig [during breaks] and go stand in front of the bandstand at the Palladium. So the jazz scene that I came up in was very much a part of what I call my Spanish heart."[155]

Corea also explains that his own learning process began with a local trumpeter named Phil Barboza who hired him despite the fact that he had little experience playing Latin music:

> And all of a sudden I'm in a band with a conga player and a timbale player, and I knew nothing about those rhythms. The conga player, his name is Bill Fitch and is a great, great conga player who later played with Cal Tjader and did a bunch of other stuff, fortunately sat me down and introduced me through recordings and he played a little piano himself. So he showed me how to play those Montuno grooves on the piano and played me some Tito Puente and Eddie Palmieri records. And I was really captured, because it was a great complement to this seriousness of the jazz that I was into up until that point.[156]

Eventually Corea would work with Paco de Lucia and deepen his understanding of flamenco forms, and he attributes his success with de Lucia to his Latin jazz days working and recording with Mongo Santamaria, Cal Tjader, and Herbie Mann.

Jazz icon Dexter Gordon explained his appreciation for Latin music: "Around the time that I worked with Machito, I used to live in East Harlem and I used to go by the place called the Park Palace, you know where all the bands used to play Tito Puente, Pacheco, Macho, you know all the bands, so I got a chance to hear a lot of the guys. So I understand a little, not too much, you know, but I'm a fan."[157] Another Machito employee was African American jazz musician Leslie Johnakins, who was at first confused by the presence of three drummers and exactly where his part fit into the syncopated mix of drums, bass, and piano.

This was a common issue for Machito, who explained: "during the rehearsals we would often have to stop because most of the musicians were foreigners except for Mario [Bauzá] because phrasing is most important, music is not all the same."[158]

NEW YORK AS A SERIOUS "POSTGRADUATE" EXPERIENCE FOR ASPIRING LATIN MUSICIANS

The noted Colombian saxophonist Justo Almario began to study at the Berklee School of Music in 1969. Shortly thereafter he worked as a substitute in Duke Ellington's band and later came to live in New York where he worked with Mongo Santamaria, Ismael Miranda, and many others before moving to the West Coast in 1978.[159] However, for a number of musicians New York City was a place to hone their craft by improving their musicianship, playing in reading bands, studying privately with noted classical and jazz pedagogues, and work with the some of the best musicians in the world. The experiences of two Dominican musicians, Crispín Fernández and Juan Colón, exemplify this view of New York City as the ultimate site for the "post-graduate" study of Latin music.

After his period of study in New York, Crispín Fernández Minaya (b. 1946) became a flautist with the National Symphonic Orchestra of the Dominican Republic as well as a saxophone professor at the National Conservatory of Music. Fernández had a solid career in his home country, was familiar with the work of many US jazz artists, and had seen how local legends such as Tavito Vásquez and Choco de León spoke of jazz and improvisation.[160] As a musician, he saw many musical parallels between American bebop and Dominican merengue as executed on the saxophone.

Fernández first visited the Big Apple with the bandleader Johnny Ventura, who he worked with from 1967–69. Fernández remembered that during his first visit he was at a gig in the Bronx talking with Kako Bastar and Ricardo Ray, and that he asked them about the possibilities of working in New York as a saxophonist. They explained that there were very few groups that used saxophone apart from groups like Tito Puente and Machito, because the majority of the salsa groups used trumpets and trombones.[161] During this first visit, Fernández knew he would eventually return to stay on his next trip, but he went home and continued to work throughout the Dominican Republic. In 1969 he told Ventura on their return trip that he wanted to stay in "New York to study, to succeed as an artist, and find teachers . . . to work on [his] embouchure and I want to leave so that I can study."[162] He spent roughly eight years in New York, from 1969–1976/77, and remains grateful for his time spent where he would "begin the hard chore of trying to become a musician of great magnitude."[163] He believes that he acquired a variety of skills in New York that would open doors for him. One of the first important lessons was that he had to play all of the saxophones. He had turned down work thinking that he only played alto and not tenor, like his hero Tavito Vásquez, but soon he was told and learned that "here you play everything."[164] During a class at City College, Fernández learned another important lesson, that it is harder to create an improvisation, organize and shape it, than it is to simply stand up and play something.[165]

Living on Ralph Avenue in Brooklyn, he took English classes, and later moved to Manhattan. Fernández began classical flute lessons with Henry Slotnik, a Russian teacher. He also took some composition and harmony classes with Nicolás Rodríguez for ten dollars per lesson. Rodríguez taught Fernández European classical concepts including counterpoint in Spanish, as well as ideas of practicing small diatonic groupings of notes. Fernández also met Alberto Socarrás during this time when accompanying a friend to a lesson, but Fernández did not study with Socarrás. He also took clarinet lessons and improved despite having a bad teacher.

Rodríguez brought Fernández to study with Slotnick, a student of Jorge Barrera. In the beginning of each lesson, Fernández would sit and talk with his teacher for half an hour and then they would work on technique during the second half hour. Remarkably, the professional musician was told that he was playing the flute badly and thinking about it incorrectly. The professor explained that Fernández needed to crawl before he could walk with the instrument, and the lessons were as practical as they were philosophical and metaphysical, like life itself. At home, Fernández's practice time was divided into three one-hour blocks: first, sound; second, the mechanism of the instrument (scales, keys, articulations, groups of notes); third, interpretation of styles. And to this day, Fernández maintains this practice. With this deliberate practice and dedication, Fernández made huge strides in his flute playing; however, he started skipping lessons and not preparing for them, for which his teacher admonished him. Realizing that Slotnik had his best interest at heart, Fernández rededicated himself to his teacher and his practice. After two and a half or three years of study, his flute teacher told him that he could audition for the seat with the Dominican symphony, but that if he studied with him for three more years that he could successfully audition for any symphony. He later earned a chair in the Dominican symphony.

Fernández took courses at Jazzmobile for a fee of thirty-five dollars a year, where he studied with Frank Foster, Frank Strozier, and Jimmy Owens on Saturdays from 9am to 5pm. He would augment these studies by joining the reading sessions previously discussed at Lynn Oliver's studio on 89th Street. Fernández enjoyed the variety of reading settings that Oliver and his wife organized. On

Monday nights, he would go to the Village Vanguard to hear the Thad Jones-Mel Lewis band perform. There he first encountered Joe Henderson, Eddie Daniels, and many others. While Fernández felt that he learned a lot about US jazz culture during this time, he also wanted to improve his reading of syncopated music. The Dominican saxophonist Mario Rivera had been living in New York for some time and was highly respected among both jazz and Latin musicians, working consistently with Dizzy Gillespie, Tito Puente, Machito, and many others. Rivera invited Fernández to join him at Tito Puente's rehearsals playing third alto saxophone, as the Puente book had a repertoire of over six hundred pieces. Fernández had a steady gig at the Havana-San Juan Friday to Sunday, but from Monday to Thursday, he played the third alto sax chair with Puente without pay, using it as a means to further his education. One night, Mario Bauzá saw him playing with Puente's band and subsequently invited him to play with Machito's band. Fernández learned a lot with Mario Bauzá and met many great players in the band. Fernández felt that both Puente's band and Machito's were characterized by jazz musicians who wanted to play Latin music, but also by Latin musicians who wanted to play jazz.

All told, Fernández treated his period of study as if it were a job to be worked at eight hours a day. In his own words he said, "I came to New York to study," and he did so from Monday to Friday and even stopped dating in order to focus on his goals.[166] His practice routine lasted from 8am to noon, with a break until 2pm, followed by more practice and study until 6pm: "this was the era during which I progressed the most."[167] At one point, Fernández started to fear that he was getting immersed in another culture so totally that he would lose his own identity both musically and culturally. He noticed this first with getting lost between genres that emphasized feels on two and four versus one and three, but also with peers telling him to forget about Latin music. During a recording session for a merengue by a noted arranger, he played a solo that was heavily influenced by John Coltrane, thoroughly disappointing everyone who expected a more *típico* performance since he was primarily known as musician who had been steeped in the tradition of Dominican merengue. This made him rethink what he was doing and realize that he would have to "marry all of these cultures" rather than change his own; he would continue his classes and studies, but not change himself.[168] In his own words, he came to the United States "not to further 'Dominicanize' [himself], but to absorb American culture without changing his own culture."[169] Ultimately, what motivated Fernández to move back to the Dominican Republic was that New York City changed a lot in the time that he was there. The city had become too dangerous, everyone was carrying a gun, but "I cried when I left New York, like breaking up with a girlfriend . . . I cried for New York."[170]

JUAN COLÓN

Juan Colón is another Dominican musician who made the decision to come to New York specifically to improve his musicianship. He details many aspects of his personal journey from childhood to the present in an excellent book, *Vivencias de un músico* (2014), that documents his illustrious career.[171] Colón had a solid formal musical formation in the Dominican Republic, but as a performer he was largely focused on merengue recording and working with Rafael Solano and Fausto Rey. He came to New York City for the first time in 1969, where he spent time with Mario Rivera, who gave him a book with different scales used for jazz and demanded that Colón practice it thoroughly before returning to Rivera's house.[172] Colón came back to visit Rivera in 1970 and Rivera, pleased with his improvement, gave Colón a book of John Coltrane transcriptions to practice in every key. Back in the Dominican Republic, Colón was working with Rafael Solano and doing well financially, but the jazz bug had bitten him. Listening to saxophonists like Stan Getz, he started to understand that jazz improvisers were playing in the moment, they were "not waiting for the piano to change, nor for the bass to change, no he [Getz] was [just] playing."[173] For Colón, this was something that he didn't understand, but wanted to focus on. A local trumpeter named Hector DeLeón, who had worked with Tito Rodríguez, Tito Puente, and Eddie Palmieri, started to show Colón some of the basics of jazz improvisation and the relationship between scales and chord changes. Colón realized that to really understand and play jazz he would have to come to the United States, and in 1979 he came back to New York. The musician's musician, Bobby Porcelli, became his mentor and put him "on the right track."[174] Colón then studied orchestration with Panamanian bassist Guillermo Edgehill and arranging with Ray Santos, who was Colón's favorite arranger and who taught him how to write for saxophones. Colón also studied orchestration with José Antonio Molina for two years in New Jersey. Colón went to JazzMobile and noted that it was where everyone went to study and play jazz. At the same time he took jazz improvisation classes with Barry Harris and classical flute lessons with Leonny Lithz. Colón also studied with Hilton Ruiz. Like Crispín Fernández, Colón came to the realization that he could not focus on jazz exclusively due to the fact that his familial obligations took precedence over the practicing demanded by someone like Mario Rivera, and also because he was able to work extensively playing merengue in the 1980s. During the 1980s he recorded and performed with such international stars as Juan Luis Guerra, Wilfrido Vargas, Celia Cruz, Sergio Vargas, and many more. However, the jazz influence stayed deep within the fiber of his being. Colón made two recordings as a leader; particularly notable is the album of Supersax-style arrangements of his idol,

Tavito Vasquéz. Other future projects such as "The Parsley Massacre" would also bear the fruits of his study.

In New York, Colón also spent time at Lynn Oliver's, which he enjoyed immensely. He tried to bring the concept of a reading band back to the Dominican Republic when he came home for good, but he could not find a group of musicians to pursue the idea. Colón felt that the lack of interest in a reading band was due to the fact that each young musician he encountered wanted to be a soloist rather than play in a horn section or work on blending in a band. To this day, Colón remains committed to working on developing music programs within the Dominican Republic, encouraging younger musicians, and preserving the history and richness of Dominican music. Since returning permanently to the Dominican Republic a few years ago, Colón has published a number of educational books: transcriptions of Tavito Vásquez solos, a book of Mario Rivera transcriptions, and he is now finishing another on saxophone pedagogy. Colón's interest in documenting these artists and sharing their greatness with the next generation of Dominican musicians is all done with the sincere desire to perpetuate the memory of his musical mentors and heroes: Choco DeLeón, Mario Rivera, and Tavito Vásquez. In a testament to his influence as a performer and educator, Colón, his music, and his teaching were recently honored in a festival in Colombia.

AFRO-CARIBBEAN FOLKLORE AS EDUCATION

A tremendously important avenue for Spanish Caribbean musical education has been the folklore scene. This encompasses both ritual and secular music from throughout the region such as Afro-Cuban sacred batá drumming, *palo*, abakuá, secular rumba, Puerto Rican plena, danza, and bomba, jíbaro music, as well as Dominican *palos*, just to name a few. A number of formal and informal musical groups dedicated to these traditions have flourished at different times throughout the last hundred years. These include Dominican groups such as Centro Cultural Dominicano (profiled in *Latin NY*, October 1979), Grupo Folkórico Dominicano de Nueva York, Asa Difé, Puerto Rican groups such as Los Pleneros de la 110, Los Pleneros de la 21, Yomo Toro's groups, Eddy Rosa's Renacer Borinquen dedicated to *jíbaro* music, Felix Romero's Teatro Otra Cosa (Afro–Puerto Rican bomba), and groups that focused on Afro-Cuban music such as Cheveré Macún Cheveré and Los Afortunados.[175] A number of excellent musicians who were born and raised in New York City became masters of Afro-Latin folklore such as Felix Sanabria, Abraham Rodríguez, Skip Burney, Victor Jaroslav, Alberto Serrano, Eddie Bobè, Eddie Rodríguez, Willie Everich, and Abby Holiday, among others. Berta Jottar and Lisa Knauer have published

Fig 1.5. Drummers l-r: Rafael Dumont, Eddie Bobè, Felix D. Sanabria, Elliot "Yeyito." Flores female dancers l-r: Roxanne Zapatero, unknown student, Carmen Sánchez, Isa Díaz. Male dancers l-r: Alicea, Felix Romero in center, Carlos. Saint Mary's Recreation Center, Bronx, NY. Photo courtesy of the Felix Romero Archives.

Fig 1.6. Female dancers, l-r: Isa Díaz, Roxanne Zapatero, Carmen Sánchez, unknown student. Drummer Eddie Bobè; Felix Romero dancing, center. Fort Monmouth, NJ. Photo courtesy of the Felix Romero Archives.

extensively about these musicians and the folkloric scene in New York with particular attention paid to the weekly rumba in Manhattan's Central Park.[176] Additionally, many of these younger Puerto Rican, African American, and Anglo musicians spent significant time with and under the tutelage of Cuban master musicians such as Los Hermanos Dreke ("Curva" y Enrique), Virgilio Martí, and later with Manuel Martín Olivera, Felipe García Villamil, Roberto Borrell, and Orlando "Puntilla" Ríos, who arrived in New York, among many others, during the period of the 1980 Mariel Boatlift.[177]

Fig 1.7. Felix D. Sanabria, Eddie Bobè, and Rafael DuMont; female dancer Roxanne Zapatero. Fort Monmouth, NJ. Photo courtesy of the Felix Romero Archives.

Prior to 1980, Sanabria remembers taking a workshop with Totico and Gene Golden in February 1977. Golden insisted that Sanabria learn to play, sing, and dance in order to become a better rumbero and drummer overall. Sanabria also got into Afro-Haitian drumming and dance through working and studying with Canel Archer, Frizner Augustín, and Louis Celestín. During this time he also met David Coleman and John Amira. For Sanabria, beyond first seeing Grupo Folclórico, Conjunto Libre, and Típica 73 using batá drums onstage in New York in 1975:

> We were getting the more visual, hands-on, seeing and listening to *our own* brothers and sisters doing this kind of music . . . what it is, now you're not just seeing a Cuban playing, you're seeing a black American, like Gene Golden playing, you're seeing a Puerto Rican like Milton Cardona. So arguably you're really looking at your neighbors being the ones who are playing this music. Now it's not just some mysterious Tata Güines [Cuban percussionist] who we never met or . . . Jesús Pérez."[178]

The mystery of the music was being removed as this generation of New York percussionists moved closer to those making it. This musical revelation coincided with the civil rights movement and the quest for knowledge of one's roots. For Sanabria, these sentiments personally resounded with Ray Barretto's 1969 song from this time period "¿De donde vengo?" (Where am I from?).[179]

Sanabria remembers how much he and his peers treasured live performances by Los Papines, Irakere, and other groups visiting from Cuba around 1978. This also coincided with more access to Cuban records by these groups. In the meantime, Sanabria and his friends frequented rumbas by the drummers at the Douglass Houses, Goddard Riverside, Grant Houses, 104th and First Avenue and the musicians who would become Los Pleneros de la 110, as well as the drummers in the South Bronx, the Tremont Avenue drummers (also in the Bronx), and the Friday-Sunday rumbas in Central Park.[180] Sanabria remembered playing rumba from March to November in 1979 or 1980 in the park without pause, because the weather was so mild. This uninterrupted time period was one of growth for Sanabria and his peers. Burney and Sanabria would eventually teach percussion at Johnny Colón's music school around 1980, and they have since taught many musicians both formally and informally. The impact of the Mariel musicians on Sanabria, Burney, and others is explored in chapter 7.

RECORDINGS AS INSTRUCTION FOR FOLKLORIC MUSIC

Prior to the arrival of these master Cuban musicians, these young New York musicians listened to any folkloric Cuban recordings that they could get their hands on. These included third- or fourth-generation cassette copies of rumba recordings that René López brought back from Cuba. A number of commercial recordings were crucial listening and important reference points for these New York musicians. These records included Silvestre Mendez's *Oriza*, Justi Barreto's 1971 recording *Santería Barbara*, *Afrocubanos Con Los Authenticos Tambores Bata De Giraldo Rodriguez*, *Santeria Cubana*, *Santero* (featuring Celia Cruz and Mercedes Valdés), Candida Batista's *Ritmo de Santo*, Celia Cruz's *Homenaje a los santos*, Gina Martin's records, Alberto Zayas's *Afro-Frenetic: Tambores de Cuba*, Gilberto Valdés's *Rezo de Santo*, Mongo Santamaria's *Tambores Afro-Cubanos* recordings for SMC, Santamaria's *Up from the Roots*, Chano Pozo's recordings for SMC, Harold Courlander's *Cult Music of Cuba* (1951), Verna Gillis's field recordings later released as *Music of Cuba* (1985), Justi Barreto's album *Guaguanco '69*, and the seminal album *Patato y Totico*.

It is important to note that Barreto's recordings were very popular, printed multiple times by a variety of labels, and well known by many percussionists of this generation.[181] These records featured Onelio Scull, Ángel Gómez, Julito Collazo, Carlos "Patato" Valdés, Domingo Gómez, Máximo Texidor, Julia Valdés, Juan Candela, Merceditas Rojas, Nicolás Hernández, and Papito. Other recordings of music by *espiritistas* such as *La mano poderosa* by Hermano Moises and *Oración del jibarito* by Aurea L. Boyrie "La India" with Rafael Caraballo y Su Conjunto, as well as Caraballo's *Plegarias a los santos*.[182] These last records along with *Santeros Cantados* by Luz Celenia Tirado, mark a unique syncretization of Puerto Rican jíbaro music with *espiritismo* and santería that was cultivated, recorded, and marketed in New York.[183] A number of percussion-centric albums by Tito Puente were also important for aspiring musicians. Felix Sanabria stated that, for him and his musical-generational cohort, the following six records "were basically our bibles: Patato and Totico's album, *Drums and Chants* [Mongo Santamaria], *Up from the Roots* [Mongo Santamaria], *Afro Roots* [Mongo Santamaria], and *Puente in Percussion*, and *Top Percussion* [Tito Puente]." As Jottar notes, "For Yeyito, Félix Sanabria, and Eddy Bobě's generation, salsa posed the question 'Where are you from?' while rumba provided the answer 'We are Afro-Latinos'" (Félix Sanabria, personal communication, 2009). Thus, with the exception of the Nuyoricans Abe Rodríguez, who worked for Totico, Yeyito, who learned with Papaito, and Eddie Bobè, who learned with Frankie Malabé, the most prominent way that this Nuyorican generation learned traditional rumba during the 1970s was, as mentioned above, by listening to the recordings whose lead players were actually the local Cuban rumberos in New York.[184]

One major musical result of this generation of musicians was that they "they were creating a hybrid style that juxtaposed the diverse rhythmic influences of a larger Afro-Latino diaspora while developing new musical skills" such as singing Spanish and English-language music while playing multiple drums.[185] This type of innovation can be heard on the doo-wop/rumba recording of "What's Your Name?" by Totico y Sus Rumberos and in live performances by the aforementioned New York–bred musicians who would also incorporate blues, jazz, funk, and pop music. However, many of these musicians went all the way with Afro-Cuban drumming and became *omo aña* (ritual drummers), some even becoming *babalawo* (priests) in Santería. After learning largely in the park and with friends, Felix Sanabria would later win a grant where he had Puntilla teach him song by song as the master had himself learned, advancing from drum to drum in order of complexity (*okónkolo*, *itótele*, and *iyá*). Sanabria said that, "from September 21, 1985 up into the 2000s," this is exactly how he learned. In figure 1.8, a photo of the Central Park rumba around 1961, one can see the musician on the playing left playing a drum made by the drum maker Gonzalo Vergara in Cuba.

Interest in and exposure to Afro-Caribbean syncretic religions and their associated musical forms were also diffused through local media and in publications such *Santería*. *Latin NY* featured monthly articles on santería practice, seeking to explain the positive aspects of the religion and to dispel any negative stereotypes. *Latin NY* also featured a detailed interview with percussionist Milton Cardona in which he speaks about ritual drumming and his own personal involvement. The interview also includes musical transcriptions of

Fig 1.8. Central Park rumba 1961. Photo courtesy of the collection of Mark Sanders.

batá drumming.[186] In addition, exhibitions and concerts focusing on the roots of Latin music and commonalities between African diaspora music helped foster interest amongst audiences and musicians.

From all of the evidence provided in this chapter, it is clear that formal and informal Latin music education has been happening in New York for many years, certainly well before 2021. A number of specific educators such as Victoria Hernández, Maria Luisa Lecompte, Eduviges Bocanegra, Nicolás Rodríguez, and Alberto Socarrás singlehandedly taught some of the best musicians in Latin music from the 1940s to the 1980s. Through the efforts of Johnny Colón, Louis Bauzó, and Ramón Rodríguez and their music programs another two generations of Latin music professionals learned from the best musicians in the scene and went on to achieve professional success. Historical knowledge was transmitted from one generation to the next through informal listening sessions at René López's house and through informal mentorships of younger musicians by their elders. The study, performance, and consumption of Afro-Latin folkloric music also served as an important force in educating Latin musicians in New York City. It is beyond the scope of this book to discuss how this music was received country by country beyond New York, but it goes without saying that all of the musicians discussed in this study have enjoyed critical

Fig 1.9. Cover of *Santería* magazine. Photo courtesy of the collection of Henry Medina.

and commercial success beyond New York, particularly when returning to their home countries or settling outside of New York City. Finally, this chapter demonstrates how and why New York City offered musicians an extensive group of opportunities to study, learn, practice, and improve their performance of Latin music that were unavailable in other countries.

EXPRESSIONS'83
EXPRESIONES'83

A CELEBRATION OF AFRICA IN THE AMERICAS
A FESTIVAL OF DANCERS, DRUMMERS AND SINGERS
A RAINBOW OF CULTURES UNDER ONE SUN —October 13, 14, 15 & 16

PRODUCED BY THE CARIBBEAN CULTURAL CENTER/VARRCRC/
UNA PRESENTACION DE VARRCRC—
MARTA VEGA, EXECUTIVE DIRECTOR

SYMPHONY SPACE 95TH ST & B'WAY NYC

ALL PERFORMANCES UNLESS OTHERWISE INDICATED START AT 8 PM

Thursday, October 13
AFRICA—Adesanya—an exciting array of
traditional Nigerian music and dance
**UNITED STATES—Marie Brooks Dance
Research Theatre—guest artist Cheryl
Byron**—Calypsonian—a potpourri of music,
dance and song from Africa, the Caribbean
and the United States
**DOMINICAN REPUBLIC—Raices y La
Cofradia**—this exciting company brings an
array of its country's dances—"Merengue,"
"Congo" and more

Friday, October 14
BRAZIL—Jelon Vieria Dance Brazil—a taste
of Brazil from the carefree hipswinging Samba
to the fast and graceful martial art foot dance
—the Capoeira!
CUBA—Roberto Borrel y Su Kubata—a
special choreographed dance and music
presentation, Rumba del Solar, sampling of
the exciting Afro-Cuban songs and dances
created in the streets of Cuba.
**PUERTO RICO—Los Guayacanes de San
Anton**—the vibrant song, music and dance of
la Plena—direct from Puerto Rico—only New
York appearance

Saturday, October 15
HAITI—Louis Celestin—an exceptional
dancer and percussionist; world famous for his
"Banda"—a hilarious dance on the odd
subject of death!
Tabou Combo—the orchestra gives a touch
of contemporary Haiti—its powerful melodies
and extraordinary rhythms!
Miriam Dorisme and Paulette St. Lot—two of
the country's foremost singers join together in
a classic exchange of sound!
TRINIDAD—Trinidad Serenaders Steel Band
featuring **The Mighty Panther**—celebrating
their 25th anniversary.
JAMAICA—Kalabash—the swinging sounds
of Reggae rhythms of this exciting orchestra.

Sunday, October 16—2:00 p.m.
CARNAVAL—African rituals mixed with New
World Cultures gave birth to "CARNAVAL"—
experience the magic, joy, spirit, rhythms,
dances and celebration of Carnaval in the
Americas. A NEW YORK FIRST—a special joint
presentation of the music and dance
companies of Haiti, Puerto Rico, Trinidad,
Dominican Republic, Cuba and Brazil!

TICKETS: $12 & $10
AVAILABLE AT
Symphony Space
95th Street & Broadway
or Call **Chargit** at
(212) 944-9300

Additional funding has been provided by The
Department of Cultural Affairs, The New York State
Council on the Arts, The National Endowment for the
Arts, and Chemical Bank. The Center is an affiliate of
the Phelps-Stokes Fund.

Presented in cooperation with **Con Edison**

ORDER BY OCTOBER 1
AND SAVE OVER 30%
FIRST 300 ORDERS
RECEIVE FREE
T-SHIRT!

For further Information (212) 307-7420

Fig 1.10. Advertisement for Expressions in *Latin NY* magazine. Photo courtesy of Izzy Sanabria.

CHAPTER 2

STRINGS AND SKINS

Latin Music Instrument Makers in New York

Today, congas and many other hand percussion instruments are ubiquitous in pop music throughout the world. Scholars and fans of Latin music have paid almost no attention to the origins of these instruments in New York and their subsequent mass production, nor have they examined the people who built the instruments used to play Latin music in New York City and internationally. Luckily there have been folklorists, journalists, and authors outside of academia who have been exceptions to this and to whose work this chapter owes a great debt. These include Richard Blondet, Mary Kent, William Cumpiano, Miriam Fuentes, Juan Sotomayor, and Rick Mattingly, among others. This chapter seeks to unify their work into one coherent narrative.

The trajectory of Spanish Caribbean musical instruments in New York began with the importation and sales of percussion and string instruments made in Cuba, Puerto Rico, and elsewhere. It then shifted to the construction of copies of these instruments until significant changes were made in their construction, and some instruments became mass-produced. The transformation of these instruments in New York City was possible because of the partnership between practicing musicians and the instrument builders who sought their input. Through the efforts of a few builders, instruments originating in Cuban and Puerto Rican musical traditions were developed further and modified according to the needs of the musicians who played a variety of Latin music in New York City.

The following pages highlight the innovations of hand-drum builders such as Frank Mesa, Jay Bereck, and Martin Cohen. Similarly, timbales, which were originally handmade by one individual in New York City, were manufactured by a number of North American companies by the mid-1940s. These instruments and their players were featured in company catalogues alongside mostly non-Latin instruments and performers. The characteristic sound of the bass in Latin music in both New York City and throughout the rest of the world is due to the use of the Ampeg Baby Bass, an electric upright bass with a solid body that was innovated in New York City by players and the company's main product engineer. This sound is still sought after as the standard, and another electric upright bass would be made and sold by one of two New York–based Puerto Rican builders who worked for a major North American guitar company. The *cuatro* and *tres*, two instruments associated with Puerto Rican jíbaro and the Cuban son respectively, had a number of builders in New York City who would make thousands of instruments. These luthiers would forever change the means by which these instruments were made because they decreased the time it took to make them. The high level of craft these builders possessed was even solicited by two of the most in-demand classical musicians of the last century, Andrés Segovia and José Rey de la Torre. Lastly, the humble cowbell, an instrument essential to Latin music, was perfected and mass-produced in New York City. Today, it is a part of North American music and popular culture with its own "More Cowbell" skit on *Saturday Night Live*. However, its development and the range of possible tone colors were the direct result of people like Johnny Pacheco, Calixto Rivera, and Martin Cohen. Before these individuals and others made these percussion instruments, there was really only one place to get them in New York City: a pastry shop on 116th Street in Manhattan.

IMPORTATION: SIMÓN JOU'S LA MODERNA

One of the earliest, if not the first purveyor of Afro-Cuban percussion instruments since at least the 1930s, was Simón Jou Llongueras, the Spanish-born and Cuban-raised owner of La Moderna Bakery and Pastry shop (see fig. 2.1). Besides selling delicious pastries and sweets, the shop sold tumbadoras (congas), bongos (bongó drums), güiros (wood scrapers), maracas, claves, and other instruments.[1] Independent researcher Richard Blondet has been able to discover previously unknown details regarding Jou's biography, finding conflicting documentation as to his birth; he was either born "in Terassa, Spain on Sept. 17th, 1893, or in Barcelona in 1894."[2] Jou was raised in Cuba and relocated to New York City in the early 1920s after spending some time in Bordeaux, France, "where he had traveled to further hone his pastry skills."[3] Jou started working at the McAlpin Hotel before striking out on his own.[4] In 1923 Jou established the first La Moderna Bakery location in a storefront on 219 W. 116th Street and he made his home above the store. By 1933 the business moved to a space between W. 115th and W. 116th Street on Lenox Avenue.[5] The store's fame spread, and as Blondet indicates, "by the mid-1950s, syndicated columnist Dorothy Kilgallen described a Hollywood film legend's connection to 'La Moderna' Bakery."[6] Kilgallen wrote: "MARLON BRANDO buys his Conga drums in a pastry shop, of

Fig 2.1. Advertisement for Simón Jou's La Moderna from *Gráfico* newspaper.

all places—a store called La Dolcera [*sic*] Moderna at Lenox Ave. and 115th St. Behind the creampuffs and layer cakes the rear of the shop is a fascinating area, with flour-dusted bakers threading their way through a maze of skins, woods and finished drums manufactured by the owner as a hobby."[7]

In the 1940s, most of the musicians who frequented this place were percussionists such as Mongo Santamaría, Willie Bobo, and Cándido Camero.[8] Percussionist Benny Bonilla remembered that there was a backyard in the back of the building where musicians such as Mongo Santamaría, Chonguito, and José Mangual would have rumbas and jam.[9] Bonilla also indicated that this is where the celebrated vocalist Frank "Machito" Grillo would procure the maracas that looked like they had been crushed and that he was always seen playing. Bonilla remembered other interesting details about the scene at Simón's shop during a conversation with Richard Blondet and explained that he "bought his first 'conga' drum at Simon Jou's La Moderna Bakery in 1949."[10] Bonilla further explained to Blondet:

Simon's was on Lenox Ave. between 115th Street & 116th Street (in the middle of the block). He had his pastry in the front store window and on the counters inside. The owner, Simon, sold wood conga shells and bongo shells (different sizes). He also sold skins for both. All of Simon's conga/bongo shells were shipped in from Cuba. The conga and bongo shells were on shelves along the wall and an open area in the rear where many percussionists such as Jose Mangual, Mongo [Santamaria], Patato [Valdes], Sabu Martinez and others, would go to hangout and chitchat. I believe, at that time, "La Moderna" Bakery was the only supplier of Cuban drum shells, Güiros and maracas. Some others came from Mexico, but the quality was not the same.[11]

In another conversation that Blondet had with Nina Simone's former percussionist, Leopoldo Fleming Jr., he indicated that he also visited La Moderna:

> I lived in that neighborhood and had occasion to visit "Simon's," as we called it. My understanding is that the drums were imported from Cuba in marked staves and reassembled there according to demand. At least that's what I was told at the time. I had one of those drums, which was without hardware, which was the norm of the time and required heating for tuning. Hence, *"Preparen candela pa' afinar los cueros"* [Prepare some fire to tune the skins].[12]

In addition, musicians acquired their drum skins from the shop and Simón would measure the client's hand after watching him play in order to be sure to have a skin with the appropriate thickness. Blondet writes that, "by 1961, La Dulceria y Pastilleria 'LA MODERNA' was in its fourth distinct decade in Harlem,"[13] and that Jou had even opened a second shop in Brooklyn.[14] Journalist Babby Quintero chronicled Jou's sale of La Moderna to two young Puerto Ricans in 1964.[15] Jou moved to Westchester County and died after being struck by a car in 1971, but his legacy extended beyond purveying pastries and instruments.[16] As Blondet described:

> Aside from offering pastry, La Moderna served as an informal community or cultural space for the local Spanish language community. Throughout the late 1920s, Jou was a regular contributor to the Grafico publication that was launched in 1927. His column "Simonadas" was Jou's own brand of satire inspired by the entertainment artistry and then-emerging industry of the period. But La Moderna's legend would become specifically revolved around the artists who engaged in Cuban Popular Music of the first half of the 20th century.[17]

While Simón Jou's inventory was supplied by a family member directly from Cuba, it was not long before New York City–based drum makers started making tools for New York's Afro-Latin drummers.

IMITATION AND INNOVATION: FRANK MESA AND JAY BERECK, TWO NEW YORK CITY DRUM-MAKING PIONEERS

In 1957 an enterprising Puerto Rican bassist in Brooklyn named Frank Mesa started to make his own conga drums under the name Eco-tone. These drums were made of fiberglass and became the preferred brand for some great musicians such as Ray Barretto, Cándido Camero, Willie Bobo, Carlos "Patato"

Fig 2.2. Skin on Skin advertisement from *Latin NY* magazine. Photo courtesy of Izzy Sanabria.

Valdés, Frankie Malabe, and others.[18] According to Nolan Warden, "Eco-tones were endorsed by many stars including Candido, Miguelito Valdés, and the percussionists for Jimi Hendrix."[19] Mesa is said to have sold his instruments at the now-defunct Manny's Music on W. 48th Street in Manhattan, and to have stopped production in 1971.[20] Eco-tone congas had a distinct shape and often a unique finish. Eco-tone enthusiasts have compiled a number of album covers and even a clip from the movie *Superfly* that feature these distinctive-looking instruments.[21]

Another musician who became a percussion instrument artisan in the 1950s was Jay Bereck, an American Jew whose shop Skin on Skin was at 1678 Atlantic Avenue in Brooklyn. For the musicians who purchased their drums from Bereck, his Jewish heritage was irrelevant, but in a 1999 *New York Daily News* profile, it was on journalist Roberto Santiago's mind. Santiago began his article by writing:

Don't tell anybody, but many practitioners of Santeria, the West African religion, purchase their batas (Nigerian two-headed drums) from a Jewish artisan in Crown Heights. "It's almost sacrilegious to reveal that, but, yes, I make the ceremonial drums," said Jay Bereck, who has been hand making congas from scratch for some of the world's greatest Latin jazz percussionists for most of his 61 years. "And I didn't have to leave Brooklyn to do it."[22]

As I show in the chapter on Jewish involvement with Latin music in New York City, there was significant Latin musical activity in Brooklyn, and drum making falls under this category. Bereck was born July 26, 1938, in the Williamsburg section of Brooklyn, and raised in a working-class family in Borough Park. His father and mother were first-generation Americans who worked as a sheet-metal apprentice and at odd jobs respectively.[23]

Bereck also worked as a sheet-metal apprentice with National Sheet Metal from 1956–60 and played some of the first drums he built playing in an East Village mambo group. Bereck also owned a coffee shop in the East Village called Café Samarkand where he worked at night. He had partners in the coffee shop and stayed in construction until he moved to drum building full time in 1976. Aware of Santiago's interest in his being Jewish, Bereck spoke about it telling Santiago: "'The only Hispanic thing about me is my wife,' said Bereck, who recently celebrated 38 years of marriage to Maria Migenes, a nurse of Puerto Rican descent. 'It was unusual to see a Jewish guy into Afro-Cuban rhythms, but that was the only kind of music that meant anything to me.'"[24] This makes sense, as Bereck explained to Dave Easter:

"Ah, Latin music—drumming has always impressed me. Somehow or another, I always found drum music very exciting. Nobody's ever asked questions from the beginning before, so I never really think about this. Ah, I always found it really exciting. When I was a kid, I used to listen to jazz. Drum solos used to excite me ah, they had I believe, the Dick Ricardo Sugar show on the radio. My parents used to dance at Roseland every weekend, and we used to have the Latin music playing and I used to bang on the table. I'd take spoons and 'clack' them together and try."[25]

Bereck also started going to the Palladium when he got older. Around this time he acquired "A pair of really jive Bongos . . . [and] a real shitty [Zimgar] conga drum at a music store on Flatbush Avenue with what we call Mexican-style tuning, tuned from the top. I remember putting a new skin on one night, and having the hardware sort of explode and stuck in the ceiling, actually."[26] Around this time he also acquired claves, maracas, and a cowbell from a music store called Hassan's in the East Village, and learned some basic Afro-Cuban drum patterns from an African American drummer named Sabu (not Sabu Martínez) and another drummer named Don Gimble. Bereck also learned from an African American friend named Charley Campbell who had a group called Damballah. They would go to the Palladium and watch the drummers instead of dancing. Bereck would also listen to Symphony Sid's radio show with his friends to hear his idols Bill Fitch, Armando Perraza, and others.

Bereck started making drums because he didn't like the drums that were available in New York City and explained that he did not undergo any formal apprenticeship with a drum maker. Instead, he taught himself. Bereck explained: "'I studied history books, examined their construction, experimented, took them apart, fixed them,' he said. 'Then in the '70s, while there was a lapse in the construction trade, I started to take on lots of orders to make congas, bongos, batas and before I knew it, I was doing it full-time.'"[27] However, in a videotaped interview with Dan Gold from 1986, Bereck added: "What it boils down to is there's something I'm trying to accomplish. Now I might try it and not really succeed. So then I want to find out why I didn't completely succeed and that's when I start trying to do research. Many of the things I do I have not found in books."[28]

Bereck explained to Dave Easter that the Cuban drum maker Vergara was his real model for making drums:

> Vergara he was the man!! I frankly copied the shape of my Congas from the shape of his Congas. The hardware basically is the old Cuban-Style hardware, except . . . it's a lot stronger. From what I understand, he did not make his own hardware. He farmed it out to somebody—maybe various people. Ah, I came into this as a metal worker. I'm a far better metal worker than the guys who did metal work on, on those drums. Uh, as far as the woodwork is concerned, uh I believe I've managed to do a really good job on the shells.[29]

Bereck knew the process of how Vergara made his drums in depth and explained that they came from American whisky barrels used to transport sugarcane, rum, and corn in Cuba. The contents of the barrels were indicated in writing inside and would be scratched and relabeled with each reuse and shipment. Bereck knew about drums made by Vergara, Solis, and Aguerra from friends who got them at Simón Jou's La Moderna, remembering "there was a bakery uptown, ah, I think it was in East Harlem called Simone's, where they used to sell a lot of these drum, you know."[30] Bereck got started by repairing Mongo Santamaria's bongó and building unique drums that some musicians such as Tommy López initially criticized due to their shape.[31] In Larry Gold's video interviews with Bereck, the drum maker talks about how the shape of his drums evolved from ice cream cone (Valje) to watermelon (Gon-Bop), then a shape that was like a watermelon shape but with a smaller bottom, and finally an even smaller bottom with a wider belly, which became the "number four shape."[32] The Skin on Skin quinto has the third shape.[33] Some of Bereck's clients have included Mongo Santamaria, Giovanni Hidalgo, Ray Barretto, Felix Sanabria, and many other well-known percussionists. Bereck also made a number of instruments specifically for Roberto Borrell, explaining that he made him a "Comparsa bombo which is bass drum . . . ah, I made Yuka drums for him, I made Abakuá drums for him, basically I made very much the range of Afro-Cuban instruments."[34] An anonymous commenter on the percussion blog Tony's Conga Adventures recalls: "I was good friends with Jay's son David growing up in Brooklyn. As a kid I remember Jay's first shop on Smith Street before Carroll Gardens turned into a wealthy scene. They had a wood stove in their house and they would burn the scraps of ash, oak and cherry from the shop. It always smelled so great."[35]

Interestingly, Bereck himself said that he was struck by the frequency with which Afro-Cubans in New York would approach him wanting to learn to make drums. In these interactions he learned from them that their parents did not appreciate rumba and Afro-Cuban culture.[36] Bereck's daughter explained what growing up with her drum-making father was like:

> I was a young teen when he began working out the process in the base-
> ment of our Brooklyn home. There was a lot of trial and error; many trips
> to the library. I remember a discussion we had about steam pressure and
> expansion—I was taking physics at the time, but I don't think I was of much
> help :-) Jay invented and built many of the devices he uses himself, some
> of which were intended to save physical effort—make no mistake, making
> hard-wood drums by hand is physically hard, sweaty work.[37]

The quality of his instruments is well known among New York City percussionists, as well as musicians outside of the United States. Percussionist Willie Martínez explained: "Jay's congas produce voices that you cannot get from mass-produced congas. With Jay's congas, when you strike the center skin, it produces a rich bottom sound a deep bass moan that sounds just like the handmade congas made in Cuba."[38]

In one of Cara Bereck Levy's videos, drummer Victor Jaroslav talks about the lasting impact of Bereck's batá drums on the ritual drumming scene, noting that at that time there were only two sets of *fundamento* (consecrated batá) drums that were used several times a week for ceremonies. Having Bereck's batá drums to practice with allowed for ritual drummers like Jaroslav to work on their drumming so as not to lose their technique and work on the difficult music the tradition requires.[39] Bereck's daughter related an anecdote about her father that speaks to his character:

> Many years ago, my father was invited by the Smithsonian Institute to show his drums in an exhibition of folkloric musical instruments. He sent a set of cherry congas. However, when the Smithsonian wanted a set for permanent exhibition, he refused. He had a year-long waiting list of customers who had put down deposits, and he was not going to make them wait while he made a set of drums for the Smithsonian.[40]

Santiago's *New York Daily News* profile of Bereck also points out his working-class roots and consciousness:

> Bereck said that he and his assistant, Amilcar, make at least three congas per week. "I want to raise my prices, but conga players remember their poverty for too long," said Bereck, who said that if it wasn't for his wife's income, he would have had to close his workshop 25 years ago. "Congeros [*sic*] are not violinists. They don't pay thousands of dollars for their instruments nor would they if they could," Bereck said with a laugh.[41]

Bereck's drums have no identifying plaque or markings to identify them as Skin on Skin, his brand. However, according to his daughter Cara Bereck Levy, "My father signs the inside of every conga in English and Hebrew—the mark of an authentic Skin-on-Skin." Thus Bereck's Jewish identity is intrinsically bound to his art.[42] These signatures can only be seen on the inside of the drums.[43] Bereck eventually moved his shop from Brooklyn to Afton, New York, and has since retired, but his instruments and his legacy live on.

JUNIOR TIRADO, CALIXTO "CALI" RIVERA, AND JOHNNY PACHECO

Natalio "Junior" Tirado Ruiz and Calixto "Cali" Rivera were two other important Puerto Rican artisans based in New York City whose instruments are still held in high esteem by professional drummers and drum collectors alike. Tirado made unique congas and bongos in his workshop at 97 Havemeyer Street in Brooklyn.[44] In 1958 an auto mechanic and drummer named Calixto Rivera moved from Puerto Rico to the Highbridge section of the Bronx and shortly after his arrival started making his own cowbells in his apartment. Forced to leave his apartment after noise complaints, Rivera later made timbales and congas in his Bronx workshop right behind Yankee Stadium at 948 Ogden Avenue.[45] These instruments bear the label JCR Percussion, and it is widely acknowledged that one of the first Latin music recordings made in New York City using Cali's bongó bell was Cheo Feliciano's salsa hit, "Anacaona."[46] As reported in the *New York Times*, "The Metropolitan Museum of Art recently bought a set of Mr. Rivera's timbales and bells; they went on display Tuesday on the balcony of the musical instruments gallery. More typical customers over the years have included a who's who of Latino musicians—Tito Puente, Marc Anthony, Eddie Montalvo."[47] Rivera's bells are characterized by a particular tone that is recognizable by the musicians who use them, and Rivera attributed this uniqueness to how he made them and physically shaped the metal.

Also based in the Bronx, and possibly preceding both Tirado and Rivera's efforts, a young Dominican musician named Johnny Pacheco started making his own cowbells. He started because he needed them for recording sessions as a percussionist, but continued because he saw that there was a real need for cowbells in the New York City metropolitan area. Mary Kent interviewed Pacheco and he spoke about his foray into instrument making in her *Salsa Talks!* book and webpage. According to Pacheco, "New York timbales players took to tracking down horse drawn carts with the copper cowbells hanging from the horses' neck in order to snip them off. I remember one time, a horse had one hanging from its neck and I tried to cut it. The driver came and knocked the hell out of me. They caught me with the evidence. It was a beautiful bell."[48]

Pacheco also made congas in addition to bells. Kent writes:

During his stint as percussionist, Pacheco tried building a pair of congas. He did the wood work and hired someone who was working on a project for the Air Force to do the iron work. While visiting him, he found a piece of metal on the floor and Pacheco instinctively picked it up and hit it with a wrench. It let out a ring that echoed in Pacheco's ear. "Jesus Christ, I've gotta make a cowbell," he echoed back. Then Pacheco produced and sold a number of these cowbells. The first prototype bell still makes occasional guest appearances on the Pacheco bandstand.[49]

Thus, artisans made congas and cowbells and labored alone in their Brooklyn and Bronx shops before these products would be mass-produced. A similar pattern can be seen with both timbales and the electric upright basses known as Baby Basses.

TIMBALES IN NEW YORK: ORIGINS AND MASS PRODUCTION

Timbales or *pailas* have been an important part of the contemporary Latin music ensemble since the 1930s. Similar to the manufacture of congas, there is a lesser-known history for this instrument's makers in New York. The earliest known New York City–based timbales maker was a Cuban individual known as El Indio who made his instruments in a basement workshop on E. 110th Street and Madison in the early 1940s. Early clients are said to have included Ubaldo Nieto, Tito Puente, Tito Rodríguez, and Manny Oquendo. Little is known about El Indio, but Latin percussionist and instrument collector Faustino Cruz told José Rosa that El Indio had been "a very well known, respected timbalero and builder who had a great friendship with Tito Puente. Indio only built timbales for individuals that could play them well, he would ask you to play a simple pattern and if you couldn't play he wouldn't build anything for you and kick you out of his house."[50] Interestingly, the timbales that El Indio made for Tito Puente would become the model that Martin Cohen would copy and make for Puente once the Leedy company, whose instruments he had endorsed, went out of business and Puente signed an endorsement deal with Latin Percussion.[51]

Fig 2.3. A 1953 Ludwig catalogue page for timbales with musician endorsers at the bottom.

In 1944 a North American named Charles Tappan who worked in Henry Adler's percussion shop decided to make his own timbales by copying El Indio's design. His design was bought and distributed by Leedy and then the combined company of Leedy and Ludwig. The 1953 Ludwig catalogue features Humberto Morales, Chico Guerrero, Antoniano Escolies, Tito Puente, Ubaldo Nieto (see fig. 2.3).[52] The 1957 Ludwig catalogue also featured Expando conga drums and a tuneable combined bongó and timbales product called bongales.[53] Rogers was another North American company to manufacture timbales during this time period. Ubaldo Nieto, Humberto Morales, and Tito Puente were among the first musicians to be sponsored by these brands, Rogers, Leedy, Slingerland, and then Latin Percussion.

MORE MASS PRODUCTION: MARTIN COHEN'S LATIN PERCUSSION

Martin Cohen was born in January 28, 1939 in the Bronx. His father had been a fur cutter in New York City's garment district. He had worked as a waiter in the Catskills and graduated with a degree in mechanical engineering from City College.[54] As he told Rick Mattingly in an interview, he fell in love with Latin music as a teenager seeing Latin jazz at venues like Birdland. Like Jay Bereck, Cohen came from a working-class background; but unlike Bereck, Cohen did not play percussion. As he explained to Mattingly in an interview: "I wanted to get a pair of bongos . . . because Jose Mangual had made the biggest impression on me. But I couldn't find a pair of bongos because the U.S. had initiated an embargo of Cuba, and that's where the good bongos, congas, and cowbells had always come from. So I decided to make my own." Cohen also explained to Mattingly that he felt that he was initially perceived as an outsider as he moved within the community of Latin musicians:

> I did my most important research in Latin dance halls in the South Bronx, where shootings were not unknown . . . Then I would go to the after-hours clubs that began at 6:00 in the morning. I was the only non-Latino in these places that, frankly, were in the seamy side of town. A lot of people probably thought I was an undercover policeman. But I got by, primarily because I had such a love affair going with Latin music.[55]

A 1980 *People* magazine feature by Eric Levin, "What's a Nice Jewish Boy Doing as King of the Bongos? Explains Martin Cohen: 'I Was Never Nice,'" brings Cohen's Jewish identity into the forefront. Eric Levin wrote that:

Neither Cohen nor the instruments he began to experiment with were instantly accepted. "Jews were an oddity in Latin dance halls," he admits. "My first bongos were like two rotten flowerpots, and the musicians would twist my name, calling me maricón—which is slang for homosexual. I was so intent on getting across, I let it pass right by me."[56]

Although Cohen did not hide his Jewish identity and the *People* article sought to capitalize on the idea that Jewish involvement in Latin music was somehow a novelty, there was a long history of Jewish involvement with every facet of Latin music in New York City that I cover in this book and elsewhere. Perhaps the Jewish angle of the piece was thought to have helped sell the story, but Cohen seemed to have played along when he knew otherwise.

Initially, Cohen found success making instruments that were specifically for studio musicians, such as a stand-mounted bongó for Specs Powell, a *quijada* (jawbone) that would not break and that eventually became known as a vibraslap, in addition to woodblocks for musicians at Carroll Studios.[57] By 1964 he was making fiberglass congas, then cowbells, and Brazilian *cabasas* that would not break.[58] Like Bereck, Cohen was a one-person operation. He told Mattingly:

> I learned how to make hardware and how to weld.... But I never had electric welding; it was acetylene welding. I did all the work in my garage, which was separate from my house, so there was no heat. I remember being out there wearing two coats and a hooded sweatshirt, welding for hours on end to make bongo rims and side plates for congas. I often had to do things that I was told were impossible.... I didn't have an engine lathe at the time, and I had to produce threads for tuning lugs. I was told that there was no way it could be done on a drill press, but that's all I owned, so I devised a technique for producing threads on a drill press that worked wonderfully.[59]

In Steven Loza's book on Tito Puente, Cohen is quoted speaking about how he came up with his company's motto: "By this time Latin Percussion was in its infancy and I used a set of Tito's Cuban-made timbales and timbalitos as a basis for the prototype of my ribbed shell design. I based the 'Trust the Leader' promotional campaign on Tito's supreme skills as a bandleader and musician."[60]

Cohen was successful, and after he moved his business to New Jersey, he started mass manufacturing his products in Thailand. By 1980 his products, manufactured under the name Latin Percussion or LP, were everywhere. Levin writes:

> His drums carry the endorsement of Earth, Wind & Fire, Dizzy Gillespie, star studio percussionist Ralph MacDonald, Donna Summer's rhythm man

Bob Conti and Latin stalwarts like Willie Bobo, Patato Valdez and Tito Puente. "Martin was the pioneer after the Cuban embargo cut off supplies of traditional instruments," says Puente. "You can really send a message on Martin's drums."[61]

Similar to Bereck, Cohen's company also manufactured batá drums, but unlike Bereck his involvement with making these drums was not without problems. Cohen explained:

> A religion surrounds Bata drums. . . . And there is an ongoing resentment to my involvement with the drums. Some people feel I am trying to commercialize something that they hold as sacred and secret. But when I went to Cuba in 1979, I went to the home of the now-deceased grand Bata master, Jesus Perez. He opened a closet containing his sacred drums and let me look at them. He and his son played for me, and he invited me to record it. But in America, there is all this secrecy, and I've met with resistance on the part of practitioners.[62]

Another popular innovation driven by players' needs came from the in-demand percussionist Marc Quiñones's need for a stronger woodblock. In response, Cohen created the popular Jam Block made of brightly colored red or blue plastic, depending on the size and pitch.

> All of our market research told us they should be black, but we made them in red and blue. That way, they got recognition from the audience. It still amazes me that I was able to get Puerto Rican timbale players to stick a red piece of plastic on their drums, because Latinos are some of the most conservative people I've ever met when it comes to trying new things. It's only by virtue of the sound being so correctly tuned to their needs that they will buy into it.[63]

Cohen eventually sold his company, but has continued to stay at the helm of design. Many Latin Percussion products were designed to fit the needs of specific musicians, such as the "Richie Gajate bracket," a bracket that allows a drummer to use a foot pedal to play a cowbell, the Jam Block, and similar items. He posts videos filmed at his home studio of artists using his products, and he is still visible on the scene. Unlike Bereck, Cohen has his name on the Latin Percussion label affixed to the outside of his drums and he explained his thinking behind this: "I saw David Brown's name on the label of an Aston Martin car, and that told me someone named David Brown designed that car and put his name on it to be accountable . . . So I put my name on the LP labels for the same reason—so somebody would always know who to complain to if the product failed."[64]

Cohen also released several commercial recordings of artists using his instruments starting in the 1970s.[65] Since its founding in 1964, Latin Percussion remains the most recognizable name in the field of mass-produced hand percussion instruments to this day. Lastly, as seen in the education chapter, Cohen made a number of commercially released recordings with master Latin percussionists teaching aspiring students how to play traditional rhythms. He also assembled a Latin jazz ensemble and other groups around his most well-known artists to tour and record under the LP name. The how-to recordings and the ensembles no doubt helped create not only an audience for the artists playing his brand of instruments, but also a healthy consumer market of Latin percussionists.

SPANISH CARIBBEAN LUTHIERS IN NEW YORK

Luthier and folklorist William Cumpiano has indicated that there were a number of important Puerto Rican luthiers in the New York City metropolitan area, particularly in Brooklyn, Manhattan, New Jersey, and beyond; some of these included Carlos Barquero, Tito Báez, Rosendo Acosta, Efraín Ronda, Diómedes "Yomi" Matos (who made the distinctive larger-sized tres played by Mario Hernández), Marco Antonio Matías, Jorge Santiago Mendoza, William del Pilar, Freddy Mejías, Natividad Tirado, Gilberto Díaz, and the legendary Guilín.[66] These men were among the most well known to have made and repaired Spanish Caribbean string instruments, thereby serving the needs of the Spanish Caribbean musical community. For almost the entire decade of the 1990s, Cumpiano worked with Juan Sotomayor, Wilfredo Echevarría, and others to interview these important instrument builders and document their stories. Many of these interviews have appeared in a variety of self-published videos and books and are also available on the website of the Puerto Rican Cuatro Project.[67] The following information is drawn from an unpublished compilation of interviews made between 1992 and 1998 by Juan Sotomayor and transcribed by William Cumpiano except where otherwise indicated.[68]

First and foremost among these pioneers was Efraín Ronda, who was born in San Germán, Puerto Rico, on November 23, 1899. Ronda made his first cuatro at the age of fifteen from *guaraguao* and *yagrumo*, local tropical woods. He also learned about cabinetmaking from Gavino Cruz in San Germán. Ronda left Puerto Rico for Santo Domingo in 1924 and stayed for two years before settling in New York City in 1926. In Santo Domingo he learned some aspects of instrument construction from Félix León Seolviso. Once in New York City, Ronda spent many years experimenting and refining fret distances and intonation, and consulting books to improve his instruments. He made instruments for the best players in New York and Puerto Rico such as El Maestro Ladí, Bartolo Caraballo, Toñito Lugo, and others. He even composed a *décima* (ten-line, octosyllabic poem with a rhyme scheme of ABBAACCDDC) detailing his involvement with the cuatro as a builder:

> *Lector, yo no busco fama,*
> *Nunca tuve vanidad,*
> *Pero he puesto en realidad*
> *El cuatro en un pentagrama.*
> *Ise [Hice] accesible al que lo ama.*
> *Su estudio musicalmente*
> *Diseñé artísticamente.*
> *Construí perfectos cuatros,*
> *Y anduve por los teatros*
> *Con el mío gloriosamente.*

> [Reader, I am not looking for fame
> I've never been vain
> But in reality I put the cuatro in musical notation
> I made what I love accessible
> Its musical study
> I designed artistically
> I built perfect cuatros
> And I gloriously went into theaters with mine.][69]

As I discuss in the education chapter, in 1933 Ronda published the first edition of his bilingual cuatro method book, *La Antorcha: método teórico y práctico para el cuatro moderno de 10 cuerdas y el antiguo de 4 cuerdas. Único volúmen de su clase.* He explained the bilingual edition as a direct result of having had four North American students of Irish and German descent who started studying with him after seeing him perform with his group El Quinteto Ronda at New York's Apollo Theater in 1926. In 1927 Ronda opened his first shop in his wife's aunt's building. He then relocated to 1759 Lexington Avenue between 109th and 110th Streets, where he even repaired Andrés Segovia's broken guitar. Ronda's first guitars sold for thirty-five dollars each; he made his first cuatro in New York in 1928, which sold for the same price. By 1930 he had made twelve cuatros and sold eight to a friend in California for $325; each came with a case and Ronda's method book. Ronda also designed and made *vihuelas*. Ronda continued to perform and teach but would fix almost any stringed instrument for anyone. The following story offers a window into his daily routine:

I went out every day . . . my daughter would calculate and tell me, "Daddy, today you have earned yourself $100." There were days when I would earn . . . a boy came and brought me a cello that he found in a basement, God only knows how many years it had been there. And he said to me, "How much would you charge me for lessons to play this instrument?" I take out the instrument and it had the tops coming off of the body, and I tell him, "first, you have to fix this instrument. You can spend 50 dollars to repair this instrument." And he says to me, "Oh, it costs that much?" After it had been a good instrument. At least 50 dollars. Because just to put the strings on would cost 14 dollars. The four strings. And the bridge, and the [tuning] pegbox that has to be repaired . . . he said "No. Give me 50 cents to get back to where I work." And I give him 50 [cents] and he left it [the cello] with me. I fixed the cello, and an African American guy came, and asks me, "how can I find a second-hand cello?" I told him, "I have two. I have one that has the top coming up, someone put something on it to fix it. But it's not offensive, it sounds good. I have another, which is an instrument in really good condition." The one that that boy brought to me. So I sold it to him for 200 dollars.[70]

From 1936–38, Ronda studied composition at Juilliard with Greenfeller and recorded more than twenty-five of his pieces for the Complemento Berrios label in Portugal and an Italian label called Aurora. Ronda taught Carlos Barquero how to make guitars and eventually closed his shop in 1966.

Jorge Mendoza was another important Puerto Rican artisan based in New York City. Mendoza was born in Arecibo in 1930 and started making guitars at the age of thirteen. He came to New York in 1951 and returned to Puerto Rico in 1974, making instruments and cases. He believed that he was the first person to mass-produce cuatros anywhere, having started doing so in Brooklyn in 1960. Mendoza did a lot of business with a Brooklyn pawn shop on Broadway called Wild, which he pointed out was distinct from the well-known H. L. Wild musical instrument makers supply store in Manhattan. Mendoza's main source of income in New York was making Formica kitchen cabinets but then he shifted exclusively to building instruments. His productivity impressed his contemporaries and he explained to another Brooklyn-based cuatro maker, William del Pilar, that the key was to have a good system and tools so as to make a large number of the same piece. Mendoza explained to Juan Sotomayor that he didn't like to modify the cuatro, tres, or guitar design and that such modifications would always bring complaints from the clients who errone-ously requested them:

I try to avoid that those people would come back to me. You buy a cuatro from me and leave. And I don't want to see you again unless you're going to buy another one. [Laughs] In New York [City], I was afraid when the client would come back. 'This guy is already coming back with a complaint.' Everything that I can do to avoid a complaint, I do it. It doesn't matter if it's five minutes, ten minutes, an hour, it's not important, and I do it.[71]

At the time of the interview, Mendoza had calculated that his production efficiency had allowed him to make a cuatro in ten to twelve hours or less, by himself, partly because he had designed a process and all the machines to make each part. During his time in New York, Mendoza also took guitar lessons with Gregorio Ayala, who had been one of Carlos Gardel's musicians. After returning to Puerto Rico in 1974 from New York, he estimated that he had made a thousand cuatros. Other Puerto Rican instrument makers like Juan Orozco even came from New York City to observe Mendoza's process in Puerto Rico.

The Newark, New Jersey–based cuatro maker Diómedes "Yomi" Matos (b. 1940) was also an accomplished performer who has worked with Paul Simon and others since coming to the mainland in 1959.[72] He learned his craft between the ages of ten and twelve from a builder named Roque Navarro in his hometown of Camuy.[73] A 1997 profile in the *New York Times* explains that Matos was mentoring a young Puerto Rican microbiologist, Roberto Rivera, as he was building a cuatro under the auspices of the New Jersey State Council of the Arts.[74] It continues:

> He has participated in the New Jersey Folk Arts Apprenticeship Program, guiding many apprentices through the years. He has also taught in public schools and has demonstrated in local art and music festivals. In 2006, he was honored with a National Heritage Fellowship from the National Endowment for the Arts. . . . he says he loves teaching more than making the cuatros and loves to watch a student grow and learn. . . . Matos is prepared to teach students how to avoid frustration with laughter when going through the long process of learning the skills for playing or making a cuatro and says patience is the most important virtue he teaches.[75]

Thus, Matos has invested much of his energy into teaching and preserving the culture of the Puerto Rican cuatro.

Manuel Velázquez (1917–2014) was another important Puerto Rican luthier based in New York City, who is widely considered to be one of the most important guitar makers of the last hundred years. He received numerous awards and accolades for his work. Velázquez came from a cabinet-making background and dreamed of making guitars from an early age. After building his first guitar at the age of sixteen and getting orders for more, he moved to New York City in 1941. Working in the shipyard as a woodworker, Velázquez made his first guitar in New York from wood salvaged from a sunken ship.[76] When he sold his first guitar for $500, he then went out and bought wood for his next instruments.[77] In a documentary on the man and his art, Velázquez explained how he started: "I put a shelf in the dining room. I make a shelf in there and then my wife she was fighting with me because of the dust. She was cleaning and I was sanding and throwing the dust on the floor."[78]

In 1950, after building more guitars and a solid reputation, he moved his shop to 420 Third Avenue in Manhattan and received accolades from the top players of the time, including Rey de la Torre, Vladimir Bobri, Noah Wolf, and Andrés Segovia.[79] In 1963 the government of Puerto Rico asked Velázquez to create a small guitar-making factory on the island.[80] In 1972 Velázquez returned to Puerto Rico but ten years later moved back to Virginia and Florida. With his son and daughter working with him until his death, Velázquez would go on to make guitars prized by everyone from Andrés Segovia to Keith Richards.[81] This brief overview of Velázquez is not intended to diminish his stature, but rather to demonstrate how one of the greatest guitar makers of our time began making his world-class instruments in the humble confines of his New York apartment like many of the instrument builders in this chapter.

Tito Baez and Rosendo Acosta were two other Puerto Rican luthiers based in Brooklyn. According to the Puerto Rican Cuatro Project, Baez (1935–2004) was originally from Yauco and had settled in Brooklyn, where he made cuatros, requintos, and guitars "for decades."[82] He was also "a renown[ed] guitar accompanist ('segunda guitarra') who played with the Sexteto Criollo Puertorriqueño next to Israel Berrios, Neri Orta and Nieves Quintero, among others."[83]

William del Pilar was another important builder whose son still maintains his shop at 396 Atlantic Avenue in Brooklyn. Del Pilar started as a cabinetmaker in Quebradillas, Puerto Rico, before coming to New York and making instruments.[84] In an interview with the *New York Daily News*, Del Pilar's son explained:

"One day these two guys got in a fight, and one of them broke his guitar over the other guy's head. So he brought it to my dad to repair," he continued. "But he had to do it in secret, because his dad didn't think you could make a living repairing instruments." By the time William del Pilar Sr. left Puerto Rico for New York in the 1940s, he was already building his own guitars, but it wasn't until 1957 that he was able to open his own shop.[85]

Del Pilar Sr. corroborated the story in a *New York Times* interview:

...when he was a boy, "only three people played the guitar in my town, and after that guy smashed his guitar over the other man's head, I was the first one in my town to make a guitar. My father was a very good cabinet maker and I knew how to use tools," the elder Del Pilar continued. "Right away, I started figuring out how to do it. The first guitar took me six months, because I was hiding it from my father, because he didn't want me to waste time." It was no waste of time. Mr. Del Pilar began making guitars, and word spread beyond his hometown. "I started by charging $10," he said.[86]

The elder del Pilar's instruments were held in high esteem by classical guitarists, as explained by Nassau County Community College professor Stanley Solow:

> "First of all, they are beautiful; they have a warm, rich sound," Professor Solow said. "And a Del Pilar has great power, almost as though there's an amplifier inside. Then, they are put together to last," Professor Solow continued. "They don't use measuring tools, they do it by feel, with years and years of experience." . . . Professor Solow said that a Ramirez guitar like the one the master guitarist, Andres Segovia, would have played would cost around $6,000, and he said he knew of no one else in the city who makes handmade guitars of the quality of those of the Del Pilars.[87]

The elder del Pilar honed his craft on his own. He explained: "I just wet the wood and tried to make it thin so I could bend it easy. I looked at other guitars. If they sounded better I tried to do the same thing."[88]

Del Pilar Jr. came to New York as a six-year-old child in 1950 and continued to make instruments. Since that time:

> He estimates he has built at least 500 instruments, not including those he has repaired and restored. He uses woods that are at least 40 years old and it takes him a year to a year and a half to finish an order. Prices range from $1,800 to $4,500, depending on the instrument. In addition to the craftsmanship that comes from a master luthier, the guitars are built with del Pilar's complicated-sounding "Resonant Bracing System," what he considers a revolutionary new system of bracing—and the reason for the patent application that hangs in the store's front window. Bracing refers to the series of wooden braces in the body of the guitar that give it structural support. Del Pilar says his system allows the guitars to maintain their purity of tone at higher frequencies, not going flat or sharp where others might.[89]

As seen with other builders discussed earlier, there is another Segovia connection. As del Pilar Jr. explained to the *Daily News*:

> His late father built more than 1,000 guitars and fixed many more. But one repair stands out in the son's mind—that done to the guitar of the legendary

strummer Andrés Segovia of Spain, who was in New York to play a concert. "It was in 1959," del Pilar recalled. "My dad repaired it, and after he was finished we went to Segovia's concert. I remember the concert, not just because of Segovia, but because [great Brazilian composer Heitor] Villa-Lobos was in the audience, and that was the year that he passed away."[90]

This story was also corroborated by the *New York Times*, but the conclusion was not as pleasant as one would think for del Pilar Sr., who explained:

The president of the Classical Guitar Society, Vladimir Bobri, called to say that Andres Segovia was in New York and needed repairs on his guitar. "I had to go to Manhattan to get the guitar," Mr. Del Pilar recalled. "I have only two hours to bring it to my home, glue it and bring it back right away because he had a concert that night." Mr. Segovia, said William Jr., "was very, very thankful. He sent my father one of his portraits and signed it," he added. "The word got out. That was really the big break."

Not every involvement with Mr. Segovia would prove so satisfying. For little more than a year, William Jr., then twelve, had been taking guitar lessons. One day in 1959, without notice, Mr. Bobri called to ask if young William could come to Manhattan to play for Mr. Segovia. "I wasn't prepared," William Jr. said. "I had never played in front of someone before." Taken to Mr. Segovia's hotel suite, William Jr. played "Study in A" by Matteo Carcassi. "Alexander Bellow, my original teacher, had changed some of the baselines [*sic*] of the piece," William Jr. said. "Segovia said, 'First of all, you played a few wrong notes. And it could have been smoother.' He could have done a better job, been a little more considerate. I felt embarrassed. I didn't feel like playing ever again. But looking back, I'm more amused than seeing it as a bad experience. I continued to play, because I love the instrument."[91]

Thus, repairing Segovia's guitar did not mean a guaranteed fairytale ending for the younger or older del Pilar.

According to an article on the Puerto Rican Cuatro Project website by Felipe Mario Olivera Pabón, there was another luthier named Manuel Henríquez Zapata who acquired significant skills in the mainland United States and elsewhere:

When in 1948, Don Manuel came to the United States when he was 22 years of age, he met an already well known Italo-American luthier by the name of Louis Scaffa in New York City. He worked with Mr. Scaffa until 1952 when he was drafted in the United States Army. He returned to New York City

and continued working with Mr. Scaffa until 1957. Continuing his fervor for
the art of artisanry, after his daily tasks, he would go to the basement of the
home he bought in New York City and build musical instruments. He would
sell these instruments to the musicians in the Latin neighborhoods, attaining
a good reputation among the musicians of the area. After many years and
experiences, in 1980, Don Manuel decided to return to Puerto Rico this time
with the purpose of remaining and dedicating himself totally to artisanry,
specializing in string instruments.[92]

Puerto Rican craftsmen also worked for American instrument manufacturers
solving design problems and helping create new instruments. Gilbert Díaz
was an important guitar maker and repairman who came to the mainland in
1952 and started working for the Gretsch Guitar Company (and later Guild)
in 1953.[93] Díaz explained:

> I did a lot of things when I was at Gretsch. I started in the plating depart-
> ment, where I worked for about 6 months. After that I worked on cymbals,
> in the drum shop and then on to the woodshop. For some time I worked in
> the repair department and eventually I ended up in the final assembly, where
> I was responsible for the electronics in the guitars. I had a colleague who
> worked with me at Gretsch, called Hank Riddering. He went on to Guild and
> shortly after that, I applied for a position too. I was hired by Bob Bromberg,
> who was in charge at the time, and I worked in final assembly; more or less
> the same job as I had with Gretsch. After a short time I went back to Gretsch,
> because they offered to pay me more when I would come back. When they
> didn't keep their promise, I applied for a position at the post office. I lived in
> Brooklyn at the time and I was supposed to start working as a mailman in the
> Bronx the next day. Anyway, Alfred Dronge looked me up, said that I would
> have a better future working for him and tried to persuade me to come back,
> which I did. When I started, Hank Riddering was head of final assembly. It
> was just three people, Hank, Mr. Ventura and myself. After 6 months Hank
> left and I became the head of that department.

At some point production moved from New York City to Hoboken and then
to a second plant in Rhode Island. Díaz's brother Jerry also started working at
the company. According to another employee, Jim Deurloo: "Al Dronge was a
very nice guy, who cared about the product and the people who were working
for him. Especially to the key-people like Carlo Greco, Gilbert Diaz & Fred
Augusto who stayed with him for the longest time." Gil Díaz played a vital
role in the development of the company's instruments. According to Moust:

Gilbert Díaz, who had been working with DeArmond pickups when he was still with Gretsch, was responsible for the introduction of DeArmond pickups, since he found them to be superior to the single-coils that Guild was using at the time. Around 1959 the first DeArmond pickups started to appear on Guild electric hollowbodies.

Díaz was adept at solving a number of problems in creative ways. As Moust explained:

> Shortly after the introduction of the Starfire models Guild had a little incident with one of its major distributors. Gilbert Díaz, the head of "final assembly" had noticed that some instruments that were registered as Starfire II models came back to be serviced with the Starfire III model designation on the label. The difference between the two models was the addition of a Bigsby tailpiece on the Starfire III. It turned out that this distributor would order Starfire II models from Guild, then put on a Bigsby and change the roman II on the label into a III, which was fairly easy to do. By buying the Bigsby's straight from the Bigsby company the distributor would make a little more on these instruments. To prevent this practice from taking place Gilbert Díaz designed Guild's own tailpiece, which then was made by the Bigsby company. It could only be obtained from Guild and the only disadvantage was, that they had to order a minimum of 2000 pieces from Bigsby. The Guild unit was very similar to the regular Bigsby Model (a.k.a. the B-6). The shape of the bass plate was slightly altered to resemble the shape of the Guild "harp" tailpiece, near the hinge. It became available by 1961 and in later years it would be known as the B-2.

As Moust indicated toward the end of his study, Díaz was involved in many instrument prototypes throughout his many years spent at the company.[94] Díaz left the company in 1972 after the death of its founder, Alfred Dronge.

William Cumpiano is the last luthier to be included in this category, even if his time in New York City was limited to being a student of Michael Gurian's guitar-making class at the New York City Crafts Students League in 1970.[95] Cumpiano had originally come from Río Piedras, Puerto Rico, and studied at Pratt Institute, graduating in 1968. After completing his first guitar, Cumpiano joined Gurian in New Hampshire in 1971 and began his guitar-making apprenticeship. Since that time he has gone on to become one of the foremost guitar makers in the world, but he is also well known for making tiples, cuatros, requintos, and treses. Cumpiano also teaches instrument building and has written one of the most important books on guitar making, *Guitarmaking: Tradition and Technology: A Complete Reference for the Design and Construction of the*

Steel-String Folk Guitar and the Classical Guitar.[96] Cumpiano has also dedicated an enormous amount of time documenting the history of the Puerto Rican cuatro and sharing the results of his lifelong research online and in videos through the Puerto Rican Cuatro Project. He continues to teach Puerto Rican tiple-making courses throughout the United States.

THE BABY BASS: MASS PRODUCTION AND PARTNERING WITH LATIN MUSICIANS

An important aspect of the New York sound of Latin music in New York City is the bass. From a technological perspective, the role and sound of the bass was impacted greatly by performers who employed the electric upright bass, particularly the Ampeg Baby Bass. The particular sound of the instrument has long characterized Latin music made in New York City. Since its adoption in New York, it has become the required bass instrument for Latin music performance and recording throughout the world.

The idea for the electric upright bass came originally from Rudy and Ed Dopera, who developed an instrument with a fiberglass body and two magnetic pickups called the Zorko bass. Their company, Dobro, had been based in California, but later moved to Chicago and is best known for resonator guitars. The Zorko was eventually licensed to and made by the Ampeg Company, which had already achieved some success making an electric pickup for the acoustic upright bass and an accompanying amplification system. Product engineer Jess Oliver found the original Dopera brothers' pickup to be inadequate and that it would make a thump sound when played pizzicato. Oliver came up with a new design for the instrument using a diaphragm pickup to allow the instrument to have much more sustain than the original Zorko when played pizzicato.[97] Additionally, the Ampeg body was made out of an Eastman product called Butyrate that was originally used to make film.[98] Oliver explained that the material was "very vacuum formable," which allowed the company "to make enough bodies in a day for the production we needed."[99] He also explained that with a vacuum-forming machine (which he designed), he could make "something like 15 or 20 a day" whereas with fiberglass they would make one per day.[100] Although founded in Chicago, the company and its founder Everett Hull moved to New York in the early 1940s.[101] Among the first American jazz musicians to use the Ampeg Baby Bass was jazz legend Oscar Pettiford, as well as Jaime Merritt, who "played a custom-built 5-string Ampeg Baby Bass personally designed by Everett Hull."[102] In a 2011 interview with *Bassplayer*, amp designer Jess Oliver recalled that the top bassists in New York were also using the Ampeg B-15 bass amplifier. He explained to Tony Levin:

All the members of the Manhattan Bass Club [a group of top session bassists who each bought an amp to be left at a studio so all of the members could avoid cartage]. Folks like Milt Hinton, Oscar Pettiford, and George Duvivier would come to the shop, as well as Latin players like Bobby Rodriguez and Julio Andino. Charles Mingus and [classical bass giant] Gary Karr, who both had Baby Basses and did ads for us, would come by, too. And I'd attend studio dates to hear our amps—everything from a George Barnes album with 20 guitarists to a recording session with Elvis Presley, in which he listened to the pianist play the song once, and completely re-stylized it in his own way. I was also gigging on weekends, testing the B-15 and the Baby Bass.[103]

Notable early adopters of the Ampeg upright electric bass in the Spanish Caribbean context included Bobby Rodríguez, Julio Andino, Israel López "Cachao," and Victor Venegas. As Greg Hopkins notes in his history of Hull and the Ampeg company: "Hull lined up his typical stable of professional musicians behind the Baby Bass. The bass was 'field tested' by Buddy Hayes with Lawrence Welk's band; Julio Andino, with Tito Rodríguez; Bobby Rodríguez, with Tito Puente; and Frank Moore, leader of the Frank Moore Four."[104] The company also had advertisements for "the Baby Bass from around 1960, picturing Everett Hull, the instrument's developer, alongside Tito Rodriguez and legendary bassist Julio Andino."[105]

While the instrument had inherent issues regarding sound and intonation, it offered a groundbreaking solution for working musicians in the Spanish Caribbean music scene who needed the volume that amplified sound offered without sacrificing the tone associated with an upright acoustic bass. Musicians also found tricks and solutions to make the instrument sound even better, as Andy González did on over eight hundred recordings:

> The gut strings the Baby Bass [an amplified, cello-sized upright made of fiberglass or plastic] used made a thumpy sound; then somebody hipped me to strings that the jazz players used on acoustic basses. Those were tight on his upright electric, but Gonzalez located another model called solo-gauge strings, designed for brighter projection in classical orchestras. By tuning them down a note, he got the tension he was looking for, which has a lot to do with the sustain I like to hear at the bottom: You play a low note that goes "Boommmmm," and the note stays.[106]

For González, the bass is the lowest drum in a Latin music ensemble and the Ampeg Baby Bass was his instrument of choice throughout his career. As the next generation of players like Andy González and Eddie "Guagua" Rivera continued to record and perform with the Baby Bass, they influenced the adoption

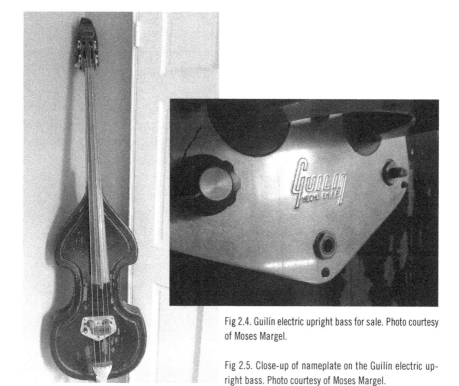

Fig 2.4. Guilín electric upright bass for sale. Photo courtesy of Moses Margel.

Fig 2.5. Close-up of nameplate on the Guilín electric upright bass. Photo courtesy of Moses Margel.

of the instrument by bassists around the world who worked in Spanish Caribbean music.[107] As I explore in the chapter on Puerto Rican and New York–born Puerto Rican musicians' musical innovations in New York City, bassists such as Salvador Cuevas, Francisco Centenno, Rubén Rodríguez, and the African American John Henry Robinson contributed their own stylistic innovations to the role of the bass in Spanish Caribbean music by incorporating slapping and popping from funk music into their recordings and performances using the electric bass guitar.

Interestingly, the electric upright bass as manufactured by Ampeg had local imitators as well. In a 1994 interview with tres player Anastasio Feliciano conducted by Juan Sotomayor, Feliciano discussed another important instrument builder named Miguel Ángel Vázquez, also known as "Guilín." Born in Manatí, Puerto Rico, in 1928, Guilín made his way to the United States, and in the 1950s earned a solid reputation among musicians and working at the Gretsch Guitar Company Factory in Brooklyn. He also made a variety of instruments including upright electric basses similar to the Ampeg Baby Bass. In the mid-1990s he returned to Manatí in the early 1990s before settling in Orlando around 1995 until his death. In the second photo, one can see the words "Hecho in P.R." [made in Puerto Rico] (see figs. 2.4 and 2.5).

As seen previously in Chapter 1, a number of New York–based Latin music magazines featured advertisements for places to formally study Latin drumming traditions, but they also featured prominently placed advertisements for drum makers and musical instrument shops. There is no question that what had originally started as simply importing instruments for musicians soon shifted to small operations in the home workshops of a few craftsmen based in New York City. These later turned in to mass production and the wide diffusion of Caribbean percussion and string instruments throughout the United States and beyond. Afro-Latin hand percussion instruments are known throughout the world today in part because of Martin Cohen's promotional efforts. These included pairing with percussion virtuosi such as Tito Puente, Cándido Camero, Carlos "Patato" Valdés, and others for endorsements and product design, and releasing recordings that sought to teach musicians how to play Afro-Latin percussion instruments as well as recordings of professional ensembles.

Unfortunately, the contributions of the original procurers and builders in the early part of this study—who had filled the needs of both professional and amateur musicians playing Latin music throughout the New York metropolitan area and beyond—have been overlooked. Even worse, some of these early pioneers, such as El Indio and Frank Mesa, had their work literally copied and imitated. They did not financially benefit from their innovations compared to those who took their designs. There is no doubt that the contributions of these lesser-known and innovative musical instrument builders helped spread the appreciation of Latin music and improved the accessibility of the musical instruments for musicians who made Latin music in New York City, while widening the consumer base for these instruments beyond New York. Finally, the depth and breadth of Puerto Rican stringed-instrument artisans extended from innovations in the making of the cuatro, an instrument of humble countryside origins, to building and repairing the finest classical guitars fitting the exacting needs of artists like Segovia and Rey de la Torre. A big guitar manufacturer with the international name recognition of Gretsch counted on the design innovations of two Puerto Rican craftsmen Guilín and Gil Díaz. There are other, similar stories of instrument builders in New York City, and future scholarship should explore them.

The most important point of this chapter is that the architects of the New York sound of Latin music used instruments built in New York by local builders to achieve their sound. The partnership between builders and musicians ensured functionality and shaped the sound of both plucked string instruments and percussion instruments. Bassists Israel "Cachao" López, Julio Andino, Bobby Rodríguez, Victor Venegas, Andy González, Eddie "Guagua" Rivera, and others made the Ampeg Baby Bass the standard in Latin music in New York City, and this sound was emulated worldwide. Many master percussionists sought out handmade hand drums built by Jay Bereck and Junior Tirado but eventually went with Frank Mesa's Eco-Tone drums before Martin Cohen's mass-produced Latin Percussion instruments became available. Such was the case for Mongo Santamaria, Tito Puente, Cándido Camero, Carlo "Patato" Valdéz, and many others. And since the success and mass production of Cohen's instruments, many artists have endorsed LP products and used the drums on countless recordings. These instruments are widely diffused internationally. While LP created its own cowbells, musicians have nevertheless continued to travel from around the world to purchase Cali Rivera's unique-sounding JCR bells in the Bronx. These bells are played and owned by many percussionists in New York City. Cuatros, treses, and guitars made by New Yorkers have been sought after by classical virtuosi and popular music icons such as Andrés Segovia, José Rey de la Torre, Yomo Toro, Edgardo Miranda, and countless others.

Thus, the history of Caribbean instrument construction and innovation in New York City developed along with musical innovations in Latin music. Like the music, the instruments changed in New York City before being more widely diffused internationally. A central theme of this study is inter-ethnic collaboration; although they did not work together as a team, a group of Cuban, Puerto Rican, Dominican, and Jewish craftsmen and some of other ethnicities transformed Caribbean musical instruments in New York City so that musicians performing Latin music here and abroad had the best tools available for musical performance and innovation. Caribbean string and percussion instruments continued to be modified and produced in the Caribbean, but New York City offered a large pool of musicians who played a wide variety of Latin music and who needed a variety of high-quality instruments, unlike builders based in the Caribbean who were only making a few types of specific instruments meant for local genres. New York City also offered opportunities for mass production that were not possible in the Caribbean.

CHAPTER 3

SONNY BRAVO, TÍPICA 73, AND THE NEW YORK SOUND

Sonny Bravo, born Elio Osácar, is a second-generation Cuban American pianist and arranger whose career has spanned seven decades in Latin music. Sonny Bravo's story epitomizes almost all of the important themes outlined throughout this book that are essential to understanding how Afro-Latin music in New York developed its distinct sound in the period 1940–90. These include the physical and metaphysical aspects of clave, the importance of folklore, musical education beyond folklore, musical biculturalism, the evolution of the anticipated bass, an emphasis on innovative music for dancers, family lineages and continuity in the New York Latin music scene, and inter-ethnic collaboration.

Bravo's upbringing and family history are tied to the history of the Cuban community in the United States in the late nineteenth century and the activities of Cuban musicians in Florida before World War II. He learned this musical history, perhaps even more so because his family had immigrated to the United States and music was an important way to keep in touch with his culture and his family. Second, as both a second-generation Cuban American musician and a second-generation musician, Bravo and his family members witnessed and partook in the major developments of Latin music in the United States. These developments include the modification and modernization of the Cuban bass pattern, a highly developed and strictly adhered-to clave sensibility, and the incorporation of specific jazz arranging techniques and other musical elements into Spanish Caribbean dance music. Third, this ongoing musical development of which he was a part, as well as his participation in the New York scene, brought him to collaborate with many non-Cuban musicians as a sideman, an arranger, and ultimately a bandleader based in New York City. Fourth, he and Johnny Rodríguez were the first Latin bandleaders from the United States to bring a pan-ethnic band to Cuba to record with Cuban counterparts, an act that was not only heavily criticized by the Cuban American community at the time, but one that had dire consequences for the band's future.[1] Lastly, Bravo has taught Cuban piano to many students in formal and informal settings since the 1970s, directly influencing how many musicians learn, listen, and perform in clave. This combination of unique characteristics illustrates how Bravo and his career exemplify the major themes in this study.

Most of the musical examples in this chapter that are used to illustrate Bravo's arranging concepts were taken directly from his scores unless otherwise indicated. I am grateful for his generosity in making them available to me. I am also grateful to Michael Eckroth for expertly transcribing the four Sonny Bravo piano solos that appear in this chapter.

FAMILIAL CONNECTIONS: SANTIAGO "ELIO" OSÁCAR, SONNY BRAVO'S FATHER

Cuba, Cuban history, and Cuban culture can frequently be better understood in the context of Cuban families and how they shaped and were shaped by history. Sonny Bravo's family is no exception; his family is the first source of clave in his life. At the end of the nineteenth century, his grandparents were neighbors in Santiago de Las Vegas, a small town just south of La Habana. As fate would have it, his grandmothers, who were good friends in Cuba, would later be neighbors again in Cayo Hueso, the Cuban name for Key West, Florida.[2] Bravo's paternal grandfather, José Osácar, a Cuban of Basque descent, would make Key West his home in the early 1900s. The African lineage in the Osácar family came to Bravo from his paternal grandmother, Ángela Colomá, described by Sonny Bravo as a *mulata*. Bravo's maternal grandfather was Enrique Douguet of Bejucal, a town that borders Santiago de Las Vegas to the south. He is listed as a cigar maker on his daughter's birth certificate. Coincidentally, Bravo's maternal grandmother, Fidelina Bravo, was Ángela Colomá's neighbor. Fidelina wrote poetry and décimas. Osácar, a Basque name sometimes spelled Ozácar and misspelled Osákar, was not an optimal stage name for a budding musician in the United States. The Douguet surname presented its own problems, and Sonny would later choose Bravo from his maternal grandmother as his stage name.

Sonny's parents, Santiago "Elio" Osácar and Elisa Douguet, were both born in Key West, Florida, in 1911 and 1910 respectively. They spoke Spanish as their first language. In the 1920s, both families relocated to the thriving Cuban community of Tampa, an important center of the nineteenth-century Cuban independence movement and well known for its place in the cigar and tobacco industry.[3] Tampa and Ybor City were also important locales for Cuban music.

Tampa's rich musical life encompassed the Italian (Neapolitan and Sicilian), Spanish (Galician and Asturian), and Cuban folk and popular music that its residents demanded for social functions, but other genres such as opera,

Fig 3.1. El Sexteto Tampeño, l-r: Tomás Osácar, Eloy, Elio Osácar, El Cubanito, Juan "Macho" Osácar, and unknown. Photo courtesy of Sonny Bravo.

zarzuela, and classical music also thrived.[4] From 1937 to 1942, the WPA made field recordings of the community to document its incredible diversity.[5] Cuban music, however, became the dominant musical style of Tampa; there were Cuban social clubs and a Cuban music school by 1917. The Cuban son is an Afro-Cuban genre that became the national genre of Cuba by the end of the 1920s, but the music was exported internationally under the name of an entirely different genre, rumba.[6] In Tampa it was actually called *son*, and was performed by expert Cuban practitioners from early on. Although son had achieved a certain level of respectability in Cuba, there is evidence that even among Afro-Cubans in Tampa it could still be provocative. In fact, according to the 1928 minutes of the Afro-Cuban Martí-Maceo Club, there was a brief ban on son because it was viewed as vulgar.[7] This is around the same time that Cuban son underwent a transformation from being a disreputable music associated with vice and ill repute to becoming celebrated as the national genre of music in the mid- to late 1920s in Cuba.[8]

This ban evidently had no effect on young Santiago "Elio" Osácar, who was performing professionally as a bassist. He can be seen at the age of seventeen or eighteen in a 1928 photo of El Sexteto Tampeño, one of the well-known bands of the time (see fig. 3.1). Elio's older brothers, Tomás, an excellent tres player, and Juan "Macho," a guitarist and vocalist, were founding members of

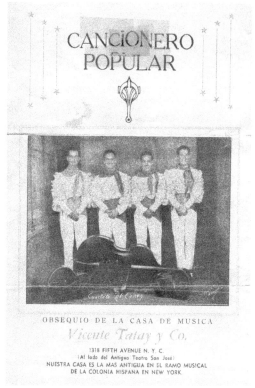

Fig 3.2. Flyer for Cuarteto Caney. l-r: Tilde, Fernando Storch, Santiago "Elio" Osácar, Johnny López (born Pereira).

El Sexteto Tampeño along with Elio.[9] Music was played at family gatherings with Elio's brothers and cousins. Another relative, Nilo Cabrera, who was Elisa's cousin from the Bravo side, was a bass player active on the Tampa scene. Bobby Rodríguez, the great bass player with Machito, Tito Puente, and Noro Morales, was another relative who will be discussed later in this chapter. There was plenty of musical work to be found locally.

Elio and Elisa were married in Tampa in 1932, approximately four years before Sonny's birth. Between 1932 and 1934 the family moved to New York City and Elio joined the famed Cuarteto and Sexteto Caney group (see figs. 3.2 and 3.3). While Osácar had only a third-grade education, he supported his family and enjoyed a successful career as a musician playing Cuban music throughout the United States.

Before looking at the impact and historical importance of Elio Osácar and the Caney Group, it is worth placing them within the context of Cuban and Afro-Cuban music in New York City. Scholars such as Christina Abreu have situated the Caney group in 1940s and 1950s Miami but have not considered

Fig 3.3. Septeto Caney. Standing l-r: Elio Osácar (bass), Rubén Berríos (piano), Ana Márquez (trumpet), Fernando Storch (tres/leader), René Martínez (guitar); kneeling l-r: Tony Negret (vocals), Alfonso "El Loco" Reyes (percussion). Photo courtesy of Sonny Bravo

their status or achievements in New York or beyond the Miami and New York scenes. While the group played Cuban son and was in fact made up of Cuban and Puerto Rican musicians, Abreu and other scholars do not explicitly identify them as an Afro-Cuban group, although they have explicitly labeled Arsenio Rodríguez, Machito, Marcelino Guerra, or Antonio Machín as such. However, the Caney group was the foremost pioneer of Cuban son in the United States; and the fact that they played the national genre of Cuban music, the Afro-Cuban son, and are not included in lists of Afro-Cuban musicians illustrates some of the problems inherent to such racial classification of music and musicians. As Abreu points out, Cubans had different experiences in the United States, largely dependent on their identification as black or white.[10] One can see musicians of all colors when looking at photos of the Caney group from its inception through its end. Additionally, Abreu points out the importance of domestic migration of Cubans within the United States from Tampa and Key West to New York.[11] The Osácar family's movements exemplify this pattern, as do those of other notable musicians, such as the vocalist Miguel Quintana, among others.

The Caney groups—in their various incarnations of *cuarteto*, *sexteto*, and *conjunto*—were led by Fernando Storch, a Cuban musician who settled in New York in the 1920s. According to an interview with Max Salazar, Elio Osácar began working with Storch around 1930 at El Toreador Restaurant at 110th Street and 5th Avenue in Manhattan.[12] The restaurant continued to be an important place for Cuban music into the mid-1930s, as evidenced by performances from Antonio Machín and others, and was praised for its authentic atmosphere.[13] By the end of the 1930s, El Torreador had become a Pan-Latin and Harlemite club that was less Cuban-centric.[14] The group was firmly established under the Caney name in early 1933 and toured nationally throughout the 1930s.[15] The band appeared regularly in New York City and had regular long-running engagements at the Havana-Madrid,[16] Club Yumurí,[17] The Latin Quarter,[18] and more prestigious venues such as Radio City Music Hall.[19] At many venues, such as the Havana Madrid, Caney provided music for Cuban floor shows with dancers and singers.[20] In 1936 Caney made their first recording for Columbia Records. and later would record for Decca, Victor, and Tico, among other labels in New York City; however, some of the Caney recordings indicate that they were actually recorded in Cuba rather than New York.[21] The band's biggest hit and theme song, "Rumba Rhapsody," sold well, opened doors at venues throughout the country, and brought opportunities to make additional recordings.[22] A May 20, 1942, *New York Post* article on New York City events shows Caney playing nightly "'Candlelight Rhumba Sessions' from 2 to 4am nightly" at Latin Quarter.[23]

Although Elio Osácar was the bass player with the legendary Cuarteto and Conjunto Caney until his death in 1957, he also made a name for himself as a bandleader in his own right. A 1938 article in the *New York Sun* praised the sound of Osácar's band:

> Elio Ozacar [*sic*] and his aggregation of hide pounders and gourd rattlers . . .
> play the sort of music that seems to cure the most homesick Cuban of any
> desire to go home. When Elio and his boys go to work you see the dancers
> bring out those special steps which shame us correspondence-course rhumba
> wigglers right back to our seats and our drinks.[24]

In February 1939 he made six recordings for Columbia and in May he made six more for Decca, all under the name Elio y Su Conjunto Moderno (see fig. 3.4).[25] These recordings were released as 78s and although the Puerto Rican vocalist Pedro Ortiz "Davilita" Davila is listed as lead vocalist, the Puerto Rican vocalist Doroteo Santiago and the legendary Cuban vocalist and bandleader Frank "Machito" Grillo share vocal duties. One of these recordings, "Yo tene un baracón," featured Mario Bauzá on trumpet.[26] This historic detail of inter-ethnic

Fig 3.4. Unknown newspaper clippings of Osácar and his Conjunto Moderno. Photo courtesy of Sonny Bravo.

collaboration in Elio Osácar's career demonstrates how, before the heyday of salsa, Cuban musicians were working with Puerto Ricans and other Caribbean peoples in the execution of Cuban music. In many ways Elio's experiences would be paralleled by those of his son.

The 1930s *son tumbao* (bass ostinato) pattern played by Elio Osácar as heard on the Caney recordings is quite different from the anticipated bass of today's son and salsa. On a number of the Caney recordings from 1936–39, Osácar is heard playing what one would identify as a "walking" bass line with consecutive quarter notes and linear movement akin to jazz. The bass part moves quite a bit more freely, rhythmically speaking; the musical model for this comes directly from the *figle* (ophicleide) or *bombardino* (euphonium) parts of nineteenth-century Cuban ensembles dedicated to the contradanza and danzón. Osácar employs a variation of the *tresillo* (dotted quarter, dotted quarter, quarter), playing on four quarter notes, and even uses consecutive eighth notes and chromaticism to connect and outline the harmony. Musical example 3.1 is a transcription of his bass part on "Cantando" demonstrating these concepts.[27] Sonny Bravo notes that the listener can also hear Elio Osácar singing the "segunda voz: '. . . *que calmes mi dolor*' in the coda."[28]

Simpler bass patterns are evident in written idiomatic musical examples from the era, such as those found in the method book *Latin-American Rhythms and Improvisations for Piano* by Noro Morales or in stock arrangements of the period.[29]

Bravo believes that his cousin Bobby Rodríguez was the first bass player who executed the anticipating pattern (see musical example 3.2), changing to the upcoming chord on beat four of the measure.[30] This view is consistent with

Musical Example 3.1. Elio Osácar's bass playing on "Cantando" [00:06–01:33]. Transcription by Benjamin Lapidus.

Musical Example 3.2. Early anticipation pattern. Transcription by Benjamin Lapidus.

other history-minded musicians such as Rodríguez's unrelated protégé Rubén Rodríguez. The shift from what Elio Osácar and Bobby Rodríguez would play to the modern anticipated bass line, two dotted quarter notes followed by a quarter note, was crystallized in Bravo's mind during a 1964 stint with José Fajardo at the El San Juan Hotel in Puerto Rico, when Bravo recalls the Cuban flute virtuoso as calling the modern bass tumbao (anticipated bass pattern) "*una cosa que se inventaron los boricuas*" (something that was invented by Puerto Ricans).[31] Bravo asserts: "Fajardo was not *just* referring to the anticipation aspect of the bass pattern but to the *syncopated* note on the beat of 2+! In other words: the tresillo pattern *sans* the first dotted quarter note on the downbeat!"[32] Musical example 3.3 demonstrates this pattern.

This view is also consistent with Peter Manuel's assertion that the guitar parts from Puerto Rican seises and aguinaldos—with their harmonic movement occurring on the last quarter note of a measure and tied to a dotted quarter note on the following measure—could very well have been the source material and reason why this pattern is ubiquitous to New York–based Spanish Caribbean music.[33] David García also examines the aforementioned bass lines (tresillo, cumbia, etc.) in pre-1940s Cuban music to show that in Arsenio Rodríguez's conjunto music there was a shift away from these patterns toward more syncopated and melodic bass patterns and that, ultimately, New York bands stayed with what is now considered to be the modern anticipated bass tumbao.[34]

Musical Example 3.3. Anticipated bass or *tresillo* without first dotted quarter note. Transcription by Benjamin Lapidus.

Fig 3.5. Sonny Bravo age 11. Photo courtesy of Sonny Bravo.

Fig 3.6. Sonny Bravo age 16 with his father Santiago "Elio" Osácar. Photo courtesy of Sonny Bravo.

LIKE FATHER, LIKE SON

Elio Osácar, a.k.a. Sonny Bravo, was born on October 7, 1936, on 111th Street and St. Nicholas Avenue in Manhattan, near the ten-block area of Lenox Avenue that was home to many Cubans.[35] At the time, his father Santiago "Elio" Osácar was constantly touring with the Caney group. For some stints mother and son would stay home, but the family traveled together as longer engagements became more frequent. As a result, Sonny attended public schools around the country. He attended kindergarten in Chicago, first grade at PS 101 in New York City, and second through fourth grades in Miami. Spanish was spoken at home; despite the fact that Sonny's parents were born in the United States, their linguistic and cultural identity was firmly Cuban. On a 1939 audio recording of a family get-together, the elder Osácar is heard singing and playing guitar while engaging with his son in conversation in Spanish peppered with English words.[36] The younger Osácar remembers that somewhere in between these frequent moves, his father performed at New York's Stork Club and other venues in Philadelphia and St. Louis while his father took a break from Caney and worked with vocalist Monchito.[37]

Elio rejoined Caney for the famous Cuarteto Caney recordings and the family continued to move back and forth between Miami and New York. Sonny attended fifth grade at PS 57 on 115th Street and Third Avenue, and for the sixth grade his mother decided she was through with moving. The family relocated to Miami where Sonny had already attended Miramar Elementary School. He

Fig 3.7. Sonny Bravo age 20 with El Conjunto Casino de Miami (1956–57), l-r: Oscar, Ramonín Eguzquiza, Gastón Delfín, Sonny Bravo (kneeling at the drum), Oscar Orta, José "Pepe" Coello. Photo courtesy of Sonny Bravo.

continued his studies at Robert E. Lee Junior High School, and graduated from Miami Senior High School, playing baseball for the Stingrays.

According to Bravo, Cubans were still in the minority in South Florida as supported by his vivid recollection of a sixth-grade talent show during which one of his classmates, Robert Gunn, played "Dixie." Bravo was a tall and timid performer who was still trying to reconcile the worlds of music and sports. He performed the Aragonaise from the Jules Massenet opera *Le Cid* on piano and received a standing ovation. In his own words he was a "shrinking violet," and had to be dragged back to the stage for an encore of a piano arrangement medley from Verdi's *Il Trovatore*, and received another standing ovation. His parents were pleased but the future Cuban piano heavyweight never gave another public recital for the rest of his junior high and high school days.

In her important study of Cuban musicians in New York City and Miami, Christina Abreu cites numerous hotels, bars, nightclubs, and social clubs that featured Cuban music in Miami during the 1940s and 1950s: the Beachcomber, the Americana, the Roney Plaza, the Brook Club, Mocambo, Hotel Saxony, Sunny Isles, the Sans Souci, the Rumba Casino, the Clover Club, Hotel Caribbean, the Hotel Cadillac, La Playa at the Hotel Lucerne, Salon Pompey at the Eden Roc Hotel, the Cha Cha Lounge, Teatro Olympia, and the Tropicana, among others.[38] Cuban performers based in Miami, New York City and in Cuba provided the music at these venues. While Sonny Bravo was aware of the music scene in New York City, he was very familiar with what was happening in Miami. He explains:

> Other *hot* spots in the '50's: Louis Varona was at Harry's American Bar (Eden Roc Hotel). Sacasas was at the Club Ronde (Fontainebleau Hotel), Fausto Curbelo was at Place Pigalle, 2 blocks from the 21 Room (Sea Gull Hotel) where I began my stint w. Caney! The Boom Boom Room (Fontainebleau Hotel) was also a hot spot! I played there with Pupi Campo *and* Fajardo![39]

In 1954 Sonny attended the University of Miami on a baseball scholarship, but in his own words: "I was using college as a stepping stone to the majors, not thinking of it as education. . . . While I was there, though, I figured I might as well study what I knew, which was music."[40] In 1955 Bravo had a baseball "tryout for a berth on the Havana Sugar Kings of the International League," a AAA team.[41] He then dropped out of school after one year "because [he] was unable to play varsity ball because of SEC rules and there was no freshman schedule as yet."[42] Bravo's baseball playing days concluded just before a second professional tryout when he suffered a career-ending injury to his pitching arm during a rainy game.

At the end of 1956 or the beginning of 1957 he made his musical professional debut, replacing the female pianist in trumpet player Gastón Delfín's Conjunto Casino de Miami. Bravo was supposed to join the group two weeks later, but his predecessor needed to leave unexpectedly. Around this time he began meeting more recent arrivals to Miami from Cuba, who were fleeing the violence that plagued the end of the Batista regime. The Conjunto Casino de Miami performed at Cuban venues throughout the city, such as the Club Cubano, Club Hispano Americano, and the Círculo Cubano. Bravo passed on all solo opportunities during his initial time with the group, as he had no piano improvisation skills. Caney's pianist, Rafael Serrano, gave him some tips throughout 1957–58 and the eager pianist soon gained confidence.

Shortly thereafter, Bravo began working with the Puerto Rican bandleader Juanito Sanabria. Sanabria had made a name for himself in New York City, but came to Miami to seek his fortune. According to Bravo, the musician's union Local 655 was quite strong and demanded that local bands would have double the size of the bands of visiting bandleaders performing in Miami.[43] This would lead to situations when there would be seven or eight trumpets in one band, but it created plenty of work. Sanabria's band alternated with visiting Cuban superstars such as Orquesta Aragón, Roberto Faz, and Benny Moré. On his breaks the young pianist would run to places like the Lido to see his idols. Bravo remembered offering to straighten Benny Moré's tie before a photo, but the legendary singer with a penchant for drinking and smoking pot told

Fig 3.8. Orquesta Riverside, 1950s. Seated l-r: Franca, Temprano, N. Arseno, Vila, Charlie; Standing l-r: T. Sosa, O. Bolivar, possibly Temprano, unknown, possibly Temprano, unknon, unknown, Gustavo "El chino." Photo courtesy of Patrick Dalmace.

the young man to leave his tie alone: "*Así es la cosa*" (this is how it is), he said, indicating that he wanted to appear disheveled.

Bravo worked with numerous musicians from the legendary Orquesta Riverside at the time and fondly remembers them to this day., Bravo not only remembers the musicians in a photo of the group (see fig. 3.8), but the groups and recordings that they participated in:

> You'll see singer Otto Bolívar, a band mate of mine when I was with Conjunto Caney in Miami, as well as Diego "Mofeta" Iborra with whom I also worked a few times in bassist "Cheo" Venero's group. I have photos! Then there's pianist Gustavo "Chino" López who was also on the scene back in the late 50's early 60's! Otto did the high voice coro in TP's [Tito Puente's] original *Dance Mania*! Check out "Mambo Gozón" from that LP. Powerful, crystal clear voice![44]

As seen from this quote, Bravo remains one of the last musical links between Cuban American musicians and Cuban musicians who were active on the Miami scene in the 1950s and early 1960s.

December 31, 1958, stands out in Bravo's memory. Benny Moré was playing at the Lido when the Cuban dictator Fulgencio Batista fell and Sonny was performing upstairs in the lounge with the Peruvian singer Gonzalo Barr. He distinctly remembered both the historical implications of the news but also that El Beny's accompanying musicians included "El Negro" Vivar, Chicho, and Cabrerita. Some of these musicians would be imprisoned during the initial years of the Cuban revolution.

Up to this point Batista's popularity was low and Fidel Castro's support came from many circles both within Cuba and beyond. In New York City, the Cuban community held events in support of the new government and local Cuban businesses supported these events. One example is the *Coronacíon de la Reina de la Reforma agraria cubana en los Estados Unidos y Sus Damas (The Corontation of the Queen of Cuban Agrarian Reform in the United States and her Court)*, a social dance on May 15, 1960, at the Statler Hilton Hotel on 33rd Street and Seventh Avenue. The program for the event shows sponsorship by local Cuban businesses such as La Barraca, the Cuban Stork Club, and Cuban American civic and political groups from Bridgeport, Connecticut, Newark and Passaic, New Jersey, and New York as well as the Cuban Consul in New York. Looking at the event activities, it appears to have possibly been a local New York Cuban American dance and social event that perhaps changed its name and orientation to reflect support for the new agrarian reform of the Cuban Revolution, or an event newly created for the era. Musicians such as Osvaldo Alén, who arrived in New York City prior to the Cuban revolution and is profiled in chapter 1, performed at these events along with Cubans coming from the island. However, there was a growing community of Cuban exiles in the immediate vicinities of New York City and Miami who established organizations aimed at toppling the new Cuban government. Exiles' political views and calls to action were expressed in exile newspapers such as *El avance cubano*. The atmosphere in the Cuban exile community was charged and would later impact Sonny Bravo's career directly.

A NEW CAREER CHAPTER

Bravo's father had a pancreatic episode June 6, 1957, while playing with Conjunto Caney at the Chateau Madrid, and died unexpectedly just a week later at Metropolitan Hospital.[45] In January 1959, Bravo was asked to take the piano chair in the Caney group during an engagement at the 21 Room of the Seagull Hotel in Miami Beach. The band still had numerous extended engagements and spent their time between New York, Pennsylvania, and Miami. The summers of 1959 and 1960 (July 4 to Labor Day) would be spent at Galen Hall in Pennsylvania. Then the band would move to New York City, taking up musical residence (Labor Day to December 1959, and January 1961) at the Chateau Madrid in the Hotel Wyndham on Sixth Avenue and 56th Street. The club and the band subsequently moved to the Lexington Hotel and finally, when the

Fig 3.9. Orquesta Fajardo early 1960s. l-r: Alberto Valdés (congas and vocals), Orestes Vilató (timbales), José Fajardo (flute), Sonny Bravo, Manolo and Manuel (violins/saxes), Berto Franco (bass). Photo courtesy of Sonny Bravo.

weather turned cold, they returned to Miami. Bravo kept this routine for two years and then started playing with Pupi Campo's brother, Mandy Campo, at the Diplomat in Hollywood, Florida, from May 1961 through July 1962. The band spent a summer (July–September 1962) in Aruba and then a long stint in Puerto Rico (October 1962–April 1963) at the San Juan Hotel.[46]

After his stint with Campo and during a trip to New York City, Nilo Sierra, a bassist for Tito Puente and Machito, took Bravo to meet José Fajardo at the Palladium so he could work with him. Fajardo commuted between Miami and New York and maintained two bands;[47] Bravo began working with him in Miami during the fall of 1963. Bravo frequently performed Saturday club dates with Fajardo in Miami. Fajardo would then travel to New York to play at Sunday matinees at places like the Hotel Taft and Monday nights at La Barraca, an important venue in New York City for Cuban and Latin music.[48] In December 1963, Bravo began a two-month engagement at the Deauville Hotel in Miami Beach. Since Fajardo was still riding a wave of success, hits, and international fame, the band then spent two weeks in Mexico in April 1964, one week in the Dominican Republic in May 1964, and one month at the El San Juan Hotel in Puerto Rico during June 1964. Fajardo stayed in Puerto Rico and Bravo traveled back to New York with his bandmate Orestes Vilató.[49]

Once Bravo moved to New York City, he continued to work with Fajardo, who had returned to New York, and as a sideman with other bandleaders such as Willie Bobo and Vicentico Valdés. Bravo's first stint with Tito Puente happened when Puente's pianist, Gil López, broke his arm in a car accident.[50] The

Fig 3.10. The bar at La Barraca, New York, April 5, 1958; l-r: José "Pepe" Fernández (owner), Rolando Laserie (vocalist), and Pancho "Rompeteclas" Cárdenas (piano). Photo by Luis Miguel, Rolando Laserie Papers, Cuban Heritage Collection, University of Miami Library.

Tito Puente Orchestra had an engagement at El Patio in Atlantic Beach and Puente needed someone to substitute for López immediately. Bravo's connection to Puente was through his cousin, Bobby Rodríguez. Saxophonist Al Abreu later suggested that Puente use Bravo for the recording *My Fair Lady Goes Latin* for the Tico label in 1964. This was not the first time Bravo and Puente had met; that happened "when the [Puente] band opened the Deauville Hotel in Miami Beach in 1958," and the two men's careers would be strongly linked in subsequent years.[51]

Bravo also began working with singer Raúl Marrero in July 1965 at a club called Los Violines an engagement that lasted through April 1966. In 1966 Bravo recorded on a session for *Queen of Latin Soul* by La Lupe and *Married Well* (Verve) by Chico O'Farrill, for which he was paid $61 per session but walked away with $46.22 after taxes and miscellaneous payroll costs.[52] During this time, he also recorded with Johnny Rodríguez and Louie Ramirez for the first time for an album entitled *Cooking with A&J* for Mardi Gras Records. Throughout 1966 Bravo worked with Nilo Sierra, Vicentico Valdés, Mauricio Smith, Bobby Valentín, and Ray Barretto before returning to work with Marrero in November 1966 at the legendary El Habana San Juan nightclub. During this engagement, Marrero convinced Bravo to start arranging.

In March 1967, Bravo was also working and recording with Rafael Cortijo and Ismael Rivera in New York. These two Puerto Rican musicians achieved worldwide success with their dancehall version of the Afro-Puerto Rican folk music styles bomba and plena. Bravo can be heard playing piano on the seminal

Fig 3.11. Rolando Laserie (standing), Arsenio Rodríguez (seated with tres), Lucho Gatica, third from left, possibly Las Hermanas Márquez, and others at La Barraca. Photo by Luis Miguel, Rolando Laserie Papers, Cuban Heritage Collection, University of Miami Library.

Fig 3.12. Cortijo Y Su Combo in Chicago, 1967: Ray Maldonado (kneeling with glasses, trumpet), Sonny Bravo (standing in back), Mongo Santamaria (in hat), Ismael Rivera, Mario Cora (two over from Ismael), Ray Armando (far right, conga). Photo courtesy of Sonny Bravo.

album *Con todos los hierros (Everything But the Kitchen Sink)*, released by Tico in 1967, and he traveled to Chicago with the band over two weekends.[53] In 1968 he would rejoin Rivera for the recording *De colores* after the brilliant singer's first of several stints in prison that plagued his career. Bravo also took a day job as an exterminator in New York City for two years because he needed more economic stability, but the job made him depressed. Seeking relief and a release, he took a gig in the Catskills and quit the exterminating job.

Thus, Bravo's performance career included stints with the best exponents of Afro-Latin music in New York City and artists who toured internationally. These groups encompassed a variety of genres such as Puerto Rican bomba, plena, New York–style mambo, Cuban charanga, and conjunto music or *música típica*. Bravo's experience playing in different groups as a sideman would prove invaluable later in his career when writing arrangements for a wide variety of groups.

THE EARLY ART OF THE ARRANGER

It was not until 1967–68 that Bravo began his second career as an arranger. He wrote his first charts for his friend Raul Marrero, a Puerto Rican bandleader and the godfather of Bravo's daughter Tamiko. Two charts, "La Hija de Lola" and "La Chica del Barrio Obrero," became major hits, and bands that covered the songs played the same arrangements.[54] This was especially true for Charlie Palmieri and Vitín Aviles. Everywhere Bravo turned, he would hear another band playing his arrangement, so he "must have been doing something right."[55] That "something right" was writing swinging and appealing arrangements; unfortunately, the pay rate for an arrangement was fifty dollars, and arrangers did not earn any publishing monies.

Interestingly, the version of the "La Hija de Lola" that Palmieri recorded on *El gigante del teclado* (see musical example 3.4) was not executed as Bravo had intended because the band's book of arrangements was burned in an accident and the musicians had to record it from memory.[56] That the musicians reinterpreted the chart is indicative of the abilities, inventiveness, and tenacity of New York–based performers of Latin music.

The descending half-step movement of the mambo (2:34–3:04) in measures 4–7 (Cm7-F7-Bm7-E7-B♭m7-E♭7-Am7-D7) is heard in Bravo's later arrangements.[57] When Palmieri plays Bravo's sequence in this recording, he eliminates the ii chord, going directly to the V chord (F7-E7-E♭7-D7). This particular harmonic and melodic motion signals a modernist view that is faithful to the tradition inherited from Caney, but reflecting New York's soundscape with its chromatic, almost jazzy lines.

Musical Example 3.4. Charlie Palmieri version of Sonny Bravo's arrangement of "La Hija de Lola," *El gigante del teclado*. Transcription by Benjamin Lapidus.

By his own admission, Bravo modeled his early arranging concept on the work of Rene Hernández, particularly the simplicity of Hernández's lines and backgrounds.[58] Austerlitz does a good job of highlighting Hernández's many qualities as a pianist and their impact on the Machito orchestra and others; these include being self-taught, employing harmonic sophistication from knowing bebop, playing and writing in clave, writing excellent bass patterns, writing uniquely for several bands, and being clave conscious, among other traits.[59] In many ways, these are among the qualities that are embodied in Bravo's work.

One of Bravo's early arrangements is of the Armando Manzanero composition "Esta tarde ví llover," written for a Raul Marrero recording session. By Bravo's own admission, this chart for three trumpets, voice, and rhythm bears the influence of the simplicity of Hernández's writing on Vicentico Valdés's version of Giraldo Piloto and Alberto Vera's "Fidelidad," arranged by Hernández for three trumpets, voice, and rhythm (see musical example 3.5). Bravo's background lines, particularly the ii-V chord progressions descending by half steps (measures 4, 6, 8) and the chromatic motion of the bass (measures 7, 12, 23), outline additional harmonies that are not present in the original composition (see musical example 3.6). The melodic motion of the horns and the simplicity of the horn voicings are clearly based on Hernández's writing style. Another idea that Bravo borrows from Hernández is the eighth-note

Musical Example 3.5. "Fidelidad" introduction, as arranged by Rene Hernández. Transcription by Benjamin Lapidus.

Musical Example 3.6. "Esta tarde ví llover" introduction, as arranged by Sonny Bravo. Transcription by Benjamin Lapidus.

rhythm of the trumpet lines. Later in his career, Bravo would return to this arrangement of Hernández's and use the intro "slightly modified, harmonically" in his accompaniment of the Cuban vocalist Xiomara Laugart on her version of "Tú mi delirio."[60] This borrowing of jazz harmony demonstrates how Cuban music served as a model for US-based performers of Cuban music. As US-based musicians learned the styles and concepts of acknowledged masters, they soon made changes within and moved beyond the Cuban templates. The harmonic modernism of Bravo's arrangement from this time period can be contrasted with the more traditionalist leaning that is heard in his earliest recorded improvisations.

Throughout his career, Sonny Bravo would continue to look to Cuba for inspiration while incorporating the music of the United States into his own vision of Cuban music. However, his contemporaries based in the United States refused to acknowledge Cuban music made after 1959. This was practical from a business standpoint as well as being politically motivated. On many Latin music albums of the period from 1959 until the late 1990s (when relations between the countries warmed), practically every Cuban composition was listed as *derechos reservados* ([all] rights reserved). This remains a popular joke among musicians when discussing a song's composer, but it served as a serious and real means by which record companies could deliberately avoid the thorny issue of royalty payments to Cuban nationals. It also did not help these composers that Cuba did not recognize international copyright law at the time, since so many Cuban compositions were being recorded and popularized in the United States and distributed throughout the world. Countless hits for a number of New York–based artists were simply listed as *derechos reservados*.

The other piece of the deliberate erasing of Cuban music was that a number of performers would not or could not return to Cuba because of the political situation. The celebrated bandleader (and Bravo's frequent employer) Tito Puente did not return to Cuba after 1959, although he had traveled there in the early 1950s. Musically, Puente did not incorporate any new genres of Cuban music nor did he adapt his concept to include any post-1959 Cuban musical trends. Others such as Cuban vocalist Celia Cruz, another Bravo employer, were outspoken against the Cuban government. Bravo worked extensively with both of these icons. And, although he and his band are emblematic of inter-ethnic collaboration in New York during the period of this study, they would be susceptible to the political realities of the Cuban/United States relationship as expressed at home in New York City, particularly in the late 1970s and early 1980s. In her book *Finding Mañana: A Memoir of Cuban Exodus*, Mirta Ojito chronicles the charged atmosphere that plagued Miami in this time period.[61] Murders of Cuban exiles who advocated for dialogue with the Cuban government and bombings of travel agencies specializing in Cuban travel as well as other businesses were quite common.[62] This violence was not limited to Miami and would also reach north to New York City. Various exile groups attempted to bomb both Cuban government officials at the United Nations and musical performances by Cuban nationals, who by extension were viewed as representing the Cuban government after 1959.[63]

SONNY BRAVO THE PIANIST

Peter Manuel has outlined several stylistic attributes of Latin (Afro-Cuban) piano improvisation that can also be applied to Sonny Bravo's playing in this period of the late 1960s. They include:

> (1) Repeated ternary-phrased, three-pitch, eighth note arpeggios, usually with doubled or tripled octaves, alternating between tonic and dominant chords . . . (2) melodies played in double, triple, or quadruple octaves . . . (3) phrases using parallel thirds or (tenths), also generally played in doubled octaves . . . (4) syncopated patterns repeating short, double-octave, right-hand phrases (usually one or two pitches) with left-hand chords . . . (5) *guajeo/montuno*-like passages; (6) block chords; (7) quasi-atonal, and often a-rhythmic nonsense riffs . . . (8) single-note right-hand runs, with occasional left-hand "comping" chords, as in mainstream jazz piano.[64]

Manuel's terminology is somewhat confusing, as it is technically impossible to play double-octaves with two hands and simultaneously accompany said phrases with left-hand chords. What Manuel characterizes as a "nonsense" riff that he transcribes from Anselmo Sacasas is actually reflective of Cuban piano giants such as Lilí (Luis Martínez Griñán), arguably the most important pianist/arranger in Cuban dance music from 1940–60, and his contemporary and friend Pedro Jústiz "Peruchín." Bravo employs this same riff to this day, and it is practically mandatory for a pianist playing in this idiom to throw this particular musical idea into the course of an improvisation. The influence of Lilí Martínez on Bravo is most obvious in two-handed ascending chromatic patterns and the Chopinesque phrasing—sometimes pushing and sometimes pulling the beat—also favored by Lilí. In an interview discussing his piano style, Bravo revealed to Robert Doerschuk the extent to which the Western European classical tradition actually informs his style, and explains that there is no difference technique-wise between salsa piano and classical music: "Not really. All my Hanon techniques come into play. There is a heavy emphasis on the wrists in salsa, and again [Heinrich] Döring [piano studies] was very helpful with that, especially when you're doing octaves."[65]

Musical Example 3.7. Sonny Bravo piano solo, "La Chica del Barrio Obrero." Transcription by Michael Eckroth.

"La Chica del Barrio Obrero," the 1968 Raúl Marrero 45rpm single on Ansonia Records, features Bravo's first recorded solo (see musical example 3.7). The personnel included Bravo's cousin Bobby Rodríguez on bass and Johnny Rodríguez on bongó.[66] Many of the characteristics Manuel enumerates can be seen in the transcription.

Fig 3.13. Louie Ramírez, Sonny Bravo, and Peter Rosaly at the recording of Bravo's solo debut. Courtesy of Sonny Bravo.

In this solo, Bravo demonstrates Manuel's first characteristic of "repeated ternary-phrased, three-pitch" ideas in double octaves.[67] The opening of the solo begins with this idea carried through measure 4 and then continued in a Chopinesque descending fashion from measures 5–8. This second idea is also quite common in Lilí Martínez Griñán's solos; Lilí was a huge influence on Bravo and many other Latin pianists and was an admitted Chopin lover who even arranged Chopin's music in Cuban son style.[68] In the next phrase, measures 9–14, Bravo plays with the rhythmic accents by pushing and pulling with his phrasing against the beat. In measures 15 through the beginning of 19, Bravo employs left-hand chords with syncopated patterns in the right hand, as Manuel suggests. In measure 20, Bravo begins working his way back to the *guajeo* (repeated piano pattern played during the *montuno* or call and response section of a song), and in measure 21 he rolls a chord on the last quarter and eighth note of the measure in a jazz or blues style. In measure 22, Bravo returns to the guajeo before ending the solo on a simple arpeggio. The cumulative effect of the solo communicates Bravo's command of the Cuban piano idiom and an ability to play with its conventions. Future solos and arrangements show a fealty to this tradition but with a greater expansion and personalization of improvising within its parameters.

In 1968 a few developments brought Bravo to record his first and only album as a single leader. Two friends, the producer Bobby Marín and the arranger Louie Ramírez—who made Bravo his pianist of choice for recording sessions—recommended Bravo to Peter Rosaly, who was the producer behind Eydie

Gorme's successful album *Canta en Español*. The result was Columbia Records' *The New York Latin Scene with Sonny Bravo: You Gotta Turn Me On*, an album of boogaloo, a late 1960s fusion of Cuban music and American rhythm and blues.[69] The songs on this album reflect the tastes of the times and the influence of those who succeeded in this format, such as Johnny Colón, Pete Rodríguez, Willie Bobo, Joe Cuba, Joe Bataan, and others. The album makes use of Spanish-language *coros* (choruses) for English popular expressions and songs like "The Tighten Up," but Bravo is only featured as an accompanist and he only has one piano solo in the entire record. The recording also features Bravo's longtime collaborators Bobby Rodríguez on bass and Johnny Rodríguez on bongó.

Not long after the release of *The New York Latin Scene with Sonny Bravo: You Gotta Turn Me On*, Bravo began to undergo a conceptual leap in his arranging and playing. This growth would take the music in new directions at the beginning of the 1970s and is marked by an advanced harmony that is not usually associated with Cuban music from that time period.

BOBBY RODRÍGUEZ: THE MISSING (FAMILY) LINK BETWEEN MODERN HARMONY AND THE BASS IN SPANISH CARIBBEAN MUSIC

Bravo's penchant for harmonic embellishment of simple chord progressions is rooted in common practice jazz harmonic substitutions, but Bravo has repeatedly denied learning jazz repertoire, practicing it as a pianist, or being able to perform idiomatically as a jazz pianist or function on a jazz gig. It was Bravo's

Fig 3.14. Sonny Bravo and Bobby Rodríguez at the corner of E. 112 Street and Lexington Avenue, Summer 1952. Photo courtesy of Sonny Bravo.

Fig 3.15. Cuarteto Marcano, l-r: Claudio Ferrer, Pedro "Piquito" Marcano, Kiki "El Moto," Luis "Lija" Ortiz, and Bobby Rodríguez (age 16). Photo courtesy of Sonny Bravo.

cousin, the renowned bassist Bobby Rodríguez (1927–2002), who showed him the harmonic substitutions that he still employs in his piano playing, particularly "don't go to a V chord without [playing] the ii."[70] Bravo often employs tritone substitutions when comping (accompanying) and, in discussing these types of subtle variations, Bravo was clear that not every bassist would catch these variations or even acknowledge them with enthusiasm.[71] Bravo singles out the 1968 José "Chombo" Silva album *Los Hits de Manzanero* as his first recording where these variations were evident, and Bobby Rodríguez plays bass on the recording.[72] Other pianists such as Gilberto "Pulpo" Colón Jr. also learned how to apply modern harmonies in the Spanish Caribbean setting through Bobby Rodríguez's tutelage.

The mystery to be solved is, where did Bobby Rodríguez get these harmonic and rhythmic ideas from and when did he begin employing them? On Rodríguez's earliest recordings in the 1940s with Cuarteto Marcano (see fig. 3.15), he can be heard playing a traditional tresillo pattern that was appropriate for the bass during that time period in Latin music.[73] After serving in World War II, Rodríguez studied bass with Bill Chartoff through the G.I. Bill.[74] Rubén Rodríguez (no relation), who was Bobby's protégé, said that Bobby also spent time with bassist Ray Brown and baritone saxophonist Cecil Payne, among others.[75] Sonny Bravo remembers taking his cousin Bobby to see Charles Mingus at Birdland because Bravo had played there during the week before with Willie

Fig 3.16. The LaSalle Cafeteria at nighttime. Photo from *Life* magazine, 1958.

Bobo's group and musicians were given complimentary entry. Multi-instrumentalist Cándido Camero remembers another location where musicians from the jazz and Latin scene would congregate after work, hang out, talk shop, and jam until 6 in the morning: the LaSalle Cafeteria at 51st Street and 7th Avenue in Manhattan (790 7th Avenue).[76] Looking at the photo in figure 3.16, one can see the cafeteria's physical proximity to Roseland and other nearby clubs, making it an ideal location for musicians to meet up. It's worth noting that in the 1940s, the LaSalle was well known as one of the "clubs-without-dues for . . . rumba musicians."[77] The LaSalle was located below an important Latin dance music venue called La Conga and both of them made headlines as early as 1939 when a fire erupted in the kitchen.[78]

Chris Washburne briefly mentions Bobby Rodríguez's connection to straight-ahead jazz musicians in his book *Sounding Salsa*, but only in the context of quoting Rodríguez's admission to supplying Charlie Parker with drugs and feeling responsible for his death.[79] Rodríguez may have been a conduit for drugs, but he was not personally responsible for Parker's death; he was truly an important and unsung catalyst for musical exchanges between Latin and jazz musicians. According to Gilberto "Pulpo" Colón Jr., Rodríguez was friendly with other jazz musicians, particularly bassists, and was

Hanging out with all the heavy guys Ron Carter, Major Holley, Richard Davis, Buster Williams, and they were doing . . . those ii-V progressions going down chromatically in the half steps. And he was hanging out with them and jamming with them, although he didn't play jazz . . . so he was privy and exposed to that by hanging out with those guys. They were his boys.[80]

Musical Example 3.8. Gilberto "Pulpo" Colón Jr. piano guajeo for "Vamonos p'al monte." Transcription by Benjamin Lapidus.

Colón posits that, since Rodríguez was playing and recording the acoustic double bass with Palmieri, Machito, and Puente before he used the Baby Bass, there was perhaps even a greater affinity to the acoustic bass in jazz. Colón states that Rodríguez got these "hipper" chord progressions from this group of jazz musicians "from hanging and listening to what they were doing with pianists that were on another level. Latin is here [lowers hand] and jazz is here [raises hand]."[81] Colón remembers doing a recording session with Rodríguez of "Vamonos p'al monte" for the album *Charanga la tapa* (1982) where he used substitute chord changes as shown in musical example 3.8. The song was recorded with the standard chord progression of i-iv-V in G minor, but on gigs Rodríguez asked Colón to play the chord changes differently.

For Colón, Rodríguez was very focused on the attack of the piano and of the bass and how the piano would complement a bass, and he demanded this of other pianists. Rodríguez's own attack on electric bass was with the thumb, rather than a standard classical pizzicato and he expected pianists to play as solidly as he did with their left hand.[82] This use of the thumb was why Rodríguez was affectionately nicknamed *dedo gordo* (fat thumb) by his peers. According to Bravo, Rodríguez was forced to switch to the electric Fender bass after his Ampeg Baby Bass and other equipment were stolen from the Tito Puente band's van; hence, the new attack with the thumb was an attempt to approximate the sound and feel of the Baby Bass on an Ampeg electric fretless bass.[83] From his years of experience playing with Charlie Palmieri and René Hernández, Rodríguez would tell Colón:

"If we're going to be a team, I can do this, if you do that [play strongly]. Otherwise, then *de que me vale* it has to be pretty? Then I gotta be rough because

I don't have an amplifier," it was acoustic bass. And, I didn't understand the concept at that time [because] I was already playing electric piano by the way . . . no touch, it's not weighted, no sustain, and it's a reproduced sound through the amplifier . . . no overtones . . . it's harder to control that type of a sound. It's harder to make that sound that he's looking for, he's seeking. So of course, in the recording it came out, but then we did gigs and it didn't come out and he was [a] real pain . . . And I don't think he was a pain . . . to be a pain, he was searching for the complement of the sounds between him and I. And that you could only get from someone who's real conscious.[84]

According to Bravo, the original chachachá bass pattern that Tito Puente used for a two-chord tonic-dominant seventh ostinato moved on beats three and four (see musical example 3.9).

Musical Example 3.9. Original chachachá pattern. Transcription by Benjamin Lapidus.

Bravo credits Bobby Rodríguez for the anticipated bass part and he explains it as "whatever the chord is on the 1st beat of the next bar may be 'anticipated' on the 4th beat of the previous bar."[85] Tying the last beat of the measure to beat 1 in the following measure is another modern innovation "whereas before it was short dry sound [attack]."[86]

Musical Example 3.10. Anticipated Bass Pattern Transcription by Benjamin Lapidus.

Musical Example 3.11. Tresillo Bass Pattern Transcription by Benjamin Lapidus.

Musical Example 3.12. Cumbia-Style Bass Pattern Transcription by Benjamin Lapidus.

These types of bass lines and what might be called cumbia-style bass lines are consistent with instructional texts of this period, such as *Latin-American Rhythms and Improvisations for Piano* by Noro Morales (1955), *How to Play Latin American Rhythm Instruments* by Humberto Morales, and the ensemble scores found in stock arrangements of the period.[87] Bravo continued to perform with his cousin in various configurations of Tito Puente's ensembles until Rodríguez's death. For Sonny Bravo, Bobby Rodríguez served as the conduit to jazz-oriented harmony and extensively shaped Bravo's harmonic sensibility. His role, however, extended beyond Bravo's musical development, as the two frequently broke musical ground on recordings and in performance, setting musical standards for the piano and bass in Latin music in New York. A perfect example of this was in Tito Puente's large ensemble and in his smaller jazz-oriented group. Lastly, Bravo is known for tapping the clave pattern with his foot while playing: "He [Rodríguez] made me realize the importance of maintaining the family practice (started by my dad) of tapping the clave pattern with our foot while playing our tumbaos!"[88] However, Bravo admits that it took him some time and practice to incorporate the foot tapping into his playing.

TÍPICA 73

In 1972 a core group of musicians played together at a weekly jam session led by Johnny Rodríguez at a Manhattan nightclub called . . . and Vinnie (see fig. 3.18). Each of these musicians had extensive experience in the realm of Spanish Caribbean dance music as sidemen playing with the top bands of the period, such as Ray Barretto, José Fajardo, Tito Puente, etc. The resulting music was really shaped by the musicians and their interactions. In my liner notes for the 2005 reissue of the Típica 73 recording *Charangueando*, I write:

> Bravo described the band's collective arranging style as follows "There were no charts then. We relied mainly on old charanga standards. I would start off with a riff . . . then Johnny [Rodríguez] would come up with a break. After the montuno René [López] would improvise a horn mambo, etc." Sonny wrote the charts out for future performances, but it really was a group effort when it came to writing the arrangements.[89]

Fig 3.17. Típica 73 at . . . and Vinnie. Standing l-r: Adalberto Santiago, Leopoldo Pineda, Sonny Bravo, Johnny Rodríguez, René López, and Joe Mannozzi; kneeling l-r: Orestes Vilató, David Pérez. Photo courtesy of Sonny Bravo.

In the spirit of this collective the musicians formed a band that functioned as a cooperative and chose its repertoire as a result of the jam sessions. In a 1977 interview, trumpeter René López explained the benefits of the cooperative arrangement to Carlos DeLeón: "You're not just a sideman. It belongs to you; you have to take care of it. That responsibility makes you want to play better."[90]

On September 23, 1972, they performed their first gig as Típica 73 at a club called La Mancha with their lineup of two trumpets and one trombone, plus rhythm section.[91] People started to notice: a 1972 listing in *New York* magazine even stated that, "On Tuesday there is a Jam Session with sidemen from a mix of the top New York Latin bands and sometimes the bandleaders themselves."[92]

Their repertoire was associated with charanga, a particular Cuban ensemble type that normally features flute, violins, and rhythm section. However, the band's initial recordings and instrumentation were actually executed with the instrumentation of a conjunto or *orquesta*.[93] Bravo had substantial experience performing this repertoire with Fajardo, as did some of the other musicians, and in subsequent years, the band would record and perform in this format. The first

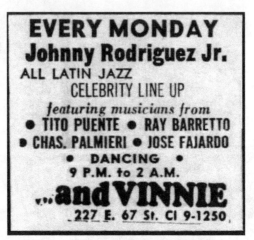

Fig 3.18. *Daily News* advertisement from March 6, 1972.

album was recorded in late 1972 and released in 1973. Típica 73's all-star roster included the Cuban-born, New York–raised *timbalero* Orestes Vilató, Bravo on piano, the Puerto Rican vocalist Adalberto Santiago, Nuyorican percussionist John "Dandy" Rodríguez Jr., Nuyorican bassist Dave Pérez, Dominican trombonist Leopoldo Pineda, Italian American trumpeter and pianist Joe Mannozzi, and Nuyorican trumpeter René López. Puerto Rican tres player Nelson Gónzalez joined shortly after the group's second LP, *La Típica '73 Vol. 2*, was released in 1974.

In Dandy, Bravo found a musical partner who also had extensive exposure to the music through his father, a legendary percussionist named John "La Vaca" Rodríguez. John Sr. performed and recorded with every major band of the 1940s, including those of Noro Morales, Tito Puente, Machito, and Tito Rodríguez, among many others. While his father was not his teacher per se, his father exposed him to contemporary Cuban records and had him sit in on gigs as a beginner. The connection to the families of Tito Puente and Tito Rodríguez also facilitated his eventual employment with those bands when he was deemed ready.[94] Bassist Nilo Sierra, a family friend, would accompany Dandy on his first trip to Puerto Rico with Tito Puente in 1962. Dandy followed in his father's footsteps and began working with Tito Puente at the age of seventeen. He also worked with Tito Rodríguez and Eddie Palmieri and, like Bravo, he made a solo recording as a co-leader in 1968 that included Bravo on half of the record.[95] Further cementing the musical and familial ties between Dandy and Bravo was the fact that Dandy played alongside Bravo's cousin Bobby Rodríguez in Puente's group and in others.

The musical sensibility of these two records separated the group instantly from their contemporaries. The repertoire alternated between originals and standards in English and in Spanish, and the renditions of standard material were filled with an embrace of humorous inside jokes, extensive musical quotations, and harmonic and stylistic choices that made the covers completely unique. Audio and video versions of their well-known rendition of "Amalia Batista" are illustrative of how their brand of musical humor always displayed respect for the tradition despite its rambunctiousness. Bravo fills his piano solo with blue notes, jazz chords, and quotations that are pretty far removed from his solo statements on previous recordings (see musical example 3.13).

Musical Example 3.13. Sonny Bravo piano solo, "Amalia Batista." Transcription by Michael Eckroth.

If one uses Bravo's first recorded solo improvisation from "La chica del barrio obrero" as a point of departure to look at his later work, it is easy to see that he is grounded in the more traditional Cuban piano school of Peruchín and Lilí Martínez, but that he has injected influences and conventions from jazz pianists into his solo improvisations.

The piano solo begins at 1:05 on the recording with a flashy scalar line played in octaves in the right hand and chords in the left hand. Then Bravo plays block chords and adds some bluesy ideas in measures 13 and 14. Beginning with measure 16 (1:15), Bravo quotes the first eight bars of the melody from Billy Strayhorn's "Take the A-Train." This is followed by a return to a traditional Cuban style of piano improvisation using octaves in the right hand and chords in the left hand starting in the pickup to measure 24 through measure 39. In measure 23, Bravo hints at what is to come in this section by rolling the notes in his left hand. Bravos uses sequences of repeated ideas in this section, particularly around the pitches C-E♭-E natural and G that begin in measure 24 and 25 and are developed throughout. Measures 30 and 31 quote the melody of

Pedro "Peruchín" Jústiz's version of Alejandro Rodríguez's "La mulata rumbera." He concludes this idea with rhythmic variations of a descending right-hand pattern centered on C-B-B♭-A in measures 36–39. With the pickup to measure 40 (1:41), Bravo quotes the beginning of the melody of Antonio Carlos Jobim's "Desafinado" with right-hand octaves and left-hand chords. After the first two measures, he plays a Cuban guajeo in measures 42 and 43 before continuing the melody in measure 44–45 and concluding it with block chords and the start of some rhythmic displacement in measures 46–47. This rhythmic displacement continues to intensify in measures 48–52. Bravo ends his solo with an idea that combines right-hand octave displacement and left-hand chords.

This recording of "Amalia Batista" is also significant because it shows how Bravo and the band incorporated a good deal of musical humor into their over-all concept. After Bravo's piano solo is finished and the band plays an idiomatic mambo, trumpeter René López follows with a scatted vocal solo (2:18–2:53) that trades phrases with non-improvised jazz-inflected horn responses. The ensemble then adds the vocal chorus "Daddy, daddy, daddy, daddy, daddy O" from Al Jolson (2:54) while López sings two more vocal improvisations. At 3:20 Nelson Gónzalez adds a humorous introduction for the band and welcomes the listener to a fictitious performance in the state of Indiana as Orestes Vilató continues with a 1920s vaudevillian impression of "Yes Sir That's My Baby" (1925), followed by López singing "Has Anybody Seen My Gal," and then Vilató's vocal impersonation of Al Jolson's "Toot Toot Tootsie" starting at 3:29. The band is rollicking and swinging behind Vilató's toy flute solo, followed by a brief trombone impression by vocalist Adalberto Santiago, and a brief mambo sec-tion before returning to the main melody. The last sound heard on the song is an audible collective sneeze. On this album, the influence of North American music is further apparent with the inclusion of two contemporary pop songs "What Are You Doing the Rest of Your Life?' and "Where Is the Love?"

TÍPICA 73 AS A VEHICLE FOR BRAVO'S ARRANGEMENTS

The influence of Bravo's initial inspiration, René Hernández, was now ex-pressed with Bravo's own personal musical voice and depth. This can be seen and heard in Bravo's arrangement of two classic René Touzet boleros, "La noche de anoche/Cada vez más" in a medley for two trumpets, trombone, vocals, and rhythm section. Here, Bravo employs one of Hernández's ideas of us-ing an interlude and a pedal point in the bass to avoid repeating the whole melody again so as to bring the vocalist back sooner, but in a later section of the form. Hernández uses this in "Fidelidad" at 01:46–01:59.[96] The arrangement begins with the ensemble playing a quote from "La noche de anoche" before the vocalist Adalberto Santiago starts singing "Cada vez más." Bravo uses the B♭ pedal in the bass at 01:49–2:05 to create some excitement and bring the ensemble directly into the melody of "La noche de anoche":

Musical Example 3.14. Sonny Bravo arrangement of "La noche de anoche/Cada vez más." Courtesy of Sonny Bravo.

Other songs from this record, like "Carahuico," have snippets of "Woody Woodpecker" heard in the piano and vocals in the Gil López arrangement. While the descarga (jam) "Watergate" takes its title from the events of the day, the music and the coros (vocal refrains) composed by Bravo are unrelated. The tres montuno (ostinato pattern) that begins the song is taken verbatim from El Niño Rivera's playing on Israel "Cachao" López's jam session recordings, but it is differentiated by use of the wah-wah pedal and a distorted sound. Vilató effectively employs vocalized percussion riffs in a conversation with himself during his timbal solo on "Descarga '73." In conclusion, Bravo's arrangements and the band's personalities crafted a highly personal and unique musical vision that was new and appealing to dancers and listeners both in New York City and beyond the United States.

Típica 73 struck new ground with their release of *La Candela* in 1975. While artists like Ray Barretto and Típica 73 had success by covering hits by Los Van Van and other Cuban artists, they were exceptions to the post-1959 sentiment of the scene. It was even more rare for Cuban groups to cover non-Cuban New York–based musicians' music, but there were a few notable exceptions.[97] These groups encountered one another at international performances in Europe, Panama, Colombia, Venezuela, and elsewhere, where they would socialize and jam.

On *La candela*, Típica 73 included a classic pre-1959 composition called "El jamaiquino" (The Jamaican) by El Niño Rivera (Andrés Echevarría), the title track by Cuba's biggest band Juan Formell and Los Van, and "La escoba barrendera," another song that had been popularized in Cuba by the charanga group

Estrellas Cubanas. In subsequent years, Bravo would adopt the drum set and the electric guitar—both of which were in vogue with his musical contemporaries in Cuba—but at this time he maintained a more traditional brass instrumentation. With the inclusion of these two particular contemporary Cuban songs, he embraced the newer Cuban dance music trends such as the *songo* rhythm, adding sacred batá drums to secular dance music, using synthesizers, and other sonic manipulation techniques.

Bravo's arrangements and Típica 73's performances of "La Candela" and "La escoba barrendera" were conceptually faithful to the original recordings and largely differed by adding new horn lines. Bravo demonstrates his highly sophisticated and personalized arranging style to make them work with his group's instrumental format. This differed from the groups who originally recorded the songs.[98] For "La Candela," the main riff is executed by the tres played through a wah-wah pedal. For this arrangement Bravo wrote all of the mambo sections, but did not change too much, his logic "If you can't do it better, don't change it, leave it alone."[99] That said, he did offer the melody played by the horns, something not found in the original. "Escoba barrendera" was essentially a transcription with the exception of a few "spots before the coro."[100] One such spot is moving the key of the song up and around to add musical excitement before settling in one key. In addition, the horn section plays the coro. Bravo uses this particular modulation technique in other arrangements such as "Que manera de sentirme bien" from the album *Salsa Encendida* (1978): the song changes keys several times during the introduction, when the first coro comes in, and finally upends a traditional carnival coro, "Siento un bombo" from major to minor for the final vamp.[101]

American jazz increasingly found its way into Bravo's arrangements and solos through frequent use of blue notes and even modal improvisations. Bravo takes more musical chances with his arrangement of "El jamaiquino" to make a serious musical statement. Unaware of El Niño Rivera's original 1958 Panart recording, Bravo used Francisco Fellove's popular version of the song as his point of departure. His arrangement of "El jamaiquino" demonstrates a fidelity to the original composition's construction while at the same time looking beyond it. Bravo employed modern harmonic innovations, rhythmic influences from contemporary North American dance music, modern signal processing, and Cuban ritual drumming.

Harmonically, many groups and arrangers in New York were emphasizing planed-fourths movement and embracing whole tone scales in their writing. This is a modal jazz concept whereby a stack of fourths "is moved up or down in step-wise fashion . . . in moments of harmonic stasis (absence of movement, such as vamps and modal playing) while retaining the notes of a given diatonic scale or mode . . . to create the sense of movement through planing even when the chords do not progress."[102] Although Bravo was eager to use quartal voicings in his arrangements, such as "La candela" and "El jamaiquino," he faced some "skepticism" from at least two of his bandmates who found it to be strange sounding. Vocalist Adalberto Santiago, who had also been a bass player for Chuíto Vélez in the 1960s, was more accustomed to singing in thirds and sixths. Bravo exhorted him to forget those days of traditional harmony in order to sing the modern arrangements. The trombonist Leopoldo Pineda also disliked Bravo's new penchant for fourths and Bravo believed that for Pineda,

> His main problem was having to "*matizar*" [to blend] with the two trumpets for a proper blend. He was used to blasting out his parts. In a quartal triad, the interval between the lead voice and the third voice is a minor seventh, not the most pleasant of sounds without the second voice. I suppose neither one of them minded the fourths between two of the three horns as long as the other horn was playing a third or a sixth.[103]

Other arrangers were also employing quartal harmony in Latin music. Gilberto "Pulpo" Colón Jr. feels that the influence of José Febles and his interest in voicing his horns like Thad Jones was part of the process.[104] For Colón this modern non-diatonic sound could be perceived as musical aggressiveness and grittiness, a New York trait that also might come from Motown and jazz.[105] The technique of parallel movement of chords with extensions was also popular among arrangers of the era. The introductions of two popular songs from this time period reflect the particular sound that was in fashion. These include Louie Cruz's arrangement of "Señor Sereno" (1972) for Orquesta Harlow and René Hernández's arrangement of "Pa' la ocha tambo" for Eddie Palmieri.[106]

Musical Example 3.15. Orquesta Harlow, mambo section, "Señor sereno." Transcription by Benjamin Lapidus.

Musical Example 3.16. Eddie Palmieri, introduction, "Pa' la ocha tambó." Transcription by Benjamin Lapidus.

Larry Harlow contends that Palmieri was the first to employ these types of chord voicings on the piano and in arrangements as a direct result of studying quartal harmony and the Schillinger system with New York guitarist Bob Bianco. Bianco was an influential musician, teacher, and author whose impact and importance is discussed in chapter 4. Palmieri has confirmed this and explains how he spread out specific clusters to create his sound.[107] Once he added these extensions, other pianists and arrangers followed suit.[108] Harlow's use of these structures in his arrangement was by way of Louie Cruz, a pianist and arranger who, by his own admission, learned some arranging techniques from books by Russ García and Van Alexander as well as other musicians.[109]

Bravo employs three—or four, depending on perspective—key changes in this arrangement, which happen pretty quickly. The song begins in E♭ and then moves to the key of A♭, then F and a brief open modal section with a return to F. For Bravo, the idea of having the band play in a different key from the vocalist offers a musical improvement in that the higher key is "brighter"; he argues that this technique makes musical sense.[110] Bravo acknowledges the fun challenge of improvising on Latin jazz songs that move through multiple key centers with Tito Puente's group, but he is adamant that this idea must serve a musical purpose in a vocal chart.

The introductory *tutti* demonstrates Bravo's ingenuity and incorporation of new harmonic ideas (0:00–0:09).[111] Here we see a whole tone harmony combined with Earth, Wind & Fire–styled horn parts:

Musical Example 3.17. "El jamaiquino," introduction, as arranged by Sonny Bravo. Courtesy of Sonny Bravo.

Bravo was also influenced by the horn parts played by Blood, Sweat and Tears as well as Kool and the Gang, whose music he loved. In the 1990s musicians in Cuba would emulate this sound decades after Bravo pioneered it in New York City.[112] After the first time that vocalist Adalberto Santiago sings the melody, Bravo has the ensemble restate the melody (0:22–0:41) using the same full ensemble texture from the introduction, almost like a shout chorus. This shout chorus is executed in the key of A♭ major. The phrase ends with another key change to F major arrived at through the final cadence of G♮ or Gmin7♭5 to C7.

Musical Example 3.18. Restatement of melody, "El jamaiquino." Courtesy of Sonny Bravo.

Then at 0:41 the instrumental ensemble responds as a choral refrain (*si se rompe se compone*) to the lead vocal line (*rómpelo*). The emphasis on quartal harmony and chromaticism is evident in this section with planed fourths moving FMaj7-E♭Maj7-D♭Maj7-E♭Maj7 in measures 1 and 2, followed by the descending chromatic movement of B7-B♭7-A7-A♭7-G7-G♭7.

Musical Example 3.19. Chromatic movement, "El jamaiquino." Courtesy of Sonny Bravo.

To leave the montuno (choral refrain) section at 1:30, Bravo uses the following figure, again played by the entire ensemble, and again a melodic idea that is not part of traditional Cuban music but reflective of North American R&B:

Musical Example 3.20. R&B riff, "El jamaiquino." Courtesy of Sonny Bravo.

After this figure, at 1:39 the piano sets up a solo section for the tres with the following quartal montuno over a C pedal in the bass. This creates an ambiguous key center that is suggestive of a modalistic solo:

Musical Example 3.21. Quartal piano riff, "El jamaiquino." Courtesy of Sonny Bravo.

The tres player Nelson González uses a wah-wah pedal over this groove, which might be considered a variant of the *mozambique* rhythm with added batá drums.[113] The solo begins at 1:42 and is accompanied by the coro (choral refrain) that is also sung using the same whole tone scale heard in the intro-duction (see musical example 3.17). The solo itself is atonal and really does not reflect the harmony in any way, but it is effective in imparting a total break with the song's melodic and harmonic motifs. After González's solo the band returns to the montuno with another bluesy and altered scale-based, non-traditional mambo figure that begins at 2:30. The traditional-styled montuno of this section also features a bluesy mambo figure from the horns at 3:31. The performance ends with the same break that introduces the arrangement. The horns play another mambo figure at 4:15 that is even bluesier and more funk-oriented than those previously offered.

In sum, the musical statement of this arrangement is quite powerful and innovative. Bravo succeeds in adding dissonances, changing the harmony, and the whole mood of the piece without losing the composer's original intentions or melodies. What is also important about this arrangement is that it updates an older classic song with new techniques. In this way, Bravo succeeds in bring-ing the tradition forward, staying in clave and incorporating new ideas within the tradition.

FURTHER EXPERIMENTATION, GROWTH, AND SEPARATION WITHIN TÍPICA 73

As he continued with his own band, Bravo was tapped for playing more tradi-tional recording sessions as a soloist. As heard in his solo (beginning at 1:47) from "Bilongo" on the 1976 album *Super Típica de Estrellas*, Bravo continued to be a tradition bearer in this style.[114] The solo employs octave runs and rhythmic excitement that are firmly within the parameters of the traditional style, but no quartal harmony or jazz quotes. This recording demonstrates how Bravo oriented his playing to fit the musical context:

chord pattern continues throughout

Musical Example 3.22. Sonny Bravo piano solo, "Bilongo." Transcription by Michael Eckroth.

After *La Candela*, Típica 73 experienced some growing pains and split into two groups. Vilató, Santiago, González, and Mannozzi formed Los Kimbos and made three albums before dissolving. Bravo continued Típica 73 in a co-leadership role with Rodríguez as the two recruited other like-minded musicians to record and perform contemporary Cuban music that was popular on the island.

1975 saw additional personnel changes with the arrival of Puerto Rican vocalist Tito Allen, Nuyorican José Grajales on timbales and congas, Cuban violinist Alfredo de la Fe, Cuban flautist/saxophonist Don Gonzalo Fernández, Cuban trumpeter Lionel Sanchez, and arrangements by Bravo, Gil López, and Louie Ramírez. The band's musical versatility was exemplified by the seamlessness of the musicians' roles: Grajales would play timbales when Rodríguez played congas and would switch to congas when Rodríguez played bongó. Thus, the shift to being a band that could record as a conjunto, orquesta, or charanga was complete. The personnel shift was also reflected in the lyrics and Bravo explained that prior to the band's split: "I had composed the coros to 'Guajira típica' as an '¿Adónde vas?' type of tune! After the 'split,' when we changed the personnel, I decided to write a *guía* [melody part] to introduce the new, more versatile format! The new lyrics tell it all!"[115] And indeed they do: the lyrics (0:00–0:38) describe the new band and its ability to perform a variety of genres in a variety of instrumental formats:

> *Hay una orquesta señores, con un sonido total,*
> *Suena a charanga, suena a conjunto, suena sensacional*
> *Arrancan con una rumba, danzón, guajira, o bembé,*
> *Oigan el nuevo sonido de la Típica 73* (2x)

[Ladies and gentlemen, there is a band, with a total sound
They sound like a charanga, a conjunto, they sound sensational
They get started with a rumba, danzón, or bembé
Hear the new sound of Típica 73] (2x)

In 1976 the band released *Rumba Caliente*, which featured more or less the same
lineup of musicians. Bravo flexed his piano chops by opening the album's title
cut with the first five bars of Rachmaninoff's Prelude in C♯ minor and some
jazz-influenced variations. The Rachmaninoff is followed by an unmetered
modal improvisation in the style of jazz pianist McCoy Tyner. Bravo brings
the band in after setting up a vamp in the style of modal jazz similar to John
Coltrane's "Impressions."

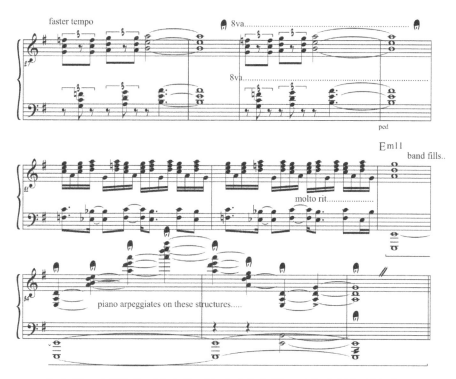

Musical Example 3.23. Piano introduction, "Rumba Caliente." Transcription by Michael Eckroth.

McCoy Tyner was one of many jazz musicians who would appear as a guest with Latin bands at the Village Gate's Salsa Meets Jazz series. John Coltrane's influence could also be heard in the saxophones of Típica 73, played by Mario Rivera and Dick Meza. Musicians who were so steeped in traditional Cuban music and other Latin styles would have absorbed jazz to such a degree from mere contact, but also because it was the state of the art at that time. Incorporating jazz concepts into an improvisation in a Latin dance music setting became accepted and a marker of the New York sound of Latin music. So as much as Bravo might refute any notion of being a jazz musician, he soaked up its language to the point of being able to use it in his own playing and arranging.

In the 1977 premiere issue of *Sangre Nueva*, Carlos DeLeón wrote a profile of Típica 73. He caught up with the band before a rehearsal in Queens for a gig in Paris. DeLeón defines what constitutes the New York sound of Spanish Caribbean music:

Without benefit of the usual media hype associated with "Superstars" (possibly because of it), Típica has been able to develop a musical repertoire that combines elements of jazz, rock, and charanga to a base of Afro-Cuban conjunto music. The result: a vibrant blend of biting horns, percussion, strings, flute, electronic synthesizer, and jazz-tinged improvisation that makes for a unique sound that captures the very essence of New York Latin music in the seventies.[116]

During this period, the band was moving back and forth between concert performances and dances, but their preference was to stay with the dancers. Trumpeter Rene López and Bravo explained that: "[Big concerts] are more removed from the people. We really enjoy a club or dance where we can see everyone dancing well; we, in turn, play better and move."[117]

In 1977, the band again changed personnel with the album *The Two Sides of Típica 73*, including Panamanian vocalist "Azuquita" (Luis Camilo Argumedes Rodríguez), Nuyorican timbalero Nicky Marrero, who also doubled on drum set, and the notable rock guitar and Cuban tres stylings of Italian American string master Harry Viggiano. Típica 73 shifted to the forefront of the salsa avant-garde with this important album. In his album liner notes, Bravo wrote that the band would continue to present a "concert" side and a "dance" side together and he promised the listener: "There will be more of the new Cuban music—more jazz/rock/latin—more concert suites—more stretching out and exploring. But there will also be more heavy dance music. As we expand our musical horizons we won't forget that Típica 73 was originally conceived as a 'dancer's' band."

Opening with Machito's percussion feature *"Bongo Fiesta,"* the album also includes Luis "Perico" Ortiz's arrangement of "It's a Gay World," and features René López's scatting and the jazz improvisations of Mexican American reedman Dick "Taco" Meza. Ortiz was another highly sought-out arranger in the New York Latin music scene who had recently come from Puerto Rico. Bravo offers a more traditional chart for "Tumba Tumbador," a song that had been a hit for his hero Benny Moré. Marrero employed an entire drum kit against a rhythmic backdrop of batá drums on a cover of Cuban powerhouse La Orquesta Ritmo Oriental's hit "Yo bailo de todo." This arrangement also features electric guitar and electric violin with wah-wah.

The most distinctive aspect of the album is the "Salsa Suite" (originally titled *Sabrosito rumbón*), Bravo's original composition and arrangement to showcase the band. Suites and concept albums were popular at that time with other Latin artists. Pianist Larry Harlow was the first to offer his own suite, *La Raza Latina*, an audio history of Latin music.[118] He followed it with another that was a Latin music response to The Who's *Tommy* called *Hommy*. Harlow's suites are each the entire length of an album.[119] *La Raza Latina* begins with an overture and continues with rumba, danzón, chachachá, son montuno, mambo, guaracha, and even disco. Before ending, the lyrics and the music suggest the past, present, and future, as well as the necessity to teach the youth about dance, culture, and roots. Bravo's suite is more compact, and the few lyrics that the suite has do not reflect any of the didactic messages of Harlow's suite; it is a showcase of the musicians in the band and the music they play.

Bravo's arrangement begins with a rumba that features the percussionists and a tradition-inspired melody. At 1:03 the whole band enters; Bravo sings the lead vocal and Azuquita sings the harmony of the verse of the song. This is followed by the minor key coro of "*sabrosito rumbón*" and Azuquita's vocal improvisations. At 2:45, there is a conga solo over two-chord vamp. Then at 3:25, the band continues with a slower rumba that includes an electric guitar. At 3:57 there is a transition to a 6/8 section that highlights the Phrygian mode, and Bravo takes a synthesizer solo until 5:20. The band then transitions to the interlude from Cachao's danzón "Cuarenta que son uno" before beginning a chachachá at 5:50 that features a flute solo by Dick "Taco" Meza that continues through 7:00. Nicky Marrero takes an extended timbal solo from that point until 7:47, when he and the horn section trade phrases. At 8:35, the whole band plays a rumba clave break to introduce the bongó solo over a fast rumba. The piece ends with the entire ensemble playing figures starting at 8:49 while the percussionists let it all out and end at 9:36.

A few musical themes, such as the danzón, were taken from previously composed music, but the overarching idea according to Bravo, was to "do a concert set and a dance set to show the versatility of the band."[120] The piece was only played once in a club off of 8th Avenue in Manhattan, but Bravo did write another version for the Fania All-Stars when his bandmates Johnny Rodríguez and Nicky Marrero were with them.

In 1978, the group released *Salsa Encendida*, another seminal recording that featured "Xiomara," the contemporary hit song by Cuban fusion/jazz/dance band Irakere. The appreciation that Bravo and his bandmates had for their Cuban counterparts was expressed vocally on another Cuban song "Que manera de sentirme bien." On this song they did something completely unheard of and even politically risky at that time in the United States: name-checking their Cuban contemporaries such as Aragón (and certain individual members of the band), Elio Revé, Juan Formell, Elena Burke, Raúl Planas, and Jesús "Chucho" Valdés. In the liner notes to the album and CD reissue, they publicly expressed their gratitude to two important Cuban musicians and an administrator who would play a key role in the group's subsequent journey to record and perform in Cuba. These three individuals helped Johnny Rodríguez set things up during a preliminary visit before the band would travel to Cuba. Bravo wrote. "*Un saludo especial para Rafael Lay, Elio Revé, y Duvalon por haber tratado a nuestro hermano con tanto afecto y cariño.*"[121] This open embrace of Cuba and its musicians was politically risky despite the opening of communication between the two countries at that time.

Alfredo de la Fé's violin was now incorporated into the brass heavy arrangements, successfully blurring the lines between charanga and orquesta. De la Fé's use of echo and wah-wah took away any strict association with the sound of the traditional charanga format; he was used more as an additional member of the rhythm section, playing guajeos with Bravo, and also served an important role as a soloist.[122] The album begins with "Baila que baila" by Ovidio Guerra and Tomás Reyes of the Cuban group Reyes 73. The album continues with "Los campeones de la salsa," an original composition and arrangement by Louie Ramírez. The song boasts, "we are the champions of salsa in New York City."[123] Bravo's arrangement "Somos dos" features a baroque-style ensemble introduction followed by a friendly vocal duel between Azuquita and José Alberto "El Canario," the group's new Dominican singer. The band was also tuned in to the musical tension between merengue and salsa musicians in New York of the time period and the need to satisfy dancers with different tastes. They recorded a merengue called "La mujer dominicana," which was the first of two merengues they would record. "Si no eres tú" features an arrangement by the veteran arranger and Mongo Santamaria band member Marty Sheller. Sheller is an important American Jewish trumpeter and arranger, previously discussed in chapter 1.

Additionally, in 1978 the band returned full circle to where they began, with the charanga repertoire at their founding jam sessions. They recorded a collection of well-known charanga songs—many of which had been popularized by Orquesta Aragón—called *Charangueando con La Típica*, but it would not be released until 1980. Because it was not released until then, many assumed that *Charangueando* was actually recorded in 1980 or was a result of the group's trip to Cuba. On April 15, 1978, the band was also featured on WNET Channel 13's *Soundstage* in a concert that featured David Amram, Dizzy Gillespie, Steve Goodman, and "members of the Chicago Symphony."[124]

CUBA 1978: A TRIP TO THE MOTHERLAND AND THE BEGINNING OF THE END

Mirta Ojito explains that conditions were such that in 1978, some openings between Cuba and the United States allowed for Cuban Americans to travel to Cuba for the first time since the revolution. From the progressive circles of New York City, a number of young Cubans like the promoter Maria Pilar "Mappy" Torres traveled to Cuba with the Antonio Maceo brigade; older exiles also returned to the island. Next to a piece on a fundraiser at a Tribeca disco for rape victims and above some other music announcements, the New York City–based publication *Latin NY* ran a small piece on legal travel to Cuba with a local operator called Guardian Tours, "a project of the Guardian radical news weekly."[125] Although it wasn't mainstream, it was possible to travel to Cuba from New York in 1978 and 1979.

With this historic moment taking place in the background, Bravo and his band achieved their musical apex in the form of collaborating with Cuban musicians in Cuba on a joint recording session. Although North American pop and jazz artists were brought to Cuba by CBS for the legendary Havana Jam concert, nothing like this recording had been planned or executed before. The seeds of the project began when Johnny Rodríguez visited Cuba with his wife in September 1977.[126] Before leaving, a friend in New York called Cuba to send word that Dandy and his wife were coming; Dandy collected four suitcases full of items for various families of friends and left via Canada.[127] When they arrived in Havana, he spent time with Rafael Lay and Pacho Alonso, and visited the flute player Gonzalo Fernández's house. This was when he first met Antonio Duvalón, who would be instrumental in facilitating Típica 73's trip and recording. As I write in the liner notes for the CD reissue of *Intercambio cultural*, it was Duvalón who suggested that Típica collaborate with a number of iconic Cuban musicians. When Rodríguez returned to New York, he pitched the idea to Sonny Bravo; Fania Records president Jerry Masucci agreed to foot the bill.[128]

Roberto Gerónimo's account in *Steppin' Out* erroneously lists the folklorist and producer René López as having been on the trip and making "all the arrangements to obtain recording time at EGREM studios in Habana"; this was not the case, as the band handled everything by themselves.[129] As mentioned earlier, Típica 73 had shared the bill with several Cuban groups such as Aragón and Revé in Mexico and Panama respectively, and had gone to see other groups like Los Hermanos Bravo while on the road, but this would be the first time they would be collaborating with Cuban colleagues in the studio. In November 1978, Típica 73, funded by Fania and armed with their arrangements, flew to Cuba via Montreal. At the airport they were greeted by Rafael Lay of Orquesta Aragón, who let Bravo know that one of Bravo's favorites, La Ritmo Oriental, was playing at the hotel where they would be staying in Cuba. Another band, Los Reyes 73, also performed for Bravo and the crew at the hotel. Típica 73 would also later record "Llévatela," a song performed for them by Los Reyes 73. At the same hotel they befriended the house band, some of whose members were working with Pello el Afrokán. In fact, the *comparsa* (carnival processional music) jam at the end of "Pa' Gozar" was actually taped at the band's hotel, the Villa Mégano near the famous Mégano club. Bravo wanted to include his field recording on the album and shocked his skeptical Cuban counterpart, Tony Taño, when he heard the quality of the portable recorder. Throughout their time in Cuba, Rodríguez relates that every major group came and played for them, including Fernando Álvarez, Quarteto D'Aida, El Conjunto de Roberto Faz, Estrellas Cubanas,

Conjunto Folclórico Nacional, as well as Conjunto Chappottín.[130] Medardo Montero was the main Cuban representative in charge of the band's visit, but Antonio Duvalón also helped behind the scenes. Bravo explained, "Típica 73 played one show outside the parking lot of the Tropicana in El Salón Mambí for the Cuban people and one more set for the apparatchiks and small tourist crowd inside the famous cabaret."[131] According to Roberto Gerónimo's account of the trip as published in *Latin NY*, there were 12,000 people in attendance who had such a good time they were "throwing large pitchers of beer while laughing and dancing nonstop and without producing any negative incident."[132] Bravo, the band, and Gerónimo were surprised by the beer throwing but were told it was a sign of approval. They were also impressed by the different way that Cubans experienced music: "Everyone marks time to *clave*, and the public has knowledge of music. Couples apart [men and women dancing], sort of a mixture of Boogaloo and the Freak, which they called Cha-Onda."[133] According to Duvalón, the last US performer to play at the Tropicana had been Nat King Cole more than twenty years earlier. Típica was so successful they were discussing a three-month contract with the Tropicana administrators.[134]

The positive energy surrounding the Típica 73 performance and recording project compared to the Fania All-Stars Cuba subsequent performance in 1979 was rooted in the fact that Típica 73 gave credit to Cuban composers on all of their recordings and that their interest seemed genuine to the Cubans.[135] The Cubans took a particular liking to Nuyorican timbalero Nicky Marrero who was, as Gerónimo writes: "Offered an additional all-expenses-paid week in Cuba (courtesy of Tinguao). He was grateful but, because of commitments in New York, had to decline."[136]

Walking around Cuba and feeling good about being able to realize their vision, the band headed to the legendary EGREM studios later that week.[137] Despite the fact that they only had an eight-track recording unit, Gerónimo reported that the recording director Tony Taño and the sound engineer Adalberto Jiménez felt that the sound was better in Cuban studios since they were made of wood and not covered with foam sound reinforcement so as to produce better acoustics.[138] The roster of Cuban musicians that recorded with the band was a dream team that included legendary standard-bearing icons of Cuban music, such as Guillermo Barreto (timbales), Félix Chappottín (trumpet), Richard Egües (flute), Felo Bacallao (vocals), Tata Güines (Congas), Niño Rivera (tres), Juan Pablo Torres (trombone), José Luis Quintana "Changuito" (percussion), as well as Raúl "Yulo" Cárdenas and Eddie Pérez on percussion. In some cases it was difficult to track these musicians down, but once they came to the studio, they were happy to contribute their time and their talent.

In Cuba, Bravo also had the opportunity to hang out with many musicians that he admired and was able to talk with them about music. At the end of

Fig 3.19. Bravo with Félix Chappottín in Cuba. Photo courtesy of Sonny Bravo.

the trip, Bravo remembered musical giants such as percussionist José Luis Quintana "Changuito" singing contemporary Cuban rumba with the two side of the clave coinciding with the *tres-dos* pattern. As he sang he exhorted Bravo to "remember," but Bravo—and most New York–based musicians and record collectors—was familiar with many versions of rumba performed by Cubans where the clave was in fact crossed and did not coincide with the tres-dos pattern.[139] Before they left for New York, Tinguao threw a huge dinner party for the band with fireworks at the home of Oscar Valdés, which also included numerous luminaries of Cuban music such as Irakere and Leo Brouwer.[140]

While the trip was a return to the ancestral homeland for Bravo and a return to the musical motherland for everyone else, it had even deeper meaning for the two Cuban-born band members, Alfredo de la Fé and Lionel Sánchez. It was de la Fé's first time in Cuba since he left eighteen years earlier. Sánchez had not been to Cuba nor seen part of his family in his hometown of Perico in twenty-one years.[141] Gerónimo writes:

Everyone in the small town knew Leonel [sic] was a member of Típica 73 and that they were in the country. When he arrived in town to visit his family, word spread quickly, and pretty soon there was a large procession of people following him who had come out to say hello and welcome him back home. It was a very happy and emotional experience for Leonel and his family.[142]

Gerónimo writes that this scenario was emblematic of the trip itself:

Leonel's return was in a way symbolic of the entire trip. It was a return to part of the family—seeing a relative we've been away from for years and getting

Fig 3.20. Bravo with Guillermo Barreto and Johnny
Rodríguez in Cuba. Photo courtesy of Sonny Bravo.

to know them again. It was also fitting that Leonel return with a band like
Típica '73, whose members, representing Cuba, Puerto Rico, Dominican
Republic and Mexico, truly reflect an Intercambio Cultural at its very best.[143]

During the second week of the trip:

> Most of the band flew home after recording the basic tracks while a num-
> ber of Cuban guest musicians were located and brought into the studio for
> their solos. . . . Due to the lack of tracks at the sessions, many parts had to be
> bounced repeatedly to accommodate all of the musicians.[144]

Johnny Rodríguez stayed with Bravo, along with vocalist Felo Barrio, as they
continued working at the EGREM studio. After the second week, Rodríguez
and Barrio left while Bravo stayed in Cuba for one more week by himself "to get
a workable mix." Angel L. Tinguao, the manager of the Villa Mégano, secured
permission for this extra time and some recording equipment was left at the
studio as a type of exchange. There was still more work left to do, and "at home,
Bravo polished the performance with Bob Ludwig after transferring the tapes
from the European system used in Cuba."[145]

The band was extremely proud and excited about their accomplishment and Fania Records released the album in 1979. In his favorable review of the album in *Latin NY*, Tony Sabournin wrote:

> *Intercambio Cultural* is not only a great LP, but it is a tangible proof of the indestructible bond existing among musicians: a link which transcends political differences or personal greed, the two factors that don't let nations of the world live in peace. Perhaps music is, indeed, the answer![146]

However, the excitement was not universally positive in the New York City area:

> Unfortunately, the reception at home was not warm and Cuban musical collaborators shunned Bravo. Cuban exile newspapers in New Jersey harshly criticized the band and published threats that Típica's "dances would end in bloodshed." Bomb threats at local performances were common and as a result, numerous band members gave notice to join other bands or simply left music altogether.[147]

Despite the reception, the band continued to record and the label released the album *Charangueando* that had been recorded earlier in 1978. In June 1979, it was announced that Cuban-born bandleader turned manager, José Curbelo, signed an agreement with Típica 73 to "lengthen their management contract with the Curbelo office for a total period of three years."[148]

In March 1980, Tony Sabournin wrote about the negative effects of the Cuba trip on Típica 73's success. After extolling the band's virtues and listing the expansiveness of their style and repertoire, he rhetorically asked the readers of *Latin NY*:

> Why isn't the *Típica 73 en Cuba* album played on commercial radio? Why does *Típica 73* continuously receive third or fourth billing behind bands which cannot stand next to them in popularity or musical prowess? Why does *Típica* seem to be ostracized from certain nightclubs and events which would enable them to expose their music to a greater audience?[149]

Sabournin reported that radio stations were afraid of alienating their Cuban audience, but he pointed out that New York–based Cuban audiences supported sold-out shows in New York by island-based artists such as Orquesta Aragón, Los Papines, and Elena Burke. Sabournin urged Hispanic media to separate "art from politics," asking rhetorically if "Anglo-geared" media prevented the American public from appreciating Russian culture. In the same article, Sabournin delineated how lack of airtime led to fewer engagements and less money, and he concluded by asking for a miracle to free the band from "the chains of adversity which are shackling them to the walls of anonymity."[150]

On June 28, 1980, dressed in the hand-sewn rumba dancer shirts seen on their controversial album cover, the band filmed a live performance at the Palm Tree nightclub slated for distribution "in several Latin American countries."[151] This film was never released and has since disappeared. Eventually, the political pressure against the band mounted and the group's recording and playing career would soon be suspended for a significant period of time. In New York City, threats of bombings and violence were serious enough to disrupt concerts by visiting Cuban musicians in the late 1970s. Bombs exploded at Avery Fisher Hall and the Cuban consulate on December 28, 1978, forcing a hasty rescheduling of Orquesta Aragon, Los Papines, and Elena Burke for the following evening at Casa de las Américas.[152] Right-wing Cubans perceived Bravo and Típica 73 as local communist sympathizers and as such, they were easy targets for anyone looking to bash Cuba. As Bravo later explained in September 2005: "Going to Cuba cost me the band, it was the kiss of death, but if I had to do it over again, I would do exactly the same! I think it's important for people to know that I have no regrets."[153]

The last hurrah for both Bravo and the band was *Into the 80s*, a collection of songs released in 1981 that featured bomba, merengue, and the band's unique combination of salsa played with horns and electric violin. Típica 73 included songs by Cuban composers on the island, such as "Tula" and "Llévatela." Puerto Rican arranger Luis "Perico" Oritz wrote the Cuban-sounding arrangement of "Llévatela." During a November 2013 rehearsal, both Bravo and Rodríguez concurred that Ortiz's arrangements of "Llévatela" and "Baile que baila" from the album *Salsa Encendida* were some of their most Cuban-sounding charts.[154] For Bravo, "'Tula' and 'Chachagüere' are the zenith of my work for Típica 73."[155] Max Salazar profiled Bravo in the May 1983 issue of *Latin NY*, but the band broke up and would not play again for many years.[156]

THE COMPOSER

Most of this chapter has been devoted to Bravo's role as a bandleader, sideman, and arranger, but he is also a composer whose compositions also reflect a deep immersion in the totality of Cuban musical history. Perhaps the best example of his composition is "Toca Alfredo Toca" from the 1979 debut solo recording by his Típica 73 bandmate Alfredo de la Fé.[157] Bravo's personal notebooks indicate that the recording sessions were June 18 and 19, 1979, and he estimates that "the *tune* was written earlier that year (*after* Cuba) & the *chart*, a month or two before the sessions, or whenever I found out about the sessions!"[158] According to Bravo, he wrote the lyrics on the melody on the way home after a gig and was in a rush to sit down at the piano to put pen to paper.[159] The lyrics, melody, and arrangement are programmatic and tailor-made for de la Fé's playing and particular personal expressive techniques:

> *Guía: Si tu crees que el violín es facil de tocar,*
> *Pregúntaselo a Alfredo, que se pasa el día entero*
> *Estudiando, afinando, buscando el sonido total, de su violín*
> *Toca Alfredo toca, tu violín lo dice todo*
> *Suena tu violín en salsa, toca Alfredo toca*
> *Ahora sabes porque Alfredo toca tan sabroso*
> *No suelta el instrumento, esta loco de contento con su wah-wah*
> *Su cajita, ha encontrado el sonido total, de su violín*
> *Toca Alfredo toca tu violín lo dice todo*
> *Suena tu violín en salsa, toca Alfredo toca*
> *Coro 1: Toca Alfredo toca, tu violín lo dice todo*
> *Coro 2: ¡Toca!*
>
> [Verse: If you think the violin is easy to play,
> Ask Alfredo about it, he spends all day,
> Studying, tuning, looking for the total sound, of his violin
> Play, Alfredo play, your violin says it all
> Play your violin in salsa, play Alfredo play
> Now you know why Alfredo plays so tastefully
> He never puts his instrument down, he's crazy with contentment with his wah-wah pedal
> His effects box, he has found the total sound of his violin
> Play, Alfredo, play, your violin says it all
> Play your violin in salsa, play, Alfredo, play
> Chorus 1: Play, Alfredo, play, your violin says it all
> Coro 2: Play!]

Bravo punctuates key moments in the lyrics, with musical devices such as de la Fé tuning his violin, playing his violin with a wah-wah pedal, using pizzicato technique, singing as he plays the violin, and having the string section and band play complicated musical figures when the lyrics discuss the total sound of his violin playing. Bravo employs a number of McCoy Tyner–esque chord voicings that make use of stacked fourths, pentatonic figures, and whole tone scales for additional musical punctuation. Puerto Rican electric bass pioneer Salvador Cuevas employs a non-traditional funk slap bass playing technique to augment the modern sound of the whole chart. The recording makes quite an impression on the listener because it manages to combine the influence of Cuban groups like La Ritmo Oriental and the modern jazz harmonic sensibilities that Bravo and his generation of musicians brought to Latin music. The following track on the album, "El casabe," features what Bravo views as one of his best solos on record. Although the song is in a minor key, the solo features many of the same ideas that Bravo employs on his 1968 "La Chica del Barrio Obrero" solo, and there is tremendous interplay between the bass and the piano—something that Eddie Palmieri and Luques Curtis employ in concert today. This song is Bravo's adaptation of Humberto Perera's "Que rico bailo yo," a song that was recorded by the Cuban group Orquesta Ritmo Oriental.[160] For this chart Bravo revoiced the original violin parts with fourths to have a more modern sound.[161] The result is a charanga sound that is unlike those of Cuba's Orquesta Aragón or its New York equivalent, Orquesta Broadway.

MUSICAL HISTORY AND MODERNITY IN SONNY BRAVO'S ARRANGEMENTS

An important part of Sonny Bravo's personal philosophy is manifest in his musical arrangements. He is interested in musically acknowledging the past while making a contemporary statement. Some of the ways that he serves this dual mission include (1) making references to original arrangements in his new arrangements either through orchestration or musical figures; (2) recording older songs that have not been treated in contemporary times; (3) evoking a particular arranger's style to provide historical reference; (4) using the entire ensemble to state a melody or refrain during the arrangement; (5) employing modern harmony in otherwise harmonically simple chord progressions; and (6) never sacrificing the goal of making music for the dancer.

Stated in a more practical way, Bravo explains: "I try to write specifically for whomever I'm writing . . . but there are some arrangers that can only write in one style, and they'll write the same for everyone. They run out of ideas and then it's bad because you hear the same thing over and over again."[162] A fantastic example that illustrates Bravo's depth as an arranger is his arrangement of Pepe Delgado's "No pienses así" from Tito Puente's album *Mambo Diablo* (1985), featuring George Shearing. By this point, Bravo had joined Puente's band permanently and the jazz leanings of the ensemble really shine in the shout chorus from this chart. Puente was very much interested in jazz and Bravo clearly captured the feel of a jazz band's ensemble feature with this musical idea.[163] The first eleven bars in musical example 3.24 occur at 1:56, where the band changes from a bolero feel to a swing feel: José Madera plays swing accents

Musical Example 3.24. "No pienses así," beginning of shout chorus. Courtesy of Sonny Bravo.

on the cymbal while he and the rhythm section continue a slow bolero feel as the horns play in cut time. Bravo's writing is impeccable.

What is interesting about the use of the shout chorus in the context of the bolero is that it demonstrates Bravo's complete understanding of jazz harmony and phrasing, despite his feeling that he himself is not a jazz musician.[164] In his own words, he could not offer "sustained improvisation" in the jazz idiom, but using the "pen to write and erase" is another thing.[165] The ideas represent solid bebop conception in their construction and outlining of the harmony and are stylistically faithful to the bebop rhythmic concepts of triplets, syncopation, and chord tunes on down beats. The idea of having a shout chorus in a bolero arrangement can be heard on Benny Moré's "Hoy como ayer," but it was not common in Cuba. Bravo applied this concept in other bolero arrangements as well such as "Alma con alma" and "Contigo en la distancia."[166]

In more recent years, Bravo has continued to update songs he has heard for many years. Arrangements for the Spanish Harlem Orchestra, the Mambo Legends, Soneros del Barrio, the Latin Giants of Jazz, and others reflect his application of advanced harmony to create musical excitement for dancers. Arrangements such as "Se formó la rumba," "Las mujeres son," "Dime si llegué a tiempo," reflect this tendency. In the case of this last piece, history is acknowledged by simply leaving out the entire horn section—two trombones, baritone saxophone—for fourteen bars except for two trumpets during the first time through the melody (after the introduction). This is done to honor the original sound of the two-trumpet version of the song recorded by Celia Cruz and Johnny Pacheco.[167] It is not uncommon for Bravo to have to explain choices and references to other musicians who might not be as historically aware, or perhaps to those who are younger than he and do not have his wealth of musical experience. These references can also come from contemporary Cuban sources. Such is the case with Bravo's arrangement of Spanish Harlem Orchestra's "Se formó la rumba." During a brief interlude before the second montuno, the horns exchange phrases with the coro over a fast mozambique rhythm. Bravo's inspiration for this section was Omar Hernández's original composition "Que sensación cuando la vi" from the 1981 Grupo Afro-Cuba recording, which used the same device of having the horns play a rumba coro, "*Traigo la mano caliente, andero, su warará*."[168] For his arrangement of "Las mujeres son" for Frankie Vasquez and Soneros del Barrio, Bravo features a section of trading fours with Nelson Gónzalez that reminds one of Orquesta Revé's version of Arsenio Rodríguez's "Ruñidera."[169] The main interlude in the chart is not a traditional mambo section but is inspired by Son 14's "Son para un sonero."[170] Bravo states that he "previously used this device on my chart of '*Lío*,' (*Intercambio Cultural*) using Herbie Hancock's 'Sun Goddess' as the interlude in lieu of a Mambo section."[171] Bravo includes an even earlier musical reference with a quote from Debussy's "Arabesque #1" at 04:10.[172]

Another instance of Bravo using an interlude instead of a mambo section and deliberately adding a reference to another arranger or arrangement can be heard in his arrangement of "El trombao original," written for Ray Viera y Su Trombao.[173] The interlude, based on Chopin's Prelude No. 20, can be heard from 3:15–3:40 followed by a unique six-bar montuno section consisting of a three-bar coro and a three-bar *soneo* (vocal improvisation section). At 4:41 the piano player Edwin Sánchez plays a piano guajeo that brings the trombones into the *moña* section that lasts through 5:18. The piano part heard during the introduction is Bravo deliberately adding a "tip of the hat to Joseíto González," as it is the exact part that González plays during the intro to Conjunto Rumbavana's 1974 recording "Te traigo mi son cubano."[174]

As seen earlier in this chapter, the Sonny Bravo arrangement concept makes use of chromatically moving ii-V progressions and jazz harmony. A few other examples of this include his original composition and arrangement of "Hot & Heavy" for Eddie Torres and the Mambo Kings Orchestra.[175] Besides the use of descending ii-V progressions and fourths, Bravo wrote the Coltrane "Giant Steps" cycle into the chart, and it is executed by pianist and bandleader Oscar Hernández. Descending chromatic ii-V progressions abound in his arrangement of "Caña Brava" (0:00–1:18, 3:16–4:58) for Alex Díaz and Son de la Calle; Bravo also employs suspended chords (the third is omitted and replaced with a fourth) at the beginning of the song's characteristic refrain to transition into the refrain.[176] On the same album, Bravo's arrangement of "Mañana of Carnaval" features Coltrane's "Giant Steps" chord changes moving at regular speed during the intro (0:00–0:17) and a chromatic descending ii-V progression, during the piano guajeo and subsequent solos (03:43–5:45), that ends before the coda.[177] In Bravo's danzón arrangement of the Beatles song "Because (*Porque*)" for Louie Ramírez y Sus Amigos, the introduction begins with a full sequence of Coltrane changes (0:00–0:14), followed by a break and a traditional three-bar paseo (0:15–0:23). The Coltrane changes come back (0:24–0:30) but move in cut time until a break (0:30–0:33), and the piano plays through the next paseo (0:34–0:42). After the melody the band returns to the introduction and the Coltrane changes and paseo (2:57–3:16). The montuno section has a descending ii-V progression for the solos and the choral refrain of the montuno proudly declares the arranger's feelings: "*este es un danzón moderno, porqué es muy original*" (this is a modern danzón, because it's very original).[178] The song ends with the Coltrane harmonic progression moving with a different rhythmic emphasis on the upbeats in cut time (5:30–5:40) before a super traditional Cuban danzón coda (5:40–5:42).[179]

Interestingly, Bravo indicated that the iconic pianist and traditionalist Charlie Palmieri felt that Bravo's arrangement was not successful because of the cut time rendering of the repetition of the intro section and the cut time upbeats at the end; the traditional danzón requires exact repeats of sections.[180] For Bravo, there was no clave jump in his arrangement as occurs in some well-known danzones by composers such as Abelardo Valdés ("Almendra"), José Urfé ("Fefita"), and Felix Reina ("Angoa"). Thus, Palmieri's critique was more about fidelity to the tradition. Bravo remembers that some musicians had difficulty adapting to the unexpected requirements of the chart during the recording session.[181]

Bravo has written for even larger ensembles and wrote a symphonic arrangement of the Noro Morales composition "Maria Cervantes" that was performed by the Dallas Symphony Orchestra. The Symphony Orchestra of Puerto Rico also performed this piece during Tito Puente's last public performance at the Centro de Bellas Artes in Santurce, Puerto Rico.

Bravo wrote three big band charts for the Latin Giants of Jazz, "No me molesto," "Gua cha rumba," "Tengo que conformarme," and one chart, "Conmigo, candela brava," for the Mambo Legends Orchestra. In his arrangement of "No me molesto," a 1950s hit for Machito and Orquesta Aragón, Bravo explodes the tight sound of the charanga for the big band texture of the Latin Giants of Jazz.[182] One recurring idea that Bravo uses in his arrangements is to connect sections with a descending altered scale/chromatic line.[183] The chord progression for the verse is changed through the use of an F dominant pedal underneath the I-vi-ii-V progression. The montuno for the chorus is also more modern than the original; Bravo achieves this by using descending ii-V7 progressions. Bravo creates an interlude to move the song to a double time "*mozan-cha,*" a combination of Mozambique and chachachá rhythms. The harmony of the interlude is also enriched and offers a quite dramatic shift from the original as well as a rhythmic shift to rumba. Lastly, Bravo adds an "*obvious* tip-of-the-hat to my mentor, René Hernández" with a nod to Hernández's arrangement of this tune for the Machito Orchestra. He does this by extending the original's two-measure unaccompanied horn break and elaborating upon it with his own trademark descending altered scale/chromatic line.

"Conmigo, candela brava" is Bravo's most personally meaningful of these four big band charts. He explains:

> Notice how I honor Tony's former band mates of La Ritmo Oriental, as well as Típica '73, when I construct a complex moña around "*Yo bailo de todo.*" Towards the end of the "background" for the flute, the saxes play an instrumental version of the coro, then all the horns. Then Frankie introduces the change of theme by bragging about his dancing. Then the bari [baritone saxophone] plays the "*conmigo tienes que bailar*" part followed by the actual coro! After a brief respite, the entire sax section riffs "*conmigo tienes que bailar*" as the trps. [trumpets] riff, "*baila, baila, José,*" having all 3 "coros" going simultaneously, and in clave! I wonder how many "listeners," *both* musicians and aficionados are aware of all this?[184]

The answer to this rhetorical question, unfortunately, is: not many. However, the level of detail, historical reference, and forethought that goes into these charts epitomizes Bravo's work and, in this way, distinguishes him from his remaining contemporaries such as Ray Santos and Juanito Márquez.

DEFENDING THE TRADITION: CLAVE AS A UNIFYING FORCE AND A STANDARD TO UPHOLD

Bravo and his music reflect eight of the ten main themes discussed in the introductory chapter: a focus on the physical and metaphysical aspects of clave; the evolution of the anticipated bass part; the importance of folklore; the emphasis on music education; musical biculturalism; the importance of

Fig 3.21. Sonny Bravo today. Photo courtesy of Gabriele Saplana.

lineages of musicians; the role of dancers; inter-ethnic collaboration; and the influence of jazz. For Sonny Bravo, the clave is a unifying force and a standard to uphold. He sees himself as personally responsible for bearing this tradition. One physical and literal manifestation of clave in Sonny Bravo's music is that he is known for tapping the clave with his foot while playing.[185] Sonny's devotion to and attention to clave is without equal and he is both affectionately and derisively labeled the "clave police." As Hector Lavoe's former musical director, Gilberto "Pulpo" Colón Jr., says of Bravo, "he listens to everything and if he feels you're wrong, he'll give it to you."[186] I personally think of him as a clave "whisperer," especially when he offers a simple solution to a mistake before a chart is recorded. However, he is a critical and discerning listener who constantly finds clave mistakes in videos and recordings, and for a fellow pianist and arranger like Colón this is important:

> He knows what [tunes] are ambiguous, what tunes fall on either 2–3 or 3–2. And that means that he dissects things and he'll tell you when there's a traffic jam in your tune [laughter]. Remember Sonny's been around . . . he is a knowledgeable cat . . . apart from being a great musician. But he's an authority on clave because he's made a career out of listening to clave to be able to do what's right within the parameters of the clave and not do anything to distract or take away from the tune. That's why I think he's good. Because there's people who do it just because people are gonna scream so you want to be able to adhere to the pattern so that nobody tells you you're wrong,

you know, [for] your ego. I think with him it's more like so it doesn't disrupt what's supposed to be going on, you know, the continuity of the piece. He's told me when I did something "*eso 'tá mal*" . . . there's a traffic jam that even the cops can't figure out.[187]

Bravo is consistently searching for ways to perfect arrangements, compositions, improvisations, and performances so that they fall in clave. By his own admission, clave "discrepancies" seem to find him rather than it appearing as though he searches them out.[188] He is adamant when his peers fail to do so and eager to point out such egregious behavior when it comes from Cuban musicians based in Cuba as well. It is possible that he holds Cuban groups to a higher standard, since Cuba is where these genres originated. He does not understand, for example, how his beloved Orquesta Aragón's classic recording of "Pare cochero" features a piano solo that quotes from Rafael Hernández's "Capullito de Alelí," and when leaving the solo to return to the montuno, the pianist plays an ascending line, but needs to play it twice to come in on the correct side of the clave.[189] He is also irritated that contemporary groups such as Los Van Van disregard the clave in hits such as "Sandunguera," as has Orquesta Aragón with a counter-clave bass part in "Porque Manuela no me pelea." He has even confronted some Cuban musicians directly when their paths cross during travels. While traveling with Tito Puente in Spain in the early 1990s, he was so upset with Adalberto Alvarez's arrangement for "Son para un sonero" that he asked Alvarez how the band could enter out of clave after the beautiful interlude toward the end of the arrangement[190]—to which Alvarez shrugged his shoulders and answered "*descuido*" (carelessness).[191]

Despite this almost religious fidelity to clave, Bravo himself is not immune to critique of clave in his own work. During some discussions with Cuban musicians on the road whose paths crossed with his, he was criticized that Típica 73 had played rumba with the clave crossed.[192] The *conguero* (conga player) for Orquesta Aragón at that time, Guillermo García, specifically told Bravo that the clave was *montao* (crossed) in "Rumba Caliente" or during the "Salsa Suite," to which Bravo responded "this is how we did it in New York City."[193] Similarly, his 1968 arrangement for "La Chica del Barrio Obrero" has a rumba section played on the wrong side of the clave, and Bravo remembers percussionist Tommy López unsuccessfully trying to set him straight at the session. Bravo continues to work on solving clave discrepancies in older recordings and compositions, without changing the phrasing of the melody too drastically. His goal is to maintain the clave from start to finish with no jumps. Some of the clave puzzles that he continues to work at include songs such as "Cubano Chant" (1956) by Ray Bryant or "Quisiera ser mi estrella" (1926) by Sexteto Habanero.[194]

Through his piano playing and musical arrangements, Sonny Bravo honors his elders while embodying and upholding the tradition of Latin music. He aims for an artistic and musical height of what can be done within the rhythmic constraints and phrasing of clave. His musical contributions also reflect a unique personal journey that has enabled him to innovate from within the tradition. Bravo represents musical innovation that is intimately tied to musical tradition by way of family. Both his father and his cousin represent this family connection as well as their having taught and worked with him throughout his lifetime. Like his father, Sonny Bravo would continue the practice of performing Cuban music with non-Cuban musicians.

Finally, Bravo's efforts to musically reconnect with his grandparents' homeland constitutes the first time in history that this happened, and the historical result is forever preserved with a recording. No one had brought a band of New York–based musicians to record in Cuba with their contemporaries at a time when that was politically more difficult. Today it is quite common to see Cuban groups performing in the United States and vice versa, but few people remember how radical and unwelcome an idea it was not so long ago. Furthermore, musicians are not threatened or in danger of hurting their livelihoods through travel to Cuba, and for many musicians it is a primary objective to study and perform there.

Bravo's role as an educator has extended for over forty years in a variety of settings including at the Harbor Conservatory, the New School, and initially for Johnny Colón's music school discussed in chapter 1. To this day Bravo maintains private piano students and has taught many important Latin pianists of a younger generation, including Ricky González, Martin Arroyo, Yeissonn Villamar, Luis Gómez, Christian Sands, Klaus Mueller, and many more. Informally, Bravo is eager to point out and discuss a variety of issues pertaining to specific arrangements and improvisations through his active participation in listservs for Latin music in both English and Spanish. In these ways, he has continued to mentor and educate musicians from around the world who are interested in what he has to say.

Sonny Bravo is as New York as the Brooklyn Bridge, but he is as Cuban and Caribbean as one can be. Bravo himself said that percussionist John Santos described him: "As Cuban as el Valle de Yumurí! It was his response to my comment that many Cuban musicians do *not* consider me Cuban because I was neither born nor raised there!"[195] Bravo also asserts his Cuban identity by wearing a Cuban national baseball team hat and jacket on gigs and in daily life.

He continues to innovate and expand the tradition as a result of his being a New Yorker of Cuban descent, and not as a result of being a Cuban in New York. While important musical figures such as Mario Bauzá, Rene Hernández,

Machito, Chano Pozo, Mongo Santamaria, Celia Cruz, and Cándido Camero made their home and base of operations in New York, it was through their contact with North American music that they made advances in their art forms. However, Sonny Bravo's contributions reflect a unique personal journey that enabled him to innovate from within the tradition because of his biculturality; in this way, he transcends labels of Cuban and American. He is as comfortable with tradition-oriented settings as he is with modern iterations and has remained open to contemporary Cuban music so as to be able to incorporate and include contemporary practice in his own work.

Bravo's family nurtured his deep understanding and mastery of traditional Cuban music, but it is also through his family and through him that one can see how in New York they changed the standard of the music rhythmically, sonically, and harmonically. His professional training and development deeply reflect the idea of the streets of New York serving as a university and a place where like-minded bicultural musicians would shape the sound of Latin music. Bravo's musical development, his identity as a Latino New Yorker, and his position as an architect of the New York sound of Latin music reflect the changes over fifty years in Latin music as performed in New York and beyond. His experience as a Cuban American musician and his connection to the past, present, and future of Latin music reflects his family's musical lineage, their history, and their important contributions to Latin music in New York City.

CHAPTER 4

"THIS GUY DOES NOT LOOK LATIN"

The Panamanian Connection, Race, Ethnicity, and Musical Identity in New York City

The below advertisement shows the New York fascination with Spanish Caribbean music and culture was not limited to Cuba. The Panamanian Village at 166 Eldridge Street opened in the early 1940s and featured a mix of jazz bands, Latin music, and Yiddish performers.[1] The exotic-sounding name of this venue demonstrates that Panama and Panamanians were viewed as interchangeable

Fig 4.1. Panamanian Village advertisement.

with other Spanish Caribbean cultures for the purposes of commercial promotion of the non–geographically specific concept of Latin music in New York. However, the Panamanian musicians in this chapter were and continue to be well prepared to handle many types of music due to their previous unique experiences in Panama. Located musically and geographically in a central point within a circum-Caribbean flow, Panama served as an incubator for jazz, Cuban, and West Indian–Caribbean music traditions. Pianist Terry Pearce asserts that playing modern salsa today is not much different from when he began in Panama:

> To be perfectly honest, it is the same stuff I've been playing since my youth back in Panama. I mean, there have been certain innovations throughout the years, but basically, it is the same swinging son montuno and mambo that I have always played. The arrangements and the messages may have changed somewhat, reflecting the different times, but the foundation and the structure have remained unchanged since the 50's.[2]

This chapter explores the unique Panamanian musical community in New York, particularly Brooklyn-based musicians, and their contributions to the development of Latin music in New York. Many of the musicians in this chapter excelled in various genres. Some worked in mainly one or two; others were more versatile. Since the 1930s, a small but substantial community of Panamanian musicians has made their home in Brooklyn. In the subsequent sixty-plus years, they have seamlessly woven themselves into the rich and diverse musical culture of New York City and excelled within Spanish Caribbean, West Indian, European, and African American musical traditions. This musical multiculturalism reflects their positioning, both by outside communities and by themselves, as Afro-Latinos, West Indians, and African Americans alternatively or simultaneously.

David García's groundbreaking study *Arsenio Rodríguez and the Transnational Flows of Latin Popular Music* examines the Afro-Cuban identity central to Rodríguez's music, its musical manifestation, and its transmission to subsequent generations of non-Cuban musicians and fans.[3] Some of the Brooklyn-based Panamanians studied in this chapter who were active in Rodríguez's ensembles had specific instruction from Arsenio and other Cuban musicians. They also performed in ensembles led by Tito Rodríguez, Tito Puente, Machito, and Louis Armstrong and were instrumental in forging the New York sound. New York City, as opposed to Panama, offered many Panamanian musicians a setting in which they could use all of their talents and work in many genres of music simultaneously.

Panamanian musicians did not have to alter their playing styles to seamlessly integrate themselves into a wide range of ensembles, create musical "moments," and conduct musical "transactions" in the type of framework for the study of black music outlined by Samuel Floyd Jr.[4] In most cases these musicians felt solidarity with the musicians and cultures that were similar to, yet distinct from, their own, such as Cuban, Puerto Rican, West Indian, and African American. When performing and recording their "own" music, their musical choices reflected their experiences.

Perhaps due to misidentification and English surnames, to date this group of musicians has been overlooked by scholars and historians of Latin music in New York City. In Panama the contribution of West Indians to the greater national culture is only recently being acknowledged. In the area of Bocas del Toro, where numerous Brooklyn-based musicians hail from, there is almost no national recognition of these musical heroes or attempts to preserve and tell their important stories.[5]

This unique group of Afro-Latin musicians who were born in Panama to parents from the English Caribbean experienced hardship and injustice as well as success and vindication, all of which are inextricably bound to a complicated history of migration, labor, segregation, and United States expansion in the Canal Zone. In Panama, West Indians and Afro-Panamanians were subjected to segregation policies and other injustices in the Canal Zone and beyond. This included the organization of "separate but equal" schools, hospitals, transportation, and stores known as the gold and silver system for whites and blacks respectively.[6] Pay scales also differed by race under this system. As Lydia Reid pointed out, the system was far from equal:

> For the brave and stalwart black workers who had been the pioneers and the backbone of all the rugged preparations of the Canal construction before this new era of demarcation of the class structure began, the drastic changes that soon followed would make theirs a totally depressing experience. Soon they would see their expectations for any professional advancement stymied.[7]

Subsequent generations of Panamanians of African descent refer to themselves as *antillanos*, which translates simply to Antilleans.[8] In the 1941 Panamanian constitution, Panamanians born to West Indian parents were unjustly singled out as not being worthy of citizenship along with Panamanians born to Jews, Hindus, Chinese, and those from the Middle East.[9] George Priestley points out that although political inclusion began to arrive to these communities in later years, particularly for the antillanos, mass migration of Panamanians to the United States was under way in the 1950s.[10] As the Canal Zone decolonized and antillanos were expelled so as not to comply with desegregation mandates, many were affected adversely in other ways. Priestley, who was my employer at Queens College and a brilliant Panamanian scholar indicates the specific causes that effected their migration to New York:

> As a result of the 1955 Remón-Eisenhower Treaty, thousands of non-U.S. citizens, mostly Antilleans and their offspring, lost their jobs, housing, and commissary-buying privileges, and were compelled to pay income taxes to the government of Panama. Second, despite significant economic growth in the Panamanian economy during the 1960s, few Antillean-Panamanians found jobs in the private sector. Third, public sector jobs were open only to a few who participated in the 1960–1968 "democratic spring," while the majority joined the ranks of the socioeconomically and politically excluded. Feeling abandoned by the United States and relatively shut out of the economic opportunities opening in Panama, thousands of Antillean-Panamanians began to migrate to the United States in the 1960s, particularly to Brooklyn.[11]

In New York City, the Panamanian community settled among English-Caribbean communities in the Brooklyn neighborhoods of Crown Heights, Flatbush, and East Flatbush. Franklin Avenue is the community's best-known focal point. Having experienced living within and negotiating a segregated system in their homeland, they were able to recognize and adapt to such a system in New York City.

According to the 2010 US Census, there were 28,200 Panamanians in New York City.[12] Today, Franklin Avenue in the Crown Heights section of Brooklyn is known as Little Panama. People looking for Panamanian cuisine often travel to Kelso at 648 Franklin Avenue, and Independence celebrations and a parade are held on October 9 each year with a march on Franklin Avenue and a street festival on Lincoln Place.[13] Although there had been mixed feelings in the community about naming the street for the Panamanian community, Panamanian residents were adamant about seeking recognition.[14] At one community board meeting that addressed the topic, a Panamanian speaker told the crowd that:

> "If you talk to someone in Panama about the United States, they say they want to come to Franklin Avenue." Panamanian businesses, social clubs, and churches persist on Franklin, particularly north of Park Place, and even those who have moved away come back on the weekends to see friends and attend services.[15]

However, cultural pride does not equal recognition, and Carlos Russell calls the Panamanian community of Crown Heights, Brooklyn visibly invisible . . . [because] most of the Panamanians living in New York—foreign and U.S.-born—are of Caribbean ancestry. In a neighborhood such as Crown Heights, where a large chunk of the population is of Caribbean descent, there is no way of telling by appearances alone if someone's ancestors came from Panama or Jamaica. "All through this system and this city, Panamanians are to be found," Russell said, "and you will never know that they're Panamanians unless you ask them."[16]

This invisibility—combined with the ability to blend in musically and culturally within Latino, African American, and West Indian social settings—manifested itself differently for each of the musicians presented in this chapter. For some it was easy to be drawn to African American culture.[17] Others have undoubtedly experienced racism and prejudice from Latinos while others felt embraced by them. As Oboler and Dzidzienyo explain:

It is important to focus on the specificity of the life experience of both Afro-Latin Americans and U.S.-born and/or raised Afro-Latinas/os . . . while the stigma of blackness is similar throughout the hemisphere, the experience of blackness is heterogeneous depending on historical and cultural characteristics as well as the demographic composition of each country.[18]

Thus, for some of the musicians profiled in this chapter, their experiences as Afro-Latinos were similar and different from one another both in New York City and Panama. All of their musical contributions have been important despite the similarities and differences in their experiences as Panamanians in New York City. This chapter makes extensive use of interviews conducted by Bobby Sanabria and Elena Martínez for a project on Afro-Latinidad; I am most grateful for their generosity with these materials. Finally, this chapter demonstrates a number of the themes discussed in the introduction, including engagement with jazz, musical biculturalism, inter-ethnic collaboration, emphasis on music education, and family lineages of musicians.

MUSICAL-HISTORICAL BACKGROUND OF PANAMANIAN MUSICIANS IN NEW YORK

Panama has a wide range of musical genres rooted in Spanish Caribbean, West Indian, indigenous, and North American music that includes a variety of unique indigenous and non-indigenous instruments and combinations. The Panamanian writer and musician Noel Foster Steward has divided Panamanian music more specifically into three categories and additional subcategories that include (1) vernacular and típica styles of folkloric music, (2) urban popular music such as jazz, calypso, Latin orquestas, and smaller Latin combos, and (3) *música popular típica*.[19] The longstanding existence of performing ensembles in this last group, such as the Banda Republicana de Panamá, the band of firefighters, the national police band (with multiple groups), the national symphony, and other groups have provided training and experience to many musicians.[20] As a result of these rich musical traditions, successful Panamanian musicians in Panama City, Bocas del Toro, and Colón were proficient in many of the aforementioned genres and had rigorous musical training. These musicians lived in Colón and played in the hotels, dancehalls, cabarets, and jazz clubs in the Canal Zone. In the Panamanian jazz documentary *Jazz Tambo*, Noel Foster highlights this circum-Caribbean flow:

> Jazz has always been in Panamá. Since the beginning of the United States, given the geographic characteristics of this country, almost all of the things get to this country. In the years during which jazz originated in the United States, in one way or another this influence arrived in Panamá.[21]

He identifies and provides addresses for more than forty venues, noting:

> All of these centers functioned during the era of the Second World War and later attended military in transit, tourists, and nationals who visited the cabarets to catch the artistic revues. In each one of these places, one, two or three musical groups would perform daily accompanying the best artists from the Americas and Europe, converting Panamá into a center of artistic spectaculars.[22]

Visiting Cuban, Puerto Rican, and New York–based musicians often performed in these venues, such as Noro Morales, Machito, Benny More, Billy Eckstine, the Nicholas Brothers, Ella Fitzgerald, Duke Ellington, Shirley Scott, and Cab Calloway.[23] Clubs such as Bop City, the Windsor, Bar Kelvin, Saint Pete, Maxim's, and Café Chase offered musicians a place to play until the morning hours and participating musicians included Americans, Panamanians, and Cubans. The proliferation of jazz in Panama followed the major trends in the United States, encompassing swing, big band, and bebop. All-night jam sessions were popular among musicians in Colón after they finished their engagements. Clubs such as the Café Krech featured bebop, while the Esquire was home to organists such as Zaggy, Frank Anderson, and Chacho de la Rosa, among others.[24] The Hammond organ seems to have had a disproportionate number of exponents in Panama when compared to other areas outside of the United States such as Cuba, Haiti, Puerto Rico, or Jamaica.[25] Other noted organ players included Neville Chan,

Avelino Muñoz, Reinaldo Alfu y su grupo, Doc Patterson (now based in Queens, New York), and Frank Anderson (who I discuss in detail below).[26] What follows are brief profiles of Panamanian musicians who were involved in jazz, as well as those who played Latin music and other genres of music.

AN EARLY PIONEER: VERNON ANDRADE

One of the first Panamanian musicians to arrive in New York City was Vernon Andrade. He is significant because he was the first musician of color (and the first Latino) to establish a residency in a New York City venue. A multi-instru-mentalist who played violin, bass, guitar, saxophones, clarinet, and other instruments, Andrade came to the United States in 1920 to study dentistry. Shortly thereafter, he joined the Deacon Johnson Orchestra as a violinist and was then discovered by Bob Douglas, the West Indian owner/operator of the Renaissance Casino and an African American basketball team of the same name.[27] From 1923 on, Andrade was the leader of the house orchestra of the Renaissance, with a six-month stint at the Savoy Ballroom after defeating other bands in a competition.[28] This places him chronologically ahead of his contemporaries Fletcher Henderson, Duke Ellington, Chick Webb, and Cab Calloway, who would have similar residencies. His tenure at the Renaissance lasted twenty-seven years. Trombonist Clyde E. B. Bernhardt, an Andrade band member, provides some details about the band's audience:

> Private organizations gave regular affairs and receptions at the Renaissance—mixed black and white political clubs, leading West Indian and Panamanian social groups, and high-powered colored associations. Andrade played for them all. He was the regular house band and sometimes worked seven nights a week, plus maybe two or three matinees.[29]

From this account, one can see that the Panamanian community was well established, active, and held musical activities. The band also worked at the Apollo. Among musicians, Andrade was considered to be "hard to please" as an employer, but always fair. Interestingly, his band consisted of musicians from a variety of Caribbean and African American locales, including Puerto Rican trumpeter Chico Carrión.[30]

In 1927 the great Afro-Cuban jazz innovator Mario Bauzá visited New York City as a sixteen-year-old clarinetist with Antonio María Romeu. In a 1993 interview, Bauzá explained that during his fifteen-day trip with Romeu, there was already at least one Pan-Latin jazz ensemble established in New York that included Panamanians:

There were Latino's [sic] playing jazz in New York City then. My cousin, Rene [Endreira] played for a band called the Santo Domingo Serenaders. It was a band made up of Dominican, Cuban, Panamanian and West Indian musicians playing jazz. I laugh when writers ask me what I think about the growing interest of this new generation of Latinos who play jazz. How can they when they don't even know that there were players before them doing what they profess to do now![31]

A contemporary of Andrade was Horatio "Ray" Durant, who played with Napoleon Zayas and led the Deep River Boys; but soon after, additional Panamanian musicians would establish themselves in New York.

PANAMANIAN PIANISTS IN NEW YORK CITY: THE FIRST WAVE

In the late 1920s, two Panamanian pianists, Luis Russell and Nicolás Rodríguez, became influential figures on the New York jazz and Latin music scenes. Luis Russell is acknowledged as a major arranger and important figure in jazz history. Hailing from Bocas del Toro, Russell was the first Panamanian musician to enjoy international success. He was an accomplished musician who played piano in silent movie houses from the age of fifteen. At seventeen he won the national lottery and used the prize money to move to New Orleans with his sister and mother.[32] There he is said to have studied with local pianist and personality Steve Lewis. From New Orleans, Russell moved to Chicago, where he worked with different bands and recorded under his own name. He came to New York with Joe "King" Oliver and soon left Oliver to start his own band. Luis Russell's band enjoyed success in New York and soon backed up Louis Armstrong live and on many important jazz recordings in the 1920–40s. Russell also recorded some of his own jazz compositions as a member of the group led by New Orleans drummer and Armstrong/Oliver collaborator Paul Barbarin. Additionally, Russell recorded under his name on the Parlophone and Apollo labels.[33]

A 1932 readers poll in the *Pittsburgh Courier* placed Russell's band in the "second division" alongside Claude Hopkins, Chick Webb, Hardy Brothers, Johnson's Happy Pals, Ike Dixon, Zack White, Jimmie Lunceford, Marion Hardy, and Fess Williams, but the writer makes it clear that these are all musically excellent bands that he had seen perform live on multiple occasions and that they each could have been and might be in the "big ten" with more support from readers.[34] A Panamanian contemporary of Russell was the pianist David Rivera, who recorded with Ike Quebec and can be heard on the track "Dolores."[35] Rivera's national reputation is evidenced in a 1944 advertisement for his appearance at the Anchor Bar: "Former pianist here, back home for a vacation with us after a successful tour with Cab Calloway's orchestra! Dave will be pleased to see his many friends once more."[36]

NICOLÁS RODRÍGUEZ

Once Luis Russell retired and Dave Rivera stopped working, it was Nicolás Rodríguez who would be the Panamanian to have the greatest impact on the New York scene. Mario Bauzá assessed and compared Luis Russell with his own Panamanian contemporary, Nicolás Rodríguez: "Rodriguez was a—more jazz-oriented than anybody else . . . Rodriguez was a better jazzman than [Luis] Russell . . . He played more in the veins of Art Tatum. And Russell played more the vein of Louis Armstrong . . . Rodriguez was more progressive . . . than Luis . . ."[37]

Nicolás Rodríguez was born September 10, 1906, in Bohío, Panama, located in the Canal Zone. He began his musical education with flute and then moved to trombone, saxophone, and banjo by high school. He started playing the piano when his piano-playing cousin moved into his house with her piano. Inspired by Louis Armstrong's "Cornet Chop Suey," Rodríguez started a small jazz group called the Broadway Syncopators. After gaining some arranging and performing experience, he decamped for New York City and arrived on April 7, 1928.[38] He immediately established himself in the center of the African American artistic and cultural life in Harlem; on his first night in New York, Rodríguez accidentally caught Duke Ellington performing. Rodríguez settled in at 74 W. 118th Street to live.[39] He frequented Willie "The Lion" Smith's performances and absorbed his style from watching. Rodríguez played at the Drake and Walker Theater backing up the likes of Bessie Smith. This theater is notable for being the first venue owned by African Americans that featured African American artists and brought in an African American crowd.[40] Shortly thereafter, he got into the musicians union based on his reading abilities, and began working with Jelly Roll Morton. In 1988 Rodríguez explained to Laurie and Peggy Wright how he hooked up with Morton:

> Anyway, one night in the club, Jelly Roll comes down and says, "You play very well." "Oh, thank you." "You want to join my band?" "Oh, no, I've just got this job." "Never mind that, this is my job too, I want you to go away with me with my big band, the big band that's upstairs." Now that was Procope, Garland, Ward Pinkett . . . nothing but the tops, William H. Moore, the tuba player, some fantastic players, and he wants me to join this band. So I had to meet them at Pennsylvania Station at 11 o'clock and we went to York, Pennsylvania. That was on 8th December 1928 and we played in York that very

first day. The next day after York, we moved to Harrisburg, where we made
our headquarters and we'd travel out from there every day . . . a couple of
hundred miles sometimes. Then we moved to Washington and did the same
from there and after that we went south.[41]

An advertisement for the York concert lists the December 8, 1928, performance
by Jelly Roll Morton's Red Hot Peppers at the Alcazar.[42] Another concert that
Rodríguez refers to in his interview with the Wrights was in Washington, Pennsylvania.[43] Rodríguez and the band members were mentioned by name, in
this case as *Goodwin* Rodriguez, in one favorable review of the Morton band's
performance in Baltimore that drew 1,200.[44]

Morton's band gave him a musical hazing, something that future Panamanian musicians would also come to experience in New York. Rodríguez explains:

> Now Jelly had three sets of books and, after we'd been going a while, Procope
> said, "Get the S Book." Now I'll tell you what the "S Book" is, it means the
> "Shit Book" and it's all the hardest things, the things you're not supposed to
> be able to play, and the first thing they called was Chicago Breakdown and
> it started with a piano solo so I didn't have no time to look it over but, as
> God is my judge, I just walked through that and everything else they called.
> After the first time I was improvising and the guys accepted me. I didn't hold
> nothing against them, they were just testing me out and when you're in a
> strange country and trying to make friends and so on, you have to accept
> things the way they are.[45]

Rodríguez rolled with the punches while his fellow musicians playfully ribbed
him as "'Ring-tail,' 'Coconut hustler,' 'Monkey chaser' and 'West Indian'" for
his Panamanian nationality.[46] At the conclusion of the Morton engagement,
Rodríguez began playing with Louis Armstrong when he wasn't using Luis
Russell's band. Then he joined Benny Carter, and Luis Russell subbed for him
on occasion. During this time, before the Machito band, Rodríguez started to
contemplate a Latin jazz group:

> After that, Socarrás who had been one of the changes in personnel, and I were
> playing with Benny at the Savoy, and we lived down in "Spanish Town" and
> walking home together one day we were saying that if we could get a band
> that could play Latin music *and* good American music we'd have it made,
> because we'd have no competition. And we worked on that, and I was writing
> these good American arrangements. I was working in a theatre during the
> day and at night in this night club. There wasn't no band at this time, but we
> were working on it.[47]

Rodríguez joined Don Redman's band from 1937–41 and mainly played Latin music for the next twenty-four years until resuming playing jazz with Louis Armstrong's All-Stars in 1961.[48] Newspaper listings from this period confirm Rodríguez's performances focusing on Latin music, particularly playing "authentic rhumbas" at Jewish venues such as the Fraternal Clubhouse.[49] Rodríguez also continued to work in non-Latin and non-jazz jobs and performed "Harlem Serenade" for a live radio broadcast on WMCA with Orlando Robeson and Wen Talbert's Choir in 1940.[50]

In 1957 Rodríguez took part in a fascinating recording of Haitian folk music sung by Jean Vincent that featured arrangements and flute work by Alberto Socarrás, Manuel Navarro (bass clarinet), Nilo Sierra (bass), Marcelino Guerra (guitar), and the percussionists Willie Bobo, Mongo Santamaria, Carlos "Patato" Valdés, and Vincent.[51] This record is representative of efforts to document Caribbean folkloric music and the pan-Caribbean nature of ensembles that would perform the music of a given country of origin. In this case the band is made up of Cubans, Puerto Ricans, a Panamanian, and a Haitian. Interestingly, Rodríguez and Socarrás performed together as a duo at a fundraising concert sponsored by the Instituto Puerto Rico to raise scholarship money for Puerto Rican students to attend Hunter College in 1954.[52] Rodríguez was also known to personally refer his students to study solfeo (sight singing and ear training/musicianship) with Socarrás. Rodríguez devoted the remainder of his career to teaching, which is discussed in chapter 1.

Another significant contemporary of Rodríguez and Russell was the Panamanian pianist Sonny White. Born in Panama as Ellerton Oswald on November 11, 1917, he made his way to the United States, where he worked as a pianist, organist, bandleader, and arranger. In the 1930s he worked in bands led by Jesse Stone, Willie Bryant, Sidney Bechet, Teddy Hill, and Frankie Newton. He made a large number of recordings with jazz vocalist Billie Holiday, including "Strange Fruit," Body and Soul," and "Fine and Mellow," to name a few. On the actual 78 rpm of "Strange Fruit" from 1939, White is credited with the piano interlude below Holiday's name. White recorded with Mezz Mezzrow on the Victor label.[53] He worked with Artie Shaw and Benny Carter before joining the US armed forces during World War II.[54] In Carter's band he shared the bandstand with Dizzy Gillespie, with whom he had previously worked in Hill's band.[55] White later worked with Big Joe Turner, Lena Horne, Dexter Gordon, Hot Lips Page, Jimmy Witherspoon, Wilbur de Paris, Eddie Barefield, and Jonah Jones.[56] White died on April 28, 1971; while he had a successful career in jazz, there is no musical record of him having worked in any Latin music groups or in the Latin music scene.

PRINCESS ORELIA: DANCER, ENTREPRENEUR, AND POET

Dancer, entertainer, manager, impresario, and poet Margarita Benskina, better known as Princess Orelia, made a name for herself as a pioneer of the "Cuban shake" starting in the 1930s at the Cotton Club. Benskina was born in Colón, Panama, on March 16, 1915. It is unclear if either of her parents, José and Amelia, were Cuban nationals, but she was educated and resided in both Panama and Cuba before coming to New York City for high school. In one Brooklyn listing, she and her dance partner were listed as Brazilian.[57] Her physical appearance was commented on in numerous reviews. In a review of her performance in the Cuban Village at the 1939 World's Fair, Floyd Snelson wrote in his Harlem column:

> At this spot, Princess Orelia, Pete and her jungle company are one of the greatest features in this Latin Quarter. The Princess is a well-known entertainer and was deservedly given this spot, which she is filling with distinction. Her svelte shape, her artistry, her smooth brown skin, all help to make her a glamorous entertainer and her act goes across with a bang.[58]

Princess Orelia personified a Pan-African and African diasporic artistic vision that moved easily between Africa, Latin American, the Caribbean, and the United States. In the 1930s, she shared the bill with Louis Armstrong and others at Connie Immerman's club, Connie's Inn.[59] She performed frequently at the Apollo Theater, the New Rockland Palace, the Elks Rendezvous, Club 845 in the Bronx, and other primarily African American venues with her dance partner, Pete. The routine was heavy on *el tornillo* (the screw), where she would spin Pete around as he lowered his body, and a routine known as "shoeing the mare," where the man stands over the woman and pretends to put hooves on her feet as though she was a horse.[60] Benskina also performed frequently with African dancer Asadata Dafora for the African Academy of Arts and Research Festival in New York at Carnegie Hall and at Jackson College in Mississippi. The association with Dafora is noteworthy because, as García points out, African performers such as Dafora were "perform[ing] the African past of their American Negro contemporaries."[61] Much of Benskina's work seemed to follow this vein, and she served as a conduit between Afro-Cuban and Caribbean music and dance and modern African American cultural practices such as jazz. García also points out that many of the members of Dafora's dance troupe were "Black American" and assumed to be from Africa. García writes that Dafora's troupe was at first made up of "African and American Negro musicians and dancers . . . the cast now included Afro-Cubans, Haitians, and Trinidadians."[62] Asadata Dafora, Paul Robeson, Katherine Dunham, "and so many others lived and carried out this need to know and perform the past of their racialized and gendered selves in order to not only understand but also survive their present under modernity's pressures of racism, sexism, and colonialism."[63]

Benskina's fluid identity as a Caribbean, Cuban, Panamanian, African, and African American seemed to work to her advantage as a performer, much like the other dancers in Dafora's troupe. Benskina often appeared in "jungle dances" and with her own African troupe during all-black revue shows, particularly at the Apollo Theater and at Carnegie Hall. She was also involved in charitable causes and benefits such as the American Women's Committee for the West Indies and other fundraisers.[64] Benskina performed nationally with her Cuban Congo dancers at venues such as the Howard Theater in Washington, DC, and at Chicago's Grand Terrace Café.[65] In 1941 she performed at the Latin Quarter in Boston with her dance partner Pete, but fidelity to national genres was not that important in these environments, even when on the bill with Cuban entertainer Desi Arnaz. Benskina moved easily between genres and cultures, but her pan-African and diaspora focus was seen as exotic and erotic by journalists and critics. Ted Watson wrote in the *Pittsburgh Courier*: "Princess Orelia and Pete has [sic] perfected the 'Dance of the Hills,' more amicably known as 'La Cumbia' which will lend wild abandon to their celebrated exotic routine."[66] During a 1941 tour to the West Coast with Pete, Benskina worked at a number clubs such as George Raft's Club Copacabana and the Paramount Theater, but the highlight was her taking part in a Hal Roach feature film called *Cuba Libre*.[67] In 1944 Benskina appeared with Pete on the same bill as Mary Lou Williams and Woodie Guthrie as part of a nationally touring musical revue in support of Eleanor Roosevelt and the New Deal.[68] At another of Roosevelt's concerts at Carnegie Hall in 1946, Benskina performed alongside a number of African percussionists.[69]

Throughout her career, Benskina also performed with calypso groups and was a featured dancer in a calypso show at the Brooklyn Academy of Music in 1947. She even dispensed culinary advice, advocating for the avocado as a tasty and nutritious Cuban fruit, never hinting that she was Panamanian rather than Cuban.[70] She continued to perform in Houston and Los Angeles at this time. In 1953 she performed with famed Cuban vocalist Miguelito Valdés at the Celebrity Club in Providence, Rhode Island.

Robin Kelley wrote: "she [Benskina] was a practitioner of West African divination. In 1956, she was ordained into 'the Spiritual Healers Fellowship' and owned and operated a *botánica*. Despite a life in nightclubs and theaters, she found a way to be spiritually grounded and to help others in need."[71] In this capacity she helped jazz saxophonist Charlie Rouse deal with addiction and personal problems.[72] In 1956 she continued to tour as a dancer but took on a managerial role for the Charlie Rouse and Julius Watkins group, Les Modes Jazz Quintet.[73] In 1959 Benskina was credited as co-composer for "1–2–3–4–0

In Syncopation" on their album *The Jazz Modes*.[74] In 1963 she collaborated again
with Charlie Rouse on the song "Un día."[75] Rouse performed in Benskina's stage
show, "Princess Orelia's Afro-Pot Purée," the same year.[76] In the 1970s, Benskina
published a number of books of her poetry; she earned a bachelor's degree from
Queens College in 1983. Throughout the 1970s and into the 1980s, *Jet* magazine
chronicled her accomplishments.

Ansonia Records recording artist and vocalist Silvia DeGrasse was another
important female Panamanian musician who made her home in New York City
in the 1960s. Although she was already an international star when she arrived,
DeGrasse performed throughout the New York metropolitan area, Las Vegas,
and Miami.[77] She was married to the Dominican vocalist Ernesto Chapuse-
aux and both enjoyed fruitful careers in the United States, Europe, and Latin
America. Princess Orelia and Silvia DeGrasse were quite different, but with
their base of operations in New York, both achieved success as Panamanian
artists and women in different eras.

THE SECOND WAVE OF PANAMANIAN MUSICIANS IN NEW YORK CITY

Wynton Kelly (1931–1971) and Frank Harris Anderson were two other important Panamanian pianists who were active in New York since the late 1940s.
Although Kelly's biographies list him as being born in Jamaica, according to
Cándido Camero he was Panamanian and spoke Spanish. In 1948 Dizzy Gillespie asked Camero to join his band one morning for a tour, but Camero
misunderstood Gillespie's instructions since his English was not that good. He
missed the tour and explained: "When Dizzy got back, his piano player, who
was Wynton Kelly, came looking for me. Wynton is Panamanian and so he
began asking me in Spanish what had happened. I told him and he started to
laugh out loud. He explained everything to me and then both of us started to
laugh."[78] Kelly was a well-respected jazz pianist whose playing can be heard on
a large number of iconic jazz recordings in the 1940s through the 1960s. While
Kelly mostly played straight-ahead jazz, he can be heard playing a montuno
figure during "All the Things You Are" with Johnny Griffin and John Coltrane.[79]

FRANK ANDERSON

Frank Harris Anderson is a great example of how Panamanian musicians in
New York City transcended nationality and musical genres. Although he was
last in Panamá in April 2004, he is also representative of the versatility and

Fig 4.2. Frank Anderson. Photo courtesy of Gary Gene Jefferson.

musical preparedness of Panamanian musicians. Born in Bocas del Toro on January 24, 1929, Anderson had Jamaican grandparents but his parents were born in Panama. The family came to Panama to work for United Fruit, picking bananas and doing other agricultural work. Anderson remembered, "I was 11 years old when I was homeless because of a fire . . . lost my piano." At the same time, he encountered discrimination at an early age when he won a radio contest and entry to the República de Bolivia school but was rejected due to racial prejudice.[80]

Anderson played his first professional job in 1943. His gigs at that time consisted of weddings and events like the governor's ball. At these events he would play a mixture of boleros, *taboga*, and American music from stock arrangements such as Count Basie's "Jumping at the Woodside." Cuban musicians would frequently visit Panamá, and Frank performed "Baltazar tiene un pollo" with the Cuban vocalist Cascarita and his band. He heard typical son montuno hits on the radio in the 1940s and 1950s. During this time he also befriended and studied with the Cuban pianist Pedro "Peruchín" Jústiz, who would often let him sit in on his gigs. Anderson also knew Cuban pianist René Hernández and his brother, who played alto saxophone.

Anderson listened to armed forces radio and occasionally would play a gig at the USO, to provide "a little entertainment for them" and receive payment in

American currency.[81] Anderson found out about Charlie Parker from hearing him play on live radio broadcasts from New York.[82] Up until that time, Anderson's only piano teacher had been his aunt Lenora, and shortly after her death in 1944, he started playing the organ.[83]

GETTING TO NEW YORK CITY: "THIS GUY DOES NOT LOOK LATIN!"

Anderson had a monthly gig on the showboat *Panama*. The captain of the SS *Panama*, which traveled between New Orleans and the Panama Canal, was a friend, and Anderson would play on the ship's radio show. The captain offered Anderson passage to the United States, but the ship had already left when Anderson decided to leave so he traveled to the US on the SS *Ancon*. The $175 voyage lasted five days and went directly from Cristóbal to New York. Anderson arrived in New York on September 2, 1948, joining his uncle, Arturo Smith, and his mother, who had made the trip before him.[84] He discovered a thriving community of Panamanians in New York City, but they "were scattered all over, [with] no center of community."[85] Anderson lived with his uncle in the Bedford-Stuyvesant section of Brooklyn. Luis Russell, who would become the godfather of Anderson's daughter, would take him around town every Sunday in 1948.

Anderson's first gig in New York was in the lobby of the McAlpin Hotel located on Broadway at 34th Street. For many years this venue featured numerous jazz, West Indian, and Latin ensembles and broadcasted their live performances on radio.[86] Accompanied by a tenor sax and drums, Anderson mostly performed Latin dance music and "did not deal much with the jazz scene," finding the dance field to be more lucrative.[87] Anderson preferred to play calypso dances in Brooklyn, Manhattan, and Boston (on Friday nights). He also worked with calypsonians because they had steady shows every weekend and during the week.[88] During this time, he remembered that Ralph MacDonald's father, Patrick, farmed out gigs and that the repertoire included songs such as Attila's "5 Year Plan."[89]

Up until this time the only piano teacher he had had was his aunt, but with his eye on entering Juilliard, Frank studied with Louis Alcuri Jr. In 1949, while he prepared for the audition, Anderson joined the musicians union at the behest of Nicolás Rodríguez and Luis Russell, and his mother signed his application because he was under age.[90] Anderson remembered social clubs and societies that would give independence dances and that there were older Panamanian musicians who were already in New York City. The repertoire at these society gigs included "jazz, waltzes, mambo, all mixed up on a 4 hour gig."[91]

Anderson played in his first all-Latin orchestra, Marcelino Guerra, at the Savoy Ballroom for one week. He then played on and off for a couple of years at the Hunt's Point Palace and the Palladium. Anderson remembered that someone in the band once said in Spanish, "This guy does not look Latin," but another musician said "careful 'cause he speaks Spanish."[92] In the late 1950s and early 1960s, Anderson played at the Palladium on Sunday, Wednesday, and Friday with a reduced version of the orchestra featuring Doc Cheatham and Mouse Randolph. According to Anderson, the Puerto Rican percussionist Moncho Leña was on these dates. Newspaper listings also corroborate the sharing of billing among Latin and West Indian groups at the Palladium for mambo-calypso events in 1957 with artists such as "The Duke of Iron, Maya Angelou, Helen Ferguson, and McClevity and his troupe . . . [alongside] Machito and Moncho Leña."[93] Other venues, such as Le Cupidon at 40 E. 58th Street, looked to capitalize on the trend of presenting Latin and West Indian bands. Promising prospective customers that "a visit to Le Cupidon is more exciting than a cruise to the Caribbean . . . and less expensive," one listing featured a variety of calypso acts, "mad mambo matinees" on Sunday afternoons, and Haitian artist Jean Vincent, among others.[94]

The calypso-mambo connection was a natural fit for musicians and dancers alike. According to promoter, record label executive, distributor, road manager, and Bronx-based record store owner Camille E. Hodge, it was Catalino Rolón who started promoting dances and events at the Palladium with calypso groups:

> What got me into music was that Milo, who's the leader of Milo & the Kings— a band from the Virgin Islands, came with the cricket team to perform in New York. The top band in Puerto Rico at the time was named Cortijo y su Combo and I mean you couldn't tell the difference between them and Milo & the Kings. That's how good Milo & the Kings were. For all the Spanish bands their aim was to play at the Palladium Ballroom in New York on 53rd Street and Broadway. When the man who was in charge of the music at the Palladium, his name was Catalina Colon [sic], saw Milo & the Kings auditioning he booked them immediately. Later [Rolón] took Milo & the Kings to the studio and recorded two 45's with them. One was called "The Ice Man," a Calypso tune, and the other was called "La Pachanga" which was Latin dance craze song.[95]

Anderson's memory of the Palladium was that "people came there to dance and they had a good time."[96] Nevertheless, he still experienced prejudice on the bandstand and remembered a wedding in Yonkers, where a Latin musician was so taken aback by Anderson's playing despite his appearance that he remarked, "Who taught you to play like that?"[97] Anderson also played with

Arsenio Rodríguez during Rodriguez's first trip to New York City, performing at the Ateneo on Prospect Park West in Brooklyn and then on a boat ride. At this time, Anderson also worked with Vicentico Valdés, but was not credited as conductor on the sessions.[98]

Anderson remembered encountering racism and the difficulties of touring during segregation. In October 1956, he was on tour and, after spending two weeks in Canada without a problem, he could not find an acceptable hotel room in Pittsburgh, and subsequently left the tour.[99] However, when playing at local venues such as the Boulevard Theater, Puerto Rico, San Juan, Jefferson, Rio Piedras, Union City, he felt that he "Never had a problem with a Latino Audience. The music was coming out right. The black community I don't remember them having a problem either."[100] When asked about how he viewed himself, Anderson replied that, "I am more like an African American."[101] This coincided with what he felt was a lack of support as a musician from within Panamanian community at the time. At one point he had a non-music job working in the customer service department at a garment store on Broadway. He recalled that many customers were racist and insisted on speaking with the white manager rather than with him, but the manager was supportive and insisted that the customer deal with Anderson. Later on, he received a great letter of reference from the employer and ultimately worked there until the place closed.

In New York, Anderson hooked up with other like-minded New York–based Panamanian musicians who played a number of styles, such as drummer Billy Cobham. He had remembered going "to his [Cobham's] father's home, every Saturday night" as a child back in Panama. Other Panamanian musicians from his youth who were also active in New York City included Mauricio Smith, Terry Pearce, and Rogelio Teran. Teran and Pearce were neighbors growing up. Anderson played the trumpet and Smith played the bugle in school band. Pearce led the house band at the Rainbow Room for many years and Teran was the first percussionist on *Saturday Night Live*. All of these musicians moved easily between jazz, Latin, classical, and Broadway playing situations.

Anderson's use of the organ in Latin music settings was also innovative in New York City. It began on a gig with Marcelino Guerra where the piano was so bad that he switched to the house organ for the remainder of the performance. The combination of organ and trombones was subsequently used on Guerra's recordings, the organ replacing the string section. On a number of studio dates in the 1950s early 1960s Anderson played boleros and other genres with Puerto Rican string virtuoso Yomo Toro using the organ and twelve-string guitar. Sessions with vocalists Andres Andino and Polito Galíndez would take place anywhere between 110th and 125th Street on 3rd Avenue and were released by Verne Records. Anderson also remembered playing sessions during this time with Johnny Pacheco on percussion.[102] In Anderson's estimation, no one else was playing organ on Latin records in New York City. In Brooklyn he worked at a number of small clubs with organs such as the Tip Top, the Coronet (which also had a piano) on Fulton Street, the KNC Lounge on Gates Avenue at Throop Avenue (where Bill Doggett started), Town Hill, Arlington Inn (the Bucket of Blood), and the Posh Lounge on Bedford Avenue and Eastern Parkway. Anderson says there were "guys who made the switch over from piano to organ" but he remained the only organist in Latin music.[103] This would lead to a recording as a bandleader as well as the formation of his own band.

BANDLEADER AND CHURCH ORGANIST

In the late 1950s, Anderson used his musical experience and eclectic taste to form a Pan-Caribbean band, Frank Anderson and his Pan-Americanos, that had from four to sixteen musicians. The band was made up of Panamanians, African Americans, and non-Latino musicians. The repertoire was varied and included calypso, Cuban music, and straight-ahead jazz, all arranged by Anderson. Unfortunately, the valise that held the music was stolen before an engagement, right in front of the Savoy Manor on 149th Street and the Grand Concourse in the Bronx. Anderson's good friend Alberto Socarrás offered a reward for its return but it never reappeared. Anderson was frustrated and never attempted to rewrite the music. The band was disbanded, but Anderson recorded his only solo album in 1965. He used the name Kip Anderson since there was already an active musician named Frank Anderson on the West Coast. The recording was produced by collaborator/employer Joe Cain for Kapp Records and had studio players; Anderson just showed up and played organ and someone else wrote all of the musical arrangements.[104] Throughout the 1970s, Anderson continued to record with artists such as Cándido Camero, Israel López "Cachao," Clark Terry, and many other important musicians.[105]

In an interview Anderson said that, "I remember visiting Pops [Louis Armstrong] in Basin Street East when I was in Birdland with Willie Bobo."[106] He also remembered that Louis Armstrong would travel everywhere with a big steamer trunk that had a tape recorder and recorded all of his concerts.[107]

Throughout his illustrious and varied career in New York City, Frank Anderson remained active as a church organist. According to the 2010 New York State Senate Legislative Resolution J6510–2009, "Honoring Mr. Frank Harris Anderson upon the occasion of celebrating his musical genius by the Panama Connection of Janes United Methodist Church":

Frank Anderson was the organist at the New Lots Reformed Church from 1959–1963; he is currently on the faculty of Borough of Manhattan

Community College in New York City and is the pianist for the International Ladies Garment Workers Union Chorus; he was the organist at Bushwick United Methodist Church from 1965–1995.[108]

ADVERSITY AND SUCCESS ON BROADWAY

As a young man, Frank Anderson had a private teacher and was preparing for an audition at Juilliard when he began to have vision problems. He soon gave up on Juilliard, as it was decided he should not strain his eyes too much by reading music. During a visit to a Russian doctor on West End Avenue, it was determined that he had retinal myopathy. The doctor asked his mother to come to his next appointment and suggested to her that Anderson become a plumber or work in a similar trade out of fear that he would not be able to earn a living. Doc Cheatham, Anderson's bandmate from Marcelino Guerra's group, accompanied him to a subsequent appointment with the eye doctor. When Cheatham told the doctor that Anderson was a great piano player, the doctor was no longer worried.[109]

Anderson's Broadway career started with playing piano at cattle call auditions for Broadway shows. These involved playing for double- and triple-threat prospects (act/sing/dance) and auditions were also held for people with no formal training who thought they could be the next big star. This work would lead to a more prominent role as a Broadway show conductor. Anderson landed his first Broadway conducting job with the show *Purlie*.[110] His next official conducting job was for six pieces in *Don't Bother Me I Can't Cope*.[111] This was followed by *A Raisin in the Sun*.[112] Anderson then did *Eubie!*, a two-piano show about Eubie Blake.[113] Anderson also remembered sight-reading the score of *The Wiz* (with Dennis Moorman on Mini Moog synth) at this time.[114] In 1976 Anderson worked on an all-black revival of *Guys and Dolls*.[115] This show traveled, and the legendary Panamanian trumpeter Victor "Vitín" Paz was also in the band. The two had met in New York City playing for the Supremes and later in Richmond, Virginia Beach, the Baltimore Civic Center, and in New Jersey.[116] Anderson's last Broadway-type revue show was a 1987 appearance with Rita Moreno at Avery Fisher Hall. He could not see the music due to the glare of the paper, but he made it through the performance because the paper had no shine and the conductor had a light in his hand that he could follow to keep time and cues. Seeing what was happening, another musician in the band who played accordion quickly took over and Frank left the theater, never telling anyone there about his sudden departure.[117]

Anderson remained actively playing and teaching as of 2018. His frequent collaborators include the great Panamanian saxophonist, Walter "Lord Gene"

Jefferson, and his wife, the incomparable vocalist Enid Lowe. Together they had a longstanding brunch gig playing Cuban music, boleros, tangos, and calypso at a Haitian restaurant/lounge near LaGuardia Airport called La Détente. The band included Panamanian bassist Donald Nicks, Nuyorican drummer Bobby Sanabria, and Colombian vocalist Hirám "El Pavo" Remón, who also spent time in the Canal Zone working for United Fruit and singing in local venues.

WALTER "GENE" JEFFERSON

Many people from a certain generation might recognize Jefferson from his years performing in the Apollo Theater house band on the television show *Showtime at the Apollo*. Like his parents, Jefferson was born in Panama, on July 14, 1931, but his grandparents were from Jamaica. He went to school on the Panamanian side of Panama City until fourth grade, and was then adopted so he could go to the American School and learn American English. Once enrolled, his new teacher chided him for his inability with English due to his Spanish pronunciation.

Jefferson's godmother took him to the Cub Scouts when he was nine, where he played ocarina and started on fife. Musicians would rehearse in his godmother's house, where there was a piano and many instruments. At the age of fourteen, his godmother bought him a mail-order *tumbadora* (conga) from Cuba that had to be tuned with a flame. Jefferson started listening to armed forces radio from a young age, in addition to Cuban artists on local radio and on CMQ, the Cuban radio station. He also enjoyed local conjunto music as played by Rubén Blades's father, a *bongosero*, and musicians such as Castaneda and Angela Hatsbill, who he would often watch perform during live broadcasts. For Jefferson, the scene in Panama rivaled Havana; he remembered that, in the 1940s, "Cuba had a lot of musicians and artists [whose] next stop was Colón then Panama City side . . . [they] stopped 2–3 days."[118]

Jefferson worked as a percussionist until he hurt his hands drumming during carnival at the age of eighteen. His mom bought him an old rejected military saxophone for about thirty dollars. Jefferson practiced enough to soon join an orchestra. He was self-taught, but then studied clarinet in high school. He got his start in Panamá, like so many great musicians, playing in the municipal bands before playing third clarinet in the *banda de bomberos* (firefighters band).[119] It was there, at his first rehearsal, that trumpet heavyweight Victor Paz told him, "¡Toca duro, coño!" [play hard, damn it!] as he tapped Jefferson on his back with his trumpet.[120] Jefferson remembered that he started playing the flute "when I got a legitimate job in a hotel."[121] He then studied at the *conservatorio* in Colón, which was fifty-seven miles away, but taught himself flute because

Fig 4.3. Walter "Gene" Jefferson as a young man.
Photo courtesy of Enid Lowe.

his teacher didn't really want to teach him. That was when he first saw the Panamanian virtuoso and his future collaborator Mauricio Smith. Eventually, Jefferson landed a coveted hotel gig performing for an international crowd. He played a variety of music including Broadway tunes with charts bought from the States, and he and the band accompanied acts that would come in singing the latest hits. Led by bassist Clarence Martin, the band consisted of three saxophones, two trumpets, and a full rhythm section with congas. During this time he played a lot of Chano Pozo's music, remembering "I was Chano Pozo," and he bought his charts: "after hearing Dizzy and Chano that was it."[122] On these gigs, Jefferson would encounter many Latino servicemen from Puerto Rico and Dominican Republic. He preferred to work steady gigs in hotels, six nights a week. At night, he remembers that many trumpet players would work these jobs with him and then would go to clubs wherever hot dance bands were playing. They would try to cut one another and Jefferson would hear who could "*pitar duro*" [motioning upwards to signal high register].[123]

During this time period, the Panamanian musician Luis Kant returned from New York playing three congas, and Jefferson could see the musical progress and innovation coming from New York.[124] At the age of twenty-eight, Jefferson decided to move to New York, reasoning: "I had nowhere else to be or do or to progress in Panama, I had the best job and from there it was down[hill]."[125] It was an easy move with his mother, aunt, and uncles already in the United States. In addition, many musicians from his youth were already in New York playing with the Ellington and Basie bands.

Another motivator for leaving Panama was discrimination. In Panama, Jefferson first felt the sting of discrimination when he was a young boy and swallowed a fishbone that got lodged in his throat. Waiting for a bus to go the hospital, a bus for whites passed him and he had to wait for one that would take nonwhites. This was when he fully grasped the segregation of the gold and silver system that took its cues from Jim Crow. Part of his decision to come to the United States was that "I'd rather be discriminated against in another man's country than in my own. And that was the pain, *el dolor*, it used to hurt."[126] Jefferson arrived in the US on June 6, 1960, and by June 16 he got a night job on Wall Street. He became a US citizen in five years; and although the professional transition was easy, culturally things were different. For a Panamanian musician, the word *lounge* meant live music in Panama and when he got out of the car for the first time from the airport, after driving into Brooklyn, he saw lights and signs for many bar/lounges, but they did not have any music.

Additionally, Jefferson was discouraged by the fact that there was not much happening in Brooklyn, especially on July 4th, a major holiday in the Canal Zone. He remembered that Americans celebrated all the important holidays in Panama. Generally speaking, Jefferson felt that "our culture was more American than Panamanian . . . [and] we celebrate everything we can get."[127] He was saddened that there was no festivity for the holiday, so he went to visit his brother in the Bronx.

For Jefferson, at that time there was really no Panamanian community per se; it was African American. In his view, the Panamanian community came after the 1960s and 1970s. His brother was in the Bronx at 891 Southern Boulevard near Hunts Point Palace, and most of his parents' relatives were in the Bronx or Harlem. He stayed in the Bronx as much as possible, especially when working with the Puerto Rican musicians and cousins Orlando and Frank Marín. Jefferson's first gig in New York was at a little club in the Bronx.

One night, Jefferson went to hear Frank Anderson's band at the Audobon Ballroom and started working with him immediately thereafter. They played "everything": *vals peruano*, cumbias, many different Caribbean musical genres, and Jefferson noted that there was a female bassist, who it turns out, was Luis Russell's wife Carline Ray: "Panama and Colombia have the same *sabor de la música* [taste of the music]. It was easy for us, at places like the San Andrés club, because we came from a central mix of people from [all over]."[128] For

Jefferson, being from Panama helped him play so many styles, "[it] gives you a different taste."[129] Anderson and Jefferson met Colombian vocalist Hiram "El Pavo" Remón at El Patio, a Colombian venue in Queens, and have worked together ever since.

With his cabaret card he subbed in Frank Anderson's band in 1965, and stuck with him from then on. Jefferson loved Anderson's arrangements, and the sidemen were mostly from the Count Basie and Duke Ellington bands when they were not on the road.[130] During this time, Jefferson was doing a good deal of studio recording work with artists based in Argentina and elsewhere. He recorded on many sessions often without knowing for whom he was working.

Thanks to his friend and countryman Mauricio Smith, Jefferson first worked with Arsenio Rodríguez when he recorded the saxophone parts on the seminal Arsenio Rodríguez album, *Quindembo/Afro Magic/La Magía de Arsenio Rodríguez*.[131] Jefferson played with Arsenio Rodríguez around New York and remembered meeting percussionist Chihuahua Martínez on one gig in the Bronx. Together they would play at parties, playing the coros (choral refrains) in Santería ritual music with Jack Hitchcock on trombone. Arsenio would call Jefferson "Jess" as he could not pronounce *Jeff*, the nickname that Mauricio Smith used. Despite frequently working with Arsenio Rodríguez, Jefferson only played with him in little clubs. He felt that:

> Arsenio's playing was the fullest. You could follow him and he was one of the most inspiring guys that you could play off of, that you could dance off of him. Arsenio's feel inspires you and puts you at a whole different level. *En el and de los golpes* [on the upbeat of the main pulse]. The music of Arsenio is for dancers . . . *Los que estan gozando no marchando* [those who are enjoying themselves not just marching to the beat].[132]

Jefferson used alto saxophone in Arsenio's music because Arsenio had heard Charlie Parker and knew jazz, so that's why he liked Gene. From a practical and sonic standpoint the alto worked: "Because [he] could stay above, on the tenor you are within. I was always finding my place there to do what was necessary to do. Arsenio was into music that pulls you, not *marcha*, [but] *más sabor*."[133]

Jefferson continued playing with Orlando Marín at clubs in Long Island and would alternate with an R&B band. Then they would have Tito Puente or Tito Rodríguez headline and they would play in between. One night Tito Rodríguez heard him and asked him to join his band, and Jefferson replaced Mauricio Smith. The band was filled with musical giants. He traveled to perform many dates during carnival in Venezuela. Victor Paz was the horn director and Manny Oquendo played timbales. Bassist Julio Andino stayed in Venezuela before the tour when he got sick, and Israel "Cachao" López was the new bass player. Marcelino Valdés was the conguero, alongside Mike Collazo and Mike "El gordo" Ríos on piano.

Jefferson loved Tito Rodríguez's band because it was for dancers. He also loved Rodríguez's discipline and his vocal interpretation. This discipline showed up in the music, both onstage and off. Rodríguez would fine his musicians for attire transgressions and in order to secure their payment, the band never went into the club until Rodríguez said to go in. Jefferson also remembers that Tito Rodríguez had a regular Wednesday rehearsal at 1pm at the Palladium.[134] Arrangers would bring in charts he had assigned them to write. Jefferson remembers one occasion when Rodríguez stopped the band and shouted, "*Aregla esa mierda*, fix that shit" to the arranger Arte Azenzer. Rodríguez would offer advice and warn Jefferson to "travel with the drummer who has to get there two hours early, not with the piano player when you have to set up 3 horns and moisten reeds."[135] Ultimately, Jefferson left the Tito Rodríguez band because he had gotten sick in Venezuela, along with four other musicians. To Jefferson, Rodríguez was nice off of the bandstand, but extremely strict onstage. Jefferson recalled that he never played opposite Tito Puente because of the billing war and their professional rivalry. Frank Anderson never noticed the rivalry and Jefferson felt that "for me . . . [they were] two different bands, two different tastes."[136] Jefferson had heard about the Palladium in Panama and when he started to perform there with Rodríguez, "it was impressive, impressive, it was like okay, I made it to the Palladium."[137]

Although Birdland was next door, Jefferson did not go to Birdland; instead he would stay in the Palladium to listen. Sometimes well-known musicians who had recordings and established names like Stan Getz would come over and sit in with Tito Rodríguez's band. Jefferson remembered that one night "we were playing and we were told, nobody get off the bandstand," and at the time United Artists was causing problems for Tito Rodríguez. Someone had a gun and shot twice on the dance floor. Another fond memory of Jefferson's was when the Tito Rodríguez band played one night at Birdland, and he was happy to be listening to John Coltrane there. Jefferson wasn't into the jam session aspect of rumba, particularly when people were showing off, but he enjoyed musical competition: "One time we played opposite Willie Bobo and there was a battle of the bands at Manhattan Center with stages set up at opposite ends."[138] During his prime, he recorded "Un cigarillo en tu boca," movie soundtracks, and a lot of what he called "*música de las Américas*" (music of the Americas). Jefferson also recorded a lot with Tito Rodríguez in a studio in Bayside, Queens. At that time, Jefferson was playing fourth tenor in Tito Rodríguez's big band because of all the heavy name players in the group.

Drawing upon his vast stylistic knowledge, Jefferson also played flute on charanga gigs. Most of his studio work was with soca and calypso bands; arrangers

Fig 4.4. Proclamation from Brooklyn Borough President in honor of Gene Jefferson. Photo courtesy of Enid Lowe.

who did work for artists in Argentina; and Argentine artists based in New York, such as Frank Valiente. Jefferson also worked in Ray Charles's band during New York City performances, and later joined the house band of the Apollo Theater, where he would meet and perform with stars for many years.

TERRY PEARCE

Another contemporary and collaborator of Anderson, Smith, and Jefferson who remains active to this day is pianist Terry Pearce. Pearce was born in Colón on August 10, 1933, and began studying music from an early age. He began working professionally with groups that played Cuban conjunto music, particularly during carnival season.[139] In 1951, at the age of seventeen, he joined Armando Boza's famed big band, which included Mauricio Smith and Victor Paz. The group played throughout all of Panama and in 1955, Pearce traveled with the group to play in Quito, Ecuador. During this time, Pearce also accompanied Cuban vocalist Benny Moré and absorbed his pianist Pedro "Peruchín" Justiz's style.[140] In an interview with Chico Álvarez for Latinjazznet.com, Pearce talked about the Cuban arrangers of the time: "All of the musicians in Armando's [Boza] band were keenly aware of everything coming out of Cuba. In fact, our specialty was always Cuban music."[141]

While Pearce and his fellow musicians played Panamanian cumbias and other traditional Panamanian music, they were also steeped in jazz. And as descendants of Afro-Caribbean workers who dug the canal, Pearce stated that they had a dual identity: "We formed the nucleus of a community separated from the larger society by race, language, religion, and culture. Many of us who migrated to the U.S. would ultimately find ourselves in a sort of duality, what with surnames names like Smith and Terry" (laughter).[142] Pearce's sentiment echoes those expressed by other Panamanian musicians profiled throughout this chapter: they were Latino and Afro-Caribbean. Pearce left Boza's band to work as a musician on a cruise ship from 1960–62 and then got his visa to immigrate to the United States, arriving in New York City on January 20, 1962.[143] Working with Bobby Woodland, who performed with the stage name Madera in order to appear more Latino, Pearce played Latin music throughout the Catskill Mountain resorts. He played "swing jazz" with Doc Cheatham in New York City from 1962–69 and also worked steadily with Willie Bobo at Birdland during this time period. Pearce subbed for René Hernández in the Machito Orchestra and performed with Chubby Checker, a gig that Mauricio Smith helped him get. Playing jazz organ in the 1970s, he had the opportunity to jam with Nell Carter on various occasions. This time period also saw him subbing in charanga bands with the likes of José Fajardo and Lou Pérez, both Cuban purists, as well as Puerto Rican bandleader Raul Argüeso. The association with Argüeso at the Roseland Ballroom lasted from 1974–88. Pearce took over the band in 1996 and continued to play there until 2001. Pearce continues to play to this day and I have performed with him in Álvarez's group.

ENID LOWE: "WE ARE BLACK AND LATINO AT THE SAME TIME."

Edna Vasola Lowe Jefferson was born on July 21, 1935, in Colón. Her mother was born in Panama and her father was born in Barbados. Lowe's grandparents were Jamaican. She grew up in Silver City in the Canal Zone, and explained that she and other Panamanians had no interaction with the Americans there. Black US Army personnel could live in the gold zone but Panamanians could not go into gold stores. They didn't have any problems since "We didn't go where they are . . . We didn't miss anything from the gold side, because we had the same thing on the silver side . . . We baked white bread and brought it over to their commissaries so they were getting the same stuff that we had."[144] Lowe explained that most music clubs were in the Panamanian side in Colón, not in the Canal Zone where there were no bars. However, she remembered that many Panamanian women married black and Hispanic G.I.'s and moved to Maryland.

Fig 4.5. Enid Lowe at 15. Photo courtesy of Enid Lowe.

Lowe remembered that Hispanic G.I.'s would hang out with Panamanians. Her husband, Gene Jefferson, would take them around the town to lounges, and each lounge always featured a trio or a quartet playing music.

Lowe's musical career began with Rex Archibold, who had a variety show on CRP, the local radio station in Colón. He asked Lowe to sing the first Sunday of every month on his radio show, but another station got jealous so she performed the first and last Sunday. Performing with Archibold, she sang for the governor and various administrators. Lowe's parents did not want her to go into clubs since she was only fifteen or sixteen years old. According to Lowe, there were many women performers, but there was no competition because they were different types of singers. Lowe wasn't very fluent in Spanish, but she listened to Cuban music, particularly Benny Moré and Celia Cruz.

Since she was too young to sing in clubs, Lowe sang at extravaganzas and balls. Musicians were respectful and would take her home at night, guarding her like big brothers. Normally, Lowe's mother wasn't too enthusiastic, but she wanted to sit next to the president and other dignitaries at the concerts when her daughter sang, so she allowed her to continue. According to Lowe,

Fig 4.6. Enid Lowe and the 60th Airborne Band. Photo courtesy of Enid Lowe.

there were all types of clubs and lounges; some were expensive, geared toward officials or foreigners. Generally speaking, Lowe felt that "you couldn't be a street person, you were brought up a certain way," and this behavioral code would accompany her throughout her life. After her tenure with Archibold, Lowe sang in a big band led by Egbert King for a radio show hosted by Cecil A. Coleman on Radio Atlántico. Lowe also sang with big bands led by Egbert King, Raymond Antoine, and Victor MacDonald, a bebop trumpet player and innovator. On weekends she gave many concerts with small and large groups in theaters such as Bobby Scarlett (drummer) for the USO and on the navy base. Lowe also sang on radio broadcasts to Europe. Lowe had early experience working in a multi-ethnic group working with the 68th US Army band, a group made up of Latino musicians who were Puerto Ricans and Dominicans that also played at the Air Force cocktail lounge. The band's repertoire consisted of boleros, pop, and show tunes.

Lowe's vocal influences included Sarah Vaughan, Ella Fitzgerald, and Carmen McRae, among others. At that time, all the great vocalists came to the El Panama Hotel, where Lowe saw Ella Fitzgerald, Hazel Scott, and others perform. The El Panama was the best gig and venue to play; Lowe performed there with Clarence Martin. She also worked with Carol Graves at Maxim's, across the street from the El Panama Hotel. Lowe was interested in American music and would stay current by listening to vocal performances by Jo Stafford and others that were being broadcasted from hotels in New York City. She identifies herself not as a jazz singer but as "a singer of songs, 'cause I do different types of music."

Fig 4.7. Gene and Enid performing in Clarence Martin's band at the El Panama Hotel 1958.
Photo courtesy of Enid Lowe.

The big bands that Lowe worked with did not use stock arrangements and wrote their own charts, so she only had one stock chart, "Tolula Ladder." According to Lowe, in Panama it was common for each big band to have one male singer and even two females (one for Latin, one for jazz). Some of the male singers that she worked with included Neville Chan, Arnold Corliss, and the bolero singer Curo Dossman. American bandleader Jan Garber and his Orchestra accompanied Lowe at the El Panama Hotel. The concert was broadcast from Panama through Europe as part of the Crusade for Freedom Concert. When she left Panama and came to New York City, Garber offered her the opportunity to work with him nationally, but she didn't want to deal with the segregation of touring in the South.

Lowe's aunt and sisters were living on 98th Street and Northern Boulevard in Corona, Queens, when she arrived in New York on May 10, 1957. Upon arriving, Lowe was unimpressed by the "dirty barn" that was Idlewild Airport. The next day in the city she saw winos and heroin addicts on the street. She wondered to herself if she had come to the right place or if she had made a mistake. However, Lowe was impressed with the abundance in the supermarkets, because in Colón access to the goods in the commissary was limited to the time that one's parents were working and had privileges to buy goods there.

She connected with a manager who wanted her to sing in supper clubs in Harlem and Manhattan. Like Gene Jefferson, Lowe thought that the New York clubs and lounges were in terrible condition compared to where she had worked in Panama. Lowe got a day job at a customs brokerage firm and was one of two black people on the job. In Lowe's estimation, her employers treated her right and she could continue to work on her music at night and go in later during the day if necessary. She started doing club dates and private parties with Gene Jefferson, Frank Anderson, and Johnny Amoroso. Lowe knew Frank Anderson as a child prodigy in Panama and he had accompanied her on some Sunday evening radio broadcasts.

Lowe married Jefferson and settled in Brooklyn, since she felt it was easier than Manhattan to get around. She remembered that at that time, Panamanians were spread out all over and would meet on Fulton Street. In the early 1970s immigration became easier, and more people started coming to Franklin Avenue. Kelso Restaurant was the one of the first Panamanian gathering spots that she remembered. Also people would come to the neighborhood to buy Panamanian lottery tickets ("*comprar chance*"). Lowe felt that Caribbean people got along in Brooklyn since they were all connected "like cousins" in terms of having relatives and family ties with each country, such as Jamaica, Trinidad, and Barbados.

Lowe's feelings about racial discrimination provide insight into the experience of being black in Panama and of being Afro-Latino in New York City. Despite the fact that she was born in Panama to a father from Barbados and a Panamanian mother, the Panamanian government made Lowe naturalize as a Panamanian before she could get her visa for the United States. This was understandably painful for her. For Lowe, New York "didn't feel strange to us at all, [because in Panama] we were the original melting pot."

She also encountered discrimination from Latinos: "especially if you had black skin, they called us *chombos*." Lowe learned numerous important values from her family that included saving a dollar for every dollar spent, prioritizing education, and that "[even if] parents could not read or write we had to learn . . . We were taught to be self-sufficient. We had no welfare, no social service, we had to get up every day and work. We didn't have anyone handing us anything." Lowe explained, "our parents taught us to be proud [and would say] Lincoln did not free us." Growing up, "we were lucky because we had a very rounded upbringing" surrounded by other people. There was an added

Fig 4.8. The couple together in New York. Photo courtesy of Enid Lowe.

incentive not to get into trouble because "people would make up a song about you, 'girl got pregnant.'"

In Lowe's view, the Panamanian community was out of view from other groups, saying, "they didn't recognize us for a good long time," but now Panamanians are more organized as a group with its "own newspaper." Lowe expressed pride for performing at the first major jazz concert in Panama May 30, 2000, *El día de la raza*, along with Gene Jefferson, Frank Anderson, and Hiram Remón. The event and the performance were a fitting venue to proclaim that "we are black and Latino at the same time." Now, in other parts of the United States such as Florida and Texas, there is a group that celebrates July 4th for all Panamanians.

Besides performing in Panama as part of *El día de la raza*, Lowe is especially proud of playing the jazz brunches at La Détente for seven years. Located at 94th St. and 23rd Avenue by LaGuardia Airport, La Détente was one of the few black-owned clubs. The owners were proud Haitians whose elegant setting attracted many big stars and personal heroes such as Lou Rawls and others. According to a review in the *New York Post*:

Local politicians and savvy travelers regard La Detente, a restaurant and banquet hall featuring Haitian Creole cuisine, as an indispensable dining destination near a Queens airport. On many occasions during the past 15 years, it may have been the only option they had. Natives of Haiti view its glitzy ballrooms as ideal for special dinners and a variety of social and business functions. Politicians deem the complex an obligatory campaign stop. And grounded passengers rightly rate it as the best eating alternative during LaGuardia layovers.[145]

Fig 4.9. Mario Bauzá dancing to Enid Lowe, Gene Jefferson, Bobby Sanabria, and Frank Anderson at La Détente. Photo courtesy of Enid Lowe.

Fig 4.10. Gene Jefferson, Frank Anderson, Enid Lowe, and the author in 2014. Courtesy of Benjamin Lapidus.

As part of the International Combo, Lowe sang in English but sang some boleros in Spanish. Video footage of the band performing at La Détente in 1995
shows a tight ensemble covering a wide range of musical genres on a stage with
a large background painting of Haitian patriots. Unfortunately, Lowe never
recorded with anyone until she sang on one of my albums.

ALPHONSO JOSEPH: "I HAD TOO MUCH TROUBLE WITH THE AMERICAN LIFE"

Born February 15, 1934, on the Pacific side of Panama City, Alphonso Joseph
sang as a child in Panama. Both of his parents were born in Panama and his
father's family was originally from a French-speaking part of Nigeria. His
grandfather was from Algeria and his mother's parents were from St. Lucia.
Joseph's grandmother, Ifemí, opened a restaurant near the Colombian border
close to Colón. The whole family was originally French-speaking due to the St.
Lucia connection and the battles over possession of St. Lucia. The family spoke
French, then English, and then Spanish; thus Joseph came up in a tri-cultural,
trilingual family. French-speaking West Indians changed their names to sound
more English, as treatment of English-speaking West Indians was perceived as
better. The original family name Coudon was French, and the patriarch's first
name, Joseph, became the new family surname.

When Alphonso Joseph came to New York in 1945, there were not many
Panamanians, but more came in mid- to late 1950s. He recalled that "there were
West Indians scattered around" when his great aunt brought him and his relatives to New York. Her friends were "a mixture of St. Lucians from her country
and some Panamanians": she married a man from Grenada, had friends from
Jamaica. She sent for Alphonso's brothers and parents, and everyone eventually
moved to Jefferson Avenue in Williamsburg. During his first three to four years
in New York, Joseph lived in Bedford-Stuyvesant, Brooklyn, remembering it as
"still a mixed neighborhood [that] then became all black." Interestingly, Joseph
did not have American friends except for a few in the building.

Initially, Joseph was interested in becoming a priest and lived in a rectory. He
joined the US Air Force in March 1953, got out in June 1954, and settled in the
Puerto Rican community of Camden, New Jersey. Joseph was grateful for this
experience, saying "So I got my chance, by the grace of God, to live the Latino
life, because I had too much trouble with the American life, the racism and all
of that, and I just wanted out of that."[146] This is when and where he learned to
play the guitar for musical genres such as merengue, mambo, chachachá, *por-
ros*, seises, and aguinaldos. He played *segunda guitarra* and it was "the Puerto
Ricans who taught me how to play all the *tumbaos*, Cuban *tumbaos*."[147]

EDUCATION AND CONNECTING WITH ARSENIO RODRÍGUEZ

Joseph moved back to Brooklyn to finish his high school diploma in 1956. Later when he started college, he did not finish his first semester in order to go out on the road with Arsenio Rodríguez. Joseph first met Arsenio once when he was playing second guitar with Charlie Rodríguez. Around 1956 or 1957, Joseph began playing an acoustic guitar that was adapted with thick bass strings to be played with the thumb. In 1958 he started to play with Alexander Korah, a Bermudan in Williamsburg who had taught many Puerto Ricans to play a variety of wind and percussion instruments. The ensemble included Puerto Ricans, Korah's family members, and Joseph. Korah was a self-identified black Jew who played dances at synagogues in the vicinity of Keap Street near Korah's house. Joseph remembers wearing yarmulkes at these gigs. Korah brought Joseph to Silver and Harland music store on Row Street on the Lower East Side. The store offered a 40 percent discount to professional musicians, and he switched to a Fender bass and an Ampeg amplifier. With his popularity and increased work, Joseph remembers that many other second guitarists started to follow his switch to electric bass. One day Joseph encountered an acoustic bass in Korah's apartment, which served as meeting place for many musicians. He bought a bass the next day and started practicing and playing with Mario Lebrón around 1960; other musicians that Joseph remembered from the Brooklyn scene included Raymond Maldonado (Richie Ray's brother), and Mario Lebrón on Nevins Street.

They played gigs accompanying Daniel Santos and alternating with a trio around Avenue A and Avenue B in Brooklyn. One night on the gig, his bass amp would not work with the electric bass so Joseph ran home to get his acoustic double bass. With the gig saved, albeit with bad intonation, Joseph began studying with local Brooklyn legend Rector Bailey on Eastern Parkway.

Bailey was a Brooklyn institution, a multi-instrumentalist who worked professionally on and taught vibraphone, bass, piano, organ, and guitar. He was multilingual and spoke Spanish, Hebrew, Yiddish, and Italian. Some of his students included Doc Pomus—Bailey brought Pomus to Brooklyn's black clubs on Fulton Street—Richie Havens, Mickey Baker, Alvin Schackman, Billy Kaye, Jason Miles, the author's father, and many others.[148] Bailey also performed and recorded on guitar with a number of musicians, including Big Joe Turner, Nat King Cole, Odelle Turner, Billie Holiday, Harry Van Walls, Randy Weston, Ruth Brown, and George Wallington. He had been a conductor at the New York City Opera Company and performed on guitar at Town Hall.[149] He worked regularly at various clubs in Brooklyn, including the Putnam Central Club, the Kingston Lounge at 120 Kingston Avenue, and Tony's Café on Grand Avenue at Dean Street.[150]

Korah brought Joseph to study at Hartnitt Studios on 42nd Street, where Charlie Parker and others had taught or studied jazz. Joseph studied harmony and theory, arranging, composition, arranging, jazz, and bass through the G.I. Bill. A concerned teacher named Joe Timpa took Joseph under his wing. Joseph focused on sight-reading as well. After a year and a half the school went bankrupt, but around 1963 someone told Joseph that Arsenio needed a bass player and gave him his number. Coincidentally, Joseph also worked with pianist Nicolás Rodríguez around this time.

Joseph went to visit Arsenio Rodríguez at a hotel on 63rd Street and Broadway. Arsenio played a C7 montuno on the tres and asked Joseph to play, but stopped him, saying "*Eso 'ta capicú*" (that's a mess); then he taught Joseph the tumbao (bass ostinato) "Mi sol do la sol sol, um, fa la" and others. Joseph then went to Arsenio's house every day for a couple of weeks, until one day Arsenio grabbed Joseph's bass to demonstrate.[151] Joseph reflected:

> He'd give me a tumbao that, you know, you had to concentrate very hard not to lose your place, because with him, you could be playing something that he gives you . . . but sometimes he would change the tumbao and he comes in with something else and he throws you off [laughter], you don't know where one is anymore! That happened to me one time.[152]

Arsenio gave Joseph a lot of freedom to come up with bass lines, but if he did not like what Joseph played he would give him his bass line. Other musicians knew that Arsenio took Joseph under his wing, and musicians like Kako would affectionately call him "*El hijo de Arsenio*" (Arsenio's son). Arsenio knew that Joseph was Panamanian, and on the scene Joseph was known as Alphonso "El Panameño"; Rodríguez once told Tito Puente, "*tengo un panameño y lo estoy preparando*" (I have a Panamanian and I am preparing him). For Joseph, playing with Arsenio Rodríguez "Was the best musical experience in Latin music that I had, it was something beyond words. I mean to see people come to those ballrooms, the place was so packed. People stopped dancing and just looked at us playing, what an honor."

Joseph remembered played engagements with Rodríguez at the Palladium, the Village Gate, El Club Cubano Inter-Americano, the Havana-San Juan, El Caborojeño, and El Condado. They also traveled to Boston and New Jersey for performances. Joseph played with Arsenio for eight years until Rodríguez passed away. Joseph hooked up with Cachao when Arsenio recorded one of his arrangements for the album *Arsenio Dice*. He recorded with acoustic bass and used the Ampeg electric upright in performance. Joseph remembered that he and Julio Andino were among the first to work with electric upright and amplifier. Eventually Arsenio would disappear to California or Chicago, and

Joseph would play Latin jazz gigs in the Catskills with Cándido Camero. The pianist in the band was Rafael Benítez (Xiomara Alfaro's husband) and Johnny Malcolm was on trumpet. The repertoire on these summer gigs included tangos, boleros, and old Cuban music. Joseph also freelanced with Johnny Zamot (Johnny Ray) at this time.

Joseph's wife Franchesca remembers that "people would stop dancing and cluster around the band" when her husband played with Arsenio. She was taken with his music and was made aware that a certain status was conferred upon being one of Arsenio Rodríguez's musicians. Many times Arsenio would call to get phone numbers and their communication was difficult and humorous since Franchesca did not speak Spanish and Arsenio did not speak English. Franchesca attended many gigs, helping her husband carry his equipment and dancing with Arsenio's brother Kiki. One time Joseph brought Arsenio a song, and Arsenio grabbed his tres and played a beautiful harmony. Joseph also remembered that Augustin Caraballoso was a Jehovah's Witness and that's how Arsenio was brought to that faith. Rodríguez wanted Joseph to come with him to California, but coincidentally he died when the Josephs discovered they would be parents. Joseph often played on local boat gigs that traveled around New York City and remembers Frank Anderson's big band and Anderson subbing on Arsenio's gig. Joseph also remembered working with Panamanians pianist Alonso Wilson, saxophonist Raymond Antoine, and saxophonist Frank Jeanmarie.

After Arsenio's death, Joseph started playing at the Cuban restaurant El Liborio with Cándido Camero and his quartet six nights a week. Cachao replaced Joseph on the El Liborio gig, but soon Joseph would sub for Cachao. Joseph said that "Arsenio gave me the style to play like Cachao," and Cachao advised Joseph "the more you become famous, the more humility is required of you and he said remember always the same faces you see when you are rising up are the same faces you see when you are falling, so be humble."[153]

Joseph remembered that René Hernández and Pupi would come to Arsenio's apartment and that they transcribed Arsenio's music. Joseph recalled that these bass lines were written out with ties from the last eighth note to a half note in the first two beats of the next measure. Arsenio would talk to Joseph about music, son, and many topics. For Joseph, Arsenio's "charts were a little disorganized, because they could not find some of the parts," so playing by ear was required.

In the late 1960s, Joseph studied classical bass in the Bronx with a Hungarian Jew named Mr. Sacar for four years, going through the whole Franz Simandl book. Both Sacar and Simandl were students of another great bass player. After a year of studying with him and not finding a symphonic group to join in Brooklyn due to racism, Joseph played Beethoven's Third Symphony with the Broadway Symphony. In 1969 Joseph moved to Teaneck, New Jersey, and later to Mount Vernon, New York. He and his then wife moved to Connecticut for the next twenty-five years. Joseph focused exclusively on symphonic music during this time period and after a "series of [religious] visions" he became an ordained minister and dedicated his music to the Lord. Among the eight pieces that he recorded on his CD, Joseph included an orchestral arrangement of a psalm as an oratorio. Joseph's son made a documentary called *La época* about the sidemen of Latin music; after Joseph fell ill in the hospital, his son went through the father's Rolodex and recognized his father's connections to Celia Cruz, Tito Puente, Cachao, and many more.[154]

Lastly, Arsenio Rodríguez was alleged to have preferred working with and hiring musicians of color for all of his groups. The fact that Joseph, Anderson, and Jefferson were all Antillanos and chosen for his groups speaks not only of their status as musicians, but also of Rodríguez's worldview and the experience of the African diaspora.

RANDY WESTON: A BROOKLYN-BORN PANAMANIAN MUSICIAN IN AFRICA

Unlike most of the musicians previously discussed in this chapter, pianist and composer Randy Weston (1926–2018) was a Brooklyn-born and -bred musician who gained Panamanian citizenship in the last decade of his life. During an appearance on the television show *Democracy Now*, Weston explained that his father "was born in Panama. He lived seven years in Cuba and he came to Brooklyn and settled in Brooklyn. My mother came from Virginia, a small town called Meredithville. And she came to New York, and they got together to produce Randy Weston."[155] Like Frank Anderson, Gene Jefferson, and Enid Lowe, Weston's father Edward was from a Jamaican family and his "paternal grandfather . . . had a bakery near the canal."[156] Edward Weston "spoke fluent Spanish" and hired newly arrived Cubans and Puerto Ricans to work in his Bedford-Stuyvesant barbershop before opening a luncheonette, where he was the cook.[157] Edward Weston's restaurant was a known spot for musicians to hang out and Randy remembered: "The guys would be hanging out at my father's restaurant, listening to the jukebox. Everybody would come by and we would discuss everything from communism in China to politics and racism, to whatever various musicians were doing."[158]

The younger Weston hung out at the Palladium and enjoyed calypso along with American blues and African American church music.[159] Weston's pride in his Pan-Caribbean background came face to face with segregation in the army, where he notes that he was placed with African Americans and not Latinos. Returning home to manage his father's restaurant, Trios, Weston took refuge from the decline in his neighborhood by traveling to Massachusetts. There, at the Music Inn, he met the percussionist Cándido Camero who had performed and recorded with Dizzy Gillespie, Charlie Parker, and many others, including Frank Anderson, Gene Jefferson, and Enid Lowe. Weston's relationship with Cándido Camero dated back to working together for three years in a trio in the early 1950s; for Weston, "the music was getting more and more into Africa"— and he would eventually set foot there.[160]

Weston soon spent considerable time performing and studying in Africa. He incorporated hand drummers into his group such as Big Black and the Brooklyn-based *babalawo* (Santería priest) Chief Bey, who was a mentor to many Latin musicians in New York City. Weston writes:

> Having Chief Bey on the tour was one of the keys to our success. I knew that in many places we were likely to encounter audiences that weren't real famil- iar with Western instruments, but I knew Chief's drum would connect with the people. My whole concept of having African drum in my band—which is still the case today—goes back to hearing Chano Pozo with Dizzy Gillespie's orchestra, and hearing people like Sabu Martinez with Art Blakey. When I heard Chano with Dizzy it was like a revelation, nobody had played music like that before. From that point on having the African or Cuban drum in my band was purely a matter of connecting with our African audiences.[161]

The Panamanian bassist Alex Blake, who often employs a unique strumming technique, was another important component of Weston's bands who "fit right into" Weston's music.[162] For Blake, Weston's approach was attractive; Blake explains:

> I couldn't really put my finger on that difference, but it felt like elements of Africa and South America. Since I was from Panama, I heard certain elements in his music that reminded me of music that I'd heard as a kid in Panama . . . I left Panama when I was seven years old and I hadn't been back to my country in about forty-five years, until I went down there to play on a festival with Randy in January 2006. That first time returning to Panama was as if I was going to Africa for the first time. My heart was racing when we landed, because I hadn't been back in so many years. As soon as we got off the plane we were whisked off to have lunch with the president. Then at the concert the audience response to our performance was incredible. Listening to Randy's music was something the Panamanians could relate to rhythmically and melodically, and their response was overwhelming.[163]

During this trip the Panamanian government offered Weston citizenship, and he connected with other notable Panamanian musicians such as Carlos Garnett,

Rubén Blades, Danilo Pérez, and his family. For Weston: "it was like we were all truly home. Everybody was telling us. 'You've got to come back, you're Panamanian now'. . . Panama was fabulous, like being home."[164]

OTHER IMPORTANT PANAMANIAN MUSICIANS WHO ENGAGED WITH JAZZ AND LATIN MUSIC

Eric Dolphy was another US-born musician whose Panamanian roots are seldom acknowledged. As a member of historic jazz groups led by Charles Mingus and John Coltrane, among others, Dolphy developed a uniquely personal style of improvisation and phrasing that influenced many musicians. His albums as a leader remain classics in the avant-garde jazz tradition. Interestingly, his only recordings playing Latin-influenced music were two albums made with the Latin Jazz Quintet.[165] These two sessions put him in the company of some of the tradition bearers of Latin music in New York who are discussed throughout this book, such as Tommy López, Felipe Díaz, Arthur Jenkins, Bobby Rodríguez, Louie Ramírez, and Juan Amalbert. Coincidentally, another Coltrane collaborator, Pharoah Sanders, also recorded with the Latin Jazz Quintet.[166]

Many other important Panamanian musicians settled in New York and contributed greatly to the music scene in both the jazz and Latin worlds. One of these greats includes multi-instrumentalist Mauricio Smith.[167] Smith was born July 11, 1931, in Colón to a Trinidadian father and a Panamanian mother. Smith's father David was his first teacher. Mauricio joined the Banda de Bomberos de Colón in his teens and later the Banda Republicana; He also played in the symphony and in the Conjunto Típico de Margarita Escala.[168] Smith first came to New York in 1957, but returned to Panama. He came back in 1959 and again returned to his country. Smith came to stay in 1961 and played with Vicentico Valdés, whom he had accompanied in Panama, at the Palladium. Smith's doubling skills and jazz chops were legendary and led him to work with the best musicians in both jazz and Latin music: Charles Mingus, Thad Jones/Mel Lewis Big Band, Clark Terry, Sonny Stitt, Dizzy Gillespie, Ray Barretto, Willie Colón, Chubby Checker, Eartha Kitt, Harry Belafonte, Joe Cuba, Gloria Estefan/Miami Sound Machine, Chico O'Farrill, and many others.[169] Smith also worked as an actor, appearing in film and television productions such as *Law and Order*, *Saturday Night Live*, *Die Hard*, and *The Cosby Show*.[170] Smith died August 3, 2002, but his musical impact remains large. His son, Mauricio Smith Jr., continues to perform on saxophone, flute, and percussion throughout New York City.

Flautist Felix Wilkins began playing at the age of seven. Inspired by Johnny Pacheco, he came to New York City in 1967 and started working with fellow Panamanian Carlos Garnett, then Willie Bobo, Mongo Santamaria, and Count

Basie.[171] Wilkins was not fond of air travel, so he focused on teaching and has taught at Brooklyn College, Panama Canal College, the National Conservatory of Music in Mexico, and the University of Panama.[172]

Carlos Garnett (b. 1938) is best known for recording on four albums and performing with Miles Davis in the early 1970s. He moved to New York City in 1962 and subsequently recorded and performed with Freddie Hubbard, Art Blakey, Andrew Hill, and Norman Connors. Since the 1970s, Garnett has released several albums as a bandleader.

Saxophonist and flautist Carlos Ward was born in Ancón, Panama, in 1940. He began his musical journey as a calypsonian ukulele player and left Panama in 1952.[173] He settled in Seattle as a teenager and learned saxophone. After joining the US Navy and attending the Navy School of Music, he went on to work with John Coltrane, Cecil Taylor, Karl Berger, Ed Blackwell, Carla Bley, Don Cherry, Don Pullen, Roswell Rudd, Abdullah Ibrahim, and Rashid Ali. He has also released a number of recordings as a bandleader.

Pianist and composer Alonso Wilson de Briano pioneered a type of calypso jazz with a Latin flavor unique to Panama. In Panama he recorded a number of songs in the 1950s and 1960s such as "Never Never," "Com-Colom," and "Me voy a Panamá."[174] Wilson's son, the bassist Santi Debriano, came to New York in 1959. Debriano studied at Wesleyan, New England Conservatory, and Union College and worked as an educator for many years. An in-demand sideman, he has performed and recorded with Sam Rivers, Don Pullen, Pharoah Sanders, Sonny Fortune, Billy Hart, Larry Coryell, Chucho Valdés, Hank Jones, Cecil Taylor, Randy Weston, Freddie Hubbard, Kirk Lightsey, and Attila Zoller, among many others.[175] He has led his own groups, most notably the Panamaniacs.

Saxophonist Jorge Sylvester arrived in New York City from Panama in 1981 and has performed with David Murray, Oliver Lake, the World Saxophone Quartet, and many others.[176] He grew up in Colón and Panama City and studied at the conservatory. Learning classical, jazz, and Caribbean music, he went on to work with Panamanian jazz legend Victor Boa. Sylvester also achieved commercial success playing calypso as a teenager in Panama. In 1976, at the age of twenty-three, he moved to Spain. Since that time he has developed a personal compositional and performance style that combines forward-thinking jazz and Afro-Latin and Afro-Caribbean music. His main group is the Afro-Caribbean Experimental Collective (ACE), which he describes as follows:

> The ACE Collective utilizes the rich spectrum of rhythms from the Caribbean and other Latin American countries as a vehicle to create new and undiscovered rhythmic melodic lines within the jazz tradition. Collective and Free improvisation is an essential part of the concept utilizing juxtaposition and retrograde as main components of the experimentation.[177]

Trumpeter Victor Paz is renowned for his technique and musicality. He backed up every major performer in many genres in Panama before coming to New York in 1963. Paz was a prized student of Carmine Caruso, who "would use Victor to demonstrate his drills in forums, master classes, etc."[178] In addition to Latin recordings with Tito Puente, Tito Rodríguez, Eddie Palmieri, the Fania All-Stars, Chico O'Farrill, and others, Paz played on a number of Broadway shows such as *Barnum*, *Cabaret*, *Cats* (ten years), *A Raisin in the Sun*, *Guys and Dolls*, *Sgt. Pepper*, Liza Minelli in *The Act*, and Marlene Dietrich.[179] Paz also recorded and performed with a who's who of American popular music: the Village People, Benny Goodman, Bob James, Stanley Turrentine, Houston Person, Joey DeFrancesco, Frank Sinatra, Nat "King" Cole, Tony Bennett, Count Basie, Benny Goodman, Lionel Hampton, Quincy Jones, Johnny Mathis, Henry Mancini, Bobby Rosengarden, Dizzy Gillespie, Ray Charles, Deodato, Ella Fitzgerald, Carmen McRae, Sammy Davis Jr., the Jackson 5, Stevie Wonder, Sarah Vaughan, Bill Evans, Stanley Turrentine, Bill Taylor, Aretha Franklin, Dione Warwick, Diana Ross [as a solo act and with the Supremes], the Temptations, the Four Tops, James Brown, Nancy Wilson, Tom Jones, Paul Anka, Peggy Lee, Cleo Laine, Gladys Knight, Shirley Basie, Bobby Darin, *The Dick Cavett Show*, Antonio Carlos Jobim, Perry Como, Duke Ellington, and others.[180] Paz returned to Panama after many decades in New York City.

Trumpeter Emilio Reales is an important Panamanian trumpeter heard on Tito Rodríguez's 1968 "Esta es mi orquesta" and a number of other seminal recordings of Latin music in New York.[181] He relocated to Puerto Rico, where he taught trumpet and recorded and/or performed with Joe Quijano, Jesus Caunedo, Sammy González, and others.

Drummer Billy Cobham (son of musician Manuel Cobham) was born in Colón, Panama, in 1947. The family moved to New York City in 1947 and he was raised in Bedford-Stuyvesant, Brooklyn. A student at New York's famed High School of Music and Art, Cobham played jazz professionally with Horace Silver, Stanley Turrentine, and Shirley Scott.[182] He then went on to work with the Brecker Brothers, John McLaughlin, Miles Davis, Jack Bruce, and the Grateful Dead.[183] His background informs Cobham's musical worldview: "'It's very, very interesting for me to hear this music and to play music like Mahavishnu Orchestra or even with Jack Bruce, but my approach is fundamentally the same,' the drummer observes. 'It's got a Latin root, and it kind of sets me off from everybody else.'"[184] Since 2002 he has collaborated with the Cuban son group Asere, and for Cobham it is a meaningful relationship that extends beyond music: "Through this relationship with Asere and the music we make together, it's helping me to connect. I'm reconnecting with my roots in Panama in order to see my future better through this clearer view of my past."[185]

Based in Queens, Rupert "Doc" Johnson is a Panamanian pianist, organist, and singer who is conscious of how the mixture of jazz and Latin music, particularly boleros, are a longstanding part of Panamanian musical experience. He feels that this musical sensibility that was happening in Panama for so long is now considered to be contemporary jazz in the United States.[186] The multifaceted approach of the Panamanian musician's musical concept was well received but also misunderstood in a *New York Times* performance review, as Josh S. Wilson wrote that Johnson, "has developed such a variety of musical personalities that, as is doubtless his intention, he can appeal to a broad range of listeners."[187]

Like his brother Alex, Russell Blake is a virtuoso bass player, but he was born and raised in Brooklyn, not Panama.[188] Russell has performed and recorded with Paquito D'Rivera, Sonny Rollins, Harry Belafonte, Chaka Khan, Angie Stone, Mary Mary, and George Coleman, and has worked on Broadway playing in *The Lion King*.[189] As seen earlier, Alex Blake was born in Panama and moved to the United States at the age of seven. "By age twelve, Alex was performing with recognized musical icons such as Mongo Santamaria, Machito (Mario Bauzá), Carlos 'Patata' [sic] Valdes, and Celia Cruz."[190] In addition to his aforementioned work and travels with Randy Weston, Alex played with "Sun Ra, Dizzy Gillespie, . . . Freddie Hubbard, Art Blakey, McCoy Tyner, Stan Getz, . . . Pharoah Sanders, and many other artists."[191]

Donald Nicks is another Panamanian bassist who has worked with both American and Latin artists such as Roy Ayers, Los Pleneros de la 21, Pepe Castillo, and Jorge Sylvester, among many others.[192]

Catherine Russell is a Grammy®-nominated jazz vocalist and the daughter of Luis Russell. Born in New York in 1956, she has recorded and performed internationally with a who's who of pop and jazz artists such as David Bowie, Steely Dan, Cyndi Lauper, Paul Simon, Rosanne Cash, Wynton Marsalis, and Dr. John, among others.

Born in Panama in 1965, Danilo Pérez has become Panama's most well-known jazz musician today. After studying at Berklee College in the 1980s, he settled in New York and went on to perform and record with Dizzy Gillespie, Jon Hendricks, Claudio Roditi, Paquito D'Rivera, Wynton Marsalis, Jack De-Johnette, Charlie Haden, Michael Brecker, Joe Lovano, Tito Puente, Tom Harrell, Gary Burton, Wayne Shorter, Roy Haynes, Steve Lacy, and many others.[193] He serves as a UNESCO Artist for Peace, has run a successful jazz festival and educational outreach program in Panama, and has been a "goodwill ambassador to UNICEF and cultural ambassador to Panama."[194] Pérez is currently the artistic director of the Global Jazz Institute at Berklee and travels around the world teaching and giving master classes.

RUBÉN BLADES: COMPOSER, VOCALIST, STATESMAN

An entire book could be written about Rubén Blades and his significance in the development of Spanish Caribbean music in New York City. Many of his most celebrated songs were written during his time in New York, which began in 1974. He has also written songs associated with other artists, such as "El cantante," popularized by Hector Lavoe. Blades's family has roots in Cuba, St. Lucia, Colombia, and Panama. His collaborations with Willie Colón, Ray Barretto, and the Fania All-Stars explored universal themes and he considers salsa to be "urban folklore." Songs such as "Pablo Pueblo," "Pedro Navaja," "Juan Pachanga," and "El número 6" speak directly to various common characters and situations in New York City life, including the subway. These songs resonate with audiences beyond New York and are beloved throughout Latin America and the Caribbean. Blades has been a champion of human rights and political self-determination; he ran unsuccessfully for president of Panama and later served as minister of tourism from 2004 to 2009. He has since returned to acting and performing full-time, showing no sign of slowing down as he enters his seventies.

PANAMANIAN MUSICIANS INVOLVED WITH LATIN AND POP MUSIC

Born in Panama City in 1933, Miguel Ángel Barcasnegras, also known as Meñique, is an important vocalist who established himself as one of the most in-demand vocalists in Panama. Since arriving in New York in 1968, he has recorded and/or performed with Arsenio Rodríguez, Kako Bastar, Tito Rodríguez, Tito Puente, Charlie Palmieri, Hector Lavoe, Vitín Avilés, Celia Cruz, La Lupe, Carlos Barberia, Ray Barretto, and many more. In the early 1980s, he left New York and lived in both Florida and Puerto Rico while continuing to perform.

Luis Camilo Argumedes Rodríguez "Azuquita" was born in Colón, Panama, and started singing professionally at the age of fifteen.[195] He lived in Puerto Rico and worked with Roberto Roena and a number of artists before moving to Los Angeles. He came to New York City in 1976 and started singing with Típica 73. Since he left Típica 73, Azuquita has spent long periods in France and shorter periods of time in New York, even recording with Los Jubilados in Cuba.

Performing and recording as Joe Panama since the 1950s, pianist David Prudhomme released a number of instrumental Latin jazz and boogaloo recordings for the Decca and Victor labels from 1955–68.[196] His group absorbed some of the key members of what would soon become the Joe Cuba Sextet in 1955.[197]

Although not as well known for his music, boxer Roberto Duran was featured prominently in *Latin NY* for his high-profile boxing matches against Sugar Ray Leonard. He can be seen playing congas with Hector Lavoe during the singer's "comeback" 1989 concert on 156th Street and Third Avenue in the Bronx.[198] Later, he would record and perform as a vocalist with his Orquesta Felicidad.[199]

Another group that bears mention is Mandrill, a Brooklyn-formed ensemble of Panamanian brothers and friends that got its start in 1968 and achieved commercial success in the 1970s with "Fencewalk." The band has released many recordings and has been sampled on many hip hop tracks.

Lastly, one of most important Panamanian figures in Latin music since the 1980s is *reguetón* superstar Edgar Armando Franco, known professionally as El General. Born in Panama and raised in Brooklyn, Franco has achieved numerous gold and platinum records and is best known for his work with C+C Music Factory, which is still played today in dancehalls around the world.

After the success of Vernon Andrade, Luis Russell, and Nick Rodríguez, many Panamanian musicians arrived New York City in waves from 1940–60 and established themselves as first-call players.[200] The ease with which these musicians navigated different genres of Latin music in New York is a testament to their musical preparation and their unique experience as Afro-Latin people in the circum-Caribbean. Among these were Frank Harris Anderson, Walter "Gene" Jefferson, Enid Lowe, Carlos Garnett,[201] Victor Paz, Mauricio Smith, Felix Wilkins, Manuel Cobham, and Doc Johnson.[202] Second-wave Panamanian Brooklyn musicians including Billy Cobham, Carlos Garnett, Carlos Ward, Jorge Sylvester, Donald Nicks, Alex Blake, Luis Camilo Argumedes "Azuquita" Rodríguez, David "Joe Panama" Prudhomme, Danilo Pérez, and Santi Debriano also made valuable musical contributions in New York and beyond. US-born Panamanian musicians such as Randy Weston, Eric Dolphy, and Russell Blake have also made great contributions to jazz in New York City and internationally. Panamanian New Yorkers have also been involved in pop music, as seen with Mandrill and Edgar Armando "El General" Franco. The next generation of Panamanian musicians is performing and recording around the world using New York City as a base of operations. These musicians include Geraldo Flores, Renato Thoms, Ricky Salas, Roberto Pitre, Alberto González, and the Conjunto Nuevo Milenio (based in Brooklyn), and others who continue the tradition of their countrymen before them by excelling in all genres of Latin music.

Collectively, the Panamanian musicians discussed in this chapter have made great contributions to the musical fabric of New York City and beyond by collaborating across ethnic lines and in some cases, despite racism. They have been musical directors and conductors of Broadway shows, members of the house band at the Apollo Theater in Harlem, educators with Juilliard degrees, and have toured and performed extensively with jazz icons such as Miles Davis, Louis Armstrong, and Dizzy Gillespie, among others. In the world of Latin music, they have performed and recorded with the godfather of salsa Arsenio Rodríguez, the Fania All-Stars, Celia Cruz, Tito Puente, NEA Jazz Master Cándido Camero, and countless others. These Panamanian musicians also have performed and recorded in the bands of numerous calypsonians both in New York City and abroad. In the case of Nick Rodríguez and Frank Anderson, they broke color barriers of the classical and Broadway worlds as African Americans, as Latinos, and as West Indians. These Panamanian New Yorkers achieved many great milestones in New York's Latin music scene and have transcended genres since their arrival. Although many Panamanian musicians have since returned to Panama, New York City has been the perfect setting for them to excel in ways that were not available to them in Panama at the time that they left.

As detailed throughout this chapter, despite these musical and professional success stories, Panamanian musicians have had to negotiate racial and cultural issues as Afro-Latinos in both their musical and nonmusical lives. Writers such as Vielka Cecilia Hoy have referred to this as "negotiating among invisibilities": always having to place themselves and define themselves among ethnic and racial groups.[203] The Panamanian musicians profiled in this chapter have had unique experiences in New York City that have bound them together and made their experience similar to yet different from that of Cuban and Puerto Rican musicians. Clearly, their experience merits continued study and analysis in terms of the history of making Latin music in New York City.

CHAPTER 5

PUERTO RICAN ENGAGEMENT WITH JAZZ AND ITS EFFECTS ON LATIN MUSIC

As chapter 4 presents Panamanian musicians as honing their craft in Panama and forming part of the circum-Caribbean sphere of Afro-Latin music, in this chapter I position Puerto Rican and Nuyorican musicians based in New York City as protagonists in this same circum-Caribbean space. Puerto Rican musicians in New York City have contributed to and expanded a number of Caribbean and North American musical genres that have become cornerstones of popular music in the United States.

To date, there has been no systematic explanation of how the modern sound of New York's Latin music was developed after World War II by these musicians. Scholarship examining Puerto Rican involvement in jazz in New York City has largely been limited to the period prior to and including the war.[1] The bulk of these and other studies has focused on the musicians who served in James Reese Europe's Harlem Hellfighters (and who I briefly discuss below). Other studies of musicians during this time period have examined groups such as Los Jardineros and other musicians who were well versed in jazz and North American popular music but unassociated with the Hellfighters.[2] Juan Flores does a good job of exploring Latin music performers of the 1960s and 1970s (the salsa generation) and placing them in the larger historical context of Latin music, but he is more concerned with social and political aspects of the music rather than mechanics or structure.[3]

This chapter explores how Puerto Rican and Nuyorican (New York–born Puerto Rican) musicians in New York City used jazz harmony, arranging, improvisation, and musical aesthetics to broaden the sound of Latin popular music from the postwar period into the 1990s and beyond. New York has arguably been the world capital of jazz from the 1940s through the present, and Puerto Rican musicians were active musical protagonists in the jazz scene. This participation in a variety of jazz styles was brought to bear on the development of Latin music in New York. Possessing a truly bicultural outlook, Puerto Rican musicians in New York fashioned a sound and an aesthetic that embraced the best elements of Spanish Caribbean music and African American musical traditions. They made innovative music for dancers while pursuing the latest musical advances and techniques and simultaneously inhabiting multiple musical and social identities. As Flores suggests, this aesthetic would become the New York sound of Latin music that was later marketed locally and internationally as salsa. This chapter also explores other themes discussed in the introduction, such as the importance of clave, the impact and extent of music education among Puerto Rican musicians, family lineages, the importance of folklore, and inter-ethnic collaboration.

HISTORICAL BACKGROUND

Generally speaking, the dominant narrative of the development of Afro-Latin dance music in New York City has a variety of tropes that point to origins in Cuba, appropriation by and inclusion of Puerto Ricans and musicians of other nationalities in New York City, and the eventual molding of a New York sound that was distinct from its Cuban ancestor through the inclusion of specific Puerto Rican musical elements, as well as funk, rhythm and blues, and jazz. Most published scholarship about Puerto Rican involvement in jazz and Latin music in the period after World War II has largely placed Puerto Ricans as adopters, copiers, or appropriators of Cuban music.[4] These authors don't explore the specific musical advances and innovations in Latin music made by Puerto Ricans and others in New York City. They repeatedly choose to measure Puerto Rican musicians and their contributions by relating them to Cuban practitioners. This narrative is also problematic because it ignores many basic historical and musical facts while leaving out the specific ways that musical change and innovations were made and incorporated into Afro-Latin music in New York. It also glosses over the specific protagonists who made these changes and the various settings where inter-ethnic collaboration took place. Angel Quintero Rivera has explored some of the ways that Puerto Rican musicians used jíbaro music, bomba, and plena in Latin music in New York, specifically in salsa.[5] In reality, these three genres enjoyed their own popularity and innovation in New York City during the time period of this study, but their incorporation and inclusion into any discussion of the development of salsa needs further explanation and will be addressed at the end of this chapter. Prior to the development of salsa as a concept or marketing term, these three genres of Puerto Rican music had their own scenes, major musical protagonists, record labels, and distinct audiences in New York City and throughout the United States;

however, the main performers in these distinct genres often came together in venues and theaters that catered primarily to Puerto Ricans and other Latinos, such as El Teatro Puerto Rico and many others.

Rather than using words like *copy* or *appropriate*, I would say that Puerto Rican musicians in New York City *modernized* and made stylistic innovations in Afro-Latin music, because many were active on the scene as professional musicians during major trends in jazz in New York City and brought various stylistic traits from jazz into Afro-Latin music. This was not motivated by a desire to sound Cuban, but rather a natural consequence of playing Afro-Latin music in the center of the jazz universe and of being active and interested in *both* jazz and Afro-Latin music. Ramón Grosfoguel and Chloé S. Georas have written that "the history of Puerto Ricans in New York City is in many ways intertwined with that of the African American community. Puerto Ricans were African Americanized in New York City, the new contact zone of colonial encounter."[6] Interestingly, in music this has played out differently.

As bicultural New Yorkers, Puerto Ricans have historically occupied a position as both "other" and "black" for white musicians; but unlike their Panamanian counterparts, they have also been accepted as whites when performing in all-white groups on the bandstand. A good example of this would be Willie Rodríguez, who joined Paul Whiteman's band in 1938 and, as Basilio Serrano writes, would later go on to record with the likes of Jack Teagarden, Art Blakey, Cal Tjader, Clark Terry, Randy Weston, Charlie Byrd, Woody Herman, Enoch Light, Stan Kenton, Art Farmer, Charles Magnante, Dizzy Gillespie, Herbie Mann, Coleman Hawkins, Sarah Vaughan, and many others.[7] Shared experiences in education and housing with the African American community in New York City have also produced a number of musical and cultural settings in which African Americans and Puerto Ricans have created music together, such as doo-wop, boogaloo, and hip hop, among other genres. As some musicians worked with white bands, others worked in African American musical groups. Juan Tizol, who composed "Caravan" and "Perdido," straddled the color divide spending time recording and performing with Duke Ellington, Harry James, Louis Bellson, Nelson Riddle, Rosemary Clooney, Bing Crosby, June Christy, Patti Dunham, Jimmy Durante, Ella Fitzgerald, Benny Carter, Woody Herman, and Nat King Cole, among others.[8] In the 1950s and thereafter, Puerto Ricans were participating as vocalists in numerous doo-wop groups.

There were Afro–Puerto Rican bandleaders in the 1960s such as Willie Bobo, as well as African American bandleaders Henry "Pucho" Brown and Joe Bataan, who was Afro-Filipino. Juan Flores wrote about the particular case of the Lebrón brothers as an example of discrimination within the community of Latin music that bears quoting in its entirety:

The Lebrón Brothers were also important to an understanding of the boogaloo phenomenon because of issues of race: they were the only explicitly
Black band, their membership and following being overwhelmingly of African
descent, whether Latino or African American. While they did not describe
themselves in terms of Blackness and are quick to point out that the band also
had lighter-skinned members, that reality was a central conditioning factor in
the social experience of the family, and it also had a bearing on their musical
tastes and fortunes. On various occasions they faced discrimination, at times
overt, as when they were turned away by the management of the Casablanca
Club because they would attract "beer-drinkers and not whisky drinkers"—in
other words, the "wrong kind of people."

Though they are not generally disposed to raise the issue, their marginal-
ization within the music industry might well have something to do with their
racial identity and humble social origins, as they were at no point included
within the Fania family, even as "poor relations." As Izzy Sanabria reflected on
the Lebrón Brothers in a 1979 article, "The Lebron Brothers were a reflection
of that time. Dark-skinned and bi-lingual, they represented the Rican with an
afro. The Rican that was caught between two worlds, 'Black' and 'Latin.' The
very things that made them successful, their funk and feeling, held them back
and made them undesirable in certain clubs. . . . The Lebron Brothers never
conformed to the standards of club owners who resented the prietos (Blacks)
con afros." Some of this experience may find expression in their highly popular song from 1982, whose title tells it all: "Sin Negros No Hay Guaguancó." Interestingly, the song's lyrics include in their naming of the Afro-based musical
genres not only the Cuban rumba guaguancó but Afro-Puerto Rican bomba
and plena as well. In any case, the deep irony of the Lebrón Brothers is that as
early proponents of the word "salsa" to describe the music, they barely even
draw a mention in the master narrative of salsa history.[9]

In terms of the Cuban/Puerto Rican dichotomy in New York City, early recordings show the extent to which Puerto Ricans and Cubans were performing
and writing for one another both in the Caribbean and in New York City as
early as the turn of the twentieth century. Puerto Rican *danzas* and *guarachas*
were recorded by Cuban orquestas and musical partnerships between Cubans,
Puerto Ricans, Dominicans, and North American musicians were forged shortly
thereafter in New York City.[10] Ruth Glasser has written about a number of these
musicians. Recordings by seminal groups such as Rafael Hernández's Cuarteto Victoria, Trio Borinquen, Don Azpiazu, and the collaborations between
Panchito Riset and Luis "Lija" Ortíz exemplify these inter-ethnic exchanges
happening between Cuban, Puerto Rican, and Dominican musicians in New
York City from early on in the development of Latin music in New York City.

Independent Latin music expert and researcher Richard Blondet has pointed out other important inter-ethnic collaborations such as "the Puerto Rican-led Orquesta Marcano [1935] featuring Jose Casillas (Dominican) on vocals; the Cuban-led 'Cuarteto Caney' [1939–41], featuring Johnny López (Puerto Rico) on vocals and Rafael Audinot (Puerto Rico) on piano; The Xavier Cugat Orchestra who featured a who's who of Cuban, Puerto Rican and Dominican musicians such as Alberto Calderon (Cuba), Esy Morales (Puerto Rico), Jorge López (Puerto Rico), Pedro Berrios (Puerto Rico), and Dioris Valladares (Dominican Republic), among others; and the Alberto Socarrás (Cuban) orchestra which included Augusto Coen [Puerto Rico], Davilita (Puerto Rico), Mano Hernández (Rafael Hernández's son on drums)."[11] Thus, Puerto Ricans have been collaborating with other Spanish Caribbean musicians for a significant period of time to create Latin music in New York.

PUERTO RICANS AND JAZZ BEFORE WORLD WAR II

Puerto Rican musicians have been active participants in North American popular music for a long time. Before discussing Puerto Rican musical activity in New York City during the period of this study, it is important to look at the preceding years and the extent to which Puerto Rican musicians have been playing (North) "American" music. In many cases, their Puerto Rican origin has been overlooked. One of the best examples of this is Rafael Escudero, who played tuba and bass. Ralph, as he was credited on various records, came to the mainland in 1914 as part of the New Amsterdam Musical Association and later became associated with the Clef Club, an important organization for African American musicians that functioned as a union and venue, among other things, in the early twentieth century.[12]

Thus, Escudero was associated with many prominent African American musicians of his era including the future musical director of the Harlem Hellfighters, James Reese Europe, who led the Clef Club Orchestra. Escudero performed and/or recorded with numerous prominent African American musicians including Duke Ellington (in Wilbur Sweatman's band), Ethel Waters, and Lucille Hegamin. Later he worked with Fletcher Henderson, Wilbur Sweatman, Don Redman and McKinney's Cotton Pickers, Kaiser Marshall, W. C. Handy, and Louis Armstrong, who "thought he was one of the finest tuba players . . . [he] had heard in years."[13] Thomas J. Hennessy wrote that Escudero "was one of the Caribbean musicians prized in New York for reading ability, technique, and legitimate tone."[14]

During World War I, Lieutenant James Reese Europe—who had led two renowned bands of African American musicians in the segregated United

States—was commissioned to assemble an all-black military band. This unit was the NY 15th National Guard, which was later converted into the 369th Infantry Regiment and fought under the French flag because of segregation. They were unofficially bestowed the moniker "Harlem Hellfighters" due to the unit's fighting prowess. In need of wind players, Europe traveled to San Juan, Puerto Rico, and took some of the best musicians from a local municipal band. The 369th Infantry Regiment Band was predominantly made up of African Americans from the United States, West Indians from the US Virgin Islands then based in the US, and Afro–Puerto Ricans from Puerto Rico as well as those who were stateside and now, officially, US citizens as a result of the Jones Act. The Puerto Rican contingent in the band included Rafael Hernández on trombone; Arturo B. Ayala, Gregorio Félix Delgado, Rafael Duchesne Mondríguez, Rafael Duchesne Nieves, Antonio Gónzalez Carcel, Jesús Hernández, Eligio Rijos, Genaro Torres, clarinets/saxophones; Sixto Benítez and José Rivera Rosa, tubas; Pablo Fuentes Más, bassoon; Ceferino Hernández on saxophones; Froilán Jiménez, and Nicholas Vásquez on baritone horns; and Eleuterio Meléndez and Francisco Meléndez on mellophone. Other musicians included Leonardo Cruz, Santiago Sánchez, and José Oller, among others.

When the band returned to New York at the end of the war, they recorded for the Pathé label after having already played many concerts in Europe. They toured as the Hellfighters before Jim Europe's death and continued a bit longer thereafter under the direction of Eugene Mikell. The majority of the Puerto Rican musicians in the 369th Infantry stayed in the US and found work with Harlem Hellfighters spinoff groups.

Rafael Hernández and numerous other Puerto Rican musicians stayed in New York and became important protagonists in the music scene. Hernández worked with composer Pedro Flores for a short time, but once the two separated they each achieved a prolific output of great music. Hernández initially stayed in New York City and led his Jolly Boys band until he was contracted to work in Cuba from 1920–24 at the Teatro Faust. He continued performing and recording in New York City, Mexico, Cuba, and throughout Latin America with his own groups. He would later return to Puerto Rico as a national hero and remains arguably the most important Puerto Rican composer in history.

Other Hellfighters continued their musical activities well after the war. Rafael Duchesne Mondríguez returned to Puerto Rico and continued his musical career teaching and composing music (for which he won many prizes) in a wide range of idioms such as symphony, zarzuela, danza, and hymns until his death in 1986. He also enjoyed a career as a clarinet soloist with the symphony.

His nephew, Rafael Duchesne Nieves, stayed in New York and had success as a composer of the song "Linda Mujer," recorded by Xavier Cugat, Chico

O'Farrill, and many others. The song is known to American audiences as "You never say yes, you never say no." He continued to perform in New York and in Europe with Noble Sissle and others until his death in the 1960s.

Gregorio Félix Delgado performed under the names of Gregory Felix and Felix Gregory. Felix performed with Fess Williams at the opening of the Savoy Ballroom, with Gerald Clark, and later recorded with Lord Invader and others under the name of Felix and the Internationals and Felix and the Cats.

Another important Afro–Puerto Rican musician who was active in the African American music scene around World War I was the violinist Angelina Rivera. Rivera's father Anthony, a clarinetist, and her sister, Santos, a bassist, were all three recruited by Will Marion Cook for his New York Syncopated Orchestra in 1919. Cook's group was made up of African American and Afro-Caribbean musicians and performed throughout Europe as the Southern Syncopated Orchestra. In October 1921, while traveling to Ireland from Scotland, the group survived an infamous shipwreck—with the exception of drummer Peter Robinson—and both Angelina and Santos can be seen with the band in a newsreel covering the event.[15] Angelina Rivera was also credited as a vocalist when Cook's band traveled.[16] Rivera would go on to perform with Spencer Williams and Josephine Baker in Paris and is featured on Baker's November 20, 1926, recordings.[17] One scholar has suggested that Django Reinhardt, the European most associated with violin- and guitar-heavy gypsy jazz, probably heard her play in France.[18] Angelina and her sisters continued to perform as the Cordoba Sisters and can be seen Roy Mack's 1931 short "A Havana Cocktail" with the Hermanos Castro Orquesta.[19]

Jazz icon and pioneer Jelly Roll Morton always accentuated the Spanish tinge in his music, though he really meant the Spanish Caribbean tinge. In addition to hiring Panamanian pianist Nicolás Rodríguez (as seen in the previous chapter), Morton used the Puerto Rican saxophonist Carmelo Jarí in his bands. Carmelo Jarí was a reed master who also performed and recorded with Clarence Williams and others in the 1920s, such as Lew Leslie's Blackbirds orchestra accompanying Adelaide Hall and the Savoy Bearcats.[20]

Multi-instrumentalist Ramón "Moncho" Usera and Louis "King" Garciá were both contemporaries of Carmelo Jarí. Usera performed alongside Jarí and in other bands such as Lew Leslie's Blackbirds and with Sydney Bechet before leading his own groups. García played trumpet with seminal jazz outfit the Original Dixieland Jazz Band, as well as with the Dorsey Brothers. Willie Rodríguez, discussed earlier, was another important Puerto Rican musician who played drum set with Paul Whiteman's group in the 1930s and also worked with well-known jazz musicians such as Dizzy Gillespie, Coleman Hawkins, Sarah Vaughan, Clark Terry, and many others.[21]

Other important Puerto Rican jazz pioneers who I will mention briefly include the aforementioned trombonist Juan Tizol and the often overlooked group Los Jardineros, who played a variety of genres including Eddie Lang/Joe Venuti–style gypsy jazz, predating Django Reinhardt's recordings by at least six years.[22] Los Jardineros was comprised of some of the best Puerto Rican musicians in New York City and they recorded for the OKeh label under the patronage of Arturo Catalá. Catalá sold the recordings in the branches of his store, El Jardín de Arte, throughout Puerto Rico, but they were also sold in New York City.[23] Fernando Arbello is another early Puerto Rican jazz pioneer who was born in Ponce and worked with bands in New York City from the 1920s until the 1960s. He worked with Chick Webb, Fats Waller, Benny Carter, and many others.

After his time in the Hellfighters, the iconic Puerto Rican composer Rafael Hernández lived in Cuba and returned to New York, writing music in many different genres. A striking example of his musical craft is a 1932 recording "Señorita," made with his Orquesta Victor Antillana featuring the Puerto Rican vocalist Davilita. The arrangement starts with a big band swing sound and vocals rendered in Spanish. The band then shifts to a Latin rhythm with the clave heard quite clearly, while the lyrics are sung in English.[24] Richard Blondet points out that the Orquesta Victor Antillano recording had "Francisco 'Paco' Tizol on bass and Rafael de la O on tenor sax, who played with African American ensembles during the 'Hot Jazz' era [of the] 1920s" and that these recordings are stylistically similar to Red Nichol's Louisiana Rhythm Kings' 1928 recording of "When You're Smiling," Duke Ellington's 1932 recording of "Swing Low," and Paul Whiteman's 1935 recording of "I Get a Kick Out of You."[25] Blondet also points out:

> They are all Fox-Trots, whereas Hernandez' "Señorita" is identified as Rumba-Fox. Thus, implying a fusion of North American popular music THEN known or identified as Jazz, with Afro-Cuban elements. In this case, the clave pattern itself. It is beyond just novelty as it is interpreted by musicians with over a decade of interpreting both North American music and Cuban rhythms, genres, etc.).[26]

Thus, as Blondet correctly suggests,

> The discussion[s] of "Latin Jazz" origins are incomplete without giving a recording such as "Senorita," among others, a fair listen. In fact, that entire era is completely ignored on account of the whole "Mario Bauza successfully develops Afro Cuban music and Jazz for the first time" rhetoric starting in 1941 with Machito.

Another important Puerto Rican jazzman is Rogelio "Ram" Ramírez (1913–1994), a pianist, organist, and composer born in San Juan who came to New York at an early age. He would be involved in the swing and bebop eras, working with Rex Stewart, John Kirby, Sid Catlett, Ella Fitzgerald, Charlie Barnet, and even T-Bone Walker. He is best known for his hit song "Lover Man" that Charlie Parker, Billie Holiday, and many others have recorded, popularized, and established as part of the jazz canon.

An interesting and early example of a Puerto Rican musician playing jazz is Ramón "Monchito" Muñoz Rodríguez. His experience shows how the development of the timbales and drum set in Latin music were intertwined with the use of the drum set in jazz. He is best known for his work with Eddie Palmieri. Born in Puerto Rico in 1932, he grew up in New York City and lived near many important Latin musicians on the Upper West Side. His father Rafael was a highly regarded professional bass player. Monchito's first big professional break came playing bongó with Gene Krupa at the age of thirteen. Max Salazar interviewed him about the experience and writes:

> In 1945, there was a club on the East side of Manhattan where the bands of Harry James, Charlie Barnet, Tommy Dorsey, Stan Kenton, and other American jazz icons appeared for two weeks at a time. "One Sunday, my father took me to the club," said Monchito. "Backstage I saw a bongo and I began to play it. Gene Krupa, whose band was the featured act, heard me and urged his manager to convince my father to let me tour with his band. My father declined the offer because I was only fifteen, still attending school, and I spoke very poor English. Mr. Krupa posed for a photo with my father and me. Months later, I went to the Strand Theatre in midtown Manhattan to see the Gene Krupa orchestra. Krupa offered me a recording date. I was recorded playing bongo on the tune 'Chiquita Banana.'"[27]

Monchito went to Puerto Rico in 1944 and started playing timbales there. In a 2000 interview with Victor Réndon he explains:

> In those days timbales were not used in Puerto Rico. I started off playing the drumset. It was not until I came to New York to play with my father that I started to learn timbales. [All of the rhythms] were played with a bell mounted on the bassdrum. [Timbales were not used because] the timbales were played in Cuba for *danzónes*. The orchestras did not use timbales in Cuba either. Of the few Cuban orchestras that I saw there was one called *Orquesta Riverside*, which was very good. They used a drummer. He would just do the band hits. He would not even play *paila* [timbales or their concomitant musical parts]. The *conguero* and *bongocero* would carry the rhythm. It was

later that the drummer started to play time. Now it's different. There are many Cuban drummers that are monsters. It was the same thing with the Latin music here in New York with the orchestras of Tito Rodríguez and Tito Puente. You heard more of the punch figures with not much fill-ins. Now drummers do a lot of fill-ins. But before, music was stricter. If the *paila* was played, it was all that you did. If you did anything else then you were wrong. Now you can change and invent.[28]

Influenced by Humberto Morales and Uba Nieto, Muñoz studied with the legendary New York jazz drum teacher Henry Adler. Muñoz tells Rendón:

He was the teacher to many heavies. He taught drummers like Louis Bellson, Buddy Rich and Ed Shaughnessy. In those years, there were no instructional independence books like the Jim Chapin book, etc. Now we have all these independence books but at that time they did not exist. He would have me play the jazz ride pattern with my right hand while playing quarter notes, triplets, etc. with my left hand. He would take horn stock arrangements such as a trumpet or saxophone part and tell me to read and play the horn part with my left hand on the snaredrum. Now, we have books that deal with that . . . He would have me keep time with the bassdrum and hi-hat. But later, he would also have me play the figures with the bassdrum or hi-hat. He was a very good teacher. He also had a store on 46th street. He had his studio there and sold Leedy drums exclusively. His technician did repairs. So all the drummers from bands such as Les Brown, Charlie Barnett, and Harry James would go there to hang out and study with Henry. They would also take their instruments there because the technician was very good.

The drummer Willie Rodríguez was Muñoz's uncle and they worked together frequently in recording sessions, or Rodríguez would send Muñoz to cover for him if he had too many jobs in the same day.[29] Rondón asked Muñoz about his setup for playing Latin music and jazz with respect to the placement of the timbales, bass drum, and cymbals. Muñoz explains:

If we didn't have to play American music we would set up the timbales directly in front of us like Uba. He would set the timbales in a sitting position with the bass drum in front and a cymbal to the right. They were not played sideways by turning the body like the way many Cuban drummers do today. That is a little uncomfortable. The timbales were placed next to the bassdrum instead of the snaredrum. If we had to play American music, then we would move the timbales out of the way and place the snaredrum just like in a regular setup. The bass drum was mainly used only for band hits or played very lightly. Sometimes I would set up the timbales to the right where the floor tom is normally placed. If I had to play something like a *bolero* I would completely turn around to play the timbales and maybe play the bassdrum with my left foot.

Muñoz elaborates on the manufacturing of cowbells and timbales, which is discussed in chapter 2, but from the above comments one can see how jazz and Latin music drummers were coming together, influencing one another, and teaching one another as they developed their styles. Muñoz further explains the jazz drumming influence in Tito Puente's band:

The first drummer that Puente used was Julito Collazo. He was told by Tito to play the hi-hat pattern (sings) and to play the hits with the band. After Julito left, Mike Collazo came into the band who was a better drumset player. Mike was much more flexible just like Willie Bobo who could play jazz well. Puente recorded a jazz album called Puente Goes Jazz. The drummer was Ted Sommer. When Willie Bobo was in the band, Puente would sometimes play those tunes towards the end of a night in which Willie would play drumset. He couldn't read music but he was a natural.[30]

Finally, when asked to assess his studies with his uncle and Henry Adler with regard to his own playing, Muñoz tells Rendón:

I studied drums here in New York but I always had to play timbales unless I went with Puente to do a show in Florida. But, when I went to Puerto Rico and started playing shows my playing on drumset developed in such a way that I had never been able to do in New York. I got good playing in all the styles. When I was in New York I would sometimes record on bongos for Steve Allen or Perry Como. It would be only like two numbers or so. Afterwards I would sit or stand next to the drummer during the rehearsal or recording looking at the music and checking out what he was doing. That helped me out tremendously in all the different genres of American music which includes playing with brushes. When I went to Puerto Rico to play shows I was prepared because I was educated in that sense.

Muñoz played drum set behind Tony Bennett, Perry Como, and Carmen McRae during their appearances in Puerto Rico.[31] These exchanges with Rendón speak specifically to the ways in which great players like Muñoz applied the best techniques and execution to whatever the musical situation dictated and that they had a high level of preparedness as well as a deep understanding of both Latin dance music and straight-ahead jazz. More importantly, Muñoz shows how ingeniously and fluidly Puerto Rican musicians negotiated these musical worlds. Beyond his prolific recording and performance career, Muñoz passed on his musical knowledge to the next generation and taught musicians like the Peruvian-born drummer Alex Acuña the essentials of clave and playing Latin music on the drumset.[32] The reader is encouraged to see Muñoz in action with Vitín Aviles and Charlie Palmieri from a 1984 video of Palmieri's hit "La hija de Lola."[33]

THE EFFECT OF JAZZ ON NEW YORK'S LATIN MUSIC AFTER WORLD WAR II

From the 1940s on, New York–born percussionists of Puerto Rican descent, such as Sabú Martínez, Ray Barretto, and Ray Mantilla, made important contributions as session and touring musicians with a wide variety of straight-ahead swing jazz outfits that are well represented on hundreds if not thousands of recordings by small jazz groups and big bands. Martínez would take Chano Pozo's place in Dizzy Gillespie's group after Chano Pozo's death, and he also collaborated with jazz drummer Art Blakey.[34] Ray Barretto maintained his Latin jazz groups separately from his Afro-Latin dance-oriented bands throughout his career. However, examples of overlapping and intertwining jazz and Latin musical aesthetics abound in his records. In an excerpt of "A Maracaibo" from Barretto's 1966 recording *El Ray Criollo* with his non-jazz, dance-oriented band, one can hear the brass section playing the main riff from George and Ira Gershwin's "Fascinating Rhythm" (1:22–1:39), and the song before "A Maracaibo" is an instrumental version of Johnny Mercer and Paul Francis Webster's "The Shadow of Your Smile."[35] This makes sense because Barretto had been immersed in both jazz and Latin music since childhood. In the Carlos Ortiz documentary on Machito, Ray Barretto explains that growing up in El Barrio (Spanish Harlem), during the day he listened to the Cuban and Puerto Rican music that his mother "loved" such as Trío Los Panchos, Machito, and Arsenio Rodríguez, but at night he would listen to Count Basie and Duke Ellington.[36] Similarly, Tito Puente has spoken about how the experience of growing up in Spanish Harlem shaped him and his music, learning Cuban music with Cubans while also seeing his favorite jazz bands in Harlem.[37]

Since these pioneers broke ground, many more Puerto Rican musicians based in New York have made outstanding musical contributions in straight-ahead jazz settings. These include Eddie Gómez (bass), Martin Rivera (bass), Ray Rivera (guitar), Hilton Ruiz (piano), Andy and Jerry González (bass and trumpet/percussion), Manolo Badrena (percussion), Gerardo Vélez (drum set and percussion), Chembo Corniel (percussion), Willie Bobo (drum set and percussion),

Jimmy Haslip (bass), Miguel Zenón (saxophone), David Sánchez (saxophone), John Benítez (bass), Bobby Sanabria (drum set and percussion), Willie Martínez (drum set and percussion), Bobby Matos (drum set and percussion), Marco Pignataro (saxophone), and the newest generation of Joel Mateo (drum set), Alex Ayala (bass), and Willie Rodríguez (drum set), among others.[38]

TITO PUENTE AND RAY SANTOS: TWO PIONEERS OF LATIN MUSIC AND THEIR INVOLVEMENT WITH JAZZ

Puerto Rican musicians incorporated a number of techniques from jazz when working with Afro-Cuban–based genres. This a direct result of participation in straight-ahead jazz bands and fluency in the jazz idiom. What is always left out of the creation story of the sound of New York salsa and mambo is the fact that, although the music captured the energy of the streets, it was, in fact, highly codified, studied, written down, and methodical. As seen in the education chapter, iconic musical architects such as Tito Puente (from 1945–47) and Ray Santos (from 1948–52) formally studied music at Juilliard, not only, as some seem to assume, at "UCLA" (University of the Corner of Lexington Avenue).[39] Tito Puente talked about the importance of reading music and musical education with Steve Loza:

> In the studio, man, you had to know how to read music. You went in and you stopped at the eighth bar and you start on the ninth, see, because most of the Latin percussion musicians didn't read much music and they always depended on the ear. Your ear can only go so far. Really, you just have to learn your profession, your instrument. This is it. You have to study . . .[40]

Puente was a complete musician who wrote his own charts and took pride in the fact that he could handle all of the arranging for his band. He told Loza:

> Well, arranger, orchestrator, percussion, vibes . . . you know I was more on the musicianship end. Meanwhile, Machito was also a singer, so he had to depend on Mario [Bauzá] and arrangers. You always need a third party to give you ideas. Not me, I was on my own thing. I'd sit down. I'd write what I wanted, or I'd ask the singer to get his keys or, "What do you think about this?" and I'd do the writing, see? That was the difference there.[41]

Like Puente, Ray Santos had a similarly serious approach to performance and writing. George Rivera asked Santos how seriously he studied, to which Santos replied:

When I moved to the Bronx I started to listen to jazz. I was a big fan of saxophone players like Coleman Hawkins, Ben Webster, and Johnny Hodges. A
friend of mine told me that we could go down to 48th Street and Broadway,
the Strand Building, and for $40.00 they would rent you a saxophone and
include 20 lessons. That was around 1945. So we went down there and sure
enough they gave us the saxophones. They were C melody saxes which are
between an alto and tenor. It looks like a small tenor and sounds like a big
alto. Anyway, I took my 20 lessons with it. Me and my friend Al Alvarez,
who later went out to Las Vegas and became a big band leader, got involved
in it. Eventually we switched up. He got a tenor and I got an alto. We caught
that music fever as young men and we stayed with it for quite a long time. I
started studying formally in 1948 . . . I attended Juilliard for four years and
graduated in 1952. While studying I would play with different bands at night.[42]

Prior to Juilliard, Santos was playing in kid big bands throughout the Bronx
and also in a hotel band in Monticello in 1946. Santos told Mark Meyers what
it was like being a student at Juilliard, who some of his classmates were, and
how his tuition was paid by his working-class parents:

MM: How much was tuition?

RS: About $400 per semester, $800 a year. My father worked as a doorman
  on Park Avenue and my mom worked in a factory that made Raggedy
  Ann dolls. I was an only child, so they could afford the tuition.

MM: Did you fit in at Juilliard?

RS: I felt out of place at first. I was around protégées who were fantastic players. But it didn't discourage me. In fact, being with them encouraged me
  to become a practice fiend to catch up, which I never did [laughs]. Phil
  Woods [pictured] was a year behind me. Teo Macero was there. So was
  Leontyne Price. I was exposed to classical music and became amazed at
  how much jazz harmony came from Stravinsky and Ravel. We'd analyze
  the scores of classical works, which got me into arranging. Eventually I
  was devoting as much time to music theory and writing as I was to practicing the saxophone.[43]

Santos would cut his teeth with Machito and Tito Rodríguez alongside other Puerto Ricans, Cubans, Dominicans, Panamanians, Mexicans, and North
Americans.[44] Santos's improvisations and arrangements exhibit a number of
jazz tendencies. Tito Rodríguez introduces Santos and praises his talent and
ambition in unambiguous terms on the 1968 recording "Ésta es mi orquesta."
Although, the recording has a featured solo and spoken introduction for each
musician in the band, it is evident that during Santos's feature the listener can

hear his comfort in both the jazz and Afro-Latin setting as an improviser applying Latin phrasing to jazz motifs (5:16–6:11).[45] In 1984 Santos began teaching
at CCNY (City College of New York, part of the CUNY system) and would
remain there for twenty-eight years.[46] Nevertheless, despite all of his training,
Santos wanted to connect with the energy of the dancing audience and he
told Steve Loza: "I used to love to memorize my parts so I could just play and
watch. That kind of energy fed . . . you'd feed off of the dancers. You see them
swinging so much; you try to get into their groove and their getting into your
groove."[47] Santos's favorite arrangements that he wrote while with Machito
included "*Cooking the Mambo* and *Azulito* which I wrote after studying with
jazz pianist Hall Overton, who hipped me to modern blues, John Coltrane and
Thelonious Monk."[48]

Reflecting on the interactions between Latin and jazz musicians, Santos
told Meyers that jazz musicians working at Birdland would come up to the
Palladium,

> All the time. Dizzy Gillespie was friendly with Mario Bauza. They had both
> played together in Cab Calloway's band in the late 1930s. Dizzy loved the
> Afro-Cuban rhythms. Milt Jackson came to play with Tito Puente. At Bird-
> land, Herbie Mann, Johnny Griffin, Zoot Sims, Howard McGhee and Brew
> Moore came.[49]

Although there have been countless books and articles written about Tito
Puente and his music, his role in the development of the modern New York
jazz-influenced sound of Afro-Latin music can't be overstated. Prior to studying
at Juilliard, Puente studied arranging and orchestration while serving in the
Navy.[50] Puente used jazz and non-jazz musicians in his groups and achieved
many major musical milestones throughout his career. I will return to Tito
Puente later in this chapter, but the connection to Juilliard is important. In his
book *Tito Puente*, author Tim McNeese discusses Puente's time at Juilliard as
an immersion in the Schillinger system—something that would later capture
Eddie Palmieri's creative imagination as well—which he studied with Richard
Bender. McNeese wrote that, "Schillinger gave Puente the tools he needed to
further his ability to write and arrange music scores . . . Juilliard offered Tito
Puente opportunities that street-level musicians could not have."[51] McNeese
noted that Puente started playing the vibraphone at Juilliard; he would become
a virtuoso on the instrument. However, Puente explained to Loza what he saw
as the limits of the classroom:

> Those lessons at that time were $15. They were very expensive. I used to pay
> $7.50 and the government paid the other $7.50. While I was studying there

I was trying to learn how to write motion picture music. I was interested in that, and graphs and all that—you know, permutation of melodies—and that's what I was really studying there. I found that I wasn't involved in that end. That wasn't really my main interest, so then I stopped studying that. I have my books and everything, but I stopped there about a year or two later and developed my style and all that by actually performing and playing, because everybody has the same books. Everybody goes to school. Everybody studies. Everybody graduates. They get a big diploma. They go home and put it up against the wall, and they just stare at it all the time. "What did you do?" Don't do nothing. You know dentists and doctors, everybody, it's the same thing. You've got to go on and practice. Take every practice and gain experience playing. It's the same thing for musicians. In those days there used to be a lot of jam sessions at places—you could hang out a lot and play—and at places where the musicians used to get together and discuss different arrangements and different tunes, or "Did you hear this record?" and all that, you know. All that is part of your growing up and gaining experience in whatever profession you're in.[52]

Clearly, Puente learned what he thought was important and made it part of his music. He successfully balanced the academy and the street to enjoy an extremely successful performance and recording career. In addition, Puente saw the value in completing an education and would later set up a scholarship fund to help young musicians complete their degrees.[53] Loza's in-depth study of Tito Puente's life and music includes the assessment by Bobby Sanabria that Puente was among the first to incorporate jazz big band breaks into his Latin drumming:

Tito made his early recordings with José Curbelo and Machito [and Tito Rodríguez], proving to be one of the first drummers in Latin music to use a combination of timbales, bass drum and cymbal to "kick" big band figures, often without bongó or conga accompaniment. Tito's concept of chart interpretation and "kicking" of figures was most likely influenced by Mario Bauzá, Machito's musical director. Bauzá had previously served as musical director for Chick Webb, whom jazz historians generally acknowledge as the first drummer to "kick" figures in a big band context.[54]

Puente's sense of biculturalism was not limited to being bilingual but also due to an identification with African American music and jazz. As he told Loza:

Well, I was very much into the black people. We used to call them "colored" people in those days, you know. I was involved with jazz, I went to black

schools—they were right there in the neighborhood. I never had any conflict with them, and musicwise, they were my heroes. Some of them were
my mentors, like Ellington and Basie at the time, and Lucky Millinder, and
Chick Webb . . . all those bands. I was a young fellow, so I used to listen to
a lot of the jazz music in those days, and all Latin music. We got that in the
neighborhood because it wasn't as exposed as the jazz music was. So I'm
very happy I got brought up with both cultures, and we really got along and
developed all our music together through all these years.[55]

Interestingly, by Puente's estimation "Latin musicians can play better jazz than
jazz musicians play in Latin."[56] However, the influence was not just one-way,
and musicians would catch each other's sets at Birdland and the Palladium:

> **Loza**: Besides Dizzy Gillespie, who were some of the other jazz musicians
> coming up to the Palladium to listen?
> **Puente**: Most all of them . . . Charlie Parker, he recorded with Machito . . . the
> trumpet player Howard McGee, very famous at the time. Oh, a lot of the
> trumpet players and jazz players . . . tenor saxophonist Dexter Gordon.
> They all used to come to the Palladium and jam with us and record. Of
> course Stan Getz and all them too.[57]

Trumpeter and conguero Jerry González echoed Puente and explained that
sometimes Latin and jazz musicians would play opposite one another at the
same venue:

> Well, the jazz cats had always been checking Tito out because of the one
> time in Birdland. It used to be Art Blakey, Tito Puente, and John Coltrane,
> all night long. Alternating sets. That's the way the shit should be. It used to
> be like Miles Davis, then Machito, then Dexter Gordon, or Art Blakey. That
> kind of Latin and jazz combination was happening at Birdland. They were
> alternating with each other.[58]

Jazz was important to Tito Puente, who in 1960 made an experimental recording with Buddy Morrow called *Revolving Bandstand* that featured two different
ensembles, one jazz and one Latin, performing arrangements that alternated
between the two ensembles literally right next to one another in the studio.[59]
Loza writes that:

> Latin jazz was invigorated because of the recording, although it was not
> released until 1963; nevertheless, Puente's newer experimentation with the
> jazz mix began directly to affect younger musicians, many of whom would be

spearheading the new salsa movement by the late sixties and early seventies. One such musician was Ray Barretto. who played congas in Puente's orchestra in 1960 and recorded on the Revolving Bandstand sessions.[60]

For Puente and many other musicians, being identified as a Latino and playing/recording jazz and Latin jazz was frustrating. As quoted in Loza's study, Puente explains that:

> I remember I went to the recording company and I went to the president and I told him I was gonna record "Lush Life." You're gonna record Duke Ellington's "Lush Life"? So I told him, "No, It's not Duke Ellington's; it's Billy Strayhorn's work 'Lush Life.'" "You're gonna record that?" "Yeah, this Puerto Rican boy's gonna record 'Lush Life,' baby." And I did it. They can't believe a Latin artist could dig into that kind of music without really going into the thing. "Donna Lee" by Charlie Parker, or Miles Davis, or Monk things, or Coltrane things: "Giant Steps."
>   We were playing Latin music to John Coltrane's "Giant Steps" . . . This is our Latin jazz interpretation.[61]

Unlike Puente, bassist Julio Andino is an unsung hero whose musical contributions to Afro-Latin music have been vastly overlooked. Although Julio Andino is best known for his work as bassist for Machito and Noro Morales, he was steeped in the world of jazz and served as an early point of connection between the jazz and the Latin worlds. Andino worked with many African American bands in Harlem and is said to have originally started in Cab Calloway's band, subbing for his friend Milt Hinton. Andino was viewed as "black" by whites when he went on tours in the South, and he experienced the indignities of segregation: this was even harmful to his health.[62] A photo of Andino playing in Calloway's band used to hang on the walls of Boys and Girls Harbor Conservatory.

Andino's jazz bass contemporaries such as Slam Stewart, Oscar Pettiford, and Milt Hinton were virtuosos in their own right. Pettiford and Stewart recorded pieces that featured the bass as the focal point and lead soloist accompanied by the jazz band, pieces like "Slammin' the Gate" (1945) or Pettiford's feature "Tricotism" (1956). Similarly, in 1941 or 1942 Julio Andino recorded his first bass feature with Machito, "El bajo de Chappottín," arranged by Tito Puente while he was serving in the U.S. Navy, for World Broadcasting transcriptions, a subsidiary of Decca. Andino's bass pyrotechnics can be heard throughout the performance and, like Stewart and Pettiford, the arrangement is built around his performance.[63] The feature was updated in 1947 as "Andino's Peachy-Kato" and recorded with Rene Hernández's Orchestra, although it was probably Machito's band. "Peachy-kato" is a play on the musical term *pizzicato*, meaning plucked not bowed. *Billboard* magazine listed "Andino's Peachy-Kato" in the Hot Jazz section for advance releases on May 14, 1949, so it must have had fairly good distribution.[64]

In the 1940s and 1950s, there were two important piano players who played both dance music and jazz-influenced improvisations in the transitional period before Latin music was marketed as salsa. Pianist and composer Noro Morales was one of the earliest Latin jazz pianists based in New York City. His virtuosity and abilities as a composer, bandleader, and improviser led to many successful recordings and performances for which he was paid very well by the standards at that time. In addition, he wrote a Latin piano method book that was published in New York in 1955. Another important musical contemporary of Morales was Joe Loco, who achieved success by being one of the first Latin artists to record American popular music hits like "Gee" and "Tenderly" in a Latin rhythmic context.

PUERTO RICAN MUSICIANS AND THE PURSUIT OF JAZZ

As I detail in chapter 1, musicians who played Latin music sought lessons in orchestration, harmony, and basic instrumental technique at local music schools and through private instruction. Pianist Gilberto "Pulpo" Colón Jr. connected with his teacher, the Panamanian jazz pianist Nicolás Rodríguez. At the same time, Colón studied solfeo with Alberto Socarrás. Like his Puerto Rican contemporaries, Socarrás had made a name for himself as a jazz flautist despite being Cuban. This combination of formal and *calle* (street) study gave players like "Pulpo" Colón a personal sound that was sought out by bandleaders such as Ray Barretto and Hector Lavoe. In fact, Ray Barretto complimented Colón's sound, because he wasn't only a great technician but his chords and solos sounded like "he had dirt under his fingernails," thus personifying this balance between school and street.[65]

Bobby Valentín is a well-known salsa bandleader, arranger, and bassist who began his career aspiring to be a great jazz trumpeter. Born in Puerto Rico, Valentín moved to New York City in 1956. In an interview with George Rivera, Valentín recalls:

> I was 15 going on 16. I went to New York and studied at George Washington H.S. in Washington Heights. I had some good teachers there and I continued studying the trumpet and music. I was also studying trumpet with Carmine Caruso privately. I also studied with Clyde Resinger. I don't know if you remember him. He's an old-timer. I use to practice on forty-eighth Street near

Manny's. There was a rehearsal studio there. I use to pay just twenty-five cents an hour. That was when I started with Joe Quijano. We had started a group with Chu Hernandez that we named *Los Satelites*. It was just a local band. Professionally I started with Joe Quijano. At the studio I mentioned before I would practice with Art Farmer, Clyde Resinger, and this classical trumpet player by the name of Louie Mucci. We would form trumpet trios and quartets. I learned a lot from those guys. I would ask them a lot of questions and they would teach me many things. That was how I learned most of the music theory I know. From the street and books. I started playing professionally in 1958 with Joe Quijano. I then went on to Willie Rosario's orchestra afterwards. I started arranging while with Willie's band.[66]

On the 1965 album *Young Man with a Horn*, Valentín is pictured on the cover with a flugelhorn, like Farmer. Although the album focused on boogaloo, there is a heavy jazz influence reflected in the material, specifically in the song selection, the horn voicings (heard on "Que pollito"), and the influence of bebop phrasing on the solo improvisations ("The Gate" and "Óyeme bien"). Valentín can be clearly heard playing an idiomatic jazz trumpet solo on Horace Silver's "Song for My Father" (1:40–2:26).[67] Valentín's next album, *El mensajero*, featured many tunes categorized on the back of the album as mambo-jazz.[68]

Johnny Colón and Joe Torres are two other important contemporaries of Valentín's. Colón's *Boogaloo Blues* and Torres's *Latino con Soul* both reflect heavy jazz and blues influences.[69] Both albums are from 1967 and both include English lyrics with Afro-Latin rhythms. Non-jazz-oriented Puerto Rican musicians performing boogaloo, shing-a-ling, and other genres combined English-language lyrics, Afro-Latin instrumentation, and North American rhythm and blues throughout the 1960s. This same formula would be updated and repeated in the 1980s and beyond by artists such as Bobby Rodríguez y La Compañia, Tito Nieves, and many others.

Finally, it is important to mention Mary Lou Williams's mentorship of pianist Hilton Ruiz (1952–2006). Born in New York to Puerto Rican parents, at eight years old Ruiz performed at Carnegie Hall as a child prodigy. Ruiz told Steven Loza that, prior to that, he had studied with Santiago Messorana on 125th Street and that he had worked through the Eslava book of solfège.[70] He studied classical piano but spent many years under the tutelage of Mary Lou Williams. Ruiz straddled the worlds of Latin and jazz music, performing with Tito Puente, Jerry González, and his own Latin jazz groups, as well as performing and recording with Rahsaan Roland Kirk, Frank Foster, Jackie MacLean, George Coleman, Marion Brown, Rashid Ali, Clark Terry, Freddie Hubbard, Joe Henderson, and Joe Newman. In 1988 Ruiz appeared on Marian McPartland's celebrated NPR show *Piano Jazz*; this was a true achievement for any jazz pianist.[71] Throughout his appearance, Ruiz demonstrates his depth as a master jazz musician. Ruiz opening with a slow jazz blues that flows into his chachachá/boogaloo composition "Home Cooking." As Ruiz and McPartland continue talking, Ruiz mentions some of the legendary jazz clubs that he worked at, including Slug's, East Village Inn, and the Five Spot with Charles Mingus for "a week or two at the absence of Don Pullen."[72] Ruiz tells McPartland that working with Mingus "was a great, great thrill and the music was just so well written, and so well organized and he was such a great, great leader."[73] When McPartland asks Ruiz "out of all the people that you have worked with, who would you say was the most influential in your life, to give you something to carry on?" Ruiz answers that it was "definitely Rahsaan Roland Kirk."[74]

Ruiz explains to McPartland that he wanted to learn how to play jazz. He met Mary Lou Williams at the age of eighteen through a pianist named Mark "Markolino" Diamond, who gave him Mary Lou Williams's card with her phone number on it. He tells McPartland:

> So I called her and I went by her house, and I played for her and she was gracious enough to accept me as a student. And on occasion I got a chance to do some copying for her. I was able to be with her when she was composing. And we were just really good friends . . . She was lovely, she was a disciplined person and she believed in feeling . . . The most important thing, the lesson that she tried to teach me, I would guess, besides all the wonderful practical lessons that I learned from her, was to try to put as much feeling into what you're doing as you can . . . She showed me how to play my first chords . . . voicings.[75]

Ruiz tells Loza that Williams taught him for free and what their lessons were like:

> So I used to go to her house every day, and she would tell me more or less what not to do. Because I was really playing, I had records, I listened to McCoy Tyner, I listened to Herbie Hancock, and I was doing my own work by listening to records. Mary Lou gave me insight on ragtime, blues, boogie-woogie, how to play authentically. I got it from a person who was really there.[76]

Ruiz also studied with other jazz pianists, such as Cedar Walton, Roland Hanna, and Barry Harris.[77] After working with Joe Newman and Frank Foster, Ruiz was getting called to play with Clark Terry, Rahsaan Roland Kirk, and others, because Newman and Foster "Actually showed me what to do. My career has been a hands-on, on-the-job training type of thing."[78] By his own estimation, before Ruiz was playing with artists like Tito Puente he really considered himself to be "more of a jazz pianist than a Latin or salsa pianist."[79] Ruiz also says: "The thing was that jazz was my real love. I wanted to become a jazz bebop piano player."[80] This experience of being musically bicultural explains why Tito Puente wanted Hilton Ruiz to be in his Latin jazz band and what being in his band did for Ruiz:

> I was 100 percent uncut bebop. I knew the bebop repertoire, I knew stride piano, I knew boogie-woogie piano, I accompanied singers like Betty Carter, I've accompanied Joe Williams, Eddie Jefferson, who made up the words to those Miles Davis songs, I was his pianist too. I was pure jazz, and that's what Tito wanted. I was a jazz pianist who also played Latin . . . I kind of went away into that because that's what I wanted to do, that was my love. I heard John Coltrane and Charlie Parker and I said I want to play this music. In order to do that I had to separate myself and learn that and then come back again. I came full circle. I rediscovered my roots again, and Tito was the one who helped me rediscover my roots. He straightened me out from all the confusion. He said let's get you down to earth, this is how it goes. You need to do this, you need to do that, and that made me even stronger. So he's my feet firmly now. I can do jazz, but I also have a working knowledge of clave that took a long time. It took a long time to learn how to play clave. Some people can't figure it out.[81]

Later in the aforementioned radio interview, McPartland and Ruiz discuss the "dark" quality of some of Ruiz's chords, as on his composition "4 West," that employ major $7^\flat 5$ voicings that sound to McPartland like Mary Lou Williams. At McPartland's behest and in honor of his teacher, Ruiz then plays a Herbie Nichols composition called "Mary's Waltz" that Williams played often. During the interview, Ruiz talks about his jazz method book, cowritten with Richard Bradley, called *Jazz and How to Play It*.[82] Ruiz explains that the book has "pieces which show how to do a certain style of playing, in other words, like if you have a minor 7th extension."[83] After demonstrating the pattern to McPartland, she suggests playing "Yesterdays" so that Ruiz can use it in the course of an improvisation. McPartland ends the exchange saying, "Wow! That's really good, because they'd also have to practice a few arpeggios and scales . . . oh boy, I think I'll get that book myself." The show concludes with Ruiz playing "one of those Latin rhythms" on their final duet of "I'll Remember April." In a 2012 story covering Ruiz's tragic death in New Orleans, he is quoted saying: "With jazz, you can incorporate everything you've listened to, from all over the world. In my music, you can hear the Latin elements, because when you're playing jazz, you can only play what you are."[84]

Another Puerto Rican musician who should be included in this discussion is eight-time Grammy® nominee Bobby Sanabria, who attended Berklee College of Music on a full scholarship and graduated in 1979. The Bronx-born Sanabria, who is on the Grand Concourse's Bronx Walk of Fame, would go on to lead his own prominent bands as well as work with many important Afro-Cuban, Puerto Rican, Brazilian, jazz, and Haitian bands in New York City. Sanabria has been most visible as an in-demand educator, teaching drum set, percussion, and leading two Afro-Cuban big bands at the New School and Manhattan School of Music. He tours with his own ensembles and gives master classes throughout the United States in addition to running the annual Roberto Ocasio Latin jazz camp in Cleveland, Ohio.

JAZZ HARMONY IN THE SOUND OF LATIN DANCE MUSIC IN NEW YORK

As we have seen from the beginning of this chapter, Puerto Rican involvement in jazz has a substantial history. Musicians at home in both jazz and Latin music found creative ways to seamlessly blend these two musical idioms in the realm of dance music. Some of these creative choices would have their analogues in other genres as well, which I discuss below. One of the most striking examples of the meeting of these two worlds in New York City is Eddie Palmieri's La Perfecta.

Until the creation of Eddie Palmieri's La Perfecta, two-trombone bands were unheard-of in Afro-Latin dance music: They did not exist in Cuba or anywhere else. However, in the jazz world, two trombone stars, J.J. Johnson and Kai Winding, formed such a group in the early 1950s and had a great deal of success. Between 1954 and 1969 they released twelve albums recorded live at jazz festivals and in the studio.[85] Achieving wide popularity with their unique sound, they made a two-trombone sound acceptable and popular. Juan Flores argues that the specific jazz influence of Kai and J.J. "and Barry Rogers's knowledge of the trombone in jazz history going back to the 1920s, would tend to differentiate La Perfecta's trombone parts from those of Mon Rivera, and it may help to explain Palmieri's intense and enduring attraction among African American audiences."[86] Eddie Palmieri adopted the two-trombone sound in La Perfecta and included a flute, so the band became a *trombanga* instead of a charanga, an ensemble with two violins and a flute. At around the same time as Palmieri's first recording with La Perfecta, vocalist Mon Rivera used a three-trombone format for *Que gente averigua*, his debut plena recording with Alegre in 1962: Barry Rogers and Mark Weinstein were affiliated with Palmieri while the third trombonist, Manolin Pazo, was not. Unlike Palmieri, future Mon Rivera recordings would have up to four trombones.

This was not the only aspect of jazz that Palmieri absorbed and used to create his own sound. As an improviser, Palmieri has often employed quotes and musical ideas from bebop and the jazz piano tradition. An early example from his long career can be heard during his solo on "Descarga Palmieri" from the 1964 album *Lo que traigo es sabroso*, where Palmieri quotes the melody line from the bridge of Sonny Stitt's "The Eternal Triangle" (2:05–2:10).[87] As seen in chapter 1, Palmieri had studied piano formally with a number of teachers such as Margaret Bonds and Claudio Saavedra, but his interest in jazz harmony and its applications to Afro-Latin dance music, and later Latin jazz, was cultivated and expanded through one-on-one lessons with guitarist Bob Bianco. It was Barry Rogers who introduced Palmieri to Bianco in 1961 or 1962. Bianco per-formed regularly as a solo act, singing and accompanying himself in a Frank Sinatra style in the Diamond Jim Brady Room at the Sheraton-Tenney hotel near LaGuardia Airport throughout the mid-1960s.[88] Prior to hooking up with Bianco, Rogers had exposed Palmieri "to Charlie Parker, Thelonious Monk, Miles Davis, McCoy Tyner, and other jazz giants, all of whom came to influence his tireless musical development."[89]

Like numerous jazz musicians, Bianco was an adherent of the Schillinger system. During twenty-five years of lessons, Palmieri learned the system for compositional technique but also expanded his harmonic vocabulary. Bianco's influence was not limited to music and, according to Flores,

> Palmieri's growing social conscience and work on developing political lyrics . . . to combine AfroCuban foundations with a jazz-oriented aesthetic . . . were fostered and catalyzed by Palmieri's longtime mentor Bob Bianco, whom he referred to as a kind of savior figure. When he found himself in the doldrums and was lacking in self-confidence he would go visit this close friend in his apartment in Queens where he would get lessons in jazz harmonies and in political economy that proved invaluable to him in his awakening to new creative possibilities. . . . Thanks to intense discussions with Bianco, Palmieri came to attend the Henry George School in Manhattan and learn the rudi-ments of socioeconomic analysis as set forth in books like George's own classic *Progress and Poverty* (1879) and Phil Grant's *The Wonderful Wealth Machine* (1963).[90]

All of this would no doubt influence his later recordings that address social justice and that many cite as historically responding to the political climate of the late 1960s/early1970s, such as *La Libertad, Justicia, Live at Sing Sing*, etc.[91]

In his numerous conversations with Palmieri, Juan Flores has noted that "Ed-die speaks continuously and reverently of the 'structures' of Afro-Cuban music, the basic principles that nourish the musical execution and product no matter what composition or musical cohort is involved."[92] In my own conversations with Palmieri, he is quick to point out how these structures create excitement, motion, climax, and ecstasy. Once, when explaining a particular arrangement with his hands in the air, Palmieri illustrated how he used "unbalanced axes" to excite the listener and this would be in the shape of a diamond. The primary axis is the "imaginary line" that moves up the side of the diamond and the coda is a balancing axis that comes down.[93] He also explained how Gershwin and others used these concepts as learned from Schillinger and how they understood them. In addition to *The Schillinger System of Musical Composition* (1946), Palmieri has discussed the influence of Schillinger's 1943 text *The Mathematical Basis of the Arts* as well as Russ García's *The Professional Arranger Composer*.

Palmieri has a thorough knowledge of chord structures and voicings that he employs throughout his arrangements, accompaniment, and improvisations. While in the early 1960s the harmonic language of John Coltrane and his pianist McCoy Tyner represented the cutting edge of jazz and has since been firmly established as part of the vocabulary, Palmieri incorporated some of their ideas as well as others from modern jazz into his arrangements and improvisations. Palmieri created musical excitement in his arrangements through his use of stacked fourths moving diatonically as well as harmonies from beyond traditional Latin music such as dominant 7♯9 chords and major 13 chords.[94] The sound of many early 1970s salsa arrangements is heavily rooted in these harmonic concepts as typified in Palmieri songs like "Pa' La Ocha Tambo" (1974) and "Oyelo que te conviene" (1975).[95] For musicians in his band like Jerry González, Palmieri's band was really playing Caribbean jazz:

> Constant piano solos, drum solos, trombones were burning out all night. *Inventando mambos* [coming up with riffs], not playing written *mambos* the same way every night. That was what the deal was, they were playing jazz but in the Caribbean tradition: respecting all the elder stuff but taking it another step. Playing modal stuff like Coltrane was playing. Eddie was playing closer to Thelonious Monk and McCoy Tyner than any other Latin pianist that I know, incorporating the traditional way of playing. That was what was happening, there was some musicians playing, thinking, and feeling, and moving, swinging.[96]

For Andy González, who also played in Palmieri's band, the connections to jazz were also obvious:

> We had a very loose, free format with Eddie Palmieri, which he started when we joined the band. Nowadays you see Eddie takes these little piano interludes and sort of flows from one tune to the next without stopping, that kind

of thing. What we were doing was taking our cue from Miles Davis who was doing that also. He would just flow from one tune to the other. So we were doing that. It was quite exciting. We were also doing collective improvisation on stage under the guise of dance music. It was thrilling.[97]

Other sought-after Puerto Rican arrangers such as Louie Cruz (1939–2015) have taken to this modern sound as well, and have even named the arranging book *First Arrangement* by Van Alexander as a source.[98] In his arrangement of "Señor sereno" (1972), Cruz also employs the sounds of modern modal jazz that pervaded the early 1970s (2:17–3:10); the passage is transcribed in chapter 3, musical example 3.15.[99]

The next generation of Puerto Rican arrangers, such as Oscar Hernández, Jose Fébles, and Luis "Perico" Ortiz, also have made use of these voicings and other harmonic techniques taken directly from jazz. Each of these arrangers can be heard applying these jazz arranging concepts to salsa and other Latin music genres on Típica 73's album *Into the 80s* (1981). The interlude of Ortiz's arrangement of "Llévatela," Febles's introduction to "La igualidad," and Hernández's chart for "Facinación" are three excellent examples of how Puerto Rican musicians updated the sound of New York Afro-Latin music through their experience with jazz.[100]

PUERTO RICAN JAZZ MEN AND SALSA

Puerto Rican musicians who were steeped in jazz—Andy and Jerry González (trumpet/percussion and bass), Ray Maldonado (trumpet), Dave Valentín (flute), Hilton Ruiz (piano), Steve Berrios (drums and percussion), Kenny Kirkland (piano), and others—often performed head to head with their colleagues and friends who only played jazz. Salsa Meets Jazz was a music series at the Village Gate that paired salsa bands with a jazz soloist, in which the Latin musicians often outshown their American counterparts who were being featured. Jazz composer and trumpeter Benjamin Bierman remembers that trumpeter Ted Curson was the jazz soloist one evening and his head whipped around when he heard Ray Maldonado play an incredible solo. When pressed for more details, Bierman explains:

When Ray played, it was a bolero, and he sounded like Clifford Brown. It was stunning. And he stood up to take the solo. And as you know, there was tension between the Latin guys and the jazz guys at those things sometimes, as the Latin cats felt like the jazz soloists were getting all the play when they were just as good. They didn't feel that way about everyone, though. And certainly not when guys like Hilton Ruiz were the soloists. But they tried to cut the jazz guys, and they often did.[101]

It is no wonder that Ray Maldonado's trumpet is heard on recordings by Stevie Wonder and other top pop groups of the era. Maldonado had been a child prodigy and, after performing "Cherry Pink and Apple Blossom White" on the *Ted Mack Amateur Hour* as an eleven-year-old boy, he studied at the Brooklyn Conservatory and later at the High School of Music and Art.[102] Many of the names mentioned above brought their jazz chops to salsa gigs, and many formally studied jazz. Andy González studied with jazz bassist Steve Swallow; his brother Jerry studied at the New York School of Music alongside Kenny Dorham. As seen in chapter 1, Puerto Rican musicians such as Al Acosta and those of other ethnicities would pay five dollars to practice their sight-reading in reading bands at Lyn Oliver's studio, where they would play through the books of jazz big bands such as Duke Ellington and Count Basie.

In another publication (and in chapter 1) I have written about a period in the early 1970s where numerous young musicians would gather at Rene López's house in the Bronx and study old recordings.[103] Eddie Palmieri insisted that any young musician head to René's house for the ongoing intensive listening sessions as an essential part of joining his band. At these listening sessions Nicky Marrero, Andy and Jerry González, Willie Garcia, Joe Santiago, Nelson González, and even Rubén Blades would sit with older musicians like Chocolate Armenteros and Marcelino Guerra, who would help them decipher the hidden aspects of the music, like a recorded shout-out to a player, or would provide historical background to a particular recording session. At the same time, Rene López explained that the relationship was reciprocal. In the liner notes to Andy González's Grammy®-nominated recording *Entre Colegas*, I write:

> For Rene, "it wasn't a one way street . . . it was mutual" in terms of the exchange of knowledge. At Rene's house they listened to *típico*, but back at Andy and Jerry's they were hipped to John Coltrane, Archie Shepp, McCoy Tyner, Thelonious Monk, and other jazz masters. Andy and Jerry were "at the center of a new movement, more in line with the jazz community." These experiences led to a major paradigm shift in Latin jazz. For Rene, up until this time there was jazz Latin, epitomized by Errol Garner, Gene Ammons, Billy Taylor, etc. who added a percussionist to the jazz group in a supporting role. In contrast, Latin jazz would be along the lines of Tito Puente, Mongo Santamaria, and Cal Tjader who played jazz standards in the Latin setting with clave-based arrangements and phrasing. "The real historic break in Latin jazz is . . . the Fort Apache [band]," led by Andy and Jerry, because they would shift from a walking bass and swing to a clave-based feel within the same

arrangement: "This was their heart, this was their experience . . . the first time the marriage between Latin and jazz becomes seamless."[104]

Jerry González has explained to me that, when listening to pieces like Monk's "Evidence," it was easy for him to hear a connection to the pieces that he, his brother, and their friends were hearing in René López's house and the jazz that he was also listening to, specifically Frank Emilio's "Gandinga, Mondongo y Sandunga."[105] This would be the framework for him and his cohorts to move between jazz and Latin music. González told Steve Loza: "We were all searching, trying to prove ourselves, expand our vocabulary in the language. I was studying Trane and Diz and all those cats at the same time I'm studying Los Muñequitos de Matanzas to get the drum thing down."[106]

For Jerry's brother Andy González, these types of musical innovations only happened because "we studied both idioms [jazz and Latin] extensively."[107] With experience in the jazz loft scene and a forward-looking view of music, the brothers teamed up with Eddie Figueroa, who ran the New Rican Village, a venue dedicated to poetry and music of the Nuyorican and Puerto Rican experience. As music director, Andy González had a venue and an outlet to experiment further, both with his band Libre (co-led with Manny Oquendo) and other ensembles that he directed.[108] Ed Morales has profiled Figueroa's importance in creating a venue for New York Puerto Rican musicians, and chapter 7 discusses how the New Rican Village's rise and fall paved the way for the Mariel Boatlift musicians and a subsequent venue, Soundscape.[109] Flores writes that, compared to the musicians who were associated with Fania Records and its roster of popular artists, those who performed at the New Rican Village, "rather than a star status, they achieved a kind of underground, cult reputation among audiences seeking more solid, innovative, and socially rooted musical offerings."[110] The venue was a meeting place and laboratory for politics, culture, and the arts, including theater, fine arts, and music. As a result, "Libre and the González brothers thus became the central musical force of a vibrant, avant-garde setting that was outside the pervasive influence of the commercial network of record labels, DJs, promoters, and club owners."[111] A look at some of the setlists and personnel in the Soundscape archives collection at the Jazz History database from weekly performances billed as New Rican Village that ocurred at Soundscape shows how integral the González brothers were to this particular scene, along with many other musicians who worked through jazz, and a variety of Cuban, Puerto Rican, and Latin American genres.[112]

Steve Loza suggests to Jerry González that his generation was perhaps more bicultural than the previous generation, which included Puente, Rodríguez, and Machito, but González maintains that the previous generation was just as bicultural:

Loza: But a lot of guys your age did get into the jazz thing, because they were getting both. You were a very bicultural generation compared to Tito Puente or Machito.

González: Both of them, just by being in New York, they got it. Even if they weren't in it, they got it.[113]

González sees the lineages of Tito Puente and Machito as having cognates in the jazz and swing world. He explains to Steve Loza:

To me it's the same parallel as Duke and the Basie band. Duke's band became more harmonically and symphonically expansive. Whereas the Basie band I would parallel to Puente, I would parallel the Duke Ellington band to Machito. Even the sound of Machito's saxophones and horns was coming out of the Duke Ellington sound, the way the saxophones were voiced and the chords that were written for the orchestra were voiced in the Duke Ellington way. But Puente was more like the Basie band, a riff band. They worked on riffs; they weren't as orchestral in the beginning as Macho. And it was more percussive: it was a riff band, man, working the band with drums . . . Bauzá was much more profoundly affected and actually played in jazz bands, like Chick Webb, Cab Calloway. Before Machito's band was even formed, Bauzá had worked that whole black big-band jazz thing, whereas Tito didn't, Tito's experience in that is not as profound as Marío's . . . Tito played a little swing but not to the extent that Bauzá did.[114]

New York–based Puerto Ricans were fluent in various aspects of US musical culture, and this was not limited to jazz. Flores explores this idea when discussing bicultural fluency and the boogaloo genre with Joe Cuba:

The legendary, irreverent bandleader explains why he and his group were ideally qualified for playing Latin music while grounding themselves in an "American" musical aesthetic. "The American-born were the proponents of boogaloo. Latin bands couldn't play it as well. You had to have the American influence to get into that bag. I'm 'Rican all the way. My bones are 'Rican, my food is 'Rican. But I was born with the American Hit Parade."[115]

Puerto Rican musicians based in New York were wide open to collaborations across genres. In his forthcoming work on "ethno jazz," David Evans points out that the Ethiopian jazz percussionist Mulatu Astatke made two albums in New York City in the mid-1960s.[116] Astatke's two Ethiopian Quintet recordings have Puerto Rican and African American musicians who sing in Spanish on tracks such as "I Faram Gami I Faram." The musical arrangement of this particular track is a guaracha and features all of the stylistic and performative expectations of the genre as executed in 1964. Other tracks on the *Afro-Latino Soul* albums feature boogaloo, guajira, and son montuno, sometimes with the sounds of animals, perhaps to invoke the image of Africa.[117] With few exceptions these recordings sound quite similar to and bear the strong influence of small-group Latin jazz instrumentals from the same era, particularly the vibes-focused sound of the Puerto Rican percussionist Joe Cuba and the American vibraphonist Cal Tjader.

While the focus of this chapter has so far been on how Puerto Rican musicians brought jazz sensibilities and concepts to Latin music, it would be careless not to look at how they also added specific Puerto Rican elements to Latin music's largely Cuban frameworks. Juan Flores has explained how the Willie Colón and Hector Lavoe album *Asalto Navideño* (1971) added "the cadences of Puerto Rican música jíbara" through the incorporation of Yomo Toro's Puerto Rican cuatro to "the familiar trombone and conga sounds of New York salsa," thus creating an internationally popular Christmas album.[118]

In addition to the cuatro and jíbaro music forms that Colón employed, Flores writes that one of the chief means by which Colón asserted Puerto Rican identity was to use "colorful Puerto Rican colloquialism and folkloric references present in most of the lyrics."[119] Thus, what writers such as Rondón had viewed as musically unsophisticated was in fact a way of strongly asserting one's Puerto Rican cultural identity and broadcasting specific linguistic and cultural codes in a setting that traditionally held Cuban models up as the standard. In this way Colón's work was groundbreaking, simple yet sophisticated, and a self-evident critique of Cuban supremacy in the practice of Latin music in New York. Furthermore, the success of the boogaloo genre was predicated on bicultural fluency, "the same back-and-forth interweaving of verbal and musical languages," in this case African American language and culture with Spanish Caribbean language and culture.[120] Flores also points out that when Eddie Palmieri won his first two Grammy® awards for Latin music, the general assumption was that the Fania label had single-handedly built the commercial success of the music.[121] However, his win also showed that "the sheer force and quality of his very idiosyncratic music" brought him, and his "fledgling" label Coco, success outside of Fania's reach.[122] I would argue that the very idiosyncrasy of Palmieri's music that Flores refers to is indeed the connection to and experimentation with jazz.

SOME FINAL THOUGHTS ON THE JAZZ INFLUENCE IN LATIN MUSIC

At its apex from 1960–85, the Latin music scene in New York and its immediate surroundings (including the distant Catskill Mountains resorts) was home to countless dancehalls and nightclubs. These venues offered formal and informal dance competitions as well as formal and informal instruction. New York City Latin dance venues provided steady work for musicians and arrangers, who competed for billing and popularity, but more importantly they allowed for the development of new sounds and musical trends as long as they met the demands and the approval of the dancers. In a 1951 live radio broadcast from the jazz club Birdland, Tito Puente illustrated this point:

> Thank you very much, ladies and gentlemen. First of all, I want you all to know it's a great pleasure for the boys and myself being down here in Bird-land for the first time. Thank you. We're trying to keep up with times musically . . . bring some of the originality of Afrocuban music, mambo music and put some modern chord changes into them . . . and try to swing as much as we can. Our next number shows a little of this. How about playing "Camille Mambo" boys? And see what I mean.[123]

With these spoken words Puente brilliantly articulates the Spanish Caribbean musicians' seemingly competing goals in New York City that they shared with many others: The idea was to continue to grow, develop, and innovate, but the dancer could not be left behind, as was the case for bebop and modern jazz made by Puente's contemporaries. Andy González noted that Bud Powell's trio was playing opposite Tito Puente at Birdland during this engagement and that Powell's 1951 composition "Un Poco Loco" was undoubtedly influenced by Puente.

Forty years later, Puente explained his approach:

> I love Latin Jazz because it gives me a chance to become creative, because I've done everything that's supposed to be done in Latin music throughout the years. I've been involved with it forty years and I've extended myself as much as I can without losing our authenticity, of our music. When you talk about mambo, chacha, merengue, or guajira, or son montuno, if you're talking about typical music, you have to always maintain the roots of that music so you don't lose the authenticity of the music. But in Latin jazz you're more flexible. What I try do in Latin jazz is become more creative, use jazz melodies and always cultivating our Latin rhythms and keeping the roots there all the time. And that makes me an exceptional arranger in the case where it gives

me a chance to do some of Monk's things and Miles Davis, and other great composers . . . Combining their music and the Latin music, you have to know how to play jazz and you have to know how to play Latin.[124]

Thus, the jazz influence in New York's Latin music was reciprocal, and Afro-Latin music equally influenced jazz in New York.[125] Researchers such as Chris Washburne have written about some of these connections, particularly through an examination of rhythmic vocabulary. Washburne cites Max Roach, in particular, as having incorporated multiple simultaneous Afro-Latin rhythm section parts into the jazz drum vocabulary and it remains striking how much other drummers such as Kenny Clarke, Roy Haynes, Elvin Jones, and many others did, too.[126] Some jazz drummers like Milford Graves and Pete "La Roca" Sims performed in the Latin percussion chairs of Latin bands. Jazz improvisers have quoted popular Afro-Latin music in their improvisations for some time; one example of many is an entire chorus of Lee Morgan's trumpet solo on "Dish-water" (5:16–5:26), which consists of the introductory figure of "El Manisero" (The Peanut Vendor): is this a nod to Louis Armstrong or the ubiquity of the Cuban composition in US musical culture?[127]

In this book and in other writings, I explore the ways in which musicians and dancers of many different ethnicities, including Cubans, Jews, Panamanians, and others, contributed to the evolution of Afro-Latin music and its practice in New York.[128] One huge part of this history is the impact of jazz on the modern sound of Afro-Latin music, and that is largely due to the musical and social biculturalism of both Puerto Ricans born in New York City and Puerto Ricans who came to New York. Puerto Rican arrangers and instrumentalists updated the sound of Afro-Latin music to reflect the best of both worlds by engaging with jazz and employing jazz concepts in a variety of ways. In the realm of traditional Afro-Latin dance music that the seamless blending with jazz created, continual musical innovation would leave a permanent effect.

At the same time, they had to face the reality that non-Latin musicians have historically been unable to play Latin music. Tito Puente explained to Steve Loza what experiencing that difference really meant for him and other musicians:

It's very difficult to put a big Latin band on the Johnny Carson Show. He doesn't need me. He has a big band of his own there. I can't go on by myself. Buddy Rich goes out there. He does it by himself, but that's jazz; they can go in. Count Basie—I've seen play by himself [on the show], but you'll never see a Latin artist go by himself. You can't, because they can't play our music, they can't interpret it. They're great musicians, naturally, but you can't play a guaguancó on Johnny Carson because the people that he caters to don't know what guaguancó or a typical Latín tune is, so you have to go with a semicommercial thing. Maybe an "Oye como va" they might understand, or a "Tico Tíco," a Brazilian thing, or "Chin Chin Chi"—Cugat type music, and that's not my music, really, so it's a challenging thing. You're in between, and then you don't know what to do. . . . So we're Latins and yet we're not. We still got to play commercial music for the masses [and shows such as] Johnny Carson. Then our Latin people put us down for playing that type of music, so we're in the middle of both sequences. And when you cater to masses you never know which way you're heading. You could become lucky or not. You have to know what direction you're going, and it's very difficult.[129]

The deep imprint that Puerto Rican musicians have left on Latin music in New York City can't be underestimated. However, for Juan Flores, the internationalization, proliferation beyond New York City, and commercialization of the New York sound of Latin music as innovated by Puerto Ricans based in New York would eventually erase this important history and contribution:

It was at that time, the later 1970s, when the story of music called salsa and the history of Latin music in and of New York City came to diverge . . . This global proliferation of salsa may be a source of pride for Latin New Yorkers as well as for Cubans and Puerto Ricans in their home countries, but the shift clearly involved the unmooring of the musical expression from its community base and social context. While the music itself remains guided by the examples set by Tito Puente, Celia Cruz, Eddie Palmieri, Willie Colón, Ray Barretto, and other New York pioneers, the meaning and reference point for the term "salsa" have mutated. Rather than convenient and commercially savvy shorthand for the varied Cuban and Nuyorican stylistic repertoire emanating from the New York setting, salsa has for several generations now served as a catchword for the "Latino" lingo of a global soundscape devoid of any particular geographic or cultural foundation.[130]

Unfortunately, the richness and great variety of music made in New York by Puerto Ricans has been ignored in favor of an incomplete retelling of the transformation of Cuban music by Puerto Ricans into Latin music and salsa. In fact, Puerto Rican New Yorkers have been involved in many genres of music beyond those associated with Cuban music; future historiography and analysis should consider the wide range of music beyond Cuban-derived styles when examining the role of Puerto Ricans in the making of Latin music and non-Latin genres in New York City. The modern sound of Latin music that was created, in part, through Puerto Rican engagement with jazz, was then spread throughout the Caribbean and the world. This valuable contribution alongside those made by Cubans, Jews, African Americans, Panamanians, Dominicans, and others, exemplifies how musicians in New York shaped the international sound of Latin music.

CHAPTER 6

"WHERE'S BARRY?"

Another Look at Jews and Latin Music in New York City

In the highly enjoyable early 1960s descarga (jam session) recordings of the Alegre All Stars, one skit stands out, in part because of its ordinary delivery, but also for what it doesn't say. Throughout the recording, in *Waiting for Godot* comic fashion, two voices ask one another for the whereabouts of particular musicians who were scheduled for the date and they provide answers to one another that range from the sublime to the ridiculous. Before the second track, the following exchange occurs:

Al Santiago: "Hey Manny, where's Barry?"
Charlie Palmieri: "Barry couldn't make it."
Al Santiago: "Oh."
Charlie Palmieri: "So Kako called Mark."
Al Santiago: "Called who?"
Charlie Palmieri: "Mark!"
Al Santiago: "Oh, okay."[1]

This particular skit is not really funny at all because there's no punch line. If there is a punch line, it's that one highly respected and beloved musician is being substituted by another. However, a closer look reveals that the first musician is a Jewish New Yorker named Barry Rogers who is considered to be the godfather of the New York Latin trombone sound: the sound that everyone emulated and is told to emulate. The second musician mentioned by name is his friend, collaborator, and fellow Jew Mark Weinstein, who worked alongside Rogers in Eddie Palmieri's seminal group La Perfecta, and who would eventually ditch the trombone for the flute. The recording in question dates from the midpoint of this book's focus of 1940–90, demonstrating how deeply Jews have been ensconced within Latin music for some time.

Scholarly focus on Latin music in the Catskill Mountains resort scene has left out the fact that Jews were sponsoring Latin dances with live bands as early as the 1930s in New York City, if not earlier. Thus, the Latin music scene in the Catskills was an extension of the New York City scene where working- and middle-class Jews could leave New York during the summer and make an affordable escape. In a previous publication, I have examined the different roles that Jews have played in the Latin music industry as performers, arrangers, producers, dancers, and radio personalities.[2] Both chapter 2 and this chapter demonstrate that working- and middle-class Jews identified with and appreciated Latin music in New York City as an outlet for enjoyment, socializing, and also for artistic expression.

As important as the contributions of Jewish sidemen and arrangers have been to Latin music, it is important to amend the historical record and examine a number of themes more closely. This chapter begins with a look at how Jews and non-Jews represented themselves in Latin music as well as inter-ethnic collaboration. Jewish engagement with Latin music took place throughout New York beyond the Palladium Ballroom, and I present the dance announcements in New York newspapers from 1947–61 in order to show the extent of activities. Next I address the impact of two important women who made major contributions to Latin music: Abbe Lane and Eydie Gormé. These two American Jewish women—one Sephardic from the Bronx, and the other Ashkenazi from Brooklyn—enjoyed long careers, and their achievements performing and recording Latin music remain overlooked in the literature to this day. While their musical and extramusical activities were fodder for the tabloids, both women were serious artists.

This chapter briefly covers Larry Harlow's career and examines another major musical protagonist, Barry Rogers. I also show how seriously one dancer, Ira Goldwasser, delved into Afro-Cuban music for his life's duration. I will begin by showing that Jewish support of Latin music in Jewish venues was quite extensive in New York City during the time of this study. It is important to mention some important people beyond the spotlight that I will not discuss here, but whose work I plan to address in the future: recording engineers Jon Fausty, Fred Weinberg, and Irv Greenbaum, who literally helped shape the sound of Latin music in New York City.

JEWISH SELF-REPRESENTATION IN LATIN MUSIC

In a previous publication, I have looked at some of the ways in which people of Chinese descent in the Spanish-speaking Caribbean have been portrayed in popular music of the region and in the diaspora, and I explored some of the ways that they chose to portray themselves.[3] In some cases, Chinese Cubans and Puerto Ricans have self-orientalized, choosing to inhabit Asian stereotypes and even exaggerate them. However, many artists have gone out of their way to embrace their heritage, acknowledging it in their art through lyrics and/or onstage presentation choices, album covers, etc., and to demonstrate that they are as competent and creative as anyone else. Both of these creative approaches exist simultaneously alongside racist representations of Asians recorded and performed by non-Chinese Latino musicians.

A similar situation regarding the representation of Jews can be found in Latin music performed and recorded in New York during the period of this study. A compilation of recordings issued by the Idelsohn Society for Musical Preservation, *It's a Scream How Levine Does the Rhumba: The Latin-Jewish Musical Story 1940s-1980s*, points to the Catskills connection with recordings that feature particular Jewish-owned or -patronized hotels in their titles. These include "Mambo La Concord" by Machito and his Afro-Cuban Orchestra, "Grossinger's Cha Cha Cha" by Tito Puente and his Orchestra,[4] and "Raleigh Ruff" by the La Plata Sextette. These recordings with Catskills resort names echo the sentiments of musician Pete Sokolow who explained to Mark Schwartz that "In the fifties, every Catskill Mountains hotel had a person come in, maybe once or twice a week to teach the cha-cha and variations to these forty-, fifty-, sixty-year-old people. And it became the Jewish national dance." After tallying up all of the legendary Latin bands and the hotels that they each played at, producer Andy Kaufman tells Schwartz: "So the Jews that went up to the Catskills also heard the music that [was] played in the most authentic styles by these bands. They weren't watered down cha-cha bands. They were the real thing."[5] The balance of the recordings on the two-CD compilation consists of a mix of Jewish musicians playing Latin music as sidemen in Cuban and Puerto Rican bands or as novelty numbers alongside non-Jewish Latin artists performing Jewish or non-Jewish songs with titles that associate them with Jewish venues in the Catskills.

Jewish artists such as Mickey Katz used the Yiddish language and Cuban rhythms to make good fun of Jewish fascination with Latin music. This is evident in his recordings of "Gehakte Mambo" (1951), "Yiddishe Mambo" (1958), and "The Wedding Samba" (1950). Irving Kaufman's "Moe the Schmo Takes a Rumba Lesson," is probably the example that is most self-orientalizing with its use of Yiddish and Yiddish-accented English and would have its Cuban Chinese analogue in Hilda Lee's recorded version of "Pachanga" in Cantonese and heavily accented English. The Barton Brothers' "Arriba" would also fall into this category with its heavy use of the clarinet and Yiddish and English banter. Ruth Wallis's "It's a Scream How Levine Does the Rumba" is a direct comedic jab at the *mambonik* (Jewish mambo aficionado) with double entendre commenting on how Mr. Levine now knows how to use his maracas. The Barry Sisters' "Channah from Havana" (1956) also uses Yiddish, klezmer, and Cuban music to make fun of a woman who returns from a trip to Havana a changed woman. Other early Jewish performers of Latin music such as Irving Fields made several novelty albums in this vein as well and continued working in the idiom.[6] Fields performed and recorded regularly until his death at 101 in 2016. Two instances of non-Jewish artists also incorporating Yiddish as a gimmick and parody are found in Al Gómez's "Sheyn Vi Di Levone" (1950), and Slim Gaillard's "Meshuganah Mambo" (1956).

NON-JEWISH PORTRAYALS OF JEWS IN LATIN MUSIC AND INTER-ETHNIC NEGOTIATION

A number of non-Jewish artists have recorded "Latinized" versions of Jewish traditional songs—both Sephardic and Ashkenazi repertoire—in a variety of formats. Some of the best known include versions of "Hava Nagila" recorded by Celia Cruz and La Sonora Matancera (1958) as well as Mon Rivera. Johnny Conquet's 1958 album *Raisins & Almonds Cha Cha Cha & Merengues* is also representative of non-Jewish Latino interpretations of Jewish music in a variety of Latin styles.[7] Pupi Campo's recording of the Tito Puente arrangement "Joe and Paul" (1949) was originally "a Yiddish radio jingle for a clothing store in Brooklyn, before being popularized as a Borscht Belt parody by Red Buttons and the Barton Brothers."[8] Another fascinating recording from 1961 is *Mazel Tov, Mis Amigos* by Juan Calle and His Landsmen on Riverside Records. In her article about a 2010 concert commemorating the album, Tamara Straus interviewed musicologist Roger Bennett from the Idelsohn Society for Musical Preservation, who called the album

> one of the greatest ruses of 20th century American pop music. Neither Juan nor his Latin Lantzmen were actually *lantzmen* (Jews), and only some were actually Latin. Juan was John Cali, an Italian American banjo picker and radio veteran best known for his work with the Vincent Lopez Orchestra. His Latin Lantzmen included some of the biggest names in '50s and '60s Latin music: conguero Ray Barretto, timbales guru Willie Rodriguez, pianist Charlie Palmieri playing alongside African American jazz greats Clark Terry, Doc Cheatham, Lou Oles and Wendell Marshall. The sole lantzman was Yiddish vocalist Ed Powell.[9]

These musicians represented some of the best in New York at the time of the recording. Another musically interesting aspect of this recording is how John

Cali used his banjo to evoke the essence of the Cuban tres or Puerto Rican cuatro.

In 1970 Johnny Pacheco would record "Shalom Malecum" [Alechem], which was a cover of Justi Barretto's legendary 1969 rumba recording, "A Nueva York." The original uses a Yoruba and Congolese phrase associated with Santería and Palo, two Afro-Cuban religions. The Pacheco cover does as well, but adds "shalom aleichem," the Hebrew version of the Congolese and Islamic greeting, "salam alekum." In the cover and the original, Barretto makes some interesting comments about the Jewish community of New York City:

> *Aquí viven más judíos que lo que tiene Israel.*
> *Ay comay, ya suelen ser, de la población un tercio, son dueños de los*
> *comercios, y cuando ellos están de fiesta, la ciudad se queda muerta,*
> *nadie se puede mover.*
> *Ay, Dios . . .*
>
> More Jews live here than what Israel has.
> Oh sister, they are usually a third of the population, they are the own-
> ers of the businesses
> And when they celebrate their holidays, the city is totally dead, and
> no one can do anything.[10]

This is, perhaps, one of the only lyrical references to Jews in Spanish Caribbean music made by Spanish Caribbean musicians in New York City, but Barretto's perception is quite revealing: the Jewish community owns all of the businesses and non-Jews can't get anything done during the Jewish holidays.

In the Caribbean, Jews were also involved in music promotion, as exemplified by Sam Rosenberg, who formed the Caribbean Jazz Society, a subsidiary of the Jazz Club of Puerto Rico. Rosenberg, "assistant manager at the Virgin Isle Hilton, was first to promote and stage concerts of Afro-Cuban and Latin-jazz in Puerto Rico and to direct a concert called 'Jazz on the Negev' that featured jazz with an Israeli flavor."[11]

In Cuba, Carlos Argentino (born Israel Vitenszteim Vurm), who performed and recorded with Cuban music icons La Sonora Matancera in the 1950s, is probably the first major Jewish recording artist to achieve mainstream success throughout the Spanish-speaking world. Larry Harlow, whose career I have documented elsewhere, is widely acknowledged as the "marvelous Jew," and since the late 1960s he has remained a powerful force in Latin music. There have also been many highly proficient artists who have adopted Latin-sounding names to seek work as Latin music performers. These include Alfred Mendelson (Alfredo Mendez), Harvey Averne (Arvito), and Alfred Levy

(Alfredito). A great number of sidemen in the top Latin bands of the era were also Jews. For the Idelsohn Society collection, Eddie Palmieri is quoted addressing this topic:

> You used Jewish musicians or you didn't have a band! They did the show bands, everything . . . They became quite astute as Latin players . . . So if you wanted quality from your timbre, your attack, your intonation, then you had to go for the American players, and they were mostly Jewish who ran the ball game . . . Jewish players wouldn't stay with any band steady. You booked 'em. Except a steady band, for a while they'd stay—Tito Puente had his four trumpets for a while. But in general, they were all doing one-nighters. Club dates is what they called them. You went to the union hall on Mondays, Wednesdays, and Fridays, and you booked everyone you could find.[12]

Jews also worked as arrangers: the Dominican-born Manny Albam, Harold Wegbreit, and Marty Sheller made important contributions to iconic recordings by Mongo Santamaria, Tito Rodríguez, Tito Puente, and the La Playa Sextet, among others.

For Latinos who worked in the Catskills, there was appreciation for being able to make their own music for a crowd who wanted to dance to it. In writing about the Sid Caesar photo that appears later in this chapter, Aurora Flores discussed the experience with one of the musicians in the photo, trumpeter "Chocolate" Armenteros, who "fondly recalls the Catskills Resorts of Upstate New York as close as he could get to Cuba without the palm trees."[13] Armenteros told her:

> For more than a decade we played steady summers with Machito at the Concord Hotel. It was like a small City in itself. We stayed in the bungalows, hanging with the rest of the entertainers, the staff and those that couldn't afford the fancy hotels . . . After the Sunday matinee show we'd all ride back to the bungalows by car and have a good old fashioned Cuban fiesta outside, roasting a pig on a spit with white rice, black beans, rum and coke. We partied together like family. My son even learned how to golf there.

Vocalist and percussionist Jimmy Sabater (1936–2012) commented on some of the funnier aspects of the cultural exchanges between Latino musicians and Jews at the resorts:

> We used to wear yarmulkes for Shabbos, man, in the dining room. In the synagogues they would have us on Friday, Saturday, or early Sunday. In the

Catskills, we'd be eating in the main dining room, certain nights, and have to put 'em on. When in Rome . . . My first year at the Pines, I made the mistake of ordering schav. The waiter told me, "Are you sure you want that?" Boy, poison in a glass! Man, that shit tasted like death on wheels. I got used to the menu, the borscht, all of that . . . but that was my first day.[14]

Thus, the relationship between Jews and Latinos working together in Latin music ran the full gamut of possibilities from positive to ambivalent and even negative. As two minority groups who often worked together, the musical relationship was a microcosm of their wider interactions in New York City. Generally speaking, during the years in this study these inter-group interactions were more positive, possibly because both groups were made up of multilingual and largely working-class immigrants, but there were differences. Economically speaking, during the first half of this study's time frame, "in 1960 . . . Puerto Rican median family income in New York City was considerably lower than even non-White median income—$3,811 against $4,437 . . . 63 per cent of the median income for all New York City families."[15] While Jews fared better economically during this same time period and had left the kinds of jobs that Puerto Ricans held, they were subject to job and educational discrimination as well as "restrictive covenant" rules that barred them from certain neighborhoods and social clubs and organizations.[16] The Jewish resorts in the Catskills were so successful precisely because there were other resorts and places that barred Jews. Historically, both groups were also only able to assimilate to a certain point within a pluralistic society. Jews were "both a religious and ethnic minority . . . and had to make the radical adaptation to the individualistic and liberal ethos of America," whereas in "Europe, Africa, and Asia [they] were the most isolated, communally organized, and encapsulated of groups."[17] By comparison, Puerto Ricans had been subjects of one colonial empire, Spain, and then another, the United States. Citizens since 1917, Puerto Ricans saw New York as a place of economic opportunity. However, Puerto Rican economic progress was much slower than that of previous immigrant groups despite a population of over a million. Thomas Sowell wrote that, "politically, Jews have historically tended to adopt, or at least to be responsive to, the viewpoint of the 'underdog'—long after that ceased to be their own position economically."[18] This could explain an affinity with Latin music on some level, but it is also simply great music, and that could have been reason enough for many Jews to get involved as performers and consumers. Some of the interview subjects in Lex Gillespie's film *The Mamboniks* posited that Latin music spoke to the Jewish soul, and throughout the film one sees how "Latin music provided the soundtrack to Jewish social events, from weddings to bar mitzvahs."[19] As seen above, within music the roles of employers and employees shifted constantly between the two groups depending on the context. This complex and nuanced relationship was not free of problems, some of which will be seen later in this chapter in the discussion of *West Side Story*.

SNAPSHOTS OF LATIN MUSIC IN JEWISH VENUES AND JEWISH-SPONSORED EVENTS

In the telling and retelling of the history of Latin music history in New York City, the focal points of Jewish participation are often limited to attending dances at the Palladium and patronizing Latin music during the summer at Jewish resorts in the Catskills. In Carlos Ortiz's documentary *Machito*, the bandleader discusses the music moving downtown akin to jazz's geographical trajectory in New York, through the patronage of Jewish fans who danced to his music at the Park Plaza prior to their four-year engagement at La Conga in 1941. He explains: "It was a crazy atmosphere—congenial, happy. That was the beginning of integration. Italian and Jewish girls came from Brooklyn and Long Island to hear us play at the Park Plaza . . . from there the typical Latin music gradually spread downtown, block by block."[20] After La Conga, Machito and many other bands would appear regularly at the Palladium.

Palladium buffs know that the venue was owned by a Jew named Maxwell Hyman, but no one mentions that he was a concentration camp survivor who had previously been a furrier and made his money in New York in the same business.[21] The Palladium angle portrays Jews as a people who initially came on a specific Jewish or "white-only" evening at the club, such as Wednesday, and then ultimately became part of a multi-ethnic force present every night of the week that ultimately helped integrate the Palladium. There were noted Jewish dancers and musicians who performed alongside Latino and African American dancers and musicians at the Palladium. Jewish mambo dancers can be seen dancing at the Palladium in films such as *Mambo Madness* and *The Mamboniks*.[22] However, there is ample historical evidence that Jewish patronage of Latin dance music, particularly "rhumba," was extensive prior to the apex of the Palladium's mambo nights. Even when the Palladium became the most well-known venue for Latin music in the mainstream media, there were many Latin music dances, concerts, and related events that continued in the Jewish community and that are well documented in newspaper advertisements. Myriad advertisements in New York City newspapers announce social dances aimed at Jewish audiences, specifically Jewish-themed events at non-Jewish venues, and venues that were not necessarily Jewish but were located in heavily Jewish neighborhoods or organized by Jewish promoters. An examination of these newspaper announcements in the *New York Post* between 1947 and 1961 shows the extent to which Latin music played by mostly Latino musicians and American "society" orchestra music played by non-Latino musicians served to draw patrons to a wide array of Jewish settings, including religious, cultural, philanthropic, humanitarian, and Zionist, as well as secular venues. Jewish iconography and transliterations of Hebrew words are peppered throughout these notices. What follows is a summary of Latin music dances and events sponsored by Jewish organizations in New York City.

1947

Announcements in the *New York Post* from 1947 show a vibrant dance scene with secular events aimed at Jewish dancers in the know such as the "'Flatbush Rumbanicks' [of the] Flatbush Rhumba League" and their February 9, 1947, *Dansant* from 2–6:30pm at the Biltmore Ballroom on Church and Flatbush Avenues. Nightclub owner Norby Walters defined the word *mambonik* as "a *trombenik* who loved mambo—*trombenik* being a Yiddish word for a bum. A knockaround guy. It was a badge of who we were, you know?"[23] Using this logic, a rumbanick is someone who loved rumba. This advertisement, and many that follow, refer to the music and dancing as rumba. The musical genre that was performed was in fact son, but it would soon be referred to as mambo. Rumba is a genre of music that is played with three drums, a pair of sticks that plays an ostinato called *guagua*, and claves. When son was exported beyond Cuba's

Fig 6.1. Flatbush Rumbaniks advertisement from the *New York Post*, 1947.

shores it was marketed as rumba. One can look at salsa in the same way, as a marketing term for the music that was mambo, son, and chachachá.

Returning to the announcement, the word *rhumba* is printed at least ten times and the text is meant to appeal to dancers who love to dance rhumba, as well as those who are indifferent to dancing rhumba, with enticing copy such as: "It should happen to you. We mean the wonderful time everyone has doing the rhumba with us. Besides what better way to keep warm . . . Come. Rhumba fan or not you'll have fun with us. Continuous dancing—Both American and Latin American Music featuring Marita and Her Rhumba Rhythm."[24] Under the mention of the Flatbush Rhumba League is an announcement for a rhumba contest. Other ads placed by the Flatbush Rhumba League indicate that the cash prizes for the rhumba and waltz contest were $100.[25]

Further down on the same page, Don Caballero and his rumba band are listed as performing with Marita Navedo at the Hi-Ho Casino on Ocean Parkway in the Manhattan Beach section of Brooklyn. This is also a secular event, but other listings point to events sponsored by a number of different Jewish organizations from across the political and religious spectrum throughout New York. The focal point of each event is dancing to Latin music. In Manhattan, Carlos Stone & His Thrilling Rumbas were announced as performing at the Hotel Almanac on W. 71st Street and Broadway for two nights, at an event sponsored by the Westchester Jewish League.[26] The Junior Mizrachi Business and Professional Group sponsored a cocktail dansant from 3–6pm on February 9, 1947, at one of Manhattan's most storied venues for Latin music, the Havana Madrid at 1650 Broadway (near 50th Street).[27] The same week, a Jewish War Veterans dance at the Saint Nicholas Arena on 66th Street and Broadway advertised an American band plus "New rhumba sensation Juan Carlos and Orchestra."[28] A gala dance on February 15, 1947, sponsored by the Joint Jewish League of Greater New York featured an American band along with "Rivera and his authentic rhumba rhythms." On Sunday, February 16, the West End Jewish League presented a gala at the Hotel Diplomat that featured an American band and "Carlos Segui and his rumba rhythm."[29] On the same evening in Brooklyn, the Jewish Group of Flatbush sponsored "4 ½ hours of thrill-packed dance music by 12 Lovely Ladies of Rhythm . . . Frances Strow & Her Debs of Swing–plus–The Authentic Afro-Cuban Rumbas of Rosita Cruz & Her Co-Ed Rumba Orchestra."[30]

An Asora-Shevat Inauguration Dance at the Fraternal Clubhouse located at 110 W. 48th Street featured "'Music as you like it' . . . 2 Orchs.—Continuous Dancing . . . Stan Pollock & His Society Orch. . . . Flores and His Rumba Orch."[31] Another explicitly Jewish dance advertised as Mogen David (Star of David) and held at the Hotel Bradford, featured "Díaz and his Caribe Rhumba Band."[32] The same weekend, the Flatbush Rhumbanicks had a Friday night dance at the Casa del Rey on Coney Island and Newkirk Avenues in Brooklyn, featuring "Julio Torres & His Entire Rumba Band! Sensation at Grossinger's, Concord, Flagler, etc."[33] This advertisement shows that there were options for non-religious Jews who were interested in pursuing their passion for Latin music in Brooklyn during the Sabbath. Finally, the center of the dance section page is a picture of bandleader Jay Chalson whose bio states that he has "the only orchestras featuring both American and Authentic Rumba Music," possibly due to the fact that his eighteen musicians such as Chino Pozo, Dioris Valladares, and Johnny McAfee came from previous employment with Xavier Cugat and Harry James.

Jewish dancers had opportunities to dance to Latin music beyond Brooklyn. Announcements from the week of April 18, 1947, show activities in Manhattan and the Bronx. The West End Jewish League sponsored a dance at the Hotel Diplomat featuring "2 Great Bands: Mark Fieldings Society Orch. and Carlos Segui Rumba Rhythms."[34] In an ad for the Tremont Terrace in the Bronx (555 E. Tremont Avenue), the text "a rendezvous for refined young men and women" is set inside a Star of David advertising a dance with "Ruby Melnick & His Popular Orchestra [plus] Eddie Lopez & His Authentic Rumbas."[35]

Back in Brooklyn, on October 3, 1947, the Jewish Group of Flatbush sponsored a two-day dance at the Biltmore Ballroom that featured Jose Vila, Sonny Rossi, and Herbie Rosen.[36] Casa Del Rey on Coney Island and Newkirk Avenues featured the Flatbush Rhumba League with their contest and music provided by Marita.[37]

The October 25, 1947, dancing section of the *New York Post* listed a number of events in Manhattan that were sponsored by different Jewish groups. The ideal billing was one band for Latin and one for North American music. The Jewish Business and Professional League sponsored a gala dance with an entrance fee of $1.25 at the Fraternal Clubhouse (110 W. 48th Street) featuring Tony Trane and his Society Orchestra as well as Felix and his Rumbavana Orchestra.[38] Two nights at the Hotel Whitehall on West End Avenue at 100th Street featured Paul Anthony's Society Orchestra and "Machito and His Great Rumbas," on a bill sponsored by the Riverside Jewish League; notice how Machito is not advertised as playing mambo.[39] Another dance at the Hotel Riverside Plaza (73rd and Broadway), sponsored by the West End Jewish League, featured Kenny Sheldon's Society Orchestra and Romulo's Rhumba Band.[40]

In late November 1947, Brooklyn remained a bastion of Latin dancing. A combined Flatbush and New York Division gathering of the Flatbush Rhumba League held a Thanksgiving dansant on Friday, November 28 at the Hotel Saint George that featured "[Ramón] Monchito and his entire sensational rhumba band," plus there were trophies for the dance contest.[41] On November 21, 1947, Young Israel of Boro Park sponsored a night of continuous dancing at the Menora Temple, a former masonic lodge on 50th Street and 14th Avenue that featured Henry Weber's orchestra playing American music and "Johnny Velazques (writer of Rock & Rye and Panama Joe) and his rhumba music."[42] "Marita the Rhumba Queen and her rhumba orchestra" were playing in the Grand Ballroom at the Menora Temple; she was on the bill with the vocalist and actor Bob Stewart.[43] Carlos Stone and his Rhumba Band were at the Hotel Almanac in Manhattan. Jay Chalson and his Rumba Sextet were performing in the Bronx at the Westover, located at 1390 Jerome Avenue near 170th Street. The musicians in his group were also given billing: "Chino, formerly with Xavier Cugat, Anita Del Castro, Dioris—direct form Lido Beach Club, Jack Boles, Juan Carlos, and Mike Frasquon."[44]

On November 30, 1947, the Eastern Parkway Chapter of Young Men and Women Division of the American Jewish Congress left their Brooklyn neighborhood to hold a dance titled "So that others may live" at Manhattan Center on 34th Street and 8th Avenue that featured Sonny Rossi and His Rhumbas.[45]

There was never a holiday or any other reason not to dance to Latin music. A "Post-Chanukah Dance" on December 27, 1947, at the Columbus Club (1 Prospect Park West in Brooklyn) offered Don Rico and his Rumba Band.[46] On the same listings page, the George Romero Rhumba Band was advertised to perform at the 16th annual Jewish War Veterans Boro Park Post #37 dance at the Hotel Saint George (Clark and Henry Street, Brooklyn) on the same night.[47] And still on the same day at 3pm, West Side Junior Hadassah offered a "Cocktail Sunday Dansant" at the Village Barn on 52 W. 8th Street that had rumba and lindy hop contests. Many other Latin band performances are listed in Jewish neighborhood "casinos" on the same date.[48]

From these 1947 events, one can clearly see that Jews were dancing to a variety of Latin bands throughout Brooklyn, Manhattan, and the Bronx. Events in the 1950s would prove to be as diverse and extensive.

1951–53

Dance listings from the period of 1951 to 1953 demonstrate how promoters accentuated the connections between their New York events and the Catskills resort summer experiences of their potential clientele. References to the hotels were at the forefront in newspaper dance listings. For example, a reunion dance for past patrons of the Laurels and Brickman hotels in the Catskills was advertised on March 9, 1951, at the Hotel Saint George and featured two nights of music with Ted Roberts and Ned Harvey playing the American music and Larry Arnez and Jose Curbelo handling the "rhumba."[49] Alongside the previous listing there were more events in Manhattan. The Young Men and Young Women's William Bernstein Memorial District of the Zionist Organization of

Fig 6.2. Machito Zionist dance advertisement from the *New York Post*, 1953.

America offered a dance at the Pythian Temple (135 W. 70th Street) with Clark Towers and Pepi Rodriguez, but also the added attraction of "The Kosher King of the Rumba, Schlepito and [his] Rumba Mambo Band."[50] Back in Brooklyn, the Lieutenant Wallace Kaufman Post of the Jewish War Veterans of United States hosted a dance at the Hotel Vanderbilt featuring live music by Guy Leeds and "Varelo & His Rumba Orch."[51] The Kingsway Jewish Community Center, where Senator Bernie Sanders and his brother attended Hebrew school, hosted a dance with George Eugene's Society Orchestra and "Chepito & His Rumbas."[52]

Numerous Zionist groups, Jewish social action groups, and a synagogue offered events in the January 30, 1953, listings. Hatikvah Hadassah B&P sponsored its annual dance with "proceeds for rehabilitation of Jewry in Israel" at the Hotel Ansonia that featured clarinetist Jerry Wild and "Julio Cortez & His Rhumba Band." Temple B'Nai Jacob held its 5th Anniversary celebration at the Hotel McAlpin with Cass Carr's Society Orchestra and "J. Velasquez & His Rhumba Orch." The Y.F.L. of G.N.Y. & The Flatbush Young Men had a dance at the Biltmore Ballroom (Church and Nostrand Avenues) with Jose Curbelo receiving top billing and a larger font than Cy Russell. The Kingsway Jewish

Center had a dance on Saturday, January 31 with George Eugene and "Chepita and His Rhumbas." At Riverside Plaza a dance sponsored by the Nathan Strauss Chartered Young Judea Chapter featured Paul Jerome and La Playa Sextet, for "society" and Latin music. Finally, Congregation B'Nai Jacob of Flatbush featured "Glenn Warren & Orchestra [and] Rhumbas by Alfredo Henna." The same page advertises an event about the McCarran Immigration Act and throughout the years offered announcements of other lectures and public discussions.[53]

The February 6, 1953, listings featured a number of Jewish dance events that were sponsored by Zionist organizations as well as Castkill hotel reunions. One of these listings makes reference to the Palladium but the music is still not called mambo. First, the Hatikvah-Bnai Zion, an American Zionist organization, sponsored a dance at the Hotel Riverside Plaza with "Jose Curbelo plus Greg Coleman."[54] On February 7, 1953, The Y.F.L. of G.N.Y. & The Flatbush Young Men sponsored a dance at the Biltmore Ballroom (Church & Nostrand Avenues in Brooklyn) featuring "Cass Carr & His Orch.—plus—P. Sanchez & His Rumbas."[55] A reunion and dance at the Hotel McAlpin for people who summered at Loch Sheldrake had Ed Stone and "Rodriguez & His Rhumba Band."[56] "Larry Spellman & his rhumba band Featuring Lou Perez on Vocals 'Direct from the Palladium'" was advertised for a Valentines Day Dance at the Hotel Woodstock on W. 43rd Street, February 8, 1953.[57]

Machito played regularly for Jewish organizations. In May 1953, "Machito & His 16 Piece Orchestra" is announced in large print with Greg Coleman and his band as playing the annual memorial dance sponsored by "N.Y.'s Largest Young Adult Chapter [of] The Maccabeans Metropolitan Fraternal Zionists," at the Hotel Riverside Plaza.[58] On May 24, 1953, Pianist "Joe Loco & His R.C.A. Orchestra [and] Emil's Society Orch.," performed at a dance hosted by B'Nai Zion and the ad features a large picture of Joe Loco with his name in large print.[59]

The column for November 6, 1953, lists several interesting events that connect to the Catskills scene as well as making explicit reference to the term *mambo* to identify both the music and the dancers. The "Steven S. Wise Chapter, Young Men & Women [of the] Fraternal Zionists Organization of America" sponsored an autumn dance at Hotel McAlpin with "Ben Rogers Society Orchestra—plus— Rodriguez Rhumba Orchestra." Promoter Harry Goldstein promoted a dance at the Trocadero (555 East Tremont Avenue) in the Bronx with Billy Hanin's Society Orchestra and Ralph Font and "His Entire Rhumba Band . . . Direct from the Raleigh Hotel."[60] The Biltmore Ballroom featured an evening of mambo music and dance that signaled the connection to many Jewish summer hotels, Jewish dancers as well as numerous Puerto Rican dancers, including Rene Touzet's music and Larry Seldin's "Mambo Fiesta & Exhibition, [with] Vera Garrett of The Concord Hotel, Killer Joe Pero [*sic*] of The Windsor Hotel, Marilyn Winters of Browns Hotel, Anibal & Joe . . . Puerto Rico's Precision Dancers, Mambo Bob

& Rose Marie, Little George Little of Fred Waring's TV Show, Marty & Cynthia of White Roe Hotel, Armando of Goldman's Hotel & Others."[61]

November 20, 1953, offered more musically hip bills from Jewish promoters and organizations. Some groups are still listed as performing rumba or rhumba. Machito was back in Brooklyn at the Pythian Temple with Bill Hanin's Society Orchestra to play the annual dance sponsored by Young Cardoza of the B'Nai Zion National Council. The Tifereth Young Men of Brooklyn hosted a dance at the Aperion (815 Kings Highway) in Brooklyn with Al Janon's Society Orchestra "plus Rodriguez & His Rhumba Mambo Band." On Sunday, November 22, 1953, the David Marcus Chartered Lodge of Young Adult Judea sponsored a dance with "Noro Morales & his rumba orchestra [and] Emil Cole & Society Orchestra," at the Hotel Riverside Plaza. The Café Old Europe (2637 Broadway) advertised its weekly "rhumba matinee" on Sundays, and also announced its complete and separate kosher catering services. Harry Goldstein offered the Stan Ross Society Orchestra, but the main billing was for an "All-Star Latin-American Orch. [featuring] Ray Davila, Jimmy La Vaca [Rodríguez], Pepi Adorno, Pepito Lopez, Lin Georgetti formerly with Jose Curbelo, Ralph Font, [and] Marcelina [sic] Guerra."[62] As seen in chapter 3, Jimmy La Vaca was John "Dandy" Rodríguez's father.

While the period of the early 1950s was considered to be the heyday of the Palladium's mambo nights, Jewish-sponsored Latin dance events from 1951–53 demonstrate breadth in the bands that performed and in the locations where they were held. These still often included "society" bands and Latin bands performing on the same bill. Most striking is that Latin bands continued to perform at events sponsored by Jewish mutual aid societies, Jewish political and Zionist organizations, and other Jewish charitable causes.

1958-61

Dance listings from 1958 to 1961 are striking because they are linked to various major holidays in the Jewish religious calendar. An April 1958 "After-[Passover] Seder Dance" in Manhattan at the Hotel Paramount (236 W. 46th Street) featured dancing until 2am and music provided by "The Pine Hill Lodge Sensation, The Ever Popular Cuban Pebble, Larry Arnez & His Latin American Society Orch."[63] Meanwhile in Jamaica, Queens, the Jamaica Jewish Center sponsored a dance with a society band along with the "Al Vega Sextet Mambo Band."[64] Tito Rodríguez, Johnny Pacheco, and the La Plata Sextette performed at the Palladium on Friday, December 9, 1960, but Brooklyn dancers could catch "Emilio Reyes and his Famous Orchestra [offering] Latin & American Music" at the Ocean Avenue Jewish Center (on the corner of Ocean Avenue and Avenue U) for $1.75 admission at 9pm.[65]

Fig 6.3. Joe Cuba Yom Kippur dance advertisement from the *New York Post*, 1961.

For Jewish audiences it seems that there was never a time not to dance, as seen in Yom Kippur (the Jewish day of atonement) dance advertisements on Friday, September 15, 1961. Yom Kippur is considered by Jews to be the most solemn holiday and it involves fasting, intense prayer, remembering deceased family members, and self-reflection. The Social League of Forest Hills, Kew Gardens, Roslyn, Port Washington, and Manhasset offered their annual "Yom Kippur Nite" cocktail dance at the Boulevard with Bill Diablo and his Latin Rhythms and The Encores society band.[66] After all of the fasting, chest-beating, and atoning there were sure to have been Jews eager to go to the Menora Temple on "Wednesday after sundown [for] the gayest nite of the year," to dance with Joe Cuba's group and the Freddy Price society band.[67]

This detailed look at dance listings in the *New York Post*, a mainstream local newspaper, clearly demonstrates that Jews sponsored and patronized a large quantity of Latin dance events throughout New York City that extended beyond the Palladium. Thus, any discussion of Jews dancing to Latin music in New York must be widened in its chronology and geography to include mainstream, well-publicized events that have been excluded from the dominant narrative that presents the Palladium and the Catskills as the focal points of Jewish patronage of Latin music in New York. Similarly, in the next section, the activities of two female artists demonstrate that there were also early Jewish superstars of Latin music in New York City who achieved mainstream stardom.

ABBE LANE AND EYDIE GORMÉ: TWO SUCCESSFUL FEMALE VOCALISTS IN LATIN MUSIC

In both the extant scholarly writings and informal off-record discussions of the history of Latin music in New York that I have heard, the names Abbe Lane and Eydie Gormé are never mentioned. It is quite possible that their omission is due to the gendered telling of this particular musical history, but it is also possible that their success was viewed disdainfully because it was global and perhaps seen as too commercial. Not coincidentally, both were married to male performers and their careers were intertwined with those of their partners. Lane was married to Xavier Cugat and Gormé was married to Steve Lawrence, but both women made names for themselves as top-notch performers. Gormé performed and recorded with a number of world-renowned Latin music artists and continued to sing until the end of her life. Lane put a significant amount of time into performing Latin music for dancers and she used her success in Latin music as a platform to pursue a successful international career as an actress.

ABBE LANE

Born Abigail Francine Lassman on December 14, 1932, Abbe Lane enjoyed international success as a singer and film and stage actress. She started performing as a six-year-old and achieved her first great commercial success while she was married to bandleader Xavier Cugat from 1952 to 1964. During this time she recorded a number of albums with him that featured her singing a variety of Latin music genres in Spanish. She also recorded albums with Sid Ramin and Tito Puente. These recordings also featured her singing in English with Latin background music. Television clips from Lane's heyday that are viewable on YouTube highlight her showmanship and her fluency in Spanish and Italian.[68] Through her performance of Latin music, Lane was able to fashion and sustain a lifelong career in television, film, and music, remaining in the public spotlight for many years.

PRIVATE LIFE IN THE PUBLIC EYE, 1949–53

After she successfully auditioned for Cugat's band, despite only having high-school Spanish, Lane's mother accompanied her daughter on the road. Lane eventually married Cugat, as her mother could not continue to travel and maintain her own marriage. As seen below, their courtship was fraught with the drama and press coverage that unfortunately accompanies many pop music protagonists.[69]

Lane's professional activities led her to perform throughout the world. Early press indicates a busy schedule that included a variety of engagements as well as personal information. In 1949 Lane's vocals were characterized as "ear beguiling" and her picture was featured in the announcement of Cugat's show at the Palace Theater in Albany.[70] Cugat's divorce from his first wife and his impending marriage to Lane made newspaper headlines May 1950.[71] The complexities of these relationships made fodder for gossip columnists, who chronicled the couples' legal affairs with such attention-grabbing headlines as "Wife Says Bandleader Has 6 Girl Friends, Band Leader Says She Has No Proof."[72] Writers held no punches when reducing Lane to a sex object. One writer went to see Cugat, but wrote that he "stayed to look at his beautiful blonde fiancée and vocalist, Abbe Lane. She's 18 and shapely. Cugat has a shape, too, I imagine, but I didn't notice it."[73] In the same article, Cugat says that Lane "respects her mother" and that every time he asked her out, Lane would defer to her mother for permission.[74] The columnist who penned this piece made many frequent comments about Lane's appearance at the expense of her musical talent.[75] Throughout this era, Lane is given prominent billing in advertisements at the Copacabana and other venues.

The *New York Post* featured an announcement from December 5, 1950, showing Lane and Cugat on a Saturday night bill at the Cascade Gardens, while Sunday night featured Miguelito Valdés accompanied by Noro Morales, Tito Puente, Catalino [Rolón], Tito and Johnny Rodríguez, Kali Karlos Alicia, Trini Reyes, Buddy Hackett, and Lenny Kent.[76] The Cascade Gardens was located at 335 Empire Boulevard at Nostrand Avenue in Brooklyn and was a hotbed for Latin music and dancing in the Jewish community. A Thanksgiving Eve Ball sponsored by the Congregation Ahavath Israel in Kingston, New York, attracted more than two thousand attendees, who overwhelmed Cugat and Lane with autograph requests.[77] Around the same time, Cugat offered a summary of different types of mambo dancers to a journalist and characterized the fourth type as

The "Abbe Lane" style: The dancer never moves or bobs the head. The rest of the anatomy, down to the hips, flips up and down in perfect rhythm with no side-sway. "I don't suppose I'll ever understand it," Xavier said, "Here's this little Abbe coming straight from Brooklyn and yet she not only dances but speaks Spanish as though she were born there."[78]

Her relationship with Cugat and his personal affairs remained in the headlines throughout their time together. This type of press coverage shows the magnitude of Lane's persona in the mainstream media. These articles also show how Lane's image was manipulated by others in the press as well as how she was able to savvily play a part in the construction of her image in the media. In January 1951, Cugat's estranged wife continued to hound him and Lane as chronicled in the national press. An episode where the former Mrs. Cugat found Lane in a state of undress in Cugat's Chicago hotel room prior to the official dissolution of the former's marriage received wide coverage.[79] A *New York Post* review of Lane and Cugat's show at the Roxy from November 11, 1951, details the pieces in the show, but also the fact that Cugat enjoys having her onstage.[80] The press coverage surrounding Cugat's divorce and Lane's state of undress when Cugat's ex-wife caught Cugat and Lane together remained in the newspapers.[81] Lane's Chicago Hotel room was robbed and thieves made off with two fur coats worth $3,000 and $1,600.[82] In June 1951, Cugat and Lane were performing on television as part of WABD's *Calvalcade of Bands*, but Cugat was not a fan of the medium and complained that it focused on looks and that the temperature of the set put the instruments out of tune.[83]

By January 1951, Cugat's ex-wife dropped Lane from her suit against Cugat, and Lane dropped her defamation of character suit against his ex-wife. A divorce agreement was finalized and the particulars were divulged in a story originating in Hollywood.[84] On May 6, 1952, Cugat and Lane got married. Their three-day honeymoon also received national coverage, which noted the age difference of fifty-two and twenty.[85] The story was also covered by none other than the legendary newspaper gossip columnist Walter Winchell.[86] An article from the *Philadelphia Enquirer* shows that venue where Lane and Cugat got married would stay open year round.[87] Cugat's show at the Hotel Statler with Lane's specific performances were well received in the *Buffalo Evening News*.[88] Cugat also became Lane's manager.

RECORDINGS 1951–53

Amidst this drama, Lane continued to perform and record with Cugat. Lane is first heard and credited with vocals on a 1951 single made with Cugat for Columbia Records called "The Wedding Samba."[89] What's fascinating about this debut for Lane and the Cugat-Lane musical partnership is that the song's main melodic material is taken from the Yiddish song, *Der Neur Shir* (the new song or melody) written by Abraham Ellstein, a major Yiddish theater and cantorial music composer and conductor who studied at Juilliard. Lane sings the lyrics in English although a few Spanish words like *señorita* are included. Cugat would later record other Jewish music such as "The Jewish Wedding Song (Trink Le Chaim)."[90] In 1953 Lane appeared as a lead and background vocalist on another Cugat 10" called *Dancetime with Cugat*.[91] On this recording, her performance of Ayrton Amorín and Ary Macedo's "Madalena" is executed in English.

INTERNATIONAL FILM AND TELEVISION STAR 1953-58

In 1953 Lane's film career started to take shape with appearances in Universal's *Wings of the Hawk* and *Ride Clear of Diablo*. One writer offered that she would take Rita Hayworth's spot in films, and in the same article Cugat is quoted as saying that after so many years of hard work as a bandleader, "Now I may buy an expensive car and devote the rest of my career to driving my wife to the studio."[92] The couple's musical performance career continued and Lane and Cugat flew back to New York for an extended engagement at Roseland.[93] They also performed at the Paramount.[94] Lane and Cugat traveled to Asia, performing to large crowds in Manila, Tokyo, and Hong Kong.[95] Cugat talked to reporter Bob Thomas about the success of his music, but it is notable that Thomas quoted Lane as saying that "a wiggle can be understood in any language."[96] Her increased involvement in film brought the couple to buy an expansive nine-acre mansion in Brentwood, complete with a 3-D movie projector and fifty-seat theater, pool with boats, exotic birds, and a mural painted by Salvador Dalí.[97] Another article from 1953 quotes Lane as writing a movie script "built around the life of the late Lupe Velez," someone whom she admired deeply.[98]

Throughout 1954, Lane received a lot of press regarding her appearance—including her physical measurements—and her choice of fashion, in addition to her movie career. In one piece she told her interviewer, "I'm half Spanish."[99] The same year, Lane and Cugat were held at gunpoint by a robber who relieved them of some $20,000 in jewelry.[100]

In 1955 Lane traveled to Italy to act in two films made in Rome. The *Brooklyn Eagle* published a piece on the Ursula Thiess and Glenn Ford film, *The Americano*, that Lane also had a role in and the tone of the article is how Lane, the hometown girl, became an international sensation and made Brooklyn proud.[101] Cugat wrote the score and performed the music that featured Lane.[102] Lane and Cugat were still performing in venues like Roseland for crowds of two thousand people.[103]

In January 1956, Lane and Cugat had a one-hour weekly television show in Rome every Sunday.[104] Lane told one reporter that the Vatican would call her when the Pope would watch the show so that she would have to "tone down all the numbers."[105] Lane also started working on another film installment of the "Bread" series with Italian film director Vittorio De Sica, with whom she had worked in another film, *Holiday Time*.[106] And in 1956, Lane sang both an English-language swing version of "Up a Lazy River" followed by a Spanish version of "Ay que lindo chachachá" backed by Cugat and his band in the Italian film *Donatella* directed by Mario Monicelli.[107] Lane also had a part in *The Wanderers* with Peter Ustinov. In addition, Lane and Cugat started a television show called *Around the World with Cugie and Abbe*. In one week, the couple appeared on US television three times, first on Ed Sullivan's show, second on their own NBC musical show, and third on Edward R. Murrow's show *Person to Person*.[108] In a number of articles from 1954–55, Lane stated that she would be wiggling less on stage and toning down her dress to be less sexual. This was not necessarily to be, as Lane can be seen doing so when performing as the character Susana Garcés alongside Cugat and singing "Me lo dijo Adela" in the 1957 Spanish film *Susana y yo*, directed by Enrique Cahen Salaberry.[109]

Lane returned to Hollywood in 1957 after achieving success in Italian cinema and making some eight films. In one interview she explains:

> I left here [Hollywood] two years ago because nobody in Hollywood could see me as anything but a band singer. I went to Italy where they have imagination about a person's talent. When they see a girl sing, they realize she could be able to act, too . . . I went to Italy at a very good time . . . the other female stars [Sophia Loren and Gina Lollobrigida] were on the wane.[110]

In the same article, Lane observed that in Italy men like "women with meat on their bones" as opposed to "the skinny types that are fashionable here."[111] She continued to express the desire to sing while pursuing her television and film career and in 1957 she also starred in the Broadway show *Oh Captain!* at the Lombardy Theater opposite Tony Randall.[112] The show was nominated for Tony Awards in six categories, but Lane later left the show, claiming she had to continue singing while doing the show because she wasn't paid enough.[113] Members of the cast scoffed at Lane's assertion. Starting in February 1957, Cugat and Lane took over Eddie Fisher's Wednesday and Friday evening fifteen-minute show called *Coke Time*, described by Cugat in the *New York Times* as "a musical travel atmosphere on the basis of 'around the world with the Cugats.'"[114] Critics enjoyed Lane and Cugat's TV show when it focused on music, but their dialogue was deemed "corny and self-consciously coy."[115]

MUSICAL PERFORMANCES AND RECORDINGS 1958–61

In the press, Lane was still judged as a sex object or questioned about her relationship with Cugat despite her individual success. In a number of articles she spoke about balancing her career goals with their relationship and how hard she had to work to advance her career. In one article she told Hal Boyle, "I want to be accepted as a rounded, accomplished actress. I wept when I didn't get the movie role of Marjorie Morningstar. I want to be looked up to and respected not be just another sex find."[116]

On January 26, 1958, Cugat and Lane appeared together on the television show *What's My Line?*[117] Later in 1958, Lane teamed up with Tito Puente for a well-received LP called *Be Mine Tonight* that Puente also is credited with conducting. Lane is in fine form throughout the record and demonstrates her vocal abilities singing in Spanish, Italian, and English in a variety of styles. In some songs like "Óyeme mama," Lane switches between Spanish and English, while on "Arrivederci Roma" she can be heard changing easily between Italian and English, with a few Spanish words as well. As Loza points out, Puente had featured a number of important female vocalists on his albums and during performances throughout his career. This puts Lane in the company of such notable artists as Celia Cruz, La Lupe, La Lloroncita, Sophy Hernández, Noraida, Millie P., Yolanda Duke, and La India, among others.[118] Lane continued to sing with Cugat and can also be heard on the 1959 album *Latin for Lovers*, which featured Lane, Dinah Shore, and others.[119]

The couple continued traveling and performing with Cugat's band throughout this time period. As detailed in the October 22, 1959, edition of the *Evans Journal* in Angola, New York, Lane and Xavier Cugat were headlining the 1959 United Community Chest–Red Cross Appeal at City Hall.[120] They also performed in Buffalo on October 21–22, 1959, at the Statler-Hilton.

It seems that many of the men who were important in Lane's life also sought to capitalize on her fame, including her father. Lane's father had a men's clothing store in Miami Beach named Abbe Lane's Men's Shop.[121] In 1959 a full-page advertisement in the *Philadelphia Enquirer* shows a picture of her with her father and Cugat above copy that screams about discounted prices.[122] The same year, Abbe Lane's "semi-liquid . . . no starch diet" as used by many in Hollywood, was offered by columnist Lydia Lane (no relation) to her readers with a self-addressed stamped envelope.[123] Lane sang in Spanish, Italian, English, and even "Hava Nagilah" in Hebrew on the 1961 album *Abbe Lane with Xavier Cugat and his Orchestra*.[124]

A 1961 *New York Times* article on Lane's film career highlighted her success in Italy and the fact that she was acting in a foreign language:

> "It happened because I'm good at languages," Miss Lane explained yesterday between rehearsals for a New Year's Eve television show. "My parents were German and Spanish—though they were born here, too—and I was able to learn Italian easily, with a Roman accent, so I'm not limited to 'foreigner' roles. In fact, I dub my own dialogue into Italian, French, and English, something not many foreign players can do. Now audiences think of me as an Italian actress . . . I was shocked to find how many Italian stars never use their own voices . . . When I act, at least people know it's me."[125]

In 1962 Lane performed "Everything's Coming Up Roses" with Cugat on the Italian television show *Il signore delle 21*, but the song's message couldn't have been further from the truth for Lane vis à vis her relationship with Cugat.[126]

THE END OF THE CUGAT AND LANE PARTNERSHIP AND BEYOND

Cugat and Lane divorced in 1964 and "Cugat's attorney did not contest the proceedings."[127] This did not spell the end of Lane's name being associated with her ex-husband, because Cugat filed a $1 million lawsuit in New York State Supreme Court against a husband-and-wife dance team that he claimed had "'corruptly and maliciously enticed' Miss Lane to break her contract with the Cugat band."[128]

At the end of 1964, Lane married Perry Leff an attorney, "theatrical agent [and] the vice president and partner of Creative Management Associates, Ltd."[129] The couple was wed in a Jewish ceremony at the Plaza Hotel in Beverly Hills, California.[130] Lane remained active as a performer in the public eye for decades. In 1966 she appeared on *The Dean Martin Show* and even returned to *What's My Line?* by herself on January 15, 1967, where she plugged her New York engagements and an appearance on *The Ed Sullivan Show*.[131]

In 1993 Lane decided to chronicle her life with Cugat, roughly thirty years after their divorce in 1964, in a fictionalized autobiography called *But Where Is Love?* Lane explained that she waited so long because "Emotionally I felt I wasn't ready to go back into my past and relive everything."[132] In an interview that ran in the *Orlando Sentinel* and elsewhere, she justified this method of writing "fiction over an autobiography for the freedom it offered."[133] Lane explained that, "I felt that I could sit back and view my characters with greater objectivity and emotional detachment if I wrote it as a novel. I felt the story could stand up . . . without there being the two protagonists of Cugat and Abbe Lane."[134] In the book, Lane talks about physical and emotional abuse and that "[she] considers her best performance to have been during her 10-year marriage to Cugat when she portrayed a happy woman, devoted to her husband and secure in her success."[135] The book does not have much information about Lane's linguistic and musical training other than the fact that she did not speak Spanish when she first auditioned and started with Cugat, but learned on the job.[136]

In her 2012 interview with Dr. Gail Gross, Lane talked about the book being developed into a Broadway show.[137] Lane made a number of television appearances throughout her career, and into the 1980s she was seen performing internationally in Chile.[138] Lane's career success and renown in Italy is such that she was immortalized as a collectible doll in a partnership with Elizabeth Arden in Milan in 2012.[139] Lane has her own star on Hollywood's Walk of Fame.[140] Abbe Lane achieved international mainstream commercial and artistic success in a few different areas, but a significant portion of her career was dedicated to performing Latin music.

EYDIE GORMÉ

Eydie Gormé is another American Jewish singer who achieved international success singing Latin music. Like Lane, Gormé was multilingual. Gormé's success included a television show, tours, a Grammy® award, and many recordings. She was born Edith Gormezano in the Bronx on August 16, 1928, into a Sephardic Jewish family of tailors from Sicily and Turkey that spoke Ladino, a dialect of Judeo-Spanish spoken by Sephardic Jews.[141] According to one account, "she and her older siblings, Corene and Robert, grew up speaking fluent Spanish [Ladino]. Ironically, she was the only one of the three not to be given music lessons, since the others had not made much use of theirs."[142]

Gormé grew up on E. 168th Street in the Bronx. She started singing as a child and "briefly worked as an interpreter for a theatrical supply export company and later as its manager" while studying economics at City College. In her obituary, the *New York Times* wrote that she had also worked as an interpreter at the United Nations after graduating from high school.[143] Prior to her foray into Latin music, Gormé sang songs associated with the American songbook and toured with a number of groups such as Tommy Tucker, Tex Beneke, and Ray Eberle.[144] Her high school classmate Ken Greengrass, with whom she used to perform, managed Gormé. Nefsky Frankfeldt writes:

> As a single act, Gorme toured the nightclub and theater circuit and made guest appearances on top radio and television programs. She signed her first recording contract with Coral Records in 1952 and soon made the Top Twenty. Through the Voice of America, she hosted her own radio show, *Cita con Eydie* [A date with Eydie], which was transmitted to Spanish-speaking countries around the world.[145]

In an interview with the *Los Angeles Times*, Gormé spoke about her fluency in foreign languages:

> "My mother only wanted to know why I wasn't singing in Spanish, Turkish, Greek and some other language," Gorme said with the sincere, hearty laugh she gives to Lawrence onstage when he tells jokes she has no doubt heard a

thousand times before. "Nine of them she spoke. I actually did a song in Turkish once. I did a couple of things like that and some cute little hits because they were like novelties."[146]

In the mid-1950s, Gormé was booked singing American pop music and was a star seen on NBC television five nights a week on Steve Allen's show. Although Gormé was not presented as a sex symbol, nevertheless she, too, like Lane, was subjected to the patriarchal gaze and structure of the entertainment industry. In one article, she discussed some important male relationships in her life, particularly Steve Allen and Jerry Lewis, as they impacted her career, but these men chose to interact with her in ways that would be considered sexist and inappropriate today.[147] These included calling her "Easy" Gormé and other comments. Gormé married a Jewish comedian and vocalist from Brooklyn, Steve Lawrence, and they enjoyed success as a vocal duo, Steve and Eydie. Their marriage took place in Las Vegas and was covered in the mainstream press.[148] The couple had met on Steve Allen's show; in 1958 Lawrence and Gormé had their own television show on NBC. In one newspaper article, Gormé stated that it was more natural to have Lawrence's name first in the billing; interestingly, the author put Gormé's name first in the headline.[149] In another article about the show, the writer reports that:

> Mrs. Lawrence has drastically curtailed her show business work. She still makes records and will, of course, do as much as Steve on their show this Summer. But she's pretty well given up night-clubbing—"I did it nine years, that's enough"—for the simple and basic reason she wants to be with Steve.[150]

The couple also appeared together on Broadway and Gormé's album *Eydie in Love* was nominated for a Grammy® in 1958. In 1960 the couple won a Grammy award for their album *We Got Us*. The couple would enjoy future success, as Nefsky Frankfeldt writes: "Her TV appearances with Lawrence have also won recognition, with a 1976 Emmy nomination for *Steve and Eydie: Our Love Is Here to Stay*, and seven Emmys in 1979 for *Steve and Eydie Celebrate Irving Berlin*."[151]

GORMÉ'S LATIN MUSIC RECORDINGS

Gormé's 1961 album of Latin American music, *I Feel So Spanish*, featured a number of well-known compositions from the Americas such as "Bésame mucho," "La Puerta," "Frenesí," "Quien sera," and "Perfidia," among others.[152] The album and the arrangers take advantage of Gormé's abilities as a vocalist in ways that

Lane was not used. On "Quien sera," Gormé switches between Spanish and English; the arrangement is arranged and performed in a Latin big band–style chachachá. "La Puerta" is accompanied by a full string orchestra and performed as a bolero. For "Frenesí," Gormé sings in a big band swing style before switching to Spanish over a chachachá setting. The arrangement of "Perfidia" applies the same setting but in reverse.

In 1962 she released *Blame It on the Bossa Nova*, which is focused on Brazilian bossa nova but is sung in English.[153] The song selection includes "One Note Samba" and "Desafinado." Gormé would later recorded a Portuguese and Spanish version of "Blame It on the Bossa Nova" called "Cúlpale la bossa nova" in 1963. The album was nominated for a Grammy® award in 1963. The Spanish-language version of the album was released throughout the Americas in 1965.

Gormé also recorded three internationally successful albums with Trio Los Panchos, perhaps the most emblematic guitar trio of its kind in the Spanish-speaking Americas. These include *Amor: Great Love Songs in Spanish* (1964), *More Amor* (1965), and *Navidad Means Christmas* (1966)—also released as *Blanca Navidad* (1966)—which featured numerous hit songs as well as traditional songs by Cuban, Mexican, and Puerto Rican composers. The group first connected with Gormé when they attended one of her performances at the Copacabana. Peter Rosaly—who also produced Sonny Bravo's only solo record for Columbia, as detailed in chapter 3—produced the first recording.[154]

In 1966 Gormé won a Grammy® Award for *If He Walked into My Life*. *Otra Vez*, released in 1969, was another of many more Spanish-language recordings. On her 1976 release *La Gorme* she was accompanied by El Nuevo Mundo Orchestra and the 1982 album *Tómame o Déjame* featured some of this material. *La Gorme* was nominated for a Grammy® Award in 1977. In 1977 she recorded an album with Puerto Rican vocalist Danny Rivera, *Muy Amigos/Close Friends*, that was nominated for a Grammy® Award that same year. Another bolero album, *De corazón a corazón*, was released in 1988. While Gormé released many records for major labels and often sang in Spanish, she also enjoyed a successful English-language career in pop music performing into her later years.

In her *New York Times* obituary Anita Gates calls Gormé "[a] lively singer with a remarkable range."[155] NPR's *All Things Considered* also ran a story on Gormé when she died that quotes critic Will Friedwald:

> "Eydie Gorme certainly deserves respect. She's one of the greatest interpreters of the American songbook," says Will Friedwald, a jazz critic and author of the book *Jazz Singing*. "If there is a 'not' on her voice it's that it's not the most distinctive sound." But then Friedwald says distinctiveness isn't everything, and that "some of the most distinctive singers are terrible." What Gorme had was the ability to bring emotional complexity to songs. Friedwald says

that the emotion was always there, even when Gorme was using her loudest belting voice. That's a skill Friedwald says is not evident in generations that followed her. "It's a big, rich, beautiful deep voice that has phenomenal tonal range, but emotional range as well," he says.[156]

I would add that Gormé can really swing. Her phrasing was excellent and relaxed. Her albums that featured arrangements that switched back and forth from swing to Latin bear this assessment. In addition, Gormé's recordings with Trio Los Panchos remain beloved throughout the Americas and their versions of songs such as "Nosotros," "Sabor a mi," and "Piel canela" remain gold standards for musicians and fans.

In many ways, Lane and Gormé were similar. Like Abbe Lane, Eydie Gormé has a star on Hollywood's Walk of Fame, but she shares it with her husband.[157] However, looking at the artistic and commercial success of these two Jewish female New Yorkers, it is difficult to understand why their contributions to Latin music during the time period of this study have been unsung. Of all the Jewish performers who tasted mainstream notoriety, none achieved more than the only two women in this elite club; the fact that their stories are missing from every narrative of Jewish involvement in Latin music is probably the result of them being viewed simply as "chick" singers who were not as important as instrumentalists or arrangers. Tucker discusses this stereotype in jazz as one that "highlighted a shortage of musical knowledge and an entertaining excess of sex appeal."[158] Yet this is also a contradiction, because the highest ideal of an instrumentalist is to sound like a human voice and vice versa.[159] Tucker points out the gendered consumption of jazz "before anyone blows a note," and a similar framework can be applied to Latin music in New York City.[160] While there were female singers and musicians, expectations were already made of women in the scene to appear a particular way.

Cugat definitely exploited this norm, which Lane seemed to accept for some time. In a 1959 RAI (Italian national television) clip, Lane is brought out to sing in a large birdcage and Cugat is seen conducting in the shadows.[161] The poignancy of this image and the eventual demise of their relationship, during which Cugat led Lane to believe she was nothing without him, among other physical and emotional abuse, speaks to the general condition of female performers at that time whose talents were exploited by male bandleaders.[162]

In contrast, Eydie Gormé seemed to have found in Steve Lawrence someone who she could perform with, who at the same time was comfortable with having her pursue her own career goals and successes. Her career as a performer was no doubt impacted by her having to negotiate being a woman in a male-dominated industry, but she achieved artistic and commercial success based on her talent and abilities.

Fig 6.4. Barry Rogers soloing with the Joe Cotto Orchestra at Teatro Puerto Rico, 1960. Miguel Millan (maracas), Joe Cotto (timbales). Photo courtesy of Richard Blondet.

BARRY ROGERS

Trombonist, tres player, producer, composer, and arranger Barry Rogers ranks high on the list of New York–based musicians who helped shaped the sound of Latin music and whose concept, style, and execution most definitively influenced players beyond New York City. Barry Rogers is unquestionably one of the architects of the heavy trombone sound of New York salsa, as evidenced on recordings by Eddie Palmieri's La Perfecta and countless other groups who mimicked his approach or hired him for his particular sound. There is a Spanish expression that states, *Dime con quien andas y te diré quién eres* (Tell me who you walk with, and I'll tell you who you are). It can be said that Barry Rogers walked among the greats, but many greats also walked with Barry Rogers.

What's fascinating about Rogers is that he did not possess a natural or prodigious technique nor was he particularly enamored of his chosen instrument, but he was able to coax a unique sound out of it that helped define a genre and a New York aesthetic through his licks and musical approach. None other than Willie Colón told David Carp in an interview how he himself quit the trumpet and switched to the trombone after falling in love with Rogers's solo on the Joe Cotto hit "Dolores":

> When I first heard a trombone solo by Barry I said, "What the hell *is* that?"
> It sounded like an elephant, it was so big and angry and powerful and just
> brilliant. I started doubling on the trumpet and trombone and then finally

I dropped the trumpet and I started a two trombone band. And that's when things really started happening because it was such a contrast from these big bands with all the saxophones. You know, the old-timers would get up and they'd have like four trumpets, five saxes, a flute player, you know, a legion of musicians on the stage. And then we'd come up and it was like one of these little rap groups, two trombones and a rhythm section. That became the standard of the salsa band now, if you listen to salsa radio now the rule is that it's a trombone band.[163]

A friend and contemporary of Rogers named Jack Hitchcock attested to the extent to which Rogers changed the expectations of the instrument:

You could almost blame Barry Rogers for what happened to trombones in Latin music. I got to love Barry a lot, man, we got very close but at the time I hated his guts. Because I was essentially a rather soft trombone player and I liked it that way. Now Eddie Palmieri was *the* hot band and Barry and José Rodrígues, they pumped that stuff out and it was *so* loud, I mean it was incredible. Then Willie Colón comes up after him and says, "That must be the way you play!" So I mean all these guys are blatting away and I finally got to play louder out of self-defense.[164]

Rogers's health and technique suffered from his battle with the horn, and colleagues like Ángel "Papo" Vásquez heeded his advice to play with the "bell into the microphone" when working in bands with heavily amplified instruments such as the electric bass.[165] Although Rogers studied technique with guru Carmine Caruso, it was his late-1970s work with classical virtuoso and "chops doctor" Vince Penzarella that perfected his technique. Penzarella remains popular to this day among musicians to solve problems with sound and technique.

Born in the Bronx May 22, 1935, Barron W. Rogers descended from a Polish Jewish family. His father William and his uncles sang in Joseph Rosenblatt's choir accompanying many of the best cantors in the region. One of his uncles, Milton, played piano professionally and was a celebrated educator.[166] Rogers's parents were public school teachers and his mother's extensive travels as a zoologist introduced him to many cultures and practices beyond Europe and the United States, particularly those of Africa, Mexico, and the Caribbean. Rogers attended Bronx Vocational High School and was heavily interested in fixing cars and hot rod culture. In an interview with David Carp, Rogers's friend Lenny Seed remembers a moment from Rogers's funeral when Michael Brecker stated, "'Barry Rogers was the first Jewish guy I ever met that knew how to fix a car.'"[167] Photographs and family testimony show that Rogers also enjoyed sailing, another activity not typically associated with New York

City Jews. It was during this period in high school that Rogers began playing in small Latin music groups in the Bronx with Johnny Pacheco, Benny
Bonilla, Rupert Branker, and Arthur Jenkins. In 1956 Rogers hooked up with
saxophonist Hugo Dickens, an African American musician who had a Latin
band that played all over the city and on the Catskills circuit. A number of
important musicians would pass through this group and go on to be active
in major bands in both the jazz and Latin scene in New York: Pete "La Roca"
Sims (drums/timbales), Phil Newsum (timbales), Larry Harlow (piano), Eddie
Diehl (guitar), Marty Sheller (trumpet), Bobby Porcelli (saxophone), Bobby
Capers (woodwinds), Hubert Laws (flute), Ted Curson (trumpet), and Rodgers
Grant (piano), among others. The group combined jazz and Afro-Cuban music
in unique ways while also playing straight Cuban music. They also reflect a
uniquely New York phenomenon of African American, Latino, Jewish, Italian,
and Anglos performing together and experimenting with Latin music. David
Carp places the Dickens band in the context of African American social clubs
of Harlem that featured Latin music in the 1950s, but the number of recordings by African American popular musicians that featured Latin rhythms was
quite impressive at that time.

Rogers's association with Palmieri dates to 1960, when the two would perform as a conjunto, removing the trumpets and adding the flute. Another Jewish New Yorker, Mark Weinstein, eventually would join as second trombonist.
Weinstein was replaced by Joe Orange, an African American, and then by José
Rodrígues, a Brazilian. The sound of the group was based on Cuban conjunto
concepts, but also took literally from the charanga when having the trombones
play string parts in the arrangements. The influence of jazz was also paramount.
As mentioned in chapter 6, the two-trombone group of Kai Winding of J.J.
Johnson was widely acclaimed in jazz and popular in the United States and
internationally. Rogers himself was a fan of Johnson and even had a chance to
play with him as a member of Jimmy Wormworth's band in 1957.[168]

Mark Weinstein explained to David Carp how Barry Rogers's musical genius would work as he described how the two would play during a typical live
performance:

> You play down the head and there'd be the first montuno, in the first montuno
> Barry would always be singing coro. And while the singer was improvising
> Barry'd turn around and during the four bars of the singer's improvisation
> he would play something for me to play, picking it up either out of the air or
> from something the singer had sung or whatever. I then had to get it from
> him in that interval and then if I didn't get it the first time he'd do it again, if
> I didn't get it the second time he was angry at me. Then I'd start playing that
> lick, Barry would join in playing the lick with me in unison, then in harmony

and then the shit would happen. Barry would then start slowly, almost the way a sitar player develops a solo, he would start to very slowly move that lick into not quite a solo but into a sequence of ever increasing sophistication.[169]

For Weinstein, this formula proved to be more successful in creating a euphoric space for the musicians and the dancers, and this euphoria surpassed larger ensembles, particularly that of Tito Puente:

> We outswung Tito's band with all of his fuckin' cymbals, with all of his trip-
> lets, with all of his sticks over his head. Because when Barry would get the
> pots on there was nothing in the world that was more exciting, *nothing,*
> *nothing!* Not all of the high notes, not all of the screaming trumpets and
> the saxophones. When Barry would start to move through a sequence of
> improvisations there was nothing in the world that was more exciting and
> the dancers loved Barry Rogers.[170]

For musicians like Marty Sheller, the success of the Palmieri and Rogers part-nership was akin to other notable cognates in the jazz world such as Duke Ellington and Billy Strayhorn. Sheller told Carp: "I think they both had the same way of thinking about harmony. That's why it's almost interchangeable, the arrangements that Barry would do and the arrangements that Eddie would do."[171]

In 1970 Rogers connected with jazz saxophone virtuoso Michael Brecker and his trumpeter brother Randy to form the successful jazz-rock outfit Dreams. The group also included Panamanian drummer Billy Cobham, who propelled Rogers to musical heights. The band disbanded in 1972, but through his connections with various members in the group who earned good livings as studio musicians, Rogers started playing recording sessions for the likes of James Taylor, Carly Simon, Aerosmith, Average White Band, Chic, Todd Rundgren, and Tina Turner, and others.[172] As Rogers continued his association with Palmieri in the studio but not onstage, he took on the role of producer for the Grammy®-nominated *Sun of Latin Music* sessions. He told Pablo Guzman:

> I produced everything except the original rhythm track, without horns and
> without the arrangement. After the rhythm track was laid down by Eddie
> and the gang, without horns and without singing, I had to go in there and
> cut it all up with a razor blade with an engineer at the Electric Lady studios
> and we pieced the entire thing together and overdid all the horns and the
> singing later.[173]

Eddie Palmieri described one performance on the record as his best: "Un Dia Bonito" is the maximum of our collaboration *ever.* I never played piano like that again and I couldn't do that again if I tried. Because it was the magic between he and I, he drew it out and I drew everything out of him too.[174]

According to Carp, "artists on whose albums Barry receives non-playing credit, whether for mixing, engineering, or producing, include Rafael Cortijo, David Lahm, Jens Wendleboe, and the Star-Scape Singers."[175] Rogers's colleague Bernard Fox felt that Rogers's work on Orquesta Broadway's *Pasaporte* was singlehandedly responsible for reinvigorating the charanga sound and scene in New York City.[176] Rogers was also contacted to produce a recording with Linda Ronstadt in the late 1980s, but unfortunately, after creating an entire work on spec, the Ronstadt team backed out and nothing could be done with the project.

In the same way that listening to music with Manny Oquendo, Rene López, and Andy González was a serious study session that served as a point of education for subsequent generations of musicians, David Carp writes that it was the same for Barry Rogers:

> Mark Weinstein maintains that those who truly understood the depth of Barry's love of music were those with whom he shared these experiences: "To be invited to Barry's house to listen to records was the guarantee of an experience that would transform your thinking about music. Barry could sit down for hours on end and play records, classical records. I remember he introduced me to this record called *Greek Island and Mountain Music*, I've just never heard anything like it. The music that I stole for *Cuban Roots*, it was on a record of a pre-Castro folkloric group that had all of the classic guaguancós and all the classic comparsas—Barry introduced me to that album. Barry introduced me to West African music, Barry introduced me to Peter Pears singing with Dennis Brain, who was this amazing French horn player. I mean you would go to Barry's house and you knew that every single record you would hear would be amazing beyond belief and that the sequence of records that you would hear would be transcendental. To listen to Barry's records with Barry was to learn more about music than you could ever want to learn from another human being."[177]

Afro-Atlantic scholar Robert Farris Thompson was a friend of Rogers who invited him to work with his Yale students. He remembered that during one visit,

> Barry discovered that I had some batá drums and to my amazement he picked them up and he knew how to play them. Ernie Ensley was with us, he showed Ernie how to do the (sings "Kun KUN KUN KUN") and he showed me how to do (sings "KON ke KON ke KON KON ke KON ke KON KON"). And then once he had the two he came in on iya and we fused and we grooved and it was very spectral because batá of course are loaded with aché.

So they started playing themselves, the notes started going in and out and it was really incredible! I've never played batá before or since, I don't know why he never explored this in his recording. But knowing Barry I think he did it as a rhythmic exercise, he had it stored in his mind and he started improvising.[178]

Interestingly, Barry Rogers also played the Cuban tres and can be heard on recordings by the Cesta All-Stars, Típica Novel ("Tierra bendita"), Eddie Palmieri ("Si las nenas me dejan, que"), Johnny Pacheco, and Pete "El Conde" Rodríguez ("Sonero"). Some musicians have recollected seeing Rogers play tres on Palmieri's gigs circa 1968. His widow, L. K. Steiner, offered some more background on Rogers and the Cuban tres:

Barry LOVED the tres! I bought him his tres as a birthday gift. It was a complete surprise. Eddie Palmieri helped me locate "the one" in the deep deep Bronx. The instrument had a history, which I knew was a requirement. I never saw him happier then when he first took that scratched up, a bit undersized, funky tres into his arms. Barry loved digging in and driving the Rhythm Section with all his heart and soul. He drove the band on trombone, but being part of the Rhythm Section and being part of that glorious loco-motion satisfied something very deep within him. (Those who knew Barry understand my choice of word here.) He venerated Arsenio Rodriguez and needless to say the magical old Cuban cuts excited him beyond description. Barry was a great innovator in the genre, but he was a traditionalist at heart. The spirit in the old Cuban music lived in him. His personality, his interests all reflected this. It was all of a piece. He was a unique person and artist. He had an ability to speak with his own voice in the music of other cultures with authenticity. He was a world musician ahead of his time.[179]

Thus, Barry Rogers was an influential musician whose individual sound and approach would become emblematic of the sound of Latin music in New York City. His sound would be imitated and employed by many trombone-centric bands throughout New York City, Cuba, Puerto Rico, Colombia, and beyond.

LARRY HARLOW, "EL JUDÍO MARAVILLOSO" (THE MARVELOUS JEW)

Larry Harlow has been perhaps the most well-known Jew to perform and record Latin music since the late 1960s. He represents the gamut of Fania productions in his various roles as bandleader, arranger, producer, session player, and composer.[180] Born Lawrence Ira Kahn on March 20, 1939, in Brooklyn, he took the stage name Harlow because his father, who was also a musician, had used the name when a doctor named Harlow had treated the elder Harlow after an automobile accident. The younger Harlow attended the High School of Music and Art and learned classic Cuban and Puerto Rican piano solos note for note after suffering embarrassment for playing non-idiomatically when he went to play with a high school Latin pickup group. As mentioned earlier, he was an alumni of the important Hugo Dickens band, and in the 1950s he lived in Cuba and spent time attending and recording performances of both secular and religious Afro-Cuban music up until the Cuban revolution in 1959. This experience became the foundation of his understanding of the Latin music that was being played in New York. Upon his return he continued to work in the New York club scene and Catskills circuit, gaining credibility as a Latin music performer. On a musical level, Harlow stated that "the Catskills were like going to school" for him and other musicians.[181] Top-name artists such as Machito, Tito Puente, and Tito Rodríguez headlined in the best resorts while up-and-coming artists who would later achieve success as bandleaders and/or sidemen, such as Larry Harlow, Barry Rogers, Joe Cuba, Sonny Bravo, Willie Torres, Eddie Palmieri, Henry "Pucho" Brown, and countless others played as opening acts or in smaller settings.

It was during a recording session that an excited percussionist permanently sealed Harlow's stage persona as *El judío maravilloso*, the marvelous Jew, exhorting Harlow to play a piano solo by shouting "¡Toca maravilloso!" (play marvelous one).[182] This name showed the influence of his mentor, *El ciego maravilloso* (the marvelous blind man), Arsenio Rodríguez, and whose music he would frequently return to and record throughout his own career. He released a string of hit records and played in Africa with the Fania All-Stars as well as at the famous Yankee Stadium concert. In 1972 Fania released Harlow's *Tribute to Arsenio Rodríguez* when his mentor passed away. The record went gold and Harlow proceeded to embark on a series of projects that would place him in the annals of Latin music.

The first such record was an adaptation of The Who's rock opera *Tommy*, which he rewrote with Heny Álvarez and titled *Hommy* (pronounced "o-mee"). In the original rock opera the protagonist is a deaf, blind, and mute pinball wizard, while in *Hommy* he was transformed into a conga virtuoso with the same physical challenges. The record was a success for a number of reasons. First, Harlow brought Cuban singer Celia Cruz out of retirement in Mexico to sing in it. Second, it was the first salsa "concept" album. Third, it was the first record recorded with DBX noise reduction, which was achieved by using 35mm movie film for tape and configured in such a way as to record sixteen tracks. Finally, it was the first time that "real" Latin music was played in a major American concert hall venue, Carnegie Hall. *Hommy* was performed at Lincoln Center on July 23, 2014, with a new orchestral overture performed by close to one hundred musicians and singers. The concert was standing room only in part because of its history. Special guest performances by Michael Stuart, Herman Olivera, Roberto Roena, Adonis Puentes, Lisette Delgado, reprised the roles of Celia Cruz and Cheo Feliciano and three days of rehearsals built many expectations among fans and musicians. Unfortunately, the concert was canceled after rain, thunder, and lightning moved in quickly after the band completed side one of the album. As one of the musicians, I ran back onstage to retrieve my instruments and to protect the original hand-copied parts that so many of us were thrilled to use because they connected us to the past.

The next major project Harlow conceived of—*La Raza Latina*—was a suite that traced the evolution of salsa from Africa to Cuba, New York, and beyond. For Harlow it was "a musician's album."[183] In July 2011 the piece had its live world premiere at Lincoln Center with Rubén Blades, Adonis Puentes, and a fifty-piece orchestra before an audience of 22,000. A number of Hollywood celebrities were in attendance and it was an incredible experience to stand on the stage and hear the crowd roaring. A subsequent performance took place at the Adrian Arsht Center for the Arts in Miami in January 2012.[184]

Another important musical and technical achievement for Harlow was *Live in Quad*:

> Recorded live at Sing Sing on January 16, 1974, the listener can hear that the musicians came to play hard from the first note. In a recent conversation, Harlow talked about this being one of his best recordings and how the enthusiasm of the largely Latino audience affected the performance positively. This was the only Latin album recorded in the quadrophonic stereo format. The basic concept was similar to today's surround-sound but the means of achieving the four channels of audio varied across formats. As good as true quad sounded, it was doomed by incompatibility and technical variations within formats. Harlow took advantage of the new technology, recording the album on location with an RCA 8-track unit and mixing the album by essentially spinning around in a suspended rattan chair that faced four speakers.[185]

Ironically, subsequent album titles such as *Yo soy latino* (I am Latino) place his identity firmly with the Latino musical world.[186] Today, Harlow is recognized as one of the founding fathers of the New York sound of modern salsa music and is credited with recording and releasing the first album to use the word *salsa* in its title in 1972.[187] Since the mid-1990s he has continued to perform with the Fania All-Stars, his own Latin Legends band, and in a Broadway show for children called *Sofrito*, for which he wrote music to accompany acclaimed storyteller and children's radio personality David González. Harlow's biggest project to date has yet to be produced, but it has been brewing for almost thirty-five years. It is a Faustian Broadway musical entitled *Mamboland*, set during the acme of popularity of the Palladium dance hall and with characters that correspond to *orishas* (deities) in the Afro-Cuban religion of Santería.

Harlow himself is a *Santero* who also wears a large Star of David on his neck. When asked if being a Jew and a Santero were in conflict and whether or not he still considered himself a Jew in terms of nationality, Harlow has consistently answered that, "you can take the boy out of Brooklyn, but not the Brooklyn out of the boy."[188] However, he adds that it is a "very personal thing" for him and that he uses divination and *ifa* to get closer to God and to avoid potential problems.[189]

Harlow served nine years on the board of governors of the National Academy of Recording Arts and Sciences (NARAS), the body that awards the Grammys®, and was instrumental in adding the Latin music category. In 2008 he was given a lifetime achievement award at the Latin Grammys (LARAS). To this day, he continues to collaborate with other artists from Japan and Miami as a producer.

IRA GOLDWASSER'S BAR MITZVAH AND HAITIAN VODOU DRUM LESSONS

In the same way that the best professional musicians who played Latin music had formal lessons and musical education, many of the best professional Latin music dancers who were known in the commercial mambo era (1943–60) had formal training, but what is seldom discussed is where and how they received this training. Ira Goldwasser exemplifies this history.

Goldwasser was born January 3, 1939, in Manhattan General Hospital (17th Street and 2nd Avenue). His three maternal uncles were excellent boogie-woogie dancers on the Lower East Side. Goldwasser's introduction to Latin music came around the age of four. He remembered dancing to 78 rpm records by Cugat and Miguelito Valdés with his sister and playing along with maracas and bongó in the house. Goldwasser remembers that in 1948, at the age of nine, his sister's boyfriend, a mambo dancer named Norman from East Harlem, brought the record "Abanaquito" to the house. For Goldwasser, that record "changed my life . . . it was like a comet hitting planet earth . . . and to this moment that's basically what we're [with his wife] doing with our lives: we're looking for the mambo . . . it's medicine."[190]

The family moved from New Jersey to Forest Hills, Queens, and in the summertime they would go to the bungalow colonies in Sullivan County in the

Fig 6.5. Sid Caesar with Machito Band. Photo from *It Happened in the Catskills* and accessed from the Latino Americans Blog.

Catskills. Goldwasser remembers many men putting on hastily prepared plays in the evenings after being gone all week. Goldwasser also remembers going to the Avon Lodge in Woodridge at the age of ten, where Sid Caesar would stay with his wife and writers from his show.[191] Caesar's wife's uncle, Arkin, owned the hotel. It was a secular crowd and environment where "Chinese food and Tito Puente was the perfect wedding, if you had that." Goldwasser would play tennis with Caesar. The writers would write the show during the week and drive back to New York City on Saturday mornings to film it. Caesar himself had been a saxophone player in bands at various hotels in the Catskills.

In this 1960 photo (see fig. 6.5) from the Myrna Katz Frommer and Harvey Frommer book *It Happened in the Catskills*, Sid Caesar is pictured playing tenor saxophone at the Concord Hotel with Chocolate Armenteros, Mario Bauzá, Frank Grillo "Machito" (standing left to right), and possibly Graciela Pérez standing at the far left offstage, Machito and the Afro-Cubans onstage behind him.

Wanting her son to be in show business, Goldwasser's mother asked Caesar for advice to take her son for dance lessons and he told her that, "there's only one place, that's the Katherine Dunham School of Dance." Goldwasser explains that this was where everyone from the Actors Studio studied. In the fall of 1949, Goldwasser began two years of studying at Dunham's school. At the school he studied "Ballet and the Dunham technique, which was a one-hour prelude to a one hour and fifteen minute session of Afrocuban or Afro-Haitian dancing that would depend upon who was leading the class . . . And there would be four to five drummers on the side." Goldwasser does not remember who the drummers were, but he knows that Chano Pozo had been there along with Francisco Aguabella. He also remembers dancing with Geoffrey Holder and Alvin Ailey. Goldwasser remembers that the very tall Holder could not "do leaps there" because the ceilings were very low in the studio space at 220 W. 43rd Street. The space had been donated by the Schubert family. Goldwasser's ballet class was twice a week and taught by Sevilla Fort, who was in Dunham's traveling company.

The Dunham technique was one hour at the barre, stretching, and Goldwasser remembers a specific pattern (almost a tango congo rhythm) played by the drummers with which the dancers' contracting and releasing was coordinated: "she isolated movements, that was basically the Dunham technique." They then rested for five minutes,

> And then the drummers would come in and we'd start. We'd follow one drum, we'd have three lines following the teacher. The [lead] dancer would begin with a basic walk and then adding to that, and just expanding completely and then we'd move around the mirror and the barre, to the back and begin again. And we would all just go around following, three lines [sings tango congo rhythm], nonstop an hour and a quarter . . . I was the only child in the class.

Goldwasser's sister did the children's classes on Saturdays, but Goldwasser stayed with the adult classes. He did the basic and intermediate classes and "learned the essence of Afro dance: to blend physically with the beat of the drum." The famed Palladium mambo dancers Augie and Margot were training at Dunham at the same time and Goldwasser remembers Augie taking ballet classes and being advised to "go into ballet." At some point, Goldwasser remembers, he stopped seeing Augie because Augie was studying in a class with Rudolph Nureyev and a Russian teacher, and "he eventually incorporated ballet at a high level into their [Augie and Margot's] act." Goldwasser remembers going to the Palladium as a youngster sometime around this time at the age of twelve in 1951. He had made "such an impression" on Augie and Margot that some eighteen years later at the age of thirty, he went to see Rolando La Serie perform at the Chateau Madrid in the Lexington Hotel and the opening act was Augie and Margot:

> The curtains open [sings mambo music] . . . Augie [is] coming out, we were ringside, and he comes right at our table, and he's doing his thing [singing

and dancing, shouts]: "Ira, where you been?" and then he goes back into his routine. . . [laughter] 'cause you known when you're eleven, twelve . . . I think I was, it was an exceptional situation, this kid [who] had nothing to do with the music and I'm very proud of that.

Goldwasser got to a point where, with the help of his mother, he got an old-time agent whose heyday had been the burlesque era. His mother sewed him a costume and Bill Cole, an instructor at the Dunham school, choreographed a one-and-a-half-minute routine to the Billy Eckstine hit "I Left My Hat in Haiti." Lenny Herman, a lawyer and weekend Latin bandleader at the Rego Park Jewish Center, accompanied him and rehearsed the routine with him at the Bal Tabarin nightclub in the afternoons. Goldwasser got a "special permission" letter from the mayor that allowed him to perform as an underage minor in adult venues as well as membership in the American Guild of Variety Artists (AGVA). Goldwasser remembers:

> The culmination of it all was at the same time somehow we got connected with a professional children's TV program [with] NBC at the Rainbow Room, and it was Star Time or Star Time Kids . . . So I had one performance on television and that was November of 1951 . . . George Scheck [father of attorney Barry Scheck] was one of the producers.

However, Goldwasser did not perform his choreographed routine on television. Instead, he performed wearing a rumba shirt with six African American youths from Harlem called the Enrico Stewart Ensemble. By this time, Goldwasser was in junior high school and his stage name was Jac E. Sawyer. Goldwasser was asked to perform at a number of clubs, but his mother would have to accompany him to the venues. The performing life proved too much for the young man and he was more inclined toward pursuing medicine. In February 1952, while studying for his bar mitzvah, he was also taking drum lessons with a vodou priest: "that's New York City," he offers, when reflecting in 2013.

Goldwasser remembers dancing to Noro Morales at the Nevele Hotel during the champagne hour in the summer of 1952. Remembering how dance styles evolved at that time, Goldwasser explains the difference between the double mambo and the chachachá, which would come a year or two later. For Goldwasser, there was never a controversy about when to move one's body weight: it was always on beat two with the slap of the conga. The major shift to dancing on one happened with Arthur Murray "getting into the act . . . everyone recognized [including] my parents . . . that it wasn't authentic." Goldwasser remembers all of the Jewish dancers dancing on two, and remembers a controversy over the "on one" and "on two" schools of thought in 1954. Goldwasser says, "I was a show business has-been at thirteen," when he danced while schoolmate Alfredito Levy was playing accompanying music at a Forest Hills High School event:

> I performed and the other kids all laughed at me because I was dancing on two. 'Cause it was easier [to dance] on one, obviously, [to] dance on two is difficult, the offbeat. So I think the whole nation was dancing one and just New York City was dancing on two, and only the insiders, not even the kids in the Jewish centers, they were probably also [dancing] on one. And maybe sporadically, the ones that went to the Bronx that hung with people of color, they danced on two. Or the people that went to the Catskills, in the Catskills we all danced like that, everyone was dancing on two.[192]

As a dancer, Goldwasser did not see the difference between the mambo step and the son step, moving on the two, forward and back, but he acknowledged a "black feel" when holding back on beat four.[193]

In the summer of 1954, at the age of fourteen, Goldwasser was a bar waiter at the National Hotel at Swan Lake. At the beginning of the summer, Goldwasser worked as a camp waiter at Sackett Lake and he heard mambo music across the lake. Next summer, at the age of fifteen, Goldwasser worked at the Laurels Country Club, owned by Ben Novak, who also owned the Fountainbleau. For the first four weeks of the summer, Goldwasser was the waiter for the the Lecuona Cuban Boys band in the main dining room. Wednesdays and Saturdays, the band would play matiness by the swimming pool. Goldwasser remembers that Cándido Camero was also there playing five congas at once. During the second half of the summer, Goldwasser was working at the Waldemere Hotel where Emilio (de Los) Reyes was the house band with Gil López on piano. De Los Reyes was a major bandleader from Cuba who had been a member of the Casino de la Playa band and then came to New York, making recordings on the Decca and Mardi-Gras labels.[194] López even taught Goldwasser a piano montuno that he remembers to this day. Part of Goldwasser's job at the Waldemere was to serve the band. Cuban Pete and Mille Donay were the resident dance team. In total, Goldwasser figures that he must have worked at some twenty-five to thirty different hotels between 1953–62, eight summers. By his own admission, Goldwasser was fired frequently, because he was hanging out late and "I was always looking for the mambo." Goldwasser says the kids who needed to work at the hotels were called mountain rats and they would go to work at the hotels in Miami during the off season. Nat Brooks, who had been the musical director of *Star Time Kids*, was at Brown's Hotel playing at the hotel nightclub. The mambo jamboree would start at 2am and Goldwasser would travel to dance there with the celebrated dance team of Pete and Millie.

Fig 6.6. Ira Goldwasser and Millie Donay dancing to Emilio Reyes, 1954. Photo courtesy of Ira Goldwasser.

With his eye on medical school, Goldwasser was advised to attend a small liberal arts school; he graduated from Bethany College in West Virginia with a degree in chemistry and biology. In 1956–57, Goldwasser chased bebop performers in Greenwich Village. After gaining entry at New York Medical College, Goldwasser was kicked out for not studying and would return to the Catskills each summer. Mambo (slow, medium, fast), chachachá, and merengue were on the menu for dancers, and Goldwasser remembers that some of the bands performing at the hotels during this period included Joe Cuba Sextet, La Playa Sextet, Randy Carlos, and Marty Stein. In 1962 Goldwasser worked in the Catskills at the same hotel as Tito Puente. But by 1963, Goldwasser felt that the mambo seemed to be losing popularity at the hotels.

Goldwasser had met his future wife, Harriet, in Holland and after getting married the couple moved to Holland in 1961, where Goldwasser went to medical school. Once in Holland, the couple got involved in promoting soul music at a small club by the Amsterdam Hilton under a bicycle shop. There was no Latin music on the scene, but people from Suriname were into Cuban music. In 1968 the couple returned to New York City and Goldwasser worked at Lenox Hill Hospital.

In July 1969, Goldwasser got involved with Felipe Luciano and the Young Lords at Metropolitan Hospital, but there was no dancing as it was considered a bourgeois activity: "we were Maoists, [with the] red book." In 1972 Goldwasser and his wife were working in the Health Revolutionary Alliance (HRA), "a white collective of doctors and nurses, health professionals" working to radicalize and organize. Goldwasser started doing group psychotherapy work with Benjamin Sadock as a resident, and then started a satellite mental health clinic and program in East Harlem. The much younger Young Lords were surprised to see the couple "dancing like our parents" when they danced at social functions. The Goldwassers also developed relationships with a number of Black Panthers. During this time period, the Goldwassers moved to 85th Street and would go out to dance at the Corso, Barney Google's, and the Cheetah, where it seemed to them that the same bands were playing all the time. Throughout this period, Harriet Goldwasser worked as a journalist and radio correspondent for socialist radio in Holland.

Goldwasser felt that there were many agent provocateurs in the movement, and by 1972 they were gradually moving away from political movements. Eventually the couple moved back to Holland in September 1975. With Ira Goldwasser's experience dealing with urban health, and the couple's continued connection to the Dutch government through Harriet, the Ministry of Justice invited Goldwasser to come back to Holland to work with heroin addicts. After clashing with the ministry over policy for drug abusers, Goldwasser transitioned in 1978 to private practice, which he has continued. Goldwasser was invited to visit Cuba in 1973 while living in New York, but could not attend due to the imminent birth of the couple's daughter. In 1980 he went to Cuba for the first time, and met with the Ministry of Health. Having gained some visibility for promoting Latin music in Amsterdam, the Goldwassers got their first opportunity to promote Latin music by becoming the managers of a local salsa band. After a half-year of success, Ira handled the M.C. duties and Harriet did the publicity for a Celia Cruz concert in Amsterdam. There was a salsa explosion in Holland in the mid-1980s, with a good club scene. After being approached by a young local radio host from Suriname to collaborate on his show, the Goldwassers transitioned from being guests to hosting their own show. Guests from throughout the country would visit the station for interviews and live public conversations about the music. Simultaneously, the Goldwasser home became a hangout for the like of Los Papines, Nicky Marrero, Santiago Alfonso (Tropicana choreographer), and others. The couple did thirteen years of radio with five years of that period being in front of a live audience. Live bands would perform into one microphone in a cultural center and charge money for admission. The band would earn five hundred guilders and jazz musicians would also perform for an hour. For Goldwasser, the idea was a re-creation of Symphony Sid's broadcasts from the Royal Roost, as well as those of Dick "Ricardo" Sugar and Art Raymond.

Goldwasser's parents retired to Puerto Rico in 1969, living there for twenty-five years, and he attributed his own involvement with Latin music and culture to his parents' appreciation of *negritúd*. Today, Goldwasser and his wife continue to travel to Cuba, Puerto Rico, and New York following the mambo with respites in between in Amsterdam. He is frequently profiled in Dutch magazines.

THE JEWISH LEGACY OF WEST SIDE STORY AND ITS RESIGNIFICATION BY LATINOS

One of the best examples of a Jewish representation of Latin music and Latino culture in New York City is the Broadway musical *West Side Story*, created by a team of Jewish New Yorkers: Jerome Robbins (Jerome Wilson Rabinowitz), Stephen Sondheim, Arthur Laurents, and Leonard Bernstein. The play and its legacy were also fraught with the complexities and consequences of racism and representation. According to Laurents, the play was initially conceived to be a version of Shakespeare's *Romeo and Juliet* with a Jewish and Catholic couple set as the tragic lovers.

Leonard Bernstein's score for *West Side Story* is one of the most recognized and celebrated scores of the American musical theater. Bernstein was a fan of Latin popular and orchestral music. And as evidenced by "The Latin American Spirit," his Young People's Concert with the New York Philharmonic, Bernstein was fully aware of the West African, indigenous, and Iberian components of Latin music.[195] Bernstein's score for *West Side Story* differentiated between the two ethnicities of each set of protagonists by using bebop for the white teenagers and Latin music for the Puerto Rican teenagers.[196] New York–born Puerto Rican percussionist, bandleader, and eight-time Grammy® nominee Bobby Sanabria points out that for "América" the rhythms that are used are a combination of Mexican *huapango* and Venezuelan *joropo*. When pushed as to why non–Puerto Rican rhythms were used, Sanabria stated, "I think that what Bernstein was trying to convey is the universality of Latin America and how these Puerto Ricans were adapting to this new life on the mainland."[197] Nevertheless, in Sanabria's own Grammy®-nominated rendering of Bernstein's score, he incorporates Puerto Rican bomba, Dominican merengue, a variety of Afro-Cuban genres (sacred batá drumming and singing for *Ochún*, mambo, chachachá, son montuno, rumba, and more), Brazilian samba, as well as modern jazz into the material. A BBC documentary on the musical discusses how Bernstein and his Chilean wife frequented the Palladium as dancers in the

1950s. This influence is featured in the mambo scene of *West Side Story*. The use of the tritone as a melodic figure throughout the score is also reflective of the cornerstone of bebop, the flatted fifth.

Sanabria wrote a well-conceived opinion piece for the National Institute of Latino Policy that addressed the debate among Puerto Ricans who articulated the view that *West Side Story* was damaging to the community and perpetuated negative stereotypes of Puerto Ricans. He pointed out many connections to the African diaspora in the Americas that personally resonated with him in the film version of *West Side Story*. These include the entrance of Bernardo Nuñez wearing black and red clothing, the colors of Elegguá, the Yoruba spirit of the crossroads discussed in the introduction. For Sanabria, Elegguá is also referenced by the "young child drawing concentric circles in chalk on the playground cement" when Riff Lorton appears in the opening scene of the film. For Sanabria, it's irrelevant if Bernstein was aware of these tropes, because "in the mythology, Elegua [*sic*] is always present whether one knows it or not." Expounding upon the musical material of the show, Sanabria posits that the use of the tritone throughout the score also signals Elegguá:

> As *Elegua* opens and closes every *Santeria* ceremony, these notes are the beginning and the end of the entire show. As stated before, these ascending three notes and their descending three note answer draw one into the other worldliness, mystery and aché that is New York City as they appear in various manifestations throughout the entire score. Three? Even the rhythmic cadence of the prologue is based on an alternating three bar melodic cadence. Guess what *Elegua*'s number is? It sets the stage for something that had never been heard or seen on the Broadway stage.[198]

The show's creators made the show with good intentions and an underlying message asking for tolerance in the face of tragedy à la *Romeo and Juliet*. The movie version of *West Side Story* featured Puerto Rican–born and New York–raised actress Rita Moreno, who would win an Oscar Award for her portrayal of Anita. However, as successful as the music was commercially and critically, the musical was problematic for Puerto Ricans and to this day remains controversial in its portrayal of Puerto Ricans. Camilla Fojas writes:

> *West Side Story* intensified the obsession with wayward teens, but added a new element: the Puerto Rican "problem," one that is as complex as it is manifold. In keeping with the logic of the musical, the characterizations of Puerto Ricans in *West Side Story* are split between good and bad, along a gendered divide. These ambivalent depictions invest the future potential of the colonial subject in the women, while the men are part of cautionary stories. The

negative depiction of Puerto Rican men corresponds to prevailing notions in
the 1950s and 1960s about Puerto Rican degeneracy, in contradistinction to
immigrants deemed assets to the host culture. . . . Unlike idealized immigrant
groups, Puerto Ricans were thought of as bringing their "culture of poverty"
to the colonial center, causing a ruination of mainstream culture rather than
an enhancement of it. This bad reputation is evident in *West Side Story* when
Lieutenant Schrank maligns Puerto Ricans by claiming that they will "turn
the whole town into a stinking pigsty." Such ideas circulated in mass culture
through news media programming that popularized the ideological work of
social scientists focused on the Puerto Rican "problem."[199]

Laura Briggs also has written extensively about what happened politically and
socially regarding the situating of Puerto Ricans in the eyes of the non–Puerto
Rican policy-making establishment. Briggs shows how specific lyrics in *West
Side Story*'s songs were deemed offensive by Puerto Ricans and Puerto Rican
media in New York City. She explains the result of the play's success: "When
Puerto Ricans who grew up in the 1950s and '60s complain that everywhere
they went, *West Side Story* provided the lens through which mainland Americans saw them, this is part of the complaint—all the boys are criminals, all the
girls are sexualized, and the island is 'overpopulated.'"[200]

Julia Foulkes writes that Puerto Rican officials on the island made their
critiques publicly:

> The Spanish-language newspapers in New York and in Puerto Rico then
> tracked the views of Puerto Rican public officials who had seen the show, in
> particular Governor Luis Muñoz Marin and former health commissioner An-
> tonio Fernos Isern. Isern came under swift indictment by *La Prensa* in New
> York and *El Mundo* in San Juan when they noted that he did not condemn
> the lyrics. Isern felt compelled to correct the record, writing in *El Mundo*
> that the press had not reported his full statement, which included a plea to
> strike the remarks about a diseased island. Muñoz Marin, on the other hand,
> shifted the inquiry in an interview, suggesting that the problem of juvenile
> delinquency was New York's and not at all specific to Puerto Ricans. The story
> could have worked just as well with any two other groups, even the original
> Jews and Catholics, he claimed. The show was in what it revealed about New
> York, not Puerto Rico.[201]

Once the musical came out and became an instant hit, the Puerto Rican government under the leadership of Governor Luis Muñoz Marín actually hired
a public relations firm to convince mainland Americans that Puerto Ricans
were not gangsters.[202]

It is against this backdrop that "America," one of the most well-known themes in *West Side Story*, is quoted by Willie Colón and Rubén Blades on their now-classic recording of "Pedro Navaja," Blades's epic tale of tragedy in New York City on their 1978 album *Siembra*. At almost eight minutes, longer than most pop and Spanish Caribbean radio hits, "Pedro Navaja" is often explained as a Spanish-language interpretation of "Mack the Knife." This explanation is due in part from the literal translation of the title, Peter Knife. Today, most Latin music fans consider it to be a masterpiece and they know the lyrics by heart. Throughout the musical performance there are sounds of sirens and at one point there is a description of events from the perspective of an urban nightly news broadcast. Harmonically, "Pedro Navaja" and "Mack the Knife" are similar in their verse sections, but the subject matter and imagery of Blade's lyrics are grittier. As the song's main protagonists, a prostitute and a thief, kill one another and lay dying in the street, a drunk man makes off with their belongings singing to himself that life is full of surprises (*"la vida te da sorpresas, sorpresas te da la vida"*). This choral refrain in the montuno (call-and-response) section allows Blades to improvise *soneos* (vocal improvisations) that deal with the violence of urban life: *"ocho millones de historias tiene la ciudad de Nueva York"* (eight million stories in New York City). Once the brilliant arrangement by Puerto Rican trumpeter and arranger Luis "Perico" Ortíz transitions to a new mambo section, there is a wordless "happy" interlude with vocables that repeat over a cycle of chromatically descending ii-V chord progressions. Then the band breaks while the chorus sings "I like to live in America" in English with a heavy Spanish accent. This is followed immediately in a responsive fashion with the trombone section playing the notes for *"la vida te da sorpresas"* and then there is a tense B7 altered chord arpeggiated by the piano:

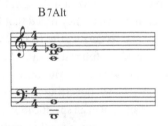

Musical Example 6.1. Chord from Pedro Navaja. Transcription by Benjamin Lapidus.

Through this simple musical statement, Blades, Colón, and Ortíz poke fun at the Broadway musical's message of tolerance, immigration, criminality, and upward mobility with the realities of life as a Latino in New York and the inner cities of the Americas. This well-known phrase from one of the world's most well-known musicals was forever hence recast with new meaning. Additionally, for

Latinos in New York and the United States as well as for Spanish speakers in the Americas, after 1978 the humor and irony of the lyric "I like to live in America" was forever entwined with the cruel reality that indeed "*la vida te da sorpresas.*"

Bernstein and Sondheim's "America" had been previously recast and resignified from the Cuban immigrant perspective many years earlier than "Pedro Navaja" on La Lupe's 1966 album *They Call Me La Lupe/A mi me llaman La Lupe.*[203] Produced by the Puerto Rican musician and producer Al Santiago for Tico Records, Chico O'Farrill's arrangement features all-new Spanish lyrics and renders the song as a samba. The lyrics of the choral refrain are changed to "Oh how beautiful America is, all the Cubans in America, we are happy in America, we are not moving from America."[204] The verses of the song talk about the Cuban immigrant experience in the United States—specifically, coming from Cuba by plane, not knowing the language but coping through singing and laughter. Another verse talks about the sadness of leaving and the hope of one day seeing Havana again. The song also speaks about working hard in the United States.

As I have written elsewhere and as exemplified with the four musical protagonists in this chapter, there is no doubt that Jewish involvement with Latin music has been ongoing, extensive, nuanced, and enduring. As a Jew who has performed and recorded a variety of Latin musical genres with groups in the United States, Cuba, Dominican Republic, Puerto Rico, South America, Europe, and Asia, I find myself in many playing situations. On occasion I am asked about my own introduction to Latin music, but more often, I am not asked anything at all and simply expected to perform my part with the required swing and feeling that the music demands. Moving to New York City at the age of fourteen, I heard and saw Latin music from throughout the Caribbean performed in my daily life, and some of the greatest musicians in Latin music lived in my neighborhood. Some of these musicians even took me under their wing. Prior to this, I was exposed to the music through my father's record collection and his piano playing. As a musician, I have been interested in and explored the roots of popular Spanish Caribbean musical genres for some time and this has informed both my performance and my scholarship. Reflecting upon all of the musicians who came before me, I am constantly in awe of the amount of discipline, craft, and hard work that is involved in writing, performing, and producing the vast body of Latin music made over the last 120 years in New York City. For the musicians who created this music, and for those who continue to do so, the primary objective has always been to create technically proficient and musically exciting dance music for a sophisticated and discerning public. The ethnicity of the musicians was less important than the quality of the swing, as demonstrated by the extent of the inter-ethnic collaboration on records and in bands from throughout the time period of this study. Jews, like Puerto Ricans, Dominicans, Panamanians, Colombians, Italians, African Americans, and others have been playing in Cuban and non-Cuban Latin bands for a long time and continue to be deeply involved in the fabric of Latin music in New York City. Recently, a large cohort of Israeli musicians, who now call New York City their home, have performed in some of the biggest Latin bands both locally and beyond. They are the latest wave of non-Latin musicians to excel in the field of Latin music. It is likely that another ethnic group or nationality will take their place as newcomers, and that can be seen with the popularity of Latin dance among Asian Americans. The music attracts so many different people because it is so satisfying and appealing. As more people are exposed to Latin music in New York, they tend to explore its variety and roots. Hopefully, this ongoing process will continue into the future. While there have of course been Jewish protagonists in Caribbean music in many other places, New York City was the place where this engagement happened in large numbers and many permutations.

CHAPTER 7

"INVASIÓN DEL 80/¡YO VINE DEL MARIEL!"

The Musical Impact of the Mariel Boatlift

Between April and September 1980, roughly 125,000 people made a perilous journey from the Port of Mariel in Cuba to Key West, Florida, and then on to Arkansas, Florida, Wisconsin, Texas, Pennsylvania, and other refugee camps before becoming permanent residents in the United States. However, the overwhelming majority of *Marielitos*, as the arrivals would become known, settled in South Florida and would go on to lead extremely productive lives, contributing positively and occupying important positions in American society. A small number of this massive group made up a cohort of musicians and dancers whose musical contributions, impact, and legacy, both in New York City and the United States, has been mostly omitted from any narrative concerning Cuban music or the development of Latin music in New York City.

This chapter discusses the immediate musical impact of the 1980 Mariel Boatlift by examining some of the dancers and musicians who arrived in New York City at that time: Orlando "Puntilla" Ríos, Manuel Martínez Olivera "*El llanero solitario*" (The Lone Ranger), Roberto Borrell, Rita Macías, Xiomara Rodríguez, Félix "Pupy" Insua, Pedro Domech, Daniel Ponce, Fernando Lavoy, Gerardo "Taboada" Fernández, Gabriel "Chinchilita" Machado, and many others. The musical activities of these and other musicians have had long-term effects on the folkloric and Latin popular dance music scenes in New York and the greater United States, not only in the performance realm but in many cases also as teachers for subsequent generations of Cuban and non-Cuban musicians, particularly Puerto Ricans in New York City. In addition, this group of artists who arrived during *El Mariel* would also serve as important points of connection for the next major wave of newly arriving musicians and dancers in the early 1990s, known as the *balseros* (raft people). Thus, the effects of this historical moment in New York's Latin music scene would be long-lasting. This chapter provides an analysis of and insight into this overlooked era of Cuban musical history in New York and how it would impact Latin music in New York and elsewhere.

Generally speaking, the Marielitos were caught between two competing narratives. The Cuban government shaped a narrative that the flotilla and mass exodus from Mariel purged Cuba of criminals, homosexuals, and other undesirables, including a surreptitious dumping of an institutionalized population with an array of serious needs. At the same time, the US media and earlier Cuban arrivals stigmatized the Marielitos for their "blackness," their criminality, and the fact that they had willingly lived in Cuba through the revolution, somehow making them unrepentant communists. Nancy Raquel Mirabál has explored the long historical narrative of Afro-Cubans in the United States and Cuba, framing the arrival of the Mariel group within a backdrop that dates to the early nineteenth century.[1] While Afro-Cubans in New York "rescripted" ideas of race from the 1930s on through a variety of organizations and activities such as El Club Cubano InterAmericano and other entities, before 1980 their numbers were not as great as those of white Cubans.[2] Compared to the arrival of previous generations, Mirabal writes that:

> In contrast to past migrations, the Mariel boatlift of 1980 and the Balseros of 1994 included a large number of Afro-Cubans. The recent migrations of Afro-Cubans again reconfigured a language of race, sexuality, culture, and gender that was not always understood or employed and among community making Cuban exiles.[3]

Looking at Ybor City and Tampa, Evelio Grillo's firsthand chronicle of growing up Afro-Cuban in the United States supports Mirabál's notion by showing how and where Afro-Cubans interacted with their African American and white Cuban counterparts in the first half of the twentieth century.[4]

Ramón Grosfoguel and Chloé S. Georas place the Mariel arrivals into the larger context with African Americans and Puerto Ricans of the era:

> During the 1980s, thousands of Cuban refugees from the Mariel migrations went to New York City from Miami. These migrants were from a more popular class background than the pre-1980s Cuban migrants. Moreover, a large number of the Marielitos were Afro-Cubans. Given the phaseout of the Cuban Refugee Program in the late 1970s, these migrants did not have access to state assistance and in turn were not cushioned against racial discrimination. As a result, the marielitos were Puerto Ricanized in New York City and "African Americanized" in Miami. They suffered a marginalization in the labor market similar to that of Puerto Ricans and Dominicans in New York City. They became part of the colonial immigrants living a social process similar to the colonial/racial subjects of the U.S. empire.[5]

In order to better understand the impact of the Mariel Boatlift on the Latin music scene in New York City, it is useful to look at music making in Cuba immediately after the revolution, the events that precipitated the Mariel boatlift, and the musical and social consequences of these events. This will show that musicians and practitioners of Afro-Cuban music and cultural traditions had additional reasons for leaving during the Mariel Boatlift that were tied to the complexity of race and identity as well freedom of religious and cultural expression.

MUSIC IN POST-REVOLUTIONARY CUBA

In his study of music in Cuba after 1959, Robin Moore describes some of the differences between the possibilities for commercial and art music versus those of Afro-Cuban folkloric music:

> By contrast, performers of folk music had relatively few options. Biases against African-derived genres especially meant that those involved with such repertoire could rarely perform in public or record. Music schools included very little instruction related to traditional music of any sort. . . . Folklore flourished in the black working-class neighborhoods of major cities and in rural towns but did not often appear on the radio or television. Its status might be likened to that of black gospel in the United States, given its strong influence on popular music but its near total invisibility for years in the marketplace.[6]

Afro-Cuban musicians and performers had significantly less access to making recordings and fewer performance venues compared to musicians who focused on art music and popular music. However, the transition toward the institutionalization of the arts—including music—took a number of significant twists and turns as venues, recording studios, manufacturing plants, radio, and television were nationalized and musicians became state employees. Moore assesses the mixed blessings of this period, writing, "the early 1960s witnessed cultural turmoil and experimentation on a magnitude that rivaled the period's political changes." Although artists started to lead the larger entities of the cultural bureaucracy, which in turn led to publication of more music and research on music, Moore concludes:

> Changes in the political sphere had negative effects on culture as well. Visas for travel became more difficult to obtain. The exodus of large segments of the middle class resulted in a lack of qualified entrepreneurs to oversee the

business of music making. Employees in charge of sound recording after 1964 demonstrated little interest in promoting artists abroad and produced fewer albums. Economic instability, campaigns of salary regulation, and the abolition of copyright and royalty payments all functioned to suppress nightlife and song composition and to encourage the departure of many performers.[7]

Many important musical protagonists left Cuba and went into exile in the United States and elsewhere, and a large number settled in New York City. Moore writes that with the establishment of state cultural institutions after 1959, "the revolution has cultivated the extraordinary gifts of many underprivileged individuals . . . from the Afro-Cuban community, [resulting] in support for research on folklore[,] . . . local performers and genres [that] far exceed[s] the relatively scanty research conducted on such themes in Puerto Rico, the Dominican Republic, and other islands."[8] Nevertheless, European art music was privileged in state-run arts schools and programs while popular and folkloric music was largely marginalized in these settings, except as Moore indicates, in conservatory percussion programs after 1979.[9]

Afro-Cuban folklore, religion, and their concomitant music were "demonstrably more visible across the island during the early 1960s, owing in part to the large number of semiprofessional ensembles that emerged as part of the Amateurs' movement."[10] This movement sought to involve as many nonprofessionals in the arts as possible and was derived from the Marxist view "that capitalism had created an unhealthy division between professional performers and workers."[11] As a result of this movement and the forming of state-sponsored groups, public presentations of traditional Afro-Cuban drumming increased significantly.[12] The Conjunto Folklórico Nacional was the "first state-funded artistic institution devoted exclusively to the performance of national [Afro-Cuban] folklore."[13] Its founding in 1962 also encouraged the pursuit of Afro-Cuban folklore in other realms, and Moore notes that popular music groups led by Pello el Afrokán, Pacho Alonso, and Enrique Bonne included more prominent Afro-Cuban drumming in the Cuban popular music of the era. There are myriad complicated issues vis à vis race and the relationship to the state's agenda that were the direct result of codifying sacred musical traditions for staged performance, but as these issues continued to be negotiated, Afro-Cuban folkloric music and dance substantially increased in visibility. However, learning these traditions in the formal conservatory setting has been historically quite limited.

Censorship of artists during 1968–73, in what is largely known as the "*quinquenio gris*" (five-year gray stretch), brought about a number of negative repercussions for some artists including internment in re-education camps, denial of visas, denial of venues to perform, and other repression.[14] Some prominent

Afro-Cuban religious informants explained point-blank to Román Orozco and Natalia Bolívar that Afro-Cuban religious ceremonies and ritual drumming were not permitted from the mid-1960s until the late 1970s.[15] The scholar and activist Serafín "Tato" Quiñones has written and spoken extensively about how his involvement with the abakuá was a direct and personal response to these injustices and persecution from authorities.[16] The music also suffered during this period, but groups like Los Van Van, Elio Revé, and others came out of this period stronger than ever, adding North American music to their sound in a variety of ways that were both obvious and not so obvious, as well as rhythms that could excite younger Cubans. Some prominent Afro-Cuban musicians in New York City have privately expressed to me the view that Cuban musicologists were recording and archiving Afro-Cuban traditions during the 1970s as a means of preserving what they viewed as worthless, invalid, or as artifacts of savagery. Moore writes: "the largely white, middle-class revolutionary leadership did not approve of African-derived religions, but they viewed them differently from Christian institutions."[17]

Regardless of faith, religious practice and communist party membership were mutually exclusive up until the early 1990s and the authorities disrupted and prohibited all religious ceremonies. In the early years of the revolution, Afro-Cuban religions were initially seen as primitive, sick, and anti-Marxist; the state prohibited artists who sang songs with religious references from performing them.[18] Orozco and Bolívar delve into some of the ways that revolutionaries who had fought against Batista were denied opportunities in the new system for being practitioners of Afro-Cuban religions.[19] In 1968 the Cuban communist party published a book called *Sectas religiosas* (religious sects), which spoke pseudo-scientifically about the dangerous qualities and problems (fraud, homosexuality, delinquency, alcoholism, drug addiction, and more) endemic to practitioners of espiritísmo, santería, palo, and abakuá.[20] However, as early as 1960 the government moved to create entities such as Teatro Nacional Cubano and the Centro de Estudios del Folclor to study Afro-Cuban folklore with "Marxist-Leninist methodology" as led by Aregliers León and Jesús Guanche.[21] In 1974 Rogelio Martínez Furé, the founder and director of the Conjunto Folklórico Nacional, articulated this methodological approach. explaining in an interview that in the Americas folklore serves "as forms of cultural resistance and manifestations of the existing class war . . . folklore, it can be said, are the most authentic manifestations of traditional popular culture in opposition to the culture of the dominant classes or [the] official culture."[22] At the same time, he explains, folklore is not synonymous with a museum of frozen culture or curious fossil[s].[23] He clearly articulates that folklore of a country can be developed "intelligently and scientifically" by removing negative folklore, which he characterizes as "superstitions, taboos without scientific foundations, idealistic conceptions about supernatural forces that govern the life of men, practices of medical quackery, coprolagnia, xenophobia, etc."[24] Thus, folklore could pursued as a serious endeavor but was separated from its spiritual meaning.

What is so puzzling about the time period of the early 1970s is that at the same time that prohibitions and restrictions were in effect, amateur Afro-Cuban folkloric ensembles spread throughout the country's provinces at the university level. One notable example was the Conjunto Folclórico Universitario, the folkloric group of the University of Havana founded in 1970 that appeared frequently on television.[25] Another folkloric group that was active at this time was the Conjunto Folklórico de Liberación '75, located in the Atarés neighborhood; many of its members, such as Juan "El Negro" Raymat, Orlando "Puntilla" Ríos, and others, would go on to perform in important folkloric groups at the national level.[26] During the same period, another percussionist, Justo Pegaito, taught classes at the Escuela de Superación Cervantes and counted notable musicians such as Mayito Rivera and Roberto Vizcaino among his students.[27] A rumbero named Changuilón also helped "Puntilla" Ríos get a percussion teaching position at la ENA with the title *Técnico auxiliar docente*.[28] While Moore has written about the absence of Afro-Cuban folklore and culture from the Cuban mass media, various musicians who lived through the era remember examples that counter this assertion, such as the weekly television show on Channel 2 called *Arte y folclór* that was dedicated to Afro-Cuban folklore and broadcast Saturdays at 7:30pm.[29] In addition, a weekly Sunday radio show on Radio Cadena Habana featured the music of Los Papines and Irakere from 1:30–2:00pm.[30] Similarly, with Cuban involvement in the Angola conflict as well as greater Cuban influence elsewhere on the continent, young Africans were coming to study in Cuba and thus, both Africa and African culture were becoming more visible. This would also be reflected in pop music recordings such as "De Cabinda a Cunene un solo pueblo" by Los Karachi, which makes direct reference to Angola and solidarity with Cuba.[31]

Moore explains how *casas de cultura* (houses of culture) were set up throughout the island, and folklore as well as other types of performances were held there.[32] Besides the aforementioned *aficionado* (amateur) events, *festivales de trabajadores* (workers' festivals) also featured folkloric groups. In the late 1970s, there was a shift toward documenting these traditions at the same time they were being seen and heard in popular music of the era. However, the state remained ambivalent about Afro-Cuban religious music and clear in its disapproval of its practice. Despite the difficulties of US-Cuba relations, some groups such as Los Papines, Afrocuba de Matanzas, Orquesta Aragón, and others made their way to New York City to perform in the late 1970s. Thus, in order to understand where the Marielitos fit into the Latin music scene of New

York, one must take into account that the story begins in Cuba with a unique and puzzling history of repression, ambivalence, and simultaneous encouragement (when stripped of religious context) of Afro-Cuban cultural expression.

CUBAN-US RELATIONS AND EVENTS THAT BROUGHT ABOUT THE MARIEL BOATLIFT

The Mariel Boatlift was precipitated by a confluence of interrelated historical events. First, in an era of repression on the island, a group of young Cuban Americans called the Antonio Maceo Brigade began traveling back to the island in 1978. Some 100,000 exiles also traveled there in 1979. At the same time, prominent Cuban exiles were engaging with the Cuban government for the release of political prisoners. Roughly three thousand prisoners were freed and their slow departure for the United States meant that with their freedom they were interacting with the general Cuban populace to the disdain of the government.[33]

Additionally, Cuban American visitors were bringing goods and gifts to their Cuban families that were not available in Cuba. Morale was also still generally low from the government's physically exhausting, resource-gobbling, and failed plan to harvest ten million tons of sugar in 1970.[34] Additionally, the war in Angola and Cuba's engagement in Africa seemed to be draining the country as well. María Teresa Vélez writes:

> During the late 1970s, the trade balance as well as the economic growth rate of Cuba had deteriorated. The last years of this decade were years of economic hardship; the standard of living had declined, food was scarce, and the housing needs of the population had gone unmet. Dissent and discontent had grown after the austerity measures the government took to cope with the emergency.[35]

Against this backdrop, on April 1, 1980, Hector Sanyustiz, Radamés Gómez, Francisco Raúl Díaz Molina, and Mercedes Álvarez crashed a bus into the grounds of the Peruvian embassy in an effort to seek asylum and leave Cuba. Soon ten to eleven thousand Cubans clamored to the embassy grounds seeking asylum. The Carter administration flew over 600 of a pledged 3,500 Cubans to Costa Rica before the Cuban government stopped the flights. Napoleón Vilabola, a Cuban American exile who had been in Cuba as part of the dialogue with the Cuban government, suggested to his old friend René Rodríguez, who had stayed in Cuba to work with government, that a flotilla should be allowed to take the Cubans out who wanted to leave.[36] After Vilabola met with Fidel

Castro in Cuba, the plan was put into action. Vilabola helped spread the message in Miami that people could return to Cuba by boat to pick up any of their relatives that wanted to leave.

On April 19, the first of many journeys would be made by a flotilla of ships between the two countries; the first boats taking evacuees to Miami left Cuba on April 21. As families traveled to the Port of Mariel, there were pro-government marches and public acts of repudiation against those who were leaving, as well as physical attacks. The encampment at the Port of Mariel was sectioned in such a way as to divide people into three groups: those claimed by family in the United States, those who had been on the grounds of the embassy, and those who had turned themselves in at police stations "declaring themselves scum, and [who] asked for a permit to leave."[37] Ojito writes that the Cuban government called this category *escoria* and it included

> Homosexuals, prostitutes, drug users, and enemies of the revolution. Castro himself manipulated the formula [for percentages of departing Cubans] every day, balancing both Washington's tolerance and Miami's innocence against his own needs to cleanse the country of "scum." He had created seven categories encompassing every possible type of person he wanted to get rid of—from *gusanos* to child molestors. If Cubans in Miami monitoring the new arrivals noticed that too many criminals were arriving in the boatlift and protested too loud, Castro would adjust his numbers, increasing the percentage of relatives and lowering the percentage of criminals for a few days. If no one protested, he would reverse the numbers.[38]

In his memoir, Paquito D'Rivera remembers a Miami meeting with one well-known neighborhood street musician and local character, Juan Charrasqueado, who had a history of mental health problems in Cuba and would wander the streets dressed as a mariachi. He remembers Charrasqueado telling him: "'Look, I wasn't doing anything wrong. I don't know why they put me on that boat and sent me here, where I don't know nobody or nothing,' the poor street musician said, confused, and disconcerted."[39]

The deliberate dumping of persons who were deemed undesirable by the Cuban government continued into May 1980, where the "majority [of the arrivals] were young, single men, many of whom admitted they had served jail time in Cuba, though their crimes ranged from attempting to leave the country illegally to having long hair or punching someone at a bar."[40] Due to racism and sensationalized press coverage, the negative reputation of the Mariel arrivals was grossly exaggerated. After arriving in the US, many of the Marielitos were moved to detention. Fighting for the unjustly held Mariel detainees, the ACLU pointed out, "only 300 were mental health patients and only 350 had committed serious felony crimes."[41] In fact in terms of actual crimes, there were only 600 felony cases out of some 125,000 people.[42]

Eventually, in December 1984, 2,746 individuals were designated for deportation from the United States back to Cuba as they were deemed undesirables.[43] This was part of an agreement under which the United States would allow some 27,000 Cuban immigrants annually, but "the agreement precipitated rioting at the federal detention centers in Oakdale, Louisiana, and Atlanta, where several thousand Cubans were being held," and the ensuing hostage crisis and property damage was the result of people who "demanded their constitutional rights, which they claimed had been denied them by so many years of confinement."[44] The situation was peacefully resolved through the intervention of the auxiliary Archbishop of Miami.[45] Although some people were freed and reunited with their families, others were deported to Cuba. By the 1990s, of the "2,400 [who] were still being detained . . . just more than 400 of them had been deported to Cuba . . . [and] approximately 100 of the Marielitos were confined in mental institutions and suffering from chronic mental illness."[46]

WHO WERE THE MARIELITOS?

James S. Olson and Judith E. Olson wrote about how the racial makeup of the Cuban American community was impacted during the Mariel Boatlift and placed it against the backdrop of earlier Cuban migration to the United States:

> In 1960 nearly 7 percent of all Cubans living in the United States were Afro-Cubans, but in 1970 that number had dropped to only 2.6 percent. More than 98 percent of the Cuban immigrants during the 1960s were white. That was hardly surprising. After the onset of the Castro revolution, most of the immigrants had been upper- and middle-class Cubans, and historically Cuban society had discriminated against black people, confining them to the lower rungs of the socioeconomic ladder. American immigration policy during the 1960s and 1970s was also biased in favor of Cubans who had family members in the United States, which also guaranteed a strong priority for whites over blacks. Finally, the Cuban revolution had provided some immediate benefits to Afro-Cubans, eliminating all forms of segregation and opening previously closed employment opportunities to them. But in the deteriorating Cuban economy, more than 40 percent of the Marielitos were Afro-Cubans. At the time of the Marielito migration in 1980, Miami's Little Havana was 99 percent white. Most of those whites carried the traditional white Cuban suspicions of Afro-Cubans. Large numbers of white Cuban Americans were prejudiced against them because of their black skin and their Santería religion.[47]

An exception to this negative reception in South Florida at the time was in found Tampa and Ybor City, an area with a historically active and vibrant Afro-Cuban community. Cuban immigrants of Afro-Cuban descent were "more likely to live in Little Havana North [Union City and West New York, New Jersey]" and not in Florida, "probably because of the feeling that racial discrimination in New York and New Jersey would not be as severe."[48] However, there was a long history with many public activities of the Afro-Cuban community in the other parts of the New York City metropolitan area, such as the Club Cubano Inter-Americano, among others, as well as other opportunities available in New York that were not available in South Florida. In light of this, it made sense that many Mariel arrivals sought to come to New York City, where there was already a large and established Afro-Caribbean and Afro-Latin community.

Cristina D. Abreu notes: "Of the 41,262 Cubans who were in New York by 1960, an estimated 28,000 had been born in Cuba. More than 25,000 were classified as 'white,' while nearly 3,000 were classified as 'black' . . . but race as constructed and imposed from above did little to diminish the cultural presence and social relevance of 'black' Cubans in and beyond *colonia cubana* [Cuban community]."[49] El Club Cubano Inter-Americano has hosted numerous social events and performances by Afro-Cuban musicians from its founding in the 1940s to the present and caters to an Afro-Cuban, Afro-Latin, Afro-Caribbean, and African American audience. Abreu points out that this "ethnic inclusiveness . . . worked to make Afro-Cuban music and musicians and Cubanness and Afrocubanness central elements of a broader Hispano/a and Latino/a identity."[50]

In the 1980s, Cuban musicians who arrived as Marielitos went on to join forces with major jazz artists and to contribute their musical talents to the heavily thriving Latin music scene in New York City, establishing themselves in genres such as charanga, salsa, merengue, son, and more. In addition, they became important teachers of Cuban folkloric music and dance. Lastly, these musicians and dancers provided Cuban and non-Cuban practitioners of Afro-Cuban religions with complete and up-to-date information on ritual and musical performance practice, whereas earlier Cuban arrivals would have shared this information with only a select few in the non-Cuban Latino community. As seen in the above historical background, Marielitos were often stigmatized for their "blackness" and the fact that they had lived in Cuba through the revolution. Some musicians embraced the Mariel identity while others sought to minimize their association with the Mariel phenomenon.

REINVIGORATION OF THE RITUAL CONTEXT:
FOLKLORE AND RELIGIOUS KNOWLEDGE

Prior to the arrival of santeros in the Mariel Boatlift, Marta Moreno Vega wrote about the effect of the Cuban revolution on the New York City–based community of santería devotees of her era:

> Since the Cuban revolution of 1959, the United States has seen a reinfusion of Africanity into its melting pot. Thousands of *santeros* have come as exiles, bringing orishas to America again. This has meant a second acculturation of Yoruba religion. This time an entirely new set of ethno-historical factors has come into play as santeros acquire North American culture and Americans feel the impact of Santería.[51]

While there were babalawos, santeras, and ritual drummers in New York City from at least the 1940s, if not earlier, there were limits on the types of religious activities possible; for example, there were no consecrated batá drums in New York until 1979.[52] An acculturation of Yoruba religion would happen again as a direct result of the Mariel arrivals, a development that steered the tradition of Afro-Cuban musical folklore and ritual music in New York City and beyond.

FELIPE GARCÍA VILLAMIL

Felipe García Villamil (b. 1931) was a former sugar worker who worked as a folkloric drummer in Cuba after the revolution before coming to the United States. Born in Matanzas, the batá drummer, drum maker, babalawo (priest), abakuá, and *palero* who had organized his own group in 1970 called Emikeké (small group).[53] Throughout her book on García Villamil, María Teresa Vélez explores how his trajectory in Afro-Cuban culture, as a musician and practitioner dedicated to a variety of religious traditions, was intertwined with the ways in which these traditions were repressed and eventually accepted by the new government, then commodified, and finally how they underwent the process of folklorization.[54]

It is unclear what the exact circumstances were that brought about García Villamil's departure from Cuba, but he explained to Vélez that the authorities told him to leave or go to prison. Like many who endured dangerously overfilled and rickety sea craft, García Villamil thought he would perish at sea. After arriving in Key West, García Villamil wound up in Wisconsin at Fort McCoy. A number of musicians in this particular refugee camp would go on to be important protagonists throughout the United States, including Jesús

Díaz, Carlos "Quinto" Eguis Águila, Esteban Alayeto a.k.a. *Siento un bombo*, as well as Gabriel "Chinchilita" Machado, who will be discussed below. While they awaited sponsorship to leave the camp, detainees were allowed to form a band and perform. According to attorney Michael Reyes, the aforementioned musicians and many others were sponsored by Ricardo González, the Cuban American owner of Madison's Cardinal Bar who "helped integrate them into Madison society in 1980," and who later organized a sister city program between Madison, Wisconsin, and Camagüey, Cuba.[55]

Another fascinating and relatively unknown story concerning the Cuban refugees held at Fort McCoy has been documented by the Chicago-based photographer Carlos Flores. One weekend in July 1980, Eddie Palmieri and his orchestra played at a concert called Carnivale, which took place at the International Amphitheater in Chicago. According to Flores, the event had many performers but a low turnout. The band flew from Chicago's O'Hare Airport to Sparta, Wisconsin, on a small plane to play a concert for the detainees sponsored by La Tremenda, WOJO-FM. Palmieri's band included Ismael Quintana (vocals), Cachete Maldonado and Little Ray Romero (percussion), Charlie "El Pirata" Cotto, Joe Santiago (bass), Tony Confresí (trumpet), Hector Aponte (vocals), and others. The detainees who had formed a band performed as well. Photographs of the event show the Palmieri band's performance as well as more personal interactions between Santiago, Palmieri, Maldonado, and Romero with detainees. One picture shows Palmieri writing something down and Flores characterizes these interactions as "exchanging information."[56]

Once released from Fort McCoy and established in Miami, García Villamil began playing ritual music with Juan Silveria a.k.a. Juan Candela. He then moved to New York City and worked with Renard Simmons. In 1983 García Villamil got his *aña* (sacred drum talisman) to New York and was thus able to play his own consecrated drums. Through various ups and downs, García Villamil eventually started teaching and formed his own group, once again calling it Emikeké:

> With Emikeké, Felipe began a new stage in his musical life, one that somewhat resembled what had happened to him in Cuba: a movement from private performances of Afro-Cuban religious music in sacred contexts to the performance of this music in public, in concerts and at lectures and demonstrations. The "new" Emikeké, which had only one Cuban member, Felipe (the others were Americans or Puerto Ricans), performed for such institutions as the Museum of Natural History and the Museum of African Art, at Lincoln Center outdoor festivals, and in lecture demonstrations in universities such as Yale, Columbia, and Rutgers. The group was also called for private religious ceremonies, predominantly Palo ceremonies, and, less

Fig 7.1. Eddie Palmieri and Ray Romero speaking with refugees at Fort McCoy. Photo courtesy of Carlos Flores.

Fig 7.2. Angel "Cachete" Maldonado (with hat) and José Santiago speaking with refugees.
Photo courtesy of Carlos Flores.

frequently to play batá for the orishas. The group dissolved in 1994 when Felipe went through a personal life crisis and left New York, establishing himself in California. . . . Felipe's experience as a cultural worker in Cuba had prepared him to deal with issues related to the "staging" of his tradition for outsiders. This skill was useful to Felipe when he organized Emikeké in New York and began "working the folklore circuit."[57]

Fig 7.3. Eddie Palmieri and band performing for refugees at Fort McCoy, L-R: Ismael Quintana, Hector Aponte, Charlie Cotto, and Eddie Palmieri. Photo courtesy of Carlos Flores.

Fig 7.4. Mariel refugee band performing at Fort McCoy. Photo courtesy of Carlos Flores.

I remember seeing García Villamil's group performing at the Museum of Natural History in the mid-1990s and I was struck by seeing his young children playing the batá. Vélez's observations about how García Villamil's new life resembled the one he had in Cuba could also be applied to many other musicians who came to New York after the Mariel Boatlift, such as Orlando "Puntilla" Ríos, Manuel Martínez Olivera, and Roberto Borrell.

Fig 7.5. Mariel refugee band performing at Fort McCoy. Photo courtesy of Carlos Flores.

Marta Moreno Vega has written that the first *tambor de fundamento* (consecrated batá drums) came to New York in 1979 and were brought by Onelio Scull and given their ritual "voice" by Papo Angarica in Cuba.[58] It is largely acknowledged that the first set of tambor de fundamento had been made, as discussed in the section on Felipe García Villamil, and was eventually consecrated and subsequently taken care of by Louis Bauzó.[59] One of the major outcomes of the arrival of the Mariel community in New York was the immediate need for consecrated batá drums to perform in religious ceremonies. Vélez writes:

> In 1982 a group of babalaos who had organized a temple in New Jersey decided to build a set of batá drums. Sixteen babalaos, during a period of five months, made a set of drums "from scratch." These babalaos either were not familiar with the secrets and restrictions of the transmission of power between sets of drums or were limited by the absence of other consecrated drums in New York.[60]

This is ritually unacceptable, because consecrated drums must be born from existing sets that have *aña* (the drum spirit). In addition, these drums were said to have been unusable for ritual situations because they had metal tuning lugs that are prohibited for rituals that require consecrated drums. Ritual drummers who came from Cuba in the Mariel saw this as sacrilegious and sent for their own *Aña* to be brought to New York City and put into consecrated drums for ritual usage. Thus, as Vélez writes, "with the arrival of drummers such as Juan

'El Negro' Raymat, Orlando 'Puntilla' Rios, Felipe García, and Alfredo 'Coyude' Vidaux, who used drums consecrated in the Cuban practice, the New York community of religious drummers began to acknowledge this as the authentic way of way placing Aña in the instruments."[61]

Interestingly, Vélez also points out that the arrival of Marielitos in New York City impacted other Afro-Cuban and Afro-Caribbean religious practices in New York, such as palo and espiritísmo practiced largely by Puerto Ricans, through exchanges of information and rituals.[62] She also explained that once ritual drummers like García Villamil got to New York:

> He found a community where a lot of ritual practice differed from and some-
> times conflicted with his. Many of the santeros in New York—especially the
> babalaos, who had acquired power and control that was not exclusively theirs
> in Cuba—felt that the wave of Cuban immigrants known as the Marielitos
> would disturb the religious practice in New York with their "innovations."[63]

In his own words, García Villamil explained how these differences were ne-gotiated or not. Sometimes the content of specific songs elicited particular responses from mounted practitioners that would not have occurred in Cuba; other times songs that were familiar in Cuba would not be known in New York, and "some of the deities seem . . . to behave differently across the ocean . . . [or] never to have crossed the ocean."[64] García Villamil described these experiences in *palo* and *santería* settings and that in New York, there was a focus on written descriptions of orally transmitted traditions and knowledge.

Vélez explained that being from Matanzas and steeped in the Afro-Cuban traditions of Matanzas, García Villamil's experience as a "minority within the Santería community" in the United States was due to the fact that the major-ity of "the Santería practices that have developed in the United States among Cubans mainly follow the Havana tradition."[65] This is most likely the reason his success and impact on the ritual music scene has differed from that of his fellow ritual drummer and Marielito, Orlando "Puntilla" Ríos.

ORLANDO "PUNTILLA" RÍOS

Born in Havana on December 26, 1947, Orlando "Puntilla" Ríos was a supremely talented drummer and a gifted singer. Before leaving in the Mariel Boatlift, he had been active in Cuba as an *abakuá*, a *rumbero*, and a *batalero*. He was a student of the famed drummer Jesús Pérez and had also learned with Pancho Quinto. According to some sources he was a percussion teacher at the National School for the Arts (ENA) from 1971–78 and performed in the best venues in

Havana, including the Tropicana and the Hotel Riviera, among others.[66] Master drummer Román Díaz remembered seeing him play with the *quinto* tied to his waist with the famous *comparsa* (carnival drum procession) Los Dandys de Belén, of which he was the musical director.[67] Also possessing deep knowledge of *Arará* (Dahomey-based Cuban) musical and religious traditions, in many ways he single-handedly transformed the Yoruba-based orisha ritual music scene in New York City and the United States through his playing and teaching.

Prior to Puntilla's arrival in New York City, the *ocha* (Santería) drumming tradition was largely secret there; elder players such as Julito Collazo, Francisco Aguabella, and Carlos "Patato" Valdéz guarded their knowledge, teaching only a select few musicians. Chano Pozo is acknowledged as the first to have played, sung, and recorded rumba as it really was. More importantly, as Rene López points out, Pozo achieved this milestone in New York City in 1947 for the SMC label, not in Cuba.[68] On his recordings he also sang in *Lucumí* (Cuban Yoruba language), and sang about Cuban Congolese-derived religious practices from palo. Robert Farris Thompson points out that this is heard in songs like "Blen Blen Blen," where he openly mentions *prendas* and spirits by name, *nganaga* and *nkisi*, for the first time on a record. Thompson also asserts that the words *Blen Blen Blen* are a Congolese "acoustic diagram . . . used to mark rhythm."[69] According to Dizzy Gillespie, Pozo also shared extensive sacred drumming information with him, too. Gillespie explained:

> Chano taught us all multirhythm; we learned from the master. On the bus, he'd give me a drum, Al McKibbon a drum, and he'd take a drum. Another guy would have a cowbell, and he'd give everybody a rhythm. We'd see how all the rhythms tied into one another, and everybody was playing something different. We'd be on the road in a bus, riding down the road, and we'd sing and play all down the highway. He'd teach us some of those Cuban chants and things like that. That's how I learned to play the congas. The chants, I mix up. I don't know one from the other, really, but they're all together. You have different ones, the Nañigo, the Ararra, the Santo and several others, and they each have their own rhythm. When you say do the Nañigo, the guy goes into that specific rhythm. They're all of African derivation.[70]

In many ways, Orlando "Puntilla" Ríos would parallel Chano Pozo in his time in New York City, but he would largely surpass him.

Puntilla described his own journey from Cuba to the United States during the Mariel Boatlift in the film *Rumba Clave Blen Blen Blen*: "None of those trips were a piece of cake. Because on boats that held 32 people he loaded 200 people. That wasn't easy. People were falling. For instance, I came in one boat made for 18, and they put in 130. Two little girls fell into the ocean."[71] It is unconscionable that 125,000 people endured a similar experience in 1980, and almost half that number again in the 1990s, but somehow their stories are not spoken of today.

Word of Puntilla's arrival in New York City spread quickly. In 1980 a young Nuyorican drummer named Felix Sanabria went to what he remembered as a brief incarnation of the New Rican Village at 116th and Second Avenue, where he first saw Puntilla at a gig with Eugenio "Totico" Arango. Prior to this Sanabria recalled his upstairs neighbor Danny Santos running up to his apartment one day after seeing a coke-bottle glasses–wearing Puntilla singing and playing at the Central Park rumba. At the New Rican Village, Sanabria recalled seeing Totico sing his rumbas and when Puntilla got on the *quinto* and also sang lead for *Elegua*, Totico was pacing up and down behind him completely stunned, with a facial expression that was wondering "where did this guy come from?"[72] Totico represented the old guard of Afro-Cuban music, having come to the United States in 1959 and recorded in the jazz and Latin realms. However, he was best known in New York and abroad for one seminal rumba recording called *Patato and Totico* that featured Israel López "Cachao" (bass), Arsenio Rodríguez (tres), Papaito Muñoz (percussion), Patato Valdéz (percussion), "Curva" Dreke, Hector and Mario Cadavieco, Panchín, Tony Mayarí, and Virgilio Martí.[73] This record has been the gold standard of rumba for New York musicians since its release in 1967 and is considered a classic. Totico's reaction to Puntilla that fabled evening was telling of the musical changes that were ahead.

Maria Teresa Vélez writes that in the ritual context, "some of the elder local drummers deemed the style of drummers like Puntilla too liberal and felt it showed many differences when compared to the older sources."[74] In most cases, prior to the Mariel Boatlift, only a few of the elder musicians such as Julito Collazo were teaching a small select group of musicians. Early ritual drummers such as Juan Candela, Francisco Aguabella, Julito Collazo, and Onelio Scull had taught Teddy Holiday and other African American drummers.[75]

Otherwise, young eager drummers like Sanabria and his friends scrounged for sources of any kind, including recordings and transcriptions. While older established Afro-Cuban and non-Cuban musicians might have felt competition from the newcomers from Cuba, the younger musicians sought them out for lessons. Young New York drummers like Felix Sanabria, Abraham Rodríguez, Skip Burney, and others did not go to Cuba until much later in life and the arrival of the Mariel Cubans was their way of going to Cuba.[76]

According to Jerry González, he "got Puntilla his first paid gig" in New York City and Puntilla himself talked about going to Soundscape "every Tuesday," where he met Andy and Jerry González.[77] In the documentary *Rumba Clave Blen Blen Blen*, Puntilla explains that every religious drummer in New York passed through "his hands" and that before his arrival "the *oro seco* did not exist here [in New York]," and that he was responsible for adding the correct rules and religious aspects into ritual drumming, adding that he "put the *batá* in the right direction" (*yo puse el tambor en una solo dirección*).[78] Fellow master drummer, collaborator, and late-1990s Cuban arrival Ogduardo "Román" Díaz explains that Puntilla's importance as a drummer is based on the fact that "he gives an open projection to batá through his skill with clave. He can go towards both sides, or just one side. The result can be heard in the work he did with Michelle Rosewoman's Nu-Yoruba."[79] This important long-term collaboration allowed Rosewoman to marry jazz harmony and Cuba religious music in creative new ways. For Díaz, playing with Puntilla when he arrived was a "dream" come true.[80]

When Puntilla arrived in New York City in 1981 after spending some time in Miami, he did not have *santo hecho* despite having been initiated and undergoing the proper rituals to work in the religion as a religious drummer. However, he actually "made santo" and became a fully devoted *santero* in the Bronx on October 13, 1984. At this occasion, his student Felix Sanabria vividly remembered him being so inspired that he was singing from his own initiation throne while Sanabria and Abraham Rodríguez played the drums for him.[81]

Prior to this ceremony, Puntilla received his *aña* (the drum spirit talisman) from another ritual drummer and drum maker named Juan "El Negro" Raymat who had also arrived in the United States from Cuba as a Marielito and who came to New York for a number of drumming rituals. Raymat was a nephew of the celebrated *babalawo* Pancho Mora, widely acknowledged as one of the first in the United States. According to Raymat, the earliest experiences of Marielito ritual drummers in New York were with devotees who were largely unfamiliar with the drumming and chant traditions of Cuba and more familiar with religiously themed recordings made by popular singers such as Celina González.[82] He assembled a crew of musicians such as Alfred "Coyude" Vidaux, who in some ways was better versed than Puntilla in ritual music. The significance of Rios and Raymat's contributions to Cuban ritual music in the United States can't be overstated. Vicky Jassey writes:

> Not only did this mass exodus bring thousands of Regla de Ocha devotees to the United States, it brought key musicians whose knowledge of rhythms, songs, rituals and drum making was unprecedented in the United States.... Two of these men, Orlando "Puntilla" Rios and Juan "El Negro" Raymat, stand out for their pioneering influence on ritual musical tradition in the United States during the 80s and 90s. Travelling frequently between New York and Miami, as well as other parts of the United States and Latin America, their impact on the fledgling religious community was immense in terms of the

new knowledge they brought from Cuba. The combined song, drumming and drum making expertise of these two men as well as their savvy approach to business changed the oricha musical ritual landscape in the United Sates where they collectively maintained a virtual monopoly over its dissemination for over a decade. . . . Both men set about training an army of Cuban, Puerto Rican and North American men to play, maintain the drums and adhere to a long list of strict protocols and taboos associated with these ritual instruments. Many of these apprentices went on to become initiated omo Añá, meaning they pledged an oath to the deity Añá and became part of an exclusive heterosexual male-only brotherhood, giving them access to playing, making and owning fundamento batá with several of them dedicating a large part of their lives to the tradition and to passing it on to the next generation.[83]

It is fitting that Puntilla named his performance group Puntilla y La Nueva Generación (the new generation), as it included his apprentices as well as a number of important dancers who came to New York City in the Mariel wave. Some of these included Roberto Borrell, Rita Macías, Pedro Domenech, and Xiomara Rodríguez; as we will see later, each would go on teach hundreds of students Cuban folkloric dance styles.

Once Puntilla's *ocha* house was established in the Bronx, some of his earliest students and supporting drummers and singers included Felix Sanabria, Gene Golden, Victor Jaroslav, Eddie Rodriguez, Victor "Papo" Sterling, Canute "Bunny" Bernard Jr., Abraham Rodriguez, Pedro "Pepe Calabaza" Valdéz, Kenneth "Skip" Burney, Carlos Sánchez, Olufemi Mitchell, Evelyn Smart, Daniel Ponce, Eddie Bobè, and Bobby Sanabria. With his students he recorded a number of important folkloric recordings in New York City that would supplant the classic *Patato y Totico* rumba album. Some of these recordings included *From La Habana to New York* (1983), the classic *Totico y Sus Rumberos* (1981), as well as various collaborations with Daniel Ponce, Michelle Rosewoman's New Yor-Uba, Kip Hanrahan, Amma McKen, and others.[84]

As a direct result of the apprenticeship with his students, many would go on to lead their own groups and document their unique musical vision combining their experiences as New Yorkers steeped in a tradition from Cuba that reflected their own personalities. One such recording by Felix Sanabria's Los Afortunados was not commercially released, but Abraham Rodríguez's *Los Inolvidables*, Eddie Bobè's *Central Park Rumba*, Emilio Barretto's *Santissimo*, and Michelle Rosewoman's Nu Yor-Uba recordings bear this hallmark. One might also argue that Puntilla's New York City collaborations with Michelle Rosewoman, along with Daniel Ponce's collaborations with jazz and rock musicians, had an influence on subsequent recordings by artists in Cuba such as those that Lázaro Ros made with Síntesis and Mezcla.

Puntilla's impact and influence took on many forms, but his music also connected back to Cubans in Cuba. Lisa Maya Knauer wrote about the significance of his 1983 album *From La Habana to New York*:

> Shortly after his arrival, *Marielito* musician Orlando "Puntilla" Ríos recorded a rumba album, *From Havana to New York*, the title capturing the sentiment of many Marielitos that they were bringing authentic Afro-Cuban culture to New York. The album featured previously unrecorded works by the Cuban rumba composer Tío Tom. Despite the embargo Puntilla sent one LP to Cuba. The circulation of that single record established Puntilla's influence on the rumba scene in Cuba in absentia, since most Cubans had never heard of Tío Tom, later acknowledged as a major rumba composer. It took Puntilla's departure for New York for Cuban audiences to hear Tío Tom's work recorded. Sending the record to Cuba set the stage for subsequent flows.[85]

Another subsequent flow was a back and forth of students moving between Pancho Quinto in Cuba and Puntilla in New York City. Kenneth Schweitzer writes: "Noting the insatiable curiosity of drummers in the New York area, Puntilla began to send U.S. American drummers to Cuba to learn how to play with Pancho and to be sworn to aña with Pancho and Enrique. As a result Pancho became one of the most internationally well-known Havana-based batá drummers."[86]

Toward the end of his life, Puntilla returned to Cuba and visited his family. René López was also there to produce a tribute album to the legendary rumbero and composer Tío Tom, who Puntilla knew well. The recording session took place at the legendary EGREM studios in Havana with some of the top-shelf rumberos based in Cuba, which included musicians from Yoruba Andavo and other groups. Although Puntilla had been visiting the island, he came to the sessions and sang and played some percussion parts (*quinto* and *catá*) on the record. The resulting CD for Smithsonian Folkways, *A Tribute to Gónzalo Acensio Tío Tom 1919–1991* (2008), is a fantastic example of Puntilla's singing and playing placed head to head with his Cuban contemporaries.[87] Upon Puntilla's passing in 2008, Nando Alvaricci had Rene López call in to his show on WBAI for a live on-air interview, during which he explained:

> It's important to know that Puntilla was a person who wherever he went to play, left his mark all the time and they would talk about it for days after he left, because he was a just a tremendous, tremendous drummer and a tremendous singer, and a very knowledgeable person of the religion and what it meant, he lived it . . . in Cuba, it was incredible the amount of respect that they had for him, in Cuba, too.[88]

On the same program, López was asked to pick some of Puntilla's recordings to share with the listeners and he chose "A una mamita" from *Totico y Sus Rumberos* because:

> "A una mamita" was considered by most of the people that know, that are really in the know about drumming, and that really know the rumba, both here and in Cuba, a lot of comments in Cuba . . . that was probably, *is* probably one of the greatest examples of *quinto* playing, you know *a perfección*, you know everything *es cada cosa en su lugar*. No over-playing, no under-playing everything stated beautifully. And if you had to tell somebody, "you want to learn how to play *quinto* in rumba" that would probably [be] one of the top examples . . . That is one of the best examples . . . of a person playing *quinto* in rumba.[89]

Totico y Sus Rumberos pays tribute to *Patato y Totico*, but it is significant because it marks the first recording with the old and new generation of New York City rumberos indicating the passing of the drumming torch. Beyond Puntilla's sublime singing and drumming, the participation of Totico, Andy and Jerry González, Gene Golden, and Abraham Rodríguez Jr. marks a new course that included Afro-Cuban ritual music as well as doo-wop. Abraham Rodríguez Jr. grew up singing jazz, soul, doo-wop, and both Cuban and Puerto Rican music. The result of his combination with the Cuban drumming tradition is a unique New York doo-wop rumba masterpiece version of Don and Juan's 1962 hit song "What's Your Name?" that is able to highlight the best of these traditions and Latin music in New York unlike any previous recording. Although he was writing about the documentary *Rumba Clave Blen Blen Blen*, Johnny Frías's assessment applies to *Totico y Sus Rumberos*:

> This approach presents the New York metropolitan area as an independent center of rumba rather than privileging Cuba as the mecca for the real culture of rumba, as is often the case. New York is thus granted its own authenticity and history, even as it has been enriched by the arrival of Cuban talent. On a side note, although the important role of Puerto Rican drummers is mentioned briefly, these musicians deserve a little more recognition.[90]

Totico y Sus Rumberos features many important Puerto Rican and non-Cuban drummers whose contributions to the scene are preserved for all history. Some of these drummers as well as other Puerto Rican and non-Cuban drummers, such as Eddie Bobè, Felix Sanabria, Abraham Rodríguez Jr., Gene Golden, Victor Jaroslav, Alberto Serrano, and Skip Burney, would go on to share their drumming and vocal talents with many musical groups and recordings as well as tour internationally as acknowledged masters of the Afro-Cuban ritual and folkloric tradition.

GABRIEL "CHINCHILITA" MACHADO: STRADDLING LATIN MUSIC AND JAZZ

Gabriel Machado is a multifaceted percussionist known affectionately as "Chinchilita." The nickname comes from his childhood likeness to the restless bird Cuban *bijirita*, known in some parts of the island as chinchilita. Machado was born September 4, 1952, in Victoria de Las Tunas, Cuba. His brothers Chato, Pare, and Ramón (who also played in the municipal band) played with him in a small group called Los Sury and then in a group called Los Armoniosos. Cristino Márquez was his first percussion teacher. Machado never studied in a conservatory setting. Although he did study music once a week in Holguín, he was proudly someone who learned in the streets and asked many questions. In the 1940s and 1950s, his father, Gabriel, was the bassist with the Gigante Miramar Orquesta, a group that played throughout Oriente (Eastern Cuba). Machado joined his father's band as a conguero (conga player) in 1969 and worked with them playing drum set for the next ten years in *bailes populares* (large outdoor dances), during carnivals and festivals, and accompanying a variety of artists.[91] Machado was also close with the legendary Cuban jazz pianist Emiliano Salvador, who would return to Puerto Padre and hang out with him. The band that Machado played with was classified as B1 under the Cuban system and he had been evaluated as a B3 musician. This evaluation system impacted the musician's pay "with A-level performers receiving the most and C-level performers the least"; it was biased toward artists with formal training and those who read Western notation.[92]

The Mariel Boatlift started during a vacation from his official, salaried work as a professional musician. Since Machado did not have any criminal history he could not be included in the first group to be taken to the Port of Mariel, but once he decided to go, he left for Havana anyway. Machado got sick during the voyage and remembers that he needed to lay down for three days. After he arrived in Key West, he was taken to Fort Chaffee. In the *refugio* Fort Chaffee, there was an orchestra led by the trumpeter/trombonist Campeón; Machado remembers meeting Pedro Domech, Rita Macías, and Xiomara Rodríguez there as well. Machado made his way to New York City on February 14, 1980, after a Cuban friend from the Bronx whose children had studied with Machado in Cuba sponsored him and helped him get settled in the Bronx, find a factory job, and eventually bring his children. Machado worked almost every day in the factory from 7am–11pm to save money to bring his family to New York City; however, his wife decided to stay in Cuba with the couple's son. There were almost no other people from Oriente when he arrived in New York. Machado's brothers, who had been playing bongó and timbal with Pío Leyva on a cruise ship, eventually decided to stay in Spain and not return to Cuba.

Almost immediately upon his arrival in New York City, Machado began working as a musician playing drum set and congas with a group of Dominican musicians led by Rafi Po. Puerto Ricans helped Machado out in every aspect in the Bronx. The factory job lasted for just one year and he lived exclusively from music thereafter, playing with many different groups.

In New York, Machado initially met few Cuban musicians from Mariel. One such friend was Ángel Pérez, a conguero and friend/admirer of Tata Güines who had played with Cubachá directed by the tresero "Maracaibo" in Cuba. Another friend was drummer Ignacio Berroa. In Machado's opinion, most Cubans wanted to stay in Miami. He had met Cuban drummer Ignacio Berroa in a recording studio called Studio 45. The two became good friends from that moment on. Berroa urged Machado to start playing timbales and Machado notes that unlike in Cuba, no groups were using drum sets in Latin music in New York when he arrived.[93]

When he was living in Oriente, Machado had no knowledge of jazz or much interest in it. It was Ignacio Berroa who brought Machado to work in Lionel Hampton's band. After joining Lionel Hampton, Machado met Buddy Rich, who lived in Hampton's building, and Machado was struck by how much Rich and the other American jazz musicians admired the Cuban musicians.

In contrast to Machado, drummer Ignacio Berroa, who also came to New York City during the Mariel Boatlift, had gotten involved in the jazz scene almost immediately. In his own words, Berroa proudly explains, "I am a Marielito, very proud to be one . . . Coincidentally, Mario Bauzá, a Cuban musician who connected Chano Pozo with Dizzy Gillespie, also connected me with Dizzy."[94]

The earliest clubs Machado remembers working at were the Dominican venues El Trocadero and El Oasis, and other clubs such as Casa Borinquen. The pay for these engagements was $100. After arriving in New York from Cuba, Machado found the music to be "*muy atrasado, atrasaísimo*" (very behind, really far behind).[95] He was surprised to hear everyone in New York playing repertoire of the 1940s and 1950s, whereas in Cuba contemporary bands like La Ritmo Oriental, Los Van Van, Irakere, and other similar groups had pushed Cuban music far ahead. Of the New York City–based groups that Machado encountered, he was most impressed by Típica 73's music and its inclusion of the modern Cuban sound. Machado worked steadily Fridays–Sundays at Los Violines in North Bergen, New Jersey (80th Street and Bergenline Avenue) with a Cuban pianist from Cienfuegos names Rafael Tomás. Machado remembers working with Regino Tellechea (a well-known bolero/*filín* singer), Fernando Lavoy, Daniel Ponce, Gerardo Martínez, and Roberto Borrell during this era. Machado appreciates Ponce's speed and power as well as his ability to play with five congas simultaneously, but he notes that Ponce could not play a simple *marcha* (keep time) on a bolero when they were recording in the studio.

Similar to his Puerto Rican counterparts, Machado was interested in North American jazz. His relationship with jazz was manifested by many years in Lionel Hampton's band (1985–2000), as well as work with the Duke Ellington Orchestra under the direction of Mercer Ellington (three years), the Carnegie Hall Jazz Orchestra under the direction of Jon Faddis, and performances with Dizzy Gillespie, Branford Marsalis, and others.

With Hampton, Machado played congas and sometimes used timbales. Machado recorded *Cooking in the Kitchen* with Milt Hinton and Ray Brown. When the band wasn't working, Hampton had the band of sixteen musicians on retainer, often paying his musicians between $100–400 weekly. Hampton's manager helped Machado with his paperwork for entry and reentry in the United States.

When Machado was not working with jazz musicians he also performed and recorded with Latin dance bands specializing in the charanga style such as Típica Novel, Charanga 76, José Fajardo, Orquesta Broadway, and Las Hermanas Márquez, as well as with Latin jazz musicians such as Paquito D'Rivera, Claudio Roditi, Oriente López, Bebo Valdés, Arturo Sandoval, Lalo Schifrin, and later with Juan Pablo Torres.

After leaving Hampton and other groups, Machado moved to West New York, New Jersey. He enjoys playing with small groups dedicated to Cuban son and views New York as part of the "*cuna de son*" (cradle of son) because he came to New York and stayed. Ultimately, Machado has expressed the view that technique is important for playing hand percussion, especially to avoid calluses and injuries. Machado was never personally interested in studying folkloric music in Cuba, but he had friends who were involved with batá drums in Santiago. He was surprised to see musicians playing batá in New York. Machado worked with Puntilla on two occasions, but he was never very interested in rumba or folklore.

PAQUITO D'RIVERA

Strictly speaking, Paquito D'Rivera is not a Marielito, as he did not leave Cuba on a vessel from the Port of Mariel. Unlike his Mariel contemporaries who came to the United States for the first time in 1980, D'Rivera first performed in New York City as an eleven-year-old saxophone prodigy at El Teatro Puerto Rico in April 1960. Also unlike his Mariel contemporaries, D'Rivera visited New York again as an adult in 1978 and 1979 when he performed and recorded with Irakere. However, he has called New York City and nearby Hudson County, New Jersey, his home since October 1980. In addition, he has been associated with a number of the Cuban musicians who came in 1980 and also with those who had been here for some time. His presence on the New York scene helps position the newly arrived Cuban musicians of his cohort.

D'Rivera's father Tito had been a revered saxophonist and music store owner who played in the military band. As a child prodigy, Paquito performed both classical and Cuban popular music from an early age. In addition to his regular studies, he took clarinet lessons at Alejandro García Caturla Music School as well as private lessons in composition, theory, and counterpoint with Félix Guerrero.[96] After many successful performances in Cuba, a 1956 law was passed that denied anyone "under the age of eighteen from working on television and radio."[97] In 1957 D'Rivera's father and manager Tito got him a contract to perform in the Dominican Republic at La Voz Dominicana, the national radio and television station. During this engagement, D'Rivera performed with the legendary saxophonist Tavito Vásquez and other well-known performers. After this engagement he signed another contract to play the Hotel del Matúm in Santiago de los Caballeros. Later that year, in August, D'Rivera performed at the Hotel Normandy in San Juan, Puerto Rico, and at El Escambrón accompanied by the Machito Orchestra. In 1960 D'Rivera and his father traveled to New York City to perform at El Teatro Puerto Rico with Rolando Laserie, Celia Cruz, and Lola Beltrán, accompanied by the Puerto Rican bandleader César Concepción.[98] As seen in other chapters of this book, it was the impresario and musician Catalino Rolón who booked him. In the early 1960s, D'Rivera attended jazz jam sessions and gigs in Havana, playing with some of the best musicians in his time, and learned from two African American musicians who had settled in Cuba, Mario Lagarde and Eddie Torriente.[99]

While D'Rivera's parents were not politically active, they were worried about his military service in 1965 and the possibility that he would be pressed into active service during an invasion.[100] At 17, he was placed in the military band, but was also required to cut sugarcane.[101] His memory of that two-and-a-half-year experience was largely negative as described in his book.[102] Jazz was a major part of his life and in Cuba jazz soon became representative of the enemy. D'Rivera recalls:

> as far as jazz was concerned, forget it. Particularly after one evening when Lieutenant Forneiro showed up unexpectedly while we were in the middle of a jam session and ordered: "Stop that immediately! I don't want to hear

another note. Compañeros, jazz music represents the enemy!" With those words, he turned off the Russian hi-fi that played albums by Bird, Dizzy, Kenton, and Miles. Thereafter, we had to listen secretly to Willis Connover's shortwave jazz program on the Voice of America. That was a very difficult time for young people because the government relentlessly persecuted every foreign manifestation of creativity, and jazz was specifically included. Unfortunately for me, jazz was one of the things that I most loved ever since I was an infant.[103]

In the 1970s, many of the places where D'Rivera previously performed were closed down and Jorge Serguera, head of the Cuban Institute of Radio and Television, censored music.[104]

After finishing his military service in 1967, D'Rivera joined La Orquesta Cubana de Música Moderna, which included some of the musicians he would later play with in Irakere, such as Chucho Valdés and Carlos Emilio Morales. A smaller offshoot of the group called Saludo Cubano toured the Soviet Bloc in 1968. Eventually, his mother grew so tired of the political situation that she left the island with her daughter and headed for Spain. Shortly after his mother's departure, D'Rivera's father also left the island, leaving Paquito and his brother Enrique with the family home in Marianao. D'Rivera's irreverence and pranks were interpreted as troublemaking by the powers that be and he was asked to leave La Orquesta Cubana de Música Moderna, but soon the new group, Irakere, took off with great success.

Many years later, D'Rivera recalled in his book that a boat filled with American jazz musicians from New York City came to Cuba in 1977. They included "Rudy Rutherford, Ron McClure, Billy Hart, Ray Mantilla, John Ore, Mickey Roker, Ben Brown, Joanne Brackeen, and Rodney Jones . . . [and] the journalist Arnold Jay Smith [and] Stan Getz."[105] Earl "Fatha" Hines was also there.[106] These musicians played at a jam session with their Cuban counterparts at the Havana Libre Hotel as well as at the Teatro Mella and the results were released under David Amram's name as *Havana-New York*.[107] The Cuban and American musicians also enjoyed some quality down time just hanging out together. The Cuban musicians at these musical exchanges included Irakere and Los Papines. Columbia Records subsequently signed Irakere, the group with whom D'Rivera had performed, for two records.

Around this time Irakere came to perform in Montreal where Paquito was reunited with his parents who had driven up from New York for one week; but they had to spend time together in secret, as the Cuban musicians were being watched closely. On a subsequent trip to New York City with Irakere, D'Rivera performed at Carnegie Hall on a bill with McCoy Tyner and Bill Evans. He also saw his parents and sister who were living in New Jersey, and musicians from his past such as Bebo Valdés (Chucho's father) and Mario Bauzá. The Cuban musicians also "participated in a jam session with Dizzy [Gillespie], Maynard Ferguson, Stan Getz, and David Amram," and traveled with them to perform at the Montreux Jazz Festival in Switzerland.[108] Before returning to Cuba, they flew back to New York City from Switzerland and D'Rivera spent time with his family in Union City, New Jersey. D'Rivera also remembered that during this visit, Dominican saxophonist Mario Rivera took him and his Cuban colleagues to a club around 168th Street where some of the best musicians in Latin music were performing, such as Victor Paz, Andy and Jerry González, and Hilton Ruiz, among others.[109] Irakere later played a US tour in twenty-two cities, and at the conclusion of the tour they recorded a second album over a period of ten days at the CBS Studio on 52nd Street.[110] This particular studio was meaningful for D'Rivera and the other musicians because Miles Davis had recorded his seminal album *Kind of Blue* there. Columbia Records subsequently released the 1979 recording of Irakere's performance at the Newport Jazz Festival. D'Rivera also remembers seeing the Thad Jones-Mel Lewis band during this visit.[111] The band received a Grammy® award in 1979 for the first Irakere recording and D'Rivera recalls Barry White giving the band the award.

March 1979 brought another contingent of US artists to perform in Cuba, including Billy Joel, Stephen Stills, Dexter Gordon, Weather Report, and Kris Kristofferson. Germane to this discussion is the performance by the Fania All-Stars, which included Puerto Rican, Nuyorican, Jewish, Dominican, and Pana-manian practitioners of Cuban-derived Latin music including Rubén Blades and Hector Lavoe. Anecdotal information regarding the group's performance was that it was not well received because Cuban audiences were more eager to hear American pop and jazz than versions of their own music played by non-Cuban musicians. D'Rivera describes Weather Report's performance, featuring Jaco Pastorius, as "music that sounded, to many of those in the audience, as if it were coming from another planet."[112]

In his memoir, D'Rivera indicates that during the time of the Mariel Boatlift, he was still trying to figure out whether he would stay or leave Cuba. He was also unsure of how he would leave. He was earning 500 pesos per month as a member of Irakere and had a car as well as access to certain comforts due to his celebrity.[113] Nevertheless, he was restless and wondered about reaching further artistic goals. Disgusted after being asked to take part in a foreign press piece to demonstrate that Cuban professionals were doing well and uninterested in leaving during the boatlift, D'Rivera was convinced by his friend Marcos Miranda to seek asylum in Spain when he was on tour with Irakere, May 6, 1980. He and his wife had agreed that he would leave her and their son behind in Cuba. Once D'Rivera left, his wife and son were harassed by government officials in a variety of ways.[114] For D'Rivera, having to deceive his colleagues during the flight from Cuba to Spain was "seven hours of anxiety, forced jokes, and repressed tears."[115] His mother flew to meet up with him in Spain and his brother Enrique, who had already gotten into trouble with the authorities and demoted from being a musician to a porter for the band, defected by leaving on a boat during the Mariel Boatlift.[116] When his defection was discovered, the authorities and neighbors visited his wife and son at home and questioned their loyalty to Cuba.[117] After six months in Madrid, D'Rivera arrived in New York City in October 1980.

Ian Michael James has written that D'Rivera's joy at being in New York, living in the Cuban neighborhood of Union City, and living freely was reflected in his music, and that in the liner notes of his record *Paquito Blowin'* D'Rivera writes: "Everyone has a 'golden dream' and ever since I was only a child, mine was to live in the United States (New York to be precise) and build there a career as a jazz musician."[118] Once in New York, D'Rivera composed and recorded songs for the son and wife he left behind in Cuba as well as a song called "Mariel" which became the title track for the album *Mariel*. James also quotes D'Rivera speaking with a reporter in Puerto Rico and reflecting on the choice he made to leave his family and his country: "It was terrible. A difficult price to pay. It's the choice between a mediocre, frustrated future and the possibility to be who I am, to fulfill myself. It's something I don't regret, but it tears me apart."[119] D'Rivera's girlfriend and future wife, the vocalist Brenda Feliciano, would eventually travel to Cuba to help facilitate D'Rivera's son and wife leaving Cuba, but they were unsuccessful until many years later. Throughout the 1980s and beyond, D'Rivera's frequent public talk and writing about Cuban politics did not seem to help his case, but his wife and son finally made it out in 1989. While his politics remained firmly against the Cuban government, he has also spoken out against racism in the Cuban exile community.[120]

In the New York City metro area, D'Rivera worked with a number of Cuban musicians who had been active since the 1950s such as Carlos Barberia, Rudy Calzado, and the vocalist Tabenito (Mario Varona), who like Calzado had sang with Jose Fajardo.[121] He also recalled using an Otley flute given to him by Raphael Prats, the grandfather of Jorge Luis Prats, in order to work with charanga groups, which were enjoying a boom. D'Rivera played flute with La Típica Novel, a charanga group led by the Jamaican and Cuban pianist Willie Ellis. In this group, Ellis would direct D'Rivera for the introduction and coda, and D'Rivera would improvise throughout the remainder of the arrangements. D'Rivera also recalled hanging out at a variety of clubs and after-hours spots such as El Pozo on Saint Nicholas Avenue and El Kikirikí. Angel "Mandarría" Pérez was among the Marielitos whom D'Rivera remembers getting caught up in trouble and ultimately losing their lives.[122] Around this time, D'Rivera subbed in Tito Puente's band and met the multi-instrumentalist Howard Levy, with whom he would subsequently record his own album.

D'Rivera also played with one of Jose Fajardo's groups at La Vilabaina on 14th Street. D'Rivera, who "grew up listening to Richard Egües and Fajardo," was essentially referencing their playing styles and going back to his roots.[123] In a documentary on the life of Israel "Cachao" López, D'Rivera states that he "fell in love again with Cuban music on the shores of the Hudson River."[124] D'Rivera remembers in the winter of 1981 playing four or five dances at the Chateau Madrid with the Carlos Barberia Orquesta, which featured the great Cuban vocalist Regino Tellechea, who had worked with Enrique Jorrín and Felipe Dulzaides in Cuba. One of the things that D'Rivera found weird and that he had never experienced in his life prior to his arrival in New York was the obsession with the clave, whether a piece of music was in 2–3 or 3–2, referring to the issue by saying that "the clave is a mystery."[125]

D'Rivera's first gig as a leader was at Verna Gillis's Soundscape. Robert Palmer wrote a good review of the concert for the *New York Times*; this caught the attention of CBS Records, and they signed him. Other musical collaborations for D'Rivera that came out of Soundscape included work with Daniel Ponce and Orlando "Puntilla" Ríos, two percussionists who came in the Mariel Boatlift and settled in New York City, as well as with Gene Golden and Babatunde.

Soundscape was also where he met the González brothers, Jorge Dalto, Hilton Ruiz, Claudio Roditi, Thiago de Mello and Brenda Feliciano. He also hooked up with players like Carlos Franzetti and Michel Camilo, with whom he would work on film scores and advertisements. He played with Alex and Russell Blake, Nicky Marrero, and Mario Rivera at places like Seventh Avenue South, where he would meet his wife, Brenda Feliciano.

In New York City, D'Rivera gained a deeper understanding of jazz as he worked through the Real Book and made the scene, noting: "I understood that in reality, one has to play less notes. Technique is like an arm: [one] can't shoot the neighbor's dog, it's to protect oneself." He also echoes Buck Clayton that music was "not what notes you play, but the ones you leave out."[126] In the early 1980s and onward, D'Rivera collaborated with many Latin American counterparts based in New York as well as with classical musicians and composer. Despite becoming an American citizen, winning six Grammy® awards, and enjoying a successful career, D'Rivera still longed for Cuba; James writes:

> He said living in exile had been difficult because "you don't belong to any place." Paquito loved New York, but during the cold winters he also dreamed of having an apartment on the Malécon to escape to. There was always something magical for him about that place where Havana met the sea, one of

many images that kept Cuba alive in his mind. "It's always there. I never left there. It's as if I'm visiting here, at least that's how I look at it," Paquito reflected, a tone of affection in his voice. "I never left."[127]

GERARDO "TABOADA" FERNÁNDEZ

Born in the Jesús de Monte neighborhood of La Habana, Gerardo Fernández (August 12, 1938–November 4, 2015) was an avid soccer player as a youngster and was given the nickname of Taboada (from the actor Julio Taboada); most who knew him called him by this name and believed it to be his surname. By his own admission Taboada was not a good student, so he started working early in life and earned a good living as a professional cigar roller for La Corona. However, he always felt some friction working within the system, and by his own description he was "apathetic." Throughout his time in Cuba, Taboada continued his work as a fast and efficient *tabacalero* who pursued music outside of work.

Luis Ortega, a guitarist and father of the famous Cuban *filín* singer Daisy Ortega, invited Taboada to sing and coached him. They performed together in a semi-professional musical group called Yacarey in 1962–63. The bandleader was Orlando Sotolongo and the group's *asesor* (advisor) was Joseito Gonzalez, the bandleader and arranger for the popular Cuban dance band Rumbavana. The band's repertoire consisted mainly of Rumbavana songs. Taboada sang coro (background vocals) and played güiro with the band before moving to another group around 1965–66, whose asesor was Cuban piano icon Guillermo Rubalcaba. Also singing in this group was Regino Tellechea, a "complete" singer who could sing boleros, guaracha, filín, and songs in English and Italian, but who later would be imprisoned and exiled from Cuba. Years later in New York City, Taboada would reunite with Tellechea in New York in a musical group called Los Dandy. In Cuba, Tellechea gave him singing tips and suggestions to improve his singing. Taboada's compadre, Ramón Gavilán Arencibia, who played güiro with Estrellas Cubanas, Pancho El Bravo, and El Combo de Kotán, taught him güiro. Taboada started playing güiro and going to rehearsals with Pancho El Bravo, Orquesta Riverside, and others after leaving Rubalcaba's group.

Taboada was among the first six hundred people to get into the Peruvian embassy during the beginning of the Mariel Boatlift. He and his wife were there for seventeen days without eating and they both received blows from sticks and kicks to the body before heading back to their home. Before leaving, he received a stinging public repudiation at the tobacco factory by friends who he had helped throughout the years: his entire one-month output of four hundred cigars a day was smashed and destroyed to make it seem that he was sabotaging his place of work. Before leaving, a friend brought him to the port in a private car and he dressed in his best clothes, looking like a government official and easily moving through security. Before leaving, he was told by one official to take a good look at Cuba, because he would never see it again. His small boat, overcrowded with sixty people, set sail for Key West. He arrived in the United States on April 26, 1980. Taboada's sister, who lived in the States, helped him get out of the processing center. He spent roughly one month in Miami, where he connected with friends from Cuba like Frank González; he started making cigars and lived on Coral Way.

After arriving in New York City from Miami, Taboada worked with Fajardo playing güiro and singing, where he met fellow Marielitos Daniel Ponce and Roberto Borrell. He replaced Fajardo's güiro player Rolando Valdés, the former owner of Orquesta Sensación. He also had a group called Trio La Verdad playing *misas esprituales* with Jesús Chaucha and Luis Rodríguez (violinist). For Taboada, the name *salsa* was "dishonest" because it hid the Cuban origins of the music. However, he recognized that there were also political factors involved in obfuscating the origins of the music.

Taboada had previously known another Mariel singer in New York, Fernando Lavoy, because he had sung in the conjunto of Taboada's brother-in-law in Cuba. He also remembered Lavoy singing with Rumbavana or Los Latinos in Cuba. At the urging of Calixto Callaba, composer of "La ignoro" and "Callejón de los rumberos," Taboada sought out and became friends with Lino Frías in New York City. He also hooked up with Juan González, who in Cuba had been the director of Conjunto Musicuba, which included the singer Mermelada. González started a group called Los Catraches with José "Chichi" Trapaga, which later would become Los Soneros and feature Lavoy. Taboada later started a conjunto called Grupo Oriza with his friend Chichi. Initially, the group rehearsed four days a week. They recorded two albums for the SAR label and played in Chicago and Washington.

Already an abakuá and having begun the first steps in Freemasonry, even being accepted into a lodge in Cuba, Taboada joined a lodge once in the United States and became a Mason. In Cuba, Taboada had been initiated into the religion of Santería, receiving his *guerreros* (warriors) and *la mano de Orunla* (the hand of Orunla), but he did not become more involved until arriving in the United States. Taboada became an *iyawo* (initiate) in 1983. Taboada was familiar with the *oro seco* and *oro cantado*, but not as a percussionist. Once in New York, he began working in the Waldorf Astoria Hotel, and had some problems with his supervisors that brought him to the Cuban Congolese-derived religion of Palo. He became a santero in 1982 and a babalawo in 1988. Taboada knew Orlando "Puntilla" Ríos in Cuba, but they did not become close until they were both in New York City.

THE MUSIC OF MARIEL IN NEW YORK CITY

For established Cuban musicians like Chico Álvarez, some of the newly arrived musicians seemed very disorganized. He remembered having this impression after seeing Fernando Lavoy singing with Alfredo "Chocolate" Armenteros at a club called Ochentas. Other Mariel musicians such as the percussionist Luis Andino transitioned from performing to teaching aspiring percussionists. The SAR label put out a number of recordings from this time, including *Los Soneros* led by Juan González, Grupo Oriza, and others. Paquito D'Rivera details a phone call with a friend who filled him in on the Mariel situation while it was still limited to the Peruvian embassy and learned that González, who had been the "director of Tejedor's conjunto," was also seeking refuge at the Peruvian embassy.[128] González eventually became the musical director of Los Kimi, one of the first Cuban groups made up of Mariel musicians who cultivated a *songo*-oriented sound. González's son was an excellent piano player who attended Manhattan School of music and held the piano chair in Los Soneros at thirteen. He would later go onto play with Machito, Celia Cruz, Marc Anthony, Tito Nieves, and many more artists touring throughout the world.[129]

The SAR/Guajiro labels made a good number of great recordings featuring Mariel musicians and Cuban musicians who were established in the United States, including the vocalist Linda Leida, Lita Branda (a Peruvian vocalist and sister of Melcochita), Roberto Torres, and others.[130] Recordings by Los Soneros, Grupo Oriza, SAR All-Stars, and Roberto Torres show a new energy, but a largely tried-and-true format of straight Cuban son, boleros, and guarachas. Fernando Lavoy *"El nariz que canta"* (the singing nose) was the lead vocalist for Los Soneros. As mentioned earlier, in Cuba he had sung with a number of groups. His vocal improvisations and compositions reflected a simultaneously humorous and macho temperament. Songs like "Cógelo Suave" and "Juana La Sin Goma" are two such examples. Unfortunately, he was murdered in the mid-1980s.

Israel Kantor is another musician who did not come in the Mariel Boatlift but was emblematic of the era. Kantor had been one of the lead vocalists with Los Van Van, often said to be Cuba's Rolling Stones. He came to the United States in 1983 and moved back and forth between Miami and New York City for the next few years, recording with a variety of New York–based artists.

FROM THE NEW RICAN TO SOUNDSCAPE: A VENUE FOR THE MUSIC OF THE MARIEL ERA

As indicated in Paquito D'Rivera's account of his early years in New York, Verna Gillis's Soundscape was an important venue for the newly arrived Cuban musicians such as D'Rivera, Puntilla, and Daniel Ponce, as well as their musically progressive counterparts who were already part of the scene, Andy and Jerry González among others. Verna Gillis is an ethnomusicologist with a PhD and the venue's name was taken from the Canadian musicologist R. Murray Shafer. Gillis and her husband opened and operated Soundscape at 500 W. 52nd Street off the corner of 10th Avenue from 1979 to 1984. Peña cites an article about the venue from Perfect Sound Forever that describes the physical space:

> It was a funky New York City HPD (Department of Housing Preservation and Development) building, probably built around 1900. HPD occupied the third floor, and there was a garbage hauling business on the first and second floors. This area of the West Side was very desolate in those days. You know the phrase "location, location, location"? Well, Tenth Avenue and 52nd Street was like the other side of the moon. Today, it's neighborhood. It was not a neighborhood in 1979.[131]

With considerable sweat equity, Gillis and her husband Andy Graves brought in a hundred chairs, built a stage, and began booking and paying groups to perform in the acoustically surprising space. The venue featured African music as well as Afro-Latin music. A number of live recordings from the venue have been released throughout the years, including performances by numerous jazz musicians.[132]

The Columbia University Radio Station WKCR 89.9FM briefly hosted the Soundscape archives.[133] Ben Young writes that, "In 1980, Tuesday nights were established as the regular weekly jam night for Afro-Latin musicians."[134] In an interview with Tomas Peña, Gillis explains:

> The early part of the week is more flexible for the musicians. So I opened the door in the summer of 1979, but something I think about is, the fact that I was in Cuba in December and January of 1979. I celebrated the New Year there. A friend (Jane Wood) and I went on a trip that was sponsored by the Center for Cuban Studies. The reason I mention this at all is that I acquired the space when I returned from Cuba. Regarding the way things went down the greatest scene of all was the Latin scene and the timing was just right.[135]

Much has been made of these intercultural and musical exchanges, but there were often moments of friction between the new Cuban arrivals and the Nuyoricans, including colorful anecdotes among musicians of that era. Gillis explains to Peña:

> There was all of this talent playing together at a time in their lives when it was possible to do so. And the reason I mention Cuba is, the Cubans were so pivotal in putting Soundscape on the map. They got all of the attention

because they were Cuban and they were newsworthy even though there were other musicians who had been playing in New York forever. So the fact that I had the space right after I came back from Cuba and it was the first place they came to. I can't take all the credit for bringing them to Soundscape. Many of them came from Eddie Figueroa's New-Rican Village. He lost the space and asked if he could use my space. It was the greatest gift that anyone could have given me. It was this ready-made music scene, and I had the place.

Thus the success of Soundscape was intrinsically tied to the demise of another important venue, The New Rican Village, which had been an important venue for Latin jazz. Looking at the sheer number of New-Rican Village–hosted events in the Soundscape archives supports this notion. As Ed Morales explains:

The New-Rican Village was the home of Afro-Caribbean music's avant-garde. It was a virtual who's who of New York Latin jazz: Hilton Ruiz, Daniel Ponce, Mario Rivera, Dave Valentin, Michel Camilo, and Andy and Jerry Gonzalez all cut their teeth there. Many of these players were members or guests with Manny Oquendo's Conjunto Libre, a group famous for a kind of jazz-influenced improvisational salsa.[136]

Noting the difference with the New Rican Village Scene, Gillis explains to Peña:

October 28, 1980. It was the evening that changed everything for everyone. All of these different alchemical things started happening, and all of those different configurations. In a certain way, everyone's life changed because it was no longer the New-Rican Village scene. It went to the next musical evolution. You see, the thing with Daniel (Ponce) and a lot of the Cubans was that Soundscape was a natural space, it wasn't a Latin club or a jazz club, so when the word got out about the Cuban musicians all of these people came to hear them it created a rivalry, jealousy and justifiable anger on the part of the guys who had been playing in the music for so long and never got a break. And then there was the enormous, complicated, psychological, emotional shit, personalities, and jealousies. I was as much a catalyst as anyone, but when I look back on it, no more or less than anybody else.[137]

Gillis explains that conflicts also arose when more jazz-oriented Latin musicians who were less interested in folkloric music mixed with the Cuban folklore heads. She said, "there were these 'clave wars,' because the Puerto Rican sense of clave is different from the Cuban sense of clave."[138]

In his profile of Gillis, Peña quotes saxophonist Enrique Fernández with regard to the venue's unique importance:

Soundscape was a coming together, a rite of passage for Latin culture in New York in the '80s. You saw and heard the music being born right in front of your eyes and ears. Remember this when you listen to these (Live From Soundscape) recordings. You are not listening to a finished musical product: for that, you can buy any of the extraordinary Latin jazz albums that come out every day. You are witnessing an experiment that worked. You are watching the mad scientists mix the glass tubes full of forbidden substances that will create life. You are in Dr. Frankenstein's laboratory watching the creature rise.[139]

Soundscape also released recordings such as *Live from Soundscape: Latin New York 1980–83* that included performances by many important musicians and groups who worked there and gave it the laboratory feeling that Fernández describes.[140]

One of the key musicians in the Soundscape scene was the percussionist Daniel Ponce, whose career seems to have rocketed to success and as quickly plummeted. Ponce arrived in New York City as a raw and powerful force steeped in the Cuban rumba scene. In Isabelle Leymarie's documentary *Latin Jazz*, he explains: "When I was in Cuba, the music that I listened to was Carnival music, comparsas, but also Yoruba [Lucumí] music. My grandfather was a musician who played Yoruba music. For this reason the great influence of Yoruba music is on my family."[141] In the same documentary, Ponce explains that playing conga in the carnival comparsa demands that the aspiring conguero develop "a good sound . . . without a microphone in the open air." His charisma and technical speed led him to work with mainstream American pop artists such as Mick Jagger, Laurie Anderson, Yoko Ono, and even to play *okónkolo* on Herbie Hancock's "Rockit." But his first musical interactions were at Soundscape. The venue also served as his actual home for some time. His first recording as a leader, *New York is Now*, declared his arrival and that of his Mariel peers in a way that could be characterized as *guapería* (one-upmanship). On the back cover of the album, Ponce states:

Before everything, I want to make clear that I arrived in this land on May 1, 1980 at 5pm through the Port of Key West. That is to say that I also came via Mariel, in other words, I am also a Marielito . . . A kiss to all of my family in Cuba especially for my son Michael Ponce Landa, missing but always with me.[142]

In this dedication section, Ponce also thanks Verna Gillis and the New York musicians Barry Rogers, Jorge Dalto, and Chocolate Armenteros. Also noticeable is the picture of Ponce's grandmother, Josefa Toledo, and the greetings to a long list of Cuban drummers and friends "both here [in New York City] and in Cuba."[143] Ponce dedicates the album to the Latin American community and the people of the United States who had given him the opportunity to make the record.

The title of the album's opening track "Invación de 80" (Invasion of 1980) chronicles his and his cohort's arrival in New York in unabashed and bragging terms. Calling the arrival of this wave of Cuban musicians an invasion, the title is a great example of *guapería*, bragging confidence and one-upmanship. The probable composer and lead vocalist on the Ponce recording, Francisco Rigores, was also a Marielito who had come through Fort Chaffee.[144] He had previously recorded a similarly themed song called "Somos cubanos" in 1982 with the Washington, DC–based Afro-Cuban folkloric group Cubanakan that featured Roberto Borrell.[145] "Somos cubanos" discusses how the Marielitos came to "harmonize" in the United States, that they were good people, not "*escoria*" (human waste); at the same time, the refrain urges fellow Marielitos to behave well ("portate bien"). The song would also be used as the theme song for Guillermo Álvarez Guedes's radio show on Clásica 92.5 FM.[146] "Invación de 80" begins with Ponce playing a virtuosic display of *quinto* (lead drum) licks. This is followed by a simple *diana* (vocables) and with the verse and a common choral refrain, *la timba no es como ayer* (the drum, or playing the drum, is not like it was in the past). After Ponce displays his chops, Rigores sings the lead canto (main verse of the song), then Orlando "Puntilla" Ríos leads the chorus and improvises in the montuno (call-and-response) section. Ponce takes another long quinto solo and then Puntilla starts a new rumba with a chant from a *pataki* [a story about the orishas in santería] about *Obatalá*, as if it were a diana. In the ritual context this can also be seen as a short anecdote, but in the rumba context it is has a different function; Puntilla also sings fragments for Obatalá during the coro of this part of the song as if it were a *pie forzado* (forced foot).[147] The diana is based on Arará/Dahomey language while the refrain uses Lucumí/Yoruba language.[148]

> **Diana**: *Guararey, Guara rara, etc.*
> **Guía 1**: *Somos los cubanos que venimos invadiendo*
> *Somos los cubanos que venimos a decirte a ti (2x)*
> *Que la timba es brava, la timba no es como ayer (2x) . . .*
> **Guía 1**: *La timba no es como ayer, rumba pa lo marivá*
> **Coro 1**: *La timba no es como ayer*
> **Guia 2 [Puntilla]**: *Criollo, Eleguá kutó junde ma wa, Mi Arere so nde ma wa . . .*
> **Coro 2**: *Abuka lo cheke, ko mo Arere gwa ma*[149]

Lead: We are the Cubans and we've come invading
We are the Cubans and we've come to say to you
That the drum [or the real swing], the drum is not like it was in the past
Lead 1: The drum is not like it was, rumba for the sea
Chorus 1: That the drum is not like it was yesterday . . .
Coro 2: With this hunchback who is working here in the house it would be
   good not to continue[150]

While *"La timba no es como ayer"* is a pretty common refrain in rumba lyrics, it can also be interpreted along the lines of "we Cubans bring the latest musical information related to Cuban music and we've invaded the scene to tell you New Yorkers and people outside of Cuba that the drum, and rumba, is not played like it was played in the old days, like you play it." This sentiment could be interpreted differently depending on who is asked, but it seems to indicate the throwing down of the rumba gantlet or at best announcing a musical invasion.[151] On his subsequent albums, *Arawe* and *Chango Te Llama*, Ponce presented a mix of Latin jazz with some of the best Cuban, Puerto Rican, Dominican, and North American musicians in New York City. In his own words, Ponce explained to Isabelle Leymarie that he was "never involved in a musical group that played jazz in Havana" and that he was surprised by what he found musically in New York, particularly funk, rock, and jazz, even recalling Luis "Perico" Ortiz's music as popular at the time of his arrival.[152]

Unfortunately, his volatile personality and other issues caused him to burn bridges with many of the musicians and supporters who had championed his career in New York. While Ponce began his career with a bang, he eventually resettled in South Florida and tragically died alone on a park bench in Miami in 2013.

THE MARIELITOS AS TEACHERS

Some of the new musical information from Cuba began making it through the folkloric community at formal performances and rehearsals, but also at regularly occurring informal gatherings. For Felix Sanabria, Mariel arrivals such as the choreographer Alberto Morgan danced for the orisha *Babaluayé* better than anyone he had ever seen; Morgan is listed as a performer on Ponce's recording *New York Now*.[153] And Kike Dreke spent a lot of time mentoring the young New York drummers like Sanabria. Dreke came in Mariel and joined his brother Curva, who can be heard singing on the important New York City rumba recording *Patato y Totico* (1967). Kike Dreke was extremely acrobatic and can be seen dancing a *rumba columbia* expertly from 3:36 to 4:38 in in the

1960 Mario Gallo directed film *Al compás de Cuba*.[154] Sanabria also remembered another great dancer who arrived in Mariel named Narciso.

As seen in chapter 1, Sanabria studied the orisha tradition formally with Puntilla, but he and his peers also learned the deeper intricacies of rumba with Manuel Martínez Olivera "*El llanero solitario*" (The Lone Ranger). Prior to his arrival in New York, Martínez is acknowledged as coining the term *guarapachangueo* upon listening to the rumba group Los Chinitos, and qualifying their unique style. Martínez was born in Marianao on January 1, 1932, and his repertoire of rumbas stretched back to songs he had learned as a child as well as some of his own compositions. He spent much of his youth in Matanzas learning the local traditions. Martínez was also a first cousin of Carlos "Patato" Valdés, whose father was a *plaza* in the *abakuá juego* of Taboada. I was lucky to perform with him regularly from 1997 to 1999 and later from 2000 to 2003 as part of Sanabria's folkloric group Los Afortunados and enjoyed his singing and musicianship immensely. *El Llanero* can be seen singing with a version of Los Afortunados made up of Skip Burney, Gene Golden, Felix Sanabria, Alberto Serrano, Paula Balan, Ernest "Chico" Álvarez, and others in many YouTube videos.[155] He died January 29, 2010, and remains an iconic figure for New York City rumberos. Los Afortunados was a folkloric group born out of one that Sanabria had started with his friend and neighbor Yeyito Flores called Cheveré Macún Cheveré. This group of Nuyorican musicians also spent time under the tutelage of master dancer and choreographer Roberto Borrell. Prior to his arrival in the United States, Borrell had been a dancer in the Conjunto Folclórico Nacional de Cuba (1968–70) and led his own folkloric music and dance ensemble called Kubatá.[156] Once he arrived in the United States in 1980, Borrell became active in the Cuban folkloric music scene and formed another version of Kubatá, which included Sanabria and his future wife Susan Richardson, Abraham Rodríguez, and other New Yorkers involved with Cuban religious and folkloric music. Other Mariel arrivals who were musicians that played with Cheveré Macún Cheveré were Estrella, and Pedro Sarmona "El Cojo." When Sanabria and his wife got married he had a number of celebrations, one of them at a small Bronx club that Puntilla owned called Santa Barbara.[157]

In a 1982 video of Borrell's group rehearsing, one can see the celebrated drummers and educators Franky Malabé and Louis Bauzó.[158] In another YouTube video from a 1980s performance by Los Afortunados, Borrell can be seen dancing the Abakuá *ireme*, but without the traditional costume.[159] After recording and performing popular music with a number of important New York–based Latin music groups, Borrell eventually settled in California and has continued teaching Cuban music and dance. One important group that Borrell recorded with as a percussionist was Los Soneros, which featured the flamboyant vocalist Fernando Lavoy.

For a Nuyorican like Sanabria, the Cubans that came in the Mariel mixed very well with the Puerto Ricans and African Americans, and Americans in general. And they opened the doors for Cuban musicians who would come during the next thirty years. For a Mariel arrival like Taboada, there were always great Cuban artists who had traveled to New York and elsewhere such as "Orlando Valiejo, Olga Guillot, Blanca Rosa Gil . . . people that were in art . . . but not in folklore."[160] Taboada, who became Sanabria's godfather, remembered seeing Puntilla perform on the previously mentioned Cuban television show *Cuba y su arte folclór*. Taboada also remembered seeing Puntilla give a class of folklore on Cuban National Television.

One musician told me that Julito Collazo told Puntilla that he could not teach batá and Puntilla disagreed, claiming that he himself had learned with legendary *bataleros* such as Pancho Quinto, Jesús Pérez, Papo Angarica, and many more and was therefore entitled to teach whomever he pleased. One of Puntilla's best students, and an excellent musician who performed and recorded with Mongo Santamaria, was Eddie Rodríguez—who purportedly sold his blood to pay for classes with Puntilla. Sanabria received his Aña ritual on September 21, 1985, and around the same time he won a $2,500–3,000 grant to study with Puntilla.

A seasoned singer and fellow Marielito like Taboada felt that he improved his voice by singing coro in Puntilla's tambor. Puntilla regarded his young and eager singers highly as they were excellent, such as Ama McKen, Olfemi Mitchell, Evelyn Smart, Abraham Rodríguez, Skip, Taboada, and Eddy Rodríguez. Rolando Creagh Alfonso even said to Taboada, "you have to respect all of those musicians [the New Yorkers] because they are your brothers."

Another Mariel arrival that has gone on to teach and perform is Vicente Sánchez. Vicente came through the Peruvian embassy during the Mariel and was in Pensacola with Puntilla; as seen in the 2013 documentary *Rumba Clave Blen Blen Blen*, one can see a wall decoration in Vicente Sánchez's house that proudly declares "Proud to be Cuban and a Marielito!"[161] In the late 1990s, he and David Oquendo were part of the first weekly Sunday rumba at La Esquina Habanera in Union City on March 23, 1996, which lasted nine years without interruption. This Grammy®-nominated group became known as Raíces Habaneras and counts several Marielitos in its midst.

Other musicians who came in Mariel and were also associated with the Grammy®-nominated Afro-Cuban folklore group Raíces Habaneras included singer, dancer, and composer Pedro Domech, who met Puntilla in 1981, as well as Xiomara Rodríguez and Rita Macías, two other dancers who went on to teach many students the dances for the orishas. The experience of these two women shows that cultural exchanges in New York City are not in one direction from Cuba to Puerto Rico. I have performed alongside both Rodríguez and Macías when they have danced with Afro–Puerto Rican folklore groups. As Rodríguez explains:

> I am very grateful for my profession. I have seen the blossoming of all my students. Many women have learned to dance to the *orishas*. I came in 1980 through Mariel . . . I dance the [Puerto Rican] bomba in a Cuban style, but I dance it because I feel it. Bomba for me is like *columbia* [a fast style of Cuban rumba]. I'm talking to you about things that no one knows. Am I right, or am I right?[162]

Thus, a core group of musicians and dancers who came to the United States during the Mariel Boatlift settled in New York City and influenced a generation of Cuban and Latin music students and performers.

The influence and groundbreaking efforts of the Mariel Cubans would have lasting repercussions as subsequent Cuban arrivals such as Félix "Pupy" Insua, Ogduardo "Román" Díaz, Pedro Pablo "Pedrito" Martínez, and others hooked up with Puntilla upon arriving from Cuba in the 1990s. Pedrito claimed that the first tambor he played with was Puntilla. Through the scholar Ivor Miller, Vicente Sánchez and Román Díaz would make the first trip ever by Cuban abakuá to visit their brethren in Nigeria.

Besides the flows that Lisa Maya Knauer has explored in her work, Robin Moore writes that the effects of the Mariel Boatlift had even broader repercussions in Cuba:

> In the aftermath of the Mariel exodus of the early 1980s, the government tried to make Cuban society more attractive to its citizens in the hopes that they would choose to stay. This was the first period since the mid-1960s in which television stations began to show video clips of foreign rock groups, for instance.[163]

The influx of important artists who came in the Mariel Boatlift was not limited to the aforementioned musicians, but rather included all of the arts. Charley Gerard points out that "Among the Marielitos were a remarkable amount of talented writers (Reynaldo Arenas, Carlos Victoria, and Andrés Reynaldo), artists (Juan Abréu, Victor Gomez, and Gilberto Ruiz Valdez), and musicians (Orlando 'Puntilla' Rios, drummer Ignacio Berroa, and conguero Daniel Ponce)."[164]

In her excellent study of Cuban musicians in New York and Miami during the 1940s and 1950s, Cristina Abreu argued that "it is necessary to study these various modes of performance simultaneously in order to understand the role black and white Cuban musicians played in shaping Cuban ethnic and broader Hispano/a and Latino/a identity."[165] Comparing the experiences of black and white Cuban musicians in New York and Miami during this time period "reveal[s] both shared understandings and significant differences in their migration experiences, their participation in the professional entertainment industries, and their construction of white, brown, and black racial identities."[166] Abreu also points out that the Cuban experience in New York in the 1940s and 1950s involved contact with African American and Puerto Ricans in Harlem, the Bronx, and Manhattan that was "sometimes friendly, sometimes hostile."[167] For Abreu, "Cuban musicians and migrants, both black and white, shaped the development of Latinidad, albeit a Latinidad that was contested and, though it usually celebrated African influences, was not always tolerant or inclusive of people of color."[168] Abreu's study is significant because it points out the historical privileging of post-1959 Cuban migration as defining the Cuban experience while burying the activities of Cubans in the United States, specifically in Miami and New York during the 1940s and 1950s, because they were seen as immigrants rather than exiles.[169]

The Afro-Cuban experience in New York prior to the Mariel Boatlift had some visible traditions. One of these traditions occurs at the Bohemian Beer Hall in Astoria, Queens, where the popular Cuban dance *Recordando el mamoncillo* (remembering the mamoncillo) [a fruit tree] takes place every year. This dance has occurred on the second Sunday of July for over thirty years. As Melba Alvarado (1919–2019), director of the Club Cubano Inter-Americano, explained in the documentary *Recordando el mamoncillo*:

> We got the idea to have a dance similar to the ones at the Tropical Brewery in Cuba. We organized this way on a Sunday afternoon with music like at the Tropical by bands that played charanga and son . . . it's a footprint of Cuban culture especially here in New York. We have planted the roots, it's well known, everyone knows what it is. There are people who have grown up with the Mamoncillo [dance].[170]

The dance takes its name from the fact that the Tropical Brewery in Havana had a mamoncillo tree near one stage and the dance was an effort to commemorate that atmosphere. The dance has particular meaning to the attendees, as one Afro-Cuban father standing with his daughter explained:

> I have always felt that I owed this to my children, because in Cuba, we were so proud of our Afro-Cuban roots [that] when we came to this country we had the good fortune to find people who felt it was important to continue our traditions. I've brought her here since she was very young. It is a sentiment that is difficult to express in words.[171]

While the Afro-Cuban experience in New York City may have been culturally rich, it was also challenging and seldom in the spotlight. For the Fosters, an Afro-Cuban family arriving in the Bronx in the early 1960s, it was a culture shock and the negotiation of being black and Latino in the social climate of their new home often meant having one's identity questioned by both their Puerto Rican and African American neighbors to different ends. In Cuba the family had been of Jamaican and Cuban heritage, in addition to having roots in Eastern Cuba.[172] One family member, Diana Foster Matsoukas, said that it wasn't until the advent of the Young Lords that she felt Afro-Latino youth openly embraced the duality of their heritage.[173]

Clearly, Cubans who arrived in 1980 with the Mariel Boatlift have also had their narrative subsumed. And although it is beyond the time frame of this book, this statement could also be correctly applied to the *balseros* (Cuban rafters who came to the United States in the early 1990s) who have made great contributions to the music scene in New York City. The musicians who came in *El Mariel* were in large numbers Afro-Cubans who were proud of their *Afrocubanidad* (of being Afro-Cuban). They brought their religious ritual and folkloric knowledge to keep them anchored in a new land after a truly harrowing migratory experience. Often this was preceded by difficult times living in Cuba after 1959. Once in the United States, and specifically in New York, these musicians helped shape a generation of Cuban ritual and folkloric drummers and dancers while simultaneously expanding their own creative vision and output, and collaborating with non-Cuban musicians to create new vibrant musical expressions.

For some people, attending the weekly multinational rumba in Central Park is still a means of holding on to an important piece of Afro-Cuban and Mariel identity. Many great rumberos still attend, such as Ruben "El Tao La Onda" González (d. 2020).[174] At the conclusion of the documentary *Rumba Clave Blen Blen Blen*, one Mariel rumbero explains:

> This is the Central Park rumba. This is one of the best parks in the world. A lot of nationalities join in this rumba. You can give me a steak sandwich with a lot of fries there, or you can give me rumba here. I go with rumba and leave you the steak sandwich and fries behind, because this is what I like, rumba. We come every Sunday to this park. I've been coming to the park to celebrate since 1980. Without this, I am not happy. This is what keeps me alive.[175]

One can see that the Afro-Cuban experience that the Marielitos brought with them in 1980 and have continued to cultivate well into the twenty-first century is another chapter in the Afro-Cuban experience in New York City that continues to develop and extend beyond the arrival of the first Afro-Cubans in

the twentieth century. The presence of the Marielito musicians has undoubtedly shaped both New York's greater Latin music scene and the Afro-Cuban
ritual and folkloric scenes as well as serving as a bridge to subsequent Cuban
arrivals in New York. Particularly interesting and important is the impact these
musicians had among Puerto Rican drummers in New York. The experience of
Marielito musicians in New York City was quite distinct from their previous
time in Cuba in that it allowed them to leave a major impact in a wide variety of
genres. This opportunity was not available to them in Cuba at the time of their
departure; in this way, New York shaped their music as much as they shaped
two generations of musicians since their arrival in 1980.

CONCLUSION
Making Latin Music in New York City

TEN IMPORTANT THEMES

Throughout this book, I have explored a variety of important and distinguishing musical factors that add detail to the narrative of Latin music in New York. My goal has been to highlight some of the specific musical aspects of New York's unique historical role in the development and innovation of Spanish Caribbean music. As mentioned in the introduction, there are at least ten specific categories of elements and themes in the preceding chapters that demonstrate how and why musicians who played Latin music in New York City directly helped shape the sound of Latin music internationally. These include (1) the physical and metaphysical aspects of clave, (2) the importance of folklore, (3) the emphasis on music education, (4) musical biculturalism and triculturalism, (5) the evolution of the anticipated bass part, (6) instrument making and its impact on performance and recording, (7) the role of dance, (8) lineages of musicians, (9) inter-ethnic collaboration, and (10) the role of jazz.

(1) Physical and Metaphysical Aspects of Clave

The emphasis on clave, a two-bar musical pattern known executed by two rounded wooden sticks called *claves*, was elevated in New York City to a highly codified musical and metaphysical level with specific musical and performance expectations. Samuel Floyd Jr. defined this rhythmic figure as emblematic of "the circum-Caribbean and the Americas."[1] Adherence to the clave is less strict in contemporary examples of Afro-Cuban–based dance music made in Cuba, Colombia, Puerto Rico, and elsewhere in comparison with New York.[2] This frequently upsets New York–based musicians of all ages who are so steeped in Afro-Cuban–based musical traditions that the principle of clave and clave direction is also applied to non-Cuban musical genres such as plena, bomba, and merengue in arrangements and performances. From the 1940s onward, New York City–based arrangers ensured that their music adhered to the clave from the moment that the pattern was initiated through the end of the piece of music. Even early Spanish Caribbean music method books published in New York City emphasized this particular point of performance practice regarding the clave: "once a rhythm is started, it is played without change throughout the entire number."[3] A clave jump or discrepancy is when a melody starts with the clave and suddenly loses its rhythmic bearing because it is not phrased with the actual beats of the clave.

New York–based musicians have repeatedly corrected instances of clave jumps and ambiguities inherent in classic Cuban compositions. One notable example is Eddie Palmieri's 1970 version of Guillermo Rodríguez Fiffe's classic Cuban composition "Bilongo" from the album *Superimposition*. The correction can be heard at 00:42 coming out of the bridge and cued with an actual clave pattern executed by Palmieri himself on the piano. Today, when the song is called on a gig, musicians will confer with one another on the bandstand as to which version they will execute: the Palmieri version or the classic *cruzao* (crossed) version that preserves the composition's clave inconstancy. This shows the deep level of clave understanding that New York musicians possess and accounts for the fact that there are musicians from Cuba and elsewhere who do not play the song with the rhythmic correction.

From early on, New York–based musicians strove to ensure that the phrasing of a given melody and its supporting parts was strictly coordinated with the clave throughout a given performance and/or recording. This adherence to the clave was neither robotic nor without a sense of swing, because the musicians and the arrangers had to keep the dancers dancing and the listener engaged. Arrangers such as Ray Santos, René Hernández, Louie Cruz, Chico O'Farrill, Sonny Bravo, Oscar Hernández, Edy Martínez, and others have exemplified this tradition, and scholars such as Paul Austerlitz, Alex Stewart, and Chris Washburne have explored this in their analyses of some of these arrangers.[4]

On a metaphysical level, musicians developed a highly sophisticated under-standing of the clave that distinguishes between "positive and negative," active and inactive, "expansive and contractive," and other "balanced opposites" or notable binary possibilities.[5] This understanding is discussed, preached, and learned in a variety of settings that demand that the successful musician have a highly developed, sensitive, and intuitive command of the concept. Chris Washburne has demonstrated the extent to which New York musicians focus on clave by playing different audio examples for musicians and then eliciting their comments to offer insight as to why the examples do or don't swing (in clave).[6] The ensuing discussion provides evidence of what musicians think and the specific musical parameters and requirements for what constitutes playing "in" and "out" of clave for them and within their musical community.

From these discussions there is no clear sense of how they personally developed this understanding and sensibility or how one would go about developing it if one did not already have it. What were some of the explicit methods and means by which these same New York–based musicians achieved the necessary mastery and intuitive sense of clave? Developing a solid sense of clave was explored in chapter 3 with Sonny Bravo and Típica 73 as well as in chapter 1. From these chapters we learn that some musicians like Sonny Bravo and Bobby Rodríguez tapped the pattern with their foot to avoid problems. Gilberto "Pulpo" Colón Jr. learned from Ray Maldonado to orient himself via the cáscara pattern played by the timbales, and all of Alberto Socarrás's students practiced executing the exercises in the Hilario Eslava book in common time and while snapping the clave pattern. Thus, the clave is crucial in the execution of Latin music in New York City and this orthodoxy is rooted in education and performance practice.

(2) Folklore

Afro-Latin folkloric music has been important to the development of popular music primarily as source material, but in the environment of New York City it served and continues to serve as both a teaching vehicle and as its own idiom of specialized performance. Historically, New York–based musicians who performed Spanish Caribbean dance music deepened their understanding of rhythm, dance, harmony, and melody through the formal and informal study of folklore. This could be as simple as clapping the clave while singing the choral refrain at an informal rumba gathering or a level of involvement requiring a long apprenticeship with a master drummer in an Afro-Caribbean sacred music such as Santería, palo, or Haitian vodou. In the folkloric setting, young musicians grounded themselves in particular genres and mastered these traditions while growing up in New York City rather than the Caribbean, yet they have still retained a level of mastery comparable to that of an indigenous master. This learning community of like-minded musicians who taught each other also served as an immediate pool of musicians ready, eager, and musically prepared to work with newly arriving masters of Afro-Latin musical folklore traditions as well as in popular Latin dance groups. As a result of the Mariel Boatlift, acknowledged masters of ritual drumming reinvigorated the existing ritual music scene and ensured the proper training of ritual and folkloric drummers from across ethnic groups. Their students would travel back and forth to Cuba, proving false the assertion that New York City and Cuba were not connected.

Chapter 1 demonstrates that folklore was not limited to the accepted image of "authentic" practitioners playing old music in an old setting. In the case of New York's Latin musicians, the emphasis on folklore also served a social purpose in creating learning communities dedicated to a variety of musical traditions. In these communities, learners would actively listen to folkloric and older popular music recordings, analyze the music and lyrics, and interact with older musicians who were present at these recording sessions, participated in them, or had intimate knowledge of the musicians and music involved. After studying and performing the music on these recordings, a group of like-minded individuals would begin to create new means of executing the music. New interpretations of folklore combined doo-wop with rumba, Cuban son, or Puerto Rican jíbaro music with *orisha* songs of Santería, rumba, and American popular song, as well as other manifestations.

Afro-Caribbean folklore in New York City has served as educational tool, social organizer, and point of departure for innovations in Latin jazz and dance music. Just as folklore and traditional music have absorbed outside elements and evolved in the Spanish Caribbean countries of origin, New York City musicians evolved unique interpretations of Spanish Caribbean folkloric musical traditions.

(3) Education beyond Folklore

It is often incorrectly assumed that musicians who perform Spanish Caribbean music, particularly Latino musicians, were entirely educated in the "University of the Street"—also known locally as "UCLA" (University of the Corner of Lexington Avenue)—and that they lacked any formal training. Clearly there were communities of folklore-focused percussionists who educated one another wherever they could find a communal space, public or private, especially on rooftops and in the parks. However, there were other learning communities that were made up of students and teachers who rigorously taught musicianship and applied instrument lessons. These musicians were able to capture the energy, philosophy, and information of the streets and convey it through their playing, but their development was highly sophisticated and codified. As seen in chapters 1 and 5–7, there were many opportunities for learning music, and a culture of studying music was prized by New York City Latin musicians and those who came from throughout the Caribbean to be a part of the scene.

The Cuban musicians Osvaldo Alén and Alberto Socarrás, along with the Panamanian pianist Nicolás Rodríguez, trained numerous musicians who remain active today. Their private students were taught through a variety of method books in the European canon as well as the popular musical traditions of Cuba, other countries, and Latin New York. Rodríguez's students also learned specific techniques to improve their performance based on their physical position relative to the instrument. Puerto Rican women such as Maria Luisa Lecompte, Eduviges Bocanegra, and Victoria Hernández played an important role as music teachers and organized public recitals for their students that were covered in the press. These noted music teachers in the Latino community emphasized musical literacy, as did the musicians.

Starting in 1962 and then through the formal establishment of the East Harlem School of Music, Johnny Colón was able to teach thousands of musicians and employ instructors that make up a who's who of Latin music, such as Charlie Palmieri and Sonny Bravo, among others. As detailed in the education chapter 1, the alumni of the school went on to perform and record with major figures in Latin music. Colón has more recently started a new youth-focused music program in Manhattan's Lower East Side. Another program at the Boys and Girls Harbor, started by Ramón Rodríguez and Louis Bauzó, has taught thousands of students who remain active in the Latin music scene. Music and Art High School was an important incubator for Latin music talent, and PS 52 in the Bronx served as meeting and rehearsal space for aspiring musicians such as Joe Torres, Orlando Marín, and others.

Many Latin musicians in New York often sought out known instrumentalists and instruction from beyond the world of Spanish Caribbean music to study instrumental technique and orchestration. Some even enrolled in and graduated from formal Western art music schools like Juilliard, Manhattan School of Music, and New York University, among others. A few examples of such instrumentalists include Bobby Rodríguez, the *tampeño* bassist who studied with Oscar Zimmerman; Andy González, who studied with Steve Swallow; and Bobby Valentín, the Puerto Rican bassist and former trumpeter who studied jazz trumpet with Art Farmer in the late 1950s.[7] Paul Austerlitz has detailed the many ways that Mario Bauzá learned jazz phrasing from Chick Webb.[8] Similarly, non-Latino musicians would learn Latin musical phrasing from their employers.[9] Finally, a large number of Spanish Caribbean musicians took part in rehearsal big bands such as Lynn Oliver's, where they would work on sight-reading and section playing of well-known arrangements with other like-minded musicians who were mostly not involved with the Latin music scene.[10]

A number of important Latin music method books, often produced by prominent Latin and non-Latin musicians, have given detailed transcriptions and technical instructions for a wide range of instruments. In addition, Martin Cohen's Latin Percussion record label released a number of instructional LPs for Latin rhythm section playing and soloing. Today, we take such books for granted thanks to YouTube, legally sanctioned music study trips to Cuba, and the acceptance of Latin music in music education from primary through university levels. Nevertheless, these first books offer us a detailed and insightful picture of how musicians conceived of their art and how the pedagogy for Latin music was first developed.

(4) Biculturalism and Beyond

In addition to their involvement in sight-reading big bands and the pursuit of greater instrumental virtuosity beyond the technical demands of Spanish Caribbean music, New York–based musicians who were active in the Latin music scene were often musically (and in many cases also socially) bicultural. Rondón mischaracterized New York in the 1960s, writing, "on the radio, the Beatles displaced guarachas, and some Latino youth abandoned Spanish in order to babble in English that no one understood."[11] However, musicians had already begun the process of embracing both Latin and North American musical and culture much earlier. Early Latino musical pioneers based in New York such as Mario Bauzá, Alberto Socarrás, Luis Russell, Rafael Escudero, and Juan Tizól worked in bands led by Chick Webb, Cab Calloway, Louis Armstrong, Benny Carter, and Duke Ellington, among others.[12] For subsequent arrivals, interaction with American popular music was inevitable and often explicitly sought out since it was only available in recorded form in their home countries, and even restricted.

For US-born musicians, musical biculturalism was the result of growing up with both Latin music and American popular music traditions and developing musical skills to be fluent within idioms such as jazz, rhythm and blues, doo-wop, soul, and other music styles. An awareness of and interest in what other musicians were doing in other genres had multiple effects. Musicians experimented and incorporated non-Latin and non-Caribbean elements into Spanish Caribbean dance music to produce genres like the boogaloo.[13] As seen in chapters 3 and 5, these elements also included contemporary sound engineering techniques, thematic ideas for recordings (such as concept albums, full-length musicals with characters, and suites with extended forms), utilizing arranging concepts that would feature particular instruments and instrumentalists as well as extending the harmonic range and sensibility of traditional son montuno song forms and their concomitant structures such as mambos, *moñas*, and *opcionales*.

For non-Latino musicians—particularly Jews, but in lesser numbers Italians, African Americans, and Anglo-Americans—there was an added degree and expectation of heightened cultural awareness. As seen in chapter 4, Panamanian musicians were often ascribed a variety of identities (Latino, West Indian, or

African American) by their musical colleagues, and they took advantage of this ambiguity to work across genres and audiences. Although the intense dancehall scene of the Catskills and New York City nightclubs served as a crucible for Latin dance music from the 1940s through the 1960s, the relationship between Jews and Latin music covered a wide range of possibilities and activities surrounding Spanish Caribbean music before, during, and after this period.

Chapter 5 shows how Puerto Rican musicians born both on the island and in the United States created and/or cultivated musical styles that expressed their belonging to both North American and Latin musical culture. Other scholarship critically examines New York creations such as boogaloo and hip hop. Puerto Rican knowledge of Cuban traditions also allowed for new forms of music that reflected these combinations such as jíbaro music with Santería and Espiritismo, as well as the mixing of Puerto Rican forms with other Cuban forms. A thorough knowledge of jazz, in particular, has left its deepest imprint on the music created and performed by Puerto Ricans in New York City that was marketed as salsa. Musicians learned these concepts as a means to further express themselves and innovate. Previous scholarly works on salsa, or Latin music in New York such as Rondón's *Libro de la salsa*, have either completely ignored these abundantly extant examples of musical creativity or dismissed them as unworthy. Thankfully, the recordings reveal the true extent to which New York–born and –based Puerto Ricans innovated many musical styles and practices in New York that were not conceived of in Cuba, Puerto Rico, or elsewhere in the Caribbean.

(5) The Evolution of the Anticipated Bass Part in New York City

The pulsating groove of the Spanish Caribbean bass line is ubiquitous and audible from storefronts and windows when driving through most busy New York City intersections. This same bass sound can also be heard when standing on a corner listening as cars with blaring stereos make their way in and out of many New York City neighborhoods. Why is this liquid sound as emblematic of New York's Spanish Caribbean heritage as a second line played by a brass band is to New Orleans?

Early recordings of Cuban music in New York City offer a good point of departure for examining the impact of New York musicians on Latin dance music, particularly with respect to the modification of the musical elements such as the anticipated bass part. The *anticipation* refers specifically to the unique and easily identifiable rhythm that the bass executes in Afro-Latin music. Peter Manuel has described it as the bass part "anticipating the harmony of the following bar."[14] While Manuel has explored how this musical characteristic evolved in a few genres of Cuban music, specific sound recordings

offer a better picture of what happened and when it happened, particularly in
New York City. Recordings made in New York City in the 1920s by the Cuban
group Sexteto and Septeto Habanero feature an ostinato played by the bass
known as the *tresillo* (dotted quarter note, dotted quarter note, quarter note).
Subsequent recordings made by Cuban musicians in New York City, such as
El Cuarteto Caney, feature the *tampeño* (Tampa-born Cuban) bassist Santiago
"Elio" Osácar, father of pianist Sonny Bravo. As seen in chapter 3, selections
such as "Cantando" and "Flor de ausencia" feature bass parts played by Osácar
that range from the tresillo to an even more active "walking" bass part during
sones and boleros.[15]

The shift away from playing the tresillo pattern starts to be heard on recordings by the great Puerto Rican pianist Noro Morales featuring the *Tampeño* bassist Bobby Rodríguez (Osácar's cousin). Rodríguez would soon drop
particular accents in subsequent recordings with the effect of smoothing out
the harmonic rhythm. By the 1960s, the anticipated bass line associated with
salsa (dotted quarter, dotted quarter, quarter tied to the dotted quarter of the
following bar) was well established. The Cuban flautist José Fajardo felt that
this was a Puerto Rican development and innovation, not a Cuban phenomenon.[16] Peter Manuel's research supports this assertion; he has suggested that
the accompanying guitar parts of Puerto Rican jíbaro music, as recorded and
performed in New York, often move with the same rhythmic cadence, and it
is possible that this helped influence the evolution of the bass in Cuban-based
dance music such as salsa and other non-Cuban genres.[17]

The influence would come directly in the form of Puerto Ricans and other
non-Cuban musicians playing Cuban-based music in New York City early in
the twentieth century. The more actively moving bass parts heard in the music
of the musically demanding tres player, composer, and Cuban son innovator
Arsenio Rodríguez were executed by his bassists Evaristo "Cuajarón" Baró,
Julio Andino, Lázaro Prieto, and later, Alfonso "El Panameño" Joseph. These
bass parts remained stylistically within the son style that Arsenio Rodríguez
represented, but these bass players changed their playing styles in different
situations beyond Rodríguez's band. New York dancers seemed to prefer the
faster tempo styles of homegrown bands such as Machito, Tito Puente, and
Tito Rodríguez. It is also likely that, because New York dancers moved differently to the mambo as performed by New York bands, the bands further
responded to the dancers' needs. Thus, the older active bass line rhythm was
bound to change. Nevertheless, the active role of the bass was expressed in
other formats within Spanish Caribbean music. As seen in chapter 5, Julio Andino's early bass features along with Bobby Rodríguez's work with Tito Puente
signal an alternative role for the upright acoustic bass as a lead instrument as
well as demonstrating technically virtuosic possibilities for the bass in Spanish

Caribbean music.[18] These songs, used as features for the bassist, echoed similar trends and characteristics of contemporary non-Latin jazz bass counterparts like Milt Hinton, Jimmy Blanton, and Slam Stewart.

Chapter 2 demonstrates that, from a technological perspective, the role and sound of the bass was impacted greatly by performers who employed the Ampeg Baby Bass that was built in New York City beginning in the early 1940s. Early adopters of the Ampeg upright electric bass in the Spanish Caribbean context needed the volume that amplified sound offered without sacrificing the tone associated with an upright acoustic bass. The result was a groundbreaking solution for working musicians in the Spanish Caribbean music scene that remains the standard and idealized sound.

(6) Instrument Making

The previously cited story of the Ampeg bass in New York City is one of many similar stories involving musical instrument builders and the construction of instruments to support the musicians who played Spanish Caribbean music. Since the 1930s, the professional musician's needs have been fulfilled by a number of luthiers and drum makers based in New York City. These instrument makers developed new technologies to improve upon the construction of traditional instruments such as basses, hand percussion (congas, batá drums, timbales, bells, bongó, chekeré, tamboras, güiras, etc.), cuatros, treses, guitars, and electric basses. New York also served as a type of research and development lab where makers could see their instruments used in a variety of contexts by a variety of professional and innovative players. Brooklyn, Manhattan, the Bronx, and neighboring New Jersey were home to variety of builders and repairmen whose instruments would become the standards to be copied and purchased for use in New York and throughout the world. Although some were able to dedicate themselves exclusively to their art, it was common to also have a full-time job and build instruments in their homes.[19]

(7) Music for Dancers

At its apex, New York and its immediate surroundings, including the satellite scene(s) in the Catskill Mountains resorts (there was also a Latino resort scene referred to as Las Villas), were home to countless dancehalls and nightclubs. Chapter 6 shows that many dances were held in Brooklyn and that these venues offered formal and informal dance competitions as well as formal and informal instruction. Other scholars have highlighted the participation of Cuban dancers during the earliest period of this study, but Puerto Ricans and Jews in New York developed a local dance technique to accommodate New York's own flavor of guaracha, son, and mambo. Augie and Margot, Mike and Millie, Ira Goldwasser, and Cuban Pete were just a few of the prominent dance teams and dancers who innovated the way that most "schooled" salsa dancers execute steps on today's dance floors around the world. These dancers studied West African and Haitian dance as well as Western ballet and incorporated these elements into their personal styles. Dancers from a variety of ethnic groups commingled and partnered throughout the scene, defying ethnic expectations and stereotypes.

(8) Family Lineages and Continuity

Another characteristic woven throughout New York's unique Spanish Caribbean musical legacy is the notion of family lineage and a resulting continuity of tradition that allows for stylistic innovation. This is discussed at length in chapter 3. In many Latin American and Caribbean islands there have been generations of families dedicated to the performance and composition of music as well as musical instrument building. New York City is quite similar, as there have been families involved in these three areas across generations. For Andy and Jerry Gónzalez, Hector Torres, Tony Cruz, Johnny "Dandy" Rodríguez, José and Gerald Madera, Sonny Bravo, Mauricio Smith Jr., Richie Bastar, Mario Grillo, Elias "Phoenix" Rivera, Ronnie Baró, Orlando Vega, Ray Coen, Orlando Fiol, Armando Fajardo, Willie and Roberto Rodríguez, and many others, seeing their parents perform and/or performing with their parents served as their earliest forms of musical education and exposure to Latin dance music. Composers and arrangers such as Mike Amadeo and Arturo O'Farrill were in a similar position to observe, listen, and learn from their fathers' activities and even work alongside them before striking out on their own. Family lineages and apprenticeships were also important in instrument building, as in chapter 2, where the Brooklyn-based luthier William Del Pilar has continued the work of his celebrated father.

(9) Inter-ethnic Collaboration

Inter-ethnic collaboration was at the core of the New York sound. All musicians, regardless of ethnicity, were expected to possess and demonstrate a wide set of skills that were grounded in the musical traditions of the Caribbean, not just those of Cuba. Looking at recordings from 1940–90, the degree to which this mixing was achieved is astounding and impressive, more so because it was not intentional: the music came first, not the nationality of the musician. Recordings by Cuarteto Victoria, Trio Borínquen, Típica 73, almost all of the SAR recordings, Fania All-Stars, Alegre All-Stars, Cesta All-Stars, and many more reflect wide participation by a number or nationalities. That said, inter-ethnic collaboration took place in a variety of ways and was not the same across the board for everyone involved. Each chapter speaks to some of the specific ways, places, and dynamics where inter-ethnic collaboration took place on the bandstand: for Típica 73 (chapter 3); for Panamanian musicians (chapter 4); in both the formal and informal "classroom" and in folklore-focused sites for Anglo (non-Latin) and Latino musicians (chapter 2); and for Jewish musicians (chapter 6). Chapter 2 focuses on musical instruments but also points out the ways in which inter-ethnic collaboration, both between Jews and Latinos and within Latino groups, brought about changes and innovations in instrument making. Future scholarship should address the immense contributions of African American and Dominican musicians to the New York sound of Latin music.

(10) Jazz

Musicians performing Latin music in New York City went out of their way to learn how to play jazz. They also participated in reading bands that were specifically for non-Latin big band jazz repertoire. This love of jazz was not limited to musicians who were active in the 1940s through the 1970s. Chapter 7 demonstrates how Mariel arrivals such as Ponce, Machado, Berroa, and others also used jazz as a means to expand their creative vision, taking part in the international jazz scene after spending time in jazz groups. Chapter 5 shows how jazz allowed Tito Puente, Sonny Bravo, Eddie Palmieri, Andy and Jerry González, and countless others to enrich Latin music and craft a personal sound. As seen in chapter 4, Panamanian musicians also gravitated to jazz before and after arriving in New York City. This was a two-way street and many non-Latin jazz musicians sought out performance opportunities with Latin musicians as well as opportunities to study Latin music and incorporate it into jazz. Far from an exhaustive list, some of the musicians in this category that have been discussed in this book include Ben Bierman, Chick Corea, Herbie Hancock, Marty Sheller, Dexter Gordon, Leslie Johnakins, and Doc Cheatham.

Shaping an International Sound Bigger than James Brown

What is the sum total of these ten previously discussed characteristics of Latin music in New York City? There is an oft-quoted expression among musicians who achieve success beyond our home turf of New York City: No one can be a prophet in their own land. In practical terms, this means getting better pay and recognition elsewhere. Juan Flores has demonstrated what this meant for New York City Latin musicians in writing about the Fania All-Stars' participation in the music extravaganza that accompanied the famed Ali-Foreman "Rumble in the Jungle" fight in 1974:

Remembering the moment when the entertainers landed in Zaire and were getting off the plane, Johnny Pacheco speaks proudly about how he outshone James Brown in the celebrities' reception by the host African fans. The thousands of Africans there to greet them "went past him [Brown]," according to the acknowledged leader of Fania, "and they started chanting 'Pa-che-co, Pa-che-co!' They went bananas, I swear to God. So he wanted to know who Pacheco was." The story of the immense popularity of Afro-Cuban music, including salsa, in Africa is a long and inspiring one, to be sure, but one can't help sense a certain special glee on Pacheco's part to have received a warmer welcome in the ancestral homeland than that towering symbol of Black diaspora expression that is James Brown. Something other than racial and cultural solidarity seems to have been at play, something having to do perhaps with commercial supremacy. In any case, this historic trip, and the Academy Award–winning film by Leon Gast years later, were an integral part in the international reach of the booming Fania empire.[20]

For Andy González and the New York City musicians in this study, there was no choosing between James Brown and Latin music, as they were part of the same continuum. In Fernando Trueba's film *Calle 54*, González explains to his colleagues—who appear throughout this book—Tito Puente, Carlos "Patato" Valdés, and Mario Rivera: "I listen to James Brown the same way that I listen to Arsenio [Rodríguez]: James Brown sets up counterpoint, it's the same thing . . . [sings "Cold Sweat" bass line] *esos son tumbaos . . . diferente . . . americano pero es tumbao* [those are tumbaos . . . different . . . American style, but it's tumbao].[21] Thus with this serious and open-minded approach, the musicians, educators, arrangers, and instrument builders profiled in these pages presented the New York sound of Latin music to the world and cemented their legacy forever on vinyl for future generations to enjoy.

GLOSSARY

abakuá	A Calibar/Cross-River Nigerian-derived Afro-Cuban secret mutual aid society and male brotherhood that enslaved and free Africans developed in Cuba based on the veneration of spirits and elders associated with the region.
aguinaldo	A genre of Puerto Rican jíbaro music with a large variety of stock melodies that identify each aguinaldo.
Aña	Literally, the spirit of the drum, a deity and talisman associated with consecrated batá drums.
anticipated bass	An important concept in Latin American and Caribbean music, whereby the bass anticipates the harmony of a given piece of music by a small difference of a beat or less in order to create syncopation.
babalawo	A male priest in the religion of Santería.
batá	A set of three hourglass-shaped drums used in Afro-Cuban Yoruba-derived sacred music and more recently in secular genres such as salsa and rumba.
bembé	An Afro-Cuban ritual setting with music associated with the Yoruba-derived religion of Santería that usually employs a bell or guataca (hoe blade) as a timeline, a tumbadora, and up to three chekeres of different sizes.
bomba	An Afro–Puerto Rican genre traditionally performed with two barrel drums called seguidor and buleador; a cuá (or fuá), the large idiophone similar to the guagua in rumba; as well as maraca and call-and-response vocals.
bongó	A two-headed drum with a small (male) and large (female) side used in a wide variety of Latin music genres.
boogaloo	A genre of music developed in New York in the early 1960s that brought together elements of Latin and African American music. Lyrics were frequently bilingual, the arrangements employed recognizable instruments and musical practices of Latin music such as congas, piano, guajeos, etc. as well as

335

handclapping and backbeat accents, as well as the use of blue notes normally associated with African American music such as soul and rhythm and blues.

cáscara   Literally *shell*. This refers to a two-bar pattern and its variants executed on the sides or shells of the timbales.

chachachá   A term coined by bandleader Enrique Jorrín for a Cuban music and dance genre developed in 1950s Havana. It is sometimes referred to as chacha, but this shortening ignores the fact that the dance emphasizes three quick steps.

clave   1. Two sticks percussed against one another in a fixed pattern. 2. The rhythmic pattern or timeline played by the two sticks (or a similar instrument) that is traditionally fixed from beginning to end and around which other musical parts are organized. Beyond Cuba, musicians refer to clave *direction* based on which side of the pattern a musical passage might begin or emphasize, particularly in discussing son, salsa, and rumba; phrasing must adhere to the pattern.

conjunto   A musical group with two trumpets, piano, Cuban tres, congas, bongó, bass, and vocalists who usually use minor percussion instruments such as güiro (gourd scraper), claves, and/ or maracas.

contradanza   A nineteenth-century European genre of dance music that spread throughout the Americas. The predecessor to the Cuban danzón and Puerto Rican danza.

coro   The choral refrain or, literally, the vocalists who sing the choral refrain during the montuno (call-and-response) section of a piece of music. This happens in a wide variety of genres of Latin American and Caribbean music as well as Latin music in New York.

cruzao/cruzado Literally *crossed*, as when a performer or a musical arrangement employs musical phrases or ideas that clash rhythmically with the dominant explicit or implicit two-bar clave pattern of a given piece of music. Thus, having musical ideas that emphasize one side of the pattern while the rest of the arrangement emphasizes the other. This creates a clash that is referred to as being crossed and demands musical correction.

cuatro   A ten-string fretted instrument with five double courses, mostly tuned in octaves: bB-eE-aA-dd-gg.

cumbia   A genre of Colombian popular dance music traditionally performed with accordion, bass, scraper, drums, and bass, as well as call-and-response vocals.

danza	A creole variety of the contradanza that had different manifestations throughout Latin America and the Caribbean. In this study, the term refers to the light-classical genre of the same name in Puerto Rico.
décima	A ten-line, octosyllabic stanza and poetry from the golden age of Spanish poetry with a rhyme scheme of ABBAACCDDC that is used in a variety of musical genres throughout the Americas. There can be variations to this rhyme scheme.
descarga	Literally *discharge*. Refers to a solo improvisation and/or a jam session among Latin musicians where the focus is to improvise.
fundamento	A concept of sacredness, but also of roots, knowledge, and moral correctness. The term is often applied by Cubans and practitioners of Santería to refer to consecrated drums, but it can also be used to qualify the righteousness or sanctity of other religious and secular practices.
guajeo	The ostinato used by a piano or tres during the montuno section of a song.
guajira	Literally a country peasant woman, but in Latin music it refers to a four- measure musical formula and tempo that can be in major or minor keys (tonic, sub-dominant, dominant, subdominant).
guía	The lead voice in a performance group executing a sung piece of music. Also the main body of a song in a number of genres that is sung before the choral refrain and call-and-response section.
güiro/güira	A Cuban gourd scraper with wide grooves played with a single stick. The Puerto Rican version has smaller spaced grooves and is played with a metal comb-like scraper. The Dominican version is called a *güira* and is made of metal and scraped with a metal scraper.
jíbaro	A type of Puerto Rican folk music that uses the five-course, ten-string guitar-like Puerto Rican cuatro, bongó, guitar, and güiro (a vegetable gourd scraper) to accompany décimas (ten-line, octosyllabic poetry with a rhyme scheme of ABBAACCDDC) and other variants of sung poetry.
mambo	A term for a section of an arrangement in Latin popular dance music where horns execute a predetermined sequence of riffs. It can also refer to a riff-heavy style of Cuban music where ostinati (repeated patterns) are performed by horns in an ensemble that is similar to a jazz big band. It can also refer a dance style from the 1950s.

maracas   Gourd rattles used in a variety of genres in Latin music.

merengue   The national genre of music of the Dominican Republic tra-
                     ditionally executed with accordion, tambora, and güira (met-
                     al scraper), marimbula, saxophone, and call-and-response
                     vocals.

montuno   A repeated ostinato section in Afro-Cuban music that can
                     employ call-and-response lyrics. Used in folkloric genres such
                     as son, changüí, and rumba, it is at the heart of salsa.

música popular típica   A term used throughout Latin America and the Carib-
                     bean to refer to traditional popular music.

pachanga   An uptempo genre of music and dance made popular in the
                     early 1960s that was performed by a flute- and violin-based
                     ensemble called a charanga.

Palo   A Congolese-derived Afro-Cuban syncretic religion that
                     enslaved and free Africans developed in Cuba based on the
                     veneration of Congolese spirits and ancestral figures.

Palos   An Afro-Dominican religious music and practice based on
                     Afro-Haitian and Congolese practices.

plena   An Afro–Puerto Rican genre of music traditionally performed
                     with three jingle-less frame drums of different sizes called
                     panderetas or panderos, güiro, and call-and-response vocals.

rumba   A secular genre of Afro-Cuban music traditionally performed
                     with three *tumbadoras* or congas of different pitches, claves,
                     and two sticks percussed on the side of a drum or cylinder
                     called guagua, as well as call-and-response vocals. Rumba can
                     also include a chekere (gourd rattle with beads).

salsa   A term to describe the New York version of Cuban-derived
                     Latin music executed and popularized starting in the 1960s. It
                     became a genre with the success of its marketing and through
                     recordings on Fania and other labels during its apex in the
                     late 1960s and early 1970s. It has since become a catchall
                     phrase for a variety of genres from across Latin America and
                     the Caribbean, no matter where it is performed.

Santería/La regla de ocha   A Yoruba-derived Afro-Cuban syncretic religion
                     that enslaved and free Africans developed in Cuba based on
                     the veneration of Yoruba orishas (spirits and ancestral fig-
                     ures) cloaked with Catholic saints.

santero   A practitioner of the Santería religion who has undergone
                     ritual obligations to receive the title. Also someone who be-
                     lieves in the Yoruba-derived religion of Santería or La regla
                     de ocha.

seis   Another genre of Puerto Rican jíbaro music with a large
                    variety of stock melodies that identify each seis.

solfège or *solfeo* The European system of assigning fixed names to scale degrees
                    for identification and practice of singing and musicianship.

son/son montuno   Established as the national genre of Cuban music in the
                    1920s and exported internationally as rumba or rhumba, son
                    is a secular Afro-Cuban popular music traditionally per-
                    formed with guitar, bass, tres, trumpet, and bongó, as well as
                    minor percussion and call-and-response vocals.

songo   A popular Cuban rhythmic pattern from the 1970s that be-
                    came more and more important in the 1980s and beyond.

timbales/paila   Creolized timpani drums used to play Latin music.

toque de santo   An Afro-Cuban ritual setting with music that is executed on
                    consecrated batá drums and conducted as per ritual obliga-
                    tion and guidelines.

tres   A Cuban instrument in the guitar family with a variety of
                    tunings, but frequently tuned gG-cc-Ee, aA-dd-F♯f♯, gG-bb-ee

tresillo   A musical figure or rhythm that employs three attacks found
                    throughout Latin music and other musical genres from
                    around the world. It is also emblematic of the musical con-
                    cept known as hemiola and it is part of the clave pattern. In
                    common time (4/4), the figure consists of a dotted quarter
                    note, followed by a dotted quarter note, and a quarter note.

tumbadora/conga   The Cuban name for Congolese-derived hand drums used
                    to execute a wide variety of musical genres in Latin music.

tumbao   This can be used interchangeably with *guajeo*, but is also used
                    to refer to the bass pattern in Latin music, as well as the fixed
                    conga pattern.

zarzuela   A light opera form from Spain, popular in nineteenth-century
                    Cuba.

NOTES

1. "Habanera tú" was the first recording made by a Cuban musician and it was made in New York by the Rosalía Gertrudis de la Concepción Díaz de Herrera, a.k.a. Chalía Herrera in 1898; Cristóbal Díaz Ayala, *Cuando salí de la Habana* (1998), 260.

2. Vernon W. Boggs and others explore a number of similar themes and protagonists in the excellent collection of essays, *Salsiology* (1992).

3. Agustín Laó-Montes, "Introduction," in Arlene Dávila and Augustín Laó-Montes, eds., *Mambo Montage: The Latinization of New York City* (New York: Columbia University Press, 2001), 1–3.

4. Laó-Montes, "Introduction," 7.

5. Samuel A. Floyd Jr., Melanie L. Zeck, and Guthrie P. Ramsey Jr., *The Transformation of Black Music* (New York: Oxford University Press, 2017), xxii.

6. Laó-Montes, "Introduction," 13.

7. Floyd et al., *The Transformation of Black Music*, xxiii.

8 Laó-Montes, "Introduction," 9.

9. Rondón, *The Book of Salsa*, 18.

10. Laó-Montes, "Introduction," 18.

11. Laó-Montes, "Introduction," 97.

12. In addition, I am not using the term Latinx to describe the musicians, music, artisans, and educators in this book because none of them use this term to refer to themselves or to the music that they perform.

13. Tim Brooks, *Lost Sounds: Blacks and the Birth of the Recording Industry, 1890–1919* (Urbana and Chicago: University of Illinois Press, 2010), 2.

14. John Storm Roberts, Interview with Mario Bauza, Jazz Oral History Project (1978), http://newarkwww.rutgers.edu/IJS/transcript_mariobauza.html. Retrieved October 4, 2012.

15. Benjamin Lapidus, "¡Toca *maravilloso!*: Larry Harlow and the Jewish connection to Latin music," in *Mazal Tov Amigos!: Jews and Popular Music in the Americas*, edited by Amalia Ran and Moshe Morad (Leiden and Boston: Brill Press, 2016), 109–21.

16. Leonardo Padura Fuentes, *Faces of Salsa: A Spoken History of the Music*, translated by Stephen J. Clark (Washington, DC: Smithsonian Books, 2003), 183–200.

17. Joe Cuba Sextet, *Wanted Dead Or Alive (Bang! Bang! Push, Push, Push)* (Tico 1146, LP, 1966).

18. Floyd et al., *The Transformation of Black Music*, xxii.

19. Gregorio Marcano, personal communication, September 4, 2019. According to Marcano, the original photo collage that contained the announcement was from his father from his father Pedro "Piquito" Marcano's collection. The collage features clippings of Johnny Seguí's groups from 1952–56.

20. Laó-Montes, "Introduction," 33.

CHAPTER 1

1. Max Salazar, *Mambo Kingdom: Latin Music in New York* (New York: Schirmer, 2002), 14.
2. Salazar, *Mambo Kingdom*, 16.
3. "Joe Quijano," Puerta de Tierra. http://www.puertadetierra.info/figuras/artistas/joe/joe_quijano.htm. Retrieved March 4, 2014.
4. "New Talent at Paul's Place," *Palm Beach Post*, Friday, September 15, 1978, B4.
5. Catherine Dower Gold, *Actividades musicales en Puerto Rico después de la Guerra Hispano-americana 1898–1910* (Victoria, BC: Trafford, [1983] 2006), 11.
6. Fernando Callejo Ferrer, *Músicos Portorriqueños* (San Juan, PR: Editores Cantero Fernandez, 1915), 255.
7. "Joe Quijano," Fundacion Nacional para la Cultura Popular. http://www.prpop.org/biografias/j_bios/JoeQuijano.shtml. Retrieved March 4, 2014.
8. Joe Quijano, personal communication, April 11, 2014. Arzencer was of Argentine background and worked with Tito Rodríguez.
9. Joe Quijano, personal communication, April 11, 2014.
10. Advertisement, Academia Maria Luisa Le Compte, *La Prensa*, February 8, 1941, 5.
11. "De Música: Concierto Estudanil," *La Prensa*, May 31, 1938, 5.
12. "Un festival artístico," *La Prensa*, March 24, 1938, 5.
13. "*De Música: alumnos infantiles en un concierto musical*," *La Prensa*, June 22, 1936, 8.
14. "Celebróse un concierto infantile en 'El Toreador,'" *La Prensa*, June 19, 1935.
15. Lorrin Thomas, *Puerto Rican Citizen: History and Political Identity in Twentieth-Century New York City* (Chicago: University of Chicago Press, 2010), 127.
16. Erasmo Vando Papers, B2F5F6, Centro de Estudios Puertorriquenos (microfilm reel).
17. "Falleció La Señora María Luisa Lecompte," *La Prensa*, March 8, 1947, 2.
18. "Falleció La Señora María Luisa Lecompte."
19. "El Festival de la Asociación Hispano Americana Pro Ciegos," *La Prensa*, July 29, 1936, 5.
20. Quijano remembered that Bocanegra's daughter, Ms. Cruz, was his teacher at PS 52.
21. Joe Quijano, personal communication, April 11, 2014.
22. Paquito Pastor, personal communication, March 14, 2014.
23. Pastor, personal communication, March 14, 2014.
24. Pastor, personal communication, March 14, 2014. He remembered her surname to be Pino.
25. Pastor, personal communication, March 14, 2014.
26. "De Música: fue un éxito el recital de la Señora Eduvigis Bocanegra Pino," *La Prensa*, June 23, 1938; "De Música: fue un éxito el recital de la Señora Eduvigis Bocanegra Pino," *La Prensa*, June 16, 1938.
27. Margo Rodríguez, personal communication, December 3, 2017.
28. *Censo Décimocuatro de Los Estados Unidos: Población—Puerto Rico*, Hoja 40.
29. Fifteenth Census of the United States, April 18, 1930. Enumeration District 31–789, Supervisor District 23, Sheet 2-A, 182.
30. "Velada Panamericana en la Bibioteca calle 110," *La Prensa*, April 16, 1941, 5. In the Erasmo Vando Papers at the Center for Puerto Rican Studies there is a 1927 photograph taken at the Wadleigh High School Auditorium on W. 115th Street. It is likely but not certain that the woman at the center of the photo is Eduviges Bocanegra.
31. Mesorana is registered as an arranger of Mesorana piano rolls for Juan Morel Campos and other composers. *Musical Compositions* No. 8 (1921). Copyright Office, Library of Congress. Retrieved April 7, 2014.
32. *La Prensa*, January 25, 1941.

33. "Banda Hispana Los Granaderos: The Sound of Music Helps Them," *New York Post*, July 26, 1960, 16.

34. Erica Y. López, "The Life and Death of Hilton Ruiz," http://www.radioelsalsero.com/2010/03/life-and-death-of-hilton-ruiz.html. Retrieved July 16, 2018.

35. These include *Farandula, Ecos del Mundo, El Diario de Nueva York, El Imparcial.*

36. *El Diario de Nueva York*, January 15, 1958.

37. Olavo Alén, personal communication, January 19, 2013.

38. "Nick Rodriguez," Louis Armstrong All Stars. http://louisarmstrongallstars.webatu.com/musicians/piano/nickrodriguez.htm. Retrieved October 4, 2012.

39. José Calero Martín and Leopoldo Valdés Quesada, *Cuba musical: album-resumen ilustrado de la historia y de la actual situación del arte musical en Cuba.* (La Habana: Imprenta de Molina, 1929), 900. See http://flutejournal.com/alberto-socarras-a-profile/ for more details on his career.

40. *Latin Lovers*, dir. Mervyn LeRoy (MGM, 1953). https://youtu.be/8q7Z_cJGdnI. Retrieved September 10, 2019.

41. Oscar Hernández, personal communication, October 10, 2011.

42. Oscar Hernández, personal communication, October 10, 2011.

43. Oscar Hernández, personal communication, October 10, 2011.

44. Oscar Hernández, personal communication, March 6, 2014.

45. Oscar Hernández, personal communication, March 6, 2014.

46. Oscar Hernández, personal communication, March 6, 2014.

47. Gilberto "Pulpo" Colón Jr., Interview, June 13, 2013.

48. Hernández landed a brief stint with Willie Colón, but kept studying.

49. Finland-based bass player Julio Romero also studied with Socarrás at this time; Other notable Soccarrás students include bassist Rubén Rodríguez, and vocalist Ronnie Baró.

50. D. Hilarión Eslava, *Método complete de solfeo sin acompañamiento* (Madrid: Lit. de S. Gonzalez, 1846).

51. Joseph P. González, personal communication, July 19, 2017.

52. Ronnie Baró, personal communication, June 6, 2013.

53. Ronnie Baró, personal communication, 2007.

54. Gilberto "Pulpo" Colón Jr., interview, June 13, 2013.

55. See the discussion of Jean Vincent, *The Soul of Haiti* in Chapter Two.

56. Gilberto "Pulpo" Colón Jr., interview, June 13, 2013.

57. Gilberto "Pulpo" Colón Jr., interview, June 13, 2013.

58. Gilberto "Pulpo" Colón Jr., interview, June 13, 2013.

59. Sergio Rivera, personal communication, June 6, 2013.

60. Rivera, personal communication, June 6, 2013.

61. Mike LeDonne and Jonathan Gold are two non-Latin players who also studied with Rodríguez.

62. Gilberto "Pulpo" Colón Jr., interview, June 13, 2013.

63. The piano part must agree with the clave as with all other instruments, and playing in a rhythmically incorrect fashion is considered *cruzao* or crossed.

64. Maldonado was proficient in jazz, Latin, and classical music. He was also an excellent percussionist who played a foot cowbell in Mongo Santamaria's band and served as musical director for Stevie Wonder for ten years.

65. Ben Bierman, personal communication, June 13, 2019.

66. Ben Bierman, interview, February 21, 2103. Bierman also studied *solfège* with Peter Randall and this made him feel connected to the Nadia Boulanger School as well.

67. Ben Bierman notebook, November 29, 1984. See also Percy Goetschius, *The Homophonic Forms of Musical Composition: An Exhaustive Treatise of the Structure and Development of Musical Forms from the Simple Phrase to the Song-Form with "Trio"* (New York: G. Schirmer, 1898).

68. Paquito Pastor, personal communication, March 14, 2014. Pastor said the same thing happened to bassist Guillermo Edgehill.

69. Pastor, personal communication, March 14, 2014.

70. Bierman, interview, February 21, 2013.

71. Bierman, interview, February 21, 2013.

72. Bierman, interview, February 21, 2013.

73. Alex Stewart, *Making the Scene: Contemporary New York City Big Band Jazz* (Berkeley: University of California Press, 2007), 248–49.

74. Interestingly, John Storm Roberts points out that Machito and Mario Bauzá hired non-Latin players to achieve a better jazz sound, but also because there were not enough high-level Latin trumpet players. John Storm Roberts, *The Latin Tinge*, 102.

75. Ben Bierman. interview, February 21, 2013.

76. Two memories included seeing Pharoah Sanders playing and just stopping to beat his chest because the music was so intense; Watching Ted Curson's head spin around as he heard Ray Maldonado play.

77. Stewart, *Making the Scene*, 240.

78. Ibid.

79. Stewart, *Making the Scene*, 46.

80. Stewart, *Making the Scene*, 246.

81. Stewart, *Making the Scene*, 253.

82. Chico Álvarez, interview, July 2, 2013. North Bergen, NJ.

83. Álvarez, interview, July 2, 2013.

84. Álvarez, interview, July 2, 2013.

85. Álvarez, interview, July 2, 2013.

86. Álvarez, interview, July 2, 2013.

87. Álvarez, interview, July 2, 2013.

88. Álvarez would marry González's daughter in 1967.

89. Álvarez, interview, July 2, 2013.

90. Cortijo was a Columbia Records artist who used the term "Afro Cuban" as early as 1935.

91. Johnny Colón, interview, February 5, 2013. During the recording session for *Boogaloo Blues*, Colón met Puerto Rican doo-wop singer José Negroni, who was with Frankie Lymon.

92. Johnny Colón, interview, February 5, 2013.

93. Johnny Colón, interview, February 5, 2013. Initially, the program was only funded in the summer, because it was a pilot program.

94. Sonny Bravo, email communication, February 25, 2013.

95. "Pulpo" Colón Jr., interview, June 13, 2013.

96. Palmieri was recovering from a quadruple bypass surgery in Puerto Rico.

97. Johnny Colón, interview, February 5, 2013.

98. Johnny Colón, interview, February 5, 2013.

99. John Brimhall, *Complete Music Theory Notebook* (Miami Beach, FL: Hansen House, 1985).

100. Johnny Colón, interview, February 5, 2013.

101. Johnny Colón, interview, February 5, 2013.

102. Johnny Colón, interview, February 5, 2013.

103. *We Like It Like That: The Story of Latin Boogaloo*. Dir. Matthew Ramírez Warren. 2014.

104. "Boys and Girls Harbor: Our Story," The Harbor. http://www.theharbor.org/our-story/history. Retrieved April 8, 2014.

105. "The Harbor Conservatory of Music in NYC Celebrates Their 30th Anniversary," Conga head.com. http://www.congahead.com/legacy/On_The_Scene/Harbor_Conservatory/30th_anniversary.htm. Retrieved April 7, 2014.

106. *Mi Mambo*. Film. 2006.

107. Randy Rojas, Luis Ayala, Al Acosta, Enrique Fernández, Hector Colón, and others.

108. *Mi Mambo*. Film. 2006.

109. *Mi Mambo*. Film. 2006.

110. Manny Oquendo (1931–2009) was an important collector and musician who worked with many important artists. He started his collection in the 1940s and spent a lot of time with Little Ray Romero, Miguelito Valdés, José Curbelo, Tito Puente, Vincetico Valdés, and Chano Pozo.

111. For Juan Flores, this group challenged the hegemony of the Fania label and its style of music, and reflected a connection to the politics of the times as well as jazz. Juan Flores, *Salsa Rising: New York Latin Music of the Sixties Generation* (New York: Oxford University Press, 2016), 224.

112. Margalit Fox, "Augie Rodriguez, 86, Half of a Mambo Team, Dies," *New York Times*, July 26, 2014. https://www.nytimes.com/2014/07/27/nyregion/augie-rodriguez-86-half-of-a-mambo-team-dies.html. Retrieved July 17, 2018.

113. Juliet McMaines, *Spinning Mambo into Salsa: Caribbean Dance in Global Commerce* (New York: Oxford University Press, 2015), 318.

114. McMaines, *Spinning Mambo into Salsa*, 318–19.

115. *The Mamboniks*, dir. Lex Gillespie (Malecón Films. 2019).

116. Daniel Goldman, *I Want to Be Ready: Improvised Dance as a Practice of Freedom* (Ann Arbor: University of Michigan Press, 2010), 36.

117. Joe Holley, "Dancer, Known as 'Cuban Pete,' Was Considered 'Maestro of the Mambo,'" *Washington Post*, January 23, 2009. http://www.washingtonpost.com/wp-dyn/content/article/2009/01/22/AR2009012203834.html?noredirect=on. Retrieved July 17, 2018.

118. Holley, "Dancer, Known as 'Cuban Pete.'"

119. *Latin NY* (September 1980): 58.

120. Among Puerto Rican folklore enthusiasts, there is substantial controversy surrounding this publication as to whether Ronda actually wrote the book or stole it from another author. Francisco Jiménez Latorre, "Aclarando las cosas," *Revista del Instituto del Cuatro Puertorriqueño* (Agosto 1975). The Puerto Rican Cuatro Project. http://www.cuatro-pr.org/es/node/131. Retrieved July 14, 2019.

121. Xavier Cugat, *Meet Mr. Cugat: Bringing "Latin America" to You in Music and Rhythms* (New York: Irving Berlin, 1943).

122. Henry Adler owned the music store where Charles Tappan worked. Tappan created modern mass-manufactured timbales in the 1940s.

123. Esy Morales recorded with Kenny Clarke and others and appeared with his band playing "Jungle Fantasy" in the film *Criss Cross* (1949), with Burt Lancaster.

124. John Amira and Steven Cornelius, *The Music of Santería: Traditional Rhythms of the Batá Drums* (Crown Point, IN: White Cliffs Media, 1992); Lois Wilcken and Frisner Augustin, *The Drums of Vodou* (Crown Point, IN: White Cliffs Media, 1992).

125. Andrew Friedman, "Field of Drums," *Village Voice*, September 5, 2000. https://www.villagevoice.com/2000/09/05/field-of-drums/, retrieved April 14, 2020.

126. Roberta L. Singer and Elena Martínez, "A South Bronx Latin Music Tale," *Centro Journal* XVI, no. 1 (Spring 2004): 195.

127. "52 Park," Place Matters. https://placematters.net/census/detail.php?id=19. Retrieved April 14, 2020.

128. Blanca Vásquez, "Mi Gente: Andy and Jerry González," *Centro Journal* 3, no. 2 (Spring 1991): 64.

129. *Calle 54*, dir. Fernando Trueba. Miramax Films. 2000.

130. Andy González, personal communication, 2015.

131. *Calle 54*.

132. Vásquez, "Mi Gente: Andy and Jerry González," 67.

133. Vásquez, "Mi Gente: Andy and Jerry González," 67.

134. Benjamin Lapidus, liner notes for Andy González, *Entre colegas* (CD, Truth Revolution Records 024, 2016).

135. Vásquez, "Mi Gente: Andy and Jerry González," 68.

136. Vásquez, "Mi Gente: Andy and Jerry González," 68

137. Vásquez, "Mi Gente: Andy and Jerry González," 65.

138. Vásquez, "Mi Gente: Andy and Jerry González," 66.

139. Vásquez, "Mi Gente: Andy and Jerry González," 66.

140. Andy González, personal communication, April 15, 2018.

141. Jerry González, personal communication, March 6, 2015.

142. Jerry González, personal communication, March 6, 2015.

143. Andrea Brachfeld, interview, July 16, 2013.

144. Andrea Brachfeld, interview, July 16, 2013.

145. Andrea Brachfeld, interview, July 16, 2013.

146. Andrea Brachfeld, interview, July 16, 2013.

147. Andrea Brachfeld, interview, July 16, 2013.

148. Andrea Brachfeld, interview, July 16, 2013.

149. Andrea Brachfeld, interview, July 16, 2013.

150. Andrea Brachfeld, interview, July 16, 2013.

151. Juan Flores indicates that Palmieri also got a good grounding in political economy through his studies with Bob Bianco and that this was audible in his politically oriented music. Flores, *Salsa Rising*, 167.

152. Flores, *Salsa Rising*, 92.

153. Historia de Richie Ray & Bobby Cruz (Contada en su propia voz). https://youtu.be/cNQZ9aisMLQ. Retrieved October 30, 2017.

154. Charley Gerard and Marty Sheller, *Salsa: The Rhythm of Latin Music* (Crown Point, IN: White Cliffs Media, [1989] 1998), 33.

155. Ron Hart, "Chick Corea Looks Back on His Long History with Latin Jazz," *Billboard*, July 12, 2019. https://www.billboard.com/articles/columns/latin/8519626/chick-corea-my-spanish-heart-antidote. Retrieved July 12, 2019.

156. Hart, "Chick Corea Looks Back on His Long History with Latin Jazz."

157. *Machito: A Latin Jazz Legacy*, dir. Carlos Ortiz (Nubia Music Society, 1987).

158. *Machito: A Latin Jazz Legacy*.

159. Rafael Bassi Labarrera, "La presencia del jazz en la música del Caribe colombiano," in *El jazz desde la perspectiva caribeña*, edited by Darío Tejeda and Rafael Emilio Yunén (Santiago de los Caballeros, Dominican Republic: Instituto de estudios caribeños, 2012), 453–75.

160. "Poncho Sánchez, Justo Almario y Crispín Fernández," in *El jazz desde la perspectiva caribeña*, edited by Darío Tejeda and Rafael Emilio Yunén (Santiago de los Caballeros, Dominican Republic: Instituto de estudios caribeños, 2012), 515.

161. Crispín Fernández Minaya, personal communication, April 8, 2017.

162. Crispín Fernández Minaya, personal communication, April 8, 2017.

163. "Poncho Sánchez, Justo Almario y Crispín Fernández," 513.

164. Crispín Fernández Minaya, personal communication, April 8, 2017.

165. "Poncho Sánchez, Justo Almario y Crispín Fernández," 515.

166. "Poncho Sánchez, Justo Almario y Crispín Fernández," 515.

167. "Poncho Sánchez, Justo Almario y Crispín Fernández," 515.

168. "Poncho Sánchez, Justo Almario y Crispín Fernández," 515.

169. "Poncho Sánchez, Justo Almario y Crispín Fernández," 515.

170. "Poncho Sánchez, Justo Almario y Crispín Fernández," 515.

171. Juan Colón, *Vivencias de un músico: sentir y existir* (Santo Domingo, Dominican Republic: Editora Corripio, 2014).

172. Juan Colón, personal communication, April 9, 2017.

173. Juan Colón, personal communication, April 9, 2017.

174. Juan Colón, personal communication, April 9, 2017.

175. Founded in 1968 and active since 1975, Teatro Otra Cosa was the first folkloric group in New York City dedicated exclusively to performing Afro-Puerto Rican bomba. Numerous drumming luminaries passed through its ranks, including Milton Cardona, Felix Sanabria, Eddie Bobè, Wilson "Chembo" Corniel, and many more.

176. Berta Jottar, "Zero Tolerance and Central Park Rumba Cabildo Politics" *Liminalities: A Journal of Performance Studies* Vol. 5, No. 4, November 2009: 1–24.

177. Berta Jottar, "From Central Park, Rumba with Love!" *Voices: The Journal of New York Folklore*, Vol. 37, Spring-Summer (2011), http://www.nyfolklore.org/pubs/voic37-1-2/rumba.html. Felix Sanabria, Susan Richardson, and Abraham Rodríguez later became members of Bauzó and Borrell's folkloric music and dance performance group, Kubatá.

178. Felix Sanabria, interview, February 8, 2013.

179. Ray Barretto, *Together* (LP, Fania 378, 1969).

180. Felix Sanabria, interview, February 8, 2013.

181. Grupo folclorico de Justi Barreto, *Santa Barbara Africana*. Santero LP-531.1969. LP; Justi Barreto, *Shango Aragua*. Echu 303. 1971. LP; Grupo folclorico de Justi Barreto, *Santería (Toques y Cantos)*. Gema LPG 1193. n.d. LP. See also: various artists, *Santero: Afro-Cuban Cult Music*. Panart LP 2060. 1957. LP; Candita Batista y Sus Tamboers Batá, *Ritmo de santo*. Maype LP 130. n.d. LP; Celia Cruz, *Homenaje a los santos*. Seeco LP 9269. 1975. LP; Grupo Afro-Cubano dirigido por Alfredo Zayas, *Afro-Frenetic Tambores de Cuba*. Panart 3053. 1961. LP; Gilberto Valdés, *Rezo de santo*. Maype 180. n.d. LP.

182. Hermano Moises, *La Mano Poderosa* (Suaritos LPS-121); Rafael Caraballo y Su Conjunto, *Santero Moderno* (Jibarito LP-129); *Plegarias a los santos* (Santero LP-329).

183. Luz Celenia Tirado y Coro con Nieves Quintero y su Conjunto, *Santeros Cantados* (Antillano LP 25).

184. Berta Jottar, "Central Park Rumba: Nuyorican Identity and the Return to African Roots," *Centro Journal* 23, no. 1 (Spring 2011): 10.

185. Jottar, "Central Park Rumba," 18.

186. "Milton Cardona," *Latin NY* (September 1983): 30.

CHAPTER 2

1. Benjamin Lapidus, "El folclor al rescate: La importancia del folclor musical caribeño en la escena de Nueva York y su impacto en el mundo," in *El folclor musical y danzario del caribe en tiempos de globalización* edited by Darío Tejeda and Rafael Emilio Yunén (Santiago de los Caballeros, Dominican Republic: Instituto de estudios caribeños, 2014): 123–33.

2. United States Social Security Death Index," database, FamilySearch (https://familysearch.org/ark:/61903/1:1:JKPF-NP1 : 20 May 2014), Simon Jou, Oct 1971; citing U.S. Social Security Administration, Death Master File, database (Alexandria, Virginia: National Technical Information Service, ongoing).

3. Richard Blondet, "Simon Jou" (unpublished, used by kind permission of the author).

4. Antonio López, *Unbecoming Blackness: The Diaspora Cultures of Afro-Cuban America* (New York: New York University Press, 2012), 228.

5. López, *Unbecoming Blackness*.

6. López, *Unbecoming Blackness*.

7. Blondet quoting Dorothy Kilgallen, "Voice of Broadway," *Schenectady Gazette*, June 7, 1956, 24.

8. Lapidus, "El folclor al rescate," 125.

9. Benny Bonilla, interview by Elena Martínez and Bobby Sanabria, Bronx, NY, July 2007.

10. Blondet, "Simon Jou."

11. Benny Bonilla, interview by Richard Blondet, March 29 and 30, 2014.

12. Leopoldo Fleming Jr., interview by Richard Blondet, March 28, 2014.

13. Blondet, "Simon Jou."

14. *La Prensa De Nueva York*, October 2, 1960, 23.

15. Babby Quintero, "En Nueva York y En Todas Partes," *El Diario-La Prensa*, June 14, 1964.

16. "Man, 78, Dies Of Injuries," *Herald Statesman*, Yonkers, NY, October 23, 1971, 10.

17. Blondet, "Simon Jou."

18. Lapidus, "El folclor al rescate," 125.

19. Nolan Warden, "A History of the Conga Drum," NolanWarden.com. http://www.nolanwarden.com/Conga_Drum_History%28Warden%29.pdf. Retrieved March 21, 2018.

20. "Echo Tone Conga List," CongaPlace.com. http://www.mycongaplace.com/forum/eng/viewtopic.php?f=14&t=7559. Retrieved March 21, 2018.

21. "Echo Tone Conga List."

22. Roberto Santiago, "Moving to a Different Beat Conga-Maker Drums Up Biz in B'klyn," *New York Daily News*, August 31, 1999. http://www.nydailynews.com/archives/boroughs/moving-beat-conga-maker-drums-biz-b-klyn-article-1.847416. Retrieved March 19, 2018.

23. Dave Easter, "Interview with Jay Bereck (November 1, 1994)," *Palm-Tip-Open* (Spring 1995), 5. Information about Bereck is drawn from this interview except where otherwise indicated.

24. Santiago, "Moving to a Different Beat."

25. Easter, "Interview with Jay Bereck," 5.

26. Easter, "Interview with Jay Bereck," 6.

27. Santiago, "Moving to a Different Beat.

28. "Jay Bereck's Skin-on-Skin Part 3." https://www.youtube.com/watch?v=JdhXKdk51q4. Retrieved March 19, 2018.

29. Easter, "Interview with Jay Bereck," 7.

30. Easter, "Interview with Jay Bereck," 8.

31. Easter, "Interview with Jay Bereck," 8.

32. Jay Bereck's Skin on Skin Part 2. https://www.youtube.com/watch?v=JdhXKdk51q4. Retrieved March 19, 2018.

33. Bereck's Skin on Skin Part 2.

34. Easter, "Interview with Jay Bereck (November 1, 1994)."

35. http://congadr.blogspot.com/2008/03/maestro-jay-berek.html. Retrieved March 19, 2018.

36. Bereck's Skin on Skin Part 3.

37. Cara Bereck Levy, August 29, 2016. https://www.youtube.com/watch?v=N_ueSsUX2OI. Retrieved March 19, 2018.

38. Santiago, "Moving to a Different Beat."

39. Bereck's Skin on Skin 2.

40. Bereck's Skin on Skin 2.

41. Santiago, "Moving to a Different Beat."

42. Cara Bereck Levy, August 29, 2016.

43. "$1000 Conga Drum—Inside Skin On Skin," https://www.youtube.com/watch?v=wLoTTPMYsck. Retrieved March 19, 2018. The English and Hebrew script signatures can be seen at 12:33.

44. Lapidus, "El folclor al rescate," 126.

45. Jana Winter, "The End of an Era, to the Beat of a Drum," *New York Times*, April 16, 2006. https://www.nytimes.com/2006/04/16/nyregion/thecity/the-end-of-an-era-to-the-beat-of-a-drum .html. Retrieved March 29, 2018.

46. "The Guy Who Makes the Best Cowbells," Jazz Night in America, December 10, 2015. https://www.npr.org/event/music/459135308/the-guy-who-makes-the-best-cowbells. Retrieved March 29, 2018.

47. "The Guy Who Makes the Best Cowbells."

48. Mary Kent, "Pacheco y Su Tumbao: An Anniversary Salute," http://www.salsatalks.com/ articles/pacheco.html. Retrieved March 25, 2018.

49. Kent, "Pacheco y Su Tumbao: An Anniversary Salute."

50. José Rosa, *World Music Survey: The History of Music from Cuba, the Caribbean, South America, and the United States* (José Rosa Enterprises, 2018), 42–43.

51. Rosa, *World Music Survey*, 43.

52. Ludwig Company, 1953 Catalogue, 1. http://www.drumarchive.com/ludwig/. Retrieved March 23, 2018.

53. Ludwig Company, 1957 Catalogue, 8–9. http://www.drumarchive.com/ludwig/. Retrieved March 23, 2018.

54. David González, "Bongos, Congas, and Cameras," *New York Times*, January 13, 2011. https:// lens.blogs.nytimes.com/2011/01/13/bongos-congas-and-cameras/. Retrieved March 29, 2018.

55. Rick Mattingly, "Percussive Arts Society Hall of Fame: Martin Cohen." http://www.pas.org/ about/hall-of-fame/martin-cohen. Retrieved March 21, 2018.

56. Eric Levin, "What's a Nice Jewish Boy Doing as King of the Bongos? Explains Martin Cohen: 'I Was Never Nice,'" *People*, April 28, 1980. http://people.com/archive/whats-a-nice-jewish-boy -doing-as-king-of-the-bongos-explains-martin-cohen-i-was-never-nice-vol-13-no-17/. Retrieved March 29, 2018.

57. Mattingly, "Percussive Arts Society Hall of Fame: Martin Cohen."

58. Mattingly, "Percussive Arts Society Hall of Fame: Martin Cohen."

59. Mattingly, "Percussive Arts Society Hall of Fame: Martin Cohen."

60. Steven Loza, *Tito Puente and the Making of Latin Music* (Urbana and Chicago: University of Illinois Press, 1999), 17.

61. Levin, "What's a Nice Jewish Boy Doing as King of the Bongos?"

62. Mattingly, "Percussive Arts Society Hall of Fame: Martin Cohen."

63. Mattingly, "Percussive Arts Society Hall of Fame: Martin Cohen."

64. Mattingly, "Percussive Arts Society Hall of Fame: Martin Cohen."

65. The author appears on the recording: Various artists, *A Musical Gift of Greatness* (Latin Percussion J323, 2001).

66. William Cumpiano, personal communication, February 26, 2013. Ronda claimed that Barquero, who was active in the 1950s, was his student.

67. The Puerto Rican Cuatro Project. http://www.cuatro-pr.org. Retrieved July 16, 2019.

68. Juan Sotomayor Pérez, *Las Tradiciones Músico-Artesanales de los Instrumentos de Cuerda de Puerto Rico: Descritos a través de las entrevistas del Proyecto del Cuatro Puertorriqueño* (Northampton, MA: El proyecto del cuatro puertorriqueño, 2003).

69. "Efraín Ronda, cuatrista y artesano, segunda entrevista March 1, 1992," in Juan Sotomayor Pérez, *Las Tradiciones Músico-Artesanales de los Instrumentos de Cuerda de Puerto Rico: Descritos a través de las entrevistas del Proyecto del Cuatro Puertorriqueño* (Northampton, MA: El proyecto del cuatro puertorriqueño, 2003), 39.

70. *Yo me salia cada diá . . . mi hija calculaba, y me dice, 'papi, tu te has ganado hoy cien pesos.' Había días que me ganaba . . . vino un muchacho y me trajo un violonchelo, que lo encontró en*

un basement, que sabe Dios cuantos años estuvo ahí. Y me dijo '¿por cuánto me enseña tocar este instrumento?' Saco el instrumento y tenía las tapas despegadas, y le digo, 'primero hay que arreglar este instrumento. Tu puedes gastar cincuenta pesos pa' arreglar este instrumento. Y me dice, 'ay, ¿cuesta tanto?' Después que era un buen instrumento. Cincuenta pesos por lo menos. Porque la encordadura nada mas te va a costar catorce pesos. Las cuatro cuerdas. Y el puente que va, y el clavijero que hay que arreglarlo . . . me dijo, 'no. Dame cincuenta centavos pa' volver al sitio donde yo trabajao.' Y le doy cincuenta y me dejó aquello. Arregle el celo, y vino un moreno americano, y me dijo, '¿cómo yo puedo encontrar un violonchelo en segundas manos?' Le dije, 'yo tengo dos. Tengo uno que está arremandao la tapa, alguien le puso un remiendo. Pero que no ofende y suena bien. Y tengo otro que es un instrumento que esta en muy buenas condiciones. El que trajo el muchacho ese. Entonces se lo vendí por doscientos pesos. Juan Sotomayor Pérez, *Las Tradiciones Músico-Artesanales de los Instrumentos de Cuerda de Puerto Rico: Descritos a través de las entrevistas del Proyecto del Cuatro Puertorriqueño* (Northampton, MA: El proyecto del cuatro puertorriqueño, 2003), 39.

71. "Jorge Mendoza, artesano," *Yo trato de evitar de que venga esas personas de nuevo hacía mi. Me compras un cuatro y te vas. ¡Y no te quiero ver mas, a menos que no me vayas a comprar otro! [rié] En Nueva York yo tenía miedo cuando veía al cliente cuando volvía. 'Ese ya viene con una queja.' Todas las cosas que yo pueda hacer para evitar un complaint pues las hago. No importa, cinco minutos, diez minutos, una hora, no tiene importancia, y las hago.* Juan Sotomayor Pérez, *Las Tradiciones Músico-Artesanales de los Instrumentos de Cuerda de Puerto Rico: Descritos a través de las entrevistas del Proyecto del Cuatro Puertorriqueño* (Northampton, MA: El proyecto del cuatro puertorriqueño, 2003), 238.

72. Karen Demasters, "Passing Folk Art to a New Generation, With a Little Help From the State," *New York Times*, March 16, 1997. https://www.nytimes.com/1997/03/16/nyregion/passing -folk-art-to-a-new-generation-with-a-little-help-from-the-state.html. Retrieved March 25, 2018.

73. Kristen G. Congdon and Kara Kelley Hallmark, *America Folk Art: A Regional Reference, Volume 1* (Santa Barbara, CA: ABC-CLIO, 2012), 66.

74. Congdon and Hallmark, *America Folk Art: A Regional Reference.* Another student's cuatro-building project with Matos was filmed and posted on YouTube: https://www.youtube.com/ watch?v=deZ5Htoha7E. Retrieved March 25, 2018.

75. Congdon and Hallmark, *America Folk Art: A Regional Reference*, 66.

76. Richard Johnston, "Velázquez Guitar 1955," in *The Classical Guitar: A Complete History Featuring the Russell Cleveland Collection*, ed. John Morrish (London: Balafon Books, 1997), 44.

77. Manuel Velázquez Documentary. https://www.youtube.com/watch?v=MAbvClxqbfo . Retrieved March 25, 2018.

78. Manuel Velázquez Documentary.

79. Johnston, "Velázquez Guitar 1955," 44.

80. Johnston, "Velázquez Guitar 1955," 45.

81. "Manuel Velazquez, In His Own Words / Remembering Manuel," Guild of American Luthiers. http://www.luth.org/memoriams/mem_manuel-velazquez.html. Retrieved March 25, 2018.

82. "Tito Baez." The Puerto Rican Cuatro Project. http://www.cuatro-pr.org/node/114. Retrieved April 2, 2018.

83. "Tito Baez."

84. Greg Jahiel, "Building Guitars on a Different Frequency," *New York Daily News*, June 11, 2009. http://www.nydailynews.com/latino/building-guitars-frequency-article-1.376856. Retrieved April 2, 2018.

85. Greg Jahiel, "Building Guitars on a Different Frequency."

86. Dennis Hevesi, "Master Guitar Makers Are Leery of Their Art," *New York Times*, February 3, 1993. https://www.nytimes.com/1993/02/03/nyregion/master-guitar-makers-are-leery-of-their -art.html. Retrieved April 2, 2018.

87. Dennis Hevesi, "Master Guitar Makers Are Leery of Their Art."

88. Dennis Hevesi, "Master Guitar Makers Are Leery of Their Art."

89. Jahiel, "Building Guitars on a Different Frequency."

90. Jahiel, "Building Guitars on a Different Frequency."

91. Hevesi, "Master Guitar Makers Are Leery of Their Art."

92. Felipe Mario Olivera Pabón, "Manuel Henríquez Zapata . . . creating our instruments for over a half-century!" The Puerto Rican Cuatro Project. http://www.cuatro-pr.org/node/273. Retrieved March 25, 2018.

93. Hans Moust, *The Guild Guitar Book: The Company and the Instruments: 1952–1977* (Milwaukee, WI: Hal Leonard, 1999), 14. The following information is taken from Hans Moust's history of Guild guitars except where otherwise indicated.

94. Moust, *The Guild Guitar Book*, 165.

95. William Cumpiano, personal communication, March 28, 2018.

96. William Cumpiano and Jonathan Natelson, *Guitarmaking: Tradition and Technology: A Complete Reference for the Design and Construction of the Steel-String Folk Guitar and the Classical Guitar* (San Francisco, CA: Chronicle Books, 1987 [1994]).

97. Jess Oliver, interview, January 22, 2005. NAMM Oral History. https://www.namm.org/library/oral-history/jess-oliver. Retrieved March 23, 2018.

98. Jess Oliver, interview, January 22, 2005.

99. Jess Oliver, interview, January 22, 2005.

100. Jess Oliver, interview, January 22, 2005.

101. It is likely that Hull would have first encountered the Zorko Bass in Chicago.

102. Jymie Merritt Biography. http://mikemerritt.com/wp/?page_id=566. Retrieved March 21, 2018.

103. Chris Jisi, "The Ampeg B-15: From Inception to Resurrection," *Bassplayer*, March 13, 2011. https://www.bassplayer.com/artists/the-ampeg-b-15-from-inception-to-resurrection. Retrieved March 23, 2018.

104. Gregg Hopkins and Bill Moore, *Ampeg: The Story Behind the Sound* (Milwaukee, WI: Hal Leonard, 1999), 84.

105. Alan Lockwood, "Bass Rules: Israel 'Cachao' Lopez and Andy Gonzalez: From Mambo to Salsa: Part Seven," *Brooklyn Rail*, March 7, 2008. http://www.brooklynrail.org/2008/03/music/bass-rules-israel-cachao-lopez-and-andy-gonzalez. Retrieved September 19, 2013.

106. Lockwood, "Bass Rules."

107. "Baby Bass," Wikipedia. http://es.wikipedia.org/wiki/Baby_bass. Retrieved 19 September 2013.

CHAPTER 3

1. In May 1977, David Amram, Dizzy Gillespie, Stan Getz, Earl Hines, Ray Mantilla, and John Ore performed alongside and recorded with their Cuban contemporaries Los Papines, Oscar Valdés, Paquito D'Rivera, and Arturo Sandoval. The results were released as David Amram, *Havana/New York* (LP, Flying Fish 057, 1978). In March 1979, US-based artists including Billy Joel, Weather Report, and the New York City–based Fania All-Stars came to perform in Cuba during an event sponsored by CBS Records called Havana Jam. Numerous video clips are posted on YouTube showing musicians from both sides of the Straits of Florida jamming; however, no studio collaborations were planned or made at that time. The Fania All-Stars performed Sonny Bravo's arrangement of Guillermo Castillo's "Tres lindas cubanas" in Cuba. A number of albums that brought Cuban and foreign musicians together were made in the 1990s and beyond including *Bridge to Havana*

(recorded in 1999, but released in 2004), Isaac Delgado's *Otra Idea* and *Primera Plana*, Alfredo Rodriguez's *Cuba*, as well as numerous recordings made by Jane Bunnett, among others.

2. Bravo believes that "the elder Douguet/Bravo and Osácar/Colomá [couples] may have been married in Cuba *before* migrating to Cayo Hueso (as neighbors), then on to Tampa, *also* as neighbors . . . [and] that [the] move to from Cayo Hueso to Tampa may have been a joint family venture." Sonny Bravo, personal communication, May 24, 2017.

3. For further reading on Tampa history, see Durward Long, "The Historical Beginnings of Ybor City and Modern Tampa," *Florida Historical Quarterly* 45, no. 1 (July 1966): 31–44; Susan Greenbaum, *More than Black: Afro-Cubans in Tampa* (Gainesville: University Press of Florida, 2002); Paula Harper, "Cuba Connections: Key West. Tampa. Miami, 1870 to 1945," *Journal of Decorative and Propaganda Arts* 22, Cuba Theme Issue (1996): 278–91.

4. Emanuel Leto, *"It was a Latin town": Folk and Popular Music in Ybor City, 1900–1950*, exhibition program (Ybor City, FL: Ybor City Museum Society), 7–13.

5. Florida Folklife from the WPA Collections, 1937 to 1942, Library of Congress. http://memory .loc.gov/ammem/collections/florida/. Retrieved November 5, 2008.

6. The son is an Afro-Cuban musical genre that uses percussion, strings, vocals, and later other instruments. Rumba, on the other hand, is a highly syncopated Afro-Cuban genre that is only played with percussion instruments and voice. For more on the internationalization of the Cuban son and rumba, see Robin Moore, *Nationalizing Blackness: Afrocubanismo and Artistic Revolution in Havana, 1920–1940* (Pittsburgh: University of Pittsburgh Press, 1997).

7. Leto, *"It was a Latin town,"* 17.

8. Moore, *Nationalizing Blackness*, 39, 96.

9. Sonny Bravo, personal communication, May 24, 2017.

10. Christina D. Abreu, *Cuban Musicians and the Making of Latino New York City and Miami, 1940–1960* (Chapel Hill: University of North Carolina Press, 2015), 12–15.

11. Abreu, *Cuban Musicians*, 58.

12. Max Salazar, "El Conjunto Caney," *Latin Beat Magazine* (August 1997): 1. El Torreador opened in 1932 during Prohibition and was located at 7 West 110th Street. This location is important in the history of the development of Spanish Caribbean dance music in New York because it was next door to the famed Park Palace at 3–5 West 110th Street.

13. "El Torreador Opens its Winter Season," *Brooklyn Daily Eagle*, October 26, 1935, 10 M2.

14. George Ticker, "Mad About Manhattan," *Leader-Republican*, Gloverville and Johnston, NY, June 10, 1939, 6.

15. Ticker, "Mad About Manhattan." In Salazar's piece, Storch mentioned working with an ensemble known as Ecos de Cuba; a band called "Eco de Cuba" led by Rolando Roca was discussed as alternating with Vernon Andrade and his Syncopators at the Istmica Club in 1933 according to the *New York Age*, January 21, 1933, 9.

16. The Caney group's performances at the Havana Madrid included "free rhumba and conga instructions and music," and the club is reported to have been the first venue to have Saturday afternoon rhumba matinees in New York. "Passing By," *Brooklyn Eagle*, March 17, 1939, 10.

17. Caney appeared on the bill at the Club Yumuri on 52nd and Broadway as part of a floor show with other Cuban artists such as Panchito Riset and Eliseo Grenet. Other performers included dancers such as Antonio and Dolores, a tango singer named La Milonguita, and a dancer named Rosita Ortega. Richard Manson, "Entertainment in the Cafes," *New York Post*, November 21, 1936, 10.

18. Malcolm Johnson, "Café Life in New York: Gas Rationing May Create Big Summer Business for Restaurants Here," *New York Sun*, May 21, 1942, 23.

19. *New York Post*, January 30, 1936, 17.

20. Richard Manson, "Entertainment in the Cafes," New York Post, April 16, 1938: 10.

21. Some of the pictures of bands in Sonny Bravo's personal collection have inscriptions from Cuban musicians dedicated to his father and were obtained during his father's visits to Cuba.

22. According to Richard Spottswood's *Ethnic Music on Records, Vol. 4*, "Rhumba Rhapsody" was recorded on April 25, 1941.

23. Richard Manson, "Going Out Tonight?" *New York Post*, May 20, 1942, 43.

24. Malcolm Johnson, "Cafes and Supper Clubs: Another Bit of Cuban Comes to Broadway—Dining at the Ambassador," *New York Sun*, November 22, 1938, 12.

25. "Elio y su conjunto moderno," Diaz-Ayala Cuban and Latin American Popular Music Collection, Florida International University Libraries. http://library.fiu.edu/latinpop/SECCIONo4Mpt2.pdf. Retrieved November 5, 2008.

26. Caney's trumpet player, Montes de Oca, is erroneously given credit for this recording. Sonny Bravo, personal communication, December 4, 2012. This recording is often erroneously attributed to Caney on compilations and reissues.

27. Cuarteto Caney, *Cuarteto Caney: 1936–1939* (CD, Harlequin HQCD75, 1996).

28. Sonny Bravo, personal communication, May 25, 2017.

29. Noro Morales, *Latin-American Rhythms and Improvisations for Piano* edited by Danny Hurd, transcribed by Ben Pickering (New York: Henry Adler, 1955).

30. Bravo, personal communication, December 4, 2012.

31. This ostinato is a dotted quarter, dotted quarter, quarter tied to a dotted quarter in the next measure, etc. Bravo, personal communication, December 4, 2012.

32. Sonny Bravo, personal communication, May 25, 2017.

33. Peter Manuel, "The Anticipated Bass in Cuban Popular Music," *Latin American Music Review /Revista de Música Latinoamericana* 6(2) (Autumn-Winter 1985): 249–61.

34. David F. García, *Arsenio Rodríguez and the Transnational Flows of Latin Popular Music* (Philadelphia: Temple University Press, 2006), 43–46.

35. Abreu, *Cuban Musicians and the Making of Latino New York City and Miami*, 127.

36. Osácar family acetate, 1939.

37. Osácar's success as a musician was helped by the fact that there were venues that specialized in Cuban music beyond New York. A 1942 article in the *Philadelphia Enquirer* shows Cuban music at Jack Lynch's Walton Roof at the top of the Walton Hotel and at Shangri-La on Market Street. Rudolph Burlingame, "Clubs Offer Festive Shows for the Holidays," *Philadelphia Enquirer*, December 25, 1942, 14. The Caney group is listed as performing at the Walton Roof on December 11, 1942. Rudolph Burlingame, "Clubs Prepare S.R.O. Signs for Holidays," *Philadelphia Enquirer*, December 11, 1942.

38. Abreu, *Cuban Musicians and the Making of Latino New York City and Miami*, 196–98.

39. Sonny Bravo, personal communication, December 3, 2017. In December 1953, Bravo worked as a carpet-layer's assistant installing carpet at the soon-to-open Fountainebleau Hotel.

40. Robert L. Doerschuk, "Secrets of Salsa Rhythm: Piano with Hot Sauce," in *Salsiology: Afro-Cuban Music and the Evolution of Salsa in New York City*, edited by Vernon Boggs (New York: Empire, 1992), 313.

41. Max Salazar, "Sonny Bravo," *Latin NY* (September-October 1968): 28.

42. Sonny Bravo, personal communication, May 26, 2017.

43. This is well documented by Simon Rottenberg, "Intra-Union Disputes Over Job Control," *Quarterly Journal of Economics* 61, no. 4 (August 1947): 633.

44. Sonny Bravo, personal communication, November 28, 2012.

45. Sonny Bravo, personal communication, December 3, 2017.

46. Photograph of Mandy Campo and Band http://library.fiu.edu/latinpop/discography_photos/jpgC/photo_C.html. Retrieved November 5, 2008.

47. This was a common practice in Cuba for popular groups with too many engagements. Cándido Camero got his start playing tres for Arsenio Rodríguez in his second band.

48. Martin Burden, "Going Out Tonight?" *New York Post*, August 29, 1962, 62. Bravo remembers hearing about the Kennedy assassination during a rehearsal at La Barraca; personal communication, May 26, 2017.

49. Cárdenas was called *Rompeteclas* (keybreaker) because he played so hard, and Eddie Palmieri has acknowledged him as an early influence. Photo by Luis Miguel, Rolando Laserie Papers, Cuban Heritage Collection, University of Miami Library.

50. According to Bravo, the car was driven by Al Abreu, who later perished in another automobile accident in Puerto Rico. Sonny Bravo, personal communication, May 26, 2017.

51. Sonny Bravo, personal communication, May 26, 2017.

52. Sonny Bravo, interview, March 23, 2013.

53. This coincides with Rivera being arrested in 1961 and sentenced to five years in prison in 1962. *El Diario de Nueva York*, November 22, 1962.

54. Raul Marrero y su Orquesta Moderna, "La Chica del Barrio Obrero" (45rpm, Ansonia 45–6677 B 7900).

55. Sonny Bravo, interview, March 23, 2013.

56. Charlie Palmieri y Su Orquesta, *El gigante del teclado* (LP, Alegre CLPA 7003, 1972).

57. In Bravo's original arrangement, the harmonic progression for the first and second endings was "| Gm7 / C7 / | and the melody in the first ending was | - D – B♭ / / |." Sonny Bravo, personal communication, May 27, 2017.

58. Bravo first met Hernández as a fifteen-year-old at a rehearsal or recording session when he was visiting his cousin, the bassist Bobby Rodríguez, during the summer of 1952. Sonny Bravo, interview, March 23, 2013.

59. Paul Austerlitz, *Jazz Consciousness: Music, Race, and Humanity* (Middletown, CT: Wesleyan University Press, 2005), 66–69.

60. Sonny Bravo, personal communication, June 7, 2017; Candido & Graciela, *Inolvidable* (CD, Chesky SACD297, 2004).

61. Mirta Ojito, *Finding Mañana: A Memoir of Cuban Exodus* (New York: Penguin, 2005).

62. Miami Herald Staff, "How events in Cuba shaped and reshaped Miami," *Miami Herald*, November 26, 2016. http://www.miamiherald.com/news/nation-world/world/americas/article117205713.html. Retrieved April 5, 2018.

63. Arnold H. Lubasch, "Omega 7 Leader Accused of Plot to Kill Delegate," *New York Times*, December 29, 1983.

64. Peter Manuel, "Improvisation in Latin Dance Music," in *In The Course of Performance: Studies in the World of Musical Improvisation*, eds. Bruno Nettl and Melinda Russell (Chicago: University of Chicago Press, 1998), 139–40.

65. Doerschuk, "Secrets of Salsa Rhythm: Piano with Hot Sauce," 322.

66. Unfortunately, the original recording of this arrangement—which includes both Bravo's arrangement and piano solo, but replacing the vocal track—was pirated and released by Fruko y sus tesos.

67. Manuel, "Improvisation in Latin Dance Music," 139–40.

68. Benjamin Lapidus, *Origins of Cuban Music and Dance: Changüí* (Lanham, MD: Scarecrow Press, 2008), 109–12.

69. Sonny Bravo, *The New York Latin Scene with Sonny Bravo: You Gotta Turn Me On*, Columbia EX 5221. LP. 1968.

70. Sonny Bravo, phone interview, April 25, 2013.

71. The curious reader can see and hear this type of interplay between Bravo and Rodríguez, specifically their adding chromatic ii-V sequences to set up mambo figures or when comping

behind soloists on "TP on the Strip," the opening song of a Tito Puente concert from August 18, 1990, at the Newport Jazz Festival, https://youtu.be/LoilS-3rqqg. Retrieved August 2, 2019.

72. José "Chombo" Silva, *Los Hits de Manzanero* (LP, GEMA LPG-3067, 1968).

73. Conjunto Marcano, "Lindo Amanecer" (78rpm, Verne 0484, 1949). Bobby Rodríguez told Rubén Rodríguez that he recorded this as a teenager in 1944 and that it was his first recording. Rubén Rodríguez, personal communication, September 7, 2019.

74. Chartoff was a bassist with the New York Philharmonic from 1943–61. John Canarina, *The New York Philharmonic: From Bernstein to Maazel* (Amadeus Press, 2010), 424.

75. Rubén Rodriguez. personal communication, September 13, 2013.

76. Cándido Camero, interview, June 11, 2015.

77. Dorothy Kilgallen, "The Voice of Broadway," *Elmira Star-Gazette*, August 9, 1947, 4.

78. "Excitement at Fire: Night Club Patrons Watch Department in Action," *New York Sun*, July 1, 1939, 1.

79. Christopher Washburne, *Sounding Salsa: Performing Latin Music in New York City* (Philadelphia: Temple University Press, 2008), 130.

80. Gilberto "Pulpo" Colón Jr., interview, June 13, 2013. Bravo also mentioned that Bobby Rodríguez was friendly with bassist Al McKibbon. Bravo, personal communication, August 1, 2019.

81. Gilberto "Pulpo" Colón Jr., interview, June 13, 2013.

82. Gilberto "Pulpo" Colón Jr., interview, June 13, 2013.

83. Sonny Bravo, personal communication, May 29, 2017.

84. Sonny Bravo, personal communication, May 29, 2017.

85. Sonny Bravo, personal communication, May 29, 2017.

86. Sonny Bravo, personal communication, May 29, 2017.

87. Morales, *Latin-American Rhythms and Improvisations for Piano*, 5–9; Humberto Morales, *How to Play Latin American Rhythm Instruments* (New York: Henry Adler, 1954), 107–13.

88. Sonny Bravo, personal communication, June 3, 2017.

89. Benjamin Lapidus, liner notes, *Charangueando* (CD, [Fania 1978] Emusica, 2005).

90. Carlos DeLeón, "Salsa's Silent Giant," *Sangre Nueva* (1977): 13.

91. DeLeón, "Salsa's Silent Giant."

92. "Buenas noches" [Latin club listings], *New York*, August 7, 1972.

93. The word *charanga* derives from *charanga francesa*, a Cuban ensemble made of bowed strings, Afro-Cuban percussion, flute (and other winds in an earlier time period), piano, bass, and later vocals. The *conjunto* is comprised of two or more trumpets, bass, tres, piano, Afro-Cuban percussion, and vocals. An *orquesta* can include woodwinds and trombones in the conjunto format much like a big band.

94. Johnny Rodríguez, personal communication, December 18, 2013.

95. Johnny Rodríguez and Angel René Orquesta, *Cookin' with A&J* (LP, Mardi Gras LP-5036, 1968).

96. Vicentico Valdés, "Fidelidad," *For Listening and Dancing* (LP, Seeco SCLP 9103, 1958).

97. Rumbavana, an established Cuban band, covered Ray Barretto's "Yo vine pa' echar candela" in 1979, http://www.youtube.com/watch?v=hoqXz1-hxoY. Retrieved November 7, 2013. See the following site for an interesting comparison of the two versions: http://enrisco.blogspot.com/2010/01/yo-vine-pa-echar-candela.html. Retrieved November 7, 2013.

98. Although Bravo's point of departure for "La escoba barrendera" was actually Estrellas Cubanas, a charanga, it is interesting to compare it to the electric guitar–infused and song-based arrangement, which was contemporary with Bravo's chart, by Raúl Planas con Rumbavana: http://www.youtube.com/watch?v=drx-sDZJbnE. Tipica 73: http://www.youtube.com/watch?v=KQ2ZqWP1Bco. Retrieved November 7, 2013.

99. Bravo, interview, December 11, 2013.

100. Bravo, interview, December 11, 2013.

101. "Que manera de sentirme bien" had been previously recorded by the Cuban group Original de Manzanillo.

102. Ed Byrne, *Functional Jazz Guitar* (2010), 207. http://freejazzinstitute.com/showposts.ph p?dept=lji&topic=20090101062155_EdByrne. Retrieved May 30, 2019.

103. Sonny Bravo, personal communication, August 12, 2019.

104. Gilberto "Pulpo" Colón Jr., interview, June 13, 2013.

105. Gilberto "Pulpo" Colón Jr., interview, June 13, 2013.

106. Eddie Palmieri, *Live at Sing Sing* (1972); Larry Harlow *Live in Quad* (1974).

107. Eddie Palmieri, personal communication, December 11, 2015.

108. Larry Harlow, personal communication, December 4, 2013.

109. John Child, "Louie Cruz: To the Best of His Knowledge," http://www.descarga.com/cgi -bin/db/archives/Interview49?5azfgnRD;;474. Retrieved March 24, 2016.

110. Sonny Bravo, interview, December 11, 2013. During the interview Bravo referenced television show big bands using this technique.

111. Típica 73, "El jamaiquino," *La Candela* (1975). https://youtu.be/cFVRhvOq_GM. Retrieved July 16, 2019.

112. The particular rhythmic figure that Bravo uses in the arrangement of "El Jamaiquino" is ♫♫♫♪ and it is at the center of Blood, Sweat and Tears' 1969 hit "Spinning Wheel." Bravo freely admits to BS&T's influence in his charts and has said that it is indicative of what was musically and commercially successful and in the air at that time.

113. As performed in New York and Cuba, the mozambique rhythm differed, but there are similarities in their bell patterns. The Típica 73 rhythm is modeled on the Cuban style popularized by Pello el Afrokan, because of the *songo* stick pattern executed on the woodblock. For more discussion, see https://en.wikipedia.org/wiki/Mozambique_(music). Retrieved August 2, 2019.

114. *Pancho Cristal presenta: Super típica estrellas* (All-Art AALP-1582, 1976). This recording was produced by the Jewish Cuban exile Pancho Cristal.

115. Sonny Bravo, personal communication, June 4, 2017.

116. DeLeón, "Salsa's Silent Giant," 13.

117. DeLeón, "Salsa's Silent Giant," 13.

118. Lapidus, "¡Toca *maravilloso!*," 109–21.

119. The author was fortunate to have performed it twice with him at Lincoln Center in 2010 and again in 2012 at Miami's Adrian Arscht Center. The author also performed *Hommy* with Harlow at Lincoln Center in 2014.

120. Sonny Bravo, interview, December 11, 2013.

121. "A special greeting for Rafael Lay, Elio Revé, and Duvalón for having treated our brother with so much love and affection." Liner notes. *Salsa Encendida* (Inca JMIS 1062, 1978).

122. For an in-depth discussion of De la Fé's style and musical analysis of his improvisations, see Sam Bardfeld, *Latin Violin: How to Play Salsa, Charanga and Latin Jazz Violin* (Brooklyn, NY: Gerard and Sarzin, 2001), 63–71.

123. "*Somos los campeones de la salsa en Nueva York.*"

124. "Amram, Tipica '73, and WNET," *Latin NY* (June 1978): 11. José Alberto, the band's vocalist, was also profiled in the "Esquina dominicana" (Dominican corner) column of the same issue, 56.

125. "New Cultural Tours to Cuba Planned by Guardian Tours," *Latin NY* (October 1979): 12.

126. Roberto Gerónimo, "The Cuban Connection: Tipica '73 becomes the first U.S. band to record in Cuba in 20 years," *Steppin' Out* 12 (February 1979): 4.

127. Johnny Rodríguez, personal communication, December 18, 2013. Cultural trips to Cuba were given press in *Latin NY* and three such packages for (1) music and dance, (2) film and

graphic arts, and (3) a ten-day trip were offered by Manhattan-based Guardian Tours October 7–14, October 21–28, and December 27, 1978–January 6, 1979.

128. Lapidus, "Típica '73," essay in accompanying booklet, *Típica '73: En Cuba – Intercambio Cultural* ([Fania 1979] Emusica, forthcoming).

129. Gerónimo, "The Cuban Connection," 4.

130. Johnny Rodríguez, personal communication, December 18, 2013.

131. Lapidus, "Típica '73" essay.

132. Roberto Gerónimo, "Típica '73 triunfa en Cuba," *Latin NY* (January 1979): 60.

133. Gerónimo, "The Cuban Connection," 4.

134. Gerónimo, "The Cuban Connection," 4.

135. Johnny Rodríguez, personal communication, December 18, 2013. Later, Rodríguez made a third trip with Martin Cohen from Latin Percussion, where they brought congas for Tata Güines and timbales for Changuito, among other musicians. Tata Güines loved the fact that Dandy was a santero and that he was a light-skinned man with a *mulata* wife. He also praised Rodríguez's playing because "the bongó [was] a lost instrument in Cuba."

136. Gerónimo, "The Cuban Connection," 4.

137. Until recently, the only major studio where every major Cuban band recorded for most of the last century has been the state-owned EGREM studio.

138. Gerónimo, "Típica '73 triunfa en Cuba," 60. Rodríguez is quoted in Gerónimo's other article about the trip, saying that he and Nicky Marrero would be returning with the Fania All-Stars in February and that he would try to cut the time for such an engagement to six weeks.

139. The seminal rumba recordings of Los Muñequitos de Matanzas feature a significant number of songs where the modern expectation for accents of rumba are placed on the opposite (or incorrect) side of the clave, according to modern expectations. Musicians in New York were exposed to these recordings early on as well as folkloric recordings made in the 1940s with similar discrepancies. The adoption of cross-clave rumba by New York–based musicians was derided by many Cuban musicians.

140. Gerónimo, "The Cuban Connection," 4.

141. Gerónimo, "The Cuban Connection," 5. As Sánchez's neighbor in the 1990s, he talked about the trip with warmth.

142. Gerónimo, "The Cuban Connection," 5.

143. Gerónimo, "The Cuban Connection," 5.

144. Lapidus, "Típica '73" essay.

145. Lapidus, "Típica '73" essay.

146. Tony Sabournin, "Review. Intercambio Cultural, TIPICA 73," *Latin NY* (October 1979): 19.

147. Lapidus, "Típica '73" essay. Celia Cruz was one musician who was displeased with Bravo as a result of the trip.

148. "What's Happening: Three Year Hitch for La Típica," *Latin NY* (June 1979): 15.

149. Tony Sabournin, "Club Scene: What is Happening with Típica 73," *Latin NY* (March 1980): 54.

150. Sabournin, "Club Scene: What is Happening with Típica 73," 54.

151. "Típica filmed at Palm Tree," Club Scene, *Latin NY* (September 1980): 54.

152. Tony Sabournin, "Lincoln Center Bombed but the Band Played On: Cuba's Orquesta Aragon, Los Papines, and Elena Burke," *Latin NY* (February 1979): 28–30; Arnold H. Lubasch, "Omega 7 Leader Accused of Plot to Kill Delegate," *New York Times*, December 29, 1983.

153. Sonny Bravo, personal communication, September 29, 2005.

154. Sonny Bravo, personal communication, November 23, 2013.

155. Sonny Bravo, personal communication, June 17, 2017.

156. Max Salazar, "Sideman's Corner: Sonny Bravo, Pianist for the 80s," *Latin NY* (May 1983): 50–51.

157. Alfredo de la Fé, *Alfredo de la Fé* (LP, Criollo Records 473, 1979).

158. Sonny Bravo, personal communication, July 11, 2017.

159. Sonny Bravo, personal communication, July 7, 2017.

160. Robert Téllez, "Entrevista a Sonny Bravo," LatinaStereo.com. http://www.latinastereo.com/Noticias/ArtMID/433/ArticleID/400/Entrevista-a-Sonny-Bravo. Retrieved July 10, 2017.

161. Sonny Bravo, personal communication.

162. DeLeón, "Salsa's Silent Giant," 13.

163. In the film *For the Love of Mambo*, Bravo describes receiving the ultimate compliment from Tito Puente after Puente finished listening closely to Bravo's arrangement at a recording session. Puente tells Bravo, "'You know that line, that thing? I would have written it like that' . . . that's the supreme compliment: 'that's something I would have done.'"

164. Another bass-playing cousin in Miami, named Hank, offered to connect Bravo with Al Haig for lessons in Miami during the late 1950s when Haig was residing there, but they never transpired.

165. Sonny Bravo, interview, December 11, 2013.

166. Tito Puente, His Latin Ensemble and Orchestra, *Un Poco Loco* (Concord Jazz Picante, CJP-329, 1987); Tito Puente and His Latin Ensemble, *Sensación* (Concord Jazz Picante, CJP-301, 1986).

167. Spanish Harlem Orchestra, *Across 110th Street* (Libertad LE04–615, 2004); Celia and Johnny, *Tremendo Caché* (LP, Vaya Records VS-37, 1975).

168. Sonny Bravo, personal communication, June 25, 2017.

169. Orquesta Revé, *Rumberos Latino Americanos* (Habanacan HABCD-2407, 1992).

170. Sonny Bravo, personal communication, June 8, 2017.

171. Sonny Bravo, personal communication, June 27, 2017.

172. Soneros del Barrio, *Siguiendo la tradicion* (Digital Culture, 2003).

173. Ray Viera y Su Trombao, *Sambumbia radioactive* (Cofresi Productions, 2013).

174. Sonny Bravo, personal communication, June 30, 2017.

175. Eddie Torres and His Mambo Kings Orchestra, *Dance City* (1994).

176. Alex Díaz y Son de la Calle (2009).

177. Alex Díaz y Son de la Calle (2009).

178. Louie Ramírez y Sus Amigos, *Louie Ramírez y Sus Amigos* (Cotique 1096, 1978).

179. Louie Ramírez y Sus Amigos, *Louie Ramírez y Sus Amigos*.

180. Sonny Bravo, personal communication, July 7, 2017.

181. Sonny Bravo, personal communication, June 22, 2017.

182. "The Latin Giants of Jazz at Latin Percussion's 45th Anniversary Concert, 'No me molesto,'" YouTube. http://www.youtube.com/watch?v=ZN6QwEDSt5M. Retrieved December 10, 2013.

183. This is the same idea he urged the author to use in 2001 when recording a chachachá that shifted to a danzón rhythm.

184. Sonny Bravo, personal communication, June 8, 2017.

185. Bravo's cousin, Bobby Rodríguez, also tapped the clave with his foot while playing.

186. Gilberto "Pulpo" Colón Jr., interview, June 13, 2013.

187. Gilberto "Pulpo" Colón Jr., interview, June 13, 2013.

188. Sonny Bravo, personal communication, June 8, 2017.

189. "Pare cochero—Orquesta Aragón," YouTube. http://www.youtube.com/watch?v=q3qr8f9bAGw. 01:54- 2:14. Retrieved December 17, 2013.

190. "Orquesta Aragón—Preguntame como estoy," YouTube. See 6:30–6:35. http://www.youtube.com/watch?v=7-5yjzPub7g. Retrieved December 17, 2013.

191. Sonny Bravo, personal communication, December 11, 2013.

192. Sonny Bravo, personal communication, March 23, 2013.

193. Sonny Bravo, personal communication, March 23, 2013.

194. Sonny Bravo, personal communication, December 11, 2013.

195. Sonny Bravo, personal communication, May 19, 2018.

CHAPTER 4

1. David W. Dunlap, *From Abyssinian to Zion: A Guide to Manhattan's Houses of Worship* (New York: Columbia University Press, 2004), 530. https://books.google.com/books?id= DJJavoWxzrIC&pg=PA139&lpg=PA139&dq=The+Panamanian+Village+eldridge+street&source= bl&ots=nCwuDZDlSd&sig=MJZy3YYbiHmLDCPP_SIul-HOpk&hl=en&sa=X&ved =0ahUKEwjl4KHl7JjUAhUIooMKHfkyCUIQ6AEIMjAD#v=onepage&q=The%20Panama nian%20Village%20eldridge%20street&f=false. Retrieved June 8, 2018.

2. Chico Álvarez Peraza, "Terry Pearce Remembers The Golden Era of Dance Music In NYC," Latin Jazz Network. https://latinjazznet.com/featured/terry-pearce-remembers-the-golden-era -of-dance-music-in-nyc/. Retrieved June 2, 2017.

3. David F. García, *Arsenio Rodriguez and the Transnational Flows of Latin Popular Music* (Philadelphia: Temple University Press, 2006).

4. Floyd et al., *The Transformation of Black Music*, xxii.

5. Luis Russell, who achieved fame with Louis Armstrong and his own band, is the only musician to have his story recounted.

6. The education system was not unified until the 1970s.

7. Lydia Reid, "The Silver and Gold Roll on the Panama Canal Zone," May 1, 2008. https:// thesilverpeopleheritage.wordpress.com/2008/05/01/the-silver-and-gold-roll-on-the-panama -canal-zone/ Retrieved June 11, 2018.

8. George Priestley, "Antillean-Panamanians or Afro-Panamanians? Political Participation and the Politic of Identity During the Carter-Torrijos Treaty Negotiations," *Transforming Anthropology* 12, no. 1/2 (2004): 51.

9. Priestley, "Antillean-Panamanians or Afro-Panamanians?," 52.

10. Priestley, "Antillean-Panamanians or Afro-Panamanians?," 52.

11. Priestley, "Antillean-Panamanians or Afro-Panamanians?," 53.

12. "Panamanian Americans," Wikipedia. http://en.wikipedia.org/wiki/Panamanian_Americans. Retrieved 24 January 2014.

13. Nick Juravich, "I Love Franklin Avenue." http://ilovefranklinave.blogspot.com/2010/09/ fighting-for-franklin.html. Retrieved 24 January 2014.

14. Erin Durkin, "Neighborhood Split Over Renaming of Franklin Ave. 'Panama Way,'" *New York Daily News*, October 21, 2010. http://www.nydailynews.com/new-york/brooklyn/neighborhood -split-renaming-part-franklin-ave-panama-article-1.190840 Retrieved January 24, 2014.

15. Durkin, "Neighborhood Split Over Renaming of Franklin Ave."

16. Becky Bratu, "Local Organization and Panamanian Community Clash," October 19, 2010. http://thebrooklynink.com/2010/10/19/16476-who-was-first-on-franklin-avenue-neighbor hood-organization-and-panamanian-community-clash-over-avenue-name/. Retrieved January 24, 2014.

17. Beyond physical similarities with African Americans, it seems that Panamanians of West Indian descent historically have also shared culinary tastes. In his book *Hog and Hominy*, Frederick Douglass Opie quotes George Priestley about rent parties run by Panamanian women in Brooklyn where they would cook soul food and the Panamanian dishes side by side; these were places where Panamanians and African Americans would interact socially. Frederick Douglass Opie, *Hog and Hominy: Soul Food from Africa to America* (New York: Columbia University Press, 2013), 149.

18. Suzanne Oboler and Anani Dzidzienyo, "Flows and Counterflows," in *Neither Enemies nor Friends: Latinos, Blacks, Afro-Latinos*, edited by Anani Dzidzienyo and Suzanne Oboler (New York: Palgrave Macmillan, 2005), 17.

19. Noel Foster Steward, *Las expresiones musicales en Panamá: una aproximación* (Panama: Editorial Universitaria, 1997), 17–20.

20. Steward, *Las expresiones musicales en Panamá: una aproximación*, 27–41.

21. "Jazz siempre ha estado en Panamá. Desde que inició los estados unidos, dadas las características geográficas de este país, todas las cosas, casi, lleguen a este país. En los años que inció el jazz allá en los estados unidos de una o otra manera llegaba esa influencia aquí a Panamá. Tanto es así que a partir de los años 1926 cuando surgió Louis Armstrong y todos esos grandes músicos, Sydney Bechet y todos esos grandes músicos, en el jazz en Nueva Orleans, en Panamá también había músicos que practicaban ese genero de música."

22. Steward, *Las expresiones musicales en Panamá: una aproximación*, 153.

23. Steward, *Las expresiones musicales en Panamá: una aproximación*, 169.

24. *Tambo Jazz*, written and directed by Gerardo Maloney (La Fundación Cine/Video/Cultura y El Grupo Experimental de Cine Universitario, Panama, 1993). https://youtu.be/-JG9NsrjBA4. Retrieved June 11, 2018.

25. *Tambo Jazz*. Shirley Scott spent eight weeks in Panama when she came down with Stanley Turrentine.

26. Reynaldo Alfu y su grupo, "Mi guaguancó," http://www.youtube.com/watch?v=GFo5vXHOC-M). Retrieved January 15, 2014. http://www.latin45.com/vinyl/panama/Page-6.html. Retrieved February 28, 2014.

27. Clyde E. B. Bernhardt, *I Remember: Eighty Years of Black Entertainment, Big Bands, and the Blues: An Autobiography by Jazz Trombonist and Blues Singer Clyde E. B. Bernhardt*, as told to Sheldon Harris, Foreword by John F. Szwed (Philadelphia: University of Pennsylvania Press, 1986), 117.

28. Bernhardt, *I Remember*.

29. Bernhardt, *I Remember*, 119.

30. Bernhardt, *I Remember*, 119.

31. Bobby Sanabria, *Profile: The Legacy of Mario Bauzá* (1993), http://www.descarga.com/cgi-bin/db/archives/Profile8?QDNwE5qj;;3641066. Retrieved January 21, 2014.

32. "Feelin' the Spirit: The Luis Russell Story," Jim Cullum Riverwalk Jazz Collection. http://riverwalkjazz.stanford.edu/program/feelin-spirit-luis-russell-story. Retrieved January 21, 2014.

33. Mario García Hudson, "Los pianistas antes de Danilo Pérez," in *El jazz desde la perspectiva caribeña*, edited by Darío Tejeda and Rafael Emilio Yunén (Santiago de los Caballeros, Dominican Republic: Instituto de estudios caribeños, 2012), 478.

34. "Polls 50,000 Votes to Cop First Place; Henderson Second," *Pittsburgh Courier*, December 12, 1932, 1, 8.

35. Ike Quebec Swingtet, "Dolores," https://youtu.be/rZk2GAjjekM; Pete Weinberg. "The Jam Session," *Wilton Bulletin* (Wilton, CT), August 15, 1946, 11.

36. *Buffalo Courier Express*, July 9, 1944, 8A.

37. Sanabria, *Profile: The Legacy of Mario Bauzá*.

38. Fifteenth Census of the United States, April 7, 1930. Enumeration District 31–922, Supervisor District 24, Sheet 5-A, 174.

39. Laurie and Peggy Wright, "THAT CAT STOPPED MY SHOW COLD: An Interview with "Nick" Rodriguez," *Storyville* 135 (September 1988): 86–94.

40. Chappy Gardner, "Along the Rialto (New York)," *Pittsburgh Courier*, October 13, 1928, 3, Second Section.

41. Gardner, "Along the Rialto (New York)."

42. "Amusements," *York Dispatcher*, December 3, 1928.

43. "Peppers at Washington Gardens," *Pittsburgh Courier*, May 11, 1929.

44. "Jelly Roll Morton Draws Large Crowd at Initial Hop," *Afro-American*, Baltimore, January 26, 1929.

45. Wright, "THAT CAT STOPPED MY SHOW COLD," 86–94.

46. Wright, "THAT CAT STOPPED MY SHOW COLD," 86–94.

47. Wright, "THAT CAT STOPPED MY SHOW COLD," 86–94.

48. Wright, "THAT CAT STOPPED MY SHOW COLD," 86–94.

49. "Back Again," *New York Post*, January 3, 1948.

50. Edythe Robertson, "Orlando Robeson and Wen Talbert's Choir On 'Harlem Serenade,'" *New York Age*, September 14, 1940, 4.

51. Jean Vincent, *The Soul of Haiti* (LP, Vanguard, 1957).

52. Jorge Del Rio, "El instituto de Puerto Rico," *El Diario de Nueva York*, July 25, 1954.

53. Mario García Hudson, "Los pianistas," 478, 482–484, 487–488.

54. "Sonny White," Wikipedia, https://en.wikipedia.org/wiki/Sonny_White.

55. Gillespie, *To Be or Not to Bop*, 88.

56. Gillespie, *To Be or Not to Bop*.

57. "Bill Robinson for African Dance Festival," *Brooklyn Sun*, March 18, 1946, 27.

58. Floyd G. Snelson, "Harlem: 'Negro Capitol of the World,'" *New York Age*, May 6, 1939, 7–12.

59. Malcolm Johnson, "In the Cafes and Supper Clubs," *New York Sun*, October 26, 1935, 6.

60. Earl Leaf, *Isles of Rhythm* (New York: A.S. Barnes, 1948), 37.

61. García, *Listening for Africa*, 128. García also points out that many of the members of Dafora's dance troupe were "Black American" and assumed to be from Africa.

62. García, *Listening for Africa*, 169.

63. García, *Listening for Africa*, 172.

64. "Front and Center with Sonny," *New York Age*, October 20, 1951, 12.

65. *Pittsburgh Courier*, June 25, 1938, 21.

66. Ted Watson, "Princess Orelia and Pete to Star in Latin Quarter Revue Starting March 23," *Pittsburgh Courier*, March 22, 1941, 21.

67. "Sign Dance Team for Feature," *Pittsburgh Courier*, November 1, 1941, 21.

68. "Bandwagon: 1944," Twin Cities Music Highlights. https://twincitiesmusichighlights.net/concerts/bandwagon-1944/. Retrieved April 26, 2020.

69. Eleanor Roosevelt, "My Day," *Buffalo Courier-Express Daily Pictorial*, April 22, 1946, 8.

70. Maudine Sims Watson, "Orelia, Famed Cuban Dancer, Gives Recipe," *Pittsburgh Courier*, January 11, 1941, 8.

71. Robin Kelley, *Thelonious Monk: The Life and Times of an American Original* (New York: Free Press, 2009), 251.

72. Kelley, *Thelonious Monk*, 346.

73. HLK, "Princess Takes Over Progressive Quintet," *Pittsburgh Courier*, January 28, 1956, 26.

74. Jazz Modes, *The Jazz Modes* (LP, Atlantic 1306, 1959).

75. Charlie Rouse, *Bossa Nova Bacchanal* (LP, Blue Note 4119, 1963).

76. Kelley, *Thelonious Monk*, 346.

77. "Silvia De Grasse," Wikipedia. https://es.wikipedia.org/wiki/Silvia_De_Grasse. Retrieved April 26, 2020.

78. Bobby Sanabria, "Candido: Father of Modern Conga Drumming," *Traps* (Autumn 2007). http://www.drummagazine.com/hand-drum/post/candido-the-father-of-modern-conga-drumming/P5/. Retrieved January 22, 2014.

79. Johnny Griffin, *Blowing Session* (Blue Note, 1958).

80. Frank Anderson, personal communication, March 21, 2011.

81. Frank Anderson, interview by Bobby Sanabria and Elena Martínez, June 15, 2010.

82. Frank Anderson, interview by Bobby Sanabria and Elena Martínez, June 15, 2010.

83. According to the documentary *Tambo Jazz*, he performed on organ at the Café Krech.

84. Interestingly, Anderson did not know Wynton Kelly, but he knew Kelly's relatives.

85. Frank Anderson, interview by Bobby Sanabria and Elena Martínez, June 15, 2010.

86. *Pacific Radio News*, Volumes 2–3 (1920). https://books.google.com/books?id=7WpOAQA
AIAAJ&pg=PA289&lpg=PA289&dq=music+at+the+McAlpin+hotel&source=bl&ots=rnZz3gg
qOK&sig=JSfqX-lFUijV8yD7ztP3lvJL4X8&hl=en&sa=X&ved=0ahUKEwi8_d_7tIzUAhVL7Y
MKHWWrAxoQ6AEIWjAJ#v=onepage&q=music%20at%20the%20McAlpin%20hotel&f=false.
Retrieved April 26, 2020.

87. Frank Anderson, interview by Bobby Sanabria and Elena Martínez, June 15, 2010.

88. Frank Anderson, personal communication, March 21, 2011.

89. MacDonald was a composer and musician known for many hits such as "Just the Two of Us."

90. Coincidentally, another Panamanian, Eduardo Álvarez, who played with Joe Cotto, joined
the union that same day.

91. Frank Anderson, interview by Bobby Sanabria and Elena Martínez, June 15, 2010.

92. Frank Anderson, interview by Bobby Sanabria and Elena Martínez, June 15, 2010.

93. "Mambo-Calypso at Palladium," *New York Post*, February 5, 1957, 37.

94. "Le Cupidon," *New York Post*, February 5, 1957, 16.

95. "Interview: Camille E. Hodge." OtherSounds.com. http://othersounds.com/interview
-camille-e-hodge/.

96. Frank Anderson, interview by Bobby Sanabria and Elena Martínez, June 15, 2010.

97. Frank Anderson, interview by Bobby Sanabria and Elena Martínez, June 15, 2010.

98. Frank Anderson, personal communication, March 21, 2011. Vicentico Valdés, *Así canta el
corazón* (SCLP-9285, 1966).

99. Frank Anderson, personal communication, August 16, 2019.

100. Frank Anderson, interview by Bobby Sanabria and Elena Martínez, June 15, 2010.

101. Frank Anderson, interview by Bobby Sanabria and Elena Martínez, June 15, 2010.

102. Frank Anderson, personal communication, March 21, 2011.

103. Frank Anderson, interview by Bobby Sanabria and Elena Martínez, June 15, 2010.

104. Kip Anderson and the Tides, *Shango! Night in a Quiet Village*. Kapp Records KS-3466.
1965. LP.

105. Candido Camero, *Beautiful* (Blue Note, 1970); Joe Cain and His Orchestra, *Latin Explosion* (Time Records S2123, 1960).

106. Frank Anderson, interview by Bobby Sanabria and Elena Martínez, June 15, 2010.

107. Frank Anderson. personal communication, March 21, 2011. On two occasions Anderson
went to Armstrong's house in Corona, Queens, with a friend and spliced together reels for use
at the Armstrong museum.

108. "Honoring Mr. Frank Harris Anderson upon the occasion of celebrating his musical
genius by the Panama Connection of Janes United Methodist Church." July 19, 2010. http://open
.nysenate.gov/legislation/bill/J6510–2009. Retrieved March 2, 2011.

109. By Anderson's account he had no real vision problems until he was forty.

110. "*Purlie*," Wikipedia. http://en.wikipedia.org/wiki/Purlie. Retrieved June 10, 2013.

111. "*Don't Bother Me, I Can't Cope*," Wikipedia. http://en.wikipedia.org/wiki/Don't_Bother
_Me,_I_Can't_Cope. Retrieved June 10, 2013.

112. "*A Raisin in the Sun*," Wikipedia. http://en.wikipedia.org/wiki/A_Raisin_in_the_Sun.
Retrieved 10 June 2013.

113. "*Eubie!*," Wikipedia. http://en.wikipedia.org/wiki/Eubie! Retrieved 10 June 2013.

114. "*The Wiz*," Wikipedia. http://en.wikipedia.org/wiki/The_Wiz. Retrieved 10 June 2013.

115. "*Guys and Dolls*," Wikipedia. http://en.wikipedia.org/wiki/Guys_and_Dolls. Retrieved 10 June 2013.

116. Frank Anderson, interview by Bobby Sanabria and Elena Martínez, June 15, 2010.

117. Frank Anderson, personal communication, March 21, 2011.

118. Jefferson remembers seeing Cuban saxophonist Jose "Chombo" Silva.

119. Christopher Washburne, "Latin Music at the Apollo." *Ain't Nothing Like the Real Thing: How the Apollo Theater Shaped American Entertainment*, edited by Richard Carlin and Kinshasha Holman Conwill (Washington, DC: Smithsonian Books, 2010), 221. Interestingly, Frank Anderson felt that the Apollo was an exploitative place to work.

120. Gene Jefferson, personal communication, March 2011.

121. Gene Jefferson, interview by Bobby Sanabria and Elena Martínez, June 15, 2010.

122. Gene Jefferson, interview by Bobby Sanabria and Elena Martínez, June 15, 2010.

123. Gene Jefferson, interview by Bobby Sanabria and Elena Martínez, June 15, 2010.

124. Kant wound up singing in Julio Andino's band.

125. Gene Jefferson, interview by Bobby Sanabria and Elena Martínez, June 15, 2010.

126. Gene Jefferson, interview by Bobby Sanabria and Elena Martínez, June 15, 2010.

127. Gene Jefferson, interview by Bobby Sanabria and Elena Martínez, June 15, 2010.

128. Gene Jefferson, interview by Bobby Sanabria and Elena Martínez, June 15, 2010.

129. Gene Jefferson, interview by Bobby Sanabria and Elena Martínez, June 15, 2010.

130. Jefferson remembers when Frank's book was stolen when they were playing the Savoy in the Bronx in the early 1960s. He corroborated the story that Frank left the book in the car or by the entrance to the club and that someone swiped it quickly.

131. Arsenio Rodríguez, *Quindembo/Afro Magic/La Magía de Arsenio Rodríguez* (Epic LN24072, 1963).

132. Gene Jefferson, interview by Bobby Sanabria and Elena Martínez, June 15, 2010.

133. Gene Jefferson, interview by Bobby Sanabria and Elena Martínez, June 15, 2010.

134. A 1964 listing for the Palladium corroborates Tito Rodríguez's Wednesday night performance.

135. Gene Jefferson, interview by Bobby Sanabria and Elena Martínez, June 15, 2010.

136. Gene Jefferson, interview by Bobby Sanabria and Elena Martínez, June 15, 2010.

137. Gene Jefferson, interview by Bobby Sanabria and Elena Martínez, June 15, 2010.

138. Gene Jefferson, interview by Bobby Sanabria and Elena Martínez, June 15, 2010.

139. Chico Álvarez Peraza, "Terry Pearce Remembers the Golden Era of Dance Music in NYC," Latin Jazz Network, August 4, 2011. https://latinjazznet.com/featured/terry-pearce-remembers -the-golden-era-of-dance-music-in-nyc/. Retrieved June 2, 2017.

140. Álvarez Peraza, "Terry Pearce Remembers the Golden Era of Dance Music in NYC."

141. Álvarez Peraza, "Terry Pearce Remembers the Golden Era of Dance Music in NYC."

142. Álvarez Peraza, "Terry Pearce Remembers the Golden Era of Dance Music in NYC."

143. Álvarez Peraza, "Terry Pearce Remembers the Golden Era of Dance Music in NYC."

144. Enid Lowe, interview with Bobby Sanabria and Elena Martínez, June 15, 2010. Information and quotations in this section are from this interview unless otherwise indicated.

145. Daniel Young, "Creole Cuisine Is Taking Off: A Haitian Hub Near LaGuardia Spices Up Dinner for Weary Travelers & Locals Alike," *New York Daily News*, January 3, 1997. http://www .nydailynews.com/archives/nydn-features/creole-cuisine-haitian-hub-laguardia-spices-dinner -weary-travelers-locals-alike-article-1.752476.

146. Alphonso Joseph, interview, October 4, 2012.

147. Alphonso Joseph, interview, October 4, 2012.

148. It was believed that Bailey had some 300 students at the time of his death. Todd Bryant Weeks, "You've Got to Have Big Ears," Allegro 11, no. 2 (2011) (A.F.M. Local 802). http://www .local802afm.org/2011/02/youve-got-to-have-big-ears/.

149. "Rector Bailey, Musician and Teacher, Dies at 57," *New York Times*, April 8, 1970. http://www.nytimes.com/1970/04/08/archives/rector-bailey-musician-and-teacher-dies-at-57 .html?_r=0.

150. Willard Jenkins, "Remembering Brooklyn's Jazz Heyday," Open Sky Jazz, August 24, 2011. http://www.openskyjazz.com/2011/08/remembering-brooklyns-jazz-heyday/. Retrieved April 26, 2020.

151. Joseph remembered that Arsenio played the bass, guitar, tres, and conga extremely well.

152. Alphonso Joseph, interview, October 4, 2012.

153. Alphonso Joseph, interview, October 4, 2012.

154. *La época.* https://laepocafilm.com. Retrieved April 26, 2020.

155. "Black History Special: Jazz Legend Randy Weston on His Life and Celebration of 'African Rhythms,'" Democracy Now! February 20, 2012. http://www.democracynow.org/2012/2/20/ black_history_special_jazz_legend_randy. Retrieved January 23, 2014.

156. Randy Weston and Willard Jenkins, *African Rhythms: The Autobiography of Randy Weston* (Durham, NC: Duke University Press, 2010), 5.

157. Weston, *Autobiography*, 15.

158. Weston, *Autobiography*, 26.

159. Weston, *Autobiography*, 21.

160. Weston, *Autobiography*, 225.

161. Weston, *Autobiography*, 115.

162. Weston, *Autobiography*, 235.

163. Alex Blake, qtd. in Weston, *Autobiography*.

164. Weston, *Autobiography*, 285.

165. The Latin Jazz Quintet + Eric Dolphy, *Caribé* (Prestige 8251, 1960); Eric Dolphy and The Latin Jazz Quintet, *The Latin Jazz Quintet* (United Artists 4071, 1961).

166. The Latin Jazz Quintet, Featured Guest Artist Pharoah Sanders, Under the Direction of Juan Amalbért, *Oh! Pharoah Speak* (Trip Records 8008, 1971).

167. Smith played all flutes, saxophones, clarinet, harmonica, classical guitar, bass, vibraphone, and Latin percussion. Anthony H. McLean, "Mauricio Smith Pereira" (November 2010). http:// diadelaetnia.homestead.com/MauricioSmith.html. Retrieved March 21, 2011.

168. McLean, "Mauricio Smith Pereira."

169. McLean, "Mauricio Smith Pereira."

170. McLean, "Mauricio Smith Pereira."

171. *Tambo Jazz.*

172. Terry Carr, "Felix Wilkins: Flutist and First Amendment Champion," Jump: The Philly Music Project (June 26, 2013). http://jumpphilly.com/2013/06/26/felix-wilkins-flutist-and-first -amendment-champion/. Retrieved February 28, 2014.

173. *Tambo Jazz.*

174. "De Briano with the Alonso Wilson Quinteto - Concolon – Ecoll," YouTube. http://www .youtube.com/watch?v=z6juExvAApo. Retrieved February 28, 2014. "Alonso Wilson Quinteto, 'Never, Never, Never – AWB,'" YouTube. https://youtu.be/4JUDqv8vihw. Retrieved February 28, 2014. Música del Alma: Hot & Soulful Latin Sounds. http://latinfunk.org/blog/?cat=6. Retrieved February 28, 2014.

175. "Santi Debriano," Wikipedia. http://en.wikipedia.org/wiki/Santi_Debriano. Retrieved February 28, 2014.

176. Eric Nemeyer, "Jorge Sylvester," *Jazz Inside* (June 2012): 4.

177. Jorge Sylvester ACE Collective. http://jorgesylvesteracecollective.blogspot.com/p/about -music.html. Retrieved March 3, 2014.

178. "Victor Paz and Question to Charly," trumpetherald.com. http://www.trumpetherald.com/ forum/viewtopic.php?p=1180074. Retrieved February 28, 2014.

179. "Victor Paz," http://victorpaztrumpet.webs.com/biografa.htm. Retrieved February 28, 2014.

180. "Victor Paz," http://victorpaztrumpet.webs.com/biografa.htm. Retrieved February 28, 2014.

181. Tito Rodríguez, *Big Band Latino* (Musicor MS 6048, 1968).

182. "Biography," BillyCobham.com. http://www.billycobham.com/html/biography.php. Retrieved February 28, 2014.

183. "Biography," BillyCobham.com.

184. "Biography," BillyCobham.com.

185. "Biography," BillyCobham.com.

186. *Tambo Jazz.*

187. John S. Wilson, "Pop: Doc Johnson in Many Moods," *New York Times*, November 26, 1983. http://www.nytimes.com/1983/11/26/arts/pop-doc-johnson-in-many-moods.html.

188. Jon Liebman, "Russel Blake," For Bass Players Only, August 20, 2012. https://forbassplayersonly.com/interview-russel-blake/. Retrieved April 26, 2020.

189. Liebman, "Russel Blake."

190. Bio, AlexBlakeBass.com. https://www.alexblakebass.com/his-story. Retrieved April 26, 2020.

191. Bio, AlexBlakeBass.com.

192. "Donald Nicks," AllMusic.com. http://www.allmusic.com/artist/donald-nicks-mn0001590117. Retrieved February 28, 2014.

193. "Danilo Pérez," Wikipedia. http://en.wikipedia.org/wiki/Danilo_Pérez. Retrieved February 28, 2014.

194. "Humanitarian," DaniloPerez.com. http://www.daniloperez.com/humanitarian-new/. Retrieved February 28, 2014.

195. "Camilo Azuquita," Salsero de Acero. http://salserodeacero.com/portal/biografia-de-camilo-azuquita/; http://fr.wikipedia.org/wiki/Azuquita. Retrieved February 28, 2014.

196. Joe Panama, *The Explosive Side of Joe Panama* (Decca 4890, 1968).

197. Salazar, *Mambo Kingdom*, 241.

198. "Hector Lavoe *Inedito* En Concierto Bronx New York 1989," YouTube. http://www.youtube.com/watch?v=9i5sScaFbPo. Retrieved February 28, 2014.

199. "Orquesta Felicidad De Roberto Duran En Venezuela - Vengo Con El Sabor," YouTube. https://youtu.be/uE1f51HuU0A. Retrieved April 26, 2020.

200. "The Fraternal Clubhouse," dance announcement, *New York Post*, January 3, 1948, 11.

201. Eleanor Towe, "The Jazz Scene: In Concert Carlos Garnett and Jackie McLean—Town Hall October 8th 1976," *New York Recorder*, October 23, 1976, 10; "Black Force at University," *Greenfield (Mass.) Recorder*, July 6, 1973, 10.

202. Harcourt Tynes, "Doc Johnson's Touch on the Keys Charms His Listeners," Gannett Westchester Newspapers, November 13, 1981, 7.

203. Vielka Cecilia Hoy, "Negotiating among Invisibilities: Tales of Afro-Latinidades in the United States," in *The Afro-Latin@ Reader: History and Culture in the United States*, eds. Miriam Jiménez Román and Juan Flores (Durham, NC: Duke University Press, 2010), 426.

CHAPTER 5

1. Ruth Glasser, *My Music Is My Flag: Puerto Rican Musicians and Their New York Communities, 1917–1940* (Berkeley: University of California Press, 1997); Basilio Serrano, *Puerto Rican Pioneers in Jazz, 1900–1939: Bomba Beats to Latin Jazz* (Bloomington, IN: iUniverse, 2015).

2. Ewin Martínez Torre, "Arturito, Los Jardineros y la revolución de El Jardín del Arte," *La cancíon popular: revista de la asociación puertorriqueño de coleccionistas de música popular* 20, Año 21 (2006–2007), http://www.herencialatina.com/Los_Jardineros/Los_Jardineros.htm. Retrieved July 3, 2018.

3. Flores, *Salsa Rising*.

4. César Miguel Rondón, *The Book of Salsa*; Peter Manuel, "Puerto Rican Music and Cultural Identity: Creative Appropriation of Cuban Sources from Danza to Salsa," *Ethnomusicology* 38, no. 2, Music and Politics (Spring-Summer 1994): 249–80.

5. Angel G. Quintero Rivera, "La música jíbara en la salsa: la presencia viva del folklore," in *Cocinando suave: ensayos de salsa en Puerto Rico*, edited by César Colón Montijo (San Juan: Ediciones Callejón, 2016), 205–22; and *Salsa, sabor y control: sociología de la música tropical* (México City: Siglo XXI Editores, 1998).

6. Ramón Grosfoguel and Chloé S. Georas, "Latino Caribbean Diasporas in New York," in *Mambo Montage: The Latinization of New York City* (New York: Columbia University Press, 2001), 97.

7. Serrano, *Puerto Rican Pioneers in Jazz, 1900–1939*. Serrano also discusses Fernando Arbello, Louis "King" Garcia, Rogelio "Roger Ram" Ramirez, and Ramon Usera.

8. Basilio Serrano, "Juan Tizol: Sus talentos y sus muchos colaboradores," *Resonancias: La revista puertorriqueña de música*, Año 5/6, Num. 10/11 (2005–2006): 60–63.

9. Flores, *Salsa Rising*, 126–28.

10. Cristóbal Díaz Ayala, *San Juan-New York: Discografía de la música puertorriqueña* (San Juan, PR: Publicaciones Gaviota, 2009), 42–67.

11. Richard Blondet, personal communication, January 22, 2018.

12. Jeffrey Magee, *The Uncrowned King of Swing: Fletcher Henderson and Big Band Jazz* (New York: Oxford University Press), 31.

13. Louis Armstrong, *Louis Armstrong, in His Own Words: Selected Writings*, ed. Thomas Brothers (New York: Oxford University Press, 1999), 126.

14. Thomas J. Hennessey, *From Jazz to Swing: African-American Jazz Musicians and Their Music, 1890–1935* (Detroit: Wayne State University Press, 1994), 90.

15. Michael Parsons, "Wreck of SS Rowan: How jazz nearly didn't come to Ireland," Irish Times, January 3, 2015. https://www.irishtimes.com/life-and-style/homes-and-property/fine-art-antiques/wreck-of-ss-rowan-how-jazz-nearly-didn-t-come-to-ireland-1.2053405?mode=amp. Retrieved August 1, 2019; "SS Rowan Survivors," https://youtu.be/Jxb8y4zlyVM.

16. Howard Rye, "Visiting Firemen 15: The Southern Syncopated Orchestra" (Part 1), Storyville 142 (June 1, 1990): 144. http://archive.nationaljazzarchive.co.uk/archive/journals/storyville/storyville-142/48612. Retrieved May 10, 2016.

17. Anthony Barnett, "Angelina Rivera and Other Early Jazz and Women Violinists," Shuffle Boil, nos. 5/6, Berkeley CA, Listening Chamber (2006); http://abar.net/rivera.htm. Retrieved May 10, 2016.

18. Michael Dregni, *Django: The Life and Music of a Gypsy Legend* (New York: Oxford University Press, 2004), 284.

19. *A Havana Cocktail*, dir. Roy Mack (1931). https://youtu.be/p84FgJxqkQs. Retrieved July 19, 2019.

20. Michael Rader and K.-B. Rau, "From the Shadows: The Re-Emergence of Carmelo Jarí," *The Frog Blues & Jazz Annual No. 2: The Musicians, the Records & the Music Of The 78 Era* (Book and CD, Frog Records, 2011); Bill Reed, *Hot from Harlem: Twelve African American Entertainers, 1890–1960*, rev. ed. (Jefferson, NC: McFarland, 2010), 217–18. http://www.harlemfuss.com/pdf/published_articles/harlem_fuss_articles_from_the_shadows_carmelo_jari.pdf. Retrieved May 13, 2016. Coincidentally, Cuban flautist Alberto Socarrás recorded what is widely acknowledged as the first jazz flute solo on "Shooting the Pistol" with Williams in 1927.

21. Serrano, *Puerto Rican Pioneers in Jazz*, 1900–1939, 237–40.

22. Cristóbal Díaz Ayala, "Influencias recíprocas entre el jazz y la música caribeña," in *El jazz desde la perspectiva caribeña* edited by Darío Tejeda (Santiago de los Caballeros, Dominican Republic: Instituto de estudios caribeños, 2012), 61.

23. Martínez Torre, "Arturito, Los Jardineros," 38–39.

24. "Rafael Hernandez / Orquesta Victor Antillana - Señorita (1932)," YouTube. https://www
.youtube.com/watch?v=UnjUh0r9qG8. Retrieved January 10, 2018.

25. Richard Blondet, personal communication, October 20, 2017.

26. Richard Blondet, personal communication, January 22, 2018.

27. Salazar, *Mambo Kingdom*, 103. Gene Krupa and His Orchestra, "Chiquita Banana (The
Banana Song)/You May Not Love Me" (78rpm, Columbia 32049, 1946).

28. Victor Rendón, "Monchito Muñoz: Puerto Rico's Little Secret," *Latin Percussionist Newsletter*, Issue 11, Fall 2000. http://www.bronxconexionlatinjazz.com/blog-percussion/20-percussion
-issue-11-fall-2000. Retrieved January 10, 2018.

29. Rendón, "Monchito Muñoz: Puerto Rico's Little Secret."

30. Rendón, "Monchito Muñoz: Puerto Rico's Little Secret."

31. Salazar, *Mambo Kingdom*, 104.

32. Salazar, *Mambo Kingdom*, 104.

33. "La Hija De Lola—Vitin Aviles Y Charlie Palmieri Al Rojo Vivo Concert PR 84." https://
www.youtube.com/watch?v=0MkYiDuIM6I. Retrieved January 10, 2018.

34. Lasse Mattsson, "Sabu Martinez: Percussionist with Joie de Vivre," *Orkester Jornalen*, April
1968. http://www.hipwax.com/sabu/OJ041968.html. Retrieved June 6, 2019.

35. Ray Barretto, *El Ray Criollo* (United Artists 6543, 1966).

36. *Machito: A Latin Jazz Legacy*, dir. Carlos Ortiz (Nubia Music Society, 1987).

37. *Latin Jazz*, dirs. Isabelle Leymarie and Karim Akadiri Soumaila (Feeling Productions/la
Sept/Epic Production, France, 1991). https://youtu.be/HRYqS8z2fGk. Retrieved March 5, 2018.

38. Pignataro was born in Italy and ran the jazz program at the Conservatorio de Música de
Puerto Rico until joining the faculty at Berklee College of Music.

39. Other musicians in Puente's orbit also studied at Juilliard, such as pianist Joe Loco, a
contemporary and friend of Puente's, and Louis Bauzó, one of Puente's sidemen. Bauzó's former
codirector at the Harbor Conservatory, Ramón Rodríguez, completed his BM at Manhattan
School of Music in music theory and piano.

40. Steven Loza, *Tito Puente and the Making of Latin Music* (Urbana and Chicago: University
of Illinois Press, 1999), 36.

41. Loza, *Tito Puente and the Making of Latin Music*, 38.

42. George Rivera, "Q&A: A Conversation with Ray Santos," http://www.jazzconclave.com/
i-room/santos.htm. Retrieved May 3, 2016.

43. Ray Santos, interview by Marc Meyers, Part 1. November 19, 2009. https://www.jazzwax
.com/2009/11/interview-ray-santos-part-1.html. Retrieved July 19, 2019.

44. Although the focus of this chapter is on Puerto Rican musicians, it is important to point
out that the Machito band's main connection to jazz was through Mario Bauzá, who was coached
by Chick Webb and later Cab Calloway, so it was logical that the Machito band and its players
would lean so heavily toward jazz. The fact that the band also included prominent non-Latin
band members such as Doc Cheatham and Leslie Johnakins, among others, also highlights the
jazz influence on its sound.

45. Tito Rodríguez, *Big Band Latino* (Musicor MS 6048, 1968).

46. David González, "Keeping the Family Beat: Photographs by Rhynna M. Santos," *New York
Times*, November 4, 2018, 8.

47. Loza, *Tito Puente and the Making of Latin Music*, 91.

48. Ray Santos, interview by Marc Meyers, Part 2. November 20, 2009. https://www.jazzwax
.com/2009/11/interview-ray-santos-part-2.html. Retrieved July 19, 2019.

49. Ray Santos, interview by Marc Meyers, Part 2.

50. Loza, *Tito Puente and the Making of Latin Music*, 35.

51. Tim McNeese, *Tito Puente* (Infobase: New York, 2008), 49.

52. Loza, *Tito Puente and the Making of Latin Music*, 33–4.

53. Loza, *Tito Puente and the Making of Latin Music*, 33

54. Loza, *Tito Puente and the Making of Latin Music*, 4.

55. Loza, *Tito Puente and the Making of Latin Music*, 27.

56. Loza, *Tito Puente and the Making of Latin Music*, 31.

57. Loza, *Tito Puente and the Making of Latin Music*, 32

58. Loza, *Tito Puente and the Making of Latin Music*, 105.

59. Tito Puente and Buddy Morrow, *Revolving Bandstand* (RCA CPL1–0684, 1974).

60. Loza, *Tito Puente and the Making of Latin Music*, 165.

61. Loza, *Tito Puente and the Making of Latin Music*, 192.

62. Stuffed Animal, "Mambo Gee Gee: The Story of George Goldner and Tico Records, Part Two: ¡Qué sabroso ésta! Mambo USA, Morris Levy & Rhythm 'n' Blues," http://www.spectropop .com/tico/TICOpart2.htm. Retrieved May 10, 2016. Speaking about the Mambo USA tour, Pete Terrace said that: "Most of the musicians traveled in a bus marked 'Mambo USA,' and when we stopped to eat, we were refused because of the dark-skinned musicians. Julio Andino, our Afro-Cuban bass player, developed an ulcer . . . the discrimination [he] experienced made him ill."

63. Julio Andino's Orchestra, "Andino's Peachy-Kato" (78rpm, Coda 5100-A 1206, 1947). Solo bajo by Andino.

64. *Billboard*, May 14, 1949, 127.

65. Gilberto "Pulpo" Colón Jr., interview, Yonkers, NY, June 13, 2013.

66. George Rivera, "Q&A: A Conversation with Bobby Valentín." http://www.jazzconclave .com/i-room/valentin.htm. Retrieved January 10, 2018.

67. Bobby Valentín, *Young Man with a Horn* (Fania SLP 332, 1965).

68. Bobby Valentín y Su Orquesta, *El mensajero* (Fonseca SLP 1108, 1966).

69. Johnny Colón and His Orchestra, *Boogaloo Blues* (Cotique C 1004, 1967); Joe Torres, *Latino Con Soul* (World Pacific 21857, 1967).

70. Loza, *Tito Puente and the Making of Latin Music*, 115.

71. Hilton Ruiz on Piano Jazz. http://southcarolinapublicradio.org/post/hilton-ruiz-piano-jazz. Retrieved January 11, 2018.

72. Hilton Ruiz on Piano Jazz.

73. Hilton Ruiz on Piano Jazz.

74. Hilton Ruiz on Piano Jazz.

75. Hilton Ruiz on Piano Jazz.

76. Loza, *Tito Puente and the Making of Latin Music*, 115.

77. Loza, *Tito Puente and the Making of Latin Music*, 115.

78. Loza, *Tito Puente and the Making of Latin Music*, 115.

79. Loza, *Tito Puente and the Making of Latin Music*, 116.

80. Loza, *Tito Puente and the Making of Latin Music*, 117

81. Loza, *Tito Puente and the Making of Latin Music*, 120.

82. Richard Bradley and Hilton Ruiz, *Jazz and How to Play It* (Bradley Publications, 1989).

83. Hilton Ruiz on Piano Jazz.

84. Robin Lloyd, "The Sad and Mysterious Death of Hilton Ruiz," KNKX. November 8, 2012. http://knkx.org/post/sad-and-mysterious-death-hilton-ruiz. Retrieved January 10, 2018.

85. "Kai Winding with J.J. Johnson" (discography), DougPayne.com. http://www.dougpayne .com/kwljj.htm. Retrieved May 10, 2016.

86. Flores, *Salsa Rising*, 81.

87. Eddie Palmieri, *Lo que traigo es sabroso* (Alegre Records 832, 1964).

88. Andy Kaufman, personal communication, June 22, 2019.

89. Flores, *Salsa Rising*, 162.

90. Flores, *Salsa Rising*, 161–62.

91. Flores addresses Palmieri's political worldview and how it influenced his music as well as how Ray Barretto's musical and political views converged. Flores, *Salsa Rising*, 154–67.

92. Flores, *Salsa Rising*, 82.

93. Eddie Palmieri, personal communication, September 30, 2016.

94. Palmieri's love of major thirteenth chords dates even earlier to his admiration for Bud Powell's "Un Poco Loco." Eddie Palmieri, personal communication, December 15, 2015.

95. Eddie Palmieri with Harlem River Drive, *Recorded Live at Sing Sing* (Tico 1303, 1972); Eddie Palmieri, *Unfinished Masterpiece* (Coco 120, 1975).

96. Blanca Vásquez, "Mi Gente: Andy and Jerry González," *Centro Journal* 3, no. 2 (Spring 1991): 70.

97. Vásquez, "Mi Gente: Andy and Jerry González," 72.

98. John Child, "Louie Cruz: To the Best of His Knowledge."

99. Ismael Miranda con Orchestra Harlow, *Oportunidad* (Fania 00419, 1972).

100. Típica 73, *Into the 80s* (Fania JM 592, 1981).

101. Ben Bierman, personal communication, New York, July 30, 2016.

102. "Ray Maldonado," descarga.com. http://www.descarga.com/cgi-bin/db/archives/Profile2. Retrieved May 12, 2016.

103. Lapidus, "El folclor al rescate," 123–33.

104. Benjamin Lapidus, "Liner Notes" and "Rene López on Andy Gónzalez," Andy González, *Entre colegas* (CD, Truth Revolution Records 024, 2016).

105. Jerry González, personal communication, March 6, 2015.

106. Loza, *Tito Puente and the Making of Latin Music*, 106.

107. Vásquez, "Mi Gente: Andy and Jerry González," 76.

108. Vásquez, "Mi Gente: Andy and Jerry González," 73.

109. Ed Morales, "Places in the Puerto Rican Heart, Eddie Figueroa, and the Nuyorican Imaginary," *Centro Voices e-Magazine.* https://centropr.hunter.cuny.edu/centrovoices/letras/places -puerto-rican-heart-eddie-figueroa-and-nuyorican-imaginary. Retrieved July 30, 2018.

110. Flores, *Salsa Rising*, 227.

111. Flores, idem.

112. The Soundscape Archives are held by the Jazz History Database at Worcester Polytechnic Institute. jazzhistorydatabase.com.

113. Loza, *Tito Puente and the Making of Latin Music*, 106.

114. Loza, *Tito Puente and the Making of Latin Music*, 103.

115. Flores, *Salsa Rising*, 121.

116. David Evans, personal communication, January 2, 2019.

117. Mulatu Astatke and His Ethiopian Quintet, *Afro-Latin Soul* (Worthy Records 1014, 1966). https://www.youtube.com/watch?v=X8vVqPbru1Q. Retrieved June 11, 2019.

118. Flores, *Salsa Rising*, 199.

119. Flores, *Salsa Rising*, 145.

120. Flores, *Salsa Rising*, 112.

121. Flores, *Salsa Rising*, 206.

122. Flores, *Salsa Rising*, 207.

123. Tito Puente Orchestra, Boris Rose recording of radio broadcast from Birdland, New York (1951).

124. *Latin Jazz*, dirs. Isabelle Leymarie and Karim Akadiri Soumaila.

125. Andy González, personal communication, September 19, 2013.

126. Christopher Washburne, "The Clave of Jazz: A Caribbean Contribution to the Rhythmic Foundation of an African-American Music," *Black Music Research Journal* 17, no. 1 (1997): 78.

127. Lee Morgan, Wynton Kelly, et al., *Dizzy Atmosphere* (Specialty 2110, 1957).

128. Lapidus, "*¡Toca maravilloso!*," 109–21; Benjamin Lapidus, "*Chinita Linda*: Portrayals of Chinese and Asian Identity and Culture by Chinese and non-Chinese in Spanish Caribbean Dance Music," in *Chinese America: History & Perspective, Journal of the Chinese Historical Society of America* (2015).

129. Loza, *Tito Puente and the Making of Latin Music*, 224.

130. Flores, *Salsa Rising*, 233.

CHAPTER 6

1. Alegre All-Stars, "Peanut Vendor," *El manicero: The Alegre All Stars Vol. 2* (Alegre Records LPA 834, 1964).

2. Lapidus, "*¡Toca maravilloso!*," 109–21.

3. Lapidus, "*Chinita Linda*," 17–28.

4. Grossinger's was one of the most celebrated of the Jewish resorts in the Catskills and was one of the last to close down.

5. Mark Schwartz, "Memories from the Days of the Mamboniks," 18, from liner notes to *It's a Scream How Levine Does The Rhumba: The Latin-Jewish Musical Story 1940s-1980s* (CD, Idelsohn Society RSR 021, 2013).

6. Lapidus, "*¡Toca maravilloso!*," 115.

7. Johnny Conquet, His Piano & Orchestra, *Raisins & Almonds Cha Cha Cha & Merengues* (RCA Victor LSP 1789, 1958).

8. Mark Schwartz, "Memories from the Days of the Mamboniks," 21.

9. Tamara Straus, "Re-creation of 'Mazel Tov, Mis Amigos,'" *San Francisco Gate*, August 26, 2010. http://www.sfgate.com/entertainment/article/Re-creation-of-Mazel-Tov-Mis-Amigos-3177182.php#photo-2313203. Retrieved December 12, 2017.

10. Justi Barretto, "*A Nueva York*," *Guaguanco '69* (Gema Records LPG 3072, 1969 [1976]).

11. "'Calypso Jazz?': Jazz Society Formed Here," *Virgin Islands Daily News*, April 23, 1963, 1. https://news.google.com/newspapers?nid=757&dat=19630423&id=rW1aAAAAIBAJ&sjid=dkc DAAAAIBAJ&pg=4517,1284479. Retrieved January 2, 2018.

12. Schwartz, "Memories from the Days of the Mamboniks," 16.

13. Aurora Flores, "Jewish-Latino," Latino Americans Blog. http://www.pbs.org/latino-amer icans/en/blog/2013/08/31/Jewish-Latino/. Retrieved January 2, 2018.

14. Schwartz, "Memories from the Days of the Mamboniks," 18.

15. James W. Vander Zanden, *American Minority Relations*, 3rd ed. (New York: Ronald Press, 1972), 198.

16. Vander Zanden, *American Minority Relations*, 218.

17. John D. Buenker and Lorman A. Ratner, eds., *Multiculturalism in the United States: A Comparative Guide to Acculturation and Ethnicity* (Westport, CT: Greenwood Press, 1992), 150–51.

18. Thomas Sowell, *Ethnic America: A History* (New York: Basic Books, 1981), 95.

19. Lex Gillespie, *The Mamboniks* (Malecón Films, 2018).

20. *Machito: A Latin Jazz Legacy*, dir. Carlos Ortiz.

21. *Machito: A Latin Jazz Legacy*, dir. Carlos Ortiz.

22. *Mambo Madness*, dir. Courtney Hafela (1955). https://youtu.be/05rLL8B9g1I. Retrieved July 21, 2019.

23. Schwartz, "Memories from the Days of the Mamboniks," 17.

24. "Dancing," *New York Post*, February 7, 1947, 40.

25. "Dancing," *New York Post*, February 14, 1947, 36.

26. "Dancing," *New York Post*, February 14, 1947, 36.

27. "Dancing," *New York Post*, February 14, 1947, 36.

28. "Dancing," *New York Post*, February 14, 1947, 36.

29. "Dancing," *New York Post*, February 14, 1947, 36.

30. "Dancing," *New York Post*, February 14, 1947, 36.

31. Dancing," *New York Post*, January 9, 1948, 47.

32. Dancing," *New York Post*, January 9, 1948, 47.

33. Dancing," *New York Post*, January 9, 1948, 47.

34. Dancing," *New York Post*, April 18, 1947, 48.

35. Dancing," *New York Post*, April 18, 1947, 48.

36. Dancing," *New York Post*, October 3, 1947, 50.

37. Dancing," *New York Post*, October 3, 1947, 50.

38. Dancing," *New York Post*, October 25, 1947, 19.

39. Dancing," *New York Post*, October 25, 1947, 19.

40. Dancing," *New York Post*, October 25, 1947, 19.

41. Dancing," *New York Post*, November 20, 1947. According to independent scholar Richard Blondet, Monchito was "an orchestra leader who emerges in 1935 and continued to adapt to all of the popular fad styling (rhumba, mambo, cha cha cha, pachanga) that would emerge over the years and identify himself with it. For many years, he was the house band at the Tavern on the Green. According to vocalist Frankie Figueroa, he ['Monchito'] was Puerto Rican." Richard Blondet, personal communication, January 5, 2018.

42. Richard Blondet, personal communication, January 5, 2018.

43. Richard Blondet, personal communication, January 5, 2018.

44. Richard Blondet, personal communication, January 5, 2018. According to Blondet, "the Chino and Dioris is in reference to Chino Pozo and Dioris Valladares. Both of whom were featured with Cugat."

45. "Dancing," *New York Post*, November 29, 1947, 19.

46. "Dancing," *New York Post*, December 27, 1947, 9.

47. "Dancing," *New York Post*, December 27, 1947, 9.

48. "Dancing," *New York Post*, December 27, 1947, 9.

49. "Dancing," *New York Post*, March 9, 1951, 74.

50. "Dancing," *New York Post*, March 9, 1951, 74.

51. "Dancing," *New York Post*, March 9, 1951, 74.

52. "Dancing," *New York Post*, March 9, 1951, 74.

53. "Dancing," *New York Post*, January 30, 1953, 45.

54. "Dancing," *New York Post*, February 6, 1953, 45.

55. "Dancing," *New York Post*, February 6, 1953, 45.

56. "Dancing," *New York Post*, February 6, 1953, 45.

57. Dancing," *New York Post*, February 8, 1953, 49.

58. "Dancing," *New York Post*, May 22, 1953, 57.

59. "Dancing," *New York Post*, May 22, 1953, 57.

60. "Dancing," *New York Post*, May 22, 1953, 57.

61. "Dancing," *New York Post*, November 6, 1953, 54.

62. "Dancing," *New York Post*, November 20, 1953, 5.

63. "Dancing," *New York Post*, April 4, 1958, 26.

64. "Dancing," *New York Post*, April 4, 1958, 26.

65. "Dancing," *New York Post*, December 9, 1960, 80.

66. "Dancing," *New York Post*, September 15, 1961, 72.

67. "Dancing," *New York Post*, September 15, 1961, 72.

68. "Xavier Cugat e Abbe Lane al 'Carosello.'" https://youtu.be/E2n0X-8FaLY. Retrieved December 5, 2017.

69. "Dr. Gail Gross Interviews Abbe Lane." https://www.youtube.com/watch?v=Jm-Yo9UF05A. Retrieved January 4, 2018.

70. Edgar S. Van Olinda, "'Round Town," October 30, 1949, *Times Union*, Albany, NY.

71. "Cugat and Singer, 18, Plan to Wed in Summer," *Knickerbocker News*, Albany, NY, May 4, 1950, 44.

72. *Buffalo Evening News*, August 18, 1950, 9; the same story also ran in the *Brooklyn Eagle*, Friday August 18, 1950, 7.

73. Earl Wilson, "It Happened Last Night: Cugat Finds Rumba Dying, Likewise His Old Romance," *New York Post*, May 23, 1950, 17.

74. Wilson, "It Happened Last Night: Cugat Finds Rumba Dying, Likewise His Old Romance."

75. Earl Wilson, "It Happened Last Night: Saluting Jack Carter, The Copa's Newest Hit," *New York Post*, November 23, 1951, 17.

76. December 8, 1950, *New York Post*, 70.

77. "Ahavath Israel Ball Attracts Thousands to Auditorium Thanksgiving Eve," *Kingston Daily Freeman*, Kingston, NY, November 23, 1951, 11.

78. Jay Breen, "Cugat Jealous of Barcelona Bullfighter As He, Abbe Plan Honeymoon in Spain," *Binghamton Press*, November 29, 1951, 28.

79. "Songstress Denies Mrs. Cugat, Raiders Found Her Unclad," *Buffalo Evening News*, January 24, 1951, 58.

80. "Baby it's Warm inside the Roxy," *New York Post*, November 11, 1951, 18.

81. "Abbe Lane to See Photographs," *Binghamton Press*, January 31, 1951, 24.

82. "Abbe Lane's Furs Stolen," *Buffalo Evening News*, September 4, 1951.

83. Rex Lardner, "Lo Introducion Avec Cugat," *New York Post*, June 18, 1951, 16.

84. "Cugats Settle Divorce Claims; Abbe Lane to Drop Suit," *Brooklyn Eagle*, January 22, 1952, 7.

85. "Cugat, Abbe Lane, Wed, Start on Honeymoon," *Buffalo Evening News*, May 6, 1952, 30.

86. Walter Winchell, "Mrs. J. Nunan Rich in her own Right," *Times Union*, 1952?.

87. "Casablanca Hotel Open All Summer," *Philadelphia Enquirer*, June 1, 1952, B19.

88. "Xavier Cugat's Latin Music Sets Buffalo Dancing Rhumba," *Buffalo Evening News*, September 24, 1952, Section V 71.

89. Xavier Cugat and his Orchestra, "Wedding Samba" (78rpm, Columbia CO 42806, 1951).

90. Xavier Cugat and his Orchestra, *Xavier Cugat Today!* (Decca 4851, 1967).

91. Xavier Cugat and his Orchestra, *Dancetime with Cugat* (RCA Victor LPM-3170, 1953).

92. James Bacon, "Is Abbe Rita's Successor? Parallels Between Them Are Numerous," *Sunday Press*, Binghamton, NY, November 1, 1953, 12C.

93. "Cugat to Play at Roseland," *New York Post*, May 17, 1953, 27.

94. "Abbe Lane on Stage at N.Y. Paramount," *Brooklyn Eagle*, May 13, 1953, 11.

95. Bob Thomas, "Band Leader Strikes 'Gold': Cugat's Shimmy Tunes Give Shakes to Orient," *Binghamton Press*, May 4, 1953, 22.

96. Thomas, "Band Leader Strikes 'Gold.'"

97. Harold Heffernan, "Abbe, Xavier Cugat Buy Pretentious Home," *Long Island Star-Journal*, August 22, 1953, 10.

98. "Abbe Lane's Career Takes Many Turns," *Buffalo Courier-Express*, September 13, 1953, 23C.

99. Aline Mosby, "Singer to Drop Sweet Roles for Siren Type," *News of the Tonawandas*, Tonawanda, NY, June 28, 1954, 12.

100. "Cugat, Wife Lose $20,000 in Cash, Jewelry to Thug," *Niagara Falls Gazette*, January 21, 1954, 27.

101. "Ole for Brooklyn Girl: Abbe Lane Dances Latin Way," *Brooklyn Eagle*, January 16, 1955, 31.

102. Louise Boyka, "Brazil Jungle Scene In Color Film Feature," *Schenectady Gazette*, April 7, 1955, 26.

103. Earl Wilson, "It Happened Last Night: Mambo Doesn't Love Papa Who Needs More Lessons," *New York Post*, March 15, 1955, 17.

104. Burton Rascoe, "Radio and Television: Cugat and Abbe Go Big in Rome," *Long Island Star-Journal*, January 28, 1956, 19.

105. John Lester, "5 Marx Brothers Cast in Show," *Long Island Star-Journal*, February 18, 1957, 17.

106. Louella O. Parsons, "Career Keeps Abbe Lane Busy," *Times-Union*, March 17, 1957, B-8.

107. "Xavier Cugat—Abbe Lane nel film 'Donatella'" (1956). https://youtu.be/X8gYH3b9Cpk. Retrieved July 22, 2019.

108. Steven H. Scheuer, "Cugat, Abbe Lane Show On Way," *Citizen Register* (Ossining, NY), February 26, 1957, 11.

109. "Abbe Lane - Me lo dijo Adela - Susana y yo - (1957)." https://youtu.be/5JdZW_LpUEY. Retrieved July 22, 2019.

110. Bob Thomas, "Back After 2 Years: Hollywood Finally Ready for Abbe," *Binghamton Press*, November 20, 1957, 40.

111. Thomas, "Back After 2 Years: Hollywood Finally Ready for Abbe."

112. "Benefit on Feb. 7 to Assist School: Performance of 'Captain's Paradise' Will Augment Steiner Scholarships," *New York Times*, December 1, 1957, 109. One performance of the show served as a fundraiser for scholarships at the Rudolf Steiner School.

113. Walter Winchell, "Abbe Lane Quits 'Oh, Captain'; She Needs Money," *Buffalo Courier Express*, July 9, 1958, 12.

114. "Xavier Cugat and His Wife, Abbe Lane, Sign to Replace Eddie Fisher on N.B.C.," *New York Times*, January 25, 1957, 45.

115. Ben Gross, "Cugat and Abbe Lane Praised on Debut," *Buffalo Evening News*, February 28, 1957, 36.

116. Hal Boyle, "The Poor Man's Philosopher: Busy Abbe Lane," *Leader-Herald*, Gloversville and Johnstown, NY, April 10, 1958, 4.

117. "What's My Line? - Xavier Cugat & Abbe Lane; Edward Mulhare" (January 26, 1958). https://youtu.be/N1OHqjM4BS8. Retrieved July 22, 2019.

118. Loza, *Tito Puente*, 168.

119. Xavier Cugat and his Orchestra, *Latin for Lovers* (RCA Camden CAL-516, 1959).

120. "Abbe Lane, Cugat to Head Appeal's Kick-Off Parade," *Evans Journal*, Angola, NY, 3.

121. Burt Bacharach, "Stag Lines: The News Column for Men," *Buffalo Evening News*, January 8, 1958, 23.

122. "Abbe Lane Fine Miami Shop" *Philadelphia Enquirer*, May 17, 1959, 8.

123. Lydia Lane, "Hollywood Beauty: Jan's Looks All Her Own But Hard to Acquire," *Times-Union*, May 17, 1959, F-5.

124. *Abbe Lane with Xavier Cugat and his Orchestra* (Mercury MG 20643, 1961).

125. Euguene Archer, "Abbe Lane is Star of Films Abroad: U.S. Singer Has Appeared in Italian-Language Movies," *New York Times*, December 27, 1961, 20.

126. "Xavier Cugat - Abbe Lane a 'Il signore delle 21'" (1962). https://youtu.be/RMxY5RNUi1M. Retrieved July 22, 2019. Lane sings a chachachá version of "Malagueña salerosa" in part 2 of the video. https://youtu.be/IYxoBzLnXCw.

127. "Abbe Lane Wins Divorce," *New York Times*, June 4, 1964, 28.

128. "Cugat Sues a Dance Team for Million Over Abbe Lane," *New York Times*, June 26, 1964, 35.

129. "Perry Leff to Wed Abbe Lane," *New York Times*, November 11, 1964, 38.

130. "Perry Leff Weds Abbe Lane," *New York Times*, December 17, 1964, 48.

131. "What's My Line? - Abbe Lane; PANEL: Steve Allen, Aliza Kashi (Jan 15, 1967)." https://youtu.be/zEIbG2hG7Xg. Retrieved July 22, 2019.

132. "Abbe Lane Book Tells of Her Life With Xavier Cugat," *Orlando Sentinel*, March 11, 1993. Retrieved January 2, 2018.

133. "Abbe Lane Book Tells of Her Life With Xavier Cugat."

134. "Abbe Lane Book Tells of Her Life With Xavier Cugat."

135. "Abbe Lane Book Tells of Her Life With Xavier Cugat."

136. Abbe Lane, *But Where Is Love?* (New York: Warner/Dove Books, 1993), 94.

137. "Dr. Gail Gross Interviews Abbe Lane."

138. "Abbe Lane en Aplauso, Chile (UC-TV, 1980)," YouTube. https://youtu.be/xH5rWB9TTT8. Retrieved December 5, 2017.

139. "Superdoll_Collectables "The Immortalisation of Abbe Lane" - 25 Maggio 2012," YouTube. https://youtu.be/LtzsL9KtRq8. Retrieved December 5, 2017.

140. "Abbe Lane—Hollywood Star Walk," *Los Angeles Times*. http://projects.latimes.com/hollywood/star-walk/abbe-lane/. Retrieved January 4, 2018.

141. Anita Gates, "Eydie Gorme, Voice of Sophisticated Pop, Dies at 84," *New York Times*, August 11, 2013. http://www.nytimes.com/2013/08/12/arts/music/eydie-gorme-blame-it-on-the-bossa-nova-singer-dies-at-84.html. Retrieved January 2, 2018.

142. Gwen Nefsky Frankfeldt, "Eydie Gorme: 1928–2013," Jewish Womens's Archive Encyclopedia. https://jwa.org/encyclopedia/article/gorme-edye. Retrieved January 2, 2018.

143. Gates, "Eydie Gorme, Voice of Sophisticated Pop, Dies at 84."

144. Gates, "Eydie Gorme, Voice of Sophisticated Pop, Dies at 84."

145. Gates, "Eydie Gorme, Voice of Sophisticated Pop, Dies at 84." One November 4, 1955, recording of Gorme's Voice of America broadcast includes performances of "Besame mucho" and "Come Home": http://www.worldcat.org/title/interview-with-eydie-gorme-1955/oclc/174970577. Retrieved January 2, 2018.

146. Robert Strauss, "Together Wherever They Go," *Los Angeles Times*, April 14, 1996. http://articles.latimes.com/1996-04-14/entertainment/ca-58268_1_steve-lawrence-and-eydie-gorme. Retrieved January 4, 2018.

147. Eydie Gorme, "The Voice of Broadway: Men in Her Life Are Important," *Knickerbocker News*, October 15, 1957, 8A.

148. "Eydie Gorme, TV Singer, Wed in Vegas," *Schenectady Gazette*, December 30, 1957, 16.

149. Saul Petit, "Gormé, Lawrence, to Start own Show Today," *Niagara Falls Gazette*, July 13, 1958, T-13.

150. Dick Kleiner, "Steve and Eydie Gorme Map Program to Replace Steve Allen from Lofty Penthouse," *Utica Observer Dispatch*, July 12, 1958, 3A.

151. Frankfeldt, "Eydie Gorme: 1928–2013."

152. Eydie Gorme, *I Feel So Spanish* (United Artists 6152, 1961).

153. Eydie Gorme, *Blame it on the Bossa Nova* (Columbia CS 8812, 1962).

154. Linda Norris, "Let's Look at the Records," October 29, 1964, [EydieGorme16].

155. Gates, "Eydie Gorme, Voice of Sophisticated Pop, Dies at 84."

156. Sonari Glinton, "Remembrances: Remembering Eydie Gorme, A Vegas Singer Without the Drama," December 29, 2013. https://www.npr.org/2013/12/29/258166712/remembering-eydie-gorme-a-vegas-singer-without-the-drama. Retrieved January 2, 2017.

157. "Abbe Lane—Hollywood Star Walk," *Los Angeles Times*. http://projects.latimes.com/hollywood/star-walk/abbe-lane/. Retrieved January 4, 2018.

158. Sherrie Tucker, *Swing Shift: "All-Girl" Bands of the 1940s* (Durham, NC: Duke University Press, 2000), 6.

159. Linda Dahl, *Stormy Weather: The Music and Lives of a Century of Jazzwomen* (New York: Pantheon, 1984), 98.

160. Dahl, *Stormy Weather*, 7.

161. Abbe Lane & Orq Xavier Cugat, "Eso es el amor," Serata di gala (1959). https://www.youtube.com/watch?v=Lfff9T3vFUU. Retrieved January 5, 2018.

162. "Dr. Gail Gross Interviews Abbe Lane."

163. David Carp, "Salsa Symbiosis: Eddie Palmieri's Chief Collaborator in the Making of La Perfecta," *Centro Journal* XVI, no. 2 (2004): 55.

164. Carp, "Salsa Symbiosis," 56.

165. Carp, "Salsa Symbiosis," 56.

166. Carp, "Salsa Symbiosis," 45.

167. David Carp, "Barry Rogers, Salsero, Searcher, World Musician." https://web.archive.org/web/20070225130918/http://www.descarga.com:80/cgi-bin/db/archives/Profile42?Lh8einfm;;115. Retrieved June 1, 2017. This unsolicited memory of Barry Rogers was also shared with me by his friend and collaborator Eddy Zervigón. Interestingly, my grandfather and his brothers had a gas station, scrap yard, and fixed cars for a living and my cousins were car crazy, fixing and repairing cars all the time.

168. Hans Koert, "Jimmy Wormworth: The 1957 American Jazz Quintet in Holland," Keep (It) Swinging (blog), June 6, 2011. http://keepswinging.blogspot.com/2011/06/jimmy-wormworth-1957-american-jazz.html. Retrieved June 1, 2017. Flores 2016 also agrees with the influence of Kai and J.J.

169. Carp, "Barry Rogers."

170. Carp, "Salsa Symbiosis," 50.

171. Carp, "Salsa Symbiosis," 54.

172. David Carp, "Barry Rogers."

173. David Carp, "Salsa Symbiosis," 58.

174. Carp, "Salsa Symbiosis," 58.

175. David Carp, "Barry Rogers."

176. David Carp, "Barry Rogers."

177. David Carp, "Barry Rogers."

178. David Carp, "Barry Rogers."

179. L. K. Steiner, Facebook/personal communication, May 3, 2017.

180. An earlier version of portions of this section appear in my essay "¡Toca *maravilloso!*"

181. Larry Harlow, interview, December 7, 1996.

182. See Peter Manuel's technical analysis of Harlow's piano improvisation and a discussion of how it is emblematic of the Latin piano style of Arsenio Rodríguez, "Improvisation in Latin Dance Music," 140–42.

183. José Tapia and Izzy Sanabria, "Larry Harlow: Jewish Salsero Numero Uno," *Latin NY* (February 1978): 22.

184. The author performed in both concerts.

185. Benjamin Lapidus, "Larry Harlow" essay, in booklet accompanying *Larry Harlow, Live in Quad* (CD, [Fania 1974] Emusica 130153, 2006).

186. Larry Harlow, *Yo soy latino* (Fania 607, 1982).

187. Larry Harlow, *Salsa* (Fania 460, 1974).

188. Larry Harlow, interview, December 7, 1996. Migene González-Wippler profiled the community of Jewish Santería devotees in "Santeria Experience," a monthly column she wrote in *Latin NY* magazine. Wippler described the comfort and ease with which Jewish santeros participated in ceremonies and ritual meals that she attended in Manhattan and that "there was no discernable difference in their behavior and actions from those of Latin santeros." She also pointed out the similarity between kosher butchering and *kapporot* (Jewish ritual practiced on the eve of Yom Kippur) and animal sacrifice. Migene González-Wippler, "Jews in Santeria," *Latin NY* (April 1984): 48–49.

189. Tapia and Sanabria, "Larry Harlow," 22.

190. Ira Goldwasser, interview, New York, August 5, 2013. Information and quotations in this section are from this interview unless otherwise indicated.

191. Caesar had spent many summers in the Catskills, which he considered to be his "college" education. "Sid Caesar on performing in the Catskills - Emmytvlegends.org," YouTube. https://www.youtube.com/watch?v=kYdV3kVJY2Q. Retrieved January 2, 2018.

192. Ira Goldwasser, interview, New York, August 5, 2013.

193. Ira Goldwasser, interview, New York, August 5, 2013.

194. For more information on this important bandleader, see "de Los Reyes, Emilio (Pedro Betancourt 1920-New York 1987," Montuno Cubano. http://www.montunocubano.com/Tumbao/biographies/reyes,%20de%20los,%20emilio.%20Engl.html. Retrieved January 2, 2018.

195. "Young People's Concert: "The Latin American Spirit" / Bernstein New York Philharmonic," YouTube. https://youtu.be/ItoubZWf9No. Retrieved January 2, 2018.

196. *West Side Story—Making of a Classic*, dir. Ursula McFarlane (BBC, 2016) (14:55). https://youtu.be/3XAoZdVGGrM. Retrieved January 2, 2018.

197. *West Side Story—Making of a Classic* (26:00).

198. Bobby Sanabria, "Reimagining West Side Story," NiLP Guest Commentary, March 19, 2018. https://www.nyrealestatelawblog.com/manhattan-litigation-blog/2018/march/reimagining-west-side-story/. Retrieved July 18, 2019.

199. Camilla Fojas, *Islands of Empire: Pop Culture and U.S. Power* (Austin: University of Texas Press, 2014), 138–39.

200. Laura Briggs, *Reproducing Empire: Race, Sex, Science, and U.S. Imperialism in Puerto Rico* (Berkeley: University of California Press, 2002), 174.

201. Julia Foulkes, *A Place for Us: "West Side Story" and New York* (Chicago: University of Chicago Press, 2016), 83.

202. Alex W. Maldonado, *Teodoro Moscoso and Puerto Rico's Operation Bootstrap* (Gainesville: University Press of Florida, 1997).

203. La Lupe, *They Call Me La Lupe/A mi me llaman La Lupe* (Tico Records 1144, 1966). https://youtu.be/M65chP41-fo. Retrieved July 17, 2019.

204. *¡Ay que bonito es América, todos los cubanos en America, Somos felices en America, no nos movemos de America!*

CHAPTER 7

1. Nancy Raquel Mirabal, "Scripting Race, Finding Place: African-Americans, Afro-Cubans and the Diasporic Imaginary in the United States," in *Neither Enemies nor Friends: Latinos, Blacks, Afro-Latinos*, edited by Anani Dzidzienyo and Suzanne Oboler (New York: Palgrave Macmillan, 2005), 189–207.

2. Mirabal, "Scripting Race, Finding Place," 198.

3. Mirabal, "Scripting Race, Finding Place," 203.

4. Evelio Grillo, "Black Cuban, Black American," in *The Afro-Latin@ Reader: History and Culture in the United States*, eds. Miriam Jiménez Román and Juan Flores (Durham, NC: Duke University Press, 2010), 99–112.

5. Ramón Grosfoguel and Chloé S. Georas, "Latino Caribbean Diasporas in New York," in *Mambo Montage: The Latinization of New York City*, eds. Agustín Laó-Montes and Arlene Dávila (New York: Columbia University Press, 2001), 113–14.

6. Robin D. Moore, *Music and Revolution: Cultural Change in Socialist Cuba* (Berkeley: University of California Press, 2006), 38.

7. Moore, *Music and Revolution*, 78.

8. Moore, *Music and Revolution*, 81. Moore is correct in his comparison, but he does not take into consideration Cuba's physical and population size advantage when making this comparison.

9. Moore, *Music and Revolution*, 94.

10. Moore, *Music and Revolution*, 175.

11. Moore, *Music and Revolution*, 85. A similar movement could be seen in other Marxist countries such as China with teahouse music.

12. Moore, *Music and Revolution*, 176.

13. Moore, *Music and Revolution*, 185.

14. Moore, *Music and Revolution*, 104.

15. Román Orozco and Natalia Bolívar, *Cubasanta: Comunistas, santeros y cristianos en la isla de Fidel Castro* (Madrid: Ediciones El Pais, 1998), 392.

16. Boris González Arenas, "Si no tengo algo por lo que estar luchando, la vida pierde sentido," *Diario de Cuba*, July 19, 2017. http://www.diariodecuba.com/cuba/1500465299_32645.html. Retrieved June 19, 2019.

17. Moore, *Music and Revolution*, 204.

18. Moore, *Music and Revolution*, 213.

19. Orozco and Bolívar, *Cubasanta*, 352–55.

20. Orozco and Bolívar, *Cubasanta*, 368–70.

21. Orozco and Bolívar, *Cubasanta*, 371–72.

22. Rogelio Martínez Furé, "Dialogo Imaginario sobre Folklore," 286. [Originally in *La Gaceta de Cuba* 121 (March 1974): 12–17]. http://iihaa.usac.edu.gt/archivohemerografico/wp-content/uploads/2017/09/06_estudios_1975_martinez.pdf. Retrieved June 20, 2019.

23. Furé, "Dialogo Imaginario sobre Folklore," 287.

24. Furé, "Dialogo Imaginario sobre Folklore," 293.

25. Nora Rodríguez Calzadilla, "En el aniversario 45 del Conjunto Folclórico Universitario," *Radio Enciclopedia*, September 28, 2015. http://www.radioenciclopedia.cu/noticias/en-aniversario-45-conjunto-folclorico-universitario-20150928/. Retrieved June 18, 2019.

26. Román Díaz, personal communication, June 19, 2019. The group was founded by the grandparents of the noted dancer and teacher Freila Merencio.

27. Román Díaz, personal communication, February 10, 2019.

28. Román Díaz, personal communication, February 10, 2019.

29. Román Díaz, personal communication. June 20, 2019.

30. Román Díaz, personal communication. June 20, 2019.

31. Los Karachi, *Meteoros Del Caribe* (Siboney LD 241, 1982).

32. Moore, *Music and Revolution*, 90.

33. Ojito, *Finding Mañana*, 54, 62.

34. "Castro Describes Economic Failure," *New York Times*, July 27, 1970, 1. https://www.nytimes.com/1970/07/27/archives/castro-describes-economic-failure-premier-offers-to-resign-in.html. Retrieved July 18, 2019; Yusimi Rodríguez, "Ten Million and Forty Years Later," *Havana Times*, August 16, 2010. https://havanatimes.org/opinion/ten-million-and-forty-years-later/. Retrieved

July 18, 2019; "Azucar para crecer: The Sugar to Grow a Ten Million Ton Harvest," *Clandestina*, February 27, 2018. https://clandestina.co/blogs/clandestina-is-something-else/the-sugar-to-grow -a-ten-million-ton-harvest. Retrieved July 18, 2019.

35. María Teresa Vélez, *Drumming for the Gods: The Life and Times of Felipe García Villamil, Santero, Palero, and Abakuá* (Philadelphia: Temple University Press, 2000), 108–9.

36. Vélez, *Drumming for the Gods*, 139.

37. Vélez, *Drumming for the Gods*, 182. Interestingly, there were people, including musicians, who wanted to leave yet who upon asking were denied for exit permits.

38. Vélez, *Drumming for the Gods*, 212. Individuals with a wide array of mental health issues were also included.

39. Paquito D'Rivera, *My Sax Life* (Chicago: Northwestern University Press, 2005), 267–68.

40. Ojito, *Finding Mañana*, 240.

41. James S. Olson and Judith E. Olson, *Cuban Americans: From Trauma to Triumph* (New York: Twayne/Simon and Schuster Macmillan, 1995), 90.

42. Olson, 90.

43. Ojito, *Finding Mañana*, 258.

44. Olson, *Cuban Americans*, 90.

45. Olson, *Cuban Americans*, 90.

46. Olson, *Cuban Americans*, 91.

47. Olson, *Cuban Americans*, 84.

48. Olson, *Cuban Americans*, 94

49. Abreu, *Cuban Musicians*, 59.

50. Abreu, *Cuban Musicians*, 81.

51. Marta Moreno Vega, "The Yoruba Orisha Tradition Comes to New York City," in *The Afro-Latin@ Reader: History and Culture in the United States*, eds. Miriam Jiménez Román and Juan Flores (Durham, NC: Duke University Press, 2010), 248.

52. Vega, "The Yoruba Orisha Tradition Comes to New York City," 248.

53. Vélez, *Drumming for the Gods*, 79. This group received official support from the Consejo Nacional de Cultura.

54. Vélez, *Drumming for the Gods*, 78–108.

55. Michael Reyes, personal communication, February 8, 2018.

56. Carlos Flores, Facebook post, March 6, 2013.

57. Vélez, *Drumming for the Gods*, 112–15.

58. Vega, "The Yoruba Orisha Tradition," 248.

59. Katherine Dunham, "The Yoruba Tradition Comes to new York City," *Kaiso!: Writings by and about Katherine Dunham* (Madison: University of Wisconsin Press, 2005), 608. According to Felix Sanabria, There was a *tambor de fundamento* in New York in 1976 that had come to NYC via Puerto Rico.

60. See Vélez, *Drumming for the Gods*, 126–27, for Felipe García Villamil's description of this process and the rituals.

61. Vélez, *Drumming for the Gods*, 126–27q.

62. Vélez, *Drumming for the Gods*, 136.

63. Vélez, *Drumming for the Gods*, 142.

64. Vélez, *Drumming for the Gods*, 142–43, 151.

65. Vélez, *Drumming for the Gods*, 109.

66. "Fallece el conocido percusionista Orlando 'Puntilla' Ríos," *Cubaencuentro*, August 14, 2008. https://www.cubaencuentro.com/cultura/noticias/fallece-el-conocido-percusionista-orlando -puntilla-rios-103846. Retrieved February 21, 2018.

67. *Rumba Clave Blen Blen Blen*, dir. Arístedes Falcón Paradí (DVD, Paradí Productions, 2013).

68. *Rumba Clave Blen Blen Blen*.

69. *Rumba Clave Blen Blen Blen*.

70. Gillespie, *To Be or Not to Bop*, 319.

71. "*Ningún viaje eso fue jamoneta, porque los barcos que eran para 32 personas e metidas 200. No puede ser hamoneta, la gente caendose. Por ejemplo yo vine en uno de esos barcos, eran 18, metieron 130. Se caerón dos chiquitas por el agua.*" *Rumba Clave Blen Blen Blen*.

72. Sanabria, personal communication, May 2, 2014.

73. *Patato and Totico* (Verve Records V5037, 1967). Patato was an important drummer in Cuba and carried his fame with him to New York City when he arrived early in the 1950s. He can be seen teaching Brigitte Bardot how to dance mambo in the 1956 film *And God Created Woman*. https://www.youtube.com/watch?v=gaFTmZ4zQCU. Retrieved March 7, 2018.

74. Vélez, *Drumming for the Gods*, 147.

75. Vélez, *Drumming for the Gods*, 147. See also "Willie Ramos: A history of ritual oricha music in the United States - The Bearers of Sacred Sound," YouTube. https://youtu.be/1NaPDHcn87k. Retrieved April 28, 2020.

76. Felix Sanabria, personal communication, February 7, 2018.

77. Felix Sanabria, personal communication, February 7, 2018.

78. Felix Sanabria, personal communication, February 7, 2018.

79. *Puntilla le da una proyección abierta a batá, a través de su mecánica con la clave. Que eso se puede comunicar hacia ambos lados, o un solo lado. Tan es así que por resultado entonces se dió el trabajo de Nu Yor-Uba, el trabajo de Michelle [Rosewoman].* Felix Sanabria, personal communication, February 7, 2018.

80. Felix Sanabria, personal communication, February 7, 2018.

81. Felix Sanabria. personal communication, February 20, 2018. Sanabria, Borrell, and Puntilla can also be seen in *Latin Jazz*, Isabelle Leymarie's documentary from this time period.

82. "Juan 'El Negro' Raymat," The Bearers of Sacred Sound. http://thebearersofsacredsound .weebly.com/juan_el_negro_raymat.html. Part 2. Retrieved February 21, 2018.

83. Vicky Jassey, "Crossing the Seas: A Brief Historic Overview: Introduction." http://thebear ersofsacredsound.weebly.com/history.html. Retrieved February 21, 2018.

84. Puntilla, *From La Habana to New York* (Puntilla Folkloric Records AF-101, 1983); *Totico y Sus Rumberos* (Montuno Records MLP-515, 1981).

85. Lisa Maya Knauer, "Audiovisual Remittances and Transnational Subjectivities," in *Cuba in the Special Period: Culture and Ideology in the 1990s*, ed. Ariana Hernandez-Reguant (New York: Palgrave Macmillan, 2009), 161.

86. Kenneth Schweitzer, "The Cuban Aña Fraternity: Strategies for Cohesion," *The Yoruba God of Drumming: Transatlantic Perspectives on the Wood That Talks*, ed. Amanda Villepastour (Jackson: University Press of Mississippi, 2015), 171–91.

87. Orlando "Puntilla" Ríos y El Conjunto Todo Rumbero, *A Tribute to Gónzalo Acensio Tío Tom 1919–1991* (CD, Smithsonian Folkways 40543, 2008).

88. René López, interview by Nando Alvaricci, August 17, 2008. WBAI 99.5 FM.

89. René López, interview by Nando Alvaricci.

90. Johnny Frías, "Review: Rumba clave blen blen blen," *Latin American Music Review/Revista De Música Latinoamericana* 36, no. 1 (2015): 124–25.

91. Gabriel Machado, "Gabriel Machado 'Chinchilita' (Timbal-Conga-Bongo)." n.d.

92. Moore, *Music and Revolution*, 91.

93. Gabriel "Chinchilita" Machado, interview by author, New York, NY, July 17, 2013.

94. "*Yo soy un Marielito, muy orgulloso de ser Marielito. Casualmente, me conectó la misma persona que conectó a Chano Pozo con Dizzy Gillespie, un músico cubano llamado Mario Bauzá.*" Berroa

is fluent in both jazz and Cuban secular music and can be seen demonstrating the simultaneous execution of jazz and rumba on the drum set in the documentary *Rumba Clave Blen Blen Blen*.

95. Gabriel "Chinchilita" Machado, interview by author, New York, July 17, 2013.

96. Ian Michael James, *Ninety Miles: Cuban Journeys in the Age of Castro* (Lanham, MD: Rowman and Littlefield, 2006), 17–18.

97. D'Rivera, *My Sax Life*, 23.

98. D'Rivera, *My Sax Life*, 66. D'Rivera remembered that Celia Cruz and the entirety of La Sonora Matancera decided not to return to Cuba at that time.

99. D'Rivera, *My Sax Life*, 101–2.

100. James, *Ninety Miles*, 28.

101. James, *Ninety Miles*, 34.

102. D'Rivera, *My Sax Life*, 130.

103. D'Rivera, *My Sax Life*, 133.

104. D'Rivera, *My Sax Life*, 138.

105. D'Rivera, *My Sax Life*, 243–44.

106. D'Rivera, *My Sax Life*, 69.

107. David Amram, *Havana New York*. Flying Fish Records 70057. 1978).

108. Amram, *Havana New York*.

109. Paquito D'Rivera, personal communication, Feb. 6, 2014.

110. Video of one performance on March 23, 1979 - recorded live at the Capitol Theatre in Passaic, New Jersey can be seen at: https://www.youtube.com/watch?v=VapQAWxEGzo. Retrieved March 7, 2018.

111. D'Rivera, personal communication, Feb. 6, 2014.

112. D'Rivera, *My Sax Life*, 245.

113. James, *Ninety Miles*, 80.

114. James, *Ninety Miles*, 85–86.

115. D'Rivera, *My Sax Life*, 281.

116. D'Rivera, *My Sax Life*, 88.

117. D'Rivera, *My Sax Life*, 276.

118. James, *Ninety Miles*, 93.

119. James, *Ninety Miles*, 95.

120. James, *Ninety Miles*, 126.

121. Paquito D'Rivera, personal communication, Feb. 6, 2014.

122. Ángel Pérez unfortunately was involved in a drug-related crime that started on Delancey Street and was gunned down on the Brooklyn Bridge. The passenger in the car was paralyzed.

123. D'Rivera, personal communication, Feb. 6, 2014.

124. *Cachao . . . Como Su Ritmo No Hay Dos*, dir. Andy García (Epic Music Video, 1993).

125. D'Rivera, personal communication, February 6, 2014.

126. D'Rivera, personal communication, February 6, 2014.

127. James, *Ninety Miles*, 95.

128. D'Rivera, *My Sax Life*, 262.

129. Juan Ángel González, personal communication, April 27, 2020.

130. "Linda Leida Álvarez," Sonora Matancera. http://sonoramatancera.com/linda-leida-alvarez.html. Retrieved February 6, 2018.

131. Tomas Peña, "Soundscape, The Latin Side: In Conversation with Founder, Verna Gillis," *JazzDeLaPena*, February 20, 2018. https://jazzdelapena.com/interviews/from-the-jdp-archives-soundscape-the-latin-side/. Retrieved July 18, 2019.

132. Featured musicians included Bill Laswell, Sun Ra, the Frank Lowe Quintet, Odean Pope, Peter Brötzman, Ed Blackwell and Charles Brackeen, Don Cherry, Arthur Rhames Trio, Ed

Blackwell and Dewey Redman, Marion Brown, Derek Bailey and George Lewis, Huss and Denis Charles. Another Soundscape recording featured Muhal Richard Abrams, Barry Harris, Anthony Davis, and Mal Waldron playing Thelonius Monk's music.

133. As of this writing, the Soundscape Archives are slated to be housed at the Jazz History Database at Worcester Polytechnic Institue http://www.jazzhistorydatabase.com/index.php. Retrieved April 26, 2020.

134. "Soundscape," WKCR. https://www.cc-seas.columbia.edu/wkcr/soundscape/project. Retrieved February 5, 2018.

135. Tomas Peña, "Soundscape, The Latin Side: In Conversation with Founder, Verna Gillis," *JazzDeLaPena*, February 20, 2018. https://jazzdelapena.com/interviews/from-the-jdp-archives -soundscape-the-latin-side/. Retrieved July 18, 2019.

136. Ed Morales, "Places in the Puerto Rican Heart, Eddie Figueroa, and the Nuyorican Imaginary."

137. Tomas Peña, "Soundscape, The Latin Side."

138. Tomas Peña, "Soundscape, The Latin Side."

139. Tomas Peña, "Soundscape, The Latin Side."

140. These included Mitch Frohman & The New York Salsa/Jazz All Stars, Yomo Toro, Tito Puente, and Son De Cuba Forever. The full personnel included Louis Bauzó (bongó), Ignacio Berroa (drumset), Ray Cruz (timbales), Paquito D'Rivera (alto saxophone), Jorge Dalto (piano), Ruben Figueroa (bass), Andy González (bass), Jerry González (trumpet), Reynaldo Jorge (trombone), Louis Kahn (trombone), José Madera (piano), Joe Mannozzi (piano), Nicky Marrero (bongó), Bobby Porcelli (alto saxophone), Tito Puente (marimba and timbales), Mario Rivera (flute and saxophone), Claudio Roditi (trumpet), Dalia Silva (vocals), Orlando Silva (drums), Yomo Toro (cuatro), Victor Venegas (bass), and Chembo Corniel (congas), among others.

141. *Latin Jazz*, dirs. Isabelle Leymarie and Karim Akadiri Soumaila.

142. Liner notes for Daniel Ponce, *New York Is Now*. "*Antes de todo quiero aclarar que yo he llegado el día primero de mayo de 1980 5 m. por la puerta de Key West. Es decir que yo vine via Mariel, o sea, yo soy Marielito . . . Un beso para toda mi familia en Cuba en especial para mi hijo Michael Ponce Landa, ausente pero en mi.*"

143. Liner notes for Daniel Ponce, *New York Is Now*.

144. "STORIES Park' N Lots with Quique Aviles & Francisco Rigores." https://youtu.be/5WsSkn_ VXCo. Retrieved November 20, 2019.

145. Cubanakán, *Cubanakán* (Futuro Records NR15601, 1982).

146. David Font-Navarrete, personal communication, November 19, 2019.

147. Ogduardo "Román" Díaz, personal communication, March 7, 2018.

148. Ogduardo "Román" Díaz, personal communication, November 12, 2019.

149. *El Cancionero Rumbero* (blog). http://cancionerorumbero.blogspot.com/2009/12/invasion -del-80.html. Retrieved February 8, 2018.

150. Ogduardo "Román" Díaz, personal communication, November 12, 2019. Translation by Lázaro Pedroso and Christiane Hayashi.

151. Puntilla and Ponce can be seen performing together at the Black and White In Color Gallery in 1990: "Orlando Puntilla/ Daniel Ponce y su Rumbata: Full Video." https://www.youtube .com/watch?v=l3la726U7lg. Retrieved March 7, 2018.

152. *Latin Jazz*, dirs. Isabelle Leymarie and Karim Akadiri Soumaila.

153. *Latin Jazz*, dirs. Isabelle Leymarie and Karim Akadiri Soumaila. Sanabria also remembered the lead vocalist on "Invasión de 80" as a Marielito named Eloy.

154. *Al compas de Cuba*, dir. Mario Gallo (1960). https://youtu.be/QuI_aiDacRo. Retrieved February 8, 2018. The author met Dreke around 2000 and he was still in incredible shape.

155. "Video 1 Los Afortunados 2." https://youtu.be/1xkjc6eufwY. Retrieved February 20, 2018.

156. Bio, RobertoBorrell.com. http://www.robertoborrell.com/bio.html. Retrieved February 20, 2018.

157. Sanabria, personal communication, February 7, 2018.

158. "Ensayos Groupo Kubata 1982 Part 1." https://youtu.be/4eZFqyOoYMA. Retrieved February 20, 2018.

159. "Los Afortunados—Abakua," https://youtu.be/ECZcdrmgdOo. Retrieved February 20, 2018.

160. Gerardo "Taboada" Fernández, interview, May 2, 2014.

161. "¡Orgulloso de ser Cubano y Marielito!"

162. *"Estoy muy agradecida de mi profesion. He visto frutos de todas las personas que you he enseñado a bailar. Que yo se que hay muchas que han aprendido sobre todo los bailes de los orishas . . . Yo vine en el 80 por el Mariel . . . Yo bailo bomba, olvidate al estilo cubano, pero lo bailo, porque lo siento. La bomba para mi es como la colombia. Te estoy hablando de cosas que nadie sabe. ¿Es o no es?"*

163. Moore, *Music and Revolution*, 105.

164. Charley Gerard,

165. Abreu, *Cuban Musicians and the Making of Latino New York City and Miami*, 3.

166. Abreu, *Cuban Musicians and the Making of Latino New York City and Miami*, 4.

167. Abreu, *Cuban Musicians and the Making of Latino New York City and Miami*, 5.

168. Abreu, *Cuban Musicians and the Making of Latino New York City and Miami*, 19.

169. Abreu, *Cuban Musicians and the Making of Latino New York City and Miami*, 223–24.

170. *Recordando el mamoncillo/Remembering the Mamoncillo*, dir. Pam Sporn (Grito Productions, 2006).

171. *Recordando el mamoncillo/Remembering the Mamoncillo*.

172. Wolfgang Saxon, "Carlos A. Foster, 76, Cowboy and Role Model," *New York Times*, December 18, 1998. http://www.nytimes.com/1998/12/18/nyregion/carlos-a-foster-76-cowboy-and-role-model.html. Retrieved March 1, 2018.

173. *Cuban Roots/Bronx Stories*, dir. Pam Sporn (Grito Productions. 2000).

174. Cordelia Candelaria, *Encyclopedia of Latino Popular Culture*, Vol. 1 (Westport, CT: Greenwood, 2004), 719.

175. *"Esta es la rumba del Parque Central, unos de los mejores parques que ha dejado en todo el mundo. Esta es una rumba en que se unan todas las nacionalidades. [Si] A mi me ponen un pan con bistec allá con bastante papas fritas y me ponen una rumba aquí. Yo, pues me voy con la rumba y dejo el bistec con papas fritas. Porque a mi lo que me gusta es esto, la rumba. Todos los domingo estamos en esta parque, yo estoy aquí en esta parque desde el año 80, de 1980 en este parque celebrando esto. Y yo sin esto no soy feliz, esto es que me tiene vivo a mi."*

CONCLUSION

1. Floyd et al., *The Transformation of Black Music*, xxix.

2. There are numerous contemporary recorded examples of modern Cuban dance music and other traditional Cuban genres including *son* that abruptly shift or "jump" the clave figure once it is initiated at the beginning of the recording. New York City musicians and dancers are hyper-aware of these discrepancies and discuss them often.

3. Phil Rale, *Latin-American Rhythms for the Drummer* (1942), 30.

4. Stewart, *Making the Scene*, 236–41; Austerlitz, *Jazz Consciousness*, 42–97; Washburne, *Sounding Salsa*, 165–206.

5. Amira and Cornelius, *The Music of Santería*, 23. See also David Peñalosa with Peter Greenwood, *The Clave Matrix: Afro-Cuban Rhythm: Its Principles and African Origins* (Redway, CA: Bembe Books, 2009).

6. Christopher Washburne, "Play it 'Con Filin!': The Swing and Expression of Salsa," *Latin American Music Review* 19(2) (Autumn-Winter 1988): 160–85.

7. Andy González, personal communication, September 11, 2013. According to Rubén Rodríguez, Bobby Rodríguez was a student of Bill Chartoff, with whom he studied through the G.I. Bill after he returned from World War II. Rubén Rodríguez, personal communication, September 19, 2013, and April 20, 2012.

8. Austerlitz, *Jazz Consciousness*, 54–55.

9. Stewart, *Making the Scene*, 237.

10. Stewart, *Making the Scene*, 46–52.

11. Rondón, *The Book of Salsa*, 13.

12. Raúl Fernández, *Latin Jazz: The Perfect Combination/La combinación perfecta* (2002), 27–29.

13. Stewart, *Making the Scene*, 240–41.

14. Manuel, "The Anticipated Bass in Cuban Popular Music," 249.

15. Cuarteto Caney, *Cuarteto Caney: 1936–1939* (CD, Harlequin HQCD75, 1996). Walking in this case refers to consecutive eighth and quarter notes that do not adhere to a fixed traditional tresillo rhythm.

16. Sonny Bravo, interview, March 23, 2013.

17. Manuel, "The Anticipated Bass in Cuban Popular Music," 249–61.

18. Andino recorded two such features: "El Bajo de Chappottín" (World Transcription Records, 1942) and Julio Andino's Orchestra, "Andino's Peachy-Kato" (78rpm, Coda 5100, 1951 or 1952). This was actually Machito's Orchestra but not done under his name due to contractual restrictions. Henry Medina, personal communication, January 7, 2014. Bobby Rodríguez's first recorded solo with Tito Puente is another bass feature: Tito Puente, "El Bajo," *Dance Mania Live* (1959). http://www.youtube.com/watch?v=fwdqPD9SgcE. Retrieved January 7, 2014.

19. This applied to Latin music performers as well. Unlike jazz musicians, many musicians who worked in the New York Latin music community had and continue to have full-time jobs while they perform professionally and tour.

20. Flores, *Salsa Rising*, 190.

21. *Calle 54*, dir. Fernando Trueba. Miramax Films. 2000. González was not alone in this understanding of rhythmic counterpoint in R&B. Drummer Gregg Bissonette explains that when José Luis "Changuito" Quintana visited Los Angeles, the innovator of the Cuban songo rhythm taught him that the correct feel for songo was achieved by channeling David Garibaldi, drummer for the R&B group Tower of Power. Thus, outside of New York, Cuban musicians also recognized the rhythmic counterpoint in North American popular music and incorporated it into their own music. "Musical Drumming In Different Styles - Gregg Bissonette," Drumeo.com. https://youtu.be/yfabTGZjCEQ. Retrieved April 27, 2020.

REFERENCES

INTERVIEWS

Álvarez Peraza, Ernest "Chico." Interview by author. Audio recording. North Bergen, NJ. July 2, 2013.

Anderson, Frank. Interview by Bobby Sanabria and Elena Martínez. Video recording. Brooklyn, NY. June 15, 2010.

Bauzá, Mario. Interview by John Storm Roberts. Jazz Oral History Project. 1978.

Bierman, Ben. Interview by author. Audio recording. Brooklyn, NY. February 21, 2013.

Bierman, Ben. Interview by author. Audio recording. Brooklyn, NY. June 10, 2013.

Bonilla, Benny. Interview by Elena Martínez and Bobby Sanabria. Audio recording. Bronx, NY. July 2007.

Brachfeld, Andrea. Interview by author. Audio recording. Brooklyn, NY. July 16, 2013.

Bravo, Sonny. Interview by author. Audio recording. Yonkers, NY. December 12, 2012.

Bravo, Sonny. Interview by author. Audio recording. Yonkers, NY. March 23, 2013.

Camero, Cándido. Interview by author. Audio recording. New York, NY. June 11, 2015.

Colón, Gilberto "Pulpo," Jr. Interview by author. Audio recording. Yonkers, NY. June 13, 2013.

Colón, Johnny. Interview by author. Audio recording. New York, NY. February 5, 2013.

Fernández, Gerardo "Taboada." Interview by author. Audio recording, Miami, FL. May 2, 2014.

Fleming, Leopoldo, Jr. Interview by Richard Blondet. New York, NY. March 28, 2014.

Goldwasser, Ira. Interview by author. Audio recording. New York, NY. August 5, 2013.

Jefferson, Gene. Interview by Bobby Sanabria and Elena Martínez. Video recording. Brooklyn, NY. June 15, 2010.

Joseph, Alphonso. Interview by author. Audio recording. Connecticut. October 4, 2012.

Livelli, Vincent. Interview by author. Audio recording. New York, NY. September 28, 2012.

López, René. Interview by Nando Alvaricci. WBAI 99.5 FM. August 17, 2008.

Lowe, Enid. Interview by Bobby Sanabria and Elena Martínez. Video recording. Brooklyn, NY. June 15, 2010.

Machado, Gabriel "Chinchilita." Interview by author. Audio recording. New York, NY. July 17, 2013.

Sanabria, Felix. Interview by author. Audio recording. Brooklyn, NY. February 8, 2013.

Schaap, Phil. Interview by author. Audio recording. New York, NY. May 25, 2014.

SECONDARY SOURCES

Abreu, Christina D. *Cuban Musicians and the Making of Latino New York City and Miami, 1940–1960*. Chapel Hill: University of North Carolina Press, 2015.

Amira, John, and Steven Cornelius. *The Music of Santería: Traditional Rhythms of the Batá Drums*. Crown Point, IN: White Cliffs Media, 1992.

Armstrong, Louis. *Louis Armstrong, in His Own Words: Selected Writings*, ed. Thomas Brothers. New York: Oxford University Press, 1999.

Austerlitz, Paul. *Jazz Consciousness: Music, Race, and Humanity*. Middletown, CT: Wesleyan University Press, 2005.

Bardfeld, Sam. *Latin Violin: How to Play Salsa, Charanga and Latin Jazz Violin*. Brooklyn, NY: Gerard and Sarzin, 2001.

Barnett, Anthony. "Angelina Rivera and Other Early Jazz and Women Violinists." *Shuffle Boil* 5/6, Berkeley CA, Listening Chamber (2006). http://abar.net/rivera.htm. Retrieved May 10, 2016.

Bassi Labarrera, Rafael. "La presencia del jazz en la música del Caribe colombiano." In *El jazz desde la perspectiva caribeña*, edited by Darío Tejeda and Rafael Emilio Yunén, 453–75. Santiago de los Caballeros, Dominican Republic: Instituto de estudios caribeños, 2012.

Bernhardt, Clyde E. B. *I Remember: Eighty Years of Black Entertainment, Big Bands, and the Blues: An Autobiography by Jazz Trombonist and Blues Singer Clyde E. B. Bernhardt*, as told to Sheldon Harris, Foreword by John F. Szwed. Philadelphia: University of Pennsylvania Press, 1986.

Blondet, Richard. "Simon Jou." Unpublished. November 10, 2017.

Bradley, Richard, and Hilton Ruiz. *Jazz and How to Play It*. New York: Bradley Publications, 1989.

Briggs, Laura. *Reproducing Empire: Race, Sex, Science, and U.S. Imperialism in Puerto Rico*. Berkeley: University of California Press, 2002.

Brimhall, John. *Complete Music Theory Notebook*. Miami Beach, FL: Hansen House, 1985.

Brooks, Tim. *Lost Sounds: Blacks and the Birth of the Recording Industry, 1890–1919*. Urbana and Chicago: University of Illinois Press, 2010.

Buenker, John D., and Lorman A. Ratner, eds. *Multiculturalism in the United States: A Comparative Guide to Acculturation and Ethnicity*. Westport, CT: Greenwood Press, 1992.

Calero Martín, José, and Leopoldo Valdés Quesada. *Cuba musical: album-resumen ilustrado de la historia y de la actual situación del arte musical en Cuba*. La Habana: Imprenta de Molina, 1929.

Callejo Ferrer, Fernando. *Músicos Portorriqueños*. San Juan, PR: Editores Cantero Fernandez, 1915.

Canarina, John. *The New York Philharmonic: From Bernstein to Maazel*. Milwaukee: Amadeus Press, 2010.

Candelaria, Cordelia. *Encyclopedia of Latino Popular Culture*, vol. 1. Westport, CT: Greenwood Press, 2004.

Carp, David. "Salsa Symbiosis: Eddie Palmieri's Chief Collaborator in the Making of La Perfecta." *Centro Journal* XVI, no. 2 (2004): 42–61.

Colón, Juan. *Vivencias de un músico: sentir y existir*. Santo Domingo, Dominican Republic: Editora Corripio, 2014.

Congdon, Kristen G., and Kara Kelley Hallmark. *America Folk Art: A Regional Reference*, vol. 1. Santa Barbara, CA: ABC-CLIO, 2012.

Cugat, Xavier. *Meet Mr. Cugat: Bringing "Latin America" to You in Music and Rhythms*. New York: Irving Berlin Music Publisher, 1943.

Cumpiano, William, and Jonathan Natelson. *Guitarmaking: Tradition and Technology—A Complete Reference for the Design and Construction of the Steel-string Folk Guitar and the Classical Guitar*. San Francisco, CA: Chronicle Books, 1987 [1994].

Dahl, Linda. *Stormy Weather: The Music and Lives of a Century of Jazzwomen*. New York: Pantheon, 1984.

Dávila, Arlene, and Agustín Laó-Montes, eds. *Mambo Montage: The Latinization of New York City*. New York: Columbia University Press, 2001.

DeLeón, Carlos. "Salsa's Silent Giant." *Sangre Nueva* (1977): 13.

Díaz Ayala, Cristóbal. *Cuando salí de la Habana:1898–1997: cien años de musica cubana por el mundo*. San Juan: Fundación Musicalia, 1998.

Díaz Ayala, Cristóbal. "Influencias recíprocas entre el jazz y la música caribeña." In *El jazz desde la perspectiva caribeña*, edited by Darío Tejeda, 61. Santiago de los Caballeros, Dominican Republic: Instituto de estudios caribeños, 2012.

Díaz Ayala, Cristóbal. *San Juan-New York: Discografía de la música puertorriqueña*. San Juan, PR: Publicaciones Gaviota, 2009.

Doerschuk, Robert L. "Secrets of Salsa Rhythm: Piano with Hot Sauce." In *Salsiology: Afro-Cuban Music and the Evolution of Salsa in New York City*, edited by Vernon Boggs, 312–24. New York: Empire, 1992.

Dregni, Michael. *Django: The Life and Music of a Gypsy Legend*. New York: Oxford University Press, 2004.

D'Rivera, Paquito. *My Sax Life*. Chicago: Northwestern University Press, 2005.

Dower-Gold, Catherine. *Actividades musicales en Puerto Rico: después de la Guerra hispanoamericana 1898–1910*. Victoria, BC: Trafford, 2006 [1983].

Dunham, Katherine. "The Yoruba Tradition Comes to New York City." In *Kaiso!: Writings by and about Katherine Dunham*. Madison: University of Wisconsin Press, 2005.

Dunlap, David W. *From Abyssynian to Zion: A Guide to Manhattan's Houses of Worship*. New York: Columbia University Press, 2004.

Dzidzienyo, Anani, and Suzanne Oboler, eds. *Neither Enemies nor Friends: Latinos, Blacks, Afro-Latinos*. New York: Palgrave Macmillan, 2005.

Easter, Dave. "Interview with Jay Bereck (November 1, 1994)." *Palm-Tip-Open* (Spring 1995): 4–10.

Eslava, D. Hilarión. *Método complete de solfeo sin acompañamiento*. Madrid: Lit. de S. Gonzalez, 1846.

Fernández, Raúl. *Latin Jazz: The Perfect Combination/La combinación perfecta*. San Francisco: Chronicle Books in association with The Smithsonian Institution Traveling Exhibition, 2002.

Flores, Juan. *Salsa Rising: New York Latin Music of the Sixties Generation*. New York: Oxford University Press, 2016.

Floyd, Samuel A., Jr. Melanie L. Zeck, and Guthrie P. Ramsey Jr. *The Transformation of Black Music*. New York: Oxford University Press, 2017.

Fojas, Camilla. *Islands of Empire: Pop Culture and U.S. Power*. Austin: University of Texas Press, 2014.

Foster Steward, Noel. *Las expresiones musicales en Panamá: una aproximación*. Panama: Editorial Universitaria, 1997.

Foulkes, Julia. *A Place for Us: "West Side Story" and New York*. Chicago: University of Chicago Press, 2016.

Frías, Johnny. "Review: Rumba clave blen blen blen." *Latin American Music Review/Revista De Música Latinoamericana* 36, no. 1 (2015): 124–25.

García, David F. *Arsenio Rodríguez and the Transnational Flows of Latin Popular Music*. Philadelphia: Temple University Press, 2006.

García Hudson, Mario. "Los pianistas antes de Danilo Pérez." In *El jazz desde la perspectiva caribeña*, edited by Darío Tejeda and Rafael Emilio Yunén, 477–88. Santiago de los Caballeros, Dominican Republic: Instituto de estudios caribeños, 2012.

Gerard, Charley, and Marty Sheller. *Salsa: The Rhythm of Latin Music*. Crown Point, IN: White Cliffs Media, 1989.

Gerónimo, Roberto. "The Cuban Connection: Tipica '73 becomes the first U.S. band to record in Cuba in 20 years." *Steppin' Out* 12 (February 1979): 1–4.Gerónimo, Roberto. "Típica '73 triunfa en Cuba." *Latin NY* (January 1979): 60–61.

Gillespie, Dizzy, with Al Fraser. *To Be or Not to Bop: Memoirs of Dizzy Gillespie*. New York: Da Capo, 1979.

Glasser, Ruth. *My Music Is My Flag: Puerto Rican Musicians and Their New York Communities, 1917–1940*. Berkeley: University of California Press, 1997.

Goetschius, Percy. *The Homophonic Forms of Musical Composition: An Exhaustive Treatise of the Structure and Development of Musical Forms from the Simple Phrase to the Song-Form with "Trio."* New York: G. Schirmer, 1898.

Goldman, Daniel. *I Want to Be Ready: Improvised Dance as a Practice of Freedom*. Ann Arbor: University of Michigan Press, 2010.

González-Wippler, Migene. "Bata: Sacred Mysteries of Santeria Percussion Revealed: An Exclusive *Latin N.Y.* Interview with Milton Cardona." *Latin NY* (September 1983): 29–32.

Greenbaum, Susan. *More than Black: Afro-Cubans in Tampa*. Gainesville: University Press of Florida, 2002.

Grillo, Evelio. "Black Cuban, Black American." In *The Afro-Latin@ Reader: History and Culture in the United States*, edited by Miriam Jiménez Román and Juan Flores, 99–112. Durham, NC: Duke University Press, 2010.

Grosfoguel, Ramón, and Chloé S. Georas. "Latino Caribbean Diasporas in New York." In *Mambo Montage: The Latinization of New York City*, edited by Agustín Laó-Montes and Arlene Dávila. New York: Columbia University Press, 2001.

Harper, Paula. "Cuba Connections: Key West. Tampa. Miami, 1870 to 1945." *Journal of Decorative and Propaganda Arts* 22, Cuba Theme Issue (1996): 278–91.

Hennessey, Thomas J. *From Jazz to Swing: African-American Jazz Musicians and Their Music, 1890–1935*. Detroit: Wayne State University Press, 1994.

Hopkins, Gregg, and Bill Moore. *Ampeg: The Story Behind the Sound*. Milwaukee, WI: Hal Leonard, 1999.

Hoy, Vielka Cecilia. "Negotiating among Invisibilities: Tales of Afro-Latinidades in the United States." In *The Afro-Latin@ Reader: History and Culture in the United States*, eds. Miriam Jiménez Román and Juan Flores. Durham, NC: Duke University Press, 2010.

James, Ian Michael. *Ninety Miles: Cuban Journeys in the Age of Castro*. Lanham, MD: Rowman and Littlefield, 2006.

Johnston, Richard. "Velázquez Guitar 1955." In *The Classical Guitar: A Complete History Featuring the Russell Cleveland Collection*, edited by John Morrish, 44–45. London: Balafon Books, 1997.

Jottar, Berta. "Central Park Rumba: Nuyorican Identity and the Return to African Roots." *Centro Journal* 23, no.1 (Spring 2011): 5–29.

Jottar, Berta. "From Central Park, Rumba with Love!" *Voices: Journal of New York Folklore* 37 (Spring-Summer 2011). http://www.nyfolklore.org/pubs/voic37-1-2/rumba.html.

Jottar, Berta. "Zero Tolerance and Central Park Rumba Cabildo Politics." *Liminalities: A Journal of Performance Studies* 5, no. 4 (November 2009): 1–24.

Kelley, Robin. *Thelonious Monk: The Life and Times of an American Original*. New York: Free Press, 2009.

Knauer, Lisa Maya. "Audiovisual Remittances and Transnational Subjectivities." *Cuba in the Special Period: Culture and Ideology in the 1990s*, edited by Ariana Hernández-Reguant, 159–77. New York: Palgrave Macmillan, 2009.

Lane, Abbe. *But Where Is Love?* New York: Warner/Dove Books, 1993.

Lapidus, Benjamin. "*Chinita Linda*: Portrayals of Chinese and Asian Identity and Culture by Chinese and Non-Chinese in Spanish Caribbean Dance Music." In *Chinese America: History & Perspective, The Journal of the Chinese Historical Society of America* (2015): 17–28.

Lapidus, Benjamin. "*El folclor al rescate: La importancia del folclor musical caribeño en la escena de Nueva York y su impacto en el mundo*." In *El folclor musical y danzario del caribe en tiempos de globalización*, edited by Darío Tejeda, 123–33. Santiago de los Caballeros, Dominican Republic: Instituto de estudios caribeños, 2014.

Lapidus, Benjamin. Liner notes. *Charangueando*. CD, [Fania 1978] Emusica, 2005.

Lapidus, Benjamin. "Liner Notes" and "Rene López on Andy Gónzalez." Andy González, *Entre colegas*. CD, Truth Revolution Records 024, 2016.

Lapidus, Benjamin. *Origins of Cuban Music and Dance: Changüí* (Lanham, MD: Scarecrow) (2008).

Lapidus, Benjamin. "Típica '73" essay in accompanying booklet. *Típica '73: En Cuba—Intercambio Cultural*. CD, [Fania 1979] Emusica, forthcoming.

Lapidus, Benjamin. "¡Toca *maravilloso!*: Larry Harlow and the Jewish connection to Latin music." In *Mazal Tov Amigos!: Jews and Popular Music in the Americas*, edited by Amalia Ran and Moshe Morad, 109–21. Leiden and Boston: Brill Press, 2016.

Leaf, Earl. *Isles of Rhythm*. New York: A.S. Barnes, 1948.

Leto, Emanuel. "*It was a Latin town*": Folk and Popular Music in Ybor City, 1900–1950. Exhibition Program. Ybor City FL: Ybor City Museum Society.

Levin, Eric. "What's a Nice Jewish Boy Doing as King of the Bongos? Explains Martin Cohen: 'I Was Never Nice.'" *People*, April 28, 1980. http://people.com/archive/whats-a-nice-jewish -boy-doing-as-king-of-the-bongos-explains-martin-cohen-i-was-never-nice-vol-13-no-17/. Retrieved March 29, 2018.

Long, Durward. "The Historical Beginnings of Ybor City and Modern Tampa." *Florida Historical Quarterly* 45, no. 1 (July 1966): 31–44.

López, Antonio. *Unbecoming Blackness: The Diaspora Cultures of Afro-Cuban America*. New York: New York University Press, 2012.

Loza, Steven. *Tito Puente and the Making of Latin Music*. Urbana and Chicago: University of Illinois Press, 1999.

Machado, Gabriel. "Gabriel Machado 'Chinchilita' (Timbal-Conga-Bongo)." n.d.

Magee, Jeffrey. *The Uncrowned King of Swing: Fletcher Henderson and Big Band Jazz*. New York: Oxford University Press, 2005.

Maldonado, Alex W. *Teodoro Moscoso and Puerto Rico's Operation Bootstrap*. Gainesville: University Press of Florida, 1997.

Manuel, Peter. "The Anticipated Bass in Cuban Popular Music," *Latin American Music Review/ Revista de Música Latinoamericana* 6(2) (Autumn-Winter 1985): 249–61.

Manuel, Peter. "Improvisation in Latin Dance Music." In *In The Course of Performance: Studies in the World of Musical Improvisation*, edited by Bruno Nettl and Melinda Russell, 127–47. Chicago: University of Chicago Press, 1998.

Manuel, Peter. "Puerto Rican Music and Cultural Identity: Creative Appropriation of Cuban Sources from Danza to Salsa." *Ethnomusicology* 38, no. 2, Music and Politics (Spring-Summer 1994): 249–80.

Martínez Torre, Ewin. "Arturito, Los Jardineros y la revolución de El Jardín del Arte." *La canción popular: revista de la asociación puertorriqueño de coleccionistas de música popular* 20, no. 21 (2006–2007): 33–44.

McMaines, Juliet. *Spinning Mambo into Salsa: Caribbean Dance in Global Commerce*. New York: Oxford University Press, 2015.

McNeese, Tim. *Tito Puente*. New York: Chelsea House, 2008.

Mestas, María del Carmen. *Pasión de rumbero*. La Habana: Editorial Pablo de la Torriente, 1998.

Mirabal, Nancy Raquel. "Scripting Race, Finding Place: African-Americans, Afro-Cubans and the Diasporic Imaginary in the United States." In *Neither Enemies nor Friends: Latinos, Blacks, Afro-Latinos*, edited by Anani Dzidzienyo and Suzanne Oboler, 189–207. New York: Palgrave Macmillan, 2005.

Moore, Robin D. *Music and Revolution: Cultural Change in Socialist Cuba*. Berkeley: University of California Press, 2006.

Moore, Robin D. *Nationalizing Blackness: Afrocubanismo and Artistic Revolution in Havana, 1920–1940*. Pittsburgh: University of Pittsburgh Press, 1997.

Morales, Humberto. *How to Play Latin American Rhythm Instruments*. New York: Henry Adler, 1954.

Morales, Noro. *Latin-American Rhythms and Improvisations for Piano*, edited by Danny Hurd. Transcribed by Ben Pickering. New York: Henry Adler, 1955.

Ojito, Mirta. *Finding Mañana: A Memoir of Cuban Exodus*. New York: Penguin, 2005.

Olson, James S., and Judith E. Olson. *Cuban Americans: From Trauma to Triumph*. New York: Twayne/Simon and Schuster Macmillan, 1995.

Opie, Frederick Douglass. *Hog and Hominy: Soul Food from Africa to America*. New York: Columbia University Press, 2013.

Orozco, Román, and Natalia Bolívar. *Cubasanta: Comunistas, santeros y cristianos en la isla de Fidel Castro*. Madrid: Ediciones El Pais, 1998.

Padura Fuentes, Leonardo. *Faces of Salsa: A Spoken History of the Music*, translated by Stephen J. Clark. Washington, DC: Smithsonian Books, 2003.

Peñalosa, David, with Peter Greenwood. *The Clave Matrix: Afro-Cuban Rhythm: Its Principles and African Origins*. Redway, CA: Bembe Books, 2009.

"Poncho Sánchez, Justo Almario y Crispín Fernández." In *El jazz desde la perspectiva caribeña*, edited by Darío Tejeda and Rafael Emilio Yunén, 507–16. Santiago de los Caballeros, Dominican Republic: Instituto de estudios caribeños, 2012.

Priestley, George. "Antillean-Panamanians or Afro-Panamanians? Political Participation and the Politics of Identity During the Carter-Torrijos Treaty Negotiations." *Transforming Anthropology* 12, no. 1/2 (2004): 50–67.

Quintero Rivera, Ángel G. "La música jíbara en la salsa: la presencia viva del folklore." In *Cocinando suave: ensayos de salsa en Puerto Rico*, edited by César Colón Montijo, 205–22. San Juan, PR: Ediciones Callejón, 2016.

Quintero Rivera, Ángel G. *Salsa, sabor y control: sociología dela música tropical*. México City: Siglo XXI Editores, 1998.

Rader, Michael, and K.-B. Rau. "From the Shadows: The Re-Emergence of Carmelo Jarí." *The Frog Blues & Jazz Annual No. 2: The Musicians, the Records and the Music of the 78 Era*. Book and CD, Frog Records, 2011. http://www.harlem-fuss.com/pdf/published_articles/harlem_fuss_articles_from_the_shadows_carmelo_jari.pdf.

Rale, Phil. *Latin-American Rhythms for the Drummer*. New York: Remick Music, 1942.

Reed, Bill. *Hot from Harlem: Twelve African American Entertainers, 1890–1960*. Rev. ed. Jefferson, NC: McFarland, 2010.

Roberts, John Storm. *The Latin Tinge: The Impact of Latin American Music in the United States*. 2nd ed. New York: Oxford University Press, 1999.

Rondón, César Miguel. *The Book of Salsa: A Chronicle of Urban Music from the Caribbean to New York City*. Translated by Frances R. Aparicio with Jackie White. Chapel Hill: University of North Carolina Press, 2010.

Rosa, José. *World Music Survey: The History of Music from Cuba, the Caribbean, South America, and the United States*. José Rosa Enterprises, 2018.

Rottenberg, Simon. "Intra-Union Disputes over Job Control." *Quarterly Journal of Economics* 61, no. 4 (August 1947): 619–39.

Rye, Howard. "Visiting Firemen 15: The Southern Syncopated Orchestra (Part 1)." *Storyville* 142 (June 1, 1990): 144. https://nationaljazzarchive.org.uk/explore/journals/storyville/storyville-142/1266221-storyville-142-0010?q=Visiting%20Firemen%2015%3A%20The%20Southern%20Syncopated%20Orchestra%20%28Part%201. Retrieved May 10, 2016.

Sabournin, Tony. "Review: Intercambio Cultural, TIPICA 73." *Latin NY* (October 1979): 18–19.

Salazar, Max. "El Conjunto Caney." *Latin Beat* (August 1997): 1.

Salazar, Max. *Mambo Kingdom: Latin Music in New York*. New York: Schirmer, 2002.

Salazar, Max. "Sideman's Corner: Sonny Bravo, Pianist for the 80s." *Latin NY* (May 1983): 50–51.

Salazar, Max. "Sonny Bravo." *Latin NY* (September-October 1968): 28–29.

Salloum, Trevor, and Bobby Sanabria. *The Conga and Bongo Drum in Jazz*. Wisconsin: Mel Bay, 2016.

Schwartz, Mark. "Memories from the Days of the Mamboniks." Liner notes to *It's a Scream How Levine Does the Rhumba: The Latin-Jewish Musical Story 1940s-1980s*. CD, Idelsohn Society RSR 021, 2013.

Schweitzer, Kenneth. "The Cuban Aña Fraternity: Strategies for Cohesion." *The Yoruba God of Drumming: Transatlantic Perspectives on the Wood That Talks*, edited by Amanda Villepastour, 171–91. Jackson: University Press of Mississippi, 2015.

Serpenti, Armand. "Conversatie met de goden." *VPRO Gids*, November 13–19, 2010: 27.

Serrano, Basilio. *Puerto Rican Pioneers in Jazz, 1900–1939: Bomba Beats to Latin Jazz*. iUniverse, 2015.

Serrano, Basilio. "Juan Tizol: Sus talentos y sus muchos colaboradores." *Resonancias: La revista puertorriqueña de música* 5/6, no. 10/11 (2005–2006): 56–65.

Sotomayor Pérez, Juan. *Las Tradiciones Músico-Artesanales de los Instrumentos de Cuerda de Puerto Rico: Descritos a través de las entrevistas del Proyecto del Cuatro Puertorriqueño*. Northampton, MA: El Proyecto Del Cuatro Puertorriqueño, 2003.

Sowell, Thomas. *Ethnic America: A History*. New York: Basic Books, 1981.

Spottswood, Richard. *Ethnic Music on Records, Vol. 4: Spanish, Portuguese, Phillipine, Basque*. Urbana and Chicago: University of Illinois Press, 1990.

Stewart, Alex. *Making the Scene: Contemporary New York City Big Band Jazz*. Berkeley: University of California Press, 2007.

Thomas, Lorrin. *Puerto Rican Citizen: History and Political Identity in Twentieth-Century New York City*. Chicago: University of Chicago Press, 2010.

Thompson, Donald, and Martha Moreno de Schwartz. *James Reese Europe's Hellfighters Band and the Puerto Rican Connection*. Parcha Press, 2005.

Tucker, Sherrie. *Swing Shift: "All-Girl" Bands of the 1940s*. Durham, NC: Duke University Press, 2000.

Vander Zanden, James W. *American Minority Relations*. 3rd ed. New York: Ronald Press, 1972.

Vásquez, Blanca. "Mi Gente: Andy and Jerry González." *Centro Journal* 3, no. 2 (Spring 1991): 62–76.

Vélez, María Teresa. *Drumming for the Gods: The Life and Times of Felipe García Villamil, Santero, Palero, and Abakuá*. Philadelphia: Temple University Press, 2000.

Washburne, Christopher. "The Clave of Jazz: A Caribbean Contribution to the Rhythmic Foundation of an African-American Music." *Black Music Research Journal* 17, no. 1 (1997): 59–80.

Washburne, Christopher. "Latin Music at the Apollo." In *Ain't Nothing Like the Real Thing: How the Apollo Theater Shaped American Entertainment*, edited by Richard Carlin and Kinshasha Holman Conwill, 220–25. Washington, DC: Smithsonian Books, 2010.

Washburne, Christopher. *Sounding Salsa: Performing Latin Music in New York City*. Philadelphia: Temple University Press, 2008.

Weston, Randy, and Willard Jenkins. *African Rhythms: The Autobiography of Randy Weston*. Durham, NC: Duke University Press, 2010.

Wright, Laurie, and Peggy Wright. "THAT CAT STOPPED MY SHOW COLD: An Interview with "Nick" Rodriguez." *Storyville* 135 (September 1988): 86–94.

NEWSPAPER ANNOUNCEMENTS AND ARTICLES WITHOUT AUTHORS

"Abbe Lane and Charo." *People*, July 28, 1980, 66–67. Retrieved January 2, 2018.

"Abbe Lane Book Tells of Her Life with Xavier Cugat." *Orlando Sentinel*, March 11, 1993. Retrieved January 2, 2018.

"Abbe Lane Fine Miami Shop." *Philadelphia Enquirer*, May 17, 1959, 8.

"Abbe Lane on Stage at N.Y. Paramount." *Brooklyn Eagle*, May 13, 1953, 11.

"Abbe Lane to See Photographs." *Binghamton Press*, January 31, 1951, 24.

"Abbe Lane Wins Divorce." *New York Times*, June 4, 1964, 28.

"Abbe Lane, Cugat to Heads Appeal's Kick-Off Parade." *Evans Journal in Angola, NY*, October 22, 1959, 3.

"Abbe Lane's Career Takes Many Turns." *Buffalo Courier-Express*, September 13, 1953, 23C.

"Abbe Lane's Furs Stolen." *Buffalo Evening News*, Tuesday, September 4, 1951.

"Academia Maria Luisa Le Compte." Advertisement, *La Prensa*, February 8, 1941, 5.

"Ahavath Israel Ball Attracts Thousands to Auditorium Thanksgiving Eve." *Kingston Daily Freeman*, Kingston, NY, November 23, 1951, 11.

"Amram, Tipica '73, and WNET." *Latin NY* (June 1978): 11.

"Amusements." *York Dispatcher*, December 3, 1928.

"Azucar para crecer: The Sugar to Grow a Ten Million Ton Harvest." *Clandestina*, February 27, 2018. https://clandestina.co/blogs/clandestina-is-something-else/the-sugar-to-grow-a-ten -million-ton-harvest. Retrieved July 18, 2019.

"Baby it's Warm inside the Roxy." *New York Post*, November 11, 1951, 18.

"Back Again." *New York Post*, January 3, 1948.

"Banda Hispana Los Granaderos: The Sound of Music Helps Them." *New York Post*, July 26, 1960, 16.

"Benefit on Feb. 7 to Assist School: Performance of 'Captain's Paradise' Will Augment Steiner Scholarships." *New York Times*, December 1, 1957, 109.

Billboard, May 14, 1949, 127.

"Bill Robinson for African Dance Festival." *Brooklyn Sun*, March 18, 1946, 27.

"Black Force at University." *Greenfield (Mass.) Recorder*, July 6, 1973, 10.

"Buenas noches" [Latin club listings], *New York*, August 7, 1972.

Buffalo Courier Express. July 9, 1944, 8A.

"Casablanca Hotel Open All Summer." *Philadelphia Enquirer*, June 1, 1952, B19.

"Castro Describes Economic Failure." *New York Times*, July 27, 1970, 1. https://www.nytimes .com/1970/07/27/archives/castro-describes-economic-failure-premier-offers-to-resign-in .html. Retrieved July 18, 2019.

"Celebróse un concierto infantile en 'El Toreador.'" *La Prensa*, June 19, 1935.

"Cugat, Abbe Lane, Wed, Start on Honeymoon." *Buffalo Evening News*, May 6, 1952, 30.

"Cugat and Singer, 18, Plan to Wed in Summer." *Knickerbocker News*, Albany, NY, May 4, 1950, 44.

"Cugats Settle Divorce Claims; Abbe Lane to Drop Suit." *Brooklyn Eagle*, January 22, 1952, 7.

"Cugat Sues a Dance Team for Million over Abbe Lane." *New York Times*, June 26, 1964, 35.

"Cugat to Play at Roseland." *New York Post*, May 17, 1953, 27.

"Cugat, Wife Lose $20,000 in Cash, Jewelry to Thug." *Niagara Falls Gazette*, January 21, 1954, 27.

"Dancing." *New York Post*, February 7, 1947, 40.

"Dancing." *New York Post*, February 14, 1947, 36.

"Dancing." *New York Post*, January 9, 1948, 47.

"Dancing." *New York Post*, April 18, 1947, 48.

"Dancing." *New York Post*, October 3, 1947, 50.

"Dancing." *New York Post*, October 25, 1947, 19.

"Dancing." *New York Post*, November 20, 1947.

"Dancing." *New York Post*, November 29, 1947, 19.

"Dancing." *New York Post*, December 27, 1947, 9.

"Dancing." *New York Post*, March 9, 1951, 74.

"Dancing." *New York Post*, February 8, 1952, 49.

"Dancing." *New York Post*, January 30, 1953, 45.

"Dancing." *New York Post*, February 6, 1953, 45.

"Dancing." *New York Post*, May 22, 1953, 57.

"Dancing." *New York Post*, November 6, 1953, 54.

"Dancing." *New York Post*, November 20, 1953, 50.

"Dancing." *New York Post*, September 15, 1961, 72.

"De Música: alumnos infantiles en un concierto musical." *La Prensa*, June 22, 1936.

"De Música: Concierto Estudanil." *La Prensa*, May 31, 1938, 5.

"De Música: fue un éxito el recital de la Señora Eduvigis Bocanegra Pino." *La Prensa*, June 23, 1938.

"De Música: fue un éxito el recital de la Señora Eduvigis Bocanegra Pino." *La Prensa*, June 16, 1938.

El Diario de Nueva York, November 22, 1962.

"El Festival de la Asociación Hispano Americana Pro Ciegos." *La Prensa*, July 29, 1936, 5.

Erasmo Vando Papers, B2F5F6. Centro de Estudios Puertorriquenos (Microfilm Reel).

"Excitement at Fire: Night Club Patrons Watch Department in Action." *New York Sun*, July 1, 1939, 1.

"Eydie Gorme, TV Singer, Wed in Vegas." *Schenectady Gazette*, December 30, 1957, 16.

"Falleció La Señora María Luisa Lecompte." *La Prensa*, March 8, 1947, 2.

"The Fraternal Clubhouse." *New York Post*, January 3, 1948, 11.

"Front and Center with Sonny." *New York Age*, October 20, 1951, 12.

Gráfico (revista 27 febrero 1927–3 enero 1931). Jesús Colón Collection (1901–1974), Centro for Puerto Rican Studies, Hunter College, CUNY, New York.

"Jelly Roll Morton Draws Large Crowd at Initial Hop." *Afro-American*, Baltimore, January 26, 1929.

La Prensa de Nueva York, October 2, 1960, 23.

Latin NY (January 1978): 59.

"Le Cupidon." *New York Post*, February 5, 1957, 16.

"Mambo-Calypso at Palladium." *New York Post*, February 5, 1957, 37.

"Man, 78, Dies of Injuries." *Herald Statesman*, Yonkers, NY, October 23, 1971, 10.

"Mesorana." *La Prensa*, January 25, 1941, 5.

"New Cultural Tours to Cuba Planned by Guardian Tours." *Latin NY* (October 1979): 12.

"New Talent at Paul's Place." *Palm Beach Post*, September 15, 1978, B4.

New York Age, January 21, 1933, 9.

New York Post, January 30, 1936, 17.

New York Post, April 4, 1958, 26.

New York Post, December 8, 1950, 70.

New York Post, December 9, 1960, 80.

"Ole for Brooklyn Girl: Abbe Lane Dances Latin Way." *Brooklyn Eagle*, Sunday, January 16, 1955, 31.

"Passing By." *Brooklyn Eagle*, March 17, 1939, 10.

"Peppers at Washington Gardens." *Pittsburgh Courier*, May 11, 1929.

"Perry Leff to Wed Abbe Lane." *New York Times*, November 11, 1964, 38.

"Perry Leff Weds Abbe Lane." *New York Times*, December 17, 1964, 48.

Pittsburgh Courier, June 25, 1938, 21.

"Polls 50,000 Votes to Cop First Place; Henderson Second." *Pittsburgh Courier*, December 12, 1932, 1, 8.

"Rector Bailey, Musician and Teacher, Dies at 57." *New York Times*, April 8, 1970. http://www.nytimes.com/1970/04/08/archives/rector-bailey-musician-and-teacher-dies-at-57.html?_r=0.

"Sign Dance Team for Feature." *Pittsburgh Courier*, November 1, 1941, 21.

"Songstress Denies Mrs. Cugat, Raiders Found Her Unclad." *Buffalo Evening News*, Wednesday, January 24, 1951, 58.

"Típica filmed at Palm Tree." Club Scene, *Latin NY* (September 1980): 54.

"Un festival artístico." *La Prensa*, March 24, 1938, 5.

"Velada Panamericana en la Biblioteca calle 110." *La Prensa*, April 16, 1941, 5.

"What's Happening: Three Year Hitch for La Típica." *Latin NY* (June 1979): 15.

"Wife Says Bandleader Has 6 Girl Friends, Band Leader Says She Has No Proof." *Buffalo Evening News*, August 18, 1950, 9. (The same story also ran in the *Brooklyn Eagle*, August 18, 1950, 7.)

"Xavier Cugat's Latin Music Sets Buffalo Dancing Rhumba." *Buffalo Evening News*, September 24, 1952, V71.

"Xavier Cugat and His Wife, Abbe Lane, Sign to Replace Eddie Fisher on N.B.C." *New York Times*, January 25, 1957, 45.

NEWSPAPER ARTICLES WITH AUTHORS

Archer, Eugene. "Abbe Lane is Star of Films Abroad: U.S. Singer Has Appeared in Italian-Language Movies." *New York Times*, December 27, 1961, 20.

Bacharach, Burt. "Stag Lines: The News Column for Men." *Buffalo Evening News*, January 8, 1958, 23.

Bacon, James. "Is Abbe Rita's Successor? Parallels Between Them Are Numerous." *Sunday Press*, Binghamton, NY, November 1, 1953, 12C.

Boyka, Louise. "Brazil Jungle Scene In Color Film Feature." *Schenectady Gazette*, April 7, 1955, 26.

Boyle, Hal. "The Poor Man's Philosopher: Busy Abbe Lane." *Leader-Herald* (Gloversville and Johnstown, NY), April 10, 1958, 4.

Breen, Jay. "Cugat Jealous of Barcelona Bullfighter As He, Abbe Plan Honeymoon In Spain." *Binghamton Press*, November 29, 1951, 28.

Burden, Martin. "Going Out Tonight?" *New York Post*, August 29, 1962, 62.

Burlingame, Rudolph. "Clubs Offer Festive Shows for the Holidays." *Philadelphia Enquirer*, December 25, 1942, 14.

Burlingame, Rudolph. "Clubs Prepare S.R.O. Signs for Holidays." *Philadelphia Enquirer*, December 11, 1942.

Daniels, Lee A. "Lynn Oliver, Leader of Jazz Orchestras and Educator, 68." *New York Times*, July 27, 1992. https://www.nytimes.com/1992/07/27/nyregion/lynn-oliver-leader-of-jazz-orchestras-and-educator-68.html. Retrieved June 13, 2019.

Del Rio, Jorge. "El instituto de Puerto Rico." *El Diario de Nueva York*, July 25, 1954, D4.

Demasters, Karen. "Passing Folk Art to a New Generation, With a Little Help from the State." *New York Times*, March 16, 1997. https://www.nytimes.com/1997/03/16/nyregion/passing-folk-art-to-a-new-generation-with-a-little-help-from-the-state.html. Retrieved March 25, 2018.

Durkin, Erin. "Neighborhood Split Over Renaming of Franklin Ave. 'Panama Way.'" *New York Daily News*, October 21, 2010. http://www.nydailynews.com/new-york/brooklyn/neighborhood-split-renaming-part-franklin-ave-panama-article-1.190840.

"El Torreador Opens its Winter Season." *Brooklyn Daily Eagle*, October 26, 1935, 10 M2.

Fox, Margalit. "Augie Rodriguez, 86, Half of a Mambo Team, Dies." *New York Times*, July 26, 2014. https://www.nytimes.com/2014/07/27/nyregion/augie-rodriguez-86-half-of-a-mambo-team-dies.html. Retrieved July 17, 2018.

Gardner, Chappy. "Along the Rialto (New York)." *Pittsburgh Courier*, October 13, 1928, 3, Second Section.

Gates, Anita. "Eydie Gorme, Voice of Sophisticated Pop, Dies at 84," *New York Times*, August 11, 2013. http://www.nytimes.com/2013/08/12/arts/music/eydie-gorme-blame-it-on-the-bossa -nova-singer-dies-at-84.html. Retrieved January 2, 2018.

González, David. "Bongos, Congas, and Cameras." *New York Times*, January 13, 2011. https://lens .blogs.nytimes.com/2011/01/13/bongos-congas-and-cameras/. Retrieved March 29, 2018.

Gorme, Eydie. "The Voice of Broadway: Men in Her Life Are Important." *Knickerbocker News*, October 15, 1957, 8A.

Gross, Ben. "Cugat and Abbe Lane Praised on Debut." *Buffalo Evening News*, February 28, 1957, 36.

Heffernan, Harold. "Abbe, Xavier Cugat Buy Pretentious Home." *Long Island Star-Journal*, August 22, 1953, 10.

Hevesi, Dennis. "Master Guitar Makers Are Leery of Their Art." *New York Times*, February 3, 1993. https://www.nytimes.com/1993/02/03/nyregion/master-guitar-makers-are-leery-of-their-art .html. Retrieved April 2, 2018.

HLK. "Princess Takes Over Progressive Quintet." *Pittsburgh Courier*, January 28, 1956, 26.

Holley, Joe. "Dancer, Known as 'Cuban Pete,' Was Considered 'Maestro of the Mambo.'" *Washington Post*, January 23, 2009. http://www.washingtonpost.com/wp-dyn/content/article/2009/01/22/ AR2009012203834.html?noredirect=on. Retrieved July 17, 2018.

Jahiel, Greg. "Building Guitars on a Different Frequency." *New York Daily News*, June 11, 2009. http://www.nydailynews.com/latino/building-guitars-frequency-article-1.376856. Retrieved April 2, 2018.

Johnson, Malcolm. "Café Life in New York: Gas Rationing May Create Big Summer Business for Restaurants Here." *New York Sun*, May 21, 1942, 23.

Johnson, Malcolm. "Cafes and Supper Clubs: Another Bit of Cuban Comes to Broadway—Dining at the Ambassador." New York Sun, November 22, 1938, 12.

Johnson, Malcolm. "In the Cafes and Supper Clubs." *New York Sun*, October 26, 1935, 6.

Kilgallen, Dorothy. "The Voice of Broadway." *Elmira Star-Gazette*, August 9, 1947, 4.

Kilgallen, Dorothy. "Voice of Broadway." *Schenectady Gazette*, June 7, 1956, 24.

Kleiner, Dick. "Steve and Eydie Gorme Map Program to Replace Steve Allen from Lofty Penthouse." *Utica Observer Dispatch*, July 12, 1958, 3A.

Lane, Lydia. "Hollywood Beauty: Jan's Looks All Her Own But Hard to Acquire." *Albany Times-Union*, May 17, 1959, F-5.

Lardner, Rex. "Lo Introducion Avec Cugat." *New York Post*, June 18, 1951, 16.

Lester, John. "5 Marx Brothers Cast in Show." *Long Island Star-Journal*, February 18, 1957, 17.

Lubasch, Arnold H. "Omega 7 Leader Accused of Plot to Kill Delegate." *New York Times*, December 29, 1983, B7.

Manson, Richard. "Going Out Tonight?" *New York Post*, May 20, 1942, 43.

Manson, Richard. "Entertainment in the Cafes." *New York Post*, April 16, 1938, 10.

Manson, Richard. "Entertainment in the Cafes." *New York Post*, November 21, 1936, 10.

Miami Herald Staff. "How events in Cuba shaped and reshaped Miami." *Miami Herald*, November 26, 2016. http://www.miamiherald.com/news/nation-world/world/americas/article117205713 .html. Retrieved April 5, 2018.

Morales, Ed. "Places in the Puerto Rican Heart, Eddie Figueroa, and the Nuyorican Imaginary." *Centro Voices e-Magazine*. https://centropr.hunter.cuny.edu/centrovoices/letras/ places-puerto-rican-heart-eddie-figueroa-and-nuyorican-imaginary.

Mosby, Aline. "Singer to Drop Sweet Roles for Siren Type." *News of the Tonawandas,* (Tonawanda, NY), June 28, 1954, 12.

Nefsky Frankfeldt, Gwen. "Eydie Gorme: 1928–2013." *Jewish Women's Archive Encyclopedia*. https:// jwa.org/encyclopedia/article/gorme-edye. Retrieved January 2, 2018.

Norris, Linda. "Let's Look at the Records." *Chatfield* [Minnesota] *News*, November 5, 1964, 4.

Parsons, Louella O. "Career Keeps Abbe Lane Busy." *Albany Times-Union*, March 17, 1957, B-8.

Parsons, Michael. "Wreck of SS Rowan: How jazz nearly didn't come to Ireland." *Irish Times*, January 3, 2015. https://www.irishtimes.com/life-and-style/homes-and-property/fine-art-antiques/wreck-of-ss-rowan-how-jazz-nearly-didn-t-come-to-ireland-1.2053405?mode=amp. Retrieved August 1, 2019.

Petit, Saul. "Gormé, Lawrence, to Start own Show Today." *Niagara Falls Gazette*, July 13, 1958, T-13.

Quintero, Babby. "En Nueva York y En Todas Partes." *El Diario-La Prensa*, June 14, 1964.

Rascoe, Burton. "Radio and Television: Cugat and Abbe Go Big in Rome." *Long Island Star-Journal*, January 28, 1956, 19.

Robertson, Edythe. "Orlando Robeson and Wen Talbert's Choir on 'Harlem Serenade.'" *New York Age*, September 14, 1940, 4.

Rodríguez, Yusimi. "Ten Million and Forty Years Later." *Havana Times*, August 16, 2010. https://havanatimes.org/opinion/ten-million-and-forty-years-later/. Retrieved July 18, 2019.

Roosevelt, Eleanor. "My Day." *Courier-Express Daily Pictorial*, April 22, 1946. 8.

Sabournin, Tony. "Club Scene: What is Happening with Típica 73." *Latin NY* (March 1980): 54.

Sabournin, Tony. "Lincoln Center Bombed but the Band Played On: Cuba's Orquesta Aragon, Los Papines, and Elena Burke." *Latin NY* (February 1979): 28–30.

Santiago, Roberto. "Moving to a Different Beat Conga-Maker Drums Up Biz in B'klyn." *New York Daily News*, August 31, 1999. http://www.nydailynews.com/archives/boroughs/moving-beat-conga-maker-drums-biz-b-klyn-article-1.847416. Retrieved March 19, 2018.

Saxon, Wolfgang. "Carlos A. Foster, 76, Cowboy and Role Model." *New York Times*, December 18, 1998. http://www.nytimes.com/1998/12/18/nyregion/carlos-a-foster-76-cowboy-and-role-model.html. Retrieved March 1, 2018.

Scheuer, Steven H. "Cugat, Abbe Lane Show On Way." *Citizen Register* (Ossining, NY), February 26, 1957, 11.

Sheff, David. "At 80, Xavier Cugat Finds Another Latin Lovely to Take the Place of Abbe Lane and Charo," *People*, July 28, 1980. https://people.com/archive/at-80-xavier-cugat-finds-another-latin-lovely-to-take-the-place-of-abbe-lane-and-charo-vol-14-no-4/. Retrieved April 26, 2020.

Snelson, Floyd G. "Harlem: 'Negro Capitol of the World." *New York Age*, May 6, 1939, 7–12.

Strauss, Robert. "Together Wherever They Go: After four decades as a team, Steve Lawrence and Eydie Gorme are the last of a breed, with an act that features his tux, her gowns, lots of pop standards and a love that's here to stay." *Los Angeles Times*, April 14, 1996. http://articles.latimes.com/1996-04-14/entertainment/ca-58268_1_steve-lawrence-and-eydie-gorme. Retrieved January 4, 2018.

Thomas, Bob. "Back After 2 Years: Hollywood Finally Ready for Abbe." *Binghamton Press*, November 20, 1957, 40.

Thomas, Bob. "Band Leader Strikes 'Gold': Cugat's Shimmy Tunes Give Shakes to Orient." *Binghamton Press*, May 4, 1953, 22.

Ticker, George. "Mad About Manhattan." *Leader-Republican* (Gloverville and Johnstown, NY), June 10, 1939, 6.

Towe, Eleanor. "The Jazz Scene: In Concert Carlos Garnett and Jackie McLean—Town Hall October 8th 1976." *New York Recorder*, October 23, 1976, 10.

Tynes, Harcourt. "Doc Johnson's Touch on the Keys Charms His Listeners." Gannett Westchester Newspapers, November 13, 1981, 7.

Van Olinda, Edgar S. "'Round Town." October 30, 1949, *Times Union*, Albany, NY, D12.

Watson, Maudine Sims. "Orelia, Famed Cuban Dancer, Gives Recipe." *Pittsburgh Courier*, January 11, 1941, 8.

Watson, Ted. "Princess Orelia and Pete to Star in Latin Quarter Revue Starting March 23." *Pittsburgh Courier*, March 22, 1941, 21.

Weinberg, Pete. "The Jam Session." *Wilton Bulletin* (Wilton, CT), August 15, 1946, 11.

Wilson, Earl. "It Happened Last Night: Mambo Doesn't Love Papa Who Needs More Lessons." *New York Post*, March 15, 1955, 17.

Wilson, Earl. "It Happened Last Night: Saluting Jack Carter, The Copa's Newest Hit." *New York Post*, November 23, 1951, 17.

Wilson, Earl. "It Happened Last Night: Cugat Finds Rumba Dying, Likewise His Old Romance." *New York Post*, May 23, 1950, 17.

Wilson, John S. "Pop: Doc Johnson in Many Moods." *New York Times*, November 26, 1983. http://www.nytimes.com/1983/11/26/arts/pop-doc-johnson-in-many-moods.html.

Winchell, Walter. "Abbe Lane Quits 'Oh, Captain'; She Needs Money." *Buffalo Courier Express*, July 9, 1958, 12.

Winchell, Walter. "Mrs. J. Nunan Rich in her own Right." *Albany Times-Union*, Monday, April 28, 1952, 6.

Winter, Jana. "The End of an Era, to the Beat of a Drum." *New York Times*, April 16, 2006. https://www.nytimes.com/2006/04/16/nyregion/thecity/the-end-of-an-era-to-the-beat-of-a-drum.html. Retrieved March 29, 2018.

Young, Daniel. "Creole Cuisine is Taking off: A Haitian Hub Near LaGuardia Spices Up Dinner for Weary Travelers & Locals Alike." *New York Daily News*, January 3, 1997. http://www.nydailynews.com/archives/nydn-features/creole-cuisine-haitian-hub-laguardia-spices-dinner-weary-travelers-locals-alike-article-1.752476.

CENSUS DATA

Fifteenth Census of the United States, April 7, 1930. Enumeration District 31–922, Supervisor District 24, Sheet 5-A, 174.

Fifteenth Census of the United States, April 18, 1930. Enumeration District 31–789, Supervisor District 23, Sheet 2-A, 182.

Censo Décimocuatro de Los Estados Unidos: Población—Puerto Rico, Hoja 40.

"United States Social Security Death Index," database, *FamilySearch* (https://familysearch.org/ark:/61903/1:1:JKPF-NP1 : 20 May 2014), Simon Jou, Oct 1971; citing U.S. Social Security Administration, Death Master File, database (Alexandria, Virginia: National Technical Information Service, ongoing).

DISCOGRAPHY

Alegre All-Stars. "Peanut Vendor." *El manicero: The Alegre All Stars Vol. 2.* Alegre Records LPA 834. LP. 1964.

Amram, David. *Havana New York.* Flying Fish Records 70057. LP. 1978.

Andino, Julio. "Andino's Peachy-Kato." Coda 5100-A 1206. 78rpm. 1947.

Astatke, Mulatu, and His Ethiopian Quintet. *Afro-Latin Soul.* Worthy Records 1014. LP. 1966.

Batista, Candida, y Sus Tambores Bata. *Ritmo de santo.* Maype 130. 196?.

Barretto, Justi. "*A Nueva York*," *Guaguanco '69.* Gema Records. LPG 3072. LP. [1969] 1976.

Barretto, Justi. *Santeria (toques y cantos).* Gema 1193. LP. 196?. Also released as Grupo Folklorico Santero De Justi Barretto, *Santería Africana: Santa Barbara Africana.* Santero LP-531. LP. 1969; and as *Shango Aragua.* Echu 303. LP. 1971.

Barretto, Ray. *El Ray Criollo.* United Artists Records 6543. LP. 1966.

Barretto, Ray. *Together*. Fania 378. LP. 1969.

Caraballo, Rafael, y Su Conjunto. *Plegarias a los santos*. Santero LP-329. LP.Caraballo, Rafael, y Su Conjunto. *Santero Moderno*. Jibarito Records LP-129. LP.

Cruz, Celia. *Homenaje a los santos*. Seeco Records 9269. LP. 1972.

Cain, Joe, and His Orchestra. *Latin Explosion*. Time Records S2123. LP. 1960.

Camero, Cándido, and Graciela Pérez. *Inolvidable*. Chesky Records SACD297. CD. 2004.

Camero, Cándido. *Beautiful*. Blue Note BST-84357. LP. 1970.

Colón, Johnny, and His Orchestra. *Boogaloo Blues*. Cotique Records C 1004. LP. 1967.

Conquet, Johnny, His Piano and Orchestra. *Raisins and Almonds Cha Cha Cha and Merengues*. RCA Victor. LSP 1789. LP. 1958.

Cuarteto Caney. *Cuarteto Caney: 1936–1939*. Harlequin HQCD75. CD. 1996.

Cuba, Joe, Sextet. *Wanted Dead Or Alive (Bang! Bang! Push, Push, Push)*. Tico 1146. LP. 1966.

Cugat, Xavier, and his Orchestra. *Dancetime with Cugat*. RCA Victor LPM-3170. LP. 1953.

Cugat, Xavier, and his Orchestra. *Latin for Lovers*. RCA Camden CAL-516. 1959. LP.

Cugat, Xavier, and his Orchestra. *Wedding Samba*. Columbia CO 42806. 78rpm. 1951.

de la Fé, Alfredo. *Alfredo de la Fé*. Criollo Records 473. 1979. LP.

Díaz, Alex. *Son de la Calle: dedicado al padre de merengue jazz Mario Rivera*. Jazzendominicana. CD. 2009.

Dolphy, Eric, and The Latin Jazz Quintet. *The Latin Jazz Quintet*. United Artists 4071. LP. 1961.

Gorme, Eydie. *Blame It on the Bossa Nova*. Columbia CS 8812. LP. 1962.

Gorme, Eydie. *I Feel So Spanish*. United Artists 6152. LP. 1961.

Griffin, Johnny. *Blowing Session*. Blue Note CDP 7 81559 2. CD. [1958] 1988.

Grupo Afrocubano dirigido por Alfredo Zayas. *Afro Frenetic: Tambores de Cuba*. Panart 3053. LP. 1961.

Harlow, Larry. *Live in Quad*. Fania Records 00472. LP. 1974.

Hermanos Moises. *La Mano Poderosa*. Suaritos LPS-121. LP. 1960.

Jazz Modes. *The Jazz Modes*. Atlantic 1306. LP. 1959.

Krupa, Gene, and His Orchestra. "Chiquita Banana (The Banana Song)/You May Not Love Me." Columbia 32049. 78rpm. 1946.

Lane, Abbe. *Abbe Lane with Xavier Cugat and his Orchestra*. Mercury MG 20643. LP. 1961.

La Lupe. *They Call Me La Lupe/A mi me llaman La Lupe*. Tico Records 1144. 1966. LP.

Latin Jazz Quintet (Featured Guest Artist Pharoah Sanders, Under the Direction of Juan Amalbért). *Oh! Pharoah Speak*. Trip 8008. 1971. LP.

Latin Jazz Quintet + Eric Dolphy. *Caribé*. Prestige 8251. 1960. LP.

Marrero, Raul, y su Orquesta Moderna. "La Chica del Barrio Obrero." Ansonia 45–6677 B (7900). 45rpm. 1967.

Mendez, Silvestre. *Oriza (Afro-Cuban Rhythms)*. Seeco 9314. LP. 1960.

Morgan, Lee, and Wynton Kelly, et al. *Dizzy Atmosphere*. Specialty 2110. LP. 1957.

Orquesta Revé. *Rumberos Latino Americanos*. Habanacan HABCD-2407. 1992.

Osácar family acetate. 1939.

Palmieri, Charlie, y Su Orquesta. *El gigante del teclado*. Alegre CLPA 7003. LP. 1972.

Palmieri, Eddie. *Unfinished Masterpiece*. Coco 120. LP. 1975.

Palmieri, Eddie. *Recorded Live at Sing Sing*. Tico 1303. 1972. LP.

Palmieri, Eddie. *Lo que traigo es sabroso*. Alegre 832. 1964. LP.

Panama, Joe. *The Explosive Side of Joe Panama*. Decca 4890. LP. 1968.

Patato and Totico. *Patato and Totico*. Verve V5037. LP. 1967.

Ponce, Daniel. *New York Is Now*. Celluloid CELL5005. LP. 1983.

Puente, Tito, Orchestra. Boris Rose recording of radio broadcast from Birdland, New York. 1951.

Puente, Tito, His Latin Ensemble and Orchestra. *Un Poco Loco*. Concord Jazz Picante. CJP-329. CD. 1987.

Puente, Tito, and His Latin Ensemble. *Sensación*. Concord Jazz Picante. CJP-301. CD. 1986.

Ramírez, Louie, y Sus Amigos. *Louie Ramírez y Sus Amigos*. Cotique JMCS-1096. LP. 1978.

Ríos, Orlando "Puntilla." *From La Habana to New York*. Puntilla Folkloric Records AF-101. LP. 1983.

Rodríguez, Arsenio. *Quindembo/Afro Magic/La Magía de Arsenio Rodríguez*. Epic LN24072. LP. 1963.

Rodríguez, Johnny, and Angel René Orquesta. *Cookin' with A&J*. Mardi Gras LP-5036. LP. 1968.

Rodríguez, Tito. *Big Band Latino*. Musicor MS 6048. LP. 1968.

Rouse, Charlie. *Bossa Nova Bacchanal*. Blue Note 4119. LP. 1963.

Silva, José "Chombo." *Los Hits de Manzanero*. GEMA LPG-3067. 1968. LP.

Soneros del Barrio. *Siguiendo la tradicion*. Digital Culture. CD. 2011.

Spanish Harlem Orchestra. *Across 110th Street*. Libertad LE04-615. CD. 2004.

Típica 73. *Into the 80s*. Fania Records JM 592. LP. 1981.

Típica 73. *Salsa Encendida*. Inca Records JMIS 1062. CD. 1978.

Tirado, Luz Celenia, y Coro con Nieves Quintero y su Conjunto. *Santeros Cantados*. Antillano LP 25. LP.

Torres, Eddie, and His Mambo Kings Orchestra. *Dance City*. CD. 1994.

Torres, Joe. *Latino Con Soul*. World Pacific 21857. LP. 1967.

Totico y Sus Rumberos. *Totico y Sus Rumberos*. Montuno MLP-515. LP. 1981.

Valdés, Gilberto. *Rezo de Santo: Ritmo de santo de la tierra de Africa en Arara*. Maype 180. LP. 1960?

Valdés, Vicentico. *For Listening and Dancing*. Seeco SCLP 9103. LP. 1958.

Valentín, Bobby, y Su Orquesta. *El mensajero*. Fonseca SLP 1108. LP. 1966.

Valentín, Bobby, y Su Orquesta. *Young Man with a Horn*. Fania SLP 332. LP. 1965.

Various artists. *A Musical Gift of Greatness*. Latin Percussion J323. CD. 2001.

Various artists. *It's a Scream How Levine Does the Rhumba: The Latin-Jewish Musical Story 1940s–1980s*. Idelsohn Society RSR 021. CD. 2013.

Various artists. *Pancho Cristal presenta: Super típica estrellas*. All-Art AALP-1582. LP. 1976.

Various artists. *Santero—Afro Cult Music*. Panart 2060. LP. 1957.

Vincent, Jean. *The Soul of Haiti*. Vanguard. LP. 1957.

Viera, Ray, y Su Trombao. *Sambumbia radioactive*. Cofresi Productions. CD. 2013.

FILM

Al compas de Cuba. Dir. Mario Gallo. 1960. https://youtu.be/QuI_aiDacRo. Retrieved February 8, 2018.*Cachao (Como su Ritmo No Hay Dos)*. Dir. Andy García, CineSon Productions. VHS. 1993.

Calle 54, Dir. Fernando Trueba, Miramax Films. DVD. 2000.

Cuban Roots/Bronx Stories. Dir. Pam Sporn, Grito Productions. DVD. 2000.

A Havana Cocktail. Dir. Roy Mack. 1931. https://youtu.be/p84FgJxqkQs. Retrieved July 19, 2019.

Latin Jazz. Dirs. Isabelle Leymarie and Karim Akadiri Soumaila, Feeling Productions/la Sept/Epic Production. 56 minutes. France. 1991. https://www.youtube.com/watch?v=HRYqS8z2fGk. Retrieved March 5, 2018.

Machito: A Latin Jazz Legacy. Dir. Carlos Ortiz, Nubia Music Society. 1987.

Mambo Madness. Dir. Courtney Hafela. 1955. https://youtu.be/05rLL8B9g1I. Retrieved July 21, 2019.

Mamboniks, The. Dir. Lex Gillespie, Malecón Films. 2019.

Mi Mambo. Produced by Pat Jaffe and Molly McBride. 2006. Film.

Recordando el mamoncillo/Remembering the Mamoncillo. Dir. Pam Sporn, Grito Productions. DVD. 2006.

Rumba Clave Blen Blen Blen. Dir. Arístedes Falcón Paradí, Paradí Productions. DVD. 2013.

Tambo Jazz. Written and dir. Gerardo Maloney, La Fundación Cine/Video/Cultura y El Grupo Experimental de Cine Universitario. Panama. 1993.

We Like It Like That: The Story of Latin Boogaloo. Dir. Matthew Ramírez Warren. 2014.

West Side Story—Making of a Classic. Directed by Ursula McFarlane, BBC. 2016. https://youtu .be/3XAoZdVGGrM. Retrieved January 2, 2018.

INTERNET VIDEOS

Alonso Wilson. http://www.youtube.com/watch?v=z6juExvAApo. Retrieved February 28, 2014.

Black History Special: Jazz Legend Randy Weston on His Life and Celebration of "African Rhythms." http://www.democracynow.org/2012/2/20/black_history_special_jazz_legend _randy. Retrieved January 23, 2014.

Cara Bereck Levy, August 29, 2016. https://www.youtube.com/watch?v=N_ueSsUX2OI. Retrieved March 19, 2018.

Dr. Gail Gross interviews Abbe Lane. https://www.youtube.com/watch?v=Jm-Yo9UF05A. Retrieved January 4, 2018.

"Ensayos Groupo Kubata 1982 Part 1." https://youtu.be/4eZFqyOoYMA. Retrieved February 20, 2018.

"For the Love of Mambo Extended Trailer." https://youtu.be/WBHbOdTFgRs. Retrieved July 27, 2018.

"The Guy Who Makes the Best Cowbells." Jazz Night in America, December 10, 2015. https://www .npr.org/event/music/459135308/the-guy-who-makes-the-best-cowbells. Retrieved March 29, 2018.

"Historia de Richie Ray & Bobby Cruz (Contada en su propia voz)." https://youtu.be/cNQZ9a isMLQ. Retrieved October 30, 2017.

https://youtu.be/cNQZ9aisMLQ. Retrieved October 30, 2017.

"Irakere—Full Concert—03/23/79—Capitol Theatre (OFFICIAL)." March 23, 1979. https://www .youtube.com/watch?v=VapQAWxEGzo. Retrieved March 7, 2018.

Jay Bereck's Skin on Skin Part 1. https://www.youtube.com/watch?v=N_ueSsUX2OI. Retrieved March 19, 2018.

"Juan 'El Negro' Raymat." Part 2. http://thebearersofsacredsound.weebly.com/juan_el_negro_ray mat.html. Retrieved February 21, 2018.

The Latin Giants of Jazz @ L.P.'s 45th—"No Me Molesto." http://www.youtube.com/watch?v =ZN6QwEDSt5M. Retrieved December 10, 2013.

"Los Afortunados—Abakua." https://youtu.be/ECZcdrmgdOo. Retrieved February 20, 2018.

"The Making of the Puerto Rican Cuatro." https://www.youtube.com/watch?v=deZ5Htoha7E. Retrieved March 25, 2018.

"Manuel Velázquez Documentary." https://www.youtube.com/watch?v=MAbvClxqbfo. Retrieved March 25, 2018.

Orlando Puntilla/Daniel Ponce y su Rumbata at the Black and White In Color Gallery in 1990. https://www.youtube.com/watch?v=l3la726U7lg. Retrieved March 7, 2018.

Patato teaching Brigitte Bardot how to dance mambo in the 1956 film *And God Created Woman*. https://www.youtube.com/watch?v=gaFTmZ4zQCU. Retrieved March 7, 2018.

Raúl Planas con Rumbavana, "La escoba barrendera." http://www.youtube.com/watch?v =drx-sDZJbnE.

Rumbavana, "Yo vine pa' echar candela" in 1979. http://www.youtube.com/watch?v=hoqXz1-hxoY.

"SS Rowan Survivors." British Pathé. https://youtu.be/Jxb8y4zlyVM.

Tipica 73, "La escoba barrendera." http://www.youtube.com/watch?v=KQ2ZqWP1Bc0. Retrieved November 7, 2013.

Vicky Jassey. "Crossing the Seas: A Brief Historic Overview: Introduction." http://thebearersof sacredsound.weebly.com/history.html. Retrieved February 21, 2018.

"Video 1 Los Afortunados 2." https://youtu.be/1xkjc6eufwY. Retrieved February 20, 2018.

"Willie Ramos: A history of ritual oricha music in the United States—The Bearers of Sacred Sound." https://youtu.be/1NaPDHcn87k. Retrieved July 27, 2018.

Xavier Cugat e Abbe Lane al "Carosello." https://youtu.be/E2noX-8FaLY. Retrieved December 5, 2017.

"$1000 Conga Drum—Inside Skin On Skin." https://www.youtube.com/watch?v=wL0TTPMYsck. Retrieved March 19, 2018.

INTERNET SOURCES

"Abbe Lane—Hollywood Star Walk." *Los Angeles Times.* http://projects.latimes.com/hollywood/star-walk/abbe-lane/. Retrieved January 4, 2018.

"Alex Blake." Alex Blake Bass. http://www.alexblakebass.com/#/bio/4556984380. Retrieved February 28, 2014.

"Alonso Wilson." http://www.latin45.com/vinyl/panama/alonso-wilson-quinteto-never-never-awb.html. Retrieved February 28, 2014.

Alvarez Peraza, Chico. "Terry Pearce Remembers The Golden Era of Dance Music In NYC." Latin Jazz Network, August 4, 2011. https://latinjazznet.com/featured/terry-pearce-remembers-the-golden-era-of-dance-music-in-nyc/.

"Azuquita." Wikipedia (French). http://fr.wikipedia.org/wiki/Azuquita. Retrieved February 28, 2014.

"Baby bass." Wikipedia (Spanish). http://es.wikipedia.org/wiki/Baby_bass. Retrieved September 19, 2013.

"Bio." RobertoBorell.com. http://www.robertoborrell.com/bio.html. Retrieved February 20, 2018.

"Biography." BillyCobham.com. http://www.billycobham.com/html/biography.php. Retrieved February 28, 2014.

"Boys and Girls Harbor: Our Story." The Harbor. http://www.theharbor.org/our-story/history. Retrieved April 8, 2014.

Bratu, Becky. "Local Organization and Panamanian Community Clash." The Ink, October 19, 2010. http://thebrooklynink.com/2010/10/19/16476-who-was-first-on-franklin-avenue-neighborhood-organization-and-panamanian-community-clash-over-avenue-name/.

"'Calypso Jazz?': Jazz Society Formed Here." *Virgin Islands Daily News,* April 23, 1963, 1. https://news.google.com/newspapers?nid=757&dat=19630423&id=rW1aAAAAIBAJ&sjid=dkcDAAAAIBAJ&pg=4517,1284479. Retrieved January 2, 2018.

"Camilo Azuquita." Salsa de Acero. http://salserodeacero.com/portal/biografia-de-camilo-azuquita/.

El Cancionero Rumbero. http://cancionerorumbero.blogspot.com/2009/12/invasion-del-80.html. Retrieved February 8, 2018.

Carlos Flores, Facebook post, March 6, 2013.

Carp, David. "Barry Rogers, Salsero, Searcher, World Musician." Descarga.com (Internet Archive). https://web.archive.org/web/20070225130918/http://www.descarga.com:80/cgi-bin/db/archives/Profile42?Lh8einfm;;115. Retrieved June 1, 2017.

Carr, Terry. "Felix Wilkins: Flutist and First Amendment Champion." Jump: The Philly Music Project. June 26, 2013. http://jumpphilly.com/2013/06/26/felix-wilkins-flutist-and-first-amendment-champion/. Retrieved February 28, 2014.

Child, John. "Louie Cruz: To the Best of His Knowledge." Descarga.com, June 22, 2006. http://www.descarga.com/cgi-bin/db/archives/Interview49?ozVtAaLh;;12283. Retrieved May 12, 2016.

"Danilo Pérez." Wikipedia. http://en.wikipedia.org/wiki/Danilo_Pérez. Retrieved February 28, 2014.

Del Risco, Enrique. "Yo vine pa' echar candela." Enrisco (blog), January 27, 2010. http://enrisco.blogspot.com/2010/01/yo-vine-pa-echar-candela.html. Retrieved November 7, 2013.

"Don't Bother Me, I Can't Cope." Wikipedia. http://en.wikipedia.org/wiki/Don't_Bother_Me,_I_Can't_Cope. Retrieved June 10, 2013.

"Donald Nicks." AllMusic.com. http://www.allmusic.com/artist/donald-nicks-mn0001590117. Retrieved February 28, 2014.

"Echo Tone Conga List." CongaPlace.com. http://www.mycongaplace.com/forum/eng/viewtopic.php?f=14&t=7559. Retrieved March 21, 1018.

"Entrevista a Sonny Bravo." LatinaStereo.com, February 8, 2017. http://www.latinastereo.com/Noticias/ArtMID/433/ArticleID/400/Entrevista-a-Sonny-Bravo. Retrieved July 10, 2017.

Erica Y. López, "The Life and Death of Hilton Ruiz." El Salsero (blog), March 30, 2010. http://www.radioelsalsero.com/2010/03/life-and-death-of-hilton-ruiz.html. Retrieved July 16, 2018.

"Eubie!" Wikipedia. http://en.wikipedia.org/wiki/Eubie! Retrieved June 10, 2013.

"Fallece el conocido percusionista Orlando 'Puntilla' Ríos." Cubaencuentro, August 14, 2008. https://www.cubaencuentro.com/cultura/noticias/fallece-el-conocido-percusionista-orlando-puntilla-rios-103846. Retrieved February 21, 2018.

"Feelin' the Spirit: The Luis Russell Story." Jim Cullum Riverwalk Jazz Collection. http://riverwalkjazz.stanford.edu/program/feelin-spirit-luis-russell-story.

Flores, Aurora. "Jewish-Latino." Latino Americans (blog). PBS.com, August 31, 2013. http://www.pbs.org/latino-americans/en/blog/2013/08/31/Jewish-Latino/. Retrieved January 2, 2018.

"Florida Folklife from the WPA Collections, 1937 to 1942." Library of Congress. http://memory.loc.gov/ammem/collections/florida/. Retrieved November 5, 2008.

Glinton, Sonari. "Remembrances: Remembering Eydie Gorme, A Vegas Singer Without The Drama." All Things Considered, NPR, December 29, 2013. https://www.npr.org/2013/12/29/258166712/remembering-eydie-gorme-a-vegas-singer-without-the-drama. Retrieved January 2, 2017.

González Arenas, Boris. "Si no tengo algo por lo que estar luchando, la vida pierde sentido." Diario de Cuba, July 19, 2017. http://www.diariodecuba.com/cuba/1500465299_32645.html. Retrieved June 19, 2019.

"Guilin Baby Bass—Puerto Rican made Wood Body 42" Scale Circa 60's? Local NYC Pick Up." Talkbass.com. July 15, 2014. https://www.talkbass.com/threads/guilin-baby-bass-puerto-rican-made-wood-body-42-scale-circa-60s-local-nyc-pick-up.1090061/. Retrieved March 25, 2018.

"Guys and Dolls." Wikipedia. http://en.wikipedia.org/wiki/Guys_and_Dolls. Retrieved June 10, 2013.

"The Harbor Conservatory of Music in NYC Celebrates Their 30th Anniversary." Congahead.com. http://www.congahead.com/legacy/On_The_Scene/Harbor_Conservatory/30th_anniversary.htm. Retrieved April 7, 2014.

Hilton Ruiz on Piano Jazz. Marian McPartland's Piano Jazz. South Carolina Public Radio, November 23, 2015. http://southcarolinapublicradio.org/post/hilton-ruiz-piano-jazz. Retrieved January 11, 2018.

"Honoring Mr. Frank Harris Anderson upon the occasion of celebrating his musical genius by the Panama Connection of Janes United Methodist Church." New York State Senate, July 19, 2010. http://open.nysenate.gov/legislation/bill/J6510–2009. Retrieved March 2, 2011.

"Humanitarian." DaniloPerez.com. http://daniloperez.com/humanitarian/. Retrieved February 28, 2014.

"In Memoriam: Manuel Velázquez, 1917–2014." Guild of American Luthiers. http://www.luth.org/memoriams/mem_manuel-velazquez.html. Retrieved March 25, 2018.

"Interview with Verna Gillis." *Review: Art and Literature of the Americas* 23, no. 40 (1989): 24–29. http://www.tandfonline.com/doi/abs/10.1080/08905768908594274?journalCode=rrev20. Retrieved April 26, 2020.

"Interview: Camille E. Hodge." OtherSounds.com. http://othersounds.com/interview-camille-e-hodge/.

Jenkins, Willard. Remembering Brooklyn's Jazz heyday." Open Sky Jazz, August 24, 2011. http://www.openskyjazz.com/2011/08/remembering-brooklyns-jazz-heyday/.

Jisi, Chris. "The Ampeg B-15: From Inception to Resurrection." *Bassplayer*, March 13, 2011. https://www.bassplayer.com/artists/the-ampeg-b-15-from-inception-to-resurrection. Retrieved March 23, 2018.

"Joe Quijano." Fundacion Nacional para la Cultura Popular. http://www.prpop.org/biografias/j_bios/JoeQuijano.shtml. Retrieved March 4, 2014.

"Joe Quijano." Puerta de Tierra. http://www.puertadetierra.info/figuras/artistas/joe/joe_quijano.htm. Retrieved March 4, 2014.

Juravich, Nick. "I Love Franklin Avenue." http://ilovefranklinave.blogspot.com/2010/09/fighting-for-franklin.html.

"Jymie Merritt Biography." MikeMerritt.com. http://mikemerritt.com/wp/?page_id=566. Retrieved March 21, 2018.

Kent, Mary. "Pacheco y Su Tumbao: An Anniversary Salute." SalsaTalks.com. http://www.salsatalks.com/articles/pacheco.html. Retrieved March 25, 2018.

Koert, Hans. "Jimmy Wormworth: The 1957 American Jazz Quintet in Holland." Keep (It) Swinging, June 6, 2011. http://keepswinging.blogspot.com/2011/06/jimmy-wormworth-1957-american-jazz.html. Retrieved June 1, 2017.

"Linda Leida Alvarez." Sonora Matancera. http://sonoramatancera.com/linda-leida-alvarez.html. Retrieved February 6, 2018.

Lloyd, Robin. "The Sad and Mysterious Death of Hilton Ruiz." KNKX, November 8, 2012. http://knkx.org/post/sad-and-mysterious-death-hilton-ruiz. Retrieved January 10, 2018.

Lockwood, Alan. "Bass Rules: Israel "Cachao" Lopez and Andy Gonzalez: From Mambo to Salsa: Part Seven." *Brooklyn Rail*, March 7, 2008. http://www.brooklynrail.org/2008/03/music/bass-rules-israel-cachao-lopez-and-andy-gonzalez. Retrieved September 19, 2013.

Ludwig Company. 1953 catalogue. http://www.drumarchive.com/ludwig/. Retrieved March 23, 2018.

Ludwig Company. 1957 catalogue. http://www.drumarchive.com/ludwig/. Retrieved March 23, 2018.

Martínez Furé, Rogelio. "Dialogo Imaginario sobre Folklore." 286. [Originally in *La Gaceta de Cuba* 121 (March 1974): 12–17.] http://iihaa.usac.edu.gt/archivohemerografico/wp-content/uploads/2017/09/06_estudios_1975_martinez.pdf. Retrieved June 20, 2019.

Mattingly, Rick. "Percussive Arts Society Hall of Fame: Martin Cohen." Percussive Arts Society. http://www.pas.org/about/hall-of-fame/martin-cohen. Retrieved March 21, 2018.

Mattsson, Lasse. "Sabu Martinez: Percussionist with Joie de Vivre." *Orkester Jornalen*, April 1968. http://www.hipwax.com/sabu/OJ041968.html. Retrieved June 6, 2019.

McLean, Anthony H. "Mauricio Smith Pereira." Etnia Negra de Panama, November 2010. http://diadelaetnia.homestead.com/MauricioSmith.html. Retrieved March 21, 2011.

Música del Alma: Hot & Soulful Latin Sounds. http://latinfunk.org/blog/?cat=6. Retrieved February 28, 2014.

Nemeyer, Eric. "Jorge Sylvester." *Jazz Inside* (June 2012): 4–14. http://jorgesylvesteracecollective.blogspot.com/p/about-music.html. Retrieved March 3, 2014.

"Nick Rodriguez." Louis Armstrong All Stars. http://louisarmstrongallstars.webatu.com/musi cians/piano/nickrodriguez.htm. Retrieved October 4, 2012.

November 4, 1955, recording of Gormé's Voice of America broadcast, includes performances of "Besame mucho" and "Come Home." http://www.worldcat.org/title/interview-with-eydie -gorme-1955/oclc/174970577. Retrieved January 2, 2018.

Oliver, Jess. Interview. NAMM Oral History, January 22, 2005. https://www.namm.org/library/ oral-history/jess-oliver. Retrieved March 23, 2018.

Olivera Pabón, Felipe Mario. "Manuel Henríquez Zapata . . . creating our instruments for over a half-century!" The Puerto Rican Cuatro Project. http://www.cuatro-pr.org/node/273. Retrieved March 25, 2018.

Orquesta Havana Riverside. Montuno Cubano. http://www.montunocubano.com/Tumbao/bio groupes/havana%20riverside.htm. Retrieved December 4, 2012.

"Panamanian Americans." Wikipedia. http://en.wikipedia.org/wiki/Panamanian_American.

Payne, Doug. "Kai Winding with J.J. Johnson" (discography). DougPayne.com. http://www.doug payne.com/kwljj.htm. Retrieved May 10, 2016.

"Purlie." Wikipedia. http://en.wikipedia.org/wiki/Purlie. Retrieved June 10, 2013.

"A Raisin in the Sun." Wikipedia. http://en.wikipedia.org/wiki/A_Raisin_in_the_Sun. Retrieved June 10, 2013.

Reid, Lydia. "The Silver and Gold Roll on the Panama Canal Zone." Silver People Heritage Foundation, May 1, 2008. https://thesilverpeopleheritage.wordpress.com/2008/05/01/ the-silver-and-gold-roll-on-the-panama-canal-zone/.

Rendón, Victor. "Monchito Muñoz: Puerto Rico's Little Secret." Latin Percussionist Newsletter Issue 11 (Fall 2000). http://www.bronxconexionlatinjazz.com/blog-percussion/20-percussion-issue -11-fall-2000. Retrieved January 10, 2018.

Rivera, George. "Q&A: A Conversation with Bobby Valentín." Jazz con Clave. http://www.jazzcon clave.com/i-room/valentin.htm. Retrieved January 10, 2018.

Rivera, George. "Q&A: A Conversation with Ray Santos." Jazz con Clave. http://www.jazzconclave .com/i-room/santos.htm. Retrieved May 3, 2016.

Rodríguez Calzadilla, Nora. "En el aniversario 45 del Conjunto Folclórico Universitario." Radio Enciclopedia, September 28, 2015. http://www.radioenciclopedia.cu/noticias/en-aniversario -45-conjunto-folclorico-universitario-20150928/ Retrieved June 18, 2019.

"Russel Blake." For Bass Players Only. http://www.forbassplayersonly.com/Interviews/Russel -Blake.html. Retrieved February 28, 2014.

Sanabria, Bobby. "Candido: Father Of Modern Conga Drumming." Traps (Autumn 2007). http:// www.drummagazine.com/hand-drum/post/candido-the-father-of-modern-conga-drum ming/P5/. Retrieved January 20, 2016.

Sanabria, Bobby. "Reimagining West Side Story." National Institute for Latino Policy, March 19, 2018. https://www.nyrealestatelawblog.com/manhattan-litigation-blog/2018/march/reimag ining-west-side-story/. Retrieved July 18, 2019.

Sanabria, Bobby. Profile: The Legacy of Mario Bauzá (1993). Descarga.com. http://www.descarga .com/cgi-bin/db/archives/Profile8?QDNwE5qj;;3641066.

"Santi Debriano." Wikipedia. http://en.wikipedia.org/wiki/Santi_Debriano. Retrieved February 28, 2014.

"Silvia DeGrasse." Viva Panama Organization. http://www.vivapanama.org/silvia-degrasse.html.

"Sonny Bravo." Dusty Groove. http://www.dustygroove.com/item.php?id=m8fgtsc79j. Retrieved November 5, 2008.

"Sonny White." Wikipedia. https://en.wikipedia.org/wiki/Sonny_White.

Soundscape Project. WKCR. https://www.cc-seas.columbia.edu/wkcr/soundscape/project. Re trieved February 5, 2018.

Stuffed Animal. "Mambo Gee Gee: The Story of George Goldner and Tico Records, Part Two: ¡Qué sabroso ésta! Mambo USA, Morris Levy & Rhythm 'n' Blues." Spectropop. http://www.spectropop.com/tico/TICOpart2.htm. Retrieved May 10, 2016.

Tamara Straus, "Re-creation of 'Mazel Tov, Mis Amigos.'" *San Francisco Gate*, August 26, 2010. http://www.sfgate.com/entertainment/article/Re-creation-of-Mazel-Tov-Mis-Amigos-3177182.php#photo-2313203. Retrieved December 12, 2017.

"Tito Baez." The Puerto Rican Cuatro Project. http://www.cuatro-pr.org/node/114. Retrieved April 2, 2018.

"Victor Paz." TrumpetHerald.com. http://www.trumpetherald.com/forum/viewtopic.php?p=1180074. Retrieved February 28, 2014.

"Victor Paz." Victor Paz website. http://victorpaztrumpet.webs.com/biografa.htm. Retrieved February 28, 2014.

Warden, Nolan. "A History of the Conga Drum," NolanWarden.com. http://www.nolanwarden.com/Conga_Drum_History%28Warden%29.pdf. Retrieved March 21, 2018.

Weeks, Todd Bryant. "'You've Got to Have Big Ears': Billy Kaye Tells the High Notes of His Illustrious Five-decade Career." *Allegro* 111, no. 2 (February 2011). http://www.local802afm.org/2011/02/youve-got-to-have-big-ears/.

"*The Wiz*." Wikipedia. http://en.wikipedia.org/wiki/The_Wiz. Retrieved June 10, 2013.

INDEX

ABOUT THE AUTHOR

Benjamin Lapidus is a Grammy®-nominated musician and professor at John Jay College of Criminal Justice, CUNY, and The Graduate Center. As a scholar he has published widely on Latin music. He has performed and recorded throughout the world as a bandleader and supporting musician.

CPSIA information can be obtained
at www.ICGtesting.com
Printed in the USA
BVHW030456271120
594052BV00005B/11